Never By Itself Alone

Never By Itself Alone

Queer Poetry, Queer Communities in Boston and the Bay Area, 1944–Present

DAVID GRUNDY

OXFORD
UNIVERSITY PRESS

Oxford University Press is a department of the University of Oxford. It furthers
the University's objective of excellence in research, scholarship, and education
by publishing worldwide. Oxford is a registered trade mark of Oxford University
Press in the UK and certain other countries.

Published in the United States of America by Oxford University Press
198 Madison Avenue, New York, NY 10016, United States of America.

© Oxford University Press 2024

All rights reserved. No part of this publication may be reproduced, stored in
a retrieval system, or transmitted, in any form or by any means, without the
prior permission in writing of Oxford University Press, or as expressly permitted
by law, by license, or under terms agreed with the appropriate reproduction
rights organization. Inquiries concerning reproduction outside the scope of the
above should be sent to the Rights Department, Oxford University Press, at the
address above.

You must not circulate this work in any other form
and you must impose this same condition on any acquirer.

Library of Congress Cataloging-in-Publication Data
Names: Grundy, David (Poet), author.
Title: Never by itself alone : queer poetry, queer communities in Boston
and the Bay Area, 1944–present / David Grundy.
Description: New York, NY : Oxford University Press, 2024. |
Includes bibliographical references and index.
Identifiers: LCCN 2023057267 (print) | LCCN 2023057268 (ebook) |
ISBN 9780197654842 (hardback) | ISBN 9780197654866 (epub)
Subjects: LCSH: Sexual minorities' writings, American—History and criticism. |
American poetry—Massachusetts—Boston—History and criticism. |
American poetry—California—San Francisco Bay Area—History and criticism. |
American poetry—Minority authors—History and criticism. |
American poetry—20th century—History and criticism. |
American poetry—21st century—History and criticism. |
Sexual minority authors—Massachusetts—Boston. |
Sexual minority authors—California—San Francisco Bay Area. |
Sexual minorities—Massachusetts—Boston—Intellectual life. |
Sexual minorities—California—San Francisco Bay Area—Intellectual life. |
LCGFT: Literary criticism.
Classification: LCC PS153.S39 G78 2024 (print) | LCC PS153.S39 (ebook) |
DDC 811/.540992066—dc23/eng/20240312
LC record available at https://lccn.loc.gov/2023057267
LC ebook record available at https://lccn.loc.gov/2023057268

DOI: 10.1093/oso/9780197654842.001.0001

Printed by Integrated Books International, United States of America

The manufacturer's authorised representative in the EU for product safety is
Oxford University Press España S.A. of el Parque Empresarial San Fernando
de Henares, Avenida de Castilla, 2 - 28830 Madrid (www.oup.es/en)

Every faggot poet fights then on two fronts. You can't just be a queer poet, you must destroy the existing profession of poetry. You can't just be a good queer 'citizen', you must destroy the state.

—Charley Shively, 'Poetry, Cocksucking and Revolution'

Contents

Acknowledgements	xi
Abbreviations	xiii

Introduction: 'Never by itself alone'	1
Prelude	1
Chapter Summaries	5
Why Boston and the Bay?	7
Methodology and Focus	13
Questions of Publication	18
From Homosexual Tradition to Queer Lineage	23
'meet their end upon the ground'	27

PART I BEGINNINGS (1944–1969)

1. 'Homosexuals in Society': Poetry and Gay Community in the 1940s	35
Introduction	35
'The Homosexual in Society': Gay Identity and the Future of America	38
The Young and Evil	38
'The mind's / natural jungle': Race, Sexuality, and Identity	43
'One day we'll see how a black man really feels'	46
'Creating New Worlds': The Berkeley Renaissance	49
The King's Two Cities	51
From the Renaissance to the Household	57
Coda: 'Being so far abroad from what he once was'	61
2. Identity and Community in the Work of Jack Spicer	65
Introduction	65
'What have I lost?': The Berkeley Renaissance and the Mattachine	66
Spicer in Boston	68
'Five Boston cats blowing their poetry REAL hard'	68
'Poetry is public property': the *Boston Newsletter*	70
'No place to turn': The Oliver Charming Notebooks	73
Sex and the Single Poem	77
The Heads of the Town up to the Aether: Spicer's Coming Community	78
Return to San Francisco and the Spicer Circle	78
'the figure of a person at once lost and unlikely'	79
'the city we create'	81

viii CONTENTS

Open Spaces: The Magazines of the Spicer Circle	84
'An Apparition of the Late J'	84
Love Poems and Protestant Letters: *Open Space*	87
Community and Negativity in Spicer's Final Work	90
'Alone we are dangerous': Community/Revolution	90
The *Pacific Nation*	91
'People are starving': *Book of Magazine Verse*	92
Messages from Actual Conditions: Spicer's Afterlives	95

3. The Occult School of Boston (i): 'Levels above and below'
(Ed Marshall and Stephen Jonas)

	97
'An occult school, unknown'	97
'A diabolical devout': The Case of Ed Marshall	98
'Leave the word alone it is dangerous'	102
'A covering and an unloading': *Hellan, Hellan*	105
'Dialogue against Dialogue': Stephen Jonas	108
'another excursion into fantasy': Jonas' 'anti-biographies'	108
'Remember me kindly': *Love, The Poem, The Sea*	110
'From one Martian to another': Jonas and Jack Spicer	112
'Boston Lingo' and the American Idiom	116
'one completed poem': Poetry and Love	122
'in hell / already': Jonas' later work	125

4. The Occult School of Boston (ii): 'Queer Shoulders at the Wheel'
(John Wieners and Gerrit Lansing)

	131
'never forget where we come from': John Wieners	131
Early Poems: Wieners in the *Boston Newsletter*	131
'a show of junkies, cocksuckers, THIEVES': Wieners and *Measure*	137
'It is my life you save': San Francisco and *The Hotel Wentley Poems*	139
Gerrit Lansing's Gay Age of Aquarius	143
'Exuberant and restless disorder': Gerrit Lansing in New York	143
'The Burden of *SET*'	145
'Naming is gaming'	148
Coda: 'Rise, Shining Martyrs'	150

PART II GAY LIBERATION IN BOSTON (1969–1983)

5. 'A Gay Presence': John Wieners, Charley Shively, and *Fag Rag*	157
'The most loathsome publication in the English language'	157
'acts of revolution': Charley Shively	160
'New love, encountered between strangers'	165
'Hacking, stuffing and reshelving'	167
'There's a certain kind of men'	169
'The Problem of Madness'	173

CONTENTS ix

6. 'My Real Name': Racial Framings, Queer Imaginings 178
   'no cosmic ribbon' 178
   'loving he and him': Prince-Eusi Ndugu 180
   Black and Queer: Adrian Stanford 183
   Stephania Byrd: 'violence not new / but old' 191
   'to strike the spirit of my history': Maurice Kenny's Queered Spaces 197
      Gay Appropriations 204

7. 'We cannot live without our lives': From the Combahee River
   Collective to *This Bridge Called My Back* 211
   Introduction 211
   Conditions: The Combahee River Collective 212
   1979 215
      'Why Did They Die?' 215
      'A Chorale for Black Woman Voices': Audre Lorde's 'Need' 218
   From Metaphor to Movement: *This Bridge Called My Back* 224
      This Bridge and Kitchen Table Press 224
      'Making some sense of the trip' 228
      'The Bridge Poem': Kate Rushin 230
   Conclusion: Bridges to the Future, Survivals of the Past 233

PART III BAY AREA COMMUNITIES: LESBIAN FEMINISM TO THE AIDS ERA (1969–PRESENT)

8. 'She Who': Judy Grahn and Bay Area Gay Women's Liberation 239
   'A very dangerous box to fall out of' 240
   Edward the Dyke as Gender Outlaw 241
   'On the Development of a Purple Fist' 245
   The Common Woman and a Common Poetics 250
   A Woman is Talking to Death 254
   'all the sides of it' 257

9. 'The first everything': Pat Parker 259
   '& a woman was born': Parker's Early Years 259
   Coming Out and Coming to Poetry 262
   Movements in Black 266
   'I have gained many sisters': 'Womanslaughter' 270
   'Where do you go to become a non-citizen?' 274
   Conclusion: On Simplicity, Class, and Literary Judgement 278

10. 'Blasting the true story into breath': Writing, Work, and Socialist
   Feminism 281
   The Third World Student Strike, the WWU, and Asian-American
      Lesbian Writing 281
   'we are the clatter of type / in your dreams': Poetry and Work 286

X CONTENTS

'Sitting at the Machine, Thinking'	286
'Do You Read What You're Typing?'	289
'Polymorphously Perverse'	292
'No One Immune'	294
11. New Narrative, New Communities from Left Write to AIDS	298
New Narrative and the Possibility of a Gay Left	299
'Gay Sunrise'	299
'A Community of the Future': *Century of Clouds*	301
Organizing for Unity: Left Write	304
'A village common producing images': New Narrative After Left Write	306
New Narrative in the Era of AIDS	312
Enola Gay	312
The Bathhouse in the Era of AIDS	314
Of AIDS and the Undead: *Real* and *The Letters of Mina Harker*	317
'I saw something I can't remember': Kevin Killian's *Argento Series*	319
Coda: 'When politics show'	323
'Inaudible substance of catastrophe'	323
The End of Gender, Coast to Coast	328
'To tell you stories'	330
Notes	335
Works Cited	353
Index	387

Acknowledgements

For years, the memory of a number of the poets I write about in this book has been kept alive by the dedication of poets and friends of poetry, whose efforts are exemplary models of scholarship and of love, often taking place outside the academy: in particular, I want to mention Jim Dunn and Raymond Foye for John Wieners, Peter Gizzi, and the late Kevin Killian for Jack Spicer, and Joe Torra for Stephen Jonas. I owe all of them thanks for their help in the research for this book. I also wish to thank David Abel, for sharing his research on Ed Marshall; Michael Bronski, for discussions of *Fag Rag* and the Good Gay Poets; Robbie Dewhurst, Jim Dunn, Raymond Foye, Francesca Lisette, Nat Raha, and Michael Seth Stewart, for sharing their work on John Wieners; Julie Enszer, for sharing work on Pat Parker and Lynn Lonidier; Laura Moriarty, for discussing her friendship with Karen Brodine, the Berkeley Poets' Co-Operative, and the foundations of Kelsey Street Press; David Rich, for sharing research on the 'Occult School' of Boston; Sam Solomon for sharing research on Karen Brodine; and Joseph Torra, for sharing research on Stephen Jonas. Particularly heartfelt thanks are due to Dodie Bellamy, Bruce Boone, Julie Enszer, Helen Gilbert, Judy Grahn, Robert Glück, Emily Woo Yamasaki, Merle Woo, and Nellie Wong for going through a draft of this manuscript, offering factual corrections and sparing my blushes further by spotting typos. For further discussion, friendship, and sharing of work over the years, I'd also like to thank Lisa Jeschke and Luke Roberts.

This project was supported through the award of a three-year British Academy Postdoctoral Research Fellowship at the University of Warwick, without which the book could not have been completed. My thanks to those who made the time at Warwick a pleasant one, including Daniel Katz, who acted as official mentor for this project, Emma Mason, Mark Storey, and Myka Tucker-Abramson, and to the students I had the pleasure to teach. Much-needed online writing company during the lockdowns of 2020 and 2021 was provided by the self-organizing British Academy Post-Doc Writing group (Birgit Arends, Micaela Canopoli, Christian Cooijmans, Dan Eltringham, Amelia Gully, Johnny Halls, Emily MacGregor, Charmian Mansell, Sofie Narbed, Daisy Ogembo, and everyone else).

Thanks to the following for their hospitality and company on archive visits to the United States in 2022: Gabe Barboza, Susan Bee, Charles Bernstein, Michael Bronski, Brandon Brown, Christina Chalmers, Norma Cole, Jim Dunn, Simon Eales, Ciáran Finlayson, Tonya Foster, Alison Fraser, Peter Gizzi,

Robert Glück, Rob Halpern, Catherine Kelly, Mitch Manning, James Maynard, Edric Mesmer, Aaron Shurin, Eric Sneathen, Steve Seidenberg, Alli Warren, and Carolyn White. Especial thanks to Tim Wilson and Andrea Grimes at the James C. Hormel LGBTQIA Center at the San Francisco Public Library; to James Maynard, Alison Fraser, and Edric Mesmer at the University of Buffalo; and to the librarians at UC Berkeley and Boston College. Thanks too to Phil Baber, Mark O. Chamberlain, Leila Kassir, and Jonathan Skinner for inviting me to give talks on work-in-progress; to Hannah Doyle, Ris Harp, Alex Rouch, and Jacqueline Wilson at OUP; to India Gray for copy-editing; to Dharuman Bheenan at Newgen Knowledge Works for facilitating revisions, typesetting and final corrections; and to the anonymous peer reviewers for their comments on this manuscript.

Early drafts of portions of Chapter 5 appeared in *Publishing Queer: Histories of Queer Publishing and Publishing Queer Voices*, edited by Leila Kassir and Richard Espley. My thanks to them. Permissions to reprint material are granted as follows. Extracts from *Century of Clouds* and *Bruce Boone Dismembered* printed by permission of Nightboat Books. All other work by Bruce Boone published by permission of Bruce Boone. Unpublished work by Karen Brodine courtesy of the copyright holder: Karen Brodine Papers, LGBTQIA Center, San Francisco Library. Extracts from *Work Week* by Karen Brodine by permission of Kelsey Street Press. Extracts from *Woman Sitting at the Machine, Thinking* by Karen Brodine by permission of Red Letter Press. Other work by Karen Brodine by kind permission of Helen Gilbert for the Estate of Karen Brodine. Work by Robert Glück used by permission of Robert Glück. Work by Judy Grahn used by permission of Judy Grahn. Work of Pat Parker © Anastasia Durham-Parker-Brady. All rights reserved. Used with permission. Work by Charley Shively printed by permission of the Estate of Charles Shively. Work by Jack Spicer used by permission of the Estate of Jack Spicer. Work by Adrian Stanford, Stephanie Byrd, and Maurice Kenny printed by permissions of *Fag Rag* and Good Gay Poets Press. Work by John Wieners printed courtesy the Literary Estate of John Wieners, Raymond Foye, executor. Work by Merle Woo used by permission of Merle Woo. Work by Nellie Wong used by permission of Nellie Wong. The cover art is a lithograph by Fran Herndon produced for the original edition of *The Heads of the Town up to the Aether* by Jack Spicer (San Francisco, CA: The Auerhahn Society, 1962). It is reproduced by kind permission of Jack Herndon for the Estate of Fran Herndon.

I am most grateful for all these permissions, freely and generously given in a way that makes the work of scholarship so much easier. For all other work not listed here, every effort has been made to contact the rightful owners with regards to copyrights and permissions. We apologize for any inadvertent errors or omissions. All other quotations fall inside the category of fair use.

Abbreviations

ASR	Judy Grahn, *A Simple Revolution*
AMT	Judy Grahn, *Another Mother Tongue*
BBP	Bruce Boone Papers, The Poetry Collection of the University Libraries, University at Buffalo, The State University of New York
CR	Consciousness Raising
D.O.B.	Daughters of Bilitis
FSP	Freedom Socialist Party
GWL	Gay Women's Liberation
KBP	Karen Brodine Papers, James C. Hormel LGBTQIA Center, San Francisco Public Library
RPCC	Revolutionary People's Constitutional Convocation
RW	Radical Women
SFSU	San Francisco State University
THA	Judy Grahn, *The Highest Apple*
This Bridge	*This Bridge Called My Back: Writings by Radical Women of Color*
UC Berkeley	University of California, Berkeley
WWU	Women Writers Union

Introduction

'Never by itself alone'

Prelude

In the winter of 1957, Jack Spicer wrote one of many letters to friend and fellow poet Robin Blaser. Both gay men, the two were part of an informal group of writers perched between bohemian, underground, academic, and political circles, whose work grew from their sexuality in ways that were open, experimental, and bold. The letter was addressed from San Francisco—where the two had met the previous decade—to Boston—where they had both worked as librarians in the summer of 1955—Spicer's letter accompanied copies of their mutual friend Steve Jonas' chapbook *Love, The Poem, The Sea, and other pieces examined by Steve Jonas*, the first publication of the newly formed White Rabbit Press, a small-press set up, at Spicer's encouragement, by a fourth friend (and unrequited love interest), Joe Dunn. Primarily, however, Spicer's letter concerns his recently completed sequence *After Lorca*, soon to be White Rabbit's second publication. Partially made up of translations of Lorca's work—some of which are in fact original poems disguised as translations—Spicer's *After Lorca* would be framed with an introduction 'by' the deceased Lorca—a victim of fascist, homophobic violence, and an iconic figure for the group—and concludes with a letter from Spicer to Lorca positing a future in which the two become 'special comrades', the latter Walt Whitman's term implying gay male sociability.[1] Spicer's letter to Blaser frames the Lorca sequence as an integral 'serial poem' or 'book', rather than a collection of stand-alone poems, in terms that are in equal parts textual and sexual.[2] In this important passage—from which the present study derives its title— Spicer sets out his vision of the serial poem poem with characteristic, double-edged ambiguity.

> [...] There is really no single poem.
>
> That is why all my stuff from the past [...] looks foul to me. The poems belong nowhere. They are one night stands filled (the best of them) with their own emotions, but pointing nowhere, as meaningless as sex in a Turkish bath. [...]
>
> Poems should echo and reecho against each other. They should create resonances. They cannot live alone any more than we can. [...]

Never By Itself Alone. David Grundy, Oxford University Press. © Oxford University Press 2024.
DOI: 10.1093/oso/9780197654842.003.0001

2 NEVER BY ITSELF ALONE

> A poem is never to be judged by itself alone. A poem is never by itself alone.
>
> (Spicer 2008, 163–64)

Though this passage appeared in an item of personal correspondence mailed in the usual manner, Spicer had already conceived the text as poetic.[3] It was, he explained to Blaser, to form part of *Admonitions,* a collection of poems dedicated to individual friends, lovers, and would-be lovers from his social and poetic circle, including Dunn, Blaser, and Robert Duncan. 'I will send you [*Admonitions*] when complete', he wrote, adding '(I have eight of them already and there will probably be fourteen including, of course, this letter.)' (Spicer 2008, 163). Though the completed *Admonitions* circulated among the poets to whom they were dedicated, the book itself would not be officially published until 1974, nearly a decade after Spicer's early death. In some ways the definition of a 'local' book, *Admonitions* constructs a textual community that also reflects on a real-life social grouping. Here, virtually anything is territory for the poem—from personal letters to pieces of intimate advice whose true readership is limited to the single reader who receives the poem's dedication (and admonition). Spicer joked in a previous letter to Blaser: 'Do you realize that this will become a literary document if you don't burn it?' (Spicer 1987, 32). Such writing deliberately transgresses boundaries of intimacy and address, reconfiguring a private letter as public address, prose as poetry, statement of poetics as poem itself, in a quicksilver play between art and life full of queered tension.

I will return in more detail to the audacious (homo)sexuality of this passage—its apparent opposition between Turkish baths, one-night stands, and other forms of commitment—later in this study. In Spicer's books to come, the poet negotiates spaces ever more clearly identified with a queer public life in San Francisco's North Beach, with the romantic disappointments he faced in often unrequited love affairs, and with poetry's capacity to both suture and expose the wounds of thwarted desire, grief, and loss that constituted the lived experience of the queer subject in mid-century America. In Spicer's work, the blurred distinction between textuality and sexuality serves as a kind of endlessly refracted hall of mirrors (the mirror is a favourite Spicerian image).[4] Spicer's 'serial poem' is a relational concept in which poems form part of sequences, or books, and each sequence connects to other sequences to form parts of a totality. The operating principle for the rest of his work, this concept is also suggestive for the entwined relations of publication, composition and community that this book will explore.

This study offers a collective history of postwar queer poetry communities in Boston and San Francisco, charting how poets, from the Second World War to the War on Terror, have built alternative communities informed by activism and constructed around small press publishing, shared intimacy, and literary experimentation. Between 1944—the date that Spicer's friend Robert Duncan wrote 'The Homosexual in Society', often adjudged to be the first piece of literary writing to frame its author as an out, gay person to be published in the United States—and the present day, queer poets in these two cities have explored new and experimental forms of sexual and textual community. Writers such as Spicer, Duncan, Blaser, John Wieners, Stephen Jonas, Judy Grahn, Pat Parker, Karen Brodine, Kevin Killian, Camille Roy, Dodie Bellamy, and Robert Glück have brought questions of community to the fore of their poems and poems to the fore of their communities. These writers have thought creatively about the contexts, means, and materials with which poetry is written, disseminated, and lived. Informed by queer activism, from early homophile organizations such as the Mattachine Society and the Daughters of Bilitis through to the Gay Liberation Movement and responses to the AIDS crisis, and by the publishing practices of what Donald Allen influentially dubbed the 'New American Poetry', along with the mimeograph revolution, the underground activist press, and contemporary, digital forms, they sought to fight loneliness, social stigma, addiction, queerphobic violence, and the vicissitudes of state legislation in ways that were often literally life-saving. Writing of the upsurge of activism, writing, and publication in the 1970s, Michael Bronski argues:

> The main purpose of [the Gay Liberation] movement—as it was for the other radical political and social movements of the time, particularly the Black Power movement and Radical Feminism—was to *save lives*. It's impossible to overstate the truth of this. The harm caused by anti-homosexual laws, policies, and policing; by abusive family relationships; by toxic religious dogma; and by psychological and physical harassment ranging from undermined self-confidence to outright murder is incalculable. (Bronski 2019, n.p.)

As one of those poets, John Wieners, put in when interviewed for *Gay Sunshine* in 1973:

> Any kind of freedom we now have in our lives was taking ground in the conversation and mores of involved writers and artists meeting in bars, museums, and lofts—out of bounds one might say. (Wieners 1986, 302)

Without such efforts, Wieners suggests, the Gay Liberation Movement might not have happened at all. Poetry—and the intense, loving, fraught, and fractured networks of poets, publishers, and writers that nourished and supported it—served as a means for queer people to articulate that which could not yet find political expression, and to create the shift in consciousness that helped bring those political means into being. And when mass movements of queer people changed the discourse and the material reality surrounding sexuality in

4 NEVER BY ITSELF ALONE

America, poetry remained a vital means of expression, amplifying the messages of coming out, gay pride, anti-imperialism, anti-sexism, and anti-racism, of 'smash the church, smash the state!' Importantly, poetry also served to address deeper questions of community formation, desire, and love—the ambivalences, contradictions, and complexities that political discourse is not always best equipped to express. This relation between poetry and life is a motivating factor in this study: the conviction that poetry matters, and that it matters in ways that are deeper, more long-lasting, and sometimes more frightening than the official record would have us believe.

This introduction begins by outlining the book's structure and summarizing the content of the individual chapters to follow. In the section, 'Why Boston and the Bay?', I explain the rationale for the study's focus on Boston and the San Francisco Bay Area, outlining links of friendship, influence, activism, and publication between groups of queer writers in these respective locations. I then turn to questions of methodology, further outlining the book's focus and, in particular, its attention to issues of gender and racialization. This section also clarifies the book's usage of terminology. While terminology, and with it, conceptualizations of identity, shifted over time, I argue that the distinction drawn by some critics between an earlier, 'gay' and 'lesbian' identity poetics, and a later, more fluid 'queer' writing is more apparent than real.[5] Too often, such a distinction imagines earlier history to be homogeneous, and then criticizes it for being homogeneous. On the contrary, I show how much of the poetry examined in this book reads as 'queer' before it could be named as such.[6] The book acknowledges and explores tensions between groups, whether in terms of gender, racialization, political, or literary outlook. It does so as part of a conviction that examining history in its messiness challenges reified narratives and identities in ways that are immensely useful for thinking about the present state of affairs. These poets' courageous conceptualizations of alternative, multi-layered identities—from the figure of the 'Martian' in the poetry of Jack Spicer and Stephen Jonas, to the 'proto-trans' gender identifications of John Wieners and Judy Grahn's 'Edward the Dyke'—complicate our sense of the literary and sexual history which this study will place at the forefront of its enquiry.

The following section outlines the book's focus on counter-institutions of publishing from the small press to the little magazine, and their relation to queer community both locally and in terms of nationwide (and internationalist) political movements. Drawing on Adrian Stanford's poem 'Sacrifice', the introduction next provides a theoretical framework drawing on notions of the radical archive and exploring questions of poetry and the queer past. Searching for predecessors—whether in what Robert K. Martin called 'The Homosexual Tradition in American Poetry', or in Sapphic Modernism—was frequently part of these writers' disparate methodologies. Yet they also challenged reified,

INTRODUCTION 5

essentialist notions of tradition, including gay tradition (notable here, for example, is Spicer's quarrel with Walt Whitman's 'damned Calamus'; Spicer 2008, 56). This section will ask whether it is possible to speak of a queer tradition as such, and what this might mean for the ways we conduct literary study of queer texts.

Chapter Summaries

The study has been organized into three parts, each of which, broadly speaking, covers a particular historical period. The first addresses early manifestations of queer poetic community in the pre–Gay Liberation era in both Boston and the Bay Area; the second, Boston-based Gay Liberation-era community; the third, Bay Area communities from 1969 to the present day. Within these three parts, the book's eleven chapters cover periods of roughly a decade, though the later chapters in particular address overlapping periods, attesting to the difficulties of chronologizing and compartmentalizing simultaneous and often cross-pollinating activity. While the study is primarily chronological, I am mindful that queer temporalities and queer histories rarely follow a straight line, and I seek to reflect this non-linearity and imbricated complexity in the form of the book as a whole. Influenced by the Spicerian conception of the serial poem, in which individual poems are always conceived of as part of a broader totality, readings of individual poems, poets, periods, and groups will overlap and call to each other throughout.

The first chapter focuses on Robert Duncan in the 1940s; the second on the Jack Spicer circle in the 1950s and early 1960s; the third and fourth on the Boston 'Occult School'. Moving forward to the post-Stonewall period, the fifth and sixth chapters turn to the work of the Fag Rag Collective in Boston; the seventh through to the tenth, to the development of lesbian poetics in Boston and San Francisco, including the activism of the Combahee River Collective, the work of Pat Parker and Judy Grahn, and of the socialist feminist poets Karen Brodine, Merle Woo, and Nellie Wong; the eleventh, to the work of the New Narrative writers and questions of community building and the response to AIDS in the 1980s. A coda addresses subsequent legacies into the twenty-first century.

The first four chapters of the study examine what John Wieners called the 'gay presence', hitherto largely excluded from histories of mid-century American poetry, whether the New American Poetry or the mimeograph revolution. The book begins with Robert Duncan's 1944 essay, 'The Homosexual in Society', arguably the first significant public defence of homosexuality in the United States. Reprinted several times during the era of Gay Liberation, Duncan's essay is nonetheless a contentious piece which also *critiques* existent forms of

6 NEVER BY ITSELF ALONE

gay identity Duncan had encountered within bohemian artistic communities in New York. Duncan's essay is thus a complexly useful way into theorizing questions of lineage and queer temporality, poetry, and the queer past. These opening chapters focus on the poets of the Berkeley and San Francisco Renaissance—particularly Duncan and Jack Spicer—and of the 'Occult School of Boston'—particularly John Wieners and Stephen Jonas—from the 1940s through to the 1960s. Examining publications such as the magazines *Boston Newsletter, J, Measure, Open Space*, and *Set*, these chapters will address the work of these writers as a group, focusing squarely on the queer political content of their work.

From chapter 5 onwards, the book moves to post-Stonewall writing and activist communities. The fifth chapter addresses the radical, Boston-based gay anarchist newspaper *Fag Rag*, founded in 1971, and the related Good Gay Poets collective, founded the following year, whose radical reconsideration of family, private property, and the state remain both ahead of their time and timely. Wieners was again centrally involved with both enterprises, and this chapter focuses on Wieners' own misunderstood poetry of this period, as well as the radical essays of key *Fag Rag* organizer and Wieners champion Charley Shively. In the sixth chapter, I examine the work of lesser-known poets Adrian Stanford, Prince Eusi-Ndugu, Stephania Byrd, and Maurice Kenny, whose work, again published by *Fag Rag* and the Good Gay Poets, in different ways addresses the problematics of self-framing as queer racialized persons within a predominantly white publishing and activist context. The seventh chapter addresses lesbian feminist poetry activism in Boston undertaken by women of colour: most notably, the Combahee River Collective. Addressing the anthology *This Bridge Called My Back*, I suggest links between such activism in the Boston area and concurrent work on the West Coast. Part III of the book focuses principally on the lesbian poetry communities that grew up in San Francisco around the Women's Press, Kelsey Street Press, the Women Writers Union, and other organizations. Chapters eight and nine pay attention to the work of Judy Grahn and Pat Parker in the 1970s, and chapter ten to that of Karen Brodine, Merle Woo, and Nellie Wong in the 1980s. The book's eleventh and final chapter turns to the 'New Narrative' writers, whose work emerged, again in San Francisco, in the 1970s and 1980s. Challenging disciplinary and class boundaries, the works of writers such as Steve Abbott, Bruce Boone, Robert Glück, Dodie Bellamy, and Kevin Killian exist in little magazines, academic journals, gay anthologies, and even porn magazines, audaciously mixing theoretical discourse drawn from the New Left, continental philosophy, and early queer theory with queer cultures centring on camp, gossip, promiscuity, friendship, and sex. The second half of the chapter addresses the increasing impact of AIDS on the New Narrative writers through to the 1990s. A coda turns to more recent work in the lineage of

INTRODUCTION 7

the communities addressed through the rest of the book, with brief case studies of work by Rob Halpern and Eileen Myles, and the editorial practices of Kevin Killian serving to focus the argument. I end with a meditation on the high stakes of scholarship on this material, as well as the position we now face, half a century after the Stonewall uprising and in a new era of pandemic, protest, and the resurgence of the far right.

Why Boston and the Bay?

In his important study, *The San Francisco Renaissance* (1989), Michael Davidson justified his focus on 'a regional literary movement', rather than on 'larger developments in American poetry during the same period', arguing that 'deterritorializing writers for the sake of shared aesthetic continuities [. . .] loses some of the vitality produced by region and community' (Davidson 1989, xiii). Not only this, but the condemnation of the 'local' as 'minor' is a tool by which canon formation reinforces sexual, gendered, raced, and class norms. Building on Davidson's work, I seek to trouble the cut-and-dried distinction between the 'local' and the 'national', and between 'minor' and 'major' literature through detailed analyses of the networks of underground publications, personal connection, and national influence that bely the limited focus of canonical studies on mainstream publication and institutional legitimation. My principal intention, however, is to re-centre sexuality as key to such accounts. Rendering sexuality as the modality that draws together these poets in their social lives and the poetry they produced helps produce a counter-canon. Yet, crucially, this alternative literary history also suggests that what draws these poets together is not a fixed category of sexual or textual identity. Rather, it is precisely in the relentless questioning and problematizing of the 'enabling fictions' of both canons and counter-canons, of sexual identities and the attendant and intersecting identities of class, gender, and race that surround them, that their work shares its closest kindship and finds its greatest strength.

But why specifically San Francisco and Boston? By the early 1970s, San Francisco, along with New York, was widely acknowledged as one of the prime locations for America's burgeoning Gay Liberation Movement. Between 1969 and 1979, more than 30,000 (predominantly male) gay people moved to San Francisco, a movement Michael Bronski compares to the African American great migrations of the 1930s as 'vital in remaking a minority culture' (Bronski 2011, 216; D'Emilio 1992, 74–95). Particularly in the post-Stonewall period, San Francisco has formed a key locale for queer community, with queer people migrating from around the country in search of refuge from violent and widespread discrimination. As Carl Wittman wrote in his influential *Gay*

8 NEVER BY ITSELF ALONE

Manifesto: 'We have fled here from every part of the nation [. . .] By the tens of thousands, we fled small towns where to be ourselves would endanger our jobs and any hope of a decent life' (Wittman, 3).[7] Focusing on San Francisco's queer poetic heritage has much to tell us about the city, and not only in the post-Stonewall moment. San Francisco developed as a focal point for queer activity in part because of the impact of the Second World War. War mobilization saw the increased proximity of same-sex interaction within the Army, Navy, and Air Force, and demobbed sailors within coastal towns extended intimations of queer desire into the formation of tentative, provisional, but tenuous communities within the city's bars, parks, and baths (D'Emilio 1992, 74–95). Twenty years earlier, a group of young poets—Spicer, Duncan, Blaser, and Landis Everson— had anticipated and laid the groundwork for the radical shift in consciousness in the broader culture through their literary activities. Associating through universities, left-wing political circles, and the city's queer social culture, for these poets, the questions of queer identity and literature could not be easily separated.[8] In some sense, literature provided grounds for expressing that which could not find a broader mode of expression elsewhere. At the same time, these poets were open about their homosexual desire, their defiantly 'out' work running counter to the model of excavating hidden meanings, encodings, and encryptions in texts that had to sublimate or disguise the love that dare not speak its name.[9] 'Nature barely provides for it. / Men fuck men by audacity', declared Robert Duncan in 'The Venice Poem' (1948) (Duncan 2019, 221). That such a proclamation was made, not only in print but also in public readings at the University of California's Berkeley campus, is, as Daniel Katz has noted, 'little short of astonishing' (Daniel Katz, 82).

Moving beyond the paradigm of the closet as model for both literature and queer life pre-Stonewall, the first two chapters focus on San Francisco in the 1940s and 1950s in order to excavate a particular mode of—at this stage predominantly—gay male expression that was frank, open, and frequently political. San Francisco has received scholarly attention as the site of the diverse currents that made up what's come to be known as the 'San Francisco Renaissance' during the 1950s and 1960s, and the significant queer presence within such currents has been stressed—to an extent. In particular, the publication of Allen Ginsberg's 'Howl' in the 1957 'San Francisco Scene' issue of *Evergreen Review*, along with his reading of the poem at the Six Gallery Reading two years earlier, has achieved near legendary status in the history of queer American literature.[10] Yet those expecting extended discussion of Allen Ginsberg—perhaps the most preeminent gay poet of his generation, and one who at a particular point in time was closely identified with San Francisco—will not find it here. Ginsberg's 1955 reading of 'Howl' at San Francisco's Six Gallery, along with the subsequent obscenity trial after the poem was published by City Lights Books, has gone down in queer lore, and the importance of Ginsberg's example for US gay poetry cannot be underestimated. Ginsberg lived in the city from 1954 to 1957 and, for this brief period, was an important San Francisco figure, an acquaintance and interlocuter of a number of the poets addressed here, Jack Spicer and John Wieners among them. But Ginsberg's reputation as part of the Beats means, firstly, that his work has been more widely covered than theirs; secondly, given the focus on heterosexual masculinity within the group, a Beat focus risks eclipsing the more explicitly or exclusively queer poetic communities, with which Ginsberg sometimes intersected, but which his celebrity has retrospectively covered over.[11] As poet and publisher James Mitchell remarks, the 'Howl' obscenity trial is 'another element that you have to add in this long process of San Francisco gay literature'. When asked, however, if he considers Ginsberg a Bay Area writer, Mitchell laughingly replies: 'No, of course not. It's interesting that he came and lived in Berkeley for a year or two, and that he wrote his masterpiece here. Ginsberg was always an influence, but nobody could write like him' (Mitchell 2018, n.p.). Jennifer Soong has recently written on Wieners and the figure of the 'minor poet' in relation to Ginsberg's foreword to Wieners' 1986 *Selected Poems*: Wieners himself archly remarked that what distinguished his work from the Beats—with which it was sometimes identified—was that they got famous and he did not (Soong, n.p.). Beyond any one example, however, this book aims explicitly to focus on writers excluded from standard accounts, accounts which I argue have failed to trace the through lines by which US queer poetry was actually shaped: those ties of poetic and political community sometimes overlapping, sometimes in contradiction, sometimes, almost, the same thing.

Behind the work of iconic queer poets like Ginsberg, then, lies a whole host of neglected histories of queer writing. Beginning with the controversial publication of Duncan's essay 'The Homosexual in Society' in 1944 and the meeting of Duncan, Jack Spicer, Landis Everson, and Robin Blaser as students at the University of California, Berkeley, three years later, and continuing through publications such as the 'Spicer circle' magazines *J*, *Open Space*, and White Rabbit Press, these poets, who half-jokingly dubbed themselves the 'Berkeley Renaissance' both anticipated and in some ways offered an alternative vision to the better-known 'San Francisco Scene' or 'San Francisco Renaissance' more influentially framed by the *Evergreen Review*. Sharing Ginsberg's leftism and queer openness, poets like Spicer were suspicious of Ginsberg's Whitmanesque visions of democratic community and apparent pursuit of literary fame, endorsing instead a local aesthetic of community, at once more intimate and more suspicious of theorizations of identity, intimacy, and democratic love. I turn to Spicer's poetic quarrel with Ginsberg at the end of the book's second chapter.

Meanwhile, in Boston—a conservative city, with a sharp disparity between the wealthy and the poor embodied in oppressive carceral institutions such as the State Capitol or the Charles Street jail, yet with a visible gay subculture

10 NEVER BY ITSELF ALONE

surrounding venues like the Playland bar or the cruising grounds on Boston Common—a group of poets with close ties to the San Francisco poets were also making their mark. While Boston is often read as a city dominated by conservative, racist, and homophobic elites—with the exception of the thriving queer, literary upper classes of Harvard, exhaustively chronicled by Douglas Shand-Tucci—a history from below provides us with a very different story (Shand-Tucci). For Boston was also a site of radical queer, anti-war, anti-imperialist, and anti-racist activism, from the sometimes contradictory activities of Boston Mattachine founder Prescott Townsend ('a political conservative on most issues', yet 'an intellectual and cultural radical', as Charley Shively put it), through to the far left Fag Rag and Combahee River Collectives (Shively 2002, 44). With close links to the San Francisco aesthetic developed by poets such as Duncan and Spicer, Boston in the 1950s and onwards saw the emergence of a queer, working-class poetics that—as Geritt Lansing's later punning coinage, the 'Occult School' of Boston, suggests—has been written out of history even more thoroughly than that of San Francisco (Lansing 1968, 6). But, in the words of Brent Hayes Edwards, reviewing Stephen Jonas' posthumous *Selected Poems*, 'Boston in this period, as much as San Francisco, was emphatically a *gay* Boston' (Brent Hayes Edwards, 260). Shaped by encounters with alternative modes of pedagogy and community—notably, Black Mountain College, where Wieners first met Duncan—and by a revelatory reading by the poet Charles Olson at the Charles Street Meeting House in 1954, Wieners, Jonas, and Ed Marshall established a close-knit community, later to include the visiting Blaser and Spicer and the irrepressible Lansing. With Jonas dispensing reading lists, books, wisdom, and illicit drugs from his apartment, whose window he left permanently open for friends and acquaintances to stop by, during the 1950s and 1960s the Boston poets enacted a more vernacular mode of poetry and poetics (Jonas 1994, introduction by Torra, 2). Purloining books from the public library, obtaining money through mail order fraud, and making use of illegal drugs, they embraced the mystical agencies they believed could be found in street life, criminality, and queer sociality, as I'll explore in the book's third and fourth chapters.

By contrast, the San Francisco poets were in part shaped by the university, meeting while students at Berkeley, where they fell under the influence of teachers such as poet Josephine Miles and scholars Leonard Wolf and Ernst Kantorowicz, the latter of whom provided a living link to the *George-kreis*, a homosexual poetic cult surrounding poet Stefan George in 1920s Germany, which—despite its dubious political valence—served as one model for gay poetic community. But they were equally shaped by anarchist and pacifist communities, World War II–era draft dodging, and the non-academic settings of the San Francisco Poetry Center and the underground artworld,

INTRODUCTION   11

manifesting in later attempts to organize artistic collectives such as the King Ubu Gallery or a proposed 'White Rabbit College' (see Jarnot, 126–28; Miriam Nichols, 100; Killian and Ellingham, 192–94). In such endeavours—and in later endeavours such as Robert Glück's workshops at the Small Press Traffic Bookstore in San Francisco and Jack Powers' Boston-based Stone Soup series, where Wieners taught a class on Massachusetts poetry—poetry, learning, and queer community were interlinked in ways that challenged the conservative clampdown on universities in the age of the Red and Lavender Scares. While Blaser would go on to a career as an academic, the younger poets more often than not fell afoul of the academy's literary and sexual conservatism.[12] Along with Kantorowicz, Spicer famously quit a teaching job at the University of California which would have required him to sign a nationalist 'Loyalty Oath'. Opposed to the stifling intellectual atmosphere increasingly governing academia, these poets also opposed the concomitant conservatism of a literary culture increasingly reliant on New Critical orthodoxy, as well as to the elite nature of much queer writing by upper-class men, which lacked a working-class sensibility.

This focus on class raises an important point. Readers may be more familiar with queer scenes in New York, which has assumed a far greater prominence in wider cultural depictions and literary-historical accounts. Boston and, in particular, San Francisco, however, were likewise important gay centres. Placed on both coasts, these cities thrived as queer spots during the geographical dispersal that, as John D'Emilio has argued, fostered the spread of separate queer communities in coastal cities to which sailors and others serving in the forces were based or disembarked (D'Emilio 2012). Boston was a city both with significant, racialized class disparities and a centuries-long history of political activism with the Transcendentalists, the abolition movement, and the labour movement. The scene of widespread gay migration in the post-Stonewall era, during which it came to be termed a 'gay mecca', San Francisco had also been the scene of significant social struggle, from conscientious objectors in the 1940s to Berkeley radicalism and the Black Panthers in Oakland in the 1960s and, in the 1970s, the fight against Proposition 8, the assassination of Harvey Milk, and the White Night Riots. Too often, accounts have treated the city's gay history and culture and its radical racial politics separately, but the radical, internationalist leftist side of the city's gay history has been emphasized in Emily Hobson's recent study *Lavender and Red*. Likewise, in Boston, the activities of the writers and collectives I address here, such as *Fag Rag* and the Combahee River Collective, emerge from a long lineage.

In literary terms, I do not propose in this book that the writers examined here—writers who lived, passed through, or were published in these cities—evince a single aesthetic of place akin to designations such as the 'San Francisco Scene'. However, the work examined here differs from that associated with New York. The New York School, for instance—one of the city's best-known queer poetry movements—evinced cosmopolitanism and intersections with the seats of economic and cultural power at the height of the Cold War. Boston and San Francisco poets, by contrast, emphasized regionalism, which at times evinced a radical breaking away from US cultural values (Jack Spicer's notion of a breakaway 'city state', for instance), or figured themselves in relation to struggles at once local and national, as in the work of the Combahee River Collective, who fought violence against women in Boston in conjunction with poets based outside the city, such as Audre Lorde.

For a poet such as Jack Spicer, who spent some time in New York, the queer poetries that flourished there offered a vision sharply marked off from the working-class focus of Boston poetry. During the 1950s and 1960s, the poets of the 'Berkeley Renaissance' and the 'Occult School' of Boston had many connections to New York and to better-known queer poetry scenes around the poets of the New York School or countercultures around figures such as Ginsberg. Their world, however, was often different: marginal to or even, in Spicer's case, opposed to an aesthetic more closely tied—in the case of the New York School— to the artworld. What the poets of Boston and San Francisco offer that existing accounts of New York queer writing—at least in this nascent phase—do not, is a profoundly class-based perspective: one which knows that what Wieners called 'a poetry of the lower class', is doubly sometimes quadruply, marginalized for reasons of class, gender, race, and sexuality. This book thus puts forward an alternative set of geographical coordinates and literary landmarks: from Duncan's 'The Homosexual in Society' to the *Boston Newsletter*, Wieners' *Hotel Wentley Poems* to *Fag Rag*, Judy Grahn's *Edward the Dyke* to Pat Parker's *Child of Myself*, the Combahee River Collective Manifesto to *This Bridge Called My Back*. By doing so, it provides a new angle on the queer poetic communities that have thrived throughout the United States and an important corrective to decades of historical erasure. Focusing on these two cities enables close attention to the development of specific communities, which in turn shows that the 'local' is never merely local: a metonymic approach whereby the local leads to the national and international. Such examples, along with the emergence of the Combahee River Collective in Boston—a movement now central to the spread of the term 'identity politics', with great ramifications for the political organizing and theory of the past few decades—suggest that the intersections of race, class, gender, place and, most crucial of all, poetry, might be adapted and extended towards a whole host of societal formations that extend well' to 'race, class, gender, place and poetry might be extended towards a whole host of societal formations that extend well beyond the boundaries of any one city or any one time period.

INTRODUCTION   13

Methodology and Focus

The approach deployed throughout this study is in equal parts textual, literary historical, theoretical, and archival. Rather than providing a contextual background to removed textual objects, subsuming text to context or context to text, I argue that socialization takes place within the language of the poems themselves and that reading these poems can sharpen and deepen accounts of queer socialities in America more broadly. On the one hand, my approach focuses on close readings of texts too often only glanced at in a cursory manner. At the same time, I seek to pay attention to the contexts in which texts appeared: to the material history of those texts, as well as to the texts in and of themselves. Consequently, a significant focus will be on counter-institutions of publishing and the relation of publication to queer community, both locally and in terms of national currents. These publications—from privately distributed chapbooks, newsletters, and little magazines to newspapers with much larger print-runs—frame these texts in ways that have been little explored, and I aim to show how such framings contribute to our understanding of the poetic work printed within them. I also draw on other material that remains uncollected and unpublished, from correspondence and from other ephemeral projects, as part of the less public, but no less collective, social context for these poems. Attention to radical archives emerges in part from a historicist practice, yet, as the innovative scholarship of Saidiya Hartman and others has recently shown, such a practice must recognize the historical omissions sometimes violently performed by the archive, and its framing by normative goals.[13] Rather than foreclose or conclude such work, viewing it as only a manifestation of past ephemera, I argue that reconstructing its milieu, both through archival recovery and through working with the poems' language, can open up ways of understanding the world that also point towards an unrealized future.

Focusing principally on literature and on literary history, this study nonetheless aims to show how activism is built into the core of these poems' formal operations, avoiding rigid separation between politics and art, art and lived experience, in the hope that it might be of aid, not only to literary scholars of the 'New American Poetry' and American experimental writing more broadly, but also to scholars of queer history and activism recovering the radical critique of society advanced by these poets. In doing so, it draws on prior scholarship, including Kevin Killian's work on Spicer and the Mattachine Society; poet-scholar Nat Raha's vital research on John Wieners and *Fag Rag*, which has crucially helped reposition Wieners' critical legacy in the context of Gay Liberation; Julie Enszer's exhaustive work on lesbian publishing and poetics; Michael Bronski's and Amy Hoffman's scholarly recovery of the 1970s Boston activist context of which they were participants; and Emily Hobson's *Lavender and Red*, a

14   NEVER BY ITSELF ALONE

historical survey of queer activism in San Francisco and a key work of historical recovery, re-situating queer activism within a context of internationalist, anti-racist politics.[14] Groups of the 1940s and 1950s like the Berkeley Renaissance, the Spicer circle, or the 'Occult School' of Boston may have functioned in some ways as coteries, but they were also part of broader movements, including the nascent gay activism of the Mattachine Society and other anarchist and left-wing organizations, anticipating the concerns given a broader base in the activism of succeeding decades. Accounts of Gay Liberation rightly draw attention to the major shift in consciousness, militancy, and public visibility occasioned by the July 1969 Stonewall street rebellion. At the same time, as Susan Stryker notes, too firm a distinction between 'pre-Stonewall' and 'post-Stonewall' overlooks the years of prior activity which enabled a local incident to have such a widespread impact. Similar acts of protest against extortionate and exclusionary bars—what Stryker calls 'militant foreshadowings'—occurred in Los Angeles (1959), Philadelphia (1965), and San Francisco (1966). Thus, 'Stonewall stands out as the biggest and most consequential example of a kind of event that was becoming increasingly common, rather than as a unique occurrence' (Stryker 2008, 82). Likewise, before the official emergence of Gay Liberation, queer activists had participated in feminist, New Left, and Black Power movements as members of the Freedom Riders, the Berkeley Free Speech Movement, the Black Panthers, the Young Lords, and Students for a Democratic Society (SDS) (Avicolli Mecca 2009, x). While mainstream homophile activism remained geared towards respectability politics, key activists and writers of the post-Stonewall generation such as Pat Parker and Judy Grahn had prior experience of the repressive forces of the state both in political organizing connected to civil rights and the harassment faced in their 'private lives'. Post-Stonewall groups like the Fag Rag collective combined the intimacies of local activism with the internationalist focus of a broader revolutionary project, seeing no contradiction between—for example—the abstruse, oblique, experimental poetry of John Wieners' later work and a popular anarchist programme for total liberation. Meanwhile, for poets such as Parker and Grahn, groupings surrounding lesbian literary and political publications—the women's bookstores at which poetry readings were held, women's health centres and women of colour sports teams, or modes of political radicalism associated with far-left groups like the Weather Underground—were part of a broad project for transformation inseparable from lived experience and inseparable from the work of poetry.[15] Likewise, for the New Narrative writers of a subsequent generation, left-wing, queer, and anti-racist activism took its places alongside 'transgressive' literature, pornography, and the emerging academic, theory-focused scholarship of feminism, psychoanalysis, and Marxism, as well as the emerging need to preserve, defend, and refigure community in the face of the devastation wrought by AIDS.

INTRODUCTION 15

Key to this book is the attempt to link both gay and lesbian poetry collectives in these cities and to address in detail the resultant intersections and tensions relating to class, race, and gender identity. Drawing the relatively extensive critical work on gay male poets such as Spicer and Duncan into a discussion of the relatively neglected field of lesbian writing in Boston and the Bay Area adds a crucial dimension missed in many existent studies, which tend to segregate into work on *either* lesbian *or* gay movements but which rarely bring them together. Gay male writers of the earlier generation took inspiration from lesbian modernists like Gertrude Stein and, most notably, H.D., an inspirational figure for Robert Duncan, as indicated in his unfinished life's work, the critical study *The H.D. Book*. Meanwhile, John Wieners identified himself, both in terms of literary inspiration and a more general identification, with a feminine tradition, from the iconic presence of Hollywood film stars, through to the queer lyric poems of Edna St. Vincent Millay or the recordings of singers such as Billie Holiday. But gay women were not generally part of these poets' *social* scenes, although heterosexual women were (Joanne Kyger, Carolyn Dunn, Helen Adam, and Rosario Jiménez are notable examples). It's thus not until a later period that we see the development of lesbian poetry communities of a similar scale or visibility. While Judy Grahn published pseudonymous work in *The Ladder*, the newsletter of the Mattachine Society's lesbian sister branch, the Daughters of Bilitis, the journal's conservative focus made it impossible to publish her more politically radical or formally experimental work, and there were few other venues available. Poets such as Grahn and Parker thus initially emerged from activist and writing communities associated with the Black Arts, Civil Rights, and Women's Liberation Movements, pioneering the collective self-organization of lesbian writers only once Stonewall had made broader lesbian organization possible.

My intention is not, therefore, to downplay the tensions that sometimes existed between gay and lesbian groupings, or the male dominance of earlier published traces within and outside the New American Poetry. Rather, it is to tell a broader story, in which the relations between gay, lesbian, and heterosexual groupings might be analyzed as part of a linked narrative. Thus, throughout this study, I have used the term 'queer' to signify both gay and lesbian practices, as well as self-identifications which might go beyond the conventional significations implied by those terms, and their anticipation of the expanded sense of identity which 'queer' came to designate at a later date. There are historical ramifications here. As Linda Garber has persuasively argued in her work on lesbian feminist poetries, *Identity Poetics*, rather than a split between the simple, essentialist binary designated 'gay' or 'lesbian' and the subsequent, anti-essentialist fluidity of the term 'queer', it's possible to trace the expanded potentials of 'queer' well before these were enshrined in academic discourse. Eric Sneathen, for instance, notes that Teresa de Lauretis coined the term 'queer theory' occurs in the same

16 NEVER BY ITSELF ALONE

1991 issue of the journal *Differences* as the first scholarly piece on New Narrative writing by Earl Jackson, Jr., while John Wieners' gender 'deviancy' has been read by contemporary poet-scholars Nat Raha and Tim Trace Peterson as 'proto-trans' (Sneathen 2019, n.p.; de Lauretis 1991; Earl Jackson 1991; Raha 2015, 2018, 2019; Trace Peterson 2013, 21). I thus use 'queer' to suggest the potentialities present from the earliest period of this study: acknowledging the presence of essentialism, binary thinking, gay misogyny, and other problematic elements reflective of their times, I also note that these writers often—though not unanimously—rejected modes of gay and lesbian activism that reduplicated conventional gender roles, such as the more conservative wings that took over Mattachine and the Daughters of Bilitis. Instead, they insisted that the nuclear family and the institution of gender itself were in need of dismantling, and stressed the historical construction of sexual discourse. This said, at certain points, my usage reflects contemporaneous usages of the terms 'gay'—both to mean 'gay male' and as a more general term for non-heterosexual orientation—and 'lesbian', as well as citing other terminologies, often reclaimed from hate speech, such as 'faggot', 'dyke', 'fairy', 'queen', and 'bulldagger'.[16] The origins of such usages, and their placement within source material, my own terminology, and the terminological conventions of the critical field as it currently stands, will be indicated where appropriate at individual points.

This study also proposes an intervention in literary historiography by foregrounding the role of queer writers of colour within these contexts and by critically addressing racial discourse in writing by white artists and activists. Existing literary studies of the Spicer circle, the Berkeley Renaissance, and New Narrative have tended to overlook the key question of racialization, save for passing mentions. Yet, as indicated by the fact that many groups of writers and mainly queer organizations—particularly early homophile groups—could deploy race as *comparison*, rather than as simply part of the struggle, such groups were constituted predominantly of white members. The first chapter will address the problematic use of racialized language in Robert Duncan's early figurations of homosexuality, and the third will explore the ways in which Stephen Jonas—a poet whose racialization remains highly ambiguous—was interpellated in the discourse of the poets around him. During the 1960s in particular, the Bay Area was a key scene of Black Radicalism, most famously in the activity of the Black Panther Party for Self-Defense. Racialized struggles were often invoked as points of comparison, contrast, solidarity, and defence by early homophile organizations, and these comparisons were all the more frequently invoked as Gay Liberation spread. Particularly during the upsurge of open assertions of queer identity during the 1970s, more emphatic statements of framing oneself as equally a racialized and a queer person came to the fore. As well as a critical analysis of the discourse of earlier, white-dominated communities, this study stages a recovery of neglected figures who participated in these or in adjacent scenes. In 1977, Boston saw the drafting of the Combahee River Collective statement by Barbara Smith, Demita Frazier, and Beverly Smith—a statement that arose from collective discussions dating back to 1974 and involving poets Stephania Byrd, Audre Lorde, and Cheryl Clarke, among others. We cannot understand the work that emerged from this period without taking into account the work of Black feminists, of queer women, and of men and trans people of colour, both as part of a general theoretical and activist background and as poets and writers involved in creating new conceptions of resistance, community, and literary practice.

However, as Darius Bost has recently argued, despite the representational shift slowly being made through current discourses of anti-Blackness within and outside the academy, queer subjects of colour are less often included within such schemata. For Bost, 'black gay bodies often signify as absence and negation in dominant scholarly and popular chronologies of antiblack violence, slavery, lynching, mass incarceration and police brutality', subject to a further 'marginalization within the black community [that] intensifies that precarity' (Bost, 14). Likewise, Robert Reid-Pharr has argued that the category of 'Black' bids for inclusion in the liberal nation-state by violently othering the figure of the Black queer, as scapegoat, a sign of chaos and crisis which creates boundaries around Blackness which whites can recognize (Reid-Pharr 1996, 373). The default understanding, both within white-dominated gay groupings, and Black radical groups, of homosexuality as 'white'—or, as in influential homophobic fantasies such as those presented in Eldridge Cleaver's *Soul on Ice*, as oriented towards whiteness—excludes blackness from the category of the homosexual, performing a double erasure (see Cleaver, 100–103). Such exclusions resonate all the more for female and non-cis queers. As the title to Akasha Gloria Hull, Patricia Bell-Scott, and Barbara Smith's crucial 1982 anthology sardonically put it, *All the Women Are White, All the Blacks Are Men, but Some of Us Are Brave*. Given this, across the book, I devote significant attention to poets of colour, including Stephen Jonas, Maurice Kenny, Pat Parker, Merle Woo, Adrian Stanford, Stephania Byrd, and Prince-Eusi Ndugu, along with the vital role of collective endeavours such as the Combahee River Collective and Kitchen Table Press. In many instances, these are the first extended critical discussions in print: a state of affairs that beggars belief. While, at times, these writers were fetishized and exoticized by the white writers who surrounded them—it is' to 'them. It is, however,' undeniable that, whether in confluence with or separate to white writers, they were also key figures in building a more genuinely diverse movement, and it is imperative that any study such as this places the questions their work raises at the forefront of its enquiry.

18 NEVER BY ITSELF ALONE

Questions of Publication

As suggested in the reading of the Jack Spicer's letter-cum-prose poem which opened this introduction, much of the work examined in the following book complicates, problematizes, and expands our sense of the material status of poetic texts. In making acts of intimate address public, these texts were also subject to censorship, a lack of material resources, and the force of circumstance of precariously lived lives. Often self-published in little magazines, small-press chapbooks, and even more ephemeral documents that circulated among specific social communities, such work has left material traces that are often tenuous, ephemeral, and subject to erasure. A key act of recovery staged by this book is thus to examine the counter-institutions of publishing by which these writers disseminated, circulated, and preserved their ideas. At a time when queer material could or would not be published by larger presses—at a time, indeed, when such material was illegal—it was through the small-scale, locally focused magazines created by the poets themselves that community could be built, linking small, but diverse groups of often queer poets across the country. The *samizdat*, small-press activity of presses, pamphlets, magazines, and anthologies encompassed both the poetry and activist worlds, manifesting a politics that rejected the false populism of heteropatriarchal American 'democracy' for a counterinsurgency of ink, paper, and type.

The opening chapters address the smaller, 'coterie' products of the Boston 'Occult School'—the *Boston Newsletter, Measure*, and *SET*—and the publications of the Spicer circle—White Rabbit Press, *J, Open Space*, and *Capitalist Bloodsucker*—alongside activist-focused magazines and newspapers such as *One* and *The Ladder*. In the book's later chapters, I address newspapers of the post-Stonewall period such as the San Francisco–based *Gay Sunshine* and the Boston-based *Fag Rag*, which provided crucial resources in cities marked by wealth disparity, gentrification, and the queerphobic hostility encapsulated in popular narratives by the murder of Harvey Milk. Many gay and lesbian activists at this time were turning to poetry in particular as a form of self-expression and consciousness raising, seeing an important continuity between their poetic and political activity. During the early 1970s, *Fag Rag*, its pages exploding with a polyvocal exploration of a revolutionary politics of sexuality and debates around politics, strategy, gentrification, and gender performance, placed poetry—particularly that of John Wieners—at the centre, and a related press—the Good Gay Poets—began to publish full-length books and chapbooks. These are key documents of the new gay and lesbian poetics. In San Francisco, the Women's Press Collective and the slightly later Kelsey Street Press performed similarly vital roles, in conjunction with feminist bookstores which provided much-needed distribution and served as venues

INTRODUCTION   19

for community-building readings. Likewise, New Narrative magazines such as *Mirage*, *No Apologies*, and *Soup* brought together writers from several different communities to further explore the intersections of sexually explicit queer writing, radical left-wing politics, and formal experimentation. Through foregrounding these publications, my intention is to show how publication contributed, both to a sense of queer community in particular cities and neighbourhoods, and, increasingly, to a unified, nationwide sense of collective belonging, in the Gay Liberation Movement, in the development of lesbian feminism, and in the face of the AIDS crisis. Such publications have continued to inspire the work of later writers—from Renee Gladman's *Clamour: A Dyke Zine* (1996–1999) to Evan Kennedy's Dirty Swan Projects (2010–present), Jamie Townsend's *Elderly* (2013–present), and Elana Chavez's and Tatiana Luboviski-Acosta's Cantíl reading series ('Featured Organization: Cantíl'; Troyan, n.p.).

Anthologies mark another crucial way poets and activists of a later generation strove to make links to earlier writers. These publications, which often conducted historical overviews as a means of constructing a gay and lesbian tradition, served functions that were both recuperative and forward looking. Bringing the work of gay forebears together, they gave their works a new context, seeing in them the seeds of their own new, politicized understanding in a manner that could not always be articulated, and finding in them modes of linguistic articulation that anticipated and in some senses enacted a radically transformed society. Notable here are Winston Leyland's anthology of gay men's poetry, *Angels of the Lyre*, published in 1975 as the first publication of Leyland's San Francisco-based Gay Sunshine Press; the joint issue of the *Gay Sunshine* newspaper and *Fag Rag*, published on the fifth anniversary of the Stonewall uprising the previous year; *Woman to Woman*, a collectively edited anthology (editors included Judy Grahn and Wendy Cadden), published by the Women's Press Collective in 1970; and *Amazon Poetry: An Anthology*, edited by Joan Larkin and Elly Bulkin in 1975, and republished in an expanded version as *Lesbian Poetry: Anthology* in 1981. During the beginning of the following decade, anthologies such as Gloria Anzaldúa and Cherríe Moraga's *This Bridge Called My Back*; Akasha Gloria Hull, Patricia Bell-Scott, and Barbara Smith's *All the Women Are White, All the Blacks Are Men, but Some of Us Are Brave* (1982); Barbara Smith's *Home Girls* (1983); and Michael J. Smith's *Black Men / White Men: A Gay Anthology* (1983) were also significant repositories of work by gay and lesbian poets regarding the intersections of gender, sexuality, and race. Through the first post-Stonewall decade, these anthologies helped emerging writers see themselves as part of a broader tradition and give coherence to the sometimes disparate activities of local queer writers. Michael Bronski, himself a member of the Fag Rag collective, writes:

20 NEVER BY ITSELF ALONE

> In the years immediately after Stonewall, the outpouring of gay male writing, particularly poetry, was a seismic event that literally, and literarily, reshaped gay male consciousness, language, and sense of self.
>
> Nationally, hundreds of queer newspapers, small magazines, literary journals, chapbooks, and broadsides appeared. Some short stories and essays were published, but the overwhelming majority of the work that gay liberation produced was poetry. (Bronski 2019, n.p.)

This outpouring would have been unthinkable in previous decades, and it involved the creation, not only of a new gay literature, but also of institutions to publish it. Of the anthologies listed above, it's notable that the majority were produced through gay-run small presses rather than major publishing houses. Queer poetry publications were often put out by collectively organized groups in ways that sought distribution through alternative channels—gay and feminist bookstores, distribution at conferences and other events—aimed, not at success in the literary mainstream or at the 'general reader' or 'wider audience' there courted, but at participating in and building specific sexual communities. As such, they built on the work of earlier decades, charted in the opening chapters of this study. As Julie Enszer has recently suggested:

> I think sometimes we fall into these historical narratives thinking the '70s were the revolutionary period. We have ideas about what it meant to be gay or lesbian in the mid-century of the United States. I think those ideas are only a partial picture of what was happening. (Halley, n.p.)

The centrality of the New York School to standard accounts of queer US poetry communities has come at the detriment of some of the most powerful poetic work produced since 1945. Correcting our overarching narrative, as well as giving due credit to major poets across two generations, expanding our sense of what queer poetry in the United States looked like beyond the New York School, while also revealing how queer poetry changes our narrative of North American poetry in general. While much work has been done on the 'mimeograph revolution' of the 1950s and 1960s, as well as the explosion of little magazines and chapbook publications by writers associated with Black Mountain College, the New York School and other groupings, the significant presence of Black publications such as *Umbra*, *Dasein*, and *Free Lance* is invariably overlooked in such surveys: so too, the queer presence within this movement is frequently elided. Yet it's an undeniable fact that gay men who wrote explicitly queer poetry and often formed networks of association, publication, and support were central to the currents now known as the New American Poetry. Donald Allen, the editor of the groundbreaking anthology of the same name was himself gay, and his anthology includes explicitly queer work by Robert Duncan, Jack Spicer, John Wieners, Robin Blaser, Frank O'Hara, and Allen Ginsberg, though the anthology prints few women and only one poet of colour (Amiri Baraka, then LeRoi Jones). Allen's anthology represented a turning point in the visibility of such currents, yet it is only the tip of the iceberg. More ephemeral publications— magazines, chapbooks, and other works—were produced at a prodigious rate in these two cities as the 1950s wore on: the magazines *Boston Newsletter*, *Open Space*, *J*, *Measure*, *SET*, *Capitalist Bloodsucker*, and the presses White Rabbit Press and Enkidu Surrogate. In the post-Stonewall moment, these served in part as inspiration for the wave of new magazines such as *Amazon Quarterly*, *Dykes and Gorgons*, *Gay Sunshine*, *Manroot*, and *Sebastian Quill* (San Francisco and Oakland), *Lavender Vision*, and *Fag Rag* (Boston), and the presses Good Gay Poets, Gay Sunshine Press, and the Women's Press. Many of these newer endeavours explicitly drew on the work of the earlier generation: *Fag Rag* reprinted Robert Duncan's 1944 essay 'The Homosexual in Society' in an early issue, while Judy Grahn's 'The Psychoanalysis of Edward the Dyke', written in the mid-1960s, was finally published as a chapbook by the Women's Press Collective in 1971, serving as a vital model for thinking about the disciplinary apparatus of psychiatry, gender normativity, and queer sexuality that was witty, satirical, and experimental in its form.

The literary magazines of the 1970s also drew inspiration in terms of format, style, and experimentalism from the more established magazines of the preceding decade such as *Poetry* and the *Paris Review*, as well as the experimental *Evergreen Review* and countercultural papers such as the *Berkeley Barb* and the *East Village Other*. Also of significance were the publications of the Black Arts Movement, in which poets such as Baraka combined the traditions of small press poetry publication with those of the radical pamphleteer and the Black Radical Tradition: notably, Baraka's own Jihad Productions (subsequently People's War), Dudley Randall's Broadside Press, and Haki Madhubuti (Don L. Lee)'s Third World Press (Madhubuti was a particular influence on Pat Parker (Parker 2016, introduction by Grahn, 20)). Yet, as Bronski notes, the new gay journals, whatever inspiration they took from existing countercultural and radical literary publications, also 'saw themselves as decisively breaking from non-gay journals' (Bronski 2019, n.p.). Though magazines such as *Evergreen* and the associated Grove Press printed work by gay writers—John Rechy, Jean Genet, and William Burroughs—such material in this context appeared through distorting and sensationalized frames. 'In an almost entirely heterosexual context, this work would have felt exploitative and culturally adrift. Lesbian and gay writers argued they did not need, nor want, the mainstream literary world (most of which would never print their work anyway). Gay art and literature had to create its own context, they declared' (Bronski 2019, n.p.). Increasingly, such publications

22 NEVER BY ITSELF ALONE

also blurred the lines between 'literary' journals and the 'non-literary' purview of activism, community news, and other art forms. The more activist-focussed *Fag Rag*, for instance, published a significant amount of poetry, along with news on Gay Liberation struggles in Boston, pieces on global politics, letters, and pornographic or quasi-pornographic artwork; Bay Area lesbian newsletter *Onyx* printed 'poems, drawings, political perspectives, photographs, book reviews, event listings, personals, and some business listings'.[17] In turn, publications such as *Fag Rag* and *Gay Sunshine* saw the first publications of writers associated with New Narrative writing, who, at the turn of the following decade, then went on to found their own magazines, often drawing on the audacious blend of gossip, erotic art, poetry, essays, and activist writing found, particularly in *Fag Rag*: a confluence that thus far remains largely underexamined. During the 1980s, *No Apologies*, *Mirage*, and *Soup* printed work that might veer from dense academic essays, replete with the terminology of Althusser, Voloshinov, and Marx, to passages of appropriated pornographic prose, printing in-progress work by writers like Killian, Bellamy, Glück, and Boone alongside tributes to Spicer, Wieners, Duncan, or Grahn.

Such publications also challenged the increasing focus in more mainstream gay magazines such as *The Advocate* on what was seen as a more conservative political stance, abandoning cross-issue commitments to radical politics in favour of limited civil rights gains and a more limited focus on identity issues. The sixth issue of *Fag Rag*, for example, includes an open letter to *The Advocate* over sensationalist coverage of gay criminality, describing the publication as 'on the defensive' that 'depend[s] on the establishment', and concluding: 'You want to be "gay" sexually and straight in everything else' (Fag Rag Collective 1973). Likewise, Merle Woo recalls: 'Careerists like David Goodstein, the wealthy owner of *The Advocate*, a tabloid for gay males, began to mold a tasteful, moderate image of gays that would be acceptable to non-gay sympathizers within the Democratic Party [. . .] These professional queers advocated the notion that lesbian and gay rights must be approached slowly in cautious little stages. Radicals and militants must be denounced and discredited' (Merle Woo 2009, 286). While New Narrative writer Steve Abbott—whose tireless proselytizing on behalf of queer and experimental art occurred across numerous venues—occasionally published in *The Advocate*, such cases were the exception rather than the rule. If one of the principal aims of post-Stonewall queer publishing was to establish a viable publication network outside the scope of the heterosexual mainstream, in turn, within queer culture, formally experimental writing and magazines established their own spaces as a direct challenge to the politics of larger queer publications. Rather than simply the product of alienation and isolation, in the pre-Stonewall phase, or of failing to reach a broader audience and a mass movement in the post-Stonewall phase, the marginality, ephemerality, and apparent obscurity of

INTRODUCTION   23

such publications in fact indexes their refusal of conservative, recuperative, and careerist modalities antithetical to their formal and political aims. Such aims ultimately envision not merely a different sort of literature or a different sort of publishing but an entirely transformed society—one whose creation requires that, in the words of the Boston Gay Liberation Front, 'resources and power must be taken from straight, white, heterosexual men and redistributed among the people' ('Boston GLF').

From Homosexual Tradition to Queer Lineage

The act of recovering ephemeral publication traces raises further questions about how and why one might construct alternative, counter-institutional and counter-canonical lineages, traditions and through-lines of queer writing. Designed to be accessible, cheaply, or even freely, available, such publications are now often accessible only in the institutional setting of university archives or at vastly inflated prices within the second-hand book trade. This gap between modes of publication which in different ways challenged the frameworks of copyright, cultural capital, and poetry-as-property and the more institutional access negotiated by contemporary scholars raises further methodological questions which this section seeks to outline in brief. In turn, these suggest broader problematics facing the very idea of queer lineage or queer tradition. Christopher Nealon has argued that 'in one sense, queer and tradition are entirely opposed: queerness is the very opposite of tradition, inasmuch as tradition involves the assembly of a single narrative of birth and development and serves the function of certifying forms of authenticity [. . .] hegemonic, univocal, all the more defensive for being based on historical wishes and half-truths (Nealon 2008, 617). Given this, previous attempts to formulate a gay tradition—most notably, Robert K. Martin's 1979 *The Homosexual Tradition in American Poetry*—risk creating a conception of gay tradition that is monovocal, linear, and progressive, a celebration of 'universal brotherhood grounded in the sexual affection between men' which both silences and projects onto women as 'secondary and convenient' and tends towards a 'touristic relation to the slice of the global south it cruises' (Nealon 2008, 620). For Brian Teare, the very idea of a poetic tradition rests on the 'heterosexist metaphor' of the family, a hegemonic construct entwined with attendant, exclusionary understandings of race, nation, and gender (Teare, 83–84). 'Who benefits most from a definition and practice of gay poetic tradition?' Teare asks:

Gay poets who, in mimicking the hegemonic structure of a heterosexist literary tradition, create community, history, and self-acceptance? Or the

24   NEVER BY ITSELF ALONE

straight mind, who sees such a tradition as both separate and inferior, and with such a tradition delineated can thus better police the boundaries of their own? (83)

For Teare, *any* tradition—whether straight or gay—'*needs* subordinates in order to remain dominant'—that is, in order to be understood as tradition at all. The construction of a gay tradition separate from the heterosexist canon thus ends up mimicking, within itself, the process of canon formation constructed around a centre and a margin, which is the canon's broader structural role, as the 'central lineage' of poets such as Whitman, Crane, and Ginsberg form an axis around which others are reduced to supporting or marginal roles—what Teare calls 'the margins of illegitimacy' (83). Yet the necessity of understanding one's place as a writer remains. If even counter-canons reproduce the exclusionary process of marginality by which so much work has already been excluded, how to productively inhabit the condition of the margin in a mode of collectivity and affiliation which doesn't simply reproduce hegemonic structure? One mode might, as Teare suggests, be a writerly one: a kind of playful, poetic re-inscription of poetic lineage through fantasy, absurdity, and interchangeability which nonetheless pays homage to writers of genuine influence. The third section of Teare's talk, 'Rejuvenate: A Creation Myth', thus builds an experimental queer lineage as his own homage to poet Alice Notley's 1980 essay 'Doctor Williams' Heiresses'—originally delivered as a lecture in San Francisco in 1980 (Teare, 85–87). Notley's talk traces a line of female poets bought into the world through Williams, one of whose professional tasks as a doctor was to deliver babies, in which Williams, the son of Emily Dickinson and Walt Whitman, in turn the son of Edgar Allen Poe and a goddess, sires numerous contemporaneous American poets in a panoply of gender-switching, absent parents, and 'a kind of ancestor worship' (Notley, n.p.). Teare suggests other predecessors, including Robert Duncan's suggestion in 'Rites of Participation' that a 'dramatic voice' unites reader and writer in 'the company of imagined like minds' which is trans-national and trans-historical, and the Adrienne Rich's claim in her lecture 'Poetry and Commitment': 'I don't speak these names, by the way, as a canon: they are voices mingling in a long conversation, a long turbulence, a great, vexed and often maligned tradition, in poetry as in politics [. . .] the tradition of those who have written against the silences of their time and location.' (Duncan 2012, 156; Rich 2007, 37). For Teare, the risk is that the subsequent cementation of the gains of Gay Liberation itself falls prey to the processes of 'intellectual shorthand', 'niche marketing', tokenism, and the process of literary canon-making which, by a similar process of partial inclusion, re-marginalizes the most radical political and aesthetic practices which, in many cases, were at the forefront of the initial moment of revolutionary upheaval that enabled change to take place (Teare, 87).

INTRODUCTION   25

At the same time, Rich suggests that without tradition—conceived of as a conversation, a writing *against*, rather than a writing *into* or *of* the heterosexist mainstream—'our world is unintelligible' (Rich 2007, 37). Indeed, conversely, it is precisely those writers pushed to the margins of counter-canons—particularly feminized writers and writers of colour—for whom acts of archival recovery and a rethinking of tradition might be most crucial.

In the introduction to the 1981 edition of *Lesbian Poetry: An Anthology*, Elly Bulkin once more turns to the problem of origins.[18] As Bulkin notes, within the previous decade of post-Stonewall US lesbian poetries, the search for 'foremothers' becomes one of 'uncovering' a prior tradition in the face of its silencing—tracing, for instance, the intimate friendship of Angelina Weld Grimké and Gloria T. Hull, or the mutual support offered Edna St Vincent Millay, Sara Teasdale, and Elinor Wylie. Yet this poetic-scholarly endeavour raises once more the problem of erasure. In particular:

> Uncovering a poet tradition representative of lesbians of colour and poor and working-class lesbians of all races involves, as Barbara Noda has written, the words 'lesbian', 'historical', and even 'poet'. A beginning problem is definitional, as Paula Gunn Allen makes clear in her exploration of her own American Indian [*sic*] culture: 'it is not known if those / who warred and hunted on the plains [. . .] were Lesbians / It is never known / if any woman was a lesbian'. (Bulkin 1981, xxviii[19])

Bulkin goes on to argue that, within groups 'whose historical poverty leaves them without a tradition of "literacy" (or "literacy" in English), and without a way to get their written or oral poetry reproduced and distributed'—in which, for example, certain groups may view 'the very act of writing down myths and stories [as] an act of disempowerment'—there is a 'near impossibility of doing certain kinds of historical research' (xxviii). This conditional trail of hearsay, rumour, and memory may find no discoverable written expression at all. For the poet or scholar searching for a prior line of lesbian poetry, the question of 'tradition', 'lineage', and 'influence' are complex matters. In the absence or impossibility of recovering an unknown poetic tradition, lesbian poetics becomes the revelation of already existent, if suppressed modes of being, from the works of the wealthy Gertrude Stein or H.D.—who could write without worrying about finance— to the more precarious experience recounted by Elsa Gidlow, who, during the Depression years, had to combine writing and paid work at a time when being out of work could mean starvation; who lived in the San Francisco area since the 1920s; and who became subject to the punitive surveillance of HUAC (House Un-American Activities Committee) (Bulkin 1981, xxix; Gidlow). At the same time, as Judy Grahn suggested in her 1970 'Lesbians as Bogeywomen', the

26 NEVER BY ITSELF ALONE

absences in the record might serve as tabula rasa from which both poetry and lesbian identification can be (re)written from scratch. Grahn here contrasts the example of Stein—who 'wrote because she wanted to, and she had a disciplined, sensitive mind, and [. . .] didn't have to work in a dimestore eight hours a day'— to the anonymous 'women in history who were the less fortunate counterparts of Gertrude Stein, unable to retire on papa's money', but instead 'cut off their hair and joined the merchant marine; or sneaked out west for a life of adventure as cowboys'. 'Even those who may never have thought about loving another woman in her life', she continues, 'still goes down in history as a lesbian. Every woman who steps out of line gets assigned a sexual definition: lesbian, whore, nymphomaniac, castrator, adultress.' (Grahn 1970, 36). For Grahn, the category 'lesbian' at once reflects the divide-and-conquer strategies of patriarchal power which 'set people off in separate categories, artificially, so they'll know who to be afraid of—each other', and serves as a means of self-definition, expressed in inspirational acts of living that may not have manifested in surviving poems, but which nonetheless provide inspiration for the present-day lesbian writer (37). Such 'common women' might not consider themselves poets, and might never have written a poem, but their lives attest to creativity, oppression, and survival that are the matter of poetry.

Nearly half a century after Bulkin's and Grahn's essays, decades of vital research into gay and lesbian literary history, along with the cementation of queer theory within the academy, has seen the growth of new ways of thinking about sexuality and personhood that echo and extend the 'beginning problem' of 'definition' they faced. At the same time, it's arguable that there have been losses as well as gains. In his recent scholarly work, *Evidence of Being*, for instance, critic Darius Bost argues that queer theory has 'move[d] away from archival recovery of gay and lesbian writing' accomplished by an earlier generation. Rather than recuperating or newly canonizing explicitly queer writers, such work instead aims at 'queering the traditional canon', thus preserving a strategy of partial inclusion—the queering of what is, in some cases, already canonized—and broader marginalization (Bost, 18). In certain cases, to do so can re-establish the rupture between queer writing as a critique of, alternative to, or dismantling of canonical structures, overlooking the formal and aesthetic choices made by openly queer writers and how critical work on such writers might complicate existing literary histories. In 1993, for instance, Arthur Flannigan Saint-Aubin questioned the framework of Joseph Beam and Essex Hemphill's anthology *Brother to Brother: New Writings by Black Gay Men* by arguing that queer theory had rendered the traditional divisions of gay activism redundant and that there was no need for a specifically Black gay male discourse. Indeed, while sexuality and ethnicity might serve as the basis for a struggle conceived in difference, rather than similarity, such a discourse risked reifying particular aspects of identity at the expense of (for example) gendered exclusions. For Flannigan, the book constructs a series of identities based on oppositions—heterosexual/homosexual, black/white—which obscure other elements of identity—notably, gender/class—and fail to grasp the 'complex ways' in which multiple oppressions 'interface' (Flannigan Saint-Aubin, 474–75). Yet, as Bost suggests, such criticism of what was, after all, the first widely available anthology of its kind—and certainly the first to be widely available, widely cited, and edited by a well-known Black writer—ends up once more performing the very act of exclusion of which it accuses its subject. Through such acts, which posit the objects they further marginalize as *themselves* tools of exclusion, essentialism, and the like, academic queer theory can once more enshrine the de facto universalization of whiteness, choosing not to have to reckon with the mobilization of particular Black gay, lesbian, and trans identities as political subjects. Given this, for Bost, and in the innovative recent creative-critical archival work of Black Radical scholars and poets such as Saidiya Hartman, M. NourbeSe Philip, and Alexis Pauline Gumbs, returning to the archive—in acts of recovery that take into account its absences as well as its presences—accomplishes a necessary historicizing function, providing material traces of lives and works that have been, in effect—and unlike the work of white queer writers—struck off the historical record (Hartman 2019; Philip 2008; Gumbs 2016). At the same time, it calls into question the very categories of historical knowledge, archival trace, and canonical inclusion. To recover such work should not be to bid for inclusion within the expanding framework of partial inclusion enacted as a self-defence mechanism by the liberalized canon and its gatekeepers, but to stress its difference from such constructions of hierarchy, and power, the violence which enables them and which they enable.

'meet their end upon the ground'

To further examine these questions, I'd like to turn to an obscure poem which has not, as far as I've been able to determine, received any prior critical attention but which is a vital meditation on the issues at stake. Adrian Stanford poem's 'Sacrifice' first appeared in Stanford's *Black and Queer*, published by Good Gay Poets in 1977, and opens *Brother to Brother* fourteen years later. Here is the poem in full.

Sacrifice

Had my father known
when he cast forth his offering
to the sea of my mother's womb
what creation their joy would bring

28   NEVER BY ITSELF ALONE

> would he have welcomed the man/she child in its birth
> heralding my duality as natures zenith (in human form)
> and blessed the son he held for all to see
> keeping my sister/self obscured, until
> i understood my second destiny–
> or would he have shuddered at the fate his loins possessed
> and retracting from those clashing thighs,
> let the seeds that bore such strains
> meet their end upon the ground
>
> (Stanford, 26)

The question of lineage is here not only one of as literary metaphor but also of personal survival. In Stanford's poem, it is the father who actively 'cast[s] forth his offering / to the sea of my mother's womb', and the mother whose passive waters receive it. And it is the father—or the Name-of-the-father, the law and logic underlying patriarchal narrative—who possesses the power to kill. As a person who is, as the title to his book has it, both 'Black and queer', the poem's speaker does not fit a heteropatriarchal schema based on strict gender division and on the role of the father in transmission. If his father knew of the child's 'two-sexed' nature, the poem asks, might they have symbolically killed the child before birth, through withdrawing in the act of intercourse—an allusion to the biblical narrative of Onan? (Genesis 38:8–10). This question, unanswered in the poem, is horrific in its implications: that one's own father would rather one were dead than queer.

At the same time, the poem is a reversal, or an 'inversion', of the narratives that would drive such a murderous desire, taking them to their logical limit and turning them against themselves. The discourse of heteropatriarchal procreation reaches its limit, its contradiction, when the patriarch considers committing the worst sin of all—the termination of a potential life—in order that queer life might not be born. If, as the heteropatriarchal narrative has it, it is the father's 'seeds', their self-perpetuation, that constitutes lineage, or heritage—with the mother's role reduced to that of passive 'carrier'—then the existence of the queer child means that the father contains within himself the potential for queerness, 'the seeds that bore such strains'. If this is so, even the act of 'sacrifice'—spilling those 'seeds' on the ground—will not exculpate the queer potential present even in that which is seen as the summit of the father's heteropatriarchal power, the act of conception. Stanford's subversive gesture thus overturns the sacred shibboleths of heteropatriarchal conception underlying those notions of heritage and lineage that form the bedrock of US conservative thought, whether in opposition to abortion or virulent homophobia.

Operating as it does deliberately within the terms of heteropatriarchal order, this is not so much a positive statement of identity as a provocation

INTRODUCTION   29

aimed at undermining the mythic edifice which narrates the impossibility or unconscionable nature of the two-gendered, Black gay subject. Stanford's poem imagines the precarity of beginnings, the counternarrative in which his father, gifted with prophetic insight, casts his sperm to the ground rather than create a queer child. To imagine such a state of non-being is a particularly pressing task for the one whose life is already so radically close to non-being, so radically shaped by a 'rotten / anti-black past' and by the murderous hatred of fag-bashers, of religious and secular bigots, parents, legislators, and state enforcers nationwide (Stanford, 22). The poem acts on multiple levels, a text that is painfully re-enacted whenever a queer person wonders why they were born, why they are alive; whenever a queer person dies, 'in mysterious circumstances', of state or extra-state violence, and of the depredations of AIDS which Stanford himself did not live to see.

Reading Stanford's beautiful and troubling poem prompts further reflection on its author. For all the talk of textuality, impersonality, or the death of the author, it matters that a particular marginalized person wrote this poem, and it matters that the text itself has assumed a similarly marginal status. Stanford's work provides a link to the earliest homophile organizations. His earliest publications were in pre-Stonewall gay magazines ONE and Tangents mid-way through the 1960s. Founded in January 1953 by members of the pioneering homophile organization the Mattachine Society, ONE was the first queer organization in the United States to have its own office, which functioned as a community centre. Winning a lawsuit against the US Post Office Department which had, in 1954, refused to deliver it in the mails as 'obscene' material, the magazine eventually ceased publication in 1969. Tangents was formed after a split in the magazine's editorial group and published from 1965 until 1970 (Mairead Case, n.p.).[20] Stanford's poems appear at successive stages in the history of queer publication: the homophile magazines which, for all their caution and conservatism, were vital lifelines; the radical new wave of publications emerging from Gay Liberation, here represented by the Good Gay Poets collective; and what Darius Bost terms the 'Black Gay Cultural Renaissance' of the 1980s, in Beam and Hemphill's Brother to Brother. Here, Stanford's piece, a poem about lineage and the relation of an uncertain future to a past characterized by queerphobic power and violence, is placed within the context of a fractured and tenuous, yet tenacious, historical record. The stakes of such fracture seem to repeat down generations: as Hemphill's introduction notes, he was passed a copy of Stanford's book by Beam, the volume's initial editor, several years after Stanford had passed away; Beam in turn passed away of AIDS-related complications, and the task was taken over by Hemphill, who would also die of the disease within a matter of years. 'In terms of my heritage of Negritude,' Hemphill writes, 'I found an abundance of literary texts to reinforce a positive black cultural identity, but as a black gay man there was, except for Baldwin, little to nurture me'.

30 NEVER BY ITSELF ALONE

Unbeknowst to me, Adrian Stanford's *Black and Queer* had been published by the Good Gay Poets of Boston in 1977. I would not be introduced to Stanford's work until 1985. Joseph Beam owned two copies of Stanford's *Black and Queer* and gave me one for my collection. I have treasured this gift since receiving it from Joe, who also told me Stanford was murdered in Philadelphia in 1981 [...]

For me, the evidence of black gay men creating overt homoerotic poetry begins with that small, powerful book. What I am suggesting is that black gay men have been publishing overt homoerotic verses since 1977, a mere thirteen years as of this writing. (Hemphill, xliv)

The sense that searching for a point of origin, of lineage, might be death-haunted, is crucial. These writers realize that constructing such a line is one of chosen filiation or familial replacement as much as it is of biological familial structures characterized by violence and rejection of queer progeny, taking the role of fantasy, myth, and performance, of imaginative (re)inscription of both personal autobiography and the broader origin myths that may or may not have archival records or founding texts to support them.

What does it mean that a path-breaking book such *Black and Queer* is still out of print and virtually impossible to find? And what does it mean that so little can be found about Adrian Stanford, save the fact that he was murdered in 1981? (Even the fact of this murder is already second- or even third-hand, related in Hemphill's introduction via Joseph Beam, who in the meantime had himself passed away (xliv).) And what does it mean that Hemphill's brief, but passionate, discussion of Stanford—with its claim that 'the evidence of black gay men creating *overt* homoerotic poetry begins with that small, powerful book' (xliv)—is virtually the only discussion of Stanford's work in print?

Almost nothing is known of Stanford's family, his friends, his lovers, the events of his life, save the appearance of poems in fledgling queer magazines from the mid-1960s through to the publication of *Black and Queer*. Stanford's only published writing besides the poems in magazines such as *ONE* and *The Drummer* and collected in *Black and Queer* comes in a review of work by playwright and former hustler Dotson Rader in *Evergreen Review* from 1971 and a brief column on Philadelphia gay life for *The Advocate* from 1972. The queer magazines in which Stanford published his early work—for understandable reasons—rarely published biographical notes. From a contributor biography for a 1980 issue of *The Black Scholar*, we learn that he was the son of 'the late journalist' Ted Stanford. Theodore Anthony Stanford himself published a book of poems, *Dark Harvest*, through the Philadelphia Bureau of Negro Affairs in 1936, some of which had previously appeared in W.E.B. DuBois' *The Crisis*, in poems which speak of first love, loneliness, and Promethean struggle; his journalism includes reviews of work by the historian J. A. Rogers, and a report on the funeral of Bessie

INTRODUCTION 31

Smith in *The Philadelphia Tribune*. It's possible then, to draw some connection between the generalized father of Stanford's poem and a father, himself a poet and involved in anti-racist struggles, but who, judging from the poem at least, appears to have viewed his son's sexuality with homophobic censure. Yet this trace is itself incomplete: little can be found of the elder Stanford's activities in print after the early 1940s. Adrian Stanford poured the matter of his life into his poems, but all we have left now are the poems, as the trace of that life; cited as pioneering text in gay black poetics but long out of print. Marked as pioneer, Stanford is also a kind of *x*, an absence or gap, part of a long chain of anonymity, falling off the pages of history, of transmission through and in spite of death, mourning, and absence.

Even when they self-organized in particular groups, circles, or publications— poets like Stanford were often at the *fringes* of movements, often doubly or triply marginalized for reasons of gender identity, race, or personal circumstance. Murdered in unknown circumstances (Stanford), dying of alcoholism (Jack Spicer), or cancer (Karen Brodine, Pat Parker), passing away from AIDS-related complications (Steve Abbott), falling prey to the depredations of drug use and of the mental health apparatus (John Wieners, Stephen Jonas), their manners of death, as well as their lives, provide vivid testimony of the precarity of queer life in America. Reclaiming their work cannot suture these wounds, these absences from historical record, though it can do valuable work in this direction— cases in point being Lewis Ellingham and Kevin Killian's immensely detailed reconstructive work on Spicer's biography, Killian's work on Spicer's involvement with the Bay Area Mattachine Society, and Julie Enszer's republication of the work of Stephania Byrd. Scholarship of this work must, therefore, embrace and take into account these gaps and render them a part of its method, learning from the work itself, reflecting such conceptions of non-linear, collective, and companionable form as a necessary task of solidarity with both living and dead. Such scholarship might learn from the delirious inventions of John Wieners' writing of the 1970s, with its revisions, over-layering, superimpositions, its queer impersonations, conspiracies, and blurring of the narratives of personal, private life and public, national history, which insist that we messily blur the two (Wieners 1975). It might learn from the polyphonic chorus of Judy Grahn's 'common woman' poems, in which working women, women without work, queer women, and people of colour die in the streets and are witnessed and cradled by those who put them in poems, registering their lives without hoping to contain them according to a preconceived theoretical or conceptual schema, as tokens or figural representatives, but as living humans of whose life or death flashes are preserved to spark the living to action, as act of memory and love, erotic or otherwise, but above all social (Grahn 1985). It might learn from Pat Parker's defiant refusal to be interpellated by white feminist audiences ('The first

32 NEVER BY ITSELF ALONE

thing you do is forget that i'm Black / Second, you must never forget that i'm Black' (Parker, 2016, 76) or to let fascists speak (71). It might learn from Dodie Bellamy's idea of monstrous writing that cannibalizes, eats up, and disgorges the languages of power enshrined in the academy, in class power, a linguistic *vagina dentata*, or feminized vampire, deploying the languages which deny it access to social privilege to stake out a territory of its own (Bellamy 2006, 144). It would learn from the poems and poetic texts it writes *with,* rather than simply trying to write *about* or *of.* It would seek, not to own, possess, analyze, systematize, classify, contain, but to learn from, to witness, to witness with, to listen to—to acknowledge, not only those names we *do* know but in Parker's words also:

> [. . .] all the names we forgot to say
> & all the names we didn't know
> & all the names we don't know, yet.
>
> (Parker, 'Movement in Black', 100)

PART I
BEGINNINGS (1944–1969)

Part I addresses early manifestations of queer poetic community in the pre–Gay Liberation era in both Boston and the Bay Area, including chapters on Robert Duncan in the 1940s; the Jack Spicer circle in the 1950s and early 1960s; and the poets of the Boston 'Occult School'. Examining publications such as the magazines *Boston Newsletter*, *J*, *Measure*, *Open Space*, and *Set*, these chapters emphasize the queer political content of their work.

1
'Homosexuals in Society'
Poetry and Gay Community in the 1940s

Introduction

In August 1944, an essay by a young poet named Robert Duncan appeared in the recently established left-wing journal *Politics*. Founded by editor Dwight Macdonald following his resignation from *Partisan Review* over his fellow editors' post-Pearl Harbor support for US involvement in the Second World War, *Politics* was conceived a venue for the non-aligned left, disillusioned at once by the CPUSA (Communist Party USA)'s turn to patriotism and by the information beginning to emerge about the effects of Stalinist repression in the Soviet Union. The new journal aimed to be 'scientific, materialistic, worldly, democratic, humanist—in the tradition of Rousseau, Jefferson, Darwin, Marx, Freud and Dewey' (Faas 1983, 149). The magazine had printed articles by conscientious objectors, but this new article was, if anything, more controversial in its topic. Duncan's essay stood out not only for its bold title—'The Homosexual in Society'—but for the fact that its author identified himself as queer, at a time when sodomy was a felony in every state, potentially punishable by a lengthy prison term, by hard labour, and by the 'medical' torture of the psychiatric apparatus. Duncan presently received a letter from famed literary critic John Crowe Ransom, a leading exponent of the New Criticism, and an editor with considerable influence within literary and academic circles. Ransom had previously accepted Duncan's poem 'An African Elegy' for publication in the *Kenyon Review*, the journal he'd established in 1939. Having previously been impressed by Duncan's poem—with its surreal landscape, drawn in part from Lorca, featuring the suicided Ophelia, Virginia Woolf, Desdemona, and generic images of Africa landscapes—Ransom now read the poem as a 'homosexual advertisement', its images—none of which explicitly reference homosexuality—interpreted as symbols to be decoded by gay men. In the exchange of letters that followed, Ransom—a political conservative who had contributed to the Southern Agrarians' infamous *I'll Take My Stand* in 1930—opined that homosexuality was 'biologically abnormal in the most obvious sense'; that it was more damaging than incest and polygamy; and that gay men should be sterilized, the latter something not entirely out of bounds with governmental policy.[1]

Never By Itself Alone. David Grundy, Oxford University Press. © Oxford University Press 2024.
DOI: 10.1093/oso/9780197654842.003.0002

36   NEVER BY ITSELF ALONE

Ransom's response illustrates just how courageous Duncan's essay was—even though his relative class privilege did not render him as vulnerable as many queer people without access to such a platform. It would not be until 1948 that Gore Vidal published *The City and the Pillar*, and until 1949 that James Baldwin's unjustly neglected essay 'Preservation of Innocence', appeared in the Morocco-based arts journal *Zero* (I discuss Baldwin's essay below). As Duncan's first biographer Ekbert Faas notes, Duncan's exchange with Ransom effectively 'put a sudden end to what easily might have turned into a successful literary career sanctioned by the New Critical establishment' (Faas 1983, 154). While signalling a break from a potential career within the mainstream of American letters, the essay also marked Duncan's growing dissatisfaction with the bohemian communities in which he'd been involved as a young poet in New York, where he had been something of a protegee of Anaïs Nin—herself a recent arrival to the city—and had associated with the queer modernist and surrealist circles surrounding Charles Henri Ford and (Parker Tyler, who had co-authored the pathbreaking experimental gay novel *The Young and Evil* while in Paris in 1933, and, back in New York, had since 1942 worked on the surrealist magazine *View*, in which Duncan has published early work). Duncan insisted to *Politics'* editor Dwight Macdonald that the essay be published under his own name, and it's this gesture that made the essay so important to a later generation of queer activists who emphasized the revolutionary potential of 'coming out' (See Bérubé 1990, 251). Yet the essay itself devotes as much time to attacking what Duncan calls a 'homosexual cult' of gay male artists (the essay does not discuss lesbians) who emphasize camp and upper-class affectations, thus, in Duncan's view, reinforcing the normative idea that homosexuality is 'deviant' or 'evil'. Espousing instead an anarchist, humanist universalism, Duncan argues instead that gay men should join their cause to that of the non-aligned left in a general struggle for human freedom, in order to avoid becoming sexual 'Zionists' or producing a commodified version of their own culture which performs bastardized versions of identity for the amusement of the rich. Duncan's critique was levelled at the circles around Tyler and Ford—though they were not named—as amplified in his essay 'Reviewing *View*: An Attack' in 1947 (Faas 1983, 323–27). In an angry response to 'The Homosexual in Society', Tyler wrote to MacDonald that Duncan had merely projected his own sense of neurosis and gay self-loathing onto queer communities and was 'no fit partisan of a social program' (Faas 1983, 151). For his part, the composer Virgil Thompson—part of the gay artistic scenes in New York which were Duncan's target—quipped 'he starts talking about the homosexual in society and he hasn't even got invited to any parties' (Duncan 1971, audio).

Through his residence in New York, Duncan was at the juncture of various important literary and political trajectories, scenes, and groupings: the presence the presentation of European surrealism by émigrés such as Marcel Duchamp and Salvador Dalí, in galleries and in publications such as *View*; anarchist political scenes involving major figures like Paul Goodman; the erotic-experimental literature of Nin, Henry Miller, Mina Loy, and others whom Duncan knew and alongside whom he was published. Prior to the essay's composition, Duncan tested out its ideas in conversation with both Pauline Kael—later a highly influential film critic—and Tennessee Williams (Faas 1983, 157). Its status as a central document in the self-figuration of American queer writers—especially gay male writers—should be evident. At the same time, in the essay itself, these groups—particularly those associated with Nin and with Tyler and Ford—are targets for critique as much as for affiliation. In the very act of announcing himself as gay, Duncan refused labels, which he disavowed as a reification and fetishization of performed modes of identity that limit human potential.

Though he considered authoring a book-length follow-up, Duncan was not primarily a political commentator. While he saw the question of sexuality as connected to a rejection of American imperialism and, in the next few years, the consolidation of the permanent war economy and the Red and Lavender Scares, such struggles were generally placed within an ideal poetic realm. Transformations that could not yet be given political voice on a broader stage attained a mystical form through such figures as the female muse, Augustine's City of God, Christian and ancient Greek mythology, and Duncan's own mythology of the 'field' and the 'meadow'. In this regard, Duncan's work suggests a tension that runs through the work considered in the present volume: that poetry both articulates political aspirations that cannot as yet be named within the sphere of political activism; yet that poetry also seems to stand opposed to the business of politics, so that the utopian hopes it expresses are sublimated into an ideal and textual realm. Attending to Duncan's early work, then, is not only important as a case study of a pioneering, openly gay poetry but also for the contradiction it reveals, both in early self-figurations of gay identity by gay writers and groups, and as these would continue to play out even into the Gay Liberation era. Duncan's essay is a valuable starting point, not because it offers a clear, programmatic statement of activism and community building built on fixed sexual identity, but because it exemplifies the fractious, contradictory, and diverse nature of the early attempts at queer world building in which these poets were engaged.

The chapter is structured in three principal sections. First reading Duncan's apparently paradoxical condemnation of a 'homosexual cult' in his 1944 essay, I then turn to the structures of analogy by which Duncan figures minoritized identities. For Duncan, I argue, race is *like* homosexuality, but the two are not *coincident*. (Likewise, lesbian sexuality is absent from his discourse, despite the

38 NEVER BY ITSELF ALONE

paramount importance for his later work of writers such as H.D. and Gertrude Stein.) To clarify this point, I turn to the poem which Ransom rejected upon reading Duncan's essay, and to Duncan's own later comments on his exchange with Ransom about this poem, showing how Duncan uses racialised figures to figure his own psychosexual projections in ways that are telling and problematic. Duncan's work of the early 1940s emerged from his time in New York bohemian circles; his work of the decade's second half emerged from and helped define the so-called Berkeley Renaissance—in reality a small grouping of Duncan, Jack Spicer, and Robin Blaser, who envisaged in a community that was social, sexual, and poetic. I turn to Duncan's key poems of this period, 'Heavenly City, Earthly City' (1946–1947) and 'The Venice Poem' (1948), examining their attempt to transmute sexual tension, jealousy, and desire into an ideal aesthetic realm that is nonetheless also characterized by a tone of melancholy and loss. In the final section of the chapter, I briefly turn to Duncan's post-Renaissance work, as his new relationship with the man who would turn out to be his life partner, the artist Jess Collins, saw him re-articulate his poetry in relation to the 'household' and to a stable domestic setting. As I argue, this suggests both a retreat from the collective concerns of Duncan's earlier work and a self-conscious reflection on the ways in which American imperial identity colours the private as well as the public sphere. The ending of the Berkeley Renaissance was in part a result of Duncan's slow but inexorable falling out with Jack Spicer, the two poets often taking up diametrically opposed views of both poetry and gay community. In the following chapter, I read Spicer's work in more detail; in the present chapter, I turn to Duncan's final gift to Spicer, a sonnet sequence after Dante which memorializes the Berkeley Renaissance in its passing and sets sail for the open waters of a potential queer future in a gesture at once of melancholy and of hope.

'The Homosexual in Society': Gay Identity and the Future of America

The Young and Evil

Born in Oakland in the same district as Gertrude Stein, Duncan's mother died in childbirth and he was adopted by a well-off middle-class family deeply invested in occultist beliefs, who believed him to be a reincarnated citizen of the lost city of Atlantis.[2] Spending his teenage years in Bakersfield, California, to where his family had moved, Duncan's first sexual encounters occurred shortly after the death of his father in 1935. At the age of fifteen, one such sexual encounter with an older boy turned violent, and Duncan was viciously beaten: it turned out that the culprit had murdered several other gay youths in the town.

'HOMOSEXUALS IN SOCIETY' 39

Questioned by the local police, Duncan was forced to admit to his mother and a police captain that he was not an 'innocent victim' of the attack, but that, in his words, 'I wanted it, I had led him, he hadn't followed me' (Faas 1983, 47, 96). Michael Davidson has convincingly argued that this encounter formed a kind of traumatic initiation that later figures in Duncan's concept of the poetic 'field'. For Duncan, poetry and sexuality both have their basis in an initiation into mysteries and poetic secrets. These are also, however traumatic encounters, not only with sexual violence, but also with the doubled interpellative violence of the state. As Davidson notes, Duncan's 'inauguration into sexual knowledge' was thus 'accompanied by his participation in institutional discourses of sexuality that "otherize" him and which he is forced to reject' (Davidson 1992, 294). Faced with a sense of 'double marginality—being beaten and then being forced to reject his "victim" status', Duncan discovers 'an otherness within himself for which society has no map': neither willing erotic partner nor the (heterosexual) victim of (homosexual) attack (Davidson 1992, 295–96).

In 1936, Duncan entered UC Berkeley as a freshman, becoming involved in campus magazines and left politics. Duncan embarked on his first significant relationship with an instructor named Ned Fahs, dropping out of college in 1938 and following Fahs to Philadelphia, where Fahs had a teaching appointment, and subsequently, to New York. Duncan met Anaïs Nin in 1939, and the two became extremely close, sharing interests in psychoanalysis, surrealism, and the sexual research of Krafft-Ebbing, with Nin excerpting from Duncan's writing in her own work, and Duncan printing excerpts from Nin's *House of Incest* in the only published issue of *Ritual*, the magazine he co-edited with Berkeley friend Virginia Admiral in 1940 (Jarnot 2012, 61–63). Having already experienced the intertwining of violence, sex, and state power in his teenage encounter in Bakersfield, Duncan's sense of his sexuality in opposition to the state was exacerbated when he was drafted in 1941. Having broken up with Fahs, Duncan began military service at Fort Knox, Kentucky, that March. Encouraged by Nin to declare his sexuality to receive a discharge, he was temporarily placed in a military psych ward and duly discharged as a 'sexual psychopath'. Returning to New York, Duncan fell out with Nin and embarked on a brief and disastrous heterosexual marriage in 1943; increasingly, he began to distance himself from the surrealist artistic groups with which he'd thus far been associated, centring in particular on Charles Henri Ford's magazine *View*.

Ford and Parker Tyler's novel *The Young and Evil*, published in Paris in 1933, had combined misogyny, sexual openness (from threesomes to one-night stands and cruising) and racially mixed Harlem queer parties. Building on their connections with the international surrealist movement, several of whom had fled to New York following the German occupation, Ford's New York–based magazine *View*, for which Tyler contributed typography, design, and layout, was

40 NEVER BY ITSELF ALONE

founded in 1942, combining high-production values and glossy advertisements with experimental writing and art, drawing connections between writing communities and the elite world art world. Described by Tosh Berman as 'the Surrealist house magazine of the war years [. . .] that looked like a high-end fashion magazine', its aesthetic was amenable to commercialism, though it maintained controversial political stances such as conscientious objection at a time of patriotism and war mobilization on both right and left. In Steven Heller's words, 'Ford did not disdain commercial avenues of support. On the contrary, he knew not only how to navigate capitalism but how to appreciate (appropriate) its imagery, namely through the lens of camp, a "view" that converged with surrealism then and with Pop Art twenty years later' (Steven Heller 2014, 158). This combination of the commercial, the queer, and the avant-garde meant that 'View's editors thought it delusional to believe that art could ever serve any cause other than its own'.

Duncan's own 'Letter to Jack Johnson' had appeared in the magazine's March 1942 issue, alongside a veritable who's who of Anglophone modernism, including Leonora Carrington, Henry Miller, William Carlos Williams, Mina Loy, and Marianne Moore. Duncan's piece, predominantly written in prose, does not reference Johnson directly: the poem is populated instead with 'wonders', 'stars', chess, 'witch-doktor[s]' [sic], winged creatures, 'lesbian fear', 'death's sirens, death's musical women and hunger', collapsing structures, and 'the mind's waiting cellars': a world of dismemberment and unrest. 'I shall be drawn thru in music / I shall be drawn thru in pain / I shall be drawn thru in delirium', writes Duncan. This mode is very much of a piece with the magazine's invocations of delirium, apocalypse, and imagery that trod the line between subversion and the replication of racialized stereotype.[3] Within the year, Duncan, whose early work had been admired by Ford and Tyler, had fallen out of favour, Ford arguing that Duncan's writing had lost its 'automatism' and become overly formal (Faas 1983, 154). The differences were not only artistic but also political. Taylor's embrace of shock tactics and the vocabulary of 'evil' and transgression were, Duncan came to believe, a kind of avant-garde version of *National Geographic*, 'styled to dish out (as the National Geographic is styled to dish out the world as retired pensioners want to see it) experience not as it is but as the wealthy dilettante wants to see it' (Faas 1983, 324). Objecting to the commercial values and elitist class basis of the magazine, Duncan also argued that the specifically queer aspects of this exclusive social group were a betrayal of the anarchist humanism to which he espoused and in which he wished to place his own sexuality.

It was in this context that Duncan wrote 'The Homosexual in Society'. Duncan's essay at once adopts generalizing terms and is rooted in a specific social circle, a specific coterie from which it draws broader conclusions. To that extent, it can partly be read as a local skirmish by an up-and-coming young writer with an influential set of artists with ties to the art world, to international surrealism, and to literary and erotic experimentation from which he was already becoming estranged. At the same time, given the lack of any stable gay activist presence, either locally or nationally, such groupings were some of the few queer collectives to which Duncan could have access. As John D'Emilio has noted, it was the increased proximity of queer men and women to each other and the migrations afforded by military service that led to the seismic shift in queer social life whose rumblings were only just beginning to be felt in 1942 (D'Emilio 1983). Duncan thus writes on a precipice.

Duncan begins by proposing to discuss 'yet another group whose only salvation is in the struggle of all humanity for freedom and individual integrity' (Faas 1983, 319).[4] Suggesting that they have responded to societal 'persecution' and 'excommunication' by 'convert[ing] their deepest feelings into marketable oddities and sentimentalities', he argues that 'a great body of modern art is cheated by what almost amounts to a homosexual cult'. Arguing that this 'cult' of superiority manifests in 'the cultivation of a secret language, the *camp*, a tone and vocabulary that is loaded with contempt for the human', he suggests that, rather than struggling for social equality, 'homosexual propagandists [. . .] have accepted the charge of demonism', making sexuality the entire basis for artistic work, rather than simply one facet of humanity—as, he argues, sexuality was for Proust, Melville, and Hart Crane (320). In the essay's second half, Duncan turns to his own sexuality. While the syntax is, as he would later note, contorted, so that sentences seem to assume at once the perspective of a hostile 'society' and of the individual queer subject it condemns, he here argues that his previous work 'disguised [. . .] the "crime" of my own feelings [. . .] for instance, as conflicts arising from mystical sources' (321). Viewed as 'perverted' by this hostile society, Duncan took what were in fact 'simple and direct emotions and realizations' and in turn 'perverted' them into 'a mysterious realm, a mysterious relation to society'. Duncan further suggests that his own participation in queer literary circles— the 'drawing rooms and little magazines' in which came together 'a family, outrageous as it was, a community in which one was not condemned for one's homosexuality'—represented a problematic class politics, with camp affectation seeing 'my voice taking on the modulations which tell of the capitulation to snobbery and removal from "the common sort"' (322). Struck by a 'desolate feeling of wrongness', Duncan condemns the affect of a 'group language which did not allow for any feeling at all other than this self-ridicule, this gaiety [. . .] a wave surging forward, breaking into laughter and then receding, leaving a wake of disillusionment, a disbelief that extended to oneself, to life itself' (322).

If such community is inadequate, to where might 'the homosexual in society' then turn? At the time of writing, when Duncan's audience might well have included former members of various communist organizations, there was no such

42 NEVER BY ITSELF ALONE

organization for—or remotely sympathetic to—gay men and women. It's against this that Duncan's essay audaciously lays claim to homosexuality, not through the conservative model of left-wing subversion—a kind of infectious disease that diverts the American state from its heteropatriarchal destiny—nor the Stalinist model of bourgeois deviation—the ultimate in narcissistic individualism, against the communal model of family and socialist state—but as communal aspiration. Duncan opens his essay by setting out its stakes as a discussion 'of a group whose only salvation is in the struggle of all humanity for freedom and individual integrity' (319). This phrasing suggests the group to be damned—why else is it in need of 'salvation'?—is not simply that of gay men. Instead, humanity per se, as the normative category from which minorities are often excluded, is itself in need of salvation, of a not-yet-existent 'freedom and individual integrity' denied by the combination of homophobia, anti-Semitism, and anti-Black racism (to name the three examples cited in Duncan's text). Thus, we might read the statement for its implied chiastic opposite: that is to say, humanity's own salvation lies in the struggle of a group (homosexuals) itself searching for freedom and individual integrity in a manner that negates the category of sexual identity as such.

For Duncan, gay men—indeed, any minoritarian subject—must 'disown *all* the special groups (nations, religions, sexes, races) that would claim allegiance' and instead strive for the cause of universal human liberation (322). Writing in 1983, Bruce Boone argued that Duncan's essay sought to 'forc[e] all notions of community (polis) to be as inclusive as possible, and general [. . .] a sexuality that's a part of nature, not against it [. . .] This is a program of inclusiveness that hopes to be exhaustive' (Boone 1983, 82). In not only writing about but often assuming the validity of homosexual experience, Duncan was taken to violate the laws of 'universal address' by which literary universalism was coded as heteropatriarchal.[5] Duncan does not call for the self-organization of gay political groups; rather, he argues that such organization as they are currently manifested—in his example, the queer social circles of the New York art world—fetishize and reify the status imposed on them by society as a tool of repression, turning exclusion into a snobbish cult which views itself as superior to 'the common man'. Read today, the emphasis of Duncan's essay on a stringent attack on this group can read as internalized homophobia. The essay manifests a near-fanatical anti-particularity, an opposition to virtually any grouping organized around sexuality or ethnicity. The comparisons multiply: in the original essay, Duncan likens this 'cult' to the medieval Jewish ghetto; to Zionism; to African American artists who produce diluted and commodified versions of their art; and, in a 1971 aside introducing the essay at a Gay Liberation Day reading at the San Francisco Poetry Centre, to gay Nazis—presumably in reference to Ernst Röhm (Duncan 1971, audio). Such analogies are constructed almost exclusively as negative comparisons: as models of group identity which provide models to avoid, rather than alliances to be made or examples to be followed. In this sense, Duncan's essay is subject to the very critique it makes of the 'homosexual cult'. In its absence of working-class queers or queers of colour, we might have the impression that all gay men are either upper class or have aspirations towards upper-class identification, even if the essay's function is to challenge precisely this stereotype. Nowhere is there any recognition of the presence of those who are both African American and queer, both Jewish and queer; and nowhere is there any mention of female homosexuality. For Duncan, other groups serve as modes of comparisons for his own conflicted sense of sexuality as a white gay male, rather than as groups with which he and other queer people might build alliances or with which they might intersect. Such analogies thus open up a kind of gap or ellipsis, an oversight in purported universalism which cuts to the heart of the racialized and gendered problematics which continue to dog queer activism to this day. It's thus to these problematics that I now turn.

'The mind's / natural jungle': Race, Sexuality, and Identity

As noted at the start of the chapter, Duncan's dispute with John Crowe Ransom was occasioned, not simply by Duncan's essay, but by the way it caused Ransom to revise his reading of Duncan's poem 'An African Elegy', which he now rejected for publication.[6] Under the influence of Anaïs Nin, as Duncan's biographer Lisa Jarnot suggests, Duncan had written the 'African Elegy' in spring and summer 1942 (Jarnot 2012, 84). The poem continues the trope of identifying Black masculinity with exoticism and surreal disorder but is more explicit in its invocation of problematically racialized tropes. Duncan romanticizes Africa as a source of metaphors for and from the surrealist unconscious as well as for queer sexuality, in which the white gay male's identification with feminized persons and persons of colour is a source at once of forbidden excitement and of pathological terror.

For Duncan, reflecting later on the correspondence, what had offended Ransom was as much the presence of racialized figures as Duncan's sexuality—or rather, the way that the two categories mobilized each other. 'This very Southern gentleman, Ransom, was poring over a poem, and in it saw that negroes were no longer symbolic; they were actual negroes. There was a big black HE, and that sent Ransom up a tree' (Duncan 1976, 105). At this stage, for Duncan— who suddenly becomes more of a New Critic than Ransom—Ransom was in fact *correct* in his initial, laudatory reading of the poem as purely symbolic, and incorrect when fixing the figure onto a racially and sexually specific personage. The poem awakens *Ransom's* racism, with Ransom drawing the connection between racial and sexual 'deviance' in a manner Duncan had not intended. Yet if Ransom sees in the men of the poem potential lynching victims, Duncan

44 NEVER BY ITSELF ALONE

himself fails to see anything more than his own mental projections. In fact, as I'll suggest, Ransom's and Duncan's alternative interpretations of the poem—and Duncan's comments on these in later interviews—suggest racial problematics on both sides: overt racism and homophobia, in Ransom's case, and a projected identification of the white gay man with Blackness in Duncan's in a way that reinforces racial stereotyping.

The poem begins amidst wild animals in a vaguely delineated African settling—the world of 'the marvelous' immediately contrasted to the greater riches of the poet's own psyche, 'the mind's / natural jungle' (Duncan 2012, *Collected Early Poems*, 42). Explicitly set up as fantasy, this scene nonetheless reproduces racist stereotype, with spear-wielding Congolese and Swahili hunters followed by Death himself, a dog-headed Black man pursuing Virginia Woolf who, identified with Ophelia, drowns herself in a river. (The poem was written soon after Duncan received news of Woolf's death.) Masochistically awaiting impending destruction from plundering African armies, the speaker echoes the 'Negroes, Negroes' refrain from Lorca's '*El Rey de Harlem*', fantasizing African princes binding, devouring, and consuming his body. The jungle of the mind now becomes that of the body, the speaker at once Orpheus, Othello, and Death, the racialized and gendered conflict of Shakespeare's *Othello* staged as an internal conflict in which the male part of the poet's psyche seeks out and destroys its female side, only to lament this violent process of self-division (43). As the poem concludes, Duncan reflects that such imaginative speculation is potentially endless, a condition of fantasy and perpetual search which renders the marvellous a melancholic condition rather than one of psychic liberation.

In a later interview, Duncan provided a detailed sense of the poem's concerns. Written in the aftermath of a breakup and separation—'after being discarded by a first lover'—and the news of Woolf's suicide, Duncan suggests that he 'expressed [his] own world' through both the persona of the white female suicide and of Othello as a figure of possessiveness and jealousy (Duncan 1976, 96). Inspired by Lorca's poem, Duncan claims 'I flooded the poem with blacks', here functioning as menacing figures who do violence to the 'deserted and outcast' female parts of himself (97). For Duncan, the poem served as a form of self-analysis and personal purgation—as both the betrayed and jealous Othello and the Desdemona whom Othello destroys, the source and target of rage is at once located in himself and projected outwards into a series of loose and specific associations, as Woolf becomes Ophelia becomes Desdemona, and as Othello becomes a host of nameless and stereotypical 'blacks'. Duncan may have cautioned in his 1944 essay against the dangers of building up a reified identity that reflected societal condemnation, but here, race, gender, and sexuality all appear to be constructs at once fluid—in the way they are moved about in constantly shifting image registers—and fixed—in the repetition of stereotypical characterizations.

'HOMOSEXUALS IN SOCIETY' 45

Duncan's Africa is almost exclusively a literary construct, bearing little resemblance to any ancient or modern African civilization: references to the Congo and to the Swahili people merely gesture towards specificity, and the borrowing from Lorca's poem of Harlem suggests that Duncan sees little cultural difference between African Americans in New York and a generic African Blackness. This temporally and geographically vague Africa becomes the metaphor for the world of the unconscious, dreams, fantasy, prohibited sexualities—'the marvelous' and 'the mind's / natural jungle'. Within the poem, it is clear that the 'African' imagery is in fact a projection of the white speaker's psychosexual fantasies. In 1926, Sigmund Freud famously borrowed Henry Morton Stanley's colonialist description of Africa to describe the 'dark continent' of female sexuality. Quoting this phrase, Duncan, then heavily invested in psychoanalysis, both reproduces and subverts it. 'I know', he writes, 'no other continent of Africa more dark than this / dark continent of my breast' (44). For Freud, female sexuality and Africanness were elided as comparative forms of otherness; for Duncan, writing as a white gay man—a third category of 'otherness'—both terms of comparison are audaciously taken on and then repudiated within the poem's heightened dreamscape. Othering himself, Duncan both participates in and destabilizes Freud's adaptation and Stanley's original metaphor, which, as Ranjana Khanna has noted, combines sexualized figuration of the conquest of a feminized continent (sadism) with a paranoid fear of dismemberment, cannibalism, and destruction by the other (masochism) (Khanna 2003, 48–53).

Duncan's critique of the politics of *View* did not, apparently, extend to the Euro-American avant-garde's problematic fetishization of race. His writing of Blackness partook of a kind of generalized exoticism and eroticism: race became the terrain on which he played out his own 'psychodramas' (a term he later deploys to describe work of this period), fantasies, and terrors, with little sense that race might equally be the source of fantasies and terrors for those interpellated under its name. The realities of colonization are nowhere present. Instead, Duncan repeats the racist identification of Blackness with violence and with forbidden sexuality that plays out throughout American modernism, in a world where the existence of actual Black people whom the poet might encounter in any meaningful way seems null and void.

In a later interview, Duncan recalls reading the 'African Elegy' poem to the original, all-Black cast of Gertrude Stein and Virgil Thompson's *Four Saints in Three Acts*:

And when I came to the 'Negroes, negroes, all those princes' and I finish this whole thing and I'm in rapture, all those faces beaming at me, and then this great big *gorgeous* hunk of a black stud says 'Do you have any par-ti-cu-lar black gentleman in mind' [*Laughs*] and *I* thought, God! I *didn't* have any particular

46 NEVER BY ITSELF ALONE

> fellow in mind [. . .] It was Othello that was on my mind but it was a dream
> scene and I was moving it and going forward to what I was seeing. In fact, in
> that one, I find *I* am that figure. (Leyland, 87–88)[7]

Having used race as a space to project his own psychic otherness, Duncan's 'negro'
is at once generic, unable to bear the encounter with an actual individual Black
man (who in Duncan's later description is once again fetishized as a 'black stud'),
and hyper-individualized, referring only to Duncan's own interior projections.
Duncan reports this incident as if the thought of 'a particular black gentleman'
had never crossed his mind, realizing that he had expressed the sense of anguish
he felt as a social pariah through sadomasochistic images informed by the figures
of 'torturing big black men of the sort I'd read about in *The Arabian Nights*, where
a sadist comes and burns you and strips off your skin' (Duncan 1976, 106). Yet,
rather than questioning such stereotypes, either in the 1940s or in the 1970s,
when he recalled the poem three decades later, he merely notes that the analogy
is what seems to him an accurate one: 'Perhaps what I'm talking about is that
I do feel the same thing as a black treated as a pariah, and I've known it and have
suffered from it all along' (101).

As Aldon Nielsen notes, Duncan's work consistently partakes of the 'element
of exoticism' that has proved to be 'the most persistent element of the traditional
structure of racial imagery in American verse', 'appear[ing] in the poetry of
every decade of the twentieth century, and in the poetry of writers of all political
persuasions' (Nielsen, 154). For Nielsen, Duncan's 'African Elegy' 'differs very little
from [Vachel] Lindsay's 'The Congo', with Africa 'an area of darkness inhabited
by exotic primitives'.[8] Certainly, Duncan's poetry and essays of this period are
characterized by a problematically racialized discourse through which he, as did
many other white, gay male writers, sought to figure his own sexuality and that of
others. Through such structures of analogy, white authors, in Siobhan Somerville's
words, 'assume that being a person of color is "like" being gay', thus 'obscur[ing]
those who inhabit both identifications' (Somerville, 7). In the following section
I set these views in context, offering the contemporaneous and later work of James
Baldwin as contrast and corrective.

'One day we'll see how a black man really feels'

Much has been written on what Duncan thought about his own work: from
his own numerous commentaries on this work—which often exceed in length
and loquaciousness the poems themselves—to the readings by succeeding
generations of critics. There is, then, plentiful information available in Duncan's
own words and those of his interlocuters and critics of how he projected racial

and gendered identity onto his own consciousness of himself as a gay man. Yet while Duncan's views of race might be analysed for what they reveal in the psyche of whiteness, in almost none of these commentaries is the perspective of people of colour discussed or even acknowledged. And so now I wish to turn to work by a writer of colour who, while he may be amongst the most prominent and celebrated writers of the twentieth century, has faced silence and neglect, and whose early writings on the intersections of sex, race, and class are almost never discussed. In 1949, James Baldwin published an essay called 'Prison House of Innocence' in the Moroccan-based journal *Zero*. The follow-up to his much better-known essay on Richard Wright, 'Everybody's Protest Novel', this was the first essay to be published by an out gay American Black man (though race is not discussed in the essay, which explores the relations among gender identity, discourses of the 'natural', violence, and sexuality in 'hardboiled fiction').

As Douglas Field notes, while Baldwin's first essay addresses Black protest fiction and gender with no mention of homosexuality, the second addresses homosexuality and gender, with no mention of race (Field 2015, 30–31). (Ekbert Faas mentions that Baldwin was an acquaintance of Duncan's at a Woodstock artists' colony around 1945 but provides no further details [1983, 172]; it is not clear if Baldwin knew Duncan's essay, though it seems likely he would have; likewise, it's not clear to what extent Duncan went on to read Baldwin's work.) As Saidiya Hartman has recently and brilliantly shown, the post-Reconstruction afterlife of slavery has rested on gendered, racialized, and sexual categories which penalized transgressions of the family unit and reinforced stereotypes of pathologized Black sexuality (Hartman 2019; see also Somerville 2000). In turn, even with the liberalizing of discourse that took place during the period the present study begins, the split between queerness as a 'white' issue and race as a heterosexual issue continued to render queers of colour either invisible or—as in Duncan's own poetry—as fetishized objects of sexual curiosity. As John D'Emilio and Estelle Freedman note, during the late 1940s and early 1950s,

> as sexual liberalism took hold among the white middle class, it raised new issues for the maintenance of sexual order [...] But as Black urban communities grew, the Black family and Black sexual mores appeared as a convenient counterpoint, identifying the line between what was permissible and what was not. (D'Emilio and Freedman 1988, 298)

Baldwin began 'Preservation of Innocence' by demolishing the category of 'natural' and 'unnatural' as standards of judgement for sexual behaviour, arguing that the category of the homosexual served as a means of self-protection against the polymorphous nature of desire, which in actuality need not know any categorization of gender or sexuality (Baldwin 1949). Having demolished

48   NEVER BY ITSELF ALONE

the argument from nature, Baldwin illustrates this heterosexual fear through a reading of the association of sex and violence against homosexual men and women in 'hard boiled' fiction. While this essay does not mention race, even as analogy, Baldwin would go on to liken sexual and racial interpellation. In a 1971 conversation with poet Nikki Giovanni, for example, he argued: 'People invent categories in order to feel safe. White people invented black people to give white people identity [. . .] Straight cats invent faggots so they can sleep with them without becoming faggots themselves' (Baldwin and Giovanni 1973, 88–89).

Duncan's disavowal of *both* heterosexual stigmatization of homosexuality *and* nascent modes of homosexual discourse and group formation at first seems to echo the position advanced by Baldwin both during this period and later in his career, particularly in the parallels drawn between race and sexuality. In a 1984 interview with the *Village Voice*, for example, Baldwin cautions against reifying the very identity with which one has been tarred, noting: 'the word gay has always rubbed me the wrong way [. . .] What I saw of that world absolutely frightened me, bewildered me. I didn't understand the necessity of all the role playing. And in a way I still don't' (Baldwin 1984, 59). Explicitly drawing a parallel to racial identification, he argues: 'It seemed a great mistake to answer in the language of the oppressor. As long as I react as a 'nigger', as long as I protest my case on evidence or assumptions held by others, I'm simply reinforcing those assumptions' (72). Arguing for a radical difference by which a racialized African American subject experiences their sexuality—as secondary to the pre-existing interpellations of white racism—he expresses scepticism about alliances between racialized and sexualized groups: 'A black gay person who is a sexual conundrum to society is already, long before the question of sexuality comes into it, menaced and marked because he's black or she's black. The sexual question comes after the question of color; it's simply one more aspect of the danger in which all black people live' (68–69). Nonetheless, he ultimately imagines a future 'New Jerusalem' in which 'no one will have to call themselves gay. Maybe that's at the bottom of my impatience with the term. It answers a false argument, a false accusation [. . .] That is, that you have no right to be here, that you have to prove your right to be here. I'm saying I have nothing to prove. The world also belongs to me' (73). As Jonathan Ned Katz paraphrased: 'In a world in which no one identifies as gay, no one will identify as straight. That world, Baldwin suggests, divested of the homosexual/heterosexual division, will belong to all of us' (Katz 1995, 105). Likewise, though he was, as Allen Bérubé notes, one of the first writers to publicly endorse the term 'homosexual' over the slur 'queer'—to be followed by Donald Webster Cory's 1963 *The Homosexual in America*—Duncan himself rejected being identified as 'gay', even in frank and explicit discussions of his sexual experiences for publications such as *Gay Sunshine*, given in the later 1970s (Bérubé 1991, 67; Leyland 1978; Quarles 1976, 31).

Yet Baldwin's focus here and in 'Preservation of Innocence' is, in a sense, the *opposite* of Duncan's, in that it focuses on the ones who interpellate, rather than on criticizing the groups thus interpellated. While Duncan suggests that (white) homosexuals should model their political conduct on those of African Americans and Jewish activists who place these racialized identifications as secondary in their political struggles, Baldwin notes the differing levels to which one will experience their interpellation and cautions against drawing parallels between such groups (Baldwin 1984, 69). Likewise, if, in 1944, Duncan calls for the *dissolution* of an identity, that identity had barely even been established for writers of colour when Baldwin wrote 'Preservation of Innocence' five years later. Despite the stigma faced by white queer artists, Duncan's essay is nonetheless able to draw on an international cast of predecessors—Crane, Proust, and Melville. Baldwin has access to no such readily available tradition. It would take another three decades for Adrian Stanford's *Black and Queer* to be the first published book of poetry by an out Black gay male poet. 'Conversing once with Pauline Kael [Duncan's close friend] I said I intended to write on the issue, for some day some black will write on it, and then we'll really hear how a black man feels', Duncan remembered with offensive flippancy in 1976 (Duncan 1976, 101). In the meantime, Duncan, for all his humanist aspirations, speaks from within a tyrannical hold of whiteness on both conscious and unconscious mind.

'Creating New Worlds': The Berkeley Renaissance

Following the publication of 'The Homosexual in Society', Duncan was involved in anarchist circles in New York with writers such as Jackson MacLow and Paul Goodman, and Judith Malina and Julian Beck, soon to found the Living Theatre. In June 1946, he returned to Berkeley, ten years after having initially dropped out of university. Employed as a typist for the University of California, Duncan once more gravitated towards anarchist circles, including those around poet Kenneth Rexroth, and enrolled for courses at the university in 1948. Living in a student house known as 'Throckmorton Manor', in Peter Quatermain's words he 'set himself up as a kind of poetry entrepreneur', organising poetry readings, discussions, and informal lectures. Duncan later recalled the 'group of students, returning GI's and CO's, would-be Bohemians and artists [. . .] at 2029 Hearst we all drifted, making the rent and food as we could, in a kind of cooperative house' (Duncan, quoted in Jarnot 2012, 104). Ekbert Faas calls the 'Manor' a 'recently founded anti-university [. . .] Life at Throckmorton was so communal and open that tenants would hide what seemed to bourgeois rather than what might shock [. . .] There were wild parties with drinking, talking, dancing, and subsequent homosexual and heterosexual lovemaking', with Duncan involved

50   NEVER BY ITSELF ALONE

'in a hectic round of love affairs' (Faas 1983, 215). In summer 1946, Duncan met the young poet Jack Spicer at an anarchist meeting; joined by Robin Blaser, the three became each other's principal readers and interlocuters, acting as sounding board and inspiration for the poems which Duncan and Spicer were composing. (At this stage Blaser, less confident in his own work, served principally as a witness to his friends' creativity; it would not be until the following decade that he began his own writing career in earnest.[9]) Publishing in local magazines, organizing workshops at the university and informal reading groups in student accommodation, and commiserating (as well as competing) with each other in their love affairs, the three poets—along with fellow travellers such as the rich and dashing Landis Everson—saw themselves as reinventing the language and forming a new movement that would rival the world-historical impact of the Renaissance writers they studied in their university classes.

In this early phase, lasting from 1946 through to roughly 1950, the Berkeley poets, particularly Duncan, sketched out a potential community, a metonymic transposition of their own socio-sexual gatherings, based on literary self-figurations from the Knights of the Round Table to the homosexual friendships of Dante and of Elizabethan English poets such as Marlowe and Shakespeare. These elements—the social, the sexual, and the poetic—were in a kind of cyclical or circular relationship, each providing material on which the others could feed. As Duncan recounts, when he and Spicer first met, Spicer's first enquiries concerned the Albigensians, a medieval gnostic sect subject to a genocidal crusade by the medieval French Church and Crown (Spicer 1980, x). Spicer was also particularly interested in Duncan's knowledge of the circle, or *kreis*, surrounding German poet Stefan George, who, after the death in 1904 of Maximillian Kronberger, a teenage boy on whom he had fixated, had turned him into 'Maximin', the Beatrice-like devotee of a poetic cult. George's conception or a spiritual aristocracy presided over by an autocratic poet had unsettling correspondences with Nazi ideology, rendering him an immensely problematic figure, though his English-language reception had not yet revealed this aspect of his work.[10] George's influence did not lie so much in his poetry itself but in the idea of creating a community in which gay male sexuality and poetry served as mirrors for each other. The connection to George was amplified, not only by Duncan's brief earlier affair with the poet Werner Vordtriede, whose mother had been a member of groups relating to the *kreis*, but also by the presence in Berkeley of the historian Ernst Kantorowicz, a bona fide member of the *kreis* who had fled the Nazi regime and whose lectures the young poets eagerly attended (Faas 1983, 172–74).[11] Duncan was keen to adapt Kantorowicz's influential conception of the 'king's two bodies'—in which the separation between the office of kingship and the body of the person currently embodying that role rendered the office with an undying '*dignitas*'—to that of the poet.[12] Such models—opposed to the state from a conservative position that was elitist, hierarchical, and misogynist—would seem in direct contradiction to Duncan's and Spicer's avowed anarchist politics, and the overtones of megalomania they lend in particular to Duncan's work of this period remain problematic and disturbing. Yet such grandiose conceptions were in constant tension with the daily negotiations of the poets' lives as queer men in a homophobic society. Talk of spiritual aristocracy, elite circles and cults, and the dignity of kinship in effect served as a high-flown distraction from the fact that this was above all a culture organized around sexuality—the tensions and pleasures of (largely queer) sexual exchange, competition, pairings, jealousy, and the like that animate virtually all writing communities. At the same time, Duncan, Spicer, and Blaser expressed a sense of doubt and torment about such desire, as at once a vital and motivating force for their work and something which that work might seek to transcend or contradict. In this regard, Tom Parkinson identifies what he perceives as a central tension in the 'Renaissance' writers: between 'a desire to live almost totally in the imagination' and the messy business of sexual relations, filled with jealousy and competition, and often felt to be unsatisfactory (Parkinson, 103). Above all, the poets served as each other's key audients and interlocuters, actively participating in the transmutation of the messy business of romantic drama into poetry.

The King's Two Cities

Duncan's two major poems of this period, 'Heavenly City, Earthly City' (1946–1947) and 'The Venice Poem' (1948), deploy the figure of the city to explore what he later called 'psychosexual dramas' of his emotional life, along with the excitement and sense of community found at Throckmorton Manor and particularly in the meeting with Spicer and Blaser. The long title poem to *Heavenly City, Earthly City*, published by Bern Porter in 1947, was begun before Duncan's move to Berkeley, while he was living with Hamilton and Mary Tyler at Treesbank Farm in Pasadena, and worked on throughout the year. During this time, Duncan entered into an erotic competition with a friend, from whom he 'won' his lover Jerry Ackerman, and the tensions of this love triangle, along with his developing friendship with Spicer and Blaser, form its emotional backdrop. The poem opens with a sun-like figure: a 'bright and terrible disk' associated with a beauty that causes suffering and has faded along with the poet's youth, 'the city of my passion' (Duncan 2012, 84). The figure of the city as the poet's own passion, like the projected mental jungle of the 'African Elegy' once more dwells in the realm of psychic projection, whilst reaching for an Apollonian clarity in which artistic transmutation is no longer the 'sadness' of the 'marvelous' but a praise song which resolves the tension between imagined and actual, heavenly

52 NEVER BY ITSELF ALONE

and earthly, physical and spiritual desire. The city—variously described as 'city of my passion', 'earthly radiant / city of poetry' and an 'abject sexual kingdom'—is a morphing entity which seems to change form according to the poet's moods and erotic life, oscillating between despair at the loss of physical and spiritual love—the disappearance of Christ after the crucifixion, the fall of Icarus, and Orpheus' loss of Eurydice in the underworld, and his subsequent dismemberment by the Bacchae, here associated, as in the 'African Elegy', with the tearing apart of jealousy and internal conflict—and a sense of spiritual-erotic fulfilment. Duncan stages an audaciously eroticized refiguration of the Christian Easter hymn 'I Know That My Redeemer Lives': Christ's resurrection becomes an eroticized '*touch*' that '*seems to penetrate and awaken*' (86). It's impossible to tell here whether Duncan describes sexual love in spiritual terms or spiritual love in sexual terms. Such figurations were later archly criticized by Thom Gunn, who wrote: 'The figure of the lover in the earliest poems has an alarming tendency to suddenly turn into Jesus—a Jesus of the Hopkins brand, you might say' (Bertholf, 145[13]). While the poem denigrates the physical body and sexual love as 'animal' actions—'that bright confusion, love', in which 'I watch with pain my hairy self / crouchd in his abject sexual kingdom'—this kingdom also sees the speaker 'writhe in that brief ecstatic span / as if he took the sun within himself / and became a creature of the sun' (Duncan 2012, 92), leading to the poem's concluding hymn of praise in which, having been adrift in a purposeless sea, the speaker, like Odysseus, returns to a newly discovered home identified with the brotherhood of the Berkeley Renaissance:

> The wandering man returns to his city
> as if he might return to earth a light, a joy;
> and find his rest in earthly company [. . .]
> My earthly city is reveald in its beauty.
> (Duncan 2012, 94)[14]

Augustine of Hippo's *The City of God*, from which 'Heavenly City' borrows its titular conceit, counsels Christians after the sack of Rome to concern themselves with the City of God—the heavenly city, the New Jerusalem—rather than that of earthly politics and the Earthly City, Rome. While the Earthly City is associated with physical cares and pleasures, the City of God is dedicated to eternal truths. Yet the poem resolves this conflict, not through arguing for the Heavenly City and the rejection of the flesh—figured as an inert ideal, becalmed at sea—but through a transfigured Earthly City where carnal desire is embraced. Through a transformed, syncretic version of Christianity and of ancient Greek mythology, Duncan seeks to imbue homosexuality with salvific power in a synthesis of Heavenly and Earthly Cities, refigured as an aesthetic, rather than as Christian,

'HOMOSEXUALS IN SOCIETY' 53

spiritual truth. As Duncan later wrote in his statement on poetics for *The New American Poetry*: 'As Plato discovered, or St. Augustine discovered in the City of God, unrealities, fantasies, mere ideas, can never be destroyed' (Donald Allen 1961, 401). For Duncan, as he explained in one of the numerous digressions of his unfinished life's work, *The H.D. Book*, Augustine also served as a figure for the embattled group within the larger body of the empire—in Augustine's case, that of Christianity, waging for position as the empire's official religion, and in Duncan's, that of the political left, the poet in a hostile society, and the gay group.

> Augustine, when Rome fell to the Vandals in the fifth century and the Christians were accused of betraying the Empire in their disaffiliation from the war, answered in *The City of God* with the ringing affirmation of an eternity more real than historical time, a life eternal or supreme good more real than the good life of the philosopher. For Augustine [. . .] in the world beyond the household and the city, the world of human society at large 'man is separated from man by the difference of languages.' (Duncan 2012, *The H.D. Book*, 191)

Duncan notes Augustine's 'disillusionment with all the values of the Roman world' and his pacifist argument against 'just war' and the attempt to convert Rome (the Earthly City) through violence and warfare (192). In these poems, the city at once serves as the figure of community—for it was in New York and San Francisco that Duncan found artistic and social community in real life—and of the queer poets' exclusion from community. As Michael Davidson notes of the doubled city figure in Augustine, this 'image of two cities, one of saints and one of lost souls' means that 'Man lives as a citizen of both cities in a kind of suspension until the last judgment; Hell and Heaven are immanent in the literal city, one created out of daily discourse and common care' (Davidson 1977, 129). Such work seeks to resolve personal conflicts in the sphere of poetry: thus, the 'bright and terrible disk' transformed into a rapturous poem in praise of the sun.

The lover Duncan had 'won' during the composition of 'Heavenly City', student and writer Gerald ('Jerry') Ackerman, was ten years younger than Duncan, and tensions soon emerged in the relationship. Distressed by Ackerman's 'adultery' with other, younger men, from February to September 1948, these tensions informed the composition of Duncan's next major work, 'The Venice Poem'. The poem's origin in the tumultuous relationship histories of the Berkeley circle, and specifically Duncan's private life, is illustrated by the fact that the opening lines first appear in Duncan's journal alongside notes on anxiously waiting for Ackerman's return: 'Jerry's being away with someone else fucking or wanting to fuck casts panic upon me. There is no agony like these moments or hours, these unbearable stretches of time' (Duncan, quoted in Jarnot, 113–14). Yet Ekbert Faas suggests that Duncan used his jealousy as a spur to creativity, in his

54 NEVER BY ITSELF ALONE

words, 'wrest[ing] a kind of delight from the situation of Jerry's "adultery"' (Faas 1983, 257).

Lisa Jarnot notes that the Venice poem 'became a memorial of the collective erotic longings of the Berkeley Renaissance participants, and it also bore their collective influence' (Jarnot, 112). Duncan recalls composing 'The Venice Poem' in Spicer's presence, as the 'aftermath' of 'a sexual psychodrama' created a 'rhapsody that went far beyond the bounds of the decorum establisht for the art': 'his intensity in audience drew me on into reaches, wooing his listening, where over-riding / over-writing the actual events and relationships I raise figures of another realm of feeling in which visionary ejaculation and nightmare phantasy are confused' (Spicer 1980, xiii). Blaser and Spicer would come and sit with Duncan to distract him, and they became audients for the poem that developed out of this anguish—an anguish that soon came to feed the poem so that, even after his and Ackerman's temporary reconciliation, Duncan's poem—at points seeming a hymn to jealousy itself—drew strength from an aesthetic mode which at once recreated and transmuted the original feeling of despair into the source of creative energy. Poetry is the occasion for such community, and such community is the occasion for poetry. Drawing on Kantorowicz's lectures on medieval and renaissance architecture, which he infuses with homoerotic symbolism (the bell tower and ornamental lions of St Mark's standing for a penis and testicles), the poem also built on the tensions between Duncan—at once the holy fool, 'Saint William Shakespeare', the 'cross-eyed poet', and Othello—Ackerman (as Desdemona, both saint and whore) and Spicer as Iago, offering malicious advice.

This peculiar triangulation—the 'fraternity' of poets bonding over one of their number's torments in love, who then produces a kind of celebratory monument to their friendship—suggests that the queer city itself is built, not on the transformation of society, but the transmutation of negative affect through an aesthetic totality. Venice's queer history resonates in the homoerotic tensions of *Othello* and as the setting for Thomas Mann's *Death in Venice*, in which forbidden (paedophilic) male desire and plague associate with debates on irony, the body, and art. Venice is, too, a city of outsiders, in which the roots of Western capitalism develop from a city formed by exiles from other European countries. This paradoxical placement suggests the atmosphere of Duncan's poem, in which locations central to capitalism and imperialism are zones of sexual and racial ambiguity, even if Duncan's concern is not explicitly with the historical developments these might suggest. Once more, a sense of being a sexual outsider is transplanted onto racial outsiders and feminized persons. And once more, Duncan draws on Shakespeare's work, through the racialized Venetian figure of Othello (the African soldier required for military campaigns but an unnerving presence in the city itself) as a figure of jealousy; though he is not present, we might also recall Shylock, the Jewish moneylender on whose custom the city's inhabitants rely but whom they hypocritically condemn. The poem also replays some of the racialized projections of 'African Elegy'; as Lisa Jarnot notes, sections recall from Vachel Lindsay's racist poem 'The Congo', with its lurid, stereotypical invocations of 'hoodoo' ceremonies. Duncan once more 'identif[ies] sexual drama with an exotic vision of Africa': at a low point in the poem, the speaker has a vision of cannibals chewing liver and spitting bile, reciting doggerel, their drums and words whirling round in the dark as an antithesis to the realm of gods and poetry. This racialized vision at once menaces and identifies with the speaker, rendered shamefully 'primitive': 'you are shown, / naked and silly as the primeval bone' (Duncan 2012, 233). While the poem ends with a kind of elevation of self-sufficient ego to cosmic principle, with the poet crowned as infant king of a transformed world, here the image of cannibalism and shame perhaps equates the 'narcissism' of male homosexuality with the self-consumption of humans by other humans: the queer is once more aligned with that which is cast out of civilization, the terms of the comparison echoing both the sexual and racial terms of condemnation which they work through. Following these moments of shame, the poem seizes on the image of 'saint William Shakespeare' lighting candles— 'love's taper [. . .] candle of innocence / whose flame / does not die' (Duncan 2012, 237), associated with 'faith', the comfort of nursery rhymes and 'first things'—a 'devotion' which 'bears wounds' and survives 'knowledge', 'accuracy', and 'wisdom' (238). Duncan ends the poem as king of his own universe, a coda composed during a period of reconciliation with Jerry: the poet becomes "baby charmd by the bells ringing [. . .] little cross-eyed king held / secure in the centre of all things', with the poet-as-infant-king surrounded by the sound of maternal bells and phallic 'fatherly towers'.

In sharp distinction to the anarchist inflection which one might imagine Duncan would bring to such a history, 'The Venice Poem' ends with the speaker not just as poet-king, but as poet-*emperor*. As Duncan would later write in the preface to *Caesar's Gate* (1955/1972):

> I saw the city of Venice in that poem as my own and the history of its empire as
> the history of an imperialism in Poetry in which I saw my own dreams expand
> [. . .] In my vision of empire in The Venice poem I saw again the power and the
> Accumulation of Wealth, the grandeur and domination, as a poetry established
> in a pathos, a pathetic claim having knowledge of the remains of Venice, today.
> (Duncan 2012, 696)

Shakespeare's Venice thus serves as scene of economic and erotic competition, and as parallel to the ways the postwar American empire colonizes and privatizes sexual relations in the interests of state power. For Duncan, using the figure of empire as metaphor for sexual possessiveness destabilizes this root

56 NEVER BY ITSELF ALONE

of American self-figuration on both the personal and political level. In this work, imperial ambitions such as those of contemporaneous America are the products of constructions of masculine possessiveness—both heterosexual and homosexual—with psychological roots in feelings of inadequacy and a capitalist ethos of accumulation. Conversely, Duncan's own feelings of jealousy, possession, self-hatred, and torment in love, exacerbated by his homosexuality, are socially shaped by the contradictions and double-binds of the heteropatriarchal society in which he lives. Within the space of the poem, such questions can—as too in 'Heavenly City, Earthly City'—be suspended and contraries maintained as they cannot in life.

For Spicer, this ending betrayed the dynamics of the preceding poem—a false transmutation which was untrue to both the poetic and extra-poetic problematics the preceding sequence had explored, escaped through an idealistic gesture of wish fulfilment that was ultimately narcissistic, as the poet became, in Duncan's own words, 'infant emperor in his autistic universe'. In a fractious epistolary exchange later reprinted in the *Collected Books of Jack Spicer*, Spicer had earlier suggested that Duncan's vocabulary of mythic significance—his talk of a "Western Kingdom of Poetry" to which the Berkeley Renaissance poets were 'monarchs'—concealed its actual ties to social relations.

> What you do (and whenever you do it I hate you mythicly) is confuse *your* poetry with *our* poetry. In your poetry you are indeed king, having crowned yourself like Dante [. . .] You can (and probably do) give a mortgage in this crown to anyone you sleep with. You are not *our* king [. . .] and your relation with your intra-poetic feudatories has nothing to do with our inter-poetic relations. (Quoted in Faas 1983, 278)

While Spicer too believed that the poem should be more than merely an adjunct to social drama, he implies that for Duncan, the poem becomes a tool of seduction ('you can (and probably do) give a mortgage in this crown to anyone sleep with') and a careerist jockeying for position within the literary marketplace: an attempt to wield power both amongst and beyond the sexual and social relations within the community.

While models of queer 'fraternity', from the *George-kreis* to Kantorowicz's classes and the Berkeley Renaissance itself, rest on idealized images of homosocial community, these were not ideal models of political community, but governed by the jealousies, competition, and rampant egotism of young, ambitious men well capable of hurting the ones they loved. Further, the tension between elitist, homosocial models and an anarchist humanism committed to sexual liberation and gender equality plays out throughout the poetry of the Berkeley Renaissance. As such, it also reflects the historical contradictions facing these poets who lacked immediate social, political, and poetic models for a collective queerness in the face of state repression, and for whom, as Michael Davidson notes, models of the 'insular fraternity', served as modes of self-protection and self-defence against a hostile public world (Davidson 1989, 59).

Yet it was precisely this aspect of such work—'the gossip of the community', its psychosexual dramas, and those elements that seemed ethically and politically problematic—that interested a later generation of San Francisco queer writing community, that of the New Narrative writers. In the late 1970s and early 1980s Robert Glück and Bruce Boone used the work of Duncan and Spicer to suggest alternatives to what they saw as the sanitized and problematic attempt on the part of the gay community to provide relentlessly positive images to counteract what Glück described as the 'disastrous descriptions' of a homophobic society. In particular, these younger writers stressed the role of gossip in forming community and in bridging the divide between private or secret knowledge and common property, and the role of negative affects—meanness, spite, and jealousy as well as loss, mourning, and despair—in negotiating a community built around the linked fields of sex and death, Eros and Thanatos. For Boone, in his essay 'Robert Duncan and Gay Community', while the apparent contradictions of Duncan's and Spicer's work might, from the perspective of Gay Liberation, be disavowed as the product of their time, as instances of self-loathing and distrust in the absence of a broader collective means of identification, it was precisely in their negative affects that they had something to teach the present-day gay community (Boone 1983). This manifested in two apparently competing directions. Firstly, in 'The Homosexual on Society', Duncan's insistence that the community must be open to struggle on a 'universal' plane—towards the transformation of the entire field of social, sexual, and economic relations, rather than simply the concerns associated with a particular identity. Secondly, both Duncan's and Spicer's working through of negative affect—the jealousy that is, at one point, treated as a kind of deity in 'The Venice Poem', the distrust, meanness, and (in Duncan's phrase) 'refus[al] to be taken in by life' of Spicer's work (Spicer 1980). Community in Duncan's work, then, in its oscillations between local, coterie, and international, between an idealized 'commune of poetry' and the tensions of the actual social relations that surround the poem's composition, reflects the historical conditions facing the gay poet at this time, but it also suggests problematics that persist even in an era—our own—of vast symbolic, cultural, and legislative change.

From the Renaissance to the Household

Reconcilining and moving in with Jerry Ackerman after the 'The Venice Poem', Duncan's second major experiment in domesticity after his failed heterosexual

58   NEVER BY ITSELF ALONE

marriage also ended in a traumatic breakup (Faas 1983, 275). Meanwhile, Robin Blaser had been elected chairman of the Writers' Conference, a student creative writing workshop at UC Berkeley in which Ackerman, Spicer, and Duncan were all involved. Publishing *Literary Behavior*—the title a joke about the newly published Kinsey Report, *Sexual Behavior*—the group gained a reputation as a 'homosexual conspiracy' and was disbanded by faculty members, including the group's apparent allies Josephine Miles and Tom Parkinson. Duncan and Spicer were enraged at what they perceived as rampant homophobia and wrote verse satires on the events: Spicer's 'The Dunkiad' mocks Miles' criticism of the group as 'too closely knit, too limited a clique. / She said she thought their group too interfused / But I suspect she meant—they were too Greek', while Duncan's 'A Poet's Masque' presents Miles criticizing the group for 'moral indigence' and 'all the excitements of bad taste'—a critique, like Ransom's, that deliberately blurs the moral and the formalist (Spicer 2021, 76; Duncan 2019, 248). Such incidents suggested the poets' precarious relation to academia. In 1949, the University of California introduced a new rule requiring its employees to take a 'Loyalty Oath': Kantorowicz and Spicer both refused to sign and resigned their teaching positions, with Kantorowicz departing for Princeton and Spicer for Minneapolis. But the relationships of the Renaissance poets had already grown strained with Duncan and Spicer's quarrel over the ending to 'The Venice Poem'. In the face of Spicer's accusations, Duncan insisted that he, Landis Everson, Spicer, and Blaser all formed part of 'a great American School, a fraternity of poets', and that they were 'eternal lords of creation', endowed by 'the genius of the language', and 'made heirs by the greatest fraternity of poets since London circa 1600' (Faas 1983, 281). This letter reads something like special pleading at precisely the point when the physical community which he here mythologized to such an extent was in fact dispersing. By 1950, Duncan described Berkeley as now 'a wretched constriction', whose promise of transformative poetic community had abruptly vanished.

Duncan met the artist Jess Collins in Autumn 1949 at a reading on the Berkeley Campus (Tara McDowell, 122). Jess, who had worked on the Manhattan Project before resigning after the devastation of Hiroshima and Nagasaki, had transferred to the California School of Fine Arts. He and Duncan were 'married' in January 1951, and their life together gave Duncan a basis for a new mode of understanding the relation between poetry and community, in the mythic figure of the 'household' (Tara McDowell has written in detail on this phase in Duncan's work). As such, Duncan in effect exchanged one mode of queer creativity—that of the coterie, the fraternity, or the bohemian circle with its sexual and artistic experimentation serving as a kind of replacement family—with another—that of the domestic enclave, for Duncan and Jess exemplified in the pairing of Gertrude Stein and Alice B. Toklas. This idealized realm was bolstered by what McDowell calls 'the wide thick spread of inherited wealth that is a striking fact of life in the United States', as 'various forms of familial, collegial, and patron support [including an allowance from Duncan's mother and an allowance from Jess's art dealer] enabled the couple to maintain and work within the refuge of their safe-household' (McDowell, 28).

The introduction to Duncan's later collection *Bending the Bow* (1968) serves as index of Duncan's mature, post-Renaissance poetics. Community now definitively abides in poetry to an extent that exceeds the lived experience on which it draws. 'The commune of poetry becomes so real that [the poet] sounds each article in relation to parts of a great story that he knows will never be completed' (Duncan 1968, vi). For Duncan, the interplay of private and public—as it relates to his sexuality, to the cultivation of a sustainable and central domestic partnership with Jess, and to the volatile history of San Francisco as a city built, as he notes, on earthquakes—is one in which what we might call the civic, or political, voice of poetry is ultimately subsumed to a polis which exists in the 'commune' of the poem itself, where what enters are 'only words'. 'Everywhere, from whatever poem, choreographies extend into actual space. In my imagination I go through the steps the poet takes so that the area of a township appears in my reading'. Yet, ultimately, 'the boundary lines in the poem belong to the poem and not to the town'. At the same time, Duncan attended protests against the Vietnam War and was part of the Berkeley Free Speech Movement, writing passionately about them in poems such as 'The Multiversity' even as he famously castigated his long-term correspondent Denise Levertov for her own reading at an anti – Vietnam War rally, giving a reading for Gay Liberation day at which he denounced any idea of 'gay rights', and giving interviews in the gay press in which he proclaimed that he didn't see himself as gay.

In a recent essay, latter-day New Narrative writer Rob Halpern, who—as I'll examine in the book's coda—has been profoundly influenced by Duncan's work, argues that, during the 1950s, Duncan's work evolves from that of 'a faggot in conflict with his sexuality to a domesticated lover, as if he'd been following a cosmic progression from loves to Love' (Halpern 2020, n.p.). In the introduction to *The Years as Catches* (1966), Duncan argues that both his mature poetry and his mature life have found

> [a] rhythm that could contain and project the components of an emerging homosexuality in an ardor that would prepare for the development of Eros and, eventually, for that domesticated and domesticating Love that governs the creation of a household and a lasting companionship. (Duncan 2012, 30)

This adaptation of the domestic as space of refuge, with its implicit acceptance of the public/private binary central to heteropatriarchal ordering arguably marks the failure of the universalism Duncan advocated in 'The Homosexual in Society'

60 NEVER BY ITSELF ALONE

under its very name. Sexuality as a social issue—whether this be the generalized 'society' of Duncan's 1944 essay or the social community of Throckmorton Manor and the Berkeley Renaissance—is transplanted into a poetic realm that escapes society, not by negating its contradictions (which can sometimes be fatal ones) but by sidestepping then.

Duncan's 'household' in some ways represents a retreat from modes of queer community that challenge the bases of the nuclear family as the 'manifest domesticity' of an America characterized by imperial possession abroad and domestic policing as the locus of productivity at home.[15] Yet it also represents a challenge to heteropatriarchal conceptions of value, engaged through a queer modernism that emphasizes a female and feminized tradition of writing—H.D., Stein—over and against the machismo that had come to characterize American writing, from Williams to Hemingway, Pound to Olson—with what in the preface to *Bending the Bow* he called a 'girlish possibility' in men that 'embarrasses the masculinity of the reader' (Duncan 1968, vi).[16] Above all, however, the household for Duncan was a means of survival. Michael Rumaker's *Robert Duncan in San Francisco* (1978), published a couple of decades later, paints a vivid picture of the atmosphere of alienation, undercover surveillance and entrapment, distrust and hostility by which queer poets adapted various means of survival. By contrast, Duncan's mode of defence was based on his home-life with Jess. Rumaker writes:

> [I]t's important that the walls are of your own making (not those imposed from without by others) to exist and work in openly and comfortably in expansive affection and vitality; in the distance of impersonal affection that respects the singularity of the beloved, and one's own, the space to move and make in: *home*, that most powerful word, in all that it means. (Rumaker 2013, 77–78)

At the same time, Duncan continued to be plagued by the jealousy and uncertainty that had characterized his often-tormented experience of bohemian life. As Rumaker notes, Duncan's extra-marital affairs had to be carefully concealed from Jess in a replay of the familiar drama of the unfaithful husband and the stay-at-home wife (Jess punningly described himself as a 'housewaif') (43–44). Duncan himself later comments on this play of guilt and drama as a reproduction of the familial structures inherited from the heterosexual matrix (Quarles 1976). Duncan's relation to Jess, as well as its significance for his poetics, doesn't so much erase the structures of jealousy and uncertainty as displace and remove them from the community and towards the privatized space of the household. As Aaron Shurin later noted, while Duncan and Jess had many gay friends, they didn't have 'a gay community', and Duncan was later notably ambivalent about the Gay Liberation Movement, telling friends in response to the rise of the term 'gay pride' that he preferred it when it was 'gay shame'

(McDowell, 52). The 'commune' of poetry and the 'field of first permission' of the poem are textual, ideal, and imagined, able to come into existence—at least, according to Duncan's own personal bio-mythography—only when he removed himself from the gay community that had at first sustained him.

Coda: 'Being so far abroad from what he once was'

By 1962, Duncan and Spicer's relationship had soured almost beyond repair, in part due to Jess' antipathy towards Spicer's abrasive behaviour and to Spicer's increasing alcoholism. Spicer, who by this stage begun to cultivate a *kreis* of his own, felt that Duncan's domestic life betrayed their ethos, and Duncan felt that lines of Spicer's poetry were direct attacks on his own person. When Duncan's *The Opening of the Field* was published by New Directions in 1960, for instance, the fiercely anti-copyright Spicer responded by reprinting the copyright page as the cover to his own un-copyrighted small press pamphlet 'Lament for the Makers' (Killian and Ellingham, 209). But in spring 1962, Duncan wrote a series of poems, to be collected in *Roots and Branches* (1964), which returned to Spicer and to the Berkeley Renaissance as reminders of their shared quests as queer poets and the models of community they had cherished. Duncan, who rarely made visits to the North Beach area of San Francisco where Spicer spent much of his time, specifically came to hand Spicer the poems. As Kevin Killian and Lewis Ellingham write:

> In early 1962, Duncan made an unusual sortie into North Beach to show the Dante sonnets to Spicer [. . .] [Stan Persky recalls:] 'I remember Duncan bringing [the Dante poems] around to the bars; I remember Jack going outside and handing me those poems so I could read them by the light of the neon sign outside some bar. They're gorgeous, beautiful poems, and Spicer thought they were beautiful poems' [. . .] Duncan had gone to the bother and pain of a trip to North Beach to prove something to Jack. Their sense of community was never breached. (Killian and Ellingham, 226–77)

'A New Poem for Jack Spicer', printed immediately preceding the sonnets in *Roots and Branches*, serves as a kind of prelude to the sequence-in-miniature. Guided by a figure who is at once the poet's double, a lover or 'male muse', Charon, Virgil, Spicer, Ka (the ancient Egyptian concept of the soul), and Kaka (the infantile—and Artaudian—name for excrement), the speaker proceeds along a body of water that is at once the Styx, the river to hell, and the enchanted realm of poetry, of queer possibility beyond sexual and national boundaries. In a series of homophonic slippages, poetry is at once 'boat', 'body', and 'bed' and

62 NEVER BY ITSELF ALONE

then 'the lake itself, / the bewildering circling water way' (Duncan 2012, 204). These watery slippages serve as metaphoric displacements which, as befits the etymological origin of metaphor as a transport or ferrying across, confuse tenor and vehicle so that it is impossible to tell whether poetry's origin lies in the sexual (the bed) or the spiritual, the life force or the afterlife. Ultimately poetry, as that which articulates from a source which cannot be named, transports the poet beyond national identification and the imperial mendacity of America. The poem concludes:

> Lake of no shores I can name,
> Body of no day or night I can account for [. . .]
> The farthest shore is so near
> crows fly up and we know it is America.
> No crow flies. It is not America.
> From what we call Poetry
> a bird I cannot name crows.
>
> (Duncan 2014, 206)

In the following poem, the first of the Dante sonnets, Duncan turns to queer desire and its fate amongst 'the roaring waters of hell's rivers' (206). The sonnet addresses Dante's sympathetic presentation of the sodomites in Book XV of the *Inferno*, and of his master Brunetto Latini amongst them, 'a Love of which Dante does not speak unkindly'. Latini, author of perhaps the first encyclopaedia in a modern European language, was Dante's guardian and teacher after the death of his father, yet he appears in the Seventh Circle of the inferno, where it is implied that he is punished for the crime of sodomy (*Inferno*, XV.82–87.) In his 1959 afterword to 'The Homosexual in Society', Duncan likewise recalls the moment in which Latini stops to converse with Dante—though this will increase his punishment, condemned to run in a circle of fire.

It is just here, when he sees his beloved teacher, Brunetto Latini, among the sodomites, that Dante has an inspired intuition that goes beyond the law of his church and reaches toward a higher ethic: 'Were my desire all fulfilled,' he says to Brunetto, 'you had not yet been banished from human nature: for in my memory is fixed . . . the dear and kind, paternal image of you, when in the world, hour by hour, you taught me how man makes himself eternal [. . .]'

'Were my desire all fulfilled [. . .]' springs from the natural heart in the confidence of its feelings that has often been more generous than conventions and institutions. I picture that fulfillment of desire as a human state of mutual volition and aid, a shared life [. . .] Our hopes lies still in the creative imagination

'HOMOSEXUALS IN SOCIETY' 63

wherever it unifies what had been thought divided, wherever it transforms the personal experience into a communal good, 'that Brunetto Latini had not been banished from human nature'. (Duncan 2019, 12–13)[17]

For Duncan, Dante's affection for Latini serves as an index of the possibility of love and solidarity that might transcend sexual preference and social prohibition. Duncan's paraphrase of this passage in the first sonnet picks up on Dante's description of the sodomites: male lovers, gazing upon one another, seek to thread each other's eyes like the eye of a needle, a meeting 'Love has appointed there / For a joining that is not easy' (Duncan 2014, 207). In the second sonnet, Duncan extends the metaphor to that of the queer household established with Jess, the image of Jess quietly sewing in the sun picked up on as 'the thread of my leaf [. . .] wedded to the eye of its needle' (207). Both Duncan and his lover are engaged in a patchwork quilt-making which 'unites' diverse elements—such as the fragments of translations and paraphrases of Dante—'in Love's name', a 'domestic cult of Eros' which unites in a process of making that is communal, though local, poetic and erotic, 'a new definition of household and social relations'.

In the third sonnet, Duncan turns from his new context, the 'household', returning to the figure of the boat from the 'New Poem', and calling back to an earlier mode of community. Dedicated to Robin Blaser in its original printing, the poem assumes a wistful intimacy, at once celebrating and bidding farewell to the moment of the Berkeley Renaissance. Adapting Dante's sixth sonnet, in which the Florentine poet addresses Guido Cavalcanti and Lapo Gianni in a lyric *epistolae*, using his sonnet to meditate on the nature of eros and poetry's relation to love as biological and spiritual force, Duncan borrows Dante's mode of direct address and the speculative modality of the poem as an opportunity to meditate on the past. 'Robin, it would be a great thing if you, me and Jack Spicer / Were taken up in sorcery', Duncan begins (Duncan 2014, 208). Addressed to Blaser and delivered as the last of Duncan's gifts to Spicer, Duncan imagines the three poets, estranged in life, aboard the 'fairy ship' of poetry, sailing away both from the heterosexual tradition and from the past. Yet while the sonnet imagines a conditional, speculative future—'It would be a great thing if . . .'—this future is predicated on forgetting, perhaps alluding to personal conflicts, leaving only poetry as repository of thwarted ideals—'having no memory of ourselves but the poets we were / in certain verses'. The community of the three poets may, indeed, have confused the nature of love, mixing love and lust, fetishizing idealized young men who they then discard in order to melancholically lament their loss. The poem ends: 'And that each might be glad / To be so far abroad from what he was'. This travelling 'abroad' is also a travelling *away* from the moment of the Renaissance, over a decade on. The value of this nascent form of gay community was, then, in providing a point of departure which was itself departed from, at

64   NEVER BY ITSELF ALONE

once bound up with nostalgia and with an eye to the future. Harking back to the 'New Poem', with its 'lake of no shores I can name', 'the farthest shore' that both is and is not America, the figure of foreignness, identified with a community of queer poets, suggests the capacity of the poet to transcend national identification, harking back to the universalist aspirations of 'The Homosexual in Society', in which queerness is not alienation and isolation but the potential for a transformation of America itself.

Yet such aspirations could, for the moment, live only in the poetry. Soon after Spicer's grateful receipt of Duncan's poems, an angry letter from Duncan led the two to essentially break off contact, and the relation would not be repaired by the time of Spicer's death three years later. Ekbert Faas' biography ends with Duncan's figuration of himself as Odysseus returned from his wandering, beginning his new home life with Jess (Faas 1983, 285). The fairy ship had sailed—or returned home. In the following chapter, I turn in more detail to Jack Spicer's work to address alternative conceptions of queer poetic community that, by contrast, embraced a defiantly public queer ethos.

2

Identity and Community in the Work of Jack Spicer

Introduction

Following the collapse of the Berkeley Renaissance, its promise was ultimately fulfilled in very different ways by all its members. Robert Duncan increasingly turned to the domestic as a place of safety, though in subsequent years he would maintain some involvement in politics, particularly in his opposition to the Vietnam War, and maintained a presence—albeit a sometimes fractious one—within the city's thriving Gay Liberation era queer poetry scenes. Robin Blaser went on to a career within academia in Canada, having departed the United States during the time of the Vietnam draft. Jack Spicer, meanwhile, turned towards a public world of a different sort. In 1950, he refused to sign the University of California's newly imposed Loyalty Oath, which required signatories to disavow radical beliefs and communist affiliation, thus effectively scuppering his chances of a stable academic career (Killian and Ellingham, 33; 381, fn. 87). In the early 1950s, employed on the periphery of academia, first in Minnesota and then back in San Francisco, he became involved in queer bohemia and in the semi-clandestine political organizing of the Mattachine Society. A year spent in Boston from 1955 to 1956 saw him encounter the group of young queer poets later dubbed the 'Occult School of Boston', marking a turning point in his poetic work. Returning once more to California, Spicer established a group of friends and intimates known as the 'Spicer circle' in the queer bars of North Beach and the cruising grounds of Aquatic Park, a mode of community his mature poetry at once emerged from and contested until his death in 1965.

In such work, Spicer built poetics on homosexuality while questioning sexuality as a basis for identity. His poetry is peopled by figures such as 'unverts', 'spooks', 'angels', and 'Martians', which both stand in for gay men and function as something *other* than the other. It can be hard to tell whether poetry is a figure for homosexuality's otherness or homosexuality a figure for poetry's otherness: what is the tenor and what is the vehicle. Given this, the present chapter takes as its starting point Stan Persky's insistence in 1977 that Spicer's writing is incomprehensible without an 'understanding of the *social* character of homosexuality in that historical period' (Persky 1977, 121). On the one hand,

Never By Itself Alone. David Grundy, Oxford University Press. © Oxford University Press 2024.
DOI: 10.1093/oso/9780197654842.003.0003

66 NEVER BY ITSELF ALONE

Spicer's work, as Michael Davidson, Chris Nealon, Maria Damon, and others have argued, reflects the paranoia bred during the era of the Lavender Scare, as well as the contemporaneous prejudices of whiteness: masculinist, racist, misogynist, and, in particular anti-Semitic (Davidson 1989, 159; Damon 1993; Nealon 2011). On the other hand, as I'll go on to argue, his discourse is more properly *queer* and anti-identarian than gay (male) and identity-based, challenging the distinction often drawn between an earlier generation of identity-based politics under the heading 'gay and lesbian' and the later development of a more inclusive queer politics. As such, Spicer's work, while often problematic, paradoxical, and vexing, has much to tell us—even or *especially* in its faults, negativity, and paradoxes—about broader questions of queer identity, both during the period of its writing and in the present day.

This chapter begins by briefly examining the Berkeley Renaissance period, before turning to Spicer's involvement in the Mattachine and to material from the Boston period—in particular, the unfinished 'Oliver Charming' project and the collaborative *Boston Newsletter*. In these texts and in his famous conceptualisation of the 'serial poem' (from which this study takes its title), Spicer uses poetry and sexuality as unstable metaphors for each other, with the figurations of queer identity within the Mattachine re-interrogated as the basis for a new poetics. This exploration continues into Spicer's turn-of-the-decade book, *The Heads of the Town Up to the Aether*. In my reading of *Heads*, I suggest that Spicer offsets a poetics of unrequited love with a poetics of queer community, both of which provide impossible modes of being at once preserved and gone beyond in the space of poetry. Turning to Spicer's uncollected work in the 'Spicer circle' magazines *J* and *Open Space* for their fractious enactment of poetic community, I end by considering Spicer's conception of a 'Pacific Nation' and his final *Book of Magazine Verse*, with its combative attack on Allen Ginsberg. In a brief coda, I turn to later critical analyses by Bruce Boone and Stan Persky, which reflect on Spicer's legacy in the era of Gay Liberation, suggesting that Spicer's developing work at once points up the limitations of contemporaneous models of queer community and might serve as correctives to simplified visions of queer identity that followed.

'What have I lost?': The Berkeley Renaissance and the Mattachine

Spicer's first vision of queer community was that of the 'Berkeley Renaissance', emerging from his association in the late 1940s. Revelling in the elevated terms with which he, Duncan, and Blaser described their own movement, Spicer nonetheless consistently countered Duncan's idealized vision of community. This contrast is perhaps best illustrated in the 1947 poems the two wrote in competition soon after their first meeting, marking the release of conscientious objector Dick Brown from an internment camp.[1] Duncan presents Brown as Apollo, the internment camp and the 'prison' of postwar America transformed into the sacred grove of 'love's fraternity'; Spicer excludes his lovers from the Arcadian 'Poetic Paradise' via the biblical Fall of Man, the Curse of Cain, and the Fall of Icarus, ending the poem with an all-encompassing curse on 'those who know they fall, and those who weep' (Duncan 2012, 142–45, 147, 8; Spicer 1980, 7, 9). Despite these diametrically opposed figurations—echoed in his criticism of the redemptive ending of Duncan's 'The Venice Poem' the following year—he felt the collapse of the group keenly. 'What have I lost?' he asks in the turn-of-the-decade poem 'A Postscript to the Berkeley Renaissance', 'We lived in forests then, / Naked as jaybirds in the ever-real' (Spicer 2008, 45). As birds 'Breaking their cover into poetry / Up from the heart', the trio's poetry both creates and seeks to escape the self-protective enclosure of a mock-arcadian grove which 'we made [. . .] ring with sacred noise / Of gods and bears and swans and sodomy' (45). From forest grove to bird's cage, Spicer figures himself newly alone, seeking to 'sing a newer song no ghost-bird sings', one which is 'sharpened on the iron's edge' of a bird's cage (46).

Seeking at once to cement and dismantle the bonds that form an identity-based community, such early works in part reflect Spicer's own tormented early sense of sexuality, which encompassed a failed heterosexual affair and a course of psychoanalysis (Killian and Ellingham, 25–32). Following his time in Minnesota, and a largely long-distance affair with Gary Bottone, however, he became immersed in San Francisco's developing queer bohemia: in particular, the artistic community surrounding The Place gallery and bar. Employed at the San Francisco School of Fine Arts (subsequently California College of Arts), Spicer met important future correspondents (and love objects) John Allen Ryan, Allen Joyce, and Graham Mackintosh, and, along with five visual artists, co-founded the Six Gallery at which Allen Ginsberg would give his famed 1956 public reading of 'Howl' (Killian and Ellingham, 58).

Spicer also continued to reflect on the political status of gay community and state repression of the left. In 1950, Senator Joseph McCarthy had declared that anyone who opposed him was 'either a Communist or a cocksucker' (Tye, 206). And, in spring 1953, a month after the McCarthy hearings officially began, Spicer became involved with a newly formed Bay Area chapter of 'homophile' organisation the Mattachine Society. The semi-clandestine national organisation had been founded by communist labour organizer Harry Hay in Los Angeles in 1950 as an 'international fraternal order [. . .] a service and welfare organization devoted to the protection and improvement of Society's Androgynous Minority' (Hay, 96). Established in response to the arrest of queer pacifist and civil rights activist Bayard Rustin, the group's Oakland chapter was spearheaded by

68   NEVER BY ITSELF ALONE

Berkeley-based writer Gerald Brissette (Killian 2011, 17). Spicer and Blaser both attended group meetings, held at the apartment of a sympathetic heterosexual couple and attended predominantly by gay men, but also by straight men and women. The meetings, as Blaser recalled, were open and confessional, at once group therapy sessions and radical political meetings (17–18).

While more conservative tendencies in the broader organisation sought to emphasize the essential similarity between gay and straight culture, and to downplay association with radical causes such as those concerning civil rights, the Oakland chapter insisted on black-balling gay bars which discriminated against African Americans and hotly debated questions of essentialism, gender identity, and social construction, debates in which Spicer was heavily involved (22–33). During group debates, he stressed coalition building with other groups and remained sceptical as to totalizing group identification, whether by culture or by an argument from nature. He insisted, for instance, that humans were 'essentially bisexual', that sexual orientation was the result of social conditioning, and that the homo-/hetero- binary was an invention of modern Western societies (35, fn. 31). And though the group was largely white and male, he also argued for building alliances with the lesbian community—'those who are belles, butches, etc.'—and with activists of colour, an approach in tension with the gradualist approach espoused by the group's national leadership.

Spicer attended the second Mattachine convention held in Los Angeles that May, during which Hay and other members of the original group were forced out in an attempt to distance the group from 'subversive elements', deemphasizing militant action and proclaiming loyalty to US law—even though this law proclaimed homosexual acts illegal. In November, David Finn, head of the San Francisco delegation, threatened to turn over the names of participants to the FBI if the group did not explicitly repudiate the 'communistic' principles of the old leadership. Spicer, who saw Finn as a 'crypto-fascist' and had (correctly) surmised that he was an FBI informant, resigned in disgust, in effect marking the end of his involvement in activism (Feinberg, n.p.; Killian 2011, 31). In the future, he would concentrate his exploration of queerness in poetry and its attendant social environment, turning the political questions explored in the Mattachine into poetic questions— while simultaneously turning poetic questions into political ones.

Spicer in Boston

'Five Boston cats blowing their poetry REAL hard'

Having been laid off from his teaching gig at the San Francisco School of Fine Arts, Spicer surprised most who knew him when he departed for New York in August 1955. In general, he found the city intellectualy arid: missing what he called 'a sense of group creation', Spicer's desperation reached at times suicidal peaks (Spicer 1984, 146). Though he associated with the developing queer coterie around poets Frank O'Hara and John Ashbery, he was at odds with its emphases; as Joe LaSeur suggests, Spicer disliked the group's 'urbane [. . .] and campy' modes, which he found 'effete', at one point calling Ashbery a 'faggot poet' (Killian and Ellingham, 64–66, 75). At the year's end, he moved to Boston, where he found an atmosphere less sexually but more intellectually stimulating (Spicer 1984, 146, 7, 8). Robin Blaser, himself newly employed at Harvard's Widener Library, obtained a job for Spicer at the Boston Public Library: the two soon encountered a group of younger poets whose presence recalled the earlier dreams of the 'Berkeley Renaissance' but in very different terms.

Barely in their twenties, John Wieners and Joe Dunn, friends from high school, had met Stephen Jonas at a transformative reading given by Charles Olson at the Charles Street Meeting House in October 1954. Ten years older, Jonas was a voracious auto-didact who had participated in workshops held by Cid Corman, a devotee of Ezra Pound, and a defiantly out gay man of mixed heritage. Wieners and Dunn had enrolled at Black Mountain College in 1955, where they had encountered Robert Duncan—then based at the college as a teacher—and were full of plans and enthusiasm. Meanwhile, Jonas' protegee Ed Marshall—a visionary poet, street preacher, and cruising enthusiast—was a distant but important presence in New York. With the exception of Joe Dunn and his wife Carolyn, also an important part of the social group, the poets were all queer (Carolyn Dunn 2015). And in contrast to the Berkeley Renaissance, which, however bohemian, had taken place in the well-supported and upper-class milieu of the university and its environs, this new grouping—later dubbed by Gerrit Lansing the 'Occult School of Boston'—was defiantly underground (Lansing 1968). Jonas in particular resisted steady employment, used his apartment to fence stolen goods, practiced mail fraud, and lifted a voluminous book collection from the very library at which Spicer worked (Jonas 1994, 3–6). During what Dunn would later call 'that intense summer', the five poets shared work, wrote poems, and planned readings and publications (4). In September 1956, Spicer designed a poster for a reading given by the five poets throwing down the gauntlet to an *eminence grise* of American modernism, identifying instead with the nonconformist spirit associated with the late Charlie Parker. 'EZRA POUND EATS WORMS. You are invited to a poetry reading where five Boston cats are blowing their poetry REAL hard. Nothing has been so good since Bird died'. The following month, the 'five Boston cats' produced the staple-bound *Boston Newsletter*, presenting a wide range of their work in defiantly ephemeral form.

'Poetry is public property': the *Boston Newsletter*

In the absence of widespread gay activism, publication served as a model of local and sometimes national community. Robin Blaser notes that Spicer taught him how to fan himself with a copy of *One* magazine as a signal to the like-minded, and Michael Bronski observes that copies of *One* surreptitiously made their way to newsstands around the country (Killian and Ellingham, 47; Bronski 2020, n.p.). Likewise, on a more local level, the *Boston Newsletter* served both not only as a way for the group to declare their identification to and for each other as a group of poets but also a means of openly—or in clandestine fashion—reaching others. The newsletter's opening 'instructions' reflect this clandestine mode of dissemination as a means of creating community:

WHAT TO DO WITH THE BOSTON NEWSLETTER

1. Post whatever pages of it poke you in the eye in the most public place you can find—i.e. an art gallery, a bohemian bar, or a lavatory frequented by poets.
2. Type out any pages you find worth repeating and add any material you and your compatriots wish to broadcast, and send the resultant Newsletter to other poets and their lovers in other cities. Carbon paper is cheaper than blood.

(Boston Newsletter, 1)

The *Newsletter*'s third instruction—to 'burn or give away the pages you do not want to make public. <u>Do not keep them</u>'—reflects conditions of queer vulnerability and state surveillance. When the police visited Jonas' apartment searching for drugs held by Joe Dunn, they advised Jonas to destroy his collection of gay pornographic images (Jonas to Lansing 1961, n.p.).[2] And in San Francisco, the 'Howl' court case would soon follow, attended by Spicer and others from the San Francisco scene.[3] The instructions thus read as more than simply a joke, even as they are turned into a radical statement of opposition to which negotiates the public-private dichotomy facing gay men: '4. Poetry is public property. Burning or proclaiming poetry is a private necessity'. Opposed to the patronage model by which state and private philanthropy could enforce politically acceptable art, the *Newsletter* ends with a mock begging letter to the Ford Foundation. 'Upon receipt of your money, we will turn ourselves into an orchestra. Could anything be fairer? We are yours when you buy us' (*Boston Newsletter*, 32). But the *Newsletter* as a whole is defiantly committed to poetry as manifestation of a (counter)public which—of necessity—might not be able to disclose itself to the official record.

IDENTITY AND COMMUNITY IN THE WORK OF JACK SPICER   71

The original *Boston Newsletter* was the first continuously published newsletter in British America: borrowing this name suggests both joking placement within publishing history and political iconoclasm in relation to the American state (the newsletter had been a royalist mouthpiece). In contrast to its predecessor's historically weighty publication status, it's not possible to determine the exact circulation of its 1956 descendant. Indeed, given its absence from archival records, the piece challenges the boundaries of 'publication' per se.[4] The *Boston Newsletter* served as a kind of internal document of literary friendship—an affirmation of in-group identity—but also to introduce that group to others, establishing the paradoxical form of open coterie continued in the later magazines of the 'Spicer circle', which, while anti-copyright, had a limited circulation within San Francisco's North Beach. Likewise, the collective authorship of the letter and the interlinked work printed provides a suitably dialogic background for Spicer's conception of the 'serial poem', as well as anticipating Wieners' and Jonas' later roles as editors and builders of community—Wieners with *Measure* and *Fag Rag*, Jonas' with the 'magic evenings' of the 1960s—to be explored in the following chapters.

Spicer himself contributed seven poems to the newsletter, the largest number of any of the contributors. Written in San Francisco, New York, and Boston, their topics range from sexual *ennui* and cruising ('Central Park West') to the conflict between public scrutiny and private *eros* ('Dialogue between Intellect and Passion'), and the travails of unrequited love (poems for Graham Mackintosh, John Allen Ryan, and Joe Dunn). In general, Spicer's poems from this period oscillate between visions of community or (often unrequited) love and the suspended and ambivalent states present in earlier work such as the 'Arcadia' for Dick Brown. Included in the *Boston Newsletter*, 'A Prayer for Pvt. Graham Mackintosh on Halloween' had originally formed part of Spicer's 1954 correspondence with Mackintosh, his former student at the California School of Fine Arts and later a champion of his work.[5] The poem responds to Mackintosh's conscription into the US Army, addressing a prayer to 'infernal warlocks dressed in pink'—both queers and left-wing 'pinkos'— who join forces with 'white-faced boys that trick or treat' and 'nasty little girls' who 'steal the seed from dead men's loins', 'make pee-pee' on uniforms and dance on the 'conscripted' American flag (*Boston Newsletter*, 13). This infernal ensemble forms a kind of alternative family unit, opposed to the militarism that 'borrows' the 'lives' of draftees as if they were a bank loan, and Spicer enjoins this imaginary crew to 'Protect my friend from sundry harm / And rest his body in your arms'. The poem's very gay appropriation of Halloween is of a piece with the commercialized festival which itself appropriates pagan rites and enables the expression of deviant identification: the world of games,

72 NEVER BY ITSELF ALONE

play, and make-believe, turned into a realm of possibility (See also Damon 171–72).

By contrast, long-unpublished 'Goodnight', drafted in the same notebook as draft material for the *Boston Newsletter*, explores the link of poetic creativity with queerness and with suicidal ideation. Beginning with the startling line, 'Goodnight. I want to kill myself', Spicer builds on the suicides of two Berkeley acquaintances, Barton Barber, who 'jumped out of a 20 story window / while his father was buying cigars', and Donald Bliss, who 'drank a bottle of brandy / And then a little bottle of cyanide'. Kevin Killian and Lewis Ellingham suggest that Spicer had nominated these now-obscure figures as potential successors to the by now collapsed Berkeley Renaissance (Killian and Ellingham, 34). Recalling them in Boston, Spicer reckons with the loss of a close socio-poetic circle made up of principally gay men. The poem toys with the idea that Barber and Bliss might serve as queer martyrs in the mode of Hart Crane:

> Hart Crane died so that faggots could write poetry.
> And faggots have written poetry.
>
> (Spicer 2021)

Such lines seem to resonate with John Wieners' 'THAT OLD GANG OF MINE' (aka 'Hart Crane, Harry Crosby . . .'), which also appears in the *Boston Newsletter* (*Boston Newsletter*, 29). But Spicer, more so than Wieners, ponders whether such figuration must *of necessity* be sacrificial. Crane's example may have led to the democratisation of poetry—one which seems connected to the admission of homosexual experience into, and as the inspiration for, the poem. But such democratisation also reduces the stakes of such poetry, and its relevance to lived experience: 'I have discovered that anyone can write a poem [. . .] I have learned / How little poetry has to do with anything'. On the one hand, as specialized and cliquish queer modality, poetry speaks only to a limited circle; on the other hand, if anyone can write it, poetry is rendered like any other form of discourse, losing its oppositional capacity. As Spicer attempts to quote a poem by Barber, he is interrupted by further memories of Barber which seem to parody an increasingly sexualized American consumer culture—'Took a Pepsi Cola bottle up his ass / (I was in the next room)'—and by the sounds of 'you two [. . .] fucking in the next room' (Spicer was at this time living next door to Joe and Carolyn Dunn). This juxtaposition—two queer poets, one now dead, alone in their respective rooms, separated from the order of heterosexuality—reflects the societal divisions which associate the queer subject with suicidal negativity: the sexual dividing line that can sometimes make the difference between life and death.[6]

'No place to turn': The Oliver Charming Notebooks

Like the Arcadia for Dick Brown, 'Goodnight' does not resolve its double-binds and dead ends. But Spicer's next major protect would turn such contradiction into the very basis for a poetics. In early 1956, Spicer wrote to Allen Joyce:

> I'm now revising my Bacchae and writing an incredibly confused thing called *The Unvert Manifesto and Other Papers of Oliver Charming Found in the Rare Book Room of the Boston Public Library*. It started as a joke for my soldier but it's taken hold of me. (Spicer 1984, 150)[7]

Spicer's *Boston Newsletter* poems had been apprentice work: self-contained lyric poems whose metrical and rhetorical form is relatively conventional, even if their tricky delineation of queer identity is not. Drafted in the same 1956 notebook as 'Goodnight' and editorial matter for the *Boston Newsletter*, the new work was, by contrast, heavily influenced by the generic hybridity Spicer was discovering in the papers of Emily Dickinson, about which he was writing a scholarly article for the library's journal, encompassing elements of manifesto, novel, diary, and poetry (Spicer 1956; Daniel Katz 2013, 54). Spicer never completed the Charming manuscript to his satisfaction, the published version relying on a posthumous composite created by Robin Blaser. Yet, with this text, he was working his way towards a new form with which to reflect on the breaking apart of the Berkeley Renaissance, his time in the Mattachine, his encounters with queer bohemia, and the possibilities opened up by the young poets of the Occult School. The comically wordy title indicates its conceit: the cynical and rebarbative 'S'—a stand-in for Spicer himself—has discovered the handwritten papers of the Wildean 'Oliver Charming' in Spicer's real-life workplace, the Boston Public Library Rare Books room. The starting point for all the manuscripts, the so-called 'Unvert Manifesto', is an itemized list of twenty numbered statements in which Spicer defines his own neologism, the 'unvert', through the lenses of sociology, Dada, and Kurt Schwitters' *Merz*. In the following sections, excerpts from Charming's diary function as a roman-à-clef, with Graham Mackintosh appearing as 'Graham Macarel' and Joe and Carolyn Dunn as 'Mr and Mrs Doom'. These real-life figures merge freely with personages such as the fictional crusading lawyer-cum-detective Perry Mason and Emily Dickinson's New England friend and editor, Thomas Wentworth Higginson. The manuscript ends with the 'transcript of the trial of Oliver Charming', held at Spicer's favourite San Francisco haunt, a queer bar named the Black Cat. Bound and gagged, Charming, defended by Perry Mason, is placed on trial for 'the crime of angelism', the transcript ending as 'S' is sworn as the first witness (Spicer 2008, 93).

74 NEVER BY ITSELF ALONE

In blending the private form of diary entries—in which discussions of intimate matters often take parodic forms of 'sociological' discussion—and the public forms of the manifesto and the legal case, Spicer constantly tests the discursive means by which sexuality is framed. The text opposes current discursive frames for sexuality on three grounds: the sociological approach, emblematized by Richard von Krafft-Ebbing and by the Kinsey Reports; the idealist strain within the American gay poetic tradition; and the related argument from and for culture. Spicer reverses (or unverts) the Freudian truism that everything is about sexuality; in this text, sexuality is about everything, and queer identity cannot be boxed off into a minority concern. At the same time, he resists homogenizing *any* sexual identity under a universalizing umbrella, and it's here that art plays a crucial role, avoiding idealisation, reification, or condemnation by maintaining the estrangement at the heart of sexuality itself.

In particular, Spicer is concerned with the rise of sexual classification, a proliferation of discourse that, from the late nineteenth century onwards involved both liberatory and containment functions, from pathologisation with serious medical and legal consequences to the pioneering 'sexological' research, that from Krafft-Ebbing and Havelock Ellis through to Kinsey, had countered increasingly narrow definitions of acceptable sexual practice. This interest had an immediate personal connection. As 'Publications Chairman' within the Mattachine branch, Spicer had been tasked with researching an alternative name for the organisation (Killian 2011, 19). This was a task with immediate political ramifications in a context of legal prohibition and media witchhunts: the new name would need to tread a line between that which is clear to initiates and vague to outsiders—more specifically, hostile journalists and state forces (20). Seeking to avoid Wildean or 'Greek' associations which reinforced harmful stereotype, Spicer's report recommended 'Tercellan', a neologism combining the name for a male hawk in falconry ('tercel') with 'the idea of "three" or "third" in an abstract sense'. By the association with 'three', Spicer's report noted, he wished to suggest not so much the now-discredited 'myth of a third sex' (the 'invert'), as 'the presence of a third 'position', or attitude in society [. . .] evidenced by the whole Mattachine movement' (20). Spicer's replacement of 'third sex' with 'third position', or 'attitude in society' suggests queerness as *position* rather than identity. Within the 'purely' literary context of the Charming manuscript, his 'unvert' coinage went further, seeking to destabilize virtually *any* sense of identity to which the word might be attached.

The term serves as an obvious parody of Krafft-Ebing's use of the term 'invert' to describe male and female homosexuality—a term popularized by Radclyffe Hall in the 1920s, which bases its definition of same-sex desire through an inside/outside binary that Spicer seeks to challenge. If, for Krafft-Ebing and Hall, homosexuality involves masculine souls heaving in female bosoms, and vice versa,[8] Spicer's 'unvert', though located within a distinctly gay male social milieu, need not necessarily refer to queer sexuality at all. The 'Unvert Manifesto' thus begins by punning on the sociological categories (both sexual and otherwise) which rest on the Latin root word *vert(ere)*, '(to) turn'—'An unvert is neither an invert or an outvert, a pervert or a convert, an introvert or a retrovert', and it continues: 'An unvert must not be homosexual, heterosexual, bisexual, or autosexual' (Spicer 2008, 74). This definition is itself embroiled in a sexual metaphor in which tenor and vehicle are mirrored in confusing ways: the unvert 'must be metasexual. He must enjoy going to bed with his own tears' (74). In a willed impasse, the unvert 'chooses to have no place to turn'.

In part, this dead end echoes the 'faggots [who] have written poetry' in 'Goodnight': within current social conjunctures: there is no way out (or in) for the queer subject. Here Spicer's text participates in theoretical debates about the nature of male homosexuality that had played out throughout American poetry of the preceding century. As Robert K. Martin argues in *The Homosexual Tradition in American Poetry* (1979), whereas a Whitmanesque lineage emphasized physical love and queer comradeship, the Neo-Platonist 'genteel', 'academic' poetics of writers such as George Santayana advocated gay *identity* over gay *behaviour* (sexual practice). For such poets, same-sex love serves as a form of 'Uranian' or Platonic relationality that is valued precisely because it is not physical, eternal, and morally elevated over the degraded physicality of heterosexual love (Robert K. Martin 1979, 96–97). The paradoxical denial of sexual behaviour as a part of sexuality identity is turned into the basis of an aesthetic in itself: an art of sublimation, idealisation, and elitism which turns sexual prohibition into a higher good. But, while Spicer's 'unversion' likewise resists fixing identity to sexual behaviour, it does not assume de-physicalized, Platonic forms—with their correlates in an elitist contempt. Instead, it is enmeshed in a queer social milieu and deeply sceptical of the class structure and the status quo.

Countering idealist arguments, Spicer also challenges the arguments from culture that had formed an important discursive strand within the Mattachine. At the Second Mattachine Convention in 1953, he had commented: 'In the beginning I objected to the world "culture" on these grounds: when asked whether I am homosexual, I answered by asking "When?"' (Killian 2011, 261).[9] Likewise, in the Charming text, 'S' proclaims: 'We homosexuals are the only minority group that completely lacks any vestige of a separate cultural heritage. We have no songs, no folklore, even our customs are borrowed from our upper-middle-class mothers' (Spicer 2008, 78). The tone of such passages—bitchy, cutting, consistently flirting with offence—is itself close to camp: in that sense, using a mode of gay male speech to question the nature of culture and group identity itself, whilst also— to an extent—suggesting camp performativity as survival strategy and means to interrogate the given.

76 NEVER BY ITSELF ALONE

Likewise, while Spicer argues that existent queer art and culture—whether camp or the Wildean or 'Greek' aesthetic that, as he'd argued, merely reinforces stereotype—provides an inadequate basis from which to argue for a group identity, art plays a crucial role in his concept of 'unversion'. Spicer, Duncan, and Blaser had already played on the relation between art and sexuality in titling an undergraduate magazine *Literary Behavior* after the first Kinsey Report of 1948, 'On Sexual Behaviour'. The reports of 1948 and 1953 had destabilized the link between sexual acts and sexual identity—for instance, in revealing the preponderance of bisexual experience amongst nominatively heterosexual citizens—findings that had likely influenced Spicer's own arguments within the Mattachine. Yet the Charming text criticizes the Kinsey Reports for rendering the sex act banal and classifiable. Spicer's 'unverts' 'held that Kinsey was valuable evidence of the boredom of un-unverted sex—that ordinary sex has become so monotonous that it had become statistical like farm income or rolling stock totals' (Spicer 2008, 78). In literary terms, the Kinsey Report is comparable to the novels of Emile Zola—a project of societal diagnosis which forms a necessary stage in revealing that which is hidden or mystified, yet which is ultimately unsatisfactory. Spicer instead calls for a 'new Lautréamont' of sexuality—one who will restore those elements that *escape* classification, whether these be involved with the modes of sexuality defined as gay, bisexual, or straight. As well as Lautréamont, Spicer invokes the early twentieth-century avant-gardes who problematized categories of meaning-making at a time of war and conflict between capitalist powers. Through 'unversion', the sexual act is connected to 'the greatest cosmic force in the universe—Nonsense, or as we prefer to call it, MERZ'. Sex (whether homosexual or otherwise) would thus be 'frightening', destabilizing social categories and categories of the human per se 'like a dirty joke or an angel'. Decoupling sex from what Spicer calls 'the yoke of sexual meaning'—a process Daniel Katz names as 'dedomestication' (Daniel Katz 2013, 86)—Spicer's anarchic refusal of meaning does not seek to classify on the basis of culture, identity, or behaviour, as do Krafft-Ebbing, Kinsey, and the Mattachine. Rather, in line with *Merz*, 'unversion' is a definition taken so far as to become meaningless: a sexuality beyond sexuality, an identity beyond identity, a category which exceeds categorisation—even as Spicer's misogyny, anti-Semitism, and anti-Blackness—such as comparing 'camping' to a 'Jewish vaudeville joke' or 'a minstrel show impeccably played by Negroes in blackface' (Spicer 2008, 79)—reflect odious racial privileges and prejudices. With whatever sexuality such prejudices are associated, their presence in the Charming texts renders *whiteness* the ultimate and unavoidable identity category from which Spicer's text can never extricate itself.

Sex and the Single Poem

Spicer's Charming project remained unfinished. The manuscripts end with Charming on trial, defended by the (fictional) lawyer Perry Mason, who declares: 'Your honor, I have evidence to prove that my client does not exist' (Spicer 2008, 93). In this world of nonsense—reminiscent of Lewis Carroll as much as *Merz*—role-playing and performance coincide with the legal system—whose prosecution of gay men combines with the figure of the crusading lawyer, exposing the vested interests that are cloaked in the impersonal language of the law by using its very terms. Like the transcript, these purported theorisations are left hanging: the court suspended, the verdict never reached. But it was during that period that Spicer's conceptualisation of the 'serial poem'—a sequence in which individual poems are always part of a greater whole, or 'book'—finally gave him a form to explore the questions opened up in Boston. Spicer began work on perhaps his best-known text, *After Lorca*, while in Boston in late 1955, and finished it upon his return to San Francisco. In a letter sent to Robin Blaser in winter 1957, and reproduced in Spicer's succeeding book, the privately distributed *Admonitions* (1958), Spicer describes his conception of the serial poem in what is perhaps the most frequently quoted of all his statements.

> [...] There is really no single poem.
>
> That is why all my stuff from the past (except the *Elegies* and *Troilus*) looks foul to me. The poems belong nowhere. They are one night stands filled (the best of them) with their own emotions, but pointing nowhere, as meaningless as sex in a Turkish bath. [...]
>
> Poems should echo and reecho against each other. They should create resonances. They cannot live alone any more than we can. [...]
>
> A poem is never to be judged by itself alone. A poem is never by itself alone.
>
> (Spicer 2008, 163–64)

This passage, from which the present study derives its title, has been touched on in the introduction. As in 'Goodnight' and the 'Unvert Manifesto', the sexual and textual serve as each other's mirrors. Spicer appears to negatively distinguish between ephemeral sexual encounter—one-night stands and 'sex in a Turkish bath'—and the longer lasting connections of the serial poem, which some have seen as analogously linked to a monogamous, domestic relationship of the kind to which Robert Duncan had turned (Damon 1993, 159). But Spicer himself was hardly hostile to gay bars, one-night stands, cruising, or Turkish baths. Poet Stan Persky, for example, recalls that their first encounter saw him cruised by Spicer in San Francisco's Aquatic Park (Killian and Ellingham, 171). Likewise,

78 NEVER BY ITSELF ALONE

in a posthumous poem, Spicer's Occult School confidante Stephen Jonas figures White Rabbit Press—which Joe Dunn would begin at Spicer's instigation and which would publish *After Lorca*—in terms of joyously non-monogamous queer sexuality. 'White Rabbit / Press on / Promiscuous and / Come again again' (Jonas 1974). Like Spicer, Jonas applies the sexual metaphor to publishing: here, the serial poem, the relationality of poem to poem, poet to poet, person to person, is sexually charged, non-alienated, and wilfully polygamous. Jonas' poem appeared in Boston Gay Liberation magazine *Fag Rag*, a publication which, as we'll see in forthcoming chapters, firmly endorsed non-normative sexual practices like cruising, and for which 'anonymous encounters in parks, baths, bars and bathrooms' were joyous, nonjudgmental and connected to an anarchist politics.[10] Indeed, as John Emil Vincent suggests, the serial poem might equally well be understood as *equivalent* rather than *opposed* to the seriality of cruising, one-night stands, and other non-monogamous gay sexual practices and the 'sense of community' they create (Vincent 2002, 151); or at the very least, to reject binary division between different modes of *eros* (Snediker in Vincent 2011, 181). And it was to a twinned sense of queer community and serial poetics that Spicer would turn on his return to San Francisco.

The Heads of the Town up to the Aether: Spicer's Coming Community

Return to San Francisco and the Spicer Circle

Fired from his library job for breaking the spine of a rare book at the Boston Library, Spicer had left with Joe and Carolyn Dunn for San Francisco in November 1956. Working as an instructor at San Francisco State College, he encouraged Joe Dunn to begin White Rabbit Press, whose first publications— Stephen Jonas' *Love, The Poem, The Sea and Other Pieces Examined By Steve Jonas* (the retitled 'Michael Poem' from the *Boston Newsletter*) and Spicer's *After Lorca*—emerged directly from the Boston period. Spicer taught a series of workshops on 'Poetry as Magic' at the newly founded SF State Poetry Centre, with participants including Robert Duncan, John Allen Ryan, Helen Adam, and George Stanley; and embarked on what Stanley called 'a floating poets' symposium in the North Beach bars', with friends and students on the grass in Aquatic Park, and in weekly meetings at Joe and Carolyn Dunn's apartment (Killian and Ellingham, 101–102, 106–107). Such collective endeavours, generally known as the 'Spicer circle', would prove central to his poetics. The circle was both a loose-knit and a coterie enterprise. Important participants included both gay and straight men and women: the queer George Stanley, Stan

Persky—with Duncan and Blaser in some senses participants at a distance—Bill Brodecky and Lew Ellingham (later co-author of Spicer's biography); Spicer's love interests (both straight and gay) James Alexander, Russell Fitzgerald, Larry Kearney, Graham Mackintosh, and Ronnie Primack; and the heterosexual Ebbe Borregaard, Harold, Dull, Larry Fagin, Joanne Kyger, Jamie McInnis, and the couple Jim and Fran Herndon, the latter of whose illustrations for Spicer's books were a key collaborative partnership.[11] The circle maintained the paradox at the centre of the Berkeley Renaissance—a combination of radical anarchism with a conception of an elite fraternit or 'kreis' with radical anarchist politics; a community organized around gay male sexuality which included important heterosexual male and female participants.

'the figure of a person at once lost and unlikely'

Spicer increasingly stressed the role of the 'Outside' and the impersonal in the production of poetry, claiming to Blaser that his work was 'dictated' and that the poet should keep their personality out of the way as much as possible— arguments that have their roots in the 'cosmic force[s]' of *Merz* and sex in the Charming text (Killian and Ellingham, 183). Spicer would later illustrate his concept through the figure of 'Martians'—a term again with specifically queer origins, borrowed from 1950s pop culture (and attendant paranoia regarding communist invasion and the 'enemy within'), which had as its origins in a secret language Spicer had developed with John Allen Ryan, an occasional lover, spoken only by its the initiates of the 'Interplanetary Services of the Martian Anarchy' (Killian and Ellingham, 57–58).[12] But his work was also shaped by loss and personal pain. Perhaps no sequence illustrates this confluence better than *The Heads of the Town up to the Aether*, written largely in 1960 and published in 1962. The book reflects the mixed-genre form begun in the Oliver Charming and continued through Spicer's early serial poems, *After Lorca* and *Admonitions*. The poem's three sections, loosely modelled on Dante's *Divine Comedy*, move from the hell of unhappy and unrequited love ('Homage to Creeley', first published as a stand-alone chapbook in 1960), through the '*purgatorio*' of 'A Fake Novel About the Life of Arthur Rimbaud'), and finally into the 'paradise' of textuality ('A Textbook of Poetry') (Spicer 1998, 18). Only the first section consists of lineated poetry (with prose commentaries at the foot of each page that exceed the poems in length); the remainder of the book is in prose, taking the form, first of a mock-biography, and then of something approaching both instruction book and manifesto.

The book was in part prompted by Spicer's largely unrequited love for poet James ('Jim') Alexander, on whose name—'the word Jim'—the book ends

80   NEVER BY ITSELF ALONE

(Spicer 2008, 313). Its opening poem, 'Several Years Love', recalls Alexander and Spicer's former lover Russell Fitzgerald through a parody of Shakespeare's 'Sonnet 144' ('two loves had I, of comfort and despair'): 'They pushed their cocks in many places / And I'm not certain of their faces' (250). Neither of the two loves are directly named, and, as the last lines of the poem put it: 'I'm not certain of their faces / Or which I kissed or which I didn't / Or which of both of them I hadn't' (250). But the sequence frames its romantic concerns within the broader theoretical questions about the nature of language and poetry indicated by the title to its final section, 'A Textbook of Poetry'. In the Oliver Charming manuscript, Spicer's exploration of the gap between name and person is key in destabilizing questions of sexual identity. Likewise, the gap between name and person, public designation and private knowledge, forms a central conceit of *Heads*, as Spicer plays up the distinction between the name and the one named, the love object as actual person and their role within the poem. In 'the figure of Jim [...]' the Poet uses all his resistance to us to try to create the figure of a person at once lost and unlikely' (262). Alluding to Dante and to Jean Cocteau's 1950 film version of the Orpheus myth, *Heads* is constructed in part as a quest for a love lost object—the 'boy' or 'bride' aligned with Jim, Eurydice, and Beatrice (256, 262), both redeemed and cast back into the underworld through the poet's Orphic backward glance—which in itself recalls that of Lot's wife at Sodom in the paradigmatic biblical act of the destruction of queer community (Damon 1993, 198). Spicer self-consciously turns the beloved into a cipher for a poem, a point of access for the 'impersonal' realm of *Merz* and of the Outside, 'the figure of a person at once lost and unlikely' (Spicer 2008, 262). As he writes in the book's final part, echoing the terms of the Oliver Charming manuscript: 'You are only being faithful to the shadow of a word. Once lost, once found—in the horny deeps below finding [...] This is a system of metasexual metaphor. Being faithful to the nonsense of it' (304). As such, *Heads* serves both as the extension of the Charming project and the end-point of a trajectory in Spicer' work, whereby a series of younger men—from Graham Mackintosh and John Allen Ryan to Joe Dunn, and Jim Alexander—became the occasion for poetic dedications, epistles, and sequences which pivoted on figures of distance and unfulfilled desire.[13]

Stan Persky helpfully terms such dedicatees 'beloveds' rather than 'lovers', a distinction he argues was key to how Spicer's poetry reflected the 'social experience of homosexuality' in the pre–Gay Liberation era, during which romantic and sexual fulfilment was often denied in an atmosphere of paranoia and repression (Persky 1977, 123). In Spicer's case, however, this tendency to idealisation or impossibility—a key trope of love poetry in general—goes further. As Killian and Ellingham put it: 'Spicer's friends observe that he used lovers for poems and poems for lovers', turning real emotional experience into 'an abstraction, a mood, a memory' (Killian and Ellingham, 104). Friends described this as 'lov[ing] the idea more than the person'; what Duncan would call in a letter to Blaser 'the defense

IDENTITY AND COMMUNITY IN THE WORK OF JACK SPICER   81

of longing for love against the practice of love' (174, 162). In its most extreme form, as John Emil Vincent notes, 'the beloved is most appropriate when dead or absolutely unavailable' (Vincent 2002, 173). At times, Spicer suggests unfulfilled desire serves as the condition for poetry itself. Yet Spicer simultaneously critiques this idealisation of the one desired into devotional object. 'What Beatrice did did not become her own business. Dante saw to that. Sawed away the last plank anyone he loved could stand on'; '—A human love object is untrue. / Screw you. // —A divine love object is unfair' (Spicer 2008, 257, 307). Rendering the love object into a kind of transcendent creative principal—as with Dante's Beatrice or Stefan George's Maximin—does a violence to that object. Beatrice must be dead to be elevated to the quasi-divine level she assumes in Dante's poetry, with loss melancholically re-enshrined as triumph. Aware of this, Spicer's notes the poem as a 'tentative [. . .] bridge between love and the idea of love' (261). In turn, this 'awkward bridge' opens love beyond the two-person dyad. For the queer desire of Spicer's poem does not simply inhere in the figure of the beloved. Equally crucial is the desire for—and the pain involved in—social community.

'the city we create'

In March 1960, Spicer moved into a new apartment in Polk Gulch, described by Killian and Ellingham as 'a district of hardcore hustling mixed with less intense but very gay pastimes'—Polk Gulch features such as the Handle Bar, a local gay bar, appear in the sequence—whilst also 'boy-watching' in Aquatic Park (Killian and Ellingham, 188). For Robin Blaser, this physical, social community—'a loved habit of friends, bars, streets, the Broadway Tunnel, and Aquatic Park'—enabled Spicer's poetry to constitute 'a profound interrogation, an operation of language, because it is a meeting' (Spicer 1975, 286). These two modes—the 'private' space of loss and sorrow in love, and the 'public' space of Polk Gulch's queer bar life— are suggested in the juxtaposition of the first two poems in the book. 'Two Loves', with its depiction of 'the pain the poet had', is immediately followed by 'Car Song', a poem which creates a grotesquely punning space in which the cars at the cross-roads near Spicer's Polk Gulch apartment and the carriages transporting victims of the *Shoah* to the death camps align.

> Actually we are going to hell.
> We pin our puns to our backs and cross in a car
> The intersections where lovers are [. . .]
> The pun at our backs is a yellow star.
> We pin our puns on the windshield like
> We crossed each crossing in hell's despite.
>
> (Spicer 2008, 251)

82 NEVER BY ITSELF ALONE

The intersection here operates on the level of multiple puns, gesturing to what Michael Davidson notes as 'a thematics of transition: roads, paths, stairs, mirrors, trails': one which accomplishes the 'carrying across' that is at the etymological route of metaphor and rhymes with the notion of the poem as a 'tentative bridge between love and the idea of love' (Davidson 1977, 115; Spicer 2008, 261). Such transitions, however, are not so much playful or reparative as alarming and vertiginous. As the prose gloss notes: ' "Intersections" is a pun. "Yellow stars" are what the Jews wore' (Spicer 2008, 305). Spicer's puns suggest a mode of queer identity which is both borne like a cross—the Christian icon of sacrificial suffering—and which ironically appropriates the designation imposed by the Nazi regime on its Jewish citizens. These comparisons question the trope of queer martyrdom explored in 'Goodnight', along with the analogizing process by which different minority groups are first separated and then falsely compared. Intended as cautionary, they are crass in the extreme. In suggesting that the willed display of identity recalls that enforced by a genocidal regime, Spicer trivializes both the historical suffering of the Holocaust and the proud and confident display of queerness. Opposing narratives of queer victimhood, he turns group identification into racialized competition and undermines the means by which queer solidarity is performed. Yet, as Sarah Ruddy notes, Spicer's invocation of Polk Gulch—in the figure of the intersection and in the reference to the Handlebar which opens this particular poem's prose commentary—also suggests an alternative mapping of space, in which a 'public sexual culture created its own space in ways that the larger American culture in the 1950s could not' (Ruddy, 242). For Ruddy, Polk Gulch serves as 'a commodity culture on completely different terms, one in which [. . .] commerce created the common space of bodies intersecting with bodies' (241). Spicer lived 'nearly under a Bank of America vault' (Killian and Ellingham, 188), and thus 'almost literally beneath but yet completely beyond "official" commodity culture' (Ruddy, 241): a literal subculture whose modes of consumption and display both reflect and subvert that of the wider society.

Moreover, another valence of community is suggested by the allusions in 'Homage to Creeley' to Jean Cocteau's postwar updating of the Orpheus myth. In particular, Cocteau's use of the radio as a conduit for messages from the underworld serves, as many critics have noted, as perhaps the key figure for Spicer's conceptualisation of poetic inspiration and the 'Outside' (Davidson 1977, 111–13). An apparently meaninglessness stream of language with which Orpheus becomes obsessed, these messages at once resemble abstract poetry and suggest another connotation of the underworld, or 'underground': the messages to the French Resistance broadcast from London during the occupation (James S. Williams, 124–25). The world of the poem thus implicitly alludes to the world of coded messages and politicized resistance to meaning that echoes the semi-clandestine nature of the Mattachine Society. This should not imply straightforward analogies between bands of gay men and the French Resistance, just as Cocteau's own text is not a straightforward analogy. Cocteau himself had sought to protect Jewish friends from the collaborationist regime, and himself been beaten by the far right for refusing to salute the national flag, whilst also seeking protection himself from collaborationists. Likewise, in *Orphée*, the 'Zone', filmed in the ruins of an old military academy, alludes at once to the 'Occupied Zone' of the Vichy Regime and the 'Free Zone' controlled by the Resistance: a world of doubleness, secrets and passage whose stakes can be life and death (James S. Williams, 178–80, 124–25). Spicer's own intersectional zone, meanwhile, unites the worlds of romantic love, gay community, and poetry. Spicer's inversion of Blake, astutely noted by Maria Damon, turns the 'hell we build in heaven's despite'—the capacity for repression and ill-feeling to corrupt the innocence of love, particularly sexual love—into a crossing that occurs 'in hell's despite' (Damon 1993, 161–62). For Blake, possessiveness and selfishness can turn the paradisal into the hellishly jealous, competitive, and destructive; for Spicer, in spite of the paranoia, fear, and legal threat of state surveillance and homophobic violence, the queer denizens of this city are able to chart productive crossings and re-crossings, blurring the lines and carving out a space within the jaws of hell. As in his figuration of the serial poem and 'one-night stands' in the letter to Blaser, or of 'unversion' in the Oliver Charming manuscript, Spicer refuses to choose between binary options: the gay ghetto or the straight world, unrequited or fulfilled love, the realm of the real world or the realm of poetry. Instead, poetry becomes a place in which issues of queer identity, poetic inspiration, and the relation of personal desire and loss to community can be opened up to question. In the final section of *Heads*, 'A Textbook of Poetry', Spicer argues that the poem renders the city 'an unavoidable metaphor', one which is 'almost the opposite' of the physical city: a 'city redefined' which serves as a quasi-religious conglomeration—'a church. A movement of poetry' (Spicer 2008, 305–306). These two cities—roughly equivalent to Augustine's heavenly and earthly cities—are supplemented by a third: '[T]he city that we create in our bartalk or in our fuss and fury about each other is in an utterly mixed and mirrored way an image of the city. A return from exile' (306). This created city corresponds to the social community surrounding poetry: it forms the material for poetry, and poetry forms its material, though neither are exactly reducible to each other.

Ultimately, for Spicer, the principal allegiance, beyond regional, geographical, national, or sexual group, is that of poetry. In 1960, he wrote to Robert Duncan: 'It seems to me that poets have a bond of responsibility to each other even more sacred than that of lover to lover' (Daniel Katz 2013, 89). And, as John Emil Vincent notes, whatever the ostensible subjects of Spicer's serial poems— whether travails in love or narrative and mythic systems such as the outlaw legend

84   NEVER BY ITSELF ALONE

of Billy the Kid (*Billy the Kid*, 1958), Arthurian legend (*The Holy Grail*, 1962), or linguistic systems of analysis (*Language*, 1965)—they are also most often, in a self-reflexive way, about poetry itself (Vincent 2002, 153). Alongside and beyond the instability of both romantic desire and socio-sexual community, the poem assembles the ghosts of past and present loves, queer forbears, and mythological figures into a city that is at once modern San Francisco, Augustine's City of God, Dante's Florence, Socrates' Athens, Jean Cocteau's Orphic underworld, and the spaces of occupied Europe during the Nazi era (Daniel Katz 2–13, 90). This is above all a *textual* community. 'Unlike [Charles] Olson's Gloucester or [William Carlos] Williams' Patterson,' writes Michael Davidson, 'Spicer creates a city out of language' (Davidson 1977, 116). And for Spicer, this is both poetry's particular valence and its limitation: its extension beyond the physical limits of human life—with all the sociopolitical restrictions and concomitant romantic and emotional frustrations life involves—and into the community—impossible in life, but possible in the poem—of living and dead: poets, Martians, ghosts, unverts, and beloveds alike. This is a community not yet in existence, in which the movement of desire towards the love object merges with the broader 'coming community' of 'we dead men', which can currently only exist in the poem; what Daniel Benjamin calls a 'perlocutionary' community, 'calling into existence a collective that does not yet exist, or to which the speaker can only gesture but not yet belong' (Daniel Benjamin, 38).[14]

Open Spaces: The Magazines of the Spicer Circle

'An Apparition of the Late *J*'

If the 'city redefined' of *Heads* exists only in the poem, Spicer makes it clear that it would not exist at all without 'the city we create in our fuss and our bartalk': that's to say, the social world outside the poem. Prompting the composition of individual works such as *Heads*, this community also manifested in the collaborative products of the Spicer circle: notably, the magazines *J*, whose six issues were edited by Spicer and Fran Herndon from 1959 to 1960, and *Open Space*, edited by Stan Persky in 1964.[15] It was at Spicer's encouragement that Jim and Fran Herndon began *J* in 1959 (Killian and Ellingham, 165). Contributions were a combination of solicitations from Spicer and submissions to a box at The Place and Mr Otis', bars frequented by the Spicer circle. The magazine was conceived of as a cheap and local enterprise. Spicer noted to Donald Allen: '[*J*] prints poetry (or prose or drawings) by friends or friends of friends of friends of the editor [. . .] We only print 300 copies and they sell out soon' (Killian and Ellingham, 166–67). Contributions to the magazine were either pseudonymous

IDENTITY AND COMMUNITY IN THE WORK OF JACK SPICER   85

or unattributed, blurring distinctions of authorship. (Spicer's own contributions frequently appear under the name 'Mary Murphy'.[16])

Spicer's poems in *J* form an ongoing argument in miniature about poetry and its relation to love. The first issue juxtaposes Jim Alexander's 'Jack Rabbit Poems' with Spicer's own uncollected *hokku* reflecting his feelings for Alexander, placing the magazine within the orbit of Spicer's mentorship, background influence, and leadership—as well as his erotic desires—while also suggesting that poetry might both consume such personal relations and go beyond or resolve them. The third *hokku* reads:

> Loving you
> My poetry said things I don't know.
> Now
> My poetry tries to heal me.
> So im-
> Personal, so loving
> That poetry can cover both of us like a big
> Blank-
> Et.
>
> (Spicer, 'Hokkus', n.p.)

A force exterior to the lovers which protects them from the chill of the Outside, poetry is also identified with the impersonal force of the Outside itself: both 'blank' and a 'blanket', 'loving' yet devouring. In 'Epilog for Jim', the poet has been abandoned in 'The hell / Of personal relations', surrounded by the 'shadows' of birds of prey, 'buzzards wheeling in the sky'(Spicer, 'Epilog', n.p.). These birds recur in the 'Fifth Elegy', with the poet as Prometheus, his liver endlessly eaten by birds who also bring the 'messages' of dictated poetry in their 'hungry beaks'(Spicer, 'Fifth Elegy', n.p.). Here the sexual curse of Spicer's earlier 'Arcadia for Dick Brown' has become instead the burden of poetry itself. Yet personal relations are an inadequate basis for an ethics or community, eroticism or shared intimacy leading only to militarized conformity: 'Our emotions become uniforms when we talk together. My / Love your / Bonehead / Clothes' (Spicer, ['Lack of oxygen puzzles the air]', n.p.) Where personal relations harden into self-protection and falsity, poetry itself must move beyond either romantic love or a total impersonality in which no human could live.

And so, as in *Head*'s 'city we create', Spicer turns to the communities which gather around poetry, in texts concerned with the simultaneous construction and destabilisation of such community. 'New Beaches' finds a crowd gathered by the sea whose treacherous, moving surface is likened to poetry itself. Though endowed with the Christlike capacity to walk on the water, this crowd mutely

86 NEVER BY ITSELF ALONE

awaits the degraded commercial products of a compromised art, as 'froze-/ N (or un-frozen)' fish are thrown up from the water (Spicer, 'New Beaches', n.p.). In the communities that surround poetry as in poetry itself, what is thrown up from the ocean of poetry may turn out merely to be stinking fish, and sceptical vigilance is required. Meanwhile, an anonymous satirical text attributed to 'Willaim [*sic*] Morris' warns against 'the / danger of fag decadence in verse': Morris, standing in for a decorative, arts-and-crafts aesthetic, serves both as moralistic old socialist warning against 'decadence' and as part of the critique of an overly inward-facing queer coterie. Such texts are at best fraught and paradoxical: the building of community is not mere affirmation, but a process in which one must always be on one's guard against processes of ossification.

Appropriately enough, the magazine's final issue serves as a kind of premature gravestone or mausoleum. The cover illustration, 'An apparition of the late *J*', is a hypothetical map, drawn by the issue's editor, George Stanley, loosely coagulating around the 'centre republic'. As such, the map suggests the tension between the anarchist, open ethos of the Spicer circle—exemplified in Spicer's notion of a federation of linked, independent republics or 'city states' earlier expressed in the letters to Graham Mackintosh—and the influence of a hierarchical model based on charisma and leadership and Spicer's own central role as figurehead and driving force behind the enterprise. The map attests to the confusions in delineating the boundaries of community, suggesting that only when the project is ending can it be described and outlined, even as the preponderance of unattributed material in this issue suggests a resistance to mapping and classification.[17]

The issue ends with a lengthy, unattributed text, whose full title, 'GINO AND CARLO'S / A COUNTRY DANCE /—for Gordon Neal', namechecks a favourite bar of the Spicer circle. The piece juxtaposes two columns: one a satirical prose piece filled with elusive coterie references, the other a poem which raises questions of classification in more general terms.

> The Church
> The God
> The Mother
> The Father
> The Home
> The School
> (*J*, n.p.)

This list is succeeded by a series of questions at once Kinseyesque and McCarthyite, ventriloquizing both the myths of American national community and those forces they other.

> Do you like it.
> In America do you
> & are there
> To say
> Others

These questions are left unanswered. Against definitions from without that try to circumscribe community, and against other forms of community associated with family, religion, and the state, sometimes community defines itself through its silence: the ending of the issue, the 'be/leaving' that is constantly at issue in the precarious ties of poetry and queer community alike (Spicer, 'Sixth Elegy', n.p.).

Love Poems and Protestant Letters: *Open Space*

In 1964, a young sailor-turned-poet named Stan Persky began perhaps the key magazine of the Spicer circle, *Open Space*. As with *J*, entries were to be placed in a box at Gino and Carlo's. The first issue, numbered 'Issue O' and titled 'The Prospectus', came out in January 1964, announced in Persky's anonymous 'PROPOSITION':

1. A new magazine for the new year.
2. 'Open Space'—a working place.
3. To make young poets come out of hiding.
4. Take stuff from other places without the usual redtape.

The magazine sets out, like *J*, to *establish* a community, not just *reflect* one. Persky's editorials reject 'gossip and politics' for 'an aesthetic the community of poets can make' (Persky, 'Alibi'), distinguishing the magazine from 'bar set or queer coterie' and warning against careerism and the marketplace: ' "Open Space' is actual working place, is free, is for the city—it isn't meant for manuscript collectors or bookdealers who sell it as valuable merchandise—if I find anyone doing that I'll take bloody action' (Persky, 'Horns'). In the penultimate issue, Persky claimed that each issue was 'a single structure or work', and we might, indeed, read such issues, which included important in-progress sequences such as Duncan's *Passages*, Blaser's *The Holy Forest*, and Spicer's *Language*, as a kind of collective serial poem. Serial community also manifests in the section of news, reviews, and gossip, parodically titled 'Homes and Gardens', that concludes each issue, offering often acerbic and cutting reviews of poetry from the San Francisco area in terms that suggest in-reference and prior knowledge. These notes operate on distinctly Spicerian criteria: they are opiniated, they judge,

88   NEVER BY ITSELF ALONE

and they praise in equal measure. In the first issue, Persky pokes fun at a rival Spicer circle publication—Lewis Ellingham's *M*—and, despite appearing in Issue O, Allen Ginsberg is criticized in the following issue for his 'usual unintelligible histrionics'. Meanwhile, the eleventh issue satirizes Donald Allen's *New American Poetry* anthology with a mocked-up 'The Penguin Anthology of Contemporary American Verse', purportedly edited by Allen and complete with photographs of a real-life emperor penguin and a joking 'Table of Contraps', featuring Abraham Lincoln, Adolph [*sic*] Hitler and Susan Sontag, among others.

Spicer contributed the entirety of the serial poem *Language*, printed as its constituent parts were written: at the Berkeley Poetry Conference the following year, he noted that he could not have finished the sequence without this venue (Spicer 1998,166). The first issue proper begins with the first poem from the sequence, proclaiming that 'No one listens to poetry' (Spicer 2008, 373). The poem is typically paradoxical—in a community-building enterprise, Spicer emphasizes the lack of an audience, even a single auditor. Yet when the phrase recurs in its final lines, a crucial line break offers the possibility—if read as equivalent to comma—of poetry's reaching its auditor—'No / one listens to poetry' (Vincent 2002, 158). And Spicer was the only poet to submit an entry for the magazine's Valentine Day contest, the poem in question, 'Be Brave to Things', declared de facto winner. Rather than a 'one-night stand', this stand-alone, self-enclosed lyric poem is a different kind of love gift—a Valentine's Day note. Yet while the Valentine emphasizes the long-term development of the monogamous crush, 'Be Brave to Things' is addressed more broadly to the magazine and to the community Spicer hoped it could create. Punning on the Blakeian universe in a grain of sand, Spicer writes of 'hold[ing] / a tiny universe in your / hand [. . .] remnants / of what was once wide' (Spicer 1980, 89). To box up that into which one pours one's desire—as in the naming of the traditional Valentine's Day address— is to set limits on love. At the same time, the container for such 'things' is a placeholder for all the hopes poured into them: an equivalent to the 'open space' which the magazine sought to establish.

On the page, Spicer's poem is enclosed, not by a box, but by a heart. For the magazine's seventh issue, Spicer sent a sequence of nine 'Love Poems', once more addressed less to a particular beloved than to the community itself. The fifth poem suggests both the fragile limitations of a community largely built on queerness, its incompatibility with the edifice of Western culture, and scepticism towards any identification with structures of power.

> [. . .] A bunch of faggots (fasces)
> cannot be built into a log-cabin in
> which all Western Civilisation can
> cower.
>
>   (*Open Space* 7, n.p.; Spicer 2008, 384)

IDENTITY AND COMMUNITY IN THE WORK OF JACK SPICER   89

Susan Sontag's then-recent 'Notes on 'Camp" was published in *Partisan Review* that Autumn and is jokingly cited in *Open Space's* final issue: ten years later, Sontag would analyse the eroticisation of fascist imagery on the part of gay men, citing among others the work of Kenneth Anger, whose *Scorpio Rising* had appeared in 1963 and who had early on been associated with circles involving Robert Duncan and others (Sontag 1975). Likewise, in transforming the slur 'faggot' into an ancient Roman symbol for power and authority, Spicer here undermines both the violence lying within Western civilisation and the troubling identifications of queer sexuality with the very forms of state power that subjugate them. Meanwhile, the log-cabin gestures at the pioneer rhetoric of the American West, in which the 'savage' forces of otherness—including that of 'faggots'—are felt to menace. But it's unclear which side of this battle the poem takes. Spicer writes:

> [...] This
> Is the opposite of a party or a social gathering.
> It does not give much distance to go on.

On the one hand, the poem resists the ossifying forces of both (political) and (high society) parties and social gatherings. On the other, it lacks 'distance'— that is to say, perspective, scale, or longevity—and the promise held up in poetry is betrayed both by individual love object and by community: 'For you I would build a whole new / universe but you obviously find it / cheaper to rent one'. Yet the sequence as a whole ends with a kind of pledge to love that, while 'imaginary', nonetheless holds firm to the promise of the 'coming community'.

> I give you my imaginary hand and you give
> me your imaginary hand and we walk
> together (in imagination) over the earthly ground.
> (Spicer 2008, 385)

With typical contrariness, Spicer's love poems to the community appear in the same issue in which he angrily attacked the entire enterprise. In a 'Protestant Letter', Spicer addresses Persky, proclaiming himself 'sick of the tea-party first-name business, my fault as well as yours, as if *Open Space* were a Turkish bath of the imagination' (Spicer, 'Protestant Letter'). Comparing the reviews section to a 'Christian Science Monitor reporting a Sunday-School Picnic', he continues: 'Something happened. It isn't happening often enough now and I wonder if the accusation against *Open Space* is not that it is too homosexual but that it is too homogenous. Like cartons of milk'. In response, Persky chafes at Spicer's attempt to control a collective enterprise: 'Trying to figure out how

90 NEVER BY ITSELF ALONE

to be fair to you is hard, who have so often used unfairness for your way [...] It seems to me you want a world small enough so that wherever you spit you'll hit something, a world you can control' (Persky, 'A Change'). Printing Spicer's letter and his response under the title 'Report to the Stockholders', Persky witheringly implies Spicer as a kind of broker, interpellating the community of readers as investors rather than as equal participants in a community in order to challenge the power dynamics of the Spicer circle. If Spicer sought a world—or, indeed, 'a whole new / universe'—it would be short-lived. After twelve issues, Persky announced: 'As this issue concludes the one year of Open Space I was 'directed' to do (or decided to do), please do not submit manuscripts to Open Space'.

Community and Negativity in Spicer's Final Work

'Alone we are dangerous': Community/Revolution

In July the following year, Spicer returned to *Open Space* in the questions to a lecture on poetry and politics at the Berkeley Poetry Conference. Discussing the relation of poetry to politics and the social, Spicer argues that 'we belong to a community rather than a society [. . .] Every poet has to create actively his [*sic*] own community' (Spicer 1998, 167). For Spicer, *Open Space* had served as an 'artificial' means to create a community: but without the publication, 'the community has been absolutely [. . .] torn apart'. Indeed, the magazine itself had never really been 'a community, a place where you live' (Spicer 1998, 167).

This understanding of poetry's relation to community is, as in Spicer's earlier work, one characterized by double-binds: the very force that gives a certain community its strength renders it subject to fracture, barely a community at all. Yet, for Spicer, even this destructive force had a potentially revolutionary energy. In summer 1962, Spicer had published a short prose text in another Spicer circle magazine, George Stanley's *The San Francisco Capitalist Bloodsucker—N*, 'an amalgam of the *San Francisco Capitalist-Bloodsucker*, a journal of Marxist opinion, and *N*—the magazine of the future'. Stanley would later note Stanley's insistence on the importance of violent revolutionary overhaul of the entire society—what Stanley calls 'a Marxist animus, one based ultimately upon hatred and revenge against these capitalists' (Quoted in Young 2018). Yet Spicer's 'Marxism' is closer to a nihilistic anarchism, critiquing both homophobic left models of community and the American right's caricatures of communism as de-individualized uniformity. Spicer's 'Three Marxist Essays' reject the Stalinist project of constructing an ideal world-historical subject—one that had become increasingly tied to a normative conception of the family, based on anti-Semitism, homophobia, and a moralistic discourse of labour. Thus, while the American left would continue to condemn homosexuality as a bourgeois individualist deviation cut off from the family root, Spicer reverses (or unverts) the standard socialist vocabulary of unity, insisting on the revolutionary force of the individual which McCarthyism insists is denied by Marxism: 'Homosexuality is essentially being alone. Which is a fight against the capitalist bosses who do not want us to be alone. Alone we are dangerous' (Spicer 2008, 328). Rather than building on figures of unity and triumph, Spicer concentrates on precisely those elements of negativity and destruction used to criticize non-procreative homosexuality: 'Our dissatisfaction could ruin America. Our love could ruin the universe if we let it'. Such ruination destroys the unjust cosmology of straight society and might 'flower into the true revolution' (328). Such flowering, however, is then undercut, for if it occurs, 'we will be swamped by offers for beds' (328): that is to say, homosexuals will be brought back into the fold, losing precisely the revolutionary force of aloneness and negation that constitutes their revolutionary potential. Queer love is important, not because it builds up a world, but because it tears one down. Such sentiments provide little basis either for political organizing that would proceed from or incorporate the full range of sexual identities, or for a liveable intimate life— 'a community, a place where you live' (328).

The *Pacific Nation*

Nonetheless, Spicer continued to envisage alternative forms of social and political life, in terms that, despite his insistence on the local, were equally concerned with world politics. During this period, Spicer and others in his circle focused on the idea of a 'Pacific nation'. In a posthumously published interview for the San Francisco Chronicle, Spicer outlined his conception as a 'Pacific British Commonwealth formed from the Tehachapi Mountains all the way up the coast to Northern Canada and perhaps even Alaska' (Tové Neville 1965). Evincing a semi-serious anarchist political vision that combines internationalism and anti-nationalist localism, Spicer claims that California's coastal environment means that 'it isn't really part of the US' and that San Francisco should trade with 'Red China' in an independent capacity. Disavowing citizenship of the United States—a gesture harking back to his refusal to sign the Loyalty Oath in 1950— he claims: 'I would like to be in a separate country; I would like our logs and grain to be sent to people who need them'. Spicer admits the whimsical nature of his imaginings, ending the interview with, 'Nothing else I can say, but a kookie vision'. Within the Spicer circle, joking debates about ministerial appointments for the new Pacific nation suggested the playful nature of the enterprise as well as its seriousness. Stan Persky would later recall: 'we knew it was a mystical nation— but nonetheless we believed it had a reality. That this particular geographic space

92   NEVER BY ITSELF ALONE

was coherent' (Quoted in Young 2018). Indeed, Blaser, Persky, and George Stanley would later all move to Vancouver, from where Blaser and Persky edited two issues of the magazine *Pacific Nation* (Miriam Nichols 2019, 146–50).

Spicer here harks back to ideas expressed in letters to Graham Mackintosh during the immediate post-Mattachine period: a vision of linked, but self-governing city states of 'principalities'—whether San Francisco, San Mateo, or Oakland—figurations that arise, as Kevin Killian suggests, from his experience in the Mattachine of the tension between the conservative, centralized leadership and a quasi-autonomous, radical local outpost (Spicer 1970, 96; Spicer 1998, 190; Killian 2011, 31–32). The concept of the Pacific nation enables such localities to come together into a larger collective body, characterized, not by existing nationalisms, but as a space where identity might be remade. This politics, quixotic and 'kookie' as it deliberately is, should also be read against the context of the military industrial complex and US imperialism in the postwar period: from 1954, and Graham Mackintosh's Army draft during the Korean War, to 1965, and the growing anti-war movement and the increasingly frequent migration from the United States to Canada to escape the Vietnam era draft. During the Berkeley Poetry Conference of July 1965, Spicer signed an anti-war pledge, and concepts such as that of the Pacific nation bespeak a socialized otherness connected at once to queer coterie, poetic community, and world politics (Killian and Ellingham, 349, fn. 21).[18]

'People are starving': *Book of Magazine Verse*

The same month that he signed the anti-war pledge, Spicer completed his final work, the *Book of Magazine Verse*. One of his most explicitly political texts, the book contains references to Churchill and Trotsky, the assassination of John F. Kennedy, the poetry of Mao Tse-tung and the war in Vietnam, yet these world-historical references sit alongside local and specific attacks on poets from Spicer's milieu for careerism and selling out to the 'system' (for instance, by appearing on Richard O. Moore's television programme *Poetry U.S.A.*), as Duncan had' (Killian and Ellingham, 354). Like Spicer's contributions to *Open Space,* these poems seek to build a community through love as well as critique. In the ninth of his 'Ten Poems for *Downbeat*', the closing sequence of the book, Spicer echoes the 'hand in imaginary hand' of his *Open Space* love poems, juxtaposing political violence with loving relation.

> What is important is what we don't kill each other with
> And a loving hand reaches a loving hand.
> The rest of it is
> Power, guns, and bullets.
>
> (Spicer 2008, 425)

IDENTITY AND COMMUNITY IN THE WORK OF JACK SPICER   93

These lines have their political lineage in the California pacifist communities with which, in the wake of the Second World War, Spicer and Duncan had intersected. They read as at once political and anti-political gesture, suggesting that the realm of politics cannot be contested, that commitment can only be local and individual. The importance of 'what we don't kill each other' with reads as both literal and metaphorical: on the one hand, a pacificist critique written during growing consciousness of American imperial aggression in Vietnam, and, on the other hand, more locally, a desire that poetic communities might still be maintained, despite their members metaphorically stabbing each other in the back.

In the following poem—a response to Allen Ginsberg's very recent 'Kral Majales'—Spicer's figuration of love and its relation to politics is more cutting. Earlier that year, Ginsberg had fallen foul of the authorities in Czechoslovakia and Cuba, having been expelled from both countries in large part for his sexuality; during the visit to Czechoslovakia, he had been crowned 'King of May' (*Kral Majales*) by cheering crowds of students in Prague.[19] Reflecting Ginsberg's growing celebrity and identification with political presence, if not leadership per se, Ginsberg's poem of the experience sees the personal, vatic authority of the speaker juxtaposed with structures of state violence: a figuration continued into poems such as 'Wichita Vortex Sutra' (1966), alongside which it was published in the 1968 collection *Planet News*, and in which Ginsberg proclaims, 'I here declare the end of war' (Ginsberg 1968, 127). Ginsberg's poem begins by presenting capitalism and Stalinist communism as equally totalitarian forms of government; having moved through his own experiences of state repression, in its second half, Ginsberg himself serves as a kind of antithesis through his coronation by the students:

And I am the King of May, which is the power of sexual youth [. . .]
I am the King of May, which is Kral Majales in the Czechoslovakian tongue,
    [. . .]
and I am the King of May, which is old Human poesy, and 100,000 people
    chose my name.
                                        (Ginsberg 1988, 353; Ginsberg 1968, 90)

Ginsberg had read the poem—also published as a broadside by Berkeley-based Oyez Press in May 1965—in what Ralph Maud recalled as 'one of the great performances at the Berkeley Poetry Conference [. . .] received with applause and cheers', and Spicer would have been well aware of its impact (Maud, 15; Victor Coleman, 24–25). The two had maintained a combative relationship from the mid-1950s onwards: Robin Blaser reports, for instance, that when Ginsberg sought him out at Gino and Carlo's in 1963, proclaiming that he'd come 'to save

94   NEVER BY ITSELF ALONE

[Spicer's] soul', Spicer warned Ginsberg that 'he'd better watch it or he'd become a cult leader rather than a poet' (Killian and Ellingham, 275–77; Spicer 1975, 300). It is the cultish power of leadership and its confusion with poetic and political authority that is the target of Spicer's poem—even if, as his exchange with Persky in *Open Space* suggests, Spicer was well capable of pursuing such a role himself. Spicer begins by addressing Ginsberg directly.

> At least we both know how shitty the world is. You wearing a
> beard as a mask to disguise it. I wearing my tired smile. I
> don't see how you do it. One hundred thousand university
> students marching with you. Toward
> A necessity which is not love but is a name.
>
> (Spicer 2008, 426)

Recalling the gap between person and name, 'love and the idea of love' in Spicer's own work, Ginsberg's attempt to bridge such divisions is seen as an act of bad faith. Theoretically, this characterisation reflects a longer standing difference in which, as Ginsberg himself noted, Spicer's theory of 'dictation' and Ginsberg's of 'spontaneous bop prosody' represented fundamentally different impulses. While Spicer abjured 'the big lie of the personal', Ginsberg emphasized the revolutionary force of personal feeling and the salvific nature of an expanded, polymorphous queer sexuality (Killian and Ellingham, 58). For Spicer, Ginsberg's filtration of mass unrest through his own poetic coronation is an egotistical misreading of the relation between poetry and politics (and, indeed, the nature of mass action), rendering his promise of 'love' a meaningless political gesture. Spicer concludes:

> [. . .] Why
> Fight the combine of your heart and my heart or anybody's
> heart. People are starving.
>
> (Spicer 2008, 426)

The fact of material survival cannot be combatted by self-aggrandizing claims to vatic authority. Against Ginsberg's omni-sexual egotism, Spicer's poem presents a position that is not a position, at once more radical and more nihilistically defeatist. For Spicer, both poetry and sexuality must retain the frightening, the negative, and the nonsensical to avoid reification and co-option: both the negative recognition of 'how shitty the world is' in and the statement of belief in the power of a 'loving hand' that proceeds it must contain each other as dialectical counterpart.

Messages from Actual Conditions: Spicer's Afterlives

The poem for Ginsberg was the last poem Spicer wrote. Increasingly alcoholic and bitter in his later years, he was found collapsed in the elevator to his building and died in August 1965 at the age of just forty. That his writing life ended with an attack on Ginsberg—likely the most prominent out, gay leftist poet of the era—is of a piece with his work as a whole. Having in the 1950s seen the hopes for queer community briefly raised by the Mattachine Society dashed by the group's leadership coup, living through frequent disappointment in love, and unable—or unwilling—to maintain a prominent public career such as that of Ginsberg, Spicer in the 1960s had turned his hopes to poetry itself and to the small, local community, the 'Spicer circle' that surrounded it. This community regularly failed to live up to Spicer's lofty ideals—ideals which he was more than capable of using as a cover for personal quarrels. Capable of giving with one hand and taking away with the other, Spicer condemned the community he needed for failing to live up to the standards he'd set for it, while nonetheless reaffirming his disappointed commitment.

Idiosyncratic and personal as it is, Spicer's paradoxical stance—his 'private, local, populist' politics—keenly reflects the dilemmas facing queer poets during this era (Killian and Ellingham, 167). And, for later poets like New Narrative founder Bruce Boone, writing when the task of movement building amongst queer, racialized, and gendered communities had achieved a new collective potency, Spicer's 'sharpness' and 'savagery' provided salutary reminders of critical vigilance. In 1983, Boone wrote:

> [Spicer's] meanness, his nastiness [. . .] releases the texts from over-universalism. [. . .] Anger about a rotten society doesn't have to be idealistic [. . .] It's a recognition of the deformations of the world as it is now, a social inability to meet human needs (since they remain alienated) [. . .] [Spicer] wanted [. . .] his sexuality to be a rebuke, an opposite. (Boone 1983, 120, 123–24)

Emphasizing the fact that, as Boone puts it, 'this community begins as shared differences', Spicer's work thus avoids homogenisation, reification, and mystification (Boone 2020, 192). Likewise, in 1973, Stan Persky, whose role in *Open Space* had been central to Spicer's theorisation of community, returned to their quarrel in the era of Gay Liberation. Inspired by 'slave auctions' held in gay clubs, Persky's poem 'Slaves' laments what he perceives as the gay community's continuing internalisation of oppression.

96 NEVER BY ITSELF ALONE

> Sometimes I think poetry is the benumbed and
> limited expression of the limited space
> (a ghetto) we're given. Expressing real pain.
>
> (Persky 1974)

Spicer's model of dictated poetry—'a message that wants to get through / from a source we can't know'—serves as partial alternative. For the firmly materialist Persky, the model of a mysterious 'outside' risks mystification and is in fact explicable as the social world—'these messages come from the actual conditions of / slaves'. Yet Spicer's work is nonetheless salutary, for, against the 'imaginary resolution of real contradictions' that, for Althusser, constituted ideology, he refuses to let the experience of 'real pain' be exchanged for 'pat answers to / explain the messages, like: gay pride'. Spicer's poetry thus serves as a model to critique both the false consciousness that celebrates conditions of domination and a moralistic refusal to engage with the force of the negative.

For Persky as for Boone, Spicer's work, which emerges from the relative paucity of existing models for gay leftist community—and its compatibility or incompatibility with poetry—also suggests the problems with those modes of community that did subsequently develop (Persky 1977, 122). Rather than basing itself on humanist idealism, such work recognizes the incomplete nature of supposedly inclusive projects. Its challenge to fixed notions of identity, the interpellation of sexual behaviour as sexual identity, and the romanticisation of community is constructed on often rebarbative, contradictory, and destructive grounds, but the questions with which it grapples are ones that still resonate with painful clarity. In the following chapters, I return to the 'Occult School of Boston' and suggest its related but contrasting figuration of queer community, focusing on the work of Stephen Jonas, Ed Marshall, Gerrit Lansing, and John Wieners.

3

The Occult School of Boston (i)

'Levels above and below'
(Ed Marshall and Stephen Jonas)

'An occult school, unknown'

In 1968, Gerrit Lansing wrote to introduce a neglected literary movement:

> The school of Boston, in poetry, middle this century, is an occult school, unknown. What literary historian has written of [Jack] Spicer, [Robin] Blaser, [John] Wieners, [Joe] Dunn, [Ed] Marshall, [Stephen] Jonas together? [. . .] What non-epopt understands barrelling on the hill? (Lansing 1968, 6)

Over half a century since Lansing wrote these words, the 'Occult School' remains occulted. Having explored Jack Spicer's role in the group in the previous chapter, in the following two chapters, I shift focus to its other members, revealing a broader context that moves well beyond the School's existing position as occasional footnote. The early days of the Occult School resulted from a series of meetings—those of Stephen Jonas and Ed Marshall on Boston Common in 1953, and of Jonas, John Wieners, and Joe Dunn at a reading by Charles Olson the following year. These tentative groupings sparked to life with the arrival of Berkeley Renaissance exiles, Spicer and Robin Blaser. Together, the poets gathered on Beacon Hill, a historical red-light district known in the nineteenth century as 'Mount Whoredom', whose 'ass side'—to use Jonas' term—was home to a thriving queer bohemia (History Project, 174–75; Jonas 1994, 239). Here Boston gay patriarch Prescott Townsend owned a series of apartments which gave homes to the younger men he mentored, protected, and sometimes exploited: towards the end of his life, Stephen Jonas lived in one (Shively 1974; Shively 2002). And here the poets of the 'Occult School'—all, with the exception of Dunn, openly gay—gathered within the necessarily furtive world of queer subculture, envisioning poetry as zone of mystical knowledge, turning conditions of marginality and enforced secrecy into tools of power.

Producing the collaborative *Boston Newsletter* in summer 1956, the poets soon dispersed across the country but continued to cross paths in various ways in San Francisco's North Beach and New York's Lower East Side milieux of art, drugs, and

Never By Itself Alone. David Grundy, Oxford University Press. © Oxford University Press 2024.
DOI: 10.1093/oso/9780197654842.003.0004

98 NEVER BY ITSELF ALONE

queer sex; in the 'Magic Evenings' Jonas held in his Beacon Hill flat; and in the pages of Wieners' magazine *Measure* and Lansing's *Set*. Subject to imprisonment and to brutal stays in mental health institutions, the School had essentially vanished as a grouping soon after Lansing wrote his preface; Beacon Hill's queer bohemia likewise was swept aside by the forces of what is euphemistically termed 'regeneration'. Determinedly on the margins in a town dominated by conservatism, racial segregation, misogyny, and homophobia, the Occult School's poems were, as Wieners put it, 'dictated to [the city] against its will' (Wieners 1965, 129). Historically transient, theirs is not the queer poetry we've been taught to expect: pre-AIDS, pre-Stonewall, yet not in the least way closeted; experimental yet anti-elitist; coterie but defiantly lower class. Yet their work takes its place alongside the early 'homophile' activism of the Mattachine Society and the Daughters of Bilitis, and their publications *One* and *The Ladder*. Less advanced politically, it is more advanced aesthetically, and recovering this work is of paramount importance in understanding the history of queer literature at mid-century: an initiation into mysteries that can finally emerge into the light.

My analysis of the Occult School will be split over two chapters. In the first, I address the work of Ed Marshall and Stephen Jones, whose 1953 meeting represented its first flowering. In the second, I turn to Lansing and to Wieners, who, as editors, poets, and organizers, served as motivating forces in its activity and later provided keen reflections on its legacy. While Marshall's and Jonas' encounter initiated the 'School', they have since remained among its most obscure figures, in some ways exemplifying the marginality of this marginal group. The present chapter begin with Marshall's work, examining the complex interrelations between gay sexuality, sectarian Christianity and poetry in his best-known poem 'Leave the Word Alone' (1955), his chapbook *Hellan, Hellan* (1960), and in uncollected work. The chapter's second half turns to Stephen Jonas, the contradictory and enormously creative crux of the Occult School. Outlining Jonas' career, I examine his dialogue with Jack Spicer; his figurations of a gay Boston; his conception of the poem as mediating space between desire, loss, and social marginality; and his later turn to paranoiac, conspiratorial thinking, suggestive of both the strengths and pitfalls of this semi-clandestine, marginal group.

'A diabolical devout': The Case of Ed Marshall

> In a glory hole
> Anything can be seen
> —Ed Marshall, 'In a Glory Hole' (1960)

THE OCCULT SCHOOL OF BOSTON (I)   99

Poet, street preacher, and denizen of the queer underworld, Ed Marshall is not a name familiar to many readers of twentieth-century poetry.[1] Marshall's long poem 'Leave the Word Alone' (1955) was a central text for the Occult School and was named by Wieners, Allen Ginsberg, and Charles Olson as one of the great poems of the 1950s—for Wieners, of the century per se (Wieners, 126). Yet, even here, Marshall is on the fringes—'of all the members of [the] "occult school" [. . .] by far the most secret', as Robbie Dewhurst puts it (Dewhurst 2013, 40). When Jonas, Wieners, Spicer, Blaser, and Joe Dunn published the *Boston Newsletter* in the summer of 1956, Marshall had already departed for New York. Today, 'Leave the Word Alone' remains one of the more obscure poems found in Donald Allen's *The New American Poetry*: a classic hiding in plain sight.

Telling Marshall's story involves filling in certain gaps, drawing certain connections, which, like his poetry, attempt to hold together the often-contradictory forces of esoteric Christianity, gay sexuality, and poetic commitment. And if the 'occult'—as per Lansing's designation—and the search for origins go hand in hand, such origins often prove to be double, ambiguous, and polyvalent. This makes it tricky to know where to begin. In the Irving Rosenthal papers at Stanford University is a curious, not obviously 'literary' object: a small mirror which, as an appended note observes, Marshall would affix to his shoe while cruising men's rooms in order to assess the sexual prospects within adjacent cubicles. In considering Marshall's often occulted life history and often elusive poetry, the mirror serves as an apt model, reflecting to the archival scholar their own face as the object of Marshall's retrospective enquiry—a pick-up, a scoping-out, a cruising through time, without precise beginning or end. One might likewise pick out the figure of the glory hole from the poem quoted in this essay's epigraph: unpredictable successions of sensory experience through a fixed but furtive structure, brief, serial revelations that disappear almost as soon as they appear, in which, as in Marshall's poem, the red eye of a syphilitic promises danger within the temporary occupancy of a 'squatter's paradise', and in which it's important to know when to 'move on' (Marshall 1960, n.p.). Marshall's frequently associative, punning poems emerge from what he calls 'periods of long / study under the influence of any thing you name' (Marshall 1962a). bringing together flickers of the life surrounding them—the screams of fighting cats in the alley, fighting neighbours, outdoor sex with truckers or in the restroom of a bus station, a fleeting glimpse of a red eye in a glory hole—with family history, religious speculation, and American history from Aztec sacrificial procedures to the landing of the Pilgrim Fathers and the advent of a nation founded on a ruthless and genocidal Calvinism (Marshall 1960b, 1961, 1962b). Through all this, he seeks moments of poetic coherence and sexual initiation—the glory hole, the mirror, the poem—which offer often paradoxical insight into the nature of things: 'the nothingness that is everything' (Marshall 1962a).

100 NEVER BY ITSELF ALONE

Born in June 1932 in Chichester, New Hampshire, to a long-established family, the Marshalls of the Marshall's Fruit Stand company, Edward Marshall's mother, Lena, was institutionalized when he was a baby; his father affected by the Great Depression and unable to care for him, he was raised by an aunt and uncle. As a teenager, Marshall was institutionalized in the same state hospital, a few doors down from Lena, though the two never met there (Marshall 1960a, 325). Studying at the University of New Hampshire and at New England college, Henniker, New Hampshire, Marshall, like any other student, visited Boston on weekends. Sometime in 1953, as a twenty-year-old student and aspiring street preacher, he met thirty-two-year-old Stephen Jonas—poet, military veteran, and petty criminal—on Boston Common, a space for open-air preaching and for cruising, later to be the scene of Gay Liberation parades, anti-Vietnam protests, and hippie 'be-ins' at which veteran Boston gay activist Prescott Townsend operated a mimeograph machine (Shively 2002, 46). As Jonas recalls, 'you arrived to me [. . .] upon the mid-entry gate to the queens gardens holding out to me those T.S. [Eliot] poems and I shouted out [. . .] "Hell man, you've got to sea the thing"' (Jonas to Marshall, 31 July, 1957). Jonas took the twenty-year-old Marshall under his wing—the two became roommates and engaged in a relationship at once fractious and loving. Jonas' letters to Marshall through the late 1950s and Marshall's own poem 'Last of Jonas Cycle' suggest the intensity of this period, offering a combination of advice at once poetic and prosaic, cautioning against involvement in religion, and emphasizing the necessity of committing to poetry. (They were reportedly studied by Jack Spicer while he worked on his epistolary sequence 'After Lorca'.) John Wieners mentions a poem emerging directly from the relationship with Jonas entitled 'Tug of War', but the poem was lost—perhaps subject to one of Marshall's bouts of manuscript destruction, associated with periods of religious crisis (Wieners 2020, 39). In 1955, however, Marshall wrote another long poem—supposedly under the influence of meth which Jonas dropped into his coffee (Dewhurst 2014, 40)—which worked through the traumas of his family history and his connection to the mother he never knew, attracting the great enthusiasm of Jonas, Wieners, and Charles Olson. 'Leave the Word Alone'—an admitted influence on Ginsberg's 'Kaddish'—was circulated at Black Mountain College, where Wieners and Joe Dunn were students the following summer, and subsequently anthologized in Donald Allen's *The New American Poetry*. Marshall himself decided against enrolling at Black Mountain, possibly at the urging of a spiritual adviser, instead moving to New York in 1956 (Abel 2020, n.p.). Here, his work appeared in magazines such as *Measure, Yūgen*, and *Fuck You*, with a year in San Francisco resulting in a debut volume, *Hellan Hellan*, in 1960. During the early 1960s, Marshall was part of a bohemian scene on the Lower East Side involving Herbert Huncke, Irving Rosenthal, and Wieners, with whom he briefly lived. Rosenthal in particular was a champion, starting Carp and

THE OCCULT SCHOOL OF BOSTON (I) 101

Whitefish Press specifically to bring out Marshall's work: *Transit Glory* appeared in 1966, and plans for a longer selected poems entitled *Pole Vault* persisted for several years before Marshall finally pulled the plug on the project.[2] Marshall's last publications of new work appeared in 1971, and by the 1970s, he appears to have largely dissociated from literature. The last record of Marshall's involvement with the literary scene came at a reading given with Michael Rumaker at the Poetry Project in New York in 1975; in subsequent years he was involved in religious movements relating to the Episcopal and Anglican Churches. He died in the coincidentally-named Marshall, North Carolina, in 2005 (Abel 2013, n.p.).

'Raffish [and] mysterious' (Dewhurst 2014, 40), Marshall was a difficult character to pin down, the multiple valences of his life matching the difficulties in placing his work. Ginsberg later recalled Marshall's and Wieners' appearance in the Cedar Bar Tavern in the late 1950s: 'They were both gay. They were both from a sort of gay hustler's Benzedrine maybe-a-little-bit-of-junk scene' (Ginsberg 1982, n.p.). The aura of the queer *demi-monde* clearly clung to Marshall to an extent that it never did to the middle-class Ginsberg, despite the *outré* subject matter of 'Howl', or to the poets of the era's other gay groupings, the Berkeley Renaissance—Spicer, Blaser, Duncan, and Landis Everson—and the New York School—O'Hara, Schuyler, Ashbery, and others. 'Please find some bk [book] stores of occult to look into if you have nothing better to do than cruise haha' jokes Jonas in a 1957 letter, while Marshall's December 1962 biography for *Fuck You*—written in the characteristic style of editor Ed Sanders—describes Marshall as 'the famous New Hampshire poet and dope-freak. Loves to slip yohenbine to young boys' (Sanders 1962, n.p.).[3] At the same time, Marshall had the ability to move between worlds, from his career as preacher and street-corner speaker involved in various sects and branches of Christianity to his propensity for cruising. Dave Haselwood recalls: 'Ed had this incredible way of meeting people [. . .] There was this one guy [. . .] from one of the premier high society families in San Francisco. [. . .] I think he was out on the streets of San Francisco picking up guys an awful lot at that time' (Haselwood 2013, 36, 46). As well as 'picking up guys', Marshall was at times heavily involved in street-corner preaching and with various religious organizations, and would intermittently go on what friends called 'destruction kicks', attempting to collect and destroy manuscripts from friends (Abel 2020). For Jonas, Marshall's religious leanings were 'a disguise to protect your inadequacy from detection', resulting from homophobic persecution: 'Why does Edward & the Church want Authority? / Because we have been persecuted long and hard / and I want to protect myself'. 'The organized churches have joined the system and gone out after utopian rabbits', he continues. 'Write yr things I say!' (Jonas to Marshall, Feb. 1957). Marshall's religion was nonetheless hardly the Puritan variety of Jonas' imprecations. Preaching, cruising, and reading his poems in Boston Common and in New York's Union

102 NEVER BY ITSELF ALONE

and Times Squares, such spaces were for him at once zones of sex, poetry, and preaching, and his poetry likewise holds all three elements at once. While Marshall's unique, heterodox thinking struggled be assimilated to a single, pre-existing religion, it was poetry that held together diverse and competing strands, reconciling sex, poetry, religion, and the question of mental health and family history. All this can be seen in Marshall's major poem, 'Leave the Word Alone', the longest single poem in Donald Allen's hugely influential anthology *The New American Poetry*. Addressing Lena, the mother he never knew, and their shared tendency to religious calling, mental illness, and a commitment to 'the word', the poem is an act of survival and witness, in which, at times, it seems as if Marshall's very life is at stake. It's to this poem that I turn now.

'Leave the word alone it is dangerous'

In a 1965 essay draft, John Wieners proclaimed 'Leave the Word Alone', 'the first magnificent long poem of the century [. . .] And by long poem I do not mean *Maximus*, or *[T]he Cantos* or *[T]he Wasteland*, or "Venice Poem" or *From Gloucester Out* or *From Idaho Out*; but "Leave The Word Alone". Not "Kaddish" or "Howl"; but "Leave the Word Alone". Nor *Anathemata* or *In Parenthesis* but "Leave the Word Alone"' (Wieners 2015, 126).[4] Writing to Robert Creeley, Charles Olson was fascinated by the piece's New England geographies, associated with lineages of suppression and violence. For Olson, the text was a history poem, a poem of place and of the marginalized peoples who inhabit it: 'It's like the whole god damned back country started talking finally. All those faces. And tombstones. And fields. And bloody towns' (Quoted in Butterick 1983, 372). Meanwhile, Wieners calls the poem, 'the object of desire and hatred, bitterness against life and the times that produced it': record of an experience of marginalization and institutionalization, and of poetry's visionary capacity to witness and challenge such abuses (Wieners 2015, 127).

The poem begins with instruction.

> Leave the word alone it is dangerous.
> Leave the Bible alone it is dangerous.
> Leave all barbed wires alone they are
> > dangerous.
>
> (Marshall 1960, 323)

This instruction—applicable both to Marshall and to Lena—equally concerns 'the word' of religion and of poetry. The poem that follows will turn such instruction on its head, embracing the word that serves as opposition to all forms

THE OCCULT SCHOOL OF BOSTON (I)   103

of enclosure—psychiatric, systematic, dogmatic—whilst heeding its warnings of mental instability. Reconstructing Lena's biography, Marshall notes the life of hard, unremunerated labour, begun almost as soon as she married:

> With a little honey-moon   at Rye Beach they   came to the
>   farm in Chichester
>   where she slaved til 35.
>   'Get   these potatoes ready for the working men' but
>   she kept reading the Bible
>
> (325)

Bearing children is part of such 'slave' labour: Marshall himself is the physical product of relations of gendered subjugation. As the cause for his mother's escape attempt, unable to cope with a third child (323–34), Marshall—himself a non-procreative practitioner of 'Greek love'—both disrupts and continues the line of reproductive futurity, while Lena refuses the burden of domestic labour and of patriarchal ownership. Viciously punning on 'mother' as 'moo-her', Marshall likens male ownership of women to the breeding of cows:

> There aren't too many bulls, but there are harsh
>   fathers who still insist on
>   impregnation at 35 while he is 41.
>
> (323)

When Lena runs away from home, shortly after giving birth to Edward, her husband, 'Papa Harry', treats the occasion as a kind of community hunting party: 'invited all the neighbors to take part [. . .] ordered a lot of bread and / made sandwiches' (324). Having been captured and institutionalized, Lena's stay in the asylum is also haunted by the background of economic crisis:

> [. . .] catatonic, dementia-
> praecox among the wolverine
>   gang of girls who   couldn't
>   get what they wanted in the
>   29 crash.
>
> (323)

The promises of wealth and religion—that which institutionalized women desired and were everyday denied— is flattened and enclosed by disciplinary spaces. Able to resist only through 'the word'—'the Bible and her health book'— Lena is further cut off from linguistic agency.

104   NEVER BY ITSELF ALONE

Marshall himself, however, seeks to cling to the word as Lena could not.

> If I can finish this poem without cracking up and
> becoming victorious—onslaught resurrection.
>
> (323)

The Christian utopian tinge to the faith of both mother and son is shaded by a sense of danger: the poem, the 'word', might itself lead the poet to 'crack up', but if they persist, hopes and dreams may be resurrected, even as both inherited traumas—'the insanity is / in your immediate family' (329)—and repressive, patriarchal responses to non-normative behaviours are 'passed down'. Ultimately, a gesture of love and identification unites Lena's and Marshall's commitment to the 'word' against heteronormative expectation and the asylum apparatus: Lena, to continue reading her Bible and health book, Marshall to 'finish this poem'—both, refusing to 'leave the word alone'. Rescued from suicide (332) only to be locked away in silence and aloneness, Lena's wishes and desires have been systematically suppressed: in paying tribute to her, Marshall extends her line, a line both connected to genetic mental illness and to an impulse to creativity, religious fervour and the impulse to survivor. '[D]on't think this is mere journalism', cautions Marshall: '[T]his is the most painful process I have had / to go through for a long while / And I am a Christian because I know how deep / is the sore and womb from /which I came' (333). Seeking to be 'the one who could go through the trauma / and write of it', Marshall writes in place of his mother and his grandmother, attesting to their experience and to his in a female and queer counter-line to the repressive laws of patriarchal ownership, disavowal and inheritance:

> [. . .] it is not my fingers
> that writes [sic] this.
> It is Lena; it is Rhoda Straw—
> It is the sore womb and that is
> fertility.
>
> (333)

Ultimately, the 'painful process' of the poem becomes the means of 'stay[ing] out of the asylum', the 'birth' of the poem harking back to the creative impulses, not only of earlier generations but also of humankind itself: 'the bear cave by / Newfound Lake where animals — / bears, lynx have made their / imprint on Rhoda's paths' (333). Invoking Lena's mother Rhoda Straw—of Native American ancestry, 'never limited in images' (330), and associated with travel and survival—Rhoda—the road—provides the path back and forwards, away from the asylum and the barbed wire fence and towards the unbounded word.

THE OCCULT SCHOOL OF BOSTON (I)   105

'A covering and an unloading': *Hellan, Hellan*

Marshall's following of these paths took him first to Jonas—'I / get butch at times. And that is why / I can survive under Steve', he writes in 'Leave the Word Alone' (329)—and thence to New York and San Francisco, where he oscillated between preaching, poetry, and enthusiastic participation in the cities' respective queer scenes. Following a year in San Francisco, his first pamphlet, *Hellan, Hellan*, appeared through printer-poet Dave Haselwood in 1960. Having elsewhere proclaimed that 'publishing is not a gentleman's profession, it is the profession of a crook or a madman' (Haselwood 2012), Haselwood's advertising broadside self-consciously frames the book in the tradition of queer decadent writing, describing it as a 'yellow book by a diabolical devout' which 'threatens to replace *À Rebours* as the furtive reference in *Dorian Grey*'.

Hellan, Hellan itself opens with an epigraph: 'This is an infinitive; / extend it any way you want'—a kind of guide for reading and for poetic method, with subjects ranging from the conquest of Mexico, Aztec sacrificial records, and the genocidal transplantation of the puritan ethic to America (Marshall 1960b, n.p.).[5] Picking up the etymological valences of its title—'an infinitive / of the old Anglo-Saxon, meaning to bury [. . .] that anglo-Saxon root word to all hell'—the title poem is 'a covering and an unloading', recording clandestine queer sexual experience within the 'hell' of a police state. Alluding to a statement from Miguel de Unamuno's *The Tragic Sense of Life*—'Hell has been conceived as a sort of police institution, necessary in order to put fear into the world. And the worst of it is that it no longer intimidates, and therefore will have to be shut up' (Unamuno, 286)—Marshall writes:

> Hellan, Hellan the infinitive of
>   to bury—cover it over now—
>
> It is a cover job
>   all right
> Unamuno said hell and its motive
> Is to start a penal state.[6]

The poem continues by sarcastically ventriloquizing the interpellative call of the police:

> Hellan, Hellan, Hello!
> Heaven or Hell!
> WE shall get you one place or another!
> An effective police state with
>   confinement

106   NEVER BY ITSELF ALONE

> Heaven or Hell—
> physical realities?
> Well!

'Undercover' also suggests the logic of the closet, and the occulted sexual knowledge the purveyor of cruising has of ostensibly 'upright' citizens:

> Well Hello there,
> undercover
> under Chino,
>   under Ivy Leagues,
>   Crowded too tight, crowded [...]
> I know you
> I have uncovered you last week,
>   you, last night—
> Don't you remember? You had red on last
>   time—last September now done over[.]

The sexual moralism of the Pauline ethic turned on its head, the embattled band of early Christians under the Roman empire become the denizens of cruising grounds under the contemporary American empire, turning proclamations of legal and religious 'hell' into joyous hails—'Hello!'—with the threat of the asylum mocked as a sexual come-on—'Come darling, let me give you a shock treatment / feeding on ashes!' 'Hellan' becomes joyous invocation to queer sex, the poet rolling with leathermen in the heather: 'I say it is a little dirty tonight / Hea! / Soft though on that heather— / Leather! [...] Hellan, Hellan! / This is an infinitive; / extend it any way you want'. Such extension—imaginative, sexual, and textual— resolves in a rousing final calling together, within the cruising ground and open-air church that is the poem's unique terrain:

> This is a covering tonight!
> I shall encumber you—I shall encounter you all—
>   Hellan!

As Marshall had placed himself in relation to his mother's feminized and marginalized religious lineage in 'Leave the Word Alone', so here he turns his chosen terrain of poetry and gay sexuality into the domain of religion and prophecy.

Likewise, in one of Marshall's most explicitly erotic sequences, 'Times Square', printed in the postponed third issue of John Wieners' *Measure* in 1962, poetry pays ample tribute to erotic pleasure and homoerotic beauty, functioning as a means of seduction and a testament to vital forces: 'I shall continue cleaning up

THE OCCULT SCHOOL OF BOSTON (I)   107

my rhymes on my / fishing lines—/ while little fairies whistle and put on flys / and bait [. . .] the / nymphs can play and that is why it is a / swamp for the Bergsonian life-rhythm' (Marshall 1962b, 19). Imagining himself as an anthropologist in the vein of Earnest Hooton, Marshall extends Hooton's 'research methods' into the territory of sexual experience: 'an anthropologist with em- / phasis of your hands on the anatomy—Just what will the / athletes do at the greyhound [. . .] Let me see your specimens [. . .] for I let mine *participate* and dance before / me and unfold everything they've got to do—like / Rhoda who kept silent until the thunder roar' (18). Cruising, anthropology, and the renewed invocation of Rhoda Straw unite in the poem's thunderous rhythms, joyously appropriating and resisting the terms of anthropological or psychological classification.

Yet these multiple levels—akin to what Marshall himself calls 'competing / radio stations'—are barely held together within the poem, and, it would seem, much less so outside it. The last published new work by Marshall to appear in print consisted of seven poems in the magazine *Mulch* in 1971. These contain the most direct and joyous of all Marshall's poems of erotic encounter—'Give me a ring from your head— / I shall screw it! / I am coming, coming, coming / all over you!' (Marshall 1971, 77). They open, however, with a poem, 'Dramatic Silence', which attests to the silencing effect of mental illness, institutionalization, and the struggle between faith and poetics. Marshall takes up the poetic-musical 'lyre' of Greek tradition to bear witness to mental illness, to the queer chaos and defiance of his own life, uniting it with a Judaeo-Christian pun.

> The lyre of madness admitting madness
> The lyre of sickness admitting sickness.
> The lyre of seizure admitting cataleptic fits.
> The lyre of self-estrangement admitting sin
> > Stroking these to dischords—
> > then dischords
> > > then chromatics
> > > but then grace notes—
> > but only grace notes because of dischords—
> > > > disgraceful notes.
> > > > > (Marshall 1971, 74)

'Grace notes'—in sheet music, an ornament neither harmonically nor melodically essential but indicated in miniature on the score—here unite the Christian concept of grace with the 'disgrace' of sin, inverting Puritan dogma so that it is in fact the queer poet's 'disgraceful notes' that turn 'disgrace' into 'grace': indeed, that serve as the very route to grace itself. For Allen Ginsberg, Marshall's poems 'bear witness to real tears, real tragedy, real one and only life, our own self archetypes

108 NEVER BY ITSELF ALONE

honestly revealed [...] actual national grief, actual city subjectivity and personal body-lore' (Ginsberg 1972). No less than his other work, 'Dramatic Silence'— even as it suggests Marshall's interrupted relation and farewell to poetry—retains an unwavering belief as sexual as it is religious, as poetic as it is sexual. If Marshall had chosen, finally, to 'leave the word alone', these 'disgraceful notes' continue to decorate, contradict, and embellish the principal song of literary history: a refrain moving across time, a reminder of poetry's capacity to look ahead, glory hole to glory hole—'onset resurrection'.

'Dialogue against Dialogue': Stephen Jonas

'another excursion into fantasy': Jonas' 'anti-biographies'

On the fifth anniversary of the Stonewall uprising, Charley Shively reflected on a poet who 'never made it into the shiny new world of gay freedom' (Shively 1974). 'Stephen Jonas was a saint of poetry as well as of faggots', Shively writes; yet Jonas 'died of overdrinking, drugs, a broken heart, or who is to say what now that his memory has become less distinct than a stone rubbing'. Resistant to easy excerpting, Jonas' voluminous work appeared only sporadically during his lifetime, his full-length publications *Transmutations* (1966) and *Exercises for Ear* (1968) appearing in England, and despite the publication of posthumous collections, there remains much uncollected material. Such writing overspills the bounds of editorial discretion: a voluminous explosion that's messy, contradictory, and often problematic, distorting the lenses bought to bear on it, evading capture. Jonas steadfastly refuses to be fitted into neat identity categories. Never publicly associated with the politics of Gay Liberation, Jonas was of mixed ancestry, defiantly out, and a fierce critic of the American state, which he accused of grand larceny while defending himself in court on mail fraud charges. He was also prone to Poundian conspiracy thinking, anti-Semitism, and racism.

Jonas' death date—February 10, 1970—is unambiguous. (*Fag Rag* even printed his death certificate [Lives of the Poets # 3 1974, 11].) His origins are harder to trace. Jonas' friend and co-executor, Raffael de Gruttola, suggests that Jonas was born December 1921 in Atlanta, Georgia, as the African American Rufus Jones (De Gruttola, 30). His mother dying when he was a teenager, Jonas may have been raised by an uncle: his own account suggests a period with a white Protestant family in Massachusetts. Yet Jonas often span contradictory and confusing stories which David Rich has named 'anti-biographies' (Jonas 2019, 249). These served in part as compensation for Jonas' lack of knowledge of his family history, in part as challenges to the fixed modes of racial classification exemplified

THE OCCULT SCHOOL OF BOSTON (I)   109

in the one-drop rule. 'I feel I should ease your befuddlement by giving you this little tale', writes Jonas to Ed Marshall in 1956.

> There once was a boy named Luis Santos whose father had so many kids he didn't know what to do. His son Luiz was a great one for imagination—i.e. wanted to be something else. Not, surely not, a black greaser he was [...] at about sixteen while living in his dream world he met a son of a New York Quaker who taught him (Irving Fenmore Dayhof) the art of man-to-man love—he also took to his home to live and his parents took a liking to him. [...] Luis became Steve and a Quaker [...] got caught up in the Christian Science Movement and joined the Youth Movement at Boston University and later became a member of the Mother Church. [...] About this time Rufus S. Jones alias Luis Santos sometimes Stephen has worn thin his protestant efforts and drowned another person and become Jonas (the whale that swollowed [sic] the man) Or did he— —?? (Jonas to Marshall, April 1956)

Such explanations obscure as much as they reveal. Figuring himself as the biblical prophet Jonah, emerging from the belly of a whale to face up to his prophetic task, Jonas transmutes autobiographical matter to creative invention. Likewise, his poetic work suggests an eternal muddying of sources, a joy in miscegenation, both reproducing and subverting the language of racialized epithet and political prejudice in total dedication to poetry as calling.

According to de Gruttola, Jonas was in the Air Force from 1942 to 1944: given a medical discharge due to a nervous breakdown, he attended either Morehouse College or Howard University—both HBCUs—likely on the GI Bill, possibly conducting further graduate work at Emerson College and Boston University (De Gruttola, 30).[7] In the late 1940s and early 1950s, Jonas worked at the Boston Christian Science complex and at the South Boston army base in a civilian capacity, associating with Boston's queer bohemian set, including legendary gay activist Prescott Townsend. (The later poem 'Orgasm XXXIII' provides a sweeping account of this scene, including venues such as the Napoleon Club, a gay bar in the Bay Village neighbourhood, and the Barn, a space owned by Townsend which hosted theatrical performances.)[8] Discovering modernist poets such as William Carlos Williams and Robert Creeley through poet Cid Corman's show on WMEX Radio, Jonas participated in Corman's Boston-based writing group (Corman 1975). A committed poet by the time he met Marshall, Wieners, and Joe Dunn, Jonas was in many ways the most mature voice in the 'Occult School' as it came together in 1956.

Of all the School's members, Jonas was the only one to remain in Boston as the poets dispersed across the country. Writing prolifically, his work appearing in little magazines such as *Yūgen*, *Measure*, and *Set*, he resisted literary careerism.

110 NEVER BY ITSELF ALONE

Unlike most of the other members of the Occult School, Jonas was not included in Donald Allen's *New American Poetry* anthology. While Jonas' voluminous writings suggest an urge to record, he was equally committed to the ethos of local poetic community: convivial, open, transient. During the 1960s, he began to hold what he called 'Magic Evenings' on Saturday nights in his apartment on Anderson Street on Beacon Hill. Continuing the legacy of Corman's workshops and the gatherings of the Occult School, these evenings consisted of small groups of, on average, seven-to-ten people, Jonas playing records, giving tarot readings, and poets reading their work in an atmosphere of openness and generosity. As Jonas' younger friend, and now literary executor Raffael de Gruttola put it, these evenings were 'similar to a jazz cutting session where poets would come to try out their ways. A circle of regulars attended; however, anyone in town was welcome' (Jonas 1989, 23). Attendees varied from members of the Occult School such as Wieners, Lansing, and Joe Dunn, to poets associated with the faculty at nearby Tufts College such as Robert Kelly and Charles Stein; other Boston-based writers such as Carol Weston; Harvey Brown, publisher of Frontier Press and *Niagara Frontier Review*; and beginning writers and students from other Boston-area colleges (Rich 2020).

As Joseph Torra suggests, Jonas, who turned ambiguity into a strength, was able to move across class, race, and sexual lines, from Corman's workshops to the world of Prescott Townsend and the 'street people'—junkies, sex workers, addicts, and petty criminals—who were his friends (Torra 2020). An autodidact, Jonas was also a kind of unofficial teacher and mentor for a range of younger poets and hangers-on: he would often hand out reading lists to friends, and his apartment served as a kind of informal academy. Loose and informal in his approach to the dictates of private property and private space, his own or that others, Jonas would tell friends if he was out to come in through the window—'If I'm not home, come in through the window, everybody does', and, when at home, served as host, cook, and curator, his extensive record and book collection functioning as a kind of neighbourhood libary. Feeding the children of junkie friends, cooking—in his notebooks recipes jostle for space with reading lists— often with the result of late-night foraging trips to the produce dumpsters at the local market, and rewiring electricity to receive free power from his landlord's circuit, Jonas created an alternative public forum characterized by excitement, artistic discovery, generosity, and queered openness (Jonas 1994, 2). It's my hope that this sense will inform the following analysis of his life and work.

'Remember me kindly': *Love, The Poem, The Sea*

Despite his participation in Cid Corman's workshops, Jonas' connections remained limited until the emergence of the Occult School mid-decade, and the

Boston Newsletter of late summer 1956 may well represent his first publication. Yet Jonas' 'Michael Poem' is the centrepiece of the issue, its longest and most fully developed piece. The following year, it was printed in stand-alone form as the first pamphlet of Joe Dunn's White Rabbit Press, *Love, The Poem, The Sea and Other Pieces Examined by Steve Jonas*. For Torra, this is Jonas' masterpiece: 'a love poem, a statement of poetics, a statement on contemporary culture—a poem that keeps unravelling' (Torra 2020). In 1974, Charley Shively went so far as to proclaim that, here, 'Stephen Jonas wrote one of the finest love poems in any language' (Shively 1974).

Virtually nothing can discovered of the 'Michael' in question beyond a brief mention in Shively's essay—'Michael Farmer, United States Navy (August, 1956)'. Jonas turns the poem's particular occasion into self-reflexive meditation on the relations among poetry, love, and life, where it is, above all, 'the poem' that makes cohere that which in life ebbs away. Setting the distances of troubled love alongside the impending landscape of the military-industrial complex, the space race and the navy (recall that Jonas was himself a military veteran), the poem opens in medias res: '. . . not so much for receiving / stolen goods / as it were / placing the junk / dead as the world' (Jonas 1994, 102). Junk—later developed into the figure of driftwood—becomes floating, discarded matter, as well as drugs: discarded, outside, illegalized. The Homeric descent to the seashore with which Jonas' great influence, Ezra Pound, opens *The Cantos*, replays in the figure of the shoreline as place of decision, voyage and return, mixing the epic, with Jonas as Penelope to Michael's Odysseus, with lyrical lament. Somewhere between Homer and the present day, the poet is found on Washington Street—Boston's Tenderloin, a space of queer sexual pleasure, with the stores about to close. 'If in Life I am ever in Love I am consumed', Jonas proclaims, figuring love as both death wish—'that switch / blade belly thrust'—and the Dantean *Rosa Mundi*, whose seasonal blooming promises heaven (103). Love, like the oceanic flux of the sea, is something which the poem may listen to but whose meaning it can never encompass: 'The sea speaks if speech be sound / but speech is not sound / and so turns for meaning / to the poem' (102). And it this poem which 'is the child's ear / and Love is naked and unashamed'—which, unregulated, approaches closer to the mysteries of love—the 'deeper [. . .] secret' of 'the sea['s] cry' contrasted to the hubristic American space programme and its bureaucratic administration of utopia, 'a dead issue': 'visions of other worlds / accurately numbered / [. . .] plan / within a decade / to shoot the moon' (104). Addressing his beloved directly, Jonas writes:

> Mike, I have seen pieces of driftwood
> two
> so twisted together you & I

112   NEVER BY ITSELF ALONE

> would be hard put to extricate. How can I
> subject our lives to so trivial a thing
> a twisted freak thrown together in the sea of
> unconcern to be dis-
> carded on some obscure beachhead of our world?
>
> (105)

Like driftwood on the sea or birds looking for worms, 'we poor things pour /
over our signs for some parasite of meaning'. The poem ends on a bitterly
devastating note.

> It has been a lean season for you & me.
> I did not intend to write a serious poem but the Poem
> has a will all its own
> I am a poor vehicle
> a transport in summer wear
> I to be discarded also
> in the season of decline
> Love
> O self willed love
> though unworthy
> remember me kindly at the hour of decline
> know then I sacrificed all
> to say nothing.
>
> (105)

The poem concludes by predicting 'stark winter' in which to 'think what pigs
we have made of ourselves'—the lovers as Odysseus' sailors, turned to swine
by the sorceress Circe. As Shively writes: 'For Mike, Jonas pushes through
with this switch-blade belly thrust—what faggot can read it without weeping?'
(Shively 1974). Here Jonas introduces a key figure in his work: 'the Poem' as that
which holds together what in life might break apart, rejecting bureaucratized
utopian schemes, legal limits, and whatever would constrain either love or the
poem: a *memento mori* for love's passing which extends tragic poise and utopian,
loving hope.

'From one Martian to another': Jonas and Jack Spicer

During his time in Boston, poems such as these gained Jack Spicer's wholehearted
admiration. Fascinated by Jonas' racial ambiguity and underground lifestyle,

THE OCCULT SCHOOL OF BOSTON (I)   113

as Lewis Ellingham and Kevin Killian suggest, 'Jonas served as an objective correlative of Spicer's longings and fears, the outsider complete' (Killian and Ellingham, 71). Immediately bonding, the two poets continued to correspond once Spicer had left the city, dedicating and writing a string of poems to each other.[9] Jonas, along with Bob Kaufman, provided the basis for the character 'Washington Jones' in Spicer's unfinished detective novel *The Tower of Babel*, and soon after his return, Spicer told Robin Blaser that his version of Lorca's 'Ode to Walt Whitman' '[is] going to be dedicated to Steve Jonas as he taught me how to use anger (as opposed to angry irony) in a poem' (Spicer 1994; Spicer 1987, 38). While the two bonded as fellow queers, paradoxically, the poem in question directs much of its ire *against* gay men, addressed in a catalogue of sexually insulting epithets. Against the 'cocksuckers of all the worlds [. . .] Opening their flys in parks with a fever of fans', Spicer/Lorca injuncts 'the bewildered, the pure, / The classical, the appointed, the praying' to 'Lock the gates of this Bacchanalia' (Spicer 2008, 130). Such ambiguous identifications are typical of these poets' dialogue, the intimacy of epistolary address bonding across shared prejudice. In particular, as Killian and Ellingham put it, Spicer and Jonas 'rhapsodized' over their shared anti-Semitism, 'their connection becoming a *folie à deux* of spite and spleen, as each dared the other into saying more and more hateful things' (Killian and Ellingham, 71–72).

In 1957, Spicer wrote a poem for Jonas after the latter had defended himself while on trial for mail fraud. Riffing off Jonas' contention that 'the whole State is based on larceny', Spicer outlines an anti-humanist vision—'All this crap about being human'—with the very condition of being alive rendered one of perpetual theft: 'The word steals from the word, the sound from / the sound. Even / The very year of your life steals from the last one' (Spicer 2008, 192). Jonas, as truth-teller, suffers for telling the truth that everyone knows but no one acknowledges— 'Christ who didn't know that, Steve?' Jonas was easily interpolated into the 'Martian' figure key to Spicer's theories of the poetic and social 'outside'. This identification is eagerly propounded in an unpublished poem written soon after their first meeting, 'A Gentle Word from One Martian to Another' (1956), in which the two 'Martians' bond against an all-encompassing, paranoiac anti-Semitism—'These earthmen [. . .] White black, or yellow / They are Jews' (Killian and Ellingham, 72). 'With these creatures, there are no distinctions', proclaims Spicer, his racist, anti-humanist gesture redirecting the exclusionary logic of homophobia towards a new target, and concluding with a vituperative exclamation of (literal) bile: 'Puke / Of the universe'.

Jonas alludes to Spicer's poem in his own 'A Poet's Word to a Blue Painter' (1966). Citing an acquaintance 'who / speaks, naturally / with disgust of the white race / for their impositions', Jonas himself dismisses racial differentiation, 'as tho in the rat race / shades could make differences'.

114 NEVER BY ITSELF ALONE

Rats change their colors
all like chameleons
I have been
previously warned of a fellow poet
not be taken in by
their disguises
—black
yellow,
white
homosexual or Jew—all
all of them
The spew of the universe!

(Jonas 1976, 15)

Echoing Spicer's anti-humanist and anti-Semitic claims, Jonas also revises Spicer's statement—these identities are not those adopted by 'Jews' but by *any* racial or sexual identity group, including Jews. Yet Jonas picks up on the anti-Semitic trope of rats as metaphor of disease and infection, and the poem is elsewhere suffused with racial insult. Maintaining a studied ambivalence as to his own racialized identification, Jonas lashes out *as if* from the position of whiteness, while rendering whiteness a target, in an all-encompassing levelling principle.

Such poems opposed both fixed notions of racial purity and modes of performative inauthenticity which they associated with Jewishness and which they contrasted to ideals of Blackness—particularly Black music—as zone of authenticity (Jonas 1958; Jonas 1966). Yet Jonas' poem 'Cante Jondo for Soul Brother Jack Spicer' uses Blackness to praise precisely those modes of cultural transplantation, cultural parallelism and syncretism he elsewhere criticizes in anti-Semitic notions of Jewish performance and subterfuge. Interpellating Spicer as a 'soul brother', the poem's title destabilizes both Jonas' interpellation as Black and Spicer's as white. Lorca is once more the key bridging figure. The poem follows through on the connection made in Lorca's *Poeta en Nueva York* (*Poet in New York*), which links Harlem jazz and blues to *cante jondo*, or 'deep song'—a vocal style found in Andalusian flamenco music which Lorca argued was 'the only song [in Europe] that has been conserved in its pure form [. . .] the primitive songs of the oriental people' (Lorca 1980). 'Lorca (our Fedy) was 'gipsified', writes Jonas.

The blues came into Spain with the gypsies
who joined the jews & the moors in the Hollywood
hills back o' El A afta the expulsion [. . .]

THE OCCULT SCHOOL OF BOSTON (I)   115

> Flamenco came up the mississippi afta it
>   buried its black roots under a N'Orleans cat house.
>   (Jonas 1994, 161–62)

Addressing Spicer via an aside from guitarist Manita de Platas' and *cantaer* Jose Reyes' recording of 'Moritas Moras', in which one of the members of the group exclaims, '*Eso es cante moro*' ('that's Moorish singing') Jonas fuses white poet, Spanish musician, Moorish legacy, and African American blues in a single, gleefully hybrid gesture.

> Hey, Manitas, Jack Spicer says make with Meritas Moras
>   & the Cantaer intones the blues [. . .]
>   'eso es cante moro'
>   this cat is *bad*
>   'cause the blues is bad
>   from 'down home' southern Spain
>   (161)

Alluding to the hybrid roots of Spanish culture in pre-Reconqusita Moorish Spain, Jonas' poem, in Nathaniel Mackey's words, 'allies outcast orders, acknowledging hybridity and heterogeneity to entwine the heterodox [. . .] bespeak[ing] the presence and persistence of the otherwise excluded, the otherwise expelled' (Mackey, 13, 181). Linking the American South and southern Spain, the Andalusian countryside and New Orleans, Jonas blurs the lines between racial, national and cultural identification (or disidentification). Contrasting 'us latins' with 'northern insensibility', at one point Jonas jokingly exclaims: 'Spanish/ christ, i don't even speak english'. And, addressing Spicer and Lorca both: 'I adopt your style, personality—deliberately a mask'. Constructing what Eric Keenaghan terms 'imagined coalitions', racialized but anti-essentialist, which are predicated precisely against the myths of racial purity that undergird fascist politics, the poem ends in gentle tribute to the murdered Lorca, victim of fascism and homophobia (Keenaghan 2010, 10).

> weaving through the green blades
>   of fixd bayonets (poor Spain) [. . .]
> Sleepy Fedy among the olive groves
>   where I imagined they planted you
>   [. . .] red bells thru the soft wind:
>   'adiosito'
>   'good-nite'.
>   (Jonas 1994, 164)

116 NEVER BY ITSELF ALONE

'Boston Lingo' and the American Idiom

In the late 1950s, the three-way dialogue between Spicer, Lorca, and Jonas suggested one mode of queer community; the queer aesthetic of John Wieners' new magazine *Measure* provided another. 'Do you know where the fairies have come from?' wrote Wieners to Charles Olson. 'Jonas [. . .] It scares for what they can do by implication to you people' (Wieners 2020, 54). Conceiving of Wieners as Boswell to his Dr Johnson, Jonas' 'A Word on Measure', printed in the magazine's first issue, conceives of 'the Poem of the Fairy / like wings to fly off on / If we Measure / we reckon on fairydust / what rubs off the word / Measure that' (Jonas 1957, 24). On the following page, Jonas introduces a block of text which can be read either as subtitle or prose interlude, outrageously punning on poetic composition as jazz 'head' (main melody) and hand job: 'Expanding "word on measure" to include sometime that's "prose" but not always—which is the dream be it super or economy minded and or where as I could go on in the head and make this thing's head a poem but I had it down before a sort of long hand job you see I type them after I do them the first time' (25). This is a sexualized, serial poetics audaciously breaking down the boundaries between poetic artifice and lived experience. As we'll see in the following chapter, Wieners attempted in *Measure* to draw on Boston's queer, local valences, and of all the poets of the Occult School, Jonas was the most attuned to what he calls 'the music of the streets' (Jonas 1994, 155). As de Gruttola writes, Jonas was 'a city (Boston) poet [. . .] He wrote about his friends who were junkies, prostitutes, down-and-outs, poets, and others were just trying to fight the establishment' (De Gruttola, 34.) Such poems take place in apartments, on the streets, and in Boston's queer, outdoor spaces—all contested terrain. Here, Jonas delights in combining literary allusion with underworld language and incident. 'Three Versions from the Chinese', wittily turns poems from the classical Chinese—likely playing off Kenneth Rexroth's translations—to Boston's queer locales (Rexroth, 52). Variants on a poem by Ōuyáng Xiū (Ou Yang Hsiu)—who wrote under the title 'Zuiweng', or 'Old Drunkard'—present a landscape brimming with queer sexuality:

> Trees horny w/leaves
> 　　scratching their crotches
> full ov bird tweet
> 　　as the hard-on hills
> get a blow job from the east
>
> 　　　　　　　　　(Jonas 1994, 152)

Birdsongs become gay men's orgasmic cries, flowers bloom in an 'orgy' that mimics the sex around them: a queer spring pastoral delightedly taking place

THE OCCULT SCHOOL OF BOSTON (I)   117

under the noses of the law. 'On the Esplanade' transplants Tu Fu's 'By the Winding River'—to what Shively calls 'Boston's popular outdoor faggot makeout spot, near where [Jonas] lived' (Shively 1974; Rexroth, 13–14). Leaves blowing in the wind become blowjobs, and a 'pair of kingfishers [who] shack up in / the pavilion' allude both to Tu Fu's original and to Charles Olson's 'The Kingfishers', whose famous proclamation 'what does not change / is the will to change'—a statement of process both political and poetic—Jonas delightedly queers.

Yet if cruising grounds are zones of pleasure, they are also subject to state surveillance. While joyously reclaiming such spaces, Jonas also conveys the heightened sense of police harassment, gentrification, and urban 'cleansing' of illegal activity that takes place outdoors, in fractured narratives, influenced by the leaps of jazz and blues improvisation, which are at once liberating and vertiginous: on the one hand freely improvising, on the other hand, barely holding on. 'Take the next chorus we're in A flat' reports on the police's destruction of the shrubbery behind which gay men cruised on the Fenway in Boston:

> & they (the fuzz) dug up N chopped
> the shrubbery down
> in Fenway (park)
> to keep Priapus down
> & other unmentionables out
> it has been highly suggested to
> 'keep Boston clean'
>
> (Jonas 1988, 34)

Himself stopped and searched at the bus depot for ' "cruising" / or breakin' in', Jonas comes to suspects the presence of undercover police in the city's bohemian coffee houses—' "fuzz" here in plain clothes [. . .] coming on like they wuz "beats" ' (35). Juxtaposing such scenes with fractured reminiscences of institutionalization at the VA hospital in Brockton, as Jonas sardonically puts it:

> then raving myself
> I knew I wuz
> in the right place (yeah)
> a real drag

From around 1961 to 1966, Jonas worked on a sequence entitled *Exercises for Ear*: the first four poems of an eventual one-hundred-and-seventy-nine appear in the second issue of Gerrit Lansing's *Set*, and the full sequence appeared as a book in 1968. In his introduction, Lansing calls the poems 'Boston lingo tune[d] up' (Lansing 1968). Fusing local vernacular with modernist and classical strains, the

118 NEVER BY ITSELF ALONE

sequence is a series of vignettes, fragments of overheard speech, in-references, tributes and put downs. The full title describes the book's purpose through joking archaism: 'being a / primer for the beginner / in the / american idiom / by / STEPHEN JONAS / Gentleman'. Modes of aural and oral training for poet and listener, these texts resist a central, organizing point of view, establishing shifting in- and out-group positions that toy with distinctions among sexual, ethnic, and gendered groups: a parade of performances; a polyvocal, multicultural community in which boundaries are constantly being trespassed, transgressed, and set. In this regard, 'CVIII' functions as methodological statement:

> i have come to
> chew up yr language
>
> to make more palatable
> the L's & collaterals
>
> (at the service
> entrance
>
> (Jonas 1994, 72)

As the official food taster of 'the American idiom', Jonas both chews up—destroying—the language of the dominant order and makes dialectal variants 'palatable' to the ruling classes: the 'gentleman' poet reduced to the function of a servant or court attendant, somewhere between subversion and subjection. In 'XXV', however, Jonas conceives of poetry as noise, as speaking back, if not exactly speaking truth, to power:

> A music
> A spreck
>
> A formal rack-
> et in time
> a yak-yak
> a means
> of talkin' back
>
> (Jonas 1994, 36)

These are criminal poems, delighting in subverting and breaking the letter of the law. In 'A Further on the Human Condition', Jonas writes: 'this Poem / has a moral to be found / still in the journeys / of de Sade or most assuredly / among the thieves of Genet' (Jonas 1966, n.p.). Likewise, he delights in a trickster aesthetic—in 'Artful Doge' relating his pleasure at hearing that New York junkies

THE OCCULT SCHOOL OF BOSTON (I)   119

are using a stolen I.D. and credit card: 'this is truly / the promised land /—unmentioned by marx' (Jonas 1966, n.p.). In 'CXX' from *Exercises for Ear*, Jonas writes:

> i wish i were
> a bird & not
> held down to
> anything in par-
> ticular
> oh, you name it
>   (Jonas 1994, 77)

As Charley Shively notes, it was commonplace for gay men at this period to use multiple names, both a source of protection from and a source of legal retribution (Shively 1974). Jonas' adoption of multiple names, personas, and origin stories led to brushes with the law—as when he was convicted for mail order fraud after subscribing to numerous book and record clubs under assumed names. As David Rich argues, Jonas' relentless poetic and extra-poetic self-invention 'reassert[s] his own agency to define and redefine himself, to maintain mystery and reassert his right to withhold crucial details, or fabricate spurious ones' (Jonas 2019, 249).

Such messages are designed to be read only by the initiates; by those who know where to look. In his introduction to the book, Lansing argues that the *Exercises* follows the mode of the epigram, a piece of writing designed to appear as if found, in George Puttenham's words, 'upon a table, or in a windowe, or upon the wall or mantell of a chimney in some place of common resort' (Quoted in Lansing 1968). Lansing's suggestive link recalls the *Boston Newsletter*'s instructions to 'Post whatever pages of it poke you in the eye in the most public place you can find—i.e. an art gallery, a bohemian bar, or a lavatory frequented by poets'. Thus, 'XLI' speaks of 'the old golds [...] within' who are 'reawaken[ed]', in 'phallic sportings / cleft-footed revels / of scrawld / indignations / on walls / of men's rooms' (Jonas 1994, 69). This work assumes yet greater significance when we reflect that, while in jail for mail fraud, Jonas wrote streams of poems on a roll of toilet paper: sent to Jack Spicer and subsequently preserved in the pages of a copy of *Reader's Digest*, they can currently be found, along with numerous other writings on scraps of paper and cigarette packets, in Spicer's papers at UC Berkeley. Space precludes a more detailed investigation of this writing, which parallels the 'Jail Poems' written around the same time by San Francisco poet Bob Kaufman: suffice it to say that Jonas' writing in such moments is a furious dialogue against the odds, with any means to hand, and a further indication of writing's power in the face of incarceration and state violence.

120 NEVER BY ITSELF ALONE

Whether in phallic graffiti or jailhouse scrawl, then, Jonas worked improvisationally with whatever material was to hand. And *Exercises for Ear*, whose title echoes Lester Young's 'Exercise in Swing', also takes jazz as a key model (Brent Hayes Edwards, 255). Young, who frequently alluded to other players in solos peppered with quotation and melodic paraphrase, turns up in 'CXVIII' as a bona-fide modernist: '& there was "Pres" / horn horizontal aslant / blowing nothin' but / free verse' (Jonas 1994, 76). As Brent Hayes Edwards notes, Young's speech was 'as oblique and understated as his solos, and his was a highly coded language, condensed and epigrammatic' (Brent Hayes Edwards, 256). A formative influence on much language beloved of 1950s hipsters, Young, who addressed those of both genders as 'Lady', was also rumoured to be queer, nicknamed 'Miss Thing' by some in the Count Basie band, adapting the mannerisms and styles of gay men. (Gioia, n.p.) Young's ironic claim to power— the 'Pres' sobriquet, bestowed on him by Billie Holiday—at once lays claim to the political power denied him in everyday life and undercuts that power through treating it with chatty familiarity. Such slippages of gender, social position and in-group slang, all toy with linguistic meaning and its social connotations, revelling in ambiguity and the pleasure of recognizing secrets only known to the initiates. *Exercises* draws on the multiplying meanings negotiated within both subcultural and poetic discourse: the doubled valences of signifyin(g), camp and other forms of racialized and queer speech, which often rely on the line between a meaning apparent to outsiders and one revealed only to insiders.

Toilet graffiti and jazz slang are two such models. Others include young mothers in the park 'yaking the yak-yak / women yak' (Jonas 1994, 23), and, above all, the witty, double-edged discourse of 'queens' and of the queer community. Jonas' renditions find the latter to be a language already in quotation marks, characterized by performance and role play, in a language operating on several levels at once: an overheard S&M fantasy imploring the lover to impersonate an SS guard, topping from the bottom ('LXII'); a joke about the 'Greek' profile of Jonas' boyfriend Scott ('XLVI') (Jonas 1994, 40, 51). Jonas also plays with expectations of gender identity: 'LXV', for example, claims that ' . . . blues aint nuthin' / but which gender you / makin' it w'th / split' (51), and other poems deploy the gendered switches of queer and drag vernacular rendering the gap between sex and gender, biology and gender ambiguous: a drag queen 'thr[own] in the sextank /& all for trying to / live it up like a / real white woman' (Jonas 1993, 17), or 'Rudolpho (a which no gender/ 'll fit)', who seeks a Black lover to 'match [. . .] his dirty *mutandi*' (Jonas 1994, 129). Punning on the legal phrase *mutatis mutandis*—signifying that that which needs to be changed will be changed—Latin, the language of law, church, and authority, is repurposed for sexual (and racial) transgression, Rudolpho gloriously overspilling the bounds of gender. Jonas' work manifests two competing tendencies: to celebrate those

THE OCCULT SCHOOL OF BOSTON (I)   121

who overstep the bounds of designated racial, gender, or sexual identity, and
to undercut their hypocrisy and pretension—the impersonation of that which
one is not. Eviscerating queer class pretensions, 'Nubis in Nubis' pokes fun at
an inhabitant of Boston's predominantly Black suburb, Roxbury, for posing as
a 'very 'english' / gentleman', maintaining 'a nine / room cold water walk-up /
buckingham palazzo': 'the which the he-she / thinks (demented queen that /
she is) out in Chestnut Hills!' (Shively 1974). Yet if, as Shively notes, Jonas is
mocking such prejudice, he also leaves the structures from which it emerges in
place. Using racial, gender, and class reveals as stings in the tail, Jonas laughs and
mocks from every conceivable angle, in a kind of inverse lower-class solidarity
that easily turns into the opposite of solidarity.

It's thus equally true that Jonas' 'tactical misspellings' and mis-speakings can be
read in terms of Edward Kamau Brathwaite's anti-imperial 'calibanization' (Brent
Hayes Edwards, 257–58) and that the sequence serves as 'a virtual casebook for
the study of multiply directed racisms', in which 'no single racial group is liable
to emerge from the text without being insulted' (Nielsen 2004, 62). Jonas self-
reflexively undermines American rhetoric of racial purity whilst simultaneously
reinforcing its prejudices. As Brent Edwards notes, in 'CXXXVII', 'in the space
of fifteen lines, race shifts shape at least three times' (Brent Hayes Edwards, 257).
The poem reads, in full:

> the nigger
> ought to be
>   horse-
>
>   whipd
> for his
> presumptions
> but, my friend,
>
> when i look a-
>   bout me at
> this emi-
>
>   grunt dis-
> order that passes
> for White
> I'm inclined to
>   a-
>   gree
>
>   (Jonas 1994, 86)

122 NEVER BY ITSELF ALONE

At first seeming to identify with whiteness and its targeting of racialized others, Jonas then undercuts white stability via a wicked pun on the practice of racial 'passing', ending with a final statement of agreement with the Black 'presumption' it initially condemned. Tapping into racial prejudice, which it condemns by holding it up to its own standards of race purity, the poem maintains a characteristically ambivalent stance between opposing positions offensive to every conceivable group. Likewise, the early poem 'Chorale and Hymn' joyously calls out:

> Come junkies perverts
> boosters pimps prostitutes
> you hip tossers shakers you
> who mount horsemen barebacked
> you wops you hunkies you
> kikes spicks frogs you
> brits chinks Come [. . .]
> ALL COME [. . .]
> all of you Motherfuckers
> shout it loud [. . .]
> (Jonas 1994, 107–108)

Ultimately, the only identity Jonas is fully willing to assume is that of the *poet*. Exercise 'IV' opens: 'Poets barred / from Plato's utopia // take pleasure / in yr derision' (Jonas 1994, 22). Interpellated by others alternately as Black, Latino, Portuguese, or generally 'cullud', constantly living on the edge of legality, poetry provides an unchanging yet mutable system of identification in which any identity or tradition the poet chooses to assume is potentially, as Nielsen puts it, 'both garb and drag' (Nielsen 2004, 70).

'one completed poem': Poetry and Love

> At forty I want to follow my own heart's desire. [. . .] Love, I recently wrote, is a four letter word, too.
> (Jonas to Gerrit Lansing, 14 November 1961)

For Jonas, the queer socialities of the Occult School, manifested in the *Boston Newsletter* and *Measure*, along with the 'music of the streets' (Jonas 1994, 155) found in the *Exercises for Ear*, offered workable forms of community, however contradictory. The other key strain in his work sees romantic love as offering a possibility both potentially salvific and troubling. In 'A Long Poem for Jack Spicer Because He Needs It', Jonas writes 'Love has come / into our dead City / The process / swells / splits [. . .] Love comes like an / earthquake' (Jonas 1974, 56).

THE OCCULT SCHOOL OF BOSTON (I)   123

Love promises to revitalize the city, but also, like an earthquake, to destroy stable foundations: both full of promise and risking catastrophic destruction (54). Like Spicer—reported to have said that every gay poet over twenty-five feels themselves to be Verlaine in relation to a younger man's Rimbaud (Killian and Ellingham, 159)—Jonas developed a series of relationships with younger, often straight or bisexual men, whom he sought to initiate into poetry, able to take Jonas' generosity but not to return his erotic love, and often with severe drug habits. As Raffael de Gruttola notes:

> Fellow poets such as Dale Landers and Tony Sherrod were very important to him, yet at times I believe he could not reconcile their lives with his own. By this I mean he believed in their basic goodness, not realizing that many of them needed more help than his love could provide. (Jonas 1989, 24)

To Gerrit Lansing in 1961, Jonas writes of Sherrod, 'my last infatuation': 'I really must sub-consciously feel very strong emotionally for him. He is a very beautiful boy' (Jonas to Lansing, 26 November; 16 December, 1961). Originally from Knoxville, Tennessee, Sherrod had been part of the cycles around Spicer on San Francisco's North Beach in 1962 (Killian and Ellingham, 221). Lewis Ellingham describes him as 'literally beautiful, explicitly heterosexual, talkative, agreeable. He was insecure, touchy, used light drugs and drank as we all did; for jobs he drove a taxi, tended bar; while I knew him he married and fathered a child [with his wife Marie] [. . .] Tony was a bird of passage, a lovely birdquick' (402, fn. 2). From the same circle, Landers, a sometime poet whose work appeared in Sherrod's one-off magazine, *Mithrander*, died of a heroin overdose in Mexico during the early 1960s—in Gerrit Lansing's words, 'because he couldn't grok the whole truth of Jonas' expounding' (Landers, n.p.; Lansing 1968).

To his beloveds—Landers and Sherrod, as well as Ed Marshall, George Stanley, and John Fusco—Jonas wrote poems of literary and loving advice, using the address to the beloved as occasion for exposition of poetics, tool of seduction, gesture of farewell, and means of commiseration. 'A Poem for Dale Landers' (1961) opens with a vivid transmutation of the beloved's body to that of the poem, which can hold together what escapes the lover in life:

> Your body is the body of the poem,
>   and the poem is what
>   I have wanted for so long
>
> (Jonas 1989, 12)

Jonas' substitution of textual for sexual body is a necessary fiction, for no poem can mend all hurt, and fantasy cannot indefinitely substitute for reality.

124   NEVER BY ITSELF ALONE

But this is no movie this
is the real scene
no hero will come
as at the end
tall and upon a white steed,
relieving me.

(12)

Yet he must still believe that when lovers leave, the poem remains:

trying to get across to you
trying to span
as Hart Crane tried to span
that tremendous gap
the gap between
in each of our own
desolate
and daily lives.

(10)

Proffered as love gifts, such poems sublimate disconnection and unfulfilled desire, providing the strength to bear loss and the means to bridge it. This is not simply the gap between Jonas and an individual beloved, but between 'each of our own [. . .] lives', for whatever community into which it speaks.

Writing to Tony Sherrod in 'The Music Master', prosody become entwined with sexual desire in the absence of its consummation. 'Tho' I cannot offer you / my not *too* unsumptuous bed, bring / on to me yr verses', writes Jonas (1994, 154). 'You should have been my / Swinburnian "miss", he continues. Alluding to a poet whose sexual 'perversions' were notoriously encoded in the formation of innovative metrics, and figuring poetic lines as 'entwin[ing] naked / alexandrines' and 'a heaving sailor's hump', he lightly worries: 'This / will land us both [. . .] in Dante's sodom's mist'. Unable to move from prosodic sublimation to erotic fulfilment, Jonas advises Sherrod: 'Don't / chop yr things into / separate iambs / Use / the music of / the streets.' (154–55). Ultimately, in Jonas' work, it is the streets that mediate between sexual desire, prosodic sublimation, and legal persecution, even if, as Gerrit Lansing put it in a memorial poem, Jonas maintained a distinction between his love for poets such as Sherrod and Landers and the available sexuality of those streets— 'hands you chose, / Hotel Madison men's room boys, / weird high objects of yr unearthly love, / dumb credit card thieves, boosters, drunks'—dismissing the latter as 'only tricks' (Lansing 2009, 126). As I'll outline in the following chapter, for Lansing, gay hustling in New York offered a literalized 'brotherhood of man', and his poems, basically celebratory in nature, suggest sex of all kinds and in all contexts as access to occult realms. Yet, for Jonas, unreturned and idealized love was contrasted to available but degraded hustle: the poem made to bear the weight of this contradiction—along with the contradictions of class, race, and gender—felt to be unresolvable in life.

The unanswered address to the beloved combines with a sense of the smallness of the poem's audience, which Jonas both bemoans and wears as badge of honour. Shortly before his death, Jonas argued: 'the poetry audiences aren't wide enough to cope with anything like it. William Carlos Williams estimated there were ten people in the United States that could be communicated to by a poem' (Lives of the Poets # 3 1974, 10). Aware of this queer community's smallness—

> (We, and I say "We", to say I
> am limited, as at first,
> to the 'few'
> the few of your reading this)
> (Jonas 1989, 8)

—Jonas makes of it a virtue—

> We are the noble
>
> & intelligent few
>
> To understand love
>
> In the abstruse
> (Jonas 2019, 191).

Love itself is abstruse in that only the privileged few understand its philosophically difficult nature, but they also discover love *in* the abstruse—the obscure, the underground, the coterie, the criminalized margin. The abstruse is a philosophical problem, but it is also the result of political contradiction. The poetics of unrequited love fuses with the necessity of criminal secrecy and disguise, the 'streets' offering solace when love does not, the Poem replacing both, speaking to the limited circle who have ears to hear. But, for Jonas, this was not always enough.

'in hell / already': Jonas' later work

While other members of the Occult School left the city—Marshall for New York in 1956, Joe Dunn and Wieners for San Francisco the following year—Jonas steadfastly remained in Boston, finding his milieu, his inspiration, his heartbreak, and his solace in what Gerrit Lansing calls 'the Boston crevices, their histories [. . .] good affabilities' (Lansing 2009, 126). One of Jonas' closest

126 NEVER BY ITSELF ALONE

confidantes, Lansing served as his literary executor, and the two were in frequent correspondence. As de Gruttola writes, 'Gerrit was also a source of inspiration for him, and Gerrit, like John Wieners, was one of the few people whom Steve trusted and shared his thoughts with' (de Gruttola 1988, 30). Writing to Lansing in December 1961, Jonas opines: 'Oh Gerry, the beauty of language dances when it is freed from logic [...] Gerry, I think we are born with the Mark—divine spark or whatever' (Jonas to Lansing, 14 December 1961). Such intense friendships— and, until 1965, his correspondence with Jack Spicer—along with friends and loves requited and unrequited sustained him through difficult times, through 'lean season[s]' and 'dark night[s]', when the 'music of the streets' and the 'switch/ blade belly-thrust' of love could not (Jonas 1994, 105, 103).

Jonas had been discharged from the Air Force in the late 1940s after suffering a nervous breakdown, and he continued to live on a military disability check. Further hospitalized at the VA hospital in Brockton in 1959, 1960–1961, and 1963–1964, his poems, along with reports from friends and acquaintances such as Amiri Baraka, contain ominous illusions to his struggles with mental illness. In July 1963, Jonas wrote to Lansing: 'I am in the Brockton V.A. Hospital. I am trying to get out of this place and get back to writing. A letter from you as my "publisher" would help them understand my peculiar situation as a human being and a poet. Say whatever you like'. Concluding the letter, 'I don't know how many friends I lost with this latest "episode"', he poignantly wishes 'I hope you are still warm for me' (Jonas to Lansing, July 1963). Lansing and others remained warm, and Jonas continued to live in an apartment on Beacon Hill and to mentor younger poets through 'Magic Evenings' in his Beacon Hill apartment, attended by poets such as Wieners, Dunn, and Lansing, and by Robert Kelly and Carol Weston, akin to jazz 'cutting sessions where poets would come to try out their wares' (Jonas 1989, 24). Yet as the 1960s wore on, Jonas' life was increasingly devastated by drug abuse, heartbreak, and acute mental anguish, and he was increasingly immersed in Poundian, anti-Semitic conspiracy theories. A month into the new decade, Jonas died of a Glutethimide overdose—a readily available drug that, Rich suggests, may have contributed to his precarious mental state (Jonas 2019, 256).

In 'A Long Poem for Jack Spicer Because He Needs It', Jonas describes the periods between poems as 'hell'. 'Between poems I am not well [. . .] You are right Hell is / when you cant write' (Jonas 1958, 53, 57). The 'hell' of mental illness often prevented Jonas from writing, and not writing exacerbated its effects. Jonas' poems and letters alluding to periods of hospitalization and medication connected to a paranoia which exacerbated his tendency towards conspiratorial and anti-Semitic thinking. Writing to Andrew Crozier on the publication of *Exercises for Ear* in 1968, Jonas observes: 'I have not been writing for some six months. it is a long dry period. Also very painful. I think the worse is over as I have begun to write in my notebook' (Jonas to Crozier, 29 November, 1968). Much of Jonas' lengthy letter consists of political ranting: condemning 'banking

THE OCCULT SCHOOL OF BOSTON (1)   127

lice', praising George Wallace as 'the only good thing about the Presidential election' ('he at least tried to warn the people that both major political parties are controll'd by the same money factions'), and citing Pound on 'devaluation of the currency', the Adams papers, and Eustace Mullins' *The Federal Reserve Conspiracy* ('my political position is, if any, 'Federalist', which has been out of fashion since John Q. Adams' day').

Such positions also increasingly came to dominate Jonas' poetry. Around the same time that he began the *Exercises for Ear*, Jonas also initiated a series entitled *Orgasms* and continued work on the sequence—sometimes with the alternative title *Dominations*—through the decade. The *Dominations* title is here suggestive both of what Jonas perceived as the conspiratorial 'domination' of American culture by hypocrisy and nefarious economic forces and to his own attempt to 'dominate' the material, to hector, and to rant. Writing to Crozier, Jonas mentions having agreed to let Harvey Brown—a participant in his Magic Evenings—publish the first thirty of the *Orgasms* series as a book, only for Brown to return the manuscript for its 'political content', and the sequence has never been published in full. In his preface to the 1994 *Selected Poems*, Joseph Torra calls many of the *Orgasms* 'tiresome, repetitive, ugly, and hateful'. To Crozier, Jonas insists that 'any "political" stance is assumed merely "assumed" for the particular poem I'm writing at the time and is merely a mask'. Likewise, in conversation with John Wieners, René Ricard, and Gerard Malanga shortly before his death, he responds to criticism of the sequence's political tendencies by arguing that

> I'm behind a mask speaking for someone else. But people are misled that read them; they think they are my personal opinions [. . .] There's no one person, one voice going all the way through saying something. One piece of dialogue is set off against another piece of spoken dialogue [. . .] So you build up a Tower of Babel out of dialogue against dialogue.
>
> (Lives of the Poets # 3 1974, 11)

Babel—the biblical figure of the linguistic fall from grace out of an originary linguistic unity, caused by human hubris—suggests the chaos of the sequence, even as it taps into the poly-linguistic, poly-stylistic, in some ways radically democratic ethos of the *Exercises for Ear*. In 'Orgasm I', Jonas announces the freedom to travel across race, class, and gender lines found in the *Exercises*. Arguing that the poem 'comes to you', rather than being consciously planned or written by the self, there's a sense that the poem might go anywhere—'venus, mars, the kitchen sink, south station' (Jonas 1994 175). As in the *Exercises*, such freedom often comes in disguise. In the first 'Orgasm', Jonas writes, 'mask in hand, / to the wings, I beat / my retreat', and the third refers to the 'full face ov the Kabuki': the theatrical pose which is the ground for the poem of persona and performance, in turn revealing the performed nature of the self (185). Masks and

128 NEVER BY ITSELF ALONE

shifting or contradictory meanings are queer defence strategies for marginalized subjects, avoiding the legalized dictates of state scrutiny. At the same time, Jonas worries about 'the crabbed ambiguity of lost connections'. As he writes in a late poem from the sequence: 'the word is loose if not fragmentum. / the communications inaccurate if at all communicated' (170).

When Jonas visited New York in the early 1960s, he heard voices through his dental fillings and 'rambled non-stop about Pound' (Jonas 1994, 7; Jonas 2019, 23; Baraka, 238). Poems from the sequence such as the 'Oracle Bone' *Orgasm* (VII), written in July 1965 attest to his struggles with mental illness, hallucination, and emotional turmoil. Citing Spicer's poet-as-radio—'Man is a sending and receiving device' (Jonas 1994, 196)—the parade of voices appears closer to hallucinatory chaos:

> NOTE: Joe Dunn, J.B. a witch. You are lost [. . .]
> Died young and the pattern lost. [. . .]
>
> There are levels above & below. Above: Sacrifice according to
> RITES. Be serious. Below: hold yr tongue and keep yr distance. [. . .]
>
> WHISPER: Jack Spicer is the Count Ulrich
> von Lichtenstein.
>
> AN(Other Voice): O yeAH!
> Q: 'Can you point her
> exact cause of illness.
> A: Illusion.
>
> [. . .] Demons
> & devils creep up
> the fire-escape and in
> thru the kitchen window[.]
>
> (196–201)

The poem at once tries to exorcize and seeks the hidden wisdom in these clashing voices. As Jonas writes in the closing section:

> [. . .] Remember that I have
> remembered too
>
> Properly castigate by
> spelling out [. . .]

THE OCCULT SCHOOL OF BOSTON (I)   129

> Anglo-Saxon Common Law, Coke, the
> Commentaries all convergence upon
>   the Central: What's it all about
>
>   (201)

For Raffael de Gruttola, to whom Jonas dedicated the *Exercises*, Jonas saw himself as a poet-alchemist, 'transforming feelings that are hidden in the great literature of the past [...] He believed in great traditions which he felt only passed before the eyes of visionaries': counter-narratives, suppressed truths—political, economic, and religious (de Gruttola, 30; Jonas 2019, 256). The very forces which led Jonas to a queered refusal of identity—sexual, racial, poetic—combined with the deleterious effect of Ezra Pound, led him to cultish in-groups, secret theories of history, and paranoiac, anti-Semitic conspiracy theories (Ward 1990, 284–85). 'Orgasm XXIII', written in June 1968, is largely a narrative reminiscence of the Boston queer scene, a kind of *Autobiographia Literaria*. Yet the poem ends with a kind of political aside that emerges seemingly from thin air: 'on the question of coons / I shall die on the rebel side' (Jonas 1994, 239). One can read these lines in completely opposing directions: on the one hand, as identifying with the new-found militancy of the civil rights movement; on the other hand, siding with the forces of the American South, Dixie, and the 'rebels'.[10] A few lines on, Jonas ends the poem with an offensive ad-lib setting Blackness against Jewishness, as in the Spicer dialogues: '(those predisposed to a slavery democracy / for if you scratch a bit below the surface you'll find a Jew / or "investor" holdings or whatever' (239). The poem moves in contradictory directions, lashing out and seeking coherence in disorder, victim-blaming whilst also denouncing the forces that victimize.

Jonas' queer contemporaries objected to such grand historical theorizations. In conversation in 1970, René Ricard and Gerard Malanga suggested that Jonas channel the multiple voices of his poems to write a play: 'no rhetoric, just use gutter trash language' (Lives of the Poets # 3 1974, 11–12). Jonas' death foreclosed such possibilities. 'These few lines / scrabbled on sand / the tide already / coming in' read lines from a notebook fragment that may be the last thing he ever wrote (Jonas 1994, 251). Memorializing the late Charles Olson, Jonas anticipated going to his funeral. He never made it. Jonas lasted only a month into the new decade, dying on 10 February alone in his Anderson Street apartment of an overdose that Joseph Torra suggests may have been suicide (Torra 2020).

For Charley Shively, writing from 'the new, shiny world of Gay Liberation', Jonas served as 'an example, a classic tragedy—caught in the web of irreconcilable forces: his own gayness, blackness, love, beauty pitted against the Federal Reserve Bank, straight white culture, Harvard Brahmins, the police, state, American Society' (Shively 1974). Meanwhile, apparently responding to Shively's essay, John Wieners was humorously sceptical of what 'Jonas's possible

130   NEVER BY ITSELF ALONE

resurrection to the newsstand editions, outside of His coterie', might bring. For Wieners, such attention echoed the state persecution that he and Jonas faced: 'his conduct calling forth special punitive attention among those who bereft of him along *le vieux rue*, snatch on hold to last decade's *enfant cause celebre*' (Wieners 1976). Jonas' work resists a recuperative or reparative approach. While his—or Jack Spicer's—prejudices form a complex adjunct to their own conflicted sexual or racial identifications, they also, in Jonas' case, derive in large part from the influence of Ezra Pound—very much a straight white man—and from the systematic mismanagement of mental healthcare from which Wieners, too, suffered. And yet Jonas transmuted his life, his friendships, his loves, and his reading into poetry, holding to 'The Poem' as that which could, once more, 'span / that tremendous gap / the gap between / in each of our own / desolate / and daily lives'. For all their faults, Jonas' poems can still sing out with a rare and beautiful clarity. Whatever the fate of his life, whatever the social contradictions to which it gives witness, his work remains

> the whole panorama
> the whole life one which is one
> completed Poem.
>
> (Jonas 1989, 9)

4

The Occult School of Boston (ii)

'Queer Shoulders at the Wheel'
(John Wieners and Gerrit Lansing)

While both Jonas and Marshall encouraged and enlivened those around them, neither leaves an editorial record. The present chapter turns to two writers who, as magazine editors, in poems, and in essays, sought to expand the 'Occult School' from coterie to national movement, linking to broader political concerns that predated and later merged with Gay Liberation. John Wieners is perhaps the major poet of the group, yet, too often, accounts of his work have addressed it only in individual terms, overlooking his role at the centre of many important literary currents. Here, by contrast, I emphasize his role as builder of and participant in community, in the context of his little magazine *Measure* and the *Boston Newsletter*, and his best-known sequence, *The Hotel Wentley Poems* (1958).[1] Arriving in the Boston Area in the early 1960s, Gerrit Lansing developed close friendships with Wieners and Jonas, his magazine *SET* serving as a sequel to Wieners' dormant *Measure*. Reading Lansing's editorial essay 'The Burden of SET', which interprets cultural, sexual, and racial change in occult terms, and prefigures tropes central to countercultural movements later in the decade, I argue that both poets envisioned a social poetics in a generous spirit of collective queer identity. The chapter concludes by briefly turning to texts by Wieners which look back at the queer poetics of the late 1950s and early 1960s on the eve of Gay Liberation, suggesting that their combination of nostalgia and futural expectation can be productively read alongside Elizabeth Freeman's concept of 'temporal drag' to suggest how both Wieners' work and that of the Occult School as a whole manifest 'queer relations' which 'complexly exceed' both past and present (Freeman 2005, 59).

'never forget where we come from': John Wieners

Early Poems: Wieners in the *Boston Newsletter*

Growing up in suburban Milton to parents who worked service and janitorial jobs, John Wieners came to poetry through Edna St Vincent Millay: a gender-defiant identification with female poets, film stars, sex workers, and singers

Never By Itself Alone. David Grundy, Oxford University Press. © Oxford University Press 2024.
DOI: 10.1093/oso/9780197654842.003.0005

132   NEVER BY ITSELF ALONE

would continue throughout his life (Wieners 2015, 3–4).[2] Like Robert Duncan the previous decade, Wieners avoided the military draft by declaring his homosexuality, and, following his graduation from Boston College, moved with his boyfriend, Dana Durkee, into an apartment in Beacon Hill bohemia (Dewhurst 2014, 19). With Joe Dunn, a college friend, who, though straight, 'swished' in imitation of his friends (22–23), he attended a pivotal reading given by Charles Olson at the Charles Street Meeting House on September 11, 1954, at which Olson read the poem 'There Was a Youth Whose Name Was Thomas Granger', whose description of the execution of a youth convicted of sodomy prompted members of the audience to walk out.[3] Wieners, Dunn, and Stephen Jonas, who Wieners knew from the city's gay scene, stayed up all night talking, and subsequently held weekly poetry meetings at Wieners' apartment through early 1955 (Dewhurst 2013, 27). Wieners, Dunn, and his wife, Carolyn Dunn, soon followed Olson to Black Mountain College, an experimental institution in the North Carolina hills which had become a hotbed of artistic invention and alternative pedagogy (Dunn 2015). Wieners here developed friendships with writer Michael Rumaker, painter Basil King, and with Ed and Helene Dorn, among others. Back in Boston during the winter of 1955, he joined the Cambridge Poets Theatre, befriending Frank O'Hara, then in town for a residency at the Theatre, and met Jack Spicer and Ed Marshall, returning to Black Mountain for the school's final term in 1956 (Dewhurst 2014, 38). Following Black Mountain's closure, in August 1956, he and Dana moved into an apartment in the same building as Jonas. And it was here that the early encounters of the Occult School blossomed into the intense, though temporary grouping with Spicer and Robin Blaser that produced the *Boston Newsletter*.

Wieners published three poems in the *Newsletter*, each meditating on queer death and survival.[4] He later recalled reading the first, 'Ballade', to Frank O'Hara and Jack Spicer 'at the Harvard Gardens [a Cambridge bar]. And while I read my poetry in the humid summer evening of Beacon Hill, the both of them wept through the incipient rain and electric-charged air' (Wieners 1988, 80). Ten years later, shortly after Spicer himself had died, Wieners would reprint 'Ballade' with a closing dedication: 'this poem is for Jack Spicer, because he wept over it' (Wieners 1965). The poem concerns a twenty-year-old drag queen named Alice O'Brien, a tragically familiar story of domestic violence, police violence, and suicidal ideation. Scholarly enquiries have thus far yielded no information as to the real-life Alice, and, appropriately for a poem itself about queer transience, the poem's *style* is in some sense transient—words apparently left out, perhaps as manuscript errors, placeholders that were never filled, grammar in which subject, object and action become entangled and confused.[5]

The poem is by no means straightforwardly reverential. 'Alice O' Brien / would he care or be crying / at the way we're carrying on tonight', it opens, before

THE OCCULT SCHOOL OF BOSTON (II)   133

cattily commenting: 'We worked for a while together, I hated him'. Alluding to the violence of racial segregation in Boston, Alice's ex-wife is said to have died 'in a riot near Roxbury crossing', while Alice himself is subject to domestic violence: 'the lover dragged Alice down her three flights of stairs'. The regret-filled lyrics to Duke Ellington's 'I Got it Bad and that Ain't Good' thread their way through an account of Alice's demise:

> Lord above make him love me
> the way he should [. . .]
>
> Help Alice O'Brien hung himself
> in Charles Street Jail
> from his shoelaces.
>
> (Wieners 1956, n.p.)

With gruesome poignancy, Alice's swinging body recalls his posture in life, 'very gay in front of the bar', 'changing the redlight bulbs' on top of a ladder 'in his French heels'. This connection in turn triggers suspicion about the circumstances of Alice's death in the jail cell:

> though I remember
> he always wore loafers for dancing.
>
> No laces.
>
> We hear the police broke his neck

An ironized icon—'hung under the yellow lights, / swung head down / on his gay world'—Alice briefly becomes a political cause célèbre, for long-term Boston gay activist Prescott Townsend 'goes tomorrow to the burying of Alice O'Brien'. But the poem ends by shifting to a broader statement of human vulnerability—'We are all of us lost, Lawrence said'—alluding to D. H. Lawrence's long poem 'The Ship of Death', which Wieners had earlier recommended to O'Hara (Wieners 1988, 81).

> No difference
> to Alice if Alice knew
> and went dancing instead of dying
> on the laces
> from his high French heels.

134 NEVER BY ITSELF ALONE

Despite the foregoing *totentanz*, between suicide, murder, domestic abuse, and the callous disregard of others who bully the 'four-eyed runt', the poem insists that queer dancing, 'very gay in front of the bar', might replace queer dying, hung in a jail cell. No wonder Spicer and O'Hara wept.

Wieners first includes 'You Can't Kill These Machines', the second of the *Boston Newsletter* poems, in a letter to Michael Rumaker from August 1955. In the midst of a polio epidemic—'prepare an oxygen tank for my arrival' laughs Wieners—and house-hunting with Dana, hoping that the landlady won't 'care what us boys do at night', he reflects on gay identity.

> HEY—maybe that's why homosexual love or homosexual sex is SOMETHING—because it's not a blending but a give and going back, each remaining separate, yet, god knows, in contact. [...] I give all of me, dangerous or not [...] [and] I get something else added on top of me, whether it be a body or an emotion. I get *supplemented*. (Wieners 2020, 19)

Against homophobic caricatures of queer narcissism, Wieners argues for gay sex as exchange, sharing, an addition to one's self, a social act, a locus of care and protection. 'You know I say these things, as much for myself, as for you', he continues. 'I do feel though that all of us, in this, can hear this stuff from each other, it's our duty to each other, remind each other to keep holes open, mostly through our finger-tips'. 'To keep holes open' both gestures to forbidden sexual pleasure and to other gestures that encompass but also 'supplement' sexual contact, reaching out into physical and textual space in comradeship and love, bearing witness together. Such statements serve as a methodology for the connective work that Wieners' early work performs, whether in individual friendships, such as that with Rumaker, or in the other nexuses of poetry, publication, sociality, and community in which he'd soon be immersed.

The poem itself recalls an incident when Wieners, Rumaker, and painter Tom Field came across a blood-drenched car crash victim lying on the road, music continuing to play from the wrecked car's radio, and Wieners remarking in horror on the victim's resemblance to Dana (Rumaker 2012, 427–28). The register of bodily sensation, of mutual exploration and care within the letter recurs within a more straitened environment in the poem itself. Gay men's 'duty to each other, [to] remind each other to keep holes open, mostly through our finger-tips' extends to a meditation on the boundaries between the physical body and desire, love and death presented in a vocabulary of bodily connection—the holding of hands, the touching of skin—but also of seepage, of permeable holes, leaking wounds.

THE OCCULT SCHOOL OF BOSTON (II)   135

> a smashedup body by a squeezedin car
> broken chopped bones and moaning
> as blue music plays:
>> body and soul on the road
>> with blood on our arms [. . .]
> while somebody sits on him to keep his head whole
> somebody says insides are coming out his shirt.
>> (Wieners 1956, n.p.)

Addressing Dana—'You, / dying under these stars, what would it be for you / on an old road with nobody to hold'—Wieners puts aside the horror of 'this other body'—and flashes over to a scene of intimacy, its verbal elisions coyly sexual: 'Silversilk is the skin I love to / and thru our bedroom went / the whispering and laughing and lighting / of matches'. Yet these matches—fires of love—might also burn the delicate 'silversilk' of the skin, like the wings of moths drawn to a flame, returning the poem to the fear of death—'shall it be alone or together we get it'. The poem ends with an ambiguous promise:

> As long as my blood grows cold on the skin I love to
> and your good leg is on mine
> and a hundred feet up the ditch
> somebody else brushes off our mouths,
>> who cares.

Only indifference in the face of death—the blood growing cold—Wieners seems to suggest, can avert its fear and preserve the love that does exist. While this near callousness suggests that survival is predicated on indifference to suffering, the poem nonetheless extends a tender attention, combined with its letter to Rumaker, that stretches like the 'silversilk' of skin to preserve 'body and soul' on the dark highway of a homophobic America.

Wieners' final poem in the *Newsletter*, published under the title 'That Old Gang of Mine', and later, retitled and lightly revised, the first poem in the 1988 volume of uncollected works edited by Raymond Foye as *Cultural Affairs in Boston*, turns once more to the relation of sex, death, and desire in the literary context of a pair of earlier icons of American modernism, Hart Crane and poet-publisher Harry Crosby. Writing in his final journal entry, 'One is not in love unless one is prepared to die with one's beloved', Crosby died in an apparent suicide pact three days after attending a party celebrating the completion of Crane's *The Bridge*, his own death eerily anticipating Crane's suicide two years later, likely after having been beaten up by sailors to whom he'd made sexual advances (Unterecker 1969,

136   NEVER BY ITSELF ALONE

756; Fisher 2002, 501). For Wieners, Crane—as queer martyr—and Crosby—a Boston Brahmin whose decadent lifestyle belied his heritage—form potent examples of defiance within the overpowering wealth, elitism, and tradition of a city where Wieners so often found himself on 'the ass side of the hill'. Indeed, Wieners' early journals reveal his fascination with the 'Lost Generation' in general, intimately connected to his idea of writerly and Bohemian glamour. 'I fell in love with the 1920s [. . .] the disenchanted ones pulled me up by my hair. I read literal histories of the 20s by people like F. Lewis Allen [. . .] and someone called Mark Sullivan. And the world came open now' (Wieners 2015, 5).[6] Arriving at Black Mountain, Wieners, he wrote to Robert Greene, 'danced for hours, like Zelda Fitzgerald, on the deck of an old studio, to jazz and the rain through the leaves' (Wieners 2020, 8). Caresse Crosby herself had left two days before his arrival, depositing first editions of the books she and Harry Crosby had published with Black Sun Press—'impeti from the 1920's which line of electricity has fallen directly into Black Mountain College' (Wieners 2014, 12). Shortly after, Wieners wrote again to Greene, noting his presentation to class of 'an address to Hart Crane, and Harry Crosby, two suicides [. . .] written while I was stinking [i.e. drunk] on Friday, and written while I was in tears up to my knees' (11).

The poem in question takes its title from a 1923 song debuted in the Ziegfeld Follies, whose gently bittersweet farewell to 'old sweethearts and pals' transplants to a pair of suicided poets dead long before Wieners' own maturity, invoked as support for the young poet himself not to 'go over'.

> Going over the edge of
> the ships and hotel ledges
>
> Hart Crane Harry Crosby, how do you feel
> > (Wieners 1956, n.p.)

'HarryHart, this is one of your boys', Wieners announces, 'Crawling around on dirty sheets, making / love to pillows, hoping / nobody knocks on your door'. Brief resolution and commitment to life—'I mean one only cries so much [. . .] Life is worth living / love's the only value'—return to suicidal thoughts, 'the agony you saw / coming down off your New York hotel', and the poem ends ominously: 'This is jumping stuff'. As we saw in the second chapter, Jack Spicer's contemporaneous 'Goodnight' likewise reflects on the link between poetry, queerness, and suicidal ideation, yet remaining sceptical of queer martyrdom. Wieners' identification is closer. As he recalled in the prose piece 'Chop-House Memories' (1968), 'at the terminus of separate love affairs', he and Frank O'Hara took the ferry to Provincetown to visit Edwin Denby, bad weather conditions forcing them to turn around before reaching the shore.

THE OCCULT SCHOOL OF BOSTON (II)   137

As we sailed through Boston Harbor, sordid memories of lost love's jazz morning's intermingled in our devotion to each other [. . .] We both thought of suicide as the final resolution of our desire as we stood again below deck by the hectic Atlantic cutting at our feet, speaking of Hart Crane and the last words we would have in our mouths at that moment of surrender. (Wieners 1988, 80)

Crosby's and Crane's examples test the boundaries of love and death. But ultimately, for Wieners, in attesting to 'what made you go over', poetry comes to represent not so much a doomed orientation towards death as a life force, a tool of survival.

In the unpublished poem 'This', written Easter 1958 and enclosed in a letter to Charles Olson, Wieners wrote of the aim to 'force myself, to / make use / of this pain / on the inside cover of the poems / of Hart Crane' (Wieners 2014, 211). To make use of pain mitigates its effects by reaching for the addressee, real or imagined, dead or alive—as Wieners wrote to Rumaker: 'to keep holes open, mostly through our finger-tips'. From the fate of Alice O'Brien, to the car crash victim of 'You Can't Kill These Machines' and the suicides of Crane and Crosby, Wieners' *Boston Newsletter* poems construct the poem as the hand that might still the 'jumping stuff' of the one who feels themselves going over the edge. In his magazine *Measure*, Wieners would transplant this connective ethos to the broader canvas of the New American Poetry as a whole, and it's to this enterprise that the next section turns.

'a show of junkies, cocksuckers, THIEVES': Wieners and *Measure*

Following the *Boston Newsletter*, and the departure of Spicer, Blaser, and the Dunns for San Francisco, Wieners soon conceived a new magazine of his own. Writing to Olson, he initially proposed a collectively edited one-shot magazine: 'BOSTON: a blast from—etc [. . .] "The opinions expressed in this magazine do not necessarily reflect those of the city"' (Wieners 2020, 43). The project rapidly expanded through correspondent lists provided by Cid Corman, Olson, and Ginsberg to sketch out a 'new generation' encompassing the Occult School, Black Mountain, Beat, and New York poets like O'Hara. On Corman's recommendation, Wieners had taken inspiration from the magazines of an earlier queer avant-garde such as Charles Henri Ford's *Blues* at Harvard's Lamont library, where he was employed for the first half of the year, and the magazine's three issues, published in 1957, 1958, and 1962, maintained a defiantly queer, Boston underworld ethos, even as its racial and gendered oversights are marked: no women appear until the third issue, and this is a determinedly

138 NEVER BY ITSELF ALONE

male—if mostly gay—crowd (Dewhurst 2014, 45). To Charles Olson in April 1957, Wieners commented: 'It scares for what they can do by implication to you people. But I hope you say OK. Language' (54). Half-worried that such overt queerness might cause offense, Wieners also suggests that the magazine might productively 'implicate' 'you people'—presumably, heterosexuals—opening up new textual and, perhaps, sexual horizons.

During this period, Wieners, who'd studied French at Boston College, was immersed in the work of Arthur Rimbaud, translating his work and conceiving of the immediate city environment as a zone for Rimbaldian derangement and illumination. Fired from his job at the Lamont library, Wieners wrote to Robert Duncan in July 1957, referring to Louise Varèse's new translation of Rimbaud's *Illuminations* published by City Lights:

> I am / have been for the last month flooded with 'a disordering of the senses' that makes me believe in the Elect ('The secret's stashed & only I know where it is') both the damned & saved. Rimbaud: I alone have the key to this savage sideshow.[7] Boston is that now. A show of junkies, cocksuckers, outriders, THIEVES. (Wieners 2020, 71–72)

Conceiving of himself as 'a city-operative', Wieners' poems sketched out a world of forbidden assignations and queer sex, in which the entire street, inside and out, bustles with sexual energy. '[T]he dead rule / the world: the banks, bookdealers, druggists', he wrote in 'The Bridge Word', published in *Chicago Review* the following year (Wieners 1958, 13). Against such forces—'the eyes of / Boston / bleached of history', citizens of the underworld—transient spaces, vulnerable and transgressive lives—serve as the Rimbaldian 'key[s] to a savage sideshow':

> Rimbaud requires us lift
> head to every / junky [. . .]
>
> or
> Rimbaud requires us back
> alley buggered / [. . .]
> Rimbaud requires us use his room key.
> (Wieners 1958, 13–14)

And in 'Exchange of the Lady's Handmaids', set in and around Playland, Boston's oldest gay bar, he set down lines that he described to Duncan as an underworld creed: 'never / never forget where we come from, what can't be sold, or sucked / off' (Wieners 2014, 114).[8] Attaching the same lines to James Schuyler, he jokingly remarks of this fusion of Olsonian field poetics and queer subject matter: 'It cd

THE OCCULT SCHOOL OF BOSTON (II)   139

take us over the precipice [. . .] Cd fuck up the sentence as we know it, as W.S. Merwin will never know it' (Wieners 2020, 53).

Replying to Wieners, Duncan wondered if the magazine catered to 'a coterie (queer)?' (Duncan 1958, 62). Yet, while coteries were necessary forms of self-protection for gay writers, Wieners imagined larger forms of community. Riffing off Allen Ginsberg's own 'America', Wieners wrote to Ginsberg: 'There are other queer shoulders at the wheel [. . .] I hope Tangiers is good for the line and that you can choke me with a load of your stuff / and direct those you yourself are hot on to my stoop' (51). Wieners worked hard at editing and gathering his own work and that of others, yet also emphasized the ephemeral, the 'fly-by-night'—as Dave Haselwood put it, 'something that secretly happens and then disappears and appears somewhere else' (Dewhurst 214, 94, fn.378). Wieners' letters concerning *Measure* to Duncan, Olson, Schuyler, and others overflow with energy and a sense of community, yet they convey a sense of *Measure* as something too capacious to be held in print. Envisaged as quarterly until the end of the decade, only three issues of *Measure* ultimately appeared, the third delayed until 1962. As such, the magazine represents a snapshot of energetic gathering, unfinished and perhaps unfinishable. And Wieners' devotion to Rimbaldian 'derangement', and the glamour of the *demi-monde* invoked to Robert Duncan, had its dangers. Wieners wrote to Michael Rumaker: '[I am] NOT doing a bit of work but wandering everywhere in the city, dredging, crawling in the gutters baby [. . .] Also got involved with a group of on again off again addicts, who have some glamour I am prone to [. . .] Without [Dana] I would be lost, a fucking straw on the tide' (Wieners 2020, 51). In the years to come, Wieners would increasingly gravitate towards such groups, battling their waves and trying to stay afloat.

'It is my life you save': San Francisco and *The Hotel Wentley Poems*

In September 1957, Wieners and Dana moved to San Francisco, where Wieners reconnected with Joe Dunn and Michael Rumaker and developed a close and lasting friendship with poet Joanne Kyger.[9] Here, however, the complications of being young and poor were compounded by the atmosphere of constant surveillance, whether from undercover cops or homophobic landlords, and the two broke up soon after. Without a stable job, Wieners moved between friends for the next year and began using heroin (Dewhurst 2014, 62–63). Wieners' drug use, along with his queerness, led to both paranoia and the real possibility of arrest by undercover cops—'demons / who sit in blue / coats, carping / at us across the / table' (Wieners 1986, 24). To Rumaker, Wieners writes: 'I am, and become afraid, of those forces driving me. They sometimes mask as angels. Are

140 NEVER BY ITSELF ALONE

undercovermen, and we do not know we are going to be busted, until the gates are locked' (Wieners 2020, 133). In such environments, the poem becomes place of hide-out and safety—'I am going to be busted [...] What better place than / the poem to warn you?' (Dewhurst 2014, 257). The Rimbaldian 'profane illumination', the poetic uncovering of 'secrets' he'd outlined to Duncan has as its converse the state's uncovering of 'secrets' in surveillance, entrapment, drug busts.

July 1958 found Wieners staying in a room at the Hotel Wentley, an establishment in a rundown area in Polk Gulch, whose denizens included artists, drag queens, and petty criminals (Dewhurst 2014, 66). Wieners wrote *The Hotel Wentley Poems* there in a six-day burst: a still devastating sequence startling for the explicitness of its queerness, for its raw sense of desire and loss, and for the measure of its music. As much as Ginsberg's 'Howl', which had been subject to an infamous censorship trial the previous year, or the poetry of Frank O'Hara, the Wentley poems are the defining queer poems of the era. And Ginsberg himself would write: 'There is no doubt in my mind or in anyone's mind who knows these poems well that they are major American poetry and will be in anthologies in 100 years, I mean that good' (Ginsberg 1960, 125).

The sequence begins with 'A Poem for Record Players'. Referencing 'The Scene Changes', a side by Bud Powell, the legendary bebop pianist who himself suffered from racialized police harassment, mental illness, and shock therapy memorialized later in the piece 'Glass Enclosure', the poem is haunted by conditions of state violence, secrecy, and imprisonment. Yet it is also a bold statement of arrival.

> I find a pillow to
> muffle the sounds I make.
> I am engaged in taking away
> from God his sound.
>
> (Wieners 1986, 27)

In private journals, Wieners refers to Dana as 'God', here revealing another, secret 'scene', which only serves to amp up the poem's defiant blasphemy. The sounds muffled by the pillow and covered over by the record player—whether Wieners' or Dana's moans of sexual pleasure—safe from the prying ears of neighbours and landlords, become a paradoxical figure for Wieners' poetry. Likewise, at the end of the poem, Wieners announces:

> [...] oh clack your
> metal wings, god, you are
> mine now in the morning.
> I have you by the ears

THE OCCULT SCHOOL OF BOSTON (II)   141

> in the exhaust pipes of
> a thousand cars gunning
> their motors turning over
> all over town.

Once more suggesting both the Christian God and Wieners' codeword for Dana, these daring lines fuse sounds of illicit pleasure with the starting motors of the early morning rush hour, the queer world of night briefly intersecting with the sanctioned world of the work routine. Written in a state of transience—staying over in an absent friend's hotel room, adjusting to the loss of domestic stability and attendant sexual ecstasies—Wieners transmutes conditions of loss and secrecy into defiant announcement.

Writing of his experience living in the San Francisco at the time—which he describes as a virtual 'police state'—Michael Rumaker notes the isolation, fostered by guilt, shame, and legal persecution, that could all too easily prevent solidarity amongst gay writers. With 'no open ground any of us could share, no precedents for solidarity', writing itself became 'a focus and a centre, a place' (Rumaker 2013, 1976). Rumaker here singles out the central poems of the Wentley sequence, 'A Poem for the Old Man' and 'A Poem for Cocksuckers'. Written on the same day, and coming fifth and sixth in the sequence respectively, they form the most explicitly queer section within it. Reclaiming terms of degradation as indices of communal solidarity, 'A Poem for Cocksuckers' opens with an invitation into queer space for both initiated and uninitiated.[10]

> Well we can go
> in the queer bars w/
> our long hair reaching
> down to the ground and
> we can sing our songs
> of love like the black mama
> on the juke box, after all
> what have we got left.
>
> (Wieners 1986, 36)

In 1950, Senator Joseph McCarthy had told reporters, 'If you want to be against McCarthy, boys, you've got to be either a communist or a cocksucker', and the use of that stigmatized term, as well as 'queer' and 'fairy', opposes the logic of surveillance, investigation, and interrogation by parodically taking it on its own terms. As Michael Davidson notes, the poem defiantly parodies the 'slippery slope' logic of the Red and Lavender Scares, in which 'each fissure in moral character betrays larger faults beneath'—to be gay is to be a communist, to be communist

142 NEVER BY ITSELF ALONE

to be gay, to identify with or be sympathetic to African Americans is to be gay, or communist, and so on (Davidson, 61). Indeed, the claim in the poem's title—that it is 'for' cocksuckers—performatively enmeshes any straight readers as themselves potential cocksuckers. Simply to read is to be implicated (Messerli 2011). Ambiguously interpellating the reader, and resisting essentializing identifications of any type, the poem also stages identificatory moves between (white) gay men and (Black) women which repeat in the second stanza.

> On our right the fairies
> giggle in their lacquered
> voices & blow
> smoke in your eyes let them
> it's a nigger's world
> and we retain strength.

On the one hand brave and powerful in their queerness, such identifications remain problematic, not least for their use of racial slurs. Seeking to 'step into the image structure of the farthest outsider', as Aldon Nielsen puts it, Wieners identifies with a Black female presence literally disembodied—the voice of the singers on the juke box—in a racialized and gendered slippage that is at once appropriation, gender defiance, and distorted solidarity (Nielsen 1988, 157). Alluding to the torch song 'Smoke Gets in Your Eyes', whose lyrics—as rendered in a popular 1958 version by African American vocal group The Platters later that year—at once explain away and dramatically announce private grief, the smoke-blowing 'fairies' are source of succour, their protective humour—voices 'lacquered' like nail polish or hair spray—a strategy against a homophobic city and the pain of lost love. The poem ends in a more private ritual of commemoration.

> [...] Take not
> away from me the small fires
> I burn in the memory of love.
>
> (Wieners 1986, 36)

It is the collective, public world of the 'fairies' who provide 'gifts' that 'do not fail us / in our hour of / despair'. But once again, Wieners also encodes a private reference to Dana, who'd worked as a volunteer firefighter during their time together. Burning fires that suggest memorial candles in churches, the fires of love, the symbolic flames of torch songs—or, indeed, the delicate matches of 'You Can't Kill These Machines'—Wieners unites private loss and the 'fairy friends" public commiseration, in itself an act of love.

THE OCCULT SCHOOL OF BOSTON (II)   143

'A Poem for the Old Man' is more explicitly addressed to Dana: here, the socialities of queer promiscuity and of private affection between two persons do rub up against each other, Wieners at once benevolently and bitterly giving up Dana, whose 'thick chest' he had 'hero worship[ped]' to the 'hundred men' of San Francisco's queer bar scene who might 'lift him / with the enormous bale / of their desire' (37). The poem bespeaks the ambivalence between domestic monogamy and the polymorphous, polygamous pleasures of public sexuality found in much of the work examined in the early chapters of this book. Yet, if such tensions, bespeaking a wider debate within the queer community, cannot be resolved in the space of the poem, the poem is nonetheless a space—however temporary—of compensation, rest, and protection. As Wieners writes in the closing 'A Poem for the Insane':

> [...] our dreams
>
> are blue boats
> no one can bust or
> blow out to sea.

(43)

Gerrit Lansing's Gay Age of Aquarius

'Exuberant and restless disorder': Gerrit Lansing in New York

While the community-building impulses emblematized in the *Boston Newsletter* and *Measure* were short-lived, the collective gatherings of the Occult School gained renewed impetus at the turn of the decade thanks to a new arrival. Moving to the Boston area in 1961, poet and occult specialist Gerrit Lansing developed close friendships with Wieners and Jonas, editing two issues of the magazine *SET* which once more envisioned potential forms of queer community virtually unprecedented in American letters. I'll turn to Lansing's editorial essay, 'The Burden of SET', in the following section, but first, I'll outline Lansing's early career.

Born to wealthy parents in Ohio, Lansing had studied at Harvard, where he'd become friends with a group of gay poets who'd form the core of the so-called New York School (John Ashbery served as his tennis doubles partner) (Dewhurst 2014, 80).[11] By the time Wieners came to study in Black Mountain, Lansing was always part of numerous bohemian scenes in New York, where he'd moved after graduation. Part of the social circuit around Broadway lyricist John La Touche,

144   NEVER BY ITSELF ALONE

with connections to older queer literary elites—Christopher Isherwood was once a houseguest—Lansing appears in English aristocrat and travel writer Lord Kinross' (Patrick Balfour's) book on America, *The Innocents at Home*, as part of a group of bohemian artists, 'perhaps a dozen of them, all relatively poor and outwardly unconcerned about money, living for the most part in cold-water flats' (Kinross, 31). As Kinross noted, Lansing 'counterbalanced a safe University Press job with a pursuit of the esoteric and a private life of exuberant and restless disorder'. In Lansing's own words, he viewed New York as 'freedom from the American office building family home', the anonymity of the city's 'a queer mecca', offering an economic and sexual freedom he likens to 'being a tiger in the jungle' (Lansing 2012, n.p.).

Lansing, as he put it, 'led two or three different lives', frequenting both licit and illicit New York nightlife: through John La Touche, the Broadway theatre world; through the Bollingen and Eranos Foundations, Count Stefan Walewski, and Harry Smith, the occult world; and, not least, 'the poetry of the streets', the 'sexual explorations' of gay hustling and streetlife (Lansing 2015, n.p.). In the poem 'Memories of Gerrit', Wieners playfully identifies Lansing with 'Champagne in the evening, golden dawns [. . .] the geography of your soul, transporting dirty pictures / through Times Square; sado-masochism in the upper echelons of Manhattan' (Wieners 1986, 77). Lansing himself later recalled: '[W]orking in a big city (New York) in a variety of jobs, some infrequent and temporary, I sometimes had to live by my wits, which wasn't difficult if one was [a] young male and available in streets and in bars [. . .] It was easy to live "on the kindness of strangers" as Tennessee Williams puts it' (Lansing n.d.). Lansing also jokingly links his queer sexual adventures to a tradition of Enlightenment free-thinking: '[Herbert] Huncke told a friend I was / always talking about the 'brotherhood of man' / as I hustled, 44th St. West & Sixth, / or in the Rustic Bar'.[12] Like Robert Duncan in 'The Homosexual in Society', but with considerably more sexual playfulness, Lansing's queered *détournement* of the Enlightenment rhetoric of universal humanity takes it at its word, re-radicalizing its potential.

Likewise, regarding Lansing's interest in the occult, it's worth bearing in mind here the comments of Chicago surrealist Franklin Rosemont, here reproduced from his foreword to John Patrick Deveney's study *Paschal Beverly Randolph: A Nineteenth-Century Black American Spiritualist, Rosicrucian, and Sex Magician*. As Rosemont notes, in the nineteenth century, 'the international subterranean community of scholars, poets, madmen and charlatans known as 'the occult', which—and this too is significant—was one of the few milieux in which serious discussions of love was possible at the time' (Deveney 1997, xix). Occultism was, for instance, connected to the pioneering work of African Americans, such as Paschal Beverly Randolph, and to emergent strains of feminism. Given this, Rosemont stresses the need 'to try to gasp [occultists'] relation to other

THE OCCULT SCHOOL OF BOSTON (II)   145

expressions of dissidence'. As he writes: 'Occultist influence is so all-pervasive—Madame Blavatasky's impact on the 1890s Bellaymist movement is a well-known example—that to ignore them is to throw the whole picture out of focus' (Deveney 1997, xix).[13]

Working within these radical traditions, rather than the identity-based, often conservative, tendencies of then-existing homophile organizations, Lansing also anticipates the later developments of queer theory: as he put it later, 'what is now queer theory was very normal to me' (Lansing 2012, n.p.). [. . .] 'My sexual experiences I thought of as initiations into life, an education, rather than categorizable' (Lansing, n.d.). Influenced in part by a Whitmanesque vision of queered democracy, in part by the secrecy of occultist formulations, Lansing viewed his sexual encounters as no less a part of his poetics than his esoteric research or the study of writers like Olson, Pound, and Yeats, figuring sexuality as part of a pursuit of ecstasy and knowledge utterly distinct from previous figurations of queer sexual practices, whether the de-corporealized Platonist tradition identified by Robert K. Martin—against which Lansing traces a celebration of erotic physicality—or the paradigm of queer self-loathing (Martin 1979, 96–97). In Lansing's early work, sex provides a polysemous access to multiple realms that resists Manichean moral divisions and fixed identities: a 'locus where we slither out of time' (Lansing 2009, 85). In poems such as 'Bracketing in City Thickets', sailors and angels join within the 'thickets' of city cruising grounds in sacral, sexual abandon—'Our heavenly host is called to mission of derangement, / inverted postures there the rule . . .' (Lansing 2009, 47). Borrowing the Husserlian term 'bracketing' (*einklammerung* or *epoché*)—an act of suspending judgement about the natural world and instead focusing on an analysis of experience—Lansing refuses 'deri[sion]', 'pity', and moralism. Heaven and hell are not contraries, zones of legal and religious prohibition and persecution, but stops on the same subway line:

> fuck all night on Avenue Z
>
> but Bracketing-Down-The-Alphabet, they say,
> will get you a hit of heaven on Avenue A.
>
> (Lansing 2009, 47)

'The Burden of *SET*'

If it was in New York that Lansing found his queer identity, it was in the Boston area that he came to poetic maturity. Through John La Touche, Lansing befriended inventor John Hays Hammond, moving in 1960 to Hammond's home in Gloucester, MA—the so-called Hammond Castle— with artist Harry Martin,

146 NEVER BY ITSELF ALONE

who served as Hammond's chauffer and curator.[14] Here, he became close to Charles Olson, to whom he offered financial support, and met his life partner, sailor and yacht captain Deryck Burton. Having earlier met John Wieners and Stephen Jonas in New York, Lansing developed close relationships with both poets, frequently travelling to meet Jonas in Boston and establishing a lengthy correspondence, centred on shared interests in experimental writing, the occult, and identity as out queer men. Lansing would appear in the much-delayed third issue of Wieners' *Measure* and conceived the idea for a journal of his own at the turn of the decade; Wieners in turn helped him find a printer after a first choice had refused to print poems by Jonas and Ed Dorn for their 'salty' language.

Lansing's *SET* extends the interest in 'magick' expressed in *Measure's* second issue—whose epigram, 'magick is for the ones who ball, i.e. throw across', punningly links 'balling' (sex) with occult nonconformity—for a broader vision of socio-spiritual transformation anticipating countercultural discourses of the later 1960s. Writing to Jonas, Lansing noted that the title could be understood in as many as six ways: the jazz set, stance, direction, mathematical set theory, a tennis set, or the figuration of God as Set across Egyptian, Greek and Christian mythologies (Lansing 2009, 259). In particular, the attractions of set theory, with its focus on antimonies or paradoxes—encapsulated in Bertrand Russell's paradox, 'the set of all sets that are not members of themselves'—neatly fits the non-dualism key to *SET*'s methods. Capturing multiple 'stances', Lansing reads currently occulted identities—racial, gendered and sexual—as foreshadowing an epochal, pre-counter-cultural change in society as a whole.

Lansing's prose-poetic essay 'The Burden of SET', spread across the magazine's first and second issues, draws on a concept prevalent among astrological circles since late eighteenth-century France—the instantiation of a new epoch, the 'Age of Aquarius' (Lansing 1961; Lansing 1963). Prominent in the work of Yeats, Aleister Crowley, Jung, and Rudolf Steiner, the concept would soon be adopted by the counterculture, emblematized in the mass rendition of the opening song to the musical *Hair* at the 1969 Woodstock festival—itself billed as an 'Aquarian Exhibition'—and subsequently forming the basis for the 'New Age' movement.[15] Strikingly foreshadowing the counterculture's linkage of sexual, spiritual, and political transformation, Lansing's own conception of this new age operates on multiple levels: economic, racial, gendered, and sexual. In the section of the essay entitled 'The Sexual Image', Lansing proceeds, via Aleister Crowley's dictum 'all is permitted' and Whitman's conception of 'adhesiveness' (queer desire) and 'amativeness' (heterosexual desire), to outline a new sexual and gendered age.

All is permitted. Change in the Heavenly Female Power. As equality of sexes swings around, the biomechanical basis of the old differentiation is shifted. This doesn't mean everyone will be 'queer', but that as new magnetic centers astrally arise in men & women the scope of both amativeness & adhesiveness will be prodigiously enlarged. (Lansing 1963, 43)

Following this, Lansing sets out a counter-chronology encompassing both the sociological changes in sexology and definition and an esoteric, heterodox tradition emphasizing sexual and gender fluidity. The discovery of the planet Uranus here links to Karl Heinrich Ulrich's borrowing of the word 'Uranian' from Plato's *Symposium* to describe 'love of male for male', Lansing arguing in astrological terms that 'Aquarius, toward which we move, is ruled / by Uranus, according to contemporary astrologers, / & ancient Greeks saw the sign as Ganymede'. Here, even the stars themselves become emblems of gay love. As Uranus joins with Ganymede, the most beautiful of mortals, cupbearer for the Gods, epitome of androgynous, youthful male beauty and of pederasty, to 'dance [. . .] on the heavenly floor', sky becomes 'floor', heaven coming down to earth. The foreseen change equally applies to gender. 'Under the permissions', Lansing argues, 'man will be able to find woman more the original wholeness, & woman in man' (Lansing 1963. 44). Citing esoteric scripture—Babylonian, Hebrew, Orphic, and Platonic myths of an original bisexuality—and philologist Marie Delcourt's 1958 *Hermaphrodite*, he foresees 'a primordial union of male & female consciousness', an undoing of gender as currently understood. Harry Martin's striking cover illustration depicts male and female gendered bodies with a single, solar head, raising the banner of the issue's name, and, as Pierre Joris notes, Lansing's editorial within 'creates a fascinating dual layout that mirrors in a way the cover figure' (Joris, n.p.). In 1896, Belgian occultist Auguste Vanderkhov had first linked the 'Age of Aquarius' to the feminist movement (Vanderkhove, 6): likewise, while Lansing's work does not manifest an obvious interest in feminist politics—the second issue contains only one female contributor, and the first none whatsoever—it does suggest the ways occultism has historically overlapped with anti-normative gender concerns.[16]

Lansing's conception of a new age is also economic and racial. Contrasting poetry's 'labyrinths, beginnings, openings' to economic measures of value— a process which 'takes measure of value for value [. . .] makes sickness of metaphor' (40)—Lansing calls for 'economic scrutiny' (39) and criticizes 'the cultural holdon to European *humanitas*, that value-system that pinched us all' (41). Rejecting the 'value-hierarchy' of aesthetic hierarchies as 'a white spectre', he argus that 'the system of blackness toward which we are drawn arise. (The system of blackness, the Ntu of Unison, seem chaos to receding whiteness, but will prove to be 'system'.) European whiteness is sepulchre to us & European consciousness a museum' (41). As well as Carl Gustav Jung, Teilhard de Chardin and others, Lansing here draws on Janheinz Jahn's influential *Muntu* (1958/ 1961), which describes 'neo-African culture' and philosophy as a unified system

148   NEVER BY ITSELF ALONE

avoiding the dualistic and disciplinary divisions of Western thought (Jung 1971, 426; Jahn 1961, 101).[17] As with gender, Lansing interprets the dawning of a new 'aeon'—a determined astrological event that is psychic and spiritual as much as it is material and political—as a reversal of polarities: from male to female, from binary gender to hermaphroditism.

Such analysis can appear glib, particularly when one reflects that, aside from Stephen Jonas, the only writer of colour to appear in *SET* is Amiri Baraka (then LeRoi Jones), whose poem 'Short Speech to My Friends' leads off the second issue: a poem in which 'tenderness' and 'the image, of / common utopia' contrast with racial exclusion as if in gentle rebuke to the predominantly white contributors surrounding it. Baraka's intersection with queer publishing is here suggestive. Triangulating with the explicit bisexuality of *The System of Dante's Hell* (1965) and the government censorship of the journal he co-edited with Diane di Prima, *The Floating Bear*, for queer content, it suggests a markedly different side of his work to the much-noted homophobia of better-known texts. Yet, if Baraka's presence here suggests an intersection between Black Radical politics, the counterculture, and the queer avant-garde of the Occult School, such a moment is instructive both for its confluences and for its divisions, both extending and belying Lansing's utopian occult speculations. Likewise, the manifestos, roadmaps and models of queer poetic community found across the work examined in this book's first chapters—from Duncan's 'The Homosexual in Society' to Spicer's 'Unvert Manifesto', Wieners' letters concerning *Measure*, to Jonas' 'Word on Measure'—often failed to live up to their promise: proclamations of new eras which remain out of time.

'Naming is gaming'

Lansing ultimately produced only two issues of *SET*, though he continued to participate in lively artistic and intellectual dialogue with Olson and Wieners, and as part of Jonas' Magic Evenings, theorizing and reclaiming the Occult School in his 1968 preface to Jonas' *Exercises for Ear*. Following the deaths of Olson and Jonas, he left the Boston area, moving to Annapolis, Maryland, with his partner Deryck Burton. This was a time of transition and dissolution; upon arriving, Lansing would undergo treatment for alcoholism and devoted his next years to co-running the Circle West bookstore. Moving back to Gloucester in 1982, he ran Abraxas Bookstore and became a mentor and confidante to a host of younger writers, including Eileen Myles, Jim Dunn, Amanda Cook, and others, until his death in 2018. And Lansing's own poetry—both in *SET* and in the various iterations of his expanding lifework, first published as *The Heavenly Tree Grows Downward* in 1966, and in its final form as *Heavenly Tree, Northern*

THE OCCULT SCHOOL OF BOSTON (II)   149

Earth in 2009—never lets up on its utopian impulses. In poems published in *SET,* Lansing contrasts a debased public life associated with political corruption, ownership, and advertising (Lansing 2009, 178) to an alternative associated with occult rites, open-air festivities, and sexual ecstasy in which children 'Whet their knives / On their rampant private lives', heralding an emergence from fear and division to a sexual enlightenment:

> Each child takes his lovely peer
> With tender fright
> In tender fright
> They make sharp love and live in shocks of light.
>
> (198)

'Conventicles' takes its title from the assemblies of dissenting religious groups, to practices of outdoor worship and revival movements, which, as anthropologist Gwen Kennedy Neville puts it, provide:

> [A] *folk liturgy* that is both open and outdoors [which] contrasts dramatically with the liturgy of the Great Tradition, which is indoors and closed [. . .] The social organization of the folk—that of scattered, open-country community centred in the crossroads meeting [. . .] in opposition to [. . .] the feudal-economic captivity of the towns whose form of worship was that of the traditional, indoor, hierarchical state church. (Neville 2005, 45)

Here, sexual initiation provides an alternative vision of 'Religion universalized' associated with the Aquarian Age, a new mode of exploration and discovery in which the secrecy of minoritized groups contrasts possessive claims to universality and conquest, a trail of sailor's semen written onto the very stars (Lansing 2009, 194–96). Such practices serve as a model for Lansing's poetry in general: pastoral, equally committed to domestic harmony, polymorphous exploration, and a transformed vision of the polis, 'a queer *hemisphaera* [. . .] a city we once could be citizens of' (109). Figuring himself and Deryck Burton a 'the poet and the sailor, / happy criminals in love', Lansing, as in his earlier New York poems, transforms criminality and the persecution of gay sex as illicit activity into a reversed and expanded notion of domestic harmony (11). Whether in non-monogamous, polymorphous public 'play' or in the domestic relationship with Burton, queer sex establishes its own laws, counter to those of the homophobic nation. Queer sex and queered language alike rewrite and reroute the writs of homophobic law. The sequence 'The Soluble Forest', published as 'Analytic Philosophy' in 1983, states that 'naming / is gaming'; linguistic play enables an alternative understanding of law, not as prohibition but

150 NEVER BY ITSELF ALONE

as permission: 'the word of the law / is liberty, a book: [. . .] A WRIT is a route, a way and the map of a way' (Lansing 1983). In an early draft of the sequence, Lansing alludes to William Morris' utopian classic: 'The bird can takeoff, at any time. It brings news from nowhere to nowhere. It is unseizable. Wait till it sings!' (Lansing 1978, 125).

For Lansing, queerness is capable of defeating machismo and American militarism—'the strong who are strong enough to be bent, / the bent, the bending, overcome the strongest jock' (Lansing 2009, 159)—in an anarchist destruction of private property, carceral institutions, and consumerism:

> When all the malls go up in flame,
>   and jails the mighty built,
> then we the newly free proclaim
>   the Law: do what thou wilt!
>
> (177)

As 'the sympathy of all things' (Lansing 2015, n.p.), realm of 'a cosmic pansexuality' (Lansing 2009, 130), poetry holds on to a promise increasingly absent in political life, despite the achievements of Gay Liberation: from the city of night to a pastoral imaginary, the city and polis transformed, a space of play, potentiality and joy. As Lansing writes in 'Amphion', named for the Greek 'native of two lands' and builder of the city of Thebes:

> These are the gay movements, benedict
> Music of the city of earth
> City of earth
>
> (79)

Coda: 'Rise, Shining Martyrs'

Of the Occult School, Lansing lived the longest, dying in 2018 after a long and fruitful life in which he continued to serve as friend and mentor to new generations of Boston-area writers, providing a living connection to numerous trends in twentieth-century American literature, and remaining committed to a fundamentally anarchist, aesthetic approach in which queerness was not a source of shame or trauma but of celebration, fecundity, and possibility. This approach was in large part enabled by the comfortable economic background which enabled him to provide a source of moral, and at times, economic support while resolutely pursuing his own esoteric interests—mystical, sexual, poetic, convivial. Following the excitements of the late 1950s, outlined earlier in this

THE OCCULT SCHOOL OF BOSTON (II)   151

chapter, John Wieners' life unfolded according to a very different, frequently painful, trajectory. Yet, as I'll now suggest in the closing part of this chapter, Wieners too was able to turn poetry into a space of celebration and protection, as well as a record of pain and loss.

Following the publication of *The Hotel Wentley Poems*, Wieners' personal life increasingly fell apart. Intensively using heroin and peyote, friends feared him suicidal (Dewhurst 2014, 76). Arriving in New York under the influence of a drug cocktail, his erratic behaviour prompted an acquaintance to call his parents in alarm. Damaging institutionalizations followed at Medfield State Psychiatric Hospital—where his manuscripts were lost and he was threatened with electrical catheter 'treatment'—and at Bournewood Hospital in Massachusetts and Metropolitan State Hospital in Waltham—where he received thirty counts of electroshock therapy and ninety-one insulin treatments, causing extensive memory loss (Wieners 2020, 159; Dewhurst, 80–83). Wieners' intensive drug use played a role in his struggles with mental illness, but this unwilled and brutal 'treatment' amounted to medical torture. Recovering at his parents' home in Milton, family served both as protection and as cause of pain. Wieners wrote to Diane di Prima of the combination of 'apathy' and 'unrest' that saw him riding 'the waves of childhood misery, poverty and insanity. It all runs in the family' (Wieners 2020, 198). And in a journal, he observed: 'They have divided me with their small talk, with their asylums, prisons and poisons. They have crushed out the beauty' (Wieners 2015, 102). Biological family and the extended 'family' of lovers, friends, and well-wishers from queer and bohemian scenes offered support in competing ways. It would only be after his parents' death that Wieners' queer and poetry family definitively took over, sustaining him through his final decades in Boston.[18]

Wieners' great poem 'The Acts of Youth', included in a letter to Charles Olson from December 1961, oscillates between a vision of 'pain and suffering' as 'the formula all great art is made of' and 'a dream of resurrection, 'when the dark hours are done. // And we rise again in the dawn' (Wieners 2020, 169–71). Wieners seemed to be emerging into the light once more when his second book, *Ace of Pentacles*, came out in 1964, and Olson engaged him on a graduate fellowship at SUNY Buffalo the following year. Yet the Buffalo years proved unhappy. In 1966, Wieners unexpectedly began a heterosexual relationship with heiress and patron Panna Grady: 'Who would believe it? That the most notorious faggot of our times would fall, in love with the best most beautiful woman', as he wrote in a journal (Wieners 2015, 271). Spending an idyllic summer in a castle in Gloucester, he jokingly imagined himself as Panna's husband, finally assuming the role expected of him by family and society. But, after Grady terminated a pregnancy and began a relationship with Olson, devastating Wieners, his return to Buffalo saw him become an increasingly isolated figure, developing paranoid fantasies about

152   NEVER BY ITSELF ALONE

faculty member and friend Robert Creeley and his wife, Bobby Louise Hawkins. As vividly attested in letters, journals, and poems from the period, Wieners' fantasies centred on the family as seat of hidden perversion, coercion, and trauma (Wieners 2007; Wieners 2020, 239–42;Wieners 2015, 204–206, 209–10). Moving beyond literary imagination into hallucinatory delusion, these disturbing texts nonetheless accurately reflect the psychic horrors wrought by the repressive structures of heterosexuality and the violence they so often conceal.

During these periods of breakdown and recovery, Wieners reflected on his conceptions of poetry and of life, revising the Rimbaldian enthusiasms of *Measure*. 'Address of the Watchman to the Night' (1963) contrasts 'those dark eternals of the nightworld: the prostitute, the dope addict, thief and pervert', who 'band together out of fear and in need', to the 'rest, relief and redemption' that occur only 'in the form of a poem, with its order, expression and release [. . .] a cohesion of world and its cosmos down to the single syllable [. . .] The world revealed in a word' (Wieners 1973). In the preface to Jonas' *Transmutations*, Wieners finds his poetry in a vanished city, noting changes in the urban landscape, the 'regeneration' projects of a class- and race-divided Boston, as old bohemian haunts—bars, apartments, cruising spots—disappear, leaving the traces of the poets like words chalked on a wall in the rain (Wieners 1988, 31–33). This was a pivotal moment in national politics, from Malcolm X's assassination in 1965 to increased US military presence in Vietnam. In 1966 the Compton's Cafeteria riot in San Francisco would signal the queer militancy that would lead to Stonewall; Martin Luther King Jr., led a march from Roxbury to Boston Common in April to protest school segregation; and the state's public schools were officially ordered to desegregate that June. And Wieners figures the 'old haunts of these poems' as 'bombs to blow up in the face of the future, they have become the future itself: BLAST; in the face of emblems of the past we live by' (Wieners 1988, 32). Likewise, in an unpublished essay on Ed Marshall entitled 'Road of Straw', Wieners presents the poems of the Occult School as 'total evidence of that time'— counter to the evidence ploughed over by cops, psychiatrists, or homophobic literary critics, and capable of providing stability and sustenance: 'It is here in these poems that we / are welded joined together, indissoluable [*sic*] [. . .] Meet each other / again on the street of dreams, no regret' (Wieners 2015, 128). The text ends with the affectionate signoff: 'Love, John.' This love, offered to Jonas, to Ed Marshall, to those dispersed 'to the four corners / of the world', also extends a love to the present and future reader: a generously interpellative call, harking back to the queer ethos of touch from Wieners' letters to Michael Rumaker and to the closing transmutation of *The Hotel Wentley Poems*.

When Lansing coined the term 'Occult School' in 1968, he was already naming a movement that seemed to have passed into—and out of—literary history. Yet, as Wieners' texts indicate, poetry's temporalities extend beyond those of historical forgetting and material loss, preserving the hopes which set them in motion. As such, we might read them against Elizabeth Freeman's recent caution against a tendency to theorize trauma as necessarily formative of the queer subject, necessarily a part of queer life. Freeman instead proposes an 'erotohistoriography' which would trace how 'how queer relations complexly exceed the present', and 'against pain and loss' would 'posit the value of surprise, of pleasurable interruptions and momentary fulfilments from elsewhere, other times', or of what she calls 'temporal drag', 'a kind of historicist *jouissance*, a friction of dead bodies upon live ones, obsolete constructions upon emergent ones' (Freeman 2005, 59, 66). Addressing the late Jack Spicer and Stephen Jonas in his 1970 poem 'With Meaning', Wieners writes:

> Rise shining martyrs
> cut down in fire
> and darkness, [...]
>
> Yes rise shining martyrs
>
> out of your graves, tell us
> what to do, read your poems
> under springtime moonlight.
> Rise and salvage our century.

(Wieners 1986, 127)

Rising as out-of-time revenants, these ghosts also measure the distance between the world from which they came and the transformed world into which, post-Stonewall, it seemed they might come. If we view the lives of Wieners and his queer comrades—Lansing, Marshall, Jonas, Spicer, Baser—not as linear progression and disintegration, but in a spirit of out-of-time, joyous ghostliness, the possibility of their work emerges afresh, as a work that might in some small ways rise and salvage not only its century but also our own.

PART II

GAY LIBERATION IN BOSTON (1969–1983)

Part II moves forward to the post-Stonewall period. Two chapters examine the work of the Fag Rag collective in Boston, including authors John Wieners, Charley Shively, Adrian Stanford, and Stephania Byrd. The final chapter in the section focuses on the work of writers associated with the Combahee River Collective, including Audre Lorde and Kate Rushin.

5

'A Gay Presence'

John Wieners, Charley Shively, and *Fag Rag*

'The most loathsome publication in the English language'

By the early 1970s, the queer writing scenes in Boston and San Francisco surrounding Duncan, Spicer, and the poets of the 'Occult School' had been decimated by death, addiction, and mental health incarceration.[1] Yet a new generation of activists and poets, influenced by these groups, found ways to take their work forwards into the new era of Gay Liberation, as a nationwide activist resurgence was paralleled by a concurrent blooming of gay poetry. In June 1971, a group emerging from Boston Gay Liberation formed a newsletter provocatively named *Fag Rag*. With writer and activist Charley Shively at the centre, the collective was run on an anarchist, co-operative basis, with a core of members including John Mitzel and Michael Bronski, as well as visiting or occasional participants. Mirroring the publishing processes of the Women's and Black Arts Movements, *Fag Rag* formed part of an informal network of papers which spread across the country from Detroit, San Francisco, and New York. Brightly coloured and militant in both its politics and aesthetics, the magazine featured essays, letters, activist reports, poems, and explicit erotic visual art, and it was described by New Hampshire Governor Meldrim Thomson as 'the most loathsome publication in the English language' (Shively 2012).

One of the most notable of *Fag Rag*'s contributors was none other than John Wieners. In an important 2015 article for Boston quarterly *Critical Flame*, poet-critic Nat Raha argues: 'Wieners's involvement in the Gay Liberation movement (in Boston and beyond), in the radical gay anarchist newspaper *Fag Rag*, and in Boston's Mental Patients' Liberation Front, has been largely overlooked, or fundamentally misunderstood, in recent critical writing on the poet' (Raha 2015). As Raha notes in her subsequent doctoral work on Wieners: 'Alongside the consciousness-raising and action of the Mental Patients' Liberation, Wieners' poetics of the '70s pursued a radical aesthetics of liberation, exploring gay sexuality and community, queer femininity and transgressive gender expressions, avant-garde camp and a politicised psychiatric survivor consciousness' (Raha 2018, 151). Over the past few years Raha's scholarship has done much to alter this picture, particularly in its emphasis on Wieners' gender nonconforming

Never By Itself Alone. David Grundy, Oxford University Press. © Oxford University Press 2024.
DOI: 10.1093/oso/9780197654842.003.0006

158 NEVER BY ITSELF ALONE

identity and status as an incarcerated person and a psychiatric survivor (Raha 2018, 201–208; Raha 2019). This renewed focus chimes with earlier and now neglected criticism on Wieners within the pages of the Gay Liberation press, including *Fag Rag, Gay Sunshine*, and Kevin Killian's *Mirage*, by Shively, Alan Davies, and others. Such writing emphasizes Wieners' misunderstood work of this era as a vital part of the poet's oeuvre, particularly in understanding its political implications (Shively 1984; Shively 1985; Davies 1985).[2]

Following these examples, the present chapter addresses *Fag Rag* and the related Good Gay Poets Press, reading Wieners' work of the 1970s—radically performative, formally disjunctive, and experimental texts centred in working-class, non-neurotypical, and queer lived experience—alongside texts by Charley Shively which advanced a frank, explicit, and sex-positive view of sexuality. As Michael Bronski puts it, such work 'conceptualised a new way to be gay': feminist, anti-racist, and anti-imperialist in their focus, and intent on challenging conventional understandings of family, private property, and the state (Bronski 2017, n.p.).

In November 1970, the first issue of *Fag Rag* appeared as the joint *Fag Rag/ Lavender Vision*. As Sue Katz recalls, the newspaper was 'the collaboration of two Boston groups: our Stick It In The Wall Mother Fucker Collective of revolutionary, working-class feminist lesbians, and a collective of radical faeries, some lovely gender-bending guys who mixed mustaches with tutus and ball gowns with beards. If you held the newspaper in one direction, it was a dyke front page; if you flipped it over and turned it around, it was a gay boy front page' (Sue Katz 2009, n.p.). The group's playful and reactive attitude can be seen in the puns they adopted on popular New Left and Black Power slogans—from Stick It In The Wall Motherfucker, *détourning* the slogan originally taken from Amiri Baraka's poem 'Black People!' to refer to gloryholes, to the popular Fag Rag chant 'Ho, ho, homosexual, the ruling class is ineffectual; Ho, Ho, Ho Chi Minh, the NLF is going to win' (Katz n.p.; Shively 2012). The collective sought to challenge the homophobia of the left and the Women's Movement: from assertions that homosexuality was a 'bourgeois deviation' in Cuba, repeated by U.S. left groups such as the Venceremos Brigade, to Betty Friedan's McCarthyite statement, on hearing that out lesbians were to march in International Women's Day parades, 'we will not be cowed by the lavender menace' (Katz, n.p.; Shively 1972). *Lavender Vision* printed Katz's influential essay 'Smash Phallic Imperialism', which urged moving away from reproductive sexuality and towards non-exclusive, collective relationship. Following an amicable split, *Lavender Vision* put out a second and final issue, while *Fag Rag* continued as a gay male paper with a particular interest in dismantling naturalized modes of gender identity.[3]

'In some ways', write Dudley Cleninden and Adam Nagourney in their history of the Gay Rights Movement, 'the gay and lesbian community emerging in

'A GAY PRESENCE' 159

Boston and Cambridge seemed more advanced than any other in the country'
(Clendinen and Nagourney, 125). As 'perhaps the most radical journal of sexual
liberation in America', *Fag Rag* often defined themselves against what was seen
as the reformism of the Gay Rights Movement, and joining other groups in
campaigning against gentrification, legislative discrimination, and the violence
and entrapment it enabled within Boston, as well as prison reform, anti-
war activism and calls for the disbanding of the police and other state forces.
Following Carl Wittman's 1969 injunction to 'come out everywhere', 'initiate
counter community institutions', and 'free the homosexual in everyone', *Fag Rag*
expressed a frank, explicit, and sex-positive attitude which saw guilt, shame, and
sexual repression as the destructive root of masculine aggression, imperialism,
racism, and war, and advocated a vision which did not discriminate according
to body type, kink, or ageist demands. At the same time, the group were far
from biological essentialists. In one issue, Shively described what he saw as 'the
genocidal quality of the binary division'. 'The world is not black and white, man
and woman, straight and gay', he wrote. 'If "Elitism is the natural order of the
world", I want to destroy it. I do not worship nature!' (Shively 1975, 32). *Fag Rag*
insisted on the performative elements of clothing and gender and the undoing
of masculinity while being rooted in a materialist analysis of power relations.
Likewise, its visual and textual aesthetic—explicit erotic drawings alongside
articles with titles like 'Sterilize the Straights'—refused to separate radical queer
politics and antagonistic language from the 'objectivity' of theory. Unlike the
coterie aspect of the Spicer circle magazines, *J* and *Open Space*—which would
sometimes refuse to print those not from the city or even the specific area where
they were distributed—the magazine was open to its direction being determined
by the readers, in an anarchist challenge to left vanguardism or queer coterie.
In the first issue, an 'open letter to gay brothers' proclaimed 'it is up to you to
broaden the scope of the newspaper with your criticism and ideas'—soliciting
letters from prisoners and seeking to broaden its range in order to 'grow, and
relate to a wider range of people' (Fag Rag Collective, 1971).

Nonetheless, the newspaper's vision was to a large extent influenced
by founding member, long-term editorial collective member, and prolific
contributor, Charley Shively. The one constant presence through *Fag Rag's* entire
history, Shively was a controversial figure—still perhaps best remembered for
the 1977 Boston Gay Pride at which he burned, first his Harvard diploma, then
his insurance policy, a copy of the 300-year old Massachusetts State Legislature
statue which criminalized homosexuality, and—following a reading from the
Levitical prohibitions—a Bible, triggering a near riot (Clendinen and Nagourney
1999, 312). For Clendinen and Nagourney, Shively 'had become the purest kind
of sexual liberationist, an anarchist and provocateur opposed to any law or
institution or person that sought to restrict [. . .] freedom' (1999, 313). Shively's

160 NEVER BY ITSELF ALONE

editorial work, polemical essays, and advocacy of the work of poets such as Wieners, Jonas, and Spicer have thus far received little scholarly attention.[4] While Shively was also a poet, my focus here will be on his theoretical contributions, his friendship with John Wieners, and his role in contributing to the atmosphere around *Fag Rag*.

'acts of revolution': Charley Shively

Born in the improbably named Gobbler's Knob and raised in poverty in Stonelick, Ohio, Shively was, in Bronski's words, 'very nearly self-made' (Bronski 2017).[5] Shively was admitted to Harvard in 1955, which he chose because, of all the Ivy League schools that accepted him, it offered the most financial aid. Lacking the 'class affect, fashion sense or typical grooming of the typical Harvard undergraduate', his sense of both 'class consciousness [and] class resentment' grew, even as he discovered queer sex in Harvard Square, college bathrooms, and, most importantly, Cambridge itself. Shively's placement here determined his career: often too poor to go home for the holidays, he would stay alone on campus, writing poetry and venturing out for sex, trapped in an academia into which he had fought his way, yet in which, despite his subsequent teaching career, he would never quite fit. In 1961, he returned to pursue a doctorate and took advantage of a burgeoning anti-war and radical feminist movement, including the Bread and Roses collective, Cell 16, and the *No More Fun and Games* journal. Teaching at Boston State College, he graduated from Harvard the same month as the Stonewall riots and became deeply involved in the burgeoning Gay Liberation Movement. While he conducted scholarly work—notably, a six-volume edition of the work of Boston abolitionist Lysander Spooner—and was later awarded three Fulbright grants, his unconventional methods and refusal of academic norms meant that his extensive original research was often not acknowledged or presented in conventional academic forms. Shively believed that academic studies of queerness were hampered by an ethos of professionalism antithetical to the real spirit behind the work of the writers he studied. Thus, his discovery of Whitman's correspondence with male lovers was embellished with imaginative reconstructions of Whitman's erotic encounters, and his two books on Whitman, *Calamus Lovers* (1987) and *Drum Beats* (1989), were published, not by an academic press, but by Gay Sunshine.[6]

Beginning with 'Cocksucking as an Act of Revolution' (1971) and continuing through to the late 1980s, *Fag Rag* published a series of twelve essays, each bearing the subtitle 'as an act of revolution', in which Shively advanced a theory of sex, language, and liberation. Blending theory, personal reportage of sexual experiences, and fantasy, Shively's essays were not addressed to an academic audience but were intended as a consciousness-raising tool among *Fag Rag* and the broader gay left. Just as likely to reference Shively's own experiences of cruising as the works of Karl Marx, Herbert Marcuse, Mikhail Bakunin, Kate Millett, and Shulamith Firestone, these pieces attracted controversy and praise in equal measure.[7] In 1969, a group of activists had split from the Gay Liberation Front (GLF)—a left-wing coalition formed after Stonewall, and provocatively named after the Algerian and Vietnamese resistance movements—in protest over the GLF's donation of money to the Black Panther Party and its radical political stance (Bronski 2011, 210). For Bob Kohler, a key participant in Stonewall and a mentor to Marsha P. Johnson and Sylvia Rivera, the 'dirty secret' behind the new group formed by those who had split, the GAA (Gay Activists' Alliance), was that they 'wanted white power. And so they let the freaks, the artists, the poets, the drag queens, the street people, the street queens, the blacks, and the colored people [*sic*] keep the GLF' (Dong 1995). For Kohler—as for Shively and others in the Gay Liberation publication boom—being a poet could itself be an 'identity', or role, deeply connected to radical queerness and the leftist politics with which it was imbricated. To be a poet was to seek to transform the use of language and, in turn, to seek to radically transform social, sexual, and racial relations and identities. Such work, Shively believed, already existed, invoking the writing of a previous generation of poets—Duncan, Jonas, Spicer, and Wieners—whose work he wrote on, printed, and endorsed in *Fag Rag*'s pages.

The magazine's first issues published poems anonymously—as Shively notes, some of these were criticized by board members, and a letter on the second page of the second issue calls the poetry 'really terrible: like "Love Story" with a hard on'—but the collective persisted, receiving poems both from anonymous, pseudonymous, and not well-known gay men and from more established figures. In summer 1973, the fifth issue reprinted Robert Duncan's 'The Homosexual in Society', describing Duncan as 'one of America's gayest and greatest poets', and the piece itself as 'a neglected part of our historical heritage', which 'raises issues still unresolved today'. *Fag Rag*'s fifth issue as a whole marked a change of direction: the editorial distinguishes itself from the focus on gay 'news' in magazines such as *The Advocate*—which it sees as 'linear, dated, clocked and measured', conditioning its readers to 'think in terms of crises'; 'it denies us our own reality and humanness'—and instead advocates an 'emerging gay consciousness and culture', 'a medium for faggot poetry, short stories, history, plays, reviews and art no less than abstract discussions of our oppression or confessions of our misery' (2). The issue contains an essay by Shively reclaiming the queerness in Wieners' poetry, and in a prose text entitled '1972-3', Wieners himself writes that 'it seems that a period of new experimentation and confidence and excitement has broken on the shore of our sexual "minority" [...] Homophile movements grow strong and proliferate weekly, without any advertisement,

162   NEVER BY ITSELF ALONE

some out of a common need [...] We welcome the chance to come into our own, to take our place, as adults, politically potential, and emotionally capable [...] able to take our place as victor and heroes, beside our competent, newly-trained lovers' (Wieners 1973, 3). In subsequent issues, Wieners continued to contribute poems and experimental prose pieces varying from prose poetry to an 'essay' on Stephen Jonas written in a similar mode, a play (*Harlem Bodyguard*), an 'imaginary interview' between Simone de Beauvoir and Greta Garbo, and a piece of 'speculative history' on Jackie Kennedy, while Shively published several essays on Wieners' work, as well as considerations of Jonas and Spicer, both in *Fag Rag* and *Gay Sunshine*. *Fag Rag* 10 (Fall 1974) was punningly entitled '69 Poets' and printed a conversation between Jonas, Wieners, Gerard Malanga, and René Ricard, recorded shortly before Jonas' death in 1970. The issue also printed work by poets including Allen Ginsberg, Maurice Kenny, Wieners, and Shively; an interview in memoriam W. H. Auden with Auden's friend John Button; and Shively's essay 'Poetry, Cocksucking and Revolution'. (Shively was suspicious of the politics of literary celebrity, and *Fag Rag* printed his criticism of the Button interview underneath the interview itself.)

Like others on the left wing of the Gay Liberation Movement, Shively was mindful of the dangers highlighted by the GAA/GLF split, of a movement focused on civil rights and legal issues which increasingly sidelined a politics based on race, class, anti-imperialism, and the dismantling of gender. *Fag Rag* was instead inspired, in both content and visual aesthetic, by the underground publications of the anti-war, Black Power and Women's Movement, and by the 'Mimeo revolution' magazines of the 1960s. Wieners was here a key conduit, donating Shively an entire run of Ed Sanders' *Fuck You: A Magazine of the Arts*, which, from 1962 to 1965, had published sexually explicit content, including poems by Wieners and an unauthorized bootleg of W. H. Auden's sexually explicit 'A Platonic Blow'. (As the first issue proclaimed, the magazine was devoted to 'pacifism, unilateral disarmament [...] anarchism, civil disobedience' and 'indiscriminate apertural conjugation'.)

In the first moments of post-Stonewall activism, Shively had insisted, against older Mattachine activists who had argued that consciousness could only be changed after material gains had been won, that consciousness had to be changed for such gains to be possible (Shively 2012). And debates were waged within the group and the movement as a whole between 'cultural' and 'political' strategies. In San Francisco, following an editorial split, Winston Leyland's *Gay Sunshine* had moved from a primarily activist orientation towards a literary focus. And in 1974, Larry Anderson asked: 'Is *Fag Rag* a homosexual literary magazine which will publish anything of quality referring to writing style, regardless of content—written by homosexuals?' Anderson suggested that *Fag Rag might* also be 'an anti-racist, anti-masculinist publication from some gay community of thought saying there's exploitation [. . .] we don't need it here; LET'S TRY SOMETHING ELSE!' As Shively notes, *Fag Rag* continually sought to bridge this gap, blurring the boundaries between the 'gay community of thought' and 'literary magazine' experiments in literature and in life. For Shively, writing decades later, '[p]oetry and art provide a way of being both political and cultural emancipation, of fighting the revolution, and of realizing self-expression' (Shively 2012).

Fag Rag exemplifies two strains present in this book's previous chapters on Duncan, Spicer, and the Occult School: on the one hand, a local, coterie politics suspicious of careerism and the literary marketplace; on the other hand, a broader, anarchist humanism which insisted on universal emancipation and the radical overhaul of society as currently constituted. These two elements, the local and small scale and the globally transformative, were not binary opposites but intricately connected, as were radical poetics, radical politics, and queer sexual experimentation. In 1974, Shively wrote:

> Every faggot poet fights then on two fronts. You can't just be a queer poet, you must destroy the existing profession of poetry. You can't just be a good queer 'citizen', you must destroy the state. (Shively 1974, 3)

Debates played out in the Fag Rag Collective about the function of literature and the standards to be applied. Was it enough to simply present poetry that spoke of gay experience, regardless of judgements of style? On the one hand, the anarchist focus of the collective meant that anything sent to the paper would be printed, provided it did not advocate misogyny or racism, as a gesture against the elitism and competition that Shively and others saw as fostered in the literary establishment. On the other hand, Shively insisted that linguistic experimentation was a key part of queer poetry. Language was a social production and experience itself was mediated through linguistic forms: to imagine that language was a transparent window on the world would not do. Writing of the wave of sex-positive descriptions of fantasy in the first wave of post-Stonewall literature, Dennis Cooper would later argue that such work's presentation of 'a rapturous physical encounter, in the apparent belief that "getting down" embodied the ultimate act of homosexual expression' manifested 'a wearying sameness', implying 'a gay world [which] would seem to have halted its emotional and intellectual growth in high school gym class' (Cooper 1986, 51). For Cooper, instead, 'gay life is a constant experiment [. . .] its spirit, its essence, remains continually in need of definition' (123). Shively would agree. In this new wave of queer poetry, the divisions fostered by literary history and literary criticism were exploded: *Fag Rag* disavowed the competition and judgement of the academy and the literary marketplace, not in the name of a literary populism, valourizing

164 NEVER BY ITSELF ALONE

simple form or clear and 'accessible' expression, but of a radical experimentation in form as well as content, constituting a new way of being.

In 'Poetry, Cocksucking and Revolution' and 'To Speak the Unspeakable', two essays from 1974 and 1978 respectively, Shively sets forth his theories of language as revolution (Shively 1974; Shively 1978) Shively suggests, following Helène Cixous, Ella Sharper, and Ernest Jones, that language itself had its origins in erotogenic processes (Shively 1978, 10). For Shively, language encodes normative ideas of race, gender, class, and attendant power relations. Noting the reclamation of 'obscene' language as a battle against respectability politics and against the idea that a working-class person must 'clean up' their speech to move up in the world, he also acknowledges problems of definition for new and experimental sexual practices. Devoting several paragraphs to alternative words for 'gay', Shively concluding that the existing terminology is inadequate. For Shively, the grammar of the English language as such functions as a system of hetero-patriarchal domination, in which the subject 'fucks' the object. Yet, because language's origins lie in the breast and in other erotogenic modes of relation, it too might mirror Shively's notion of a kind of sexual communism which the distinction between privileged body parts and people is blurred, opposing the couple form. Responding to the controversy surrounding his article 'Cocksucking as an Act of Revolution', Shively set out his theory of the revolutionary potential of non-normative sexuality:

If sexism is the primary contradiction (sexism being the classification and stratification of people on the basis of their relations to the means of reproduction), then the creation of a sexual reality divorced totally from reproduction is revolutionary [...] I do think there is something intrinsic in the very sexual act itself taken for pleasure outside any commitment to reproduction or social order—something anarchic, dissolving society in sexual relations. (Shively 1972, 32–33)

While phantasy, dominance, and submission remain fundamental parts of sexuality as such, the negotiation of such relations constitute an anarchic flourishing. Gay identity is provisional, the aim being the unity or dissolution of gender, bodily limits, and all social hierarchy. If, then, sexuality and language as currently constituted operate on mechanisms of 'sexism', 'classification', and 'stratification', Shively suggests that poetic experimentation might form an equivalent to the sexual preponderance he seeks.

Poets speak with their tongues; they make sex not only with their mouths but with their words as well. That is the essence of poetry—not some cross word puzzle/awkward muzzle—but a licking, liking, loving to feel where words come

from. (As Bill Barber says a gay poem is one sexually attracted to other poems.)
A tongue in your ear, not directions for baking a cake or orders for conquering
Eretria or a demand for payment or an insinuation to spend money—poetry
is from the tongue, direct sexual energy. Not directed, but direct existence; in
essence, direct experience. (Shively 1974, 3)

But language alone was not the only battleground. For Shively, a commitment
to small press-style publication was concomitant to a commitment to a radical
queer anarchist politics and to a poetics of linguistic revolution. In 'Poetry,
Cocksucking and Revolution', Shively critiques the poetry business—which he
dubs 'the Imperial Poetry System'—which requires that gay poets be closeted to
achieve mainstream success, and endorses patriarchal strategies of competition
rather than of anarchic potentiality and solidarity, a kind of poetic mutual aid.

> The 'poetry world' [. . .] runs like any other Imperial Industry—grants,
> publications, books, anthologies, professorships and editorships involve
> competition, in-fighting, politics and distrust [. . .] Most establishment poets
> are faggots, but (as in the State Department, English departments, industries)
> they hold their power because of their 'discretion'. (Shively 1974, 3)

Against such a system, 'Beyond letting everyone know what you do in bed,
coming out as a faggot poet directly challenges the Imperial Poetry System'.
Fag Rag 12 announced: 'If you are published here, Little-Brown or Random
House will definitely not be knocking at your door. Harvard freshmen will not
be impressed. You will only be helping forge a gay consciousness—a weapon to
destroy the universities and publishers'. Within the orbit of *Fag Rag* and the Good
Gay Poets, these two elements—linguistic experimentation and a collaborative,
combative aesthetics of queer publishing—received their fullest exemplification
in the work of John Wieners, and in the remainder of this chapter, I will turn to
Wieners' *Behind the State Capitol* as an instantiation of what such a poetics might
look like, exploring the role of typesetting, queer collaboration, the dismantling
of binary gender identity, and the position of the psychiatric survivor.

'New love, encountered between strangers'

As we've seen, during the 1960s, Wieners had been repeatedly institutionalized,
often at the behest of his parents, who were alarmed by their son's gender
nonconforming behaviour and bohemian lifestyle. In various 'asylums', he
suffered the debilitating effects, not only of intensive recreational drug use but
also of the 'treatments' he received in asylums—whether electroshock 'therapy'

166   NEVER BY ITSELF ALONE

or heavy and debilitating doses of pharmaceuticals: 'in early morning / insulin comas, convulsions, fifty-one thousand injections' (Wieners 1975, 98). The second half of the decade had been a particular unhappy time: suffering from the disastrous outcome of his one heterosexual affair and deeply unhappy in a teaching job at the University of Buffalo, Wieners suffered several breakdowns. When the Stonewall Rebellion took place, Wieners was interned in Central Islip Hospital, Long Island, following an arrest on a forgery charge, in conditions that visitors such as the poets Bill Berkson and Anne Waldman described with horror (James C. Dunn 22; Berkson). It was here that he received a letter from Charley Shively. Establishing a tone of respectful flirtation, Shively impressed the older Wieners with his knowledge of his poetry, and Wieners relished the encounter with a younger representative of a newly flourishing queer, activist sociality after his isolation in the academic enclaves of Buffalo, writing: 'I am 5'9' and some, blue eyes, 12 teeth left, bad eyesight, etc. Your life sounds fruitful enough for a friendship' (Wieners 2014, 456). Prior to Wieners' release, the two engaged in coy flirtation, alluding to Boston cruising grounds. 'I hope to see you afterwards, or even before, if you are not too shy, as I am. I loved the poem you sent. It sort of excites me [. . .] Perhaps you could suggest some kind of meeting [. . .] I do look forward to meeting you, Charles, if only in the Fenway, by chance, under the moon, which might happen by the way. But be careful please' (Wieners 2014, 473–74[8]). The two bonded on shared class experience, Wieners thanking Shively for

> Writing so much and so well, so touchingly of your past experience[.] I could only care for you because of it. Even though I distrust as you do possibly, poverty as a means.
>
> It's interesting to see what two poor boys have to say.
>
> (462)

Upon Wieners' release, Shively took Wieners to meetings and social events of the Boston Student Homophile League, introducing him to a new circle of younger queer activists which rejuvenated his work (490–91). Through such friendships, Wieners found himself part of a new, post-Stonewall surge of gay publishing and activism in Boston, whose radical critique of American society and its institutions had been suggested in the bohemian milieux of 1960s American poetry circles but was now given an internationalist and intersectional orientation within an explicitly queer context.

Wieners' texts were at the centre of *Fag Rag*. Working-class, politically radical, and containing early manifestations of 'genderfuck', these currents offered an alternative to the dark side of identity politics and the internalized homophobia and transphobia they perpetuated. Wieners revelled in such company, his poems, essays, and other unclassifiable texts frequently appearing in *Fag Rag* under the name Jacqueline Wieners. In 1972, members of the *Fag Rag* group, again with Shively at the centre, started the Good Gay Poets Press, its name punning on Walt Whitman's designation as the 'Good Gray Poet' (Wieners 2014, 49–41). Their second publication was Wieners' joyous poem *Playboy*, recording members of the Fag Rag collective's visit to the 1972 Democratic Convention in Miami and delineating the new context Wieners had found: 'New love, encountered between strangers [. . .] I delight in sharing group feeling. / Evening vigils, drag queens, movie actors, marijuana' (Wieners 1988, 124). Having published Wieners' *Playboy*, the collective began working with Wieners on a full-length book, to collect work from the previous six years as well as new material, including work published in *Fag Rag*. This book, *Behind the State Capitol; or, Cincinnati Pike*, was eventually published in December 1975 and was Wieners' longest publication to date.[9] Highly unconventional in form and presentation, the book has been described by a later critic as 'the epitome of a form of "outsider writing"' (Stefans, 131). Rather than placing Wieners' work within the problematic lineage of 'outsider' writing, however, these poems are virtually unintelligible without considering the work's relation to queer community.

As Nat Raha writes, '*Behind the State Capitol* ought to be understood as Wieners' attempt to aesthetically express and realize a liberated Gay and psychiatric survivor consciousness—including the political potential and historical ambivalence of such struggles and the suffering that necessitates them' (Raha 2018, 194). Building on this argument, we can see that these texts are not simply records of personal pathology or individual disintegration, but manifest what Raha calls 'a transformed political consciousness that would echo in [Wieners'] formal innovations [. . .] undermining questions about what is permissible for publication as poetry' (Raha 2015, n.p.). As such, they are contributions to the re-conceptualization of identity per se, part of a fresh and active dialogue which is still of relevance today.

'Hacking, stuffing and reshelving'

Beginning around 1969, Wieners had begun experimenting with form, typography, and voicing in ways not seen in his work since very early and generally in unpublished poems. Inspired by underground publications of the 1960s mimeo revolution like Ed Sanders' *Fuck You: A Magazine of the Arts*, a complete run of which Wieners gave to Shively as inspiration, Shively saw *Fag Rag* and the Good Gay Poets as a way to 'bring total freedom to authors, allowing each of us to write whatever and however we wished. What we needed most was not respect from the straight world but respect for each other's work' (Shively

168 NEVER BY ITSELF ALONE

1985, 78). As well as much new work, *State Capitol* contained revised versions of poems that had appeared in magazines throughout the 1960s and early 1970s. Yet Wieners was not interested in preserving, collecting, or reproducing. The book is subtitled 'Cinema decoupages; verses, abbreviated prose insights': earlier poems are treated as material to be collaged and revised alongside newer, more experimental material, challenging Wieners' reputation as a writer of stand-alone lyric poems in favour of a tonally broad, gender-fluid, and generically unstable poetics. *State Capitol*'s polyvocal styles and visual appearance clearly reflected the *Fag Rag* aesthetic. The 'cinema decoupages' of the book's subtitle refer both to the book's collages—collaborations between Wieners, Shively, and John Mitzel—and to the poems, in which words, letters, and phrases are 'cut out', creating new juxtapositions and ambiguities. Wieners had worked on the manuscript for a number of years with an intern from Boston College; his edits not 'improvements' but 'hacking, stuffing and reshelving' (Shively 1985, 80). This process of revising earlier, previously published texts reflected Wieners' general practice of annotating and decoupaging his copies of his own published books for years afterwards, copies from which he would improvise at public readings. (Shively notes Wieners reading in this way at the St Mark's Poetry Project as early as 1968.) The cheapness of the book's design, resulting from the relative lack of resources for a grassroots publisher, happily merged with Wieners' own aesthetic practice and with the collective, collaborative nature of its publication. Using a rented IBM machine, the collective learned on the job. A typesetting accident created a series of chance line breaks in poems with longer lines which Wieners insisted on retaining, insisting that he would hold it against the publishers if there were *no* mistakes in the book (Shively 1985, 81). For Wieners, Alan Davies writes, 'errors are a sign of human activity, perhaps inspiring trust or sympathy, instead of misunderstanding or derision' (Davies 1985, 36). If the reader acts with a feeling for the poem's mood, an ear to its humour, its love and its terror, this becomes a collaborative process. The book's dizzying fantasy logic—in which movie stars become family members or friends or politicians, all of whom can also become the poet—reads as a kind of hyper-socialized individuality: the visible emergence of the social into the individual, or the explosion of the two, in the sexual, pathological, communitarian refusal of boundaries.

As Sam Solomon notes, during the 1970s, changed employment practices, effected by shifts in typesetting technology, saw the increased hiring of 'de-skilled' and lower-paid feminized employees—including queer people—while access to new modes of printing technology enabled the flourishing of LGBTQ + small-press literary production (Solomon 2018). *Behind the State Capitol* draws attention to the material fact of typesetting itself. In poems such as 'Aila's LASt WILL and T E S T A M E N T', Wieners deconstructs names, drawing attention to the social construction of (and performed by) language, linking the death of

'A GAY PRESENCE' 169

the immensely wealthy heiress Ailsa Mellon Bruce to economic exploitation more generally (Wieners 1975, 128). The poem is preoccupied with the letter of the law—the language that enables the 'will' of the wealthy while denying that of the poor—while 'testament' recalls the class character of testifying under compulsion (from the Lavender Scare and McCarthyism to the police station and the asylum): a queered materialism, as both writers de-naturalize the processes of labour, language, publication, and revision that too often go unremarked.[10]

These texts were also materially precarious. In July 1982, the run-down office building shared by *Fag Rag*, *Gay Community News*, and the Good Gay Poets was firebombed by a group of laid-off firemen and policemen who had set a number of arson attacks in the city, 'protesting' cuts to the emergency services (Shively 1987, 30). All but a few hundred of the remaining copies of *Behind the State Capitol* were destroyed in the fire, an event Shively would later interpret in the pages of *Gay Sunshine* as the book's 'definitive exegesis': 'Here was revealed the void, the ashes, the destruction, the devastation. John Wieners had lived it first in his mind, in his poems, in his body' (33).[11] For Shively, the very real violence faced by the book's publishers are of a piece with the violence of erasure and dismissal afforded *Behind the State Capitol* and Wieners' later work in general. Next, I'll examine how such violence suffuses both the book itself and its critical reception through Wieners' gender identity and his experience of incarceration in mental health institutions.

'There's a certain kind of men'

Throughout *Behind the State Capitol*, Wieners celebrates and performs 'as' female celebrities, first ladies, heiresses, and film stars like Lana Turner, Greta Garbo, Billie Holiday, Marlene Dietrich, Barbara Hutton, Ailsa Mellon Bruce, and, perhaps above all, Jacqueline Bouvier Kennedy Onassis. ('REAd [. . .] to 400 listeners by The Voice of Greta Garbo, 1974 / P L A Z A' [Wieners 1975, 98]). As Nat Raha notes, a gender-transgressing dimension had been present in Wieners' work from the 1950s on. 'Gender deviance buds across [this work]', writes Raha, 'with the poet's gender transgressions complexly intertwined with homosexuality, love, and psychiatric dereliction. This queer romance often situates the poet's voice and its intonation in the feminine, as relations of desire enable or fails expressions of a feminine self' (Raha 2015). Such writing 'includes numerous assertions of trans subjectivity', including 'regularly inhabiting feminine voices and personae; undertaking public "experiments" with drag and describing dragging up; and featuring drag queens and gender deviant figures in poems'. (Raha 2018, 153). Given this, Raha argues, 'descriptions of Wieners as a "gay male" poet must cognize the poet's gender non-conformity' (154). In

170 NEVER BY ITSELF ALONE

such scholarly work, the femme identifications and 'gender transgressions' of Wieners' work post-1969 in particular are now being acknowledged as what poet-editor Trace Peterson terms 'proto-trans'. Following Raha and Peterson, this chapter reads Wieners' as a 'gay femme' and 'proto-trans' identity which generally retains masculine pronouns (Raha 2015, n.p.; Peterson 2013, 21). Yet, as such scholarship emphasizes, within the queer communities who offered the few extant contemporary responses to such work, such identities were already understood, explored, and expressed. Publications like *Gay Sunshine* and *Fag Rag* took full advantage of the post-Stonewall liberation of sexual and gender identification, exploring in visuals and words genderfuck, drag and trans identities. For Shively: 'The woman-identified poet is rare even among women and perhaps unique among men. This identification gives a special cast to the gayness of John Wieners' (Shively 1977).

The gender politics expressed in publications such as *Fag Rag* and *Gay Sunshine* gave Wieners' work a new context which both celebrated gender-fluid identities and decried the medicalized torture of queer people. Within *Fag Rag*, we find images of and articles on drag and genderfuck. In the second issue, an anonymous 'essay on liberation', laid out as a poem, discusses the author's 'coming out as a transvestite': against 'straight-identified supremacy', the writer argues that 'femme-identification [. . .] is I think part of the sexual politics which show the need for and the direction of change in society [. . .] in order to maintain our reality as gay, / lesbian identification seems to me to be the goal for all of us [. . .] being femme means rejecting a lot of things we thought were defining characteristics of our personalities.' (Fag Rag 1971, 14). The following issue interviewed 'Boston's most famous drag queen', Sylvia Sydney, and Shively notes that he, Maya Silverthorne, Bunny La Rue, Wieners, and Tede Matthews— a draft dodger, poet, and activist who would go on to play a significant presence in the San Francisco queer scene—'participated in cross-dressing on stage' (Shively 2012).[12] In an essay called 'Genderfuck and its Delights', published in *Gay Sunshine* in 1974, Christopher Lonc carefully distinguished between drag performers tolerated or mocked within the 'straight world' and 'genderfuck' as a rejection of gendered social roles in general, expressed in particular (but not only) through clothing. Lonc writes:

> It is my choice to not be a man, and it is my choice to be beautiful [. . .] I want to try and show how not-normal I can be. I want to ridicule and destroy the whole cosmology of restrictive sex roles and sexual identification. (Lonc, 4)

Lonc identifies those who cross gender lines as the most militant faction within the queer movement because the first to 'get their heads bashed in' and the least able to remain 'closeted'. Lonc's work is an important part of the history of non-binary

'A GAY PRESENCE' 171

identity as it existed before currently available terminology. Emphasizing the presence of non-binary, working-class queers in the key moments of Gay Liberation such as Stonewall, it rewrites conventional feminist and queer accounts which refuse to take into account non-binary gender identities.

In the pages of *Fag Rag*, Wieners signs several texts 'Jacqueline Wieners', and anecdotes told by friends from throughout his life recount performances of femme identity, as when Wieners gave a reading at Boston College in high heels, a gold lamé jacket, and lipstick (Holladay; Berkson; Pisano, 120; Wieners 2014, 10). Poetically, Wieners' gender nonconformity is clearly present from his earliest work: examples include poems concerning drag queens—'Ballade' (1955), or 'Times Square' (1969)—and those concerning his own gender identification such as 'The Woman in Me' (1959), 'Memories of You' (1965), and 'Feminine Soliloquy' (1969) (*Boston Newsletter*; Wieners 1996, 20–21; Wieners 1988, 59–59; Wieners 1986, 159). In such texts, Wieners deploys various different vocabularies to figure his own gender nonconforming identity. In order to understand his own gender identity, Wieners at times approaches the vocabulary of 'inversion' that earlier queer writing had inherited from Richard von Krafft-Ebbing, Edward Carpenter, and Havelock Ellis. An unpublished draft of an early poem published as 'The Woman' is entitled 'The Woman in Me'; in 'Memories of You', a poem first published in *Fuck You* in 1965, he writes 'I have a woman's mind / in a man's body' (Wieners 1988, 59; 1975, 133).

Ten years later, in 'Yours to Take', Wieners writes: 'There's a certain kind of men / born to suffer as women' (Wieners 1975, 133).[13] Here, Wieners flips the construction of femininity—both as regards biological women and 'effeminate men'—through and as advertising. The opening phrases parody the advertisements for women's wear store Peck and Peck's appearing in publications such as the *New Yorker*. (Sample: 'There is a certain kind of woman who'd rather eat soutzoukakia in the Greek Isles than fondue in Stowe. For this woman, there is a certain kind of store: Peck & Peck.') As Mara Math notes: 'Those ads suggested what then passed for quirkiness and independence, spiced with a dash of sophistication, that had nothing to do with the clothing and everything to do with character—the closest exposure I had to any hint as to what elusive noncorporeal quality made women attractive' (Math, 68). Wieners' lines thus have a kind of doubled performativity, in which the apparent essentialism of the suffering homosexual is itself a wry joke on the constructions of femininity and gender created by advertising, in which the sophistication of the 'certain kind of woman' is replaced by a capacity for suffering. The Peck and Peck adverts use the particularity of the discerning female customer to reinforce normative and generalized gender roles under the guise of a liberal attitude, associating women's wear with a feminized capacity for homemaking, as well as with an individuality associated, for instance, with dressing 'not for men, not for women, but for herself'.

172   NEVER BY ITSELF ALONE

Wieners' poem presents the corollary to this apparently 'liberated' woman; the 'certain kind of men' who 'suffer as women' are 'the worst kind / who never marry and play around // with their own kind'. The ambiguous voice of the poem—which appears to take the impersonal-personal tone of the Peck and Peck's advert—describes these men as 'murderers', suggesting that their rejection of reproductive futurity has to do with their own rejection by women, and suggesting male queer identity as the result of an 'antagonism' between the sexes. The tone then changes, as the poet proclaims: 'It's the women who have struck out in their suffering.' The poem concludes, 'who can say, it's too // soon to know.' In the Peck and Peck adverts, gender itself is a commodity, associated with the correct gendered accoutrements, from the clothing being advertised to the modes of comparison with which it's advertised, surrounding lifestyle, behaviour, or other commodities. In Wieners' poem, the gendered suffering of the feminized subjects links the 'certain kind of women' to 'women', a bleak take on the humorously fatalistic logic of the advertisement. Wieners' poems, as we'll see, identify with female celebrities—singers, film stars, politicians' wives—in part due to their perceived capacity for suffering. In the pamphlet WOMAN, Wieners describes Rose and Jacqueline Onassis as 'tantamount heroines to survive the dinginess of ugly politicians who drink and brawl at others' expenses' (Wieners 1988, 102). In 'The Acts of Youth', Wieners claims 'I have always seen my life as drama' and describes himself as 'a marked man' (Wieners 1986, 62). Wieners' own identification with particular figurations of suffering, from the *poète maudite* to the songs of Billie Holiday, fits into a long tradition of gay male identification with both female glamour and female suffering—the two sometimes presented as inseparable. As Michael Bronski suggests, 'the gay male identification with female stars is either an infatuation with glamour and beauty and pain and suffering, or it could be masking a trans identity'.[14] Yet texts such as 'Yours to Take' show Wieners as intensely aware of the mediated and constructed nature of this 'inherent' capacity for suffering.

Ventriloquizing wealthy female film stars, singers, or heiresses, Wieners critiques naturalized modes of gender performance in ways that also insist on the sustaining role of fantasy and role-play over confession and autobiographical explanation. (In 1984, he quipped to Raymond Foye that he was 'borrowing heavily for my own autobiography' from the memoirs of stripper Blaze Starr [Wieners 1988, 15]). Frequently, the connective 'as', in the manner of film credits, links one person's performance 'as' another character. 'Where was I as Greta Garbo?' asks one poem, and Wieners' 'signs' an early version of 'Ailsa's Last Will and Testament' 'Gusta L. (Garbo) Gustafson', fusing the original and stage names of a notoriously reclusive Hollywood star, with the signature additionally destabilizing the idea of authentic legal record, as 'Garbo' appends her own name to heiress Ailsa Mellon Bruce's will (Wieners 1975, 72, 128; Wieners 1973, 29). Wieners often focuses on

'A GAY PRESENCE' 173

female celebrities whose glamour has faded, fodder for gossip column exposés in women's and movie magazines with titles like 'What happened to the mind of Jennifer Jones?', in which the collapse of an 'ideal' body becomes the subject of fascinated horror. Collaging the memories of his past—a high school graduation photo, a poem written in 1952, old letters, reminiscences of youth in Boston or New York—with the present, and identifying with the ageing Alida Valli, Lana Turner, or Garbo, Wieners understands the beauty standards pressed upon feminized people, whether through the heteronormative expectations of child-bearing faced by Valli or of youthful beauty within gay groupings (Wieners 1975, 16). Further, Wieners understands that the construction of glamorous Hollywood identity, through clothes, makeup, plastic surgery, and media coverage may serve to painfully alter the body in a manner of which the 'rack' of childbirth is, in a sense, merely the inverse. Like many queer people, Wieners' Hollywood spectatorship is hardly simple, identifying with its images of idealized femininity, while aware of their cruel costs and seeking to subvert the social codes they enforced through appropriative camp and experimental strategies of his own. The lives of 'the rich and the super-rich' offer a sometimes painful contrast to Wieners' own sufferings as a 'child of the working class', and the two modes—the sometimes desperate poverty of Wieners' own life ('poverty has nearly ripped my life off' [Wieners 1988, 158]) and the lives of the 'rich and super-rich'—are used to undercut each other in the interests, ultimately, of a communal, queer aesthetic which will render the movies' fantasies of pleasure more than simply pipe dreams underwritten by suffering, violence, and decline.

'The Problem of Madness'

For Wieners, such suffering results from gendered and classed norms.[15] In the mental health system of the 1950s, 1960s, and 1970s in which he found himself entangled, gender nonconforming behaviour was often punished with medicalized torture masquerading as 'treatment'. 'Aversion therapy' involved the administration of electrical shock to the genitalia of patients when they became aroused upon being shown queer pornography: combined with the homophobic prejudices of talk therapists, the practice is memorably satirized in poet Judy Grahn's 1964 *The Psychoanalysis of Edward the Dyke*.[16] Wieners himself was repeatedly 'treated' with electroshock, lithium, insulin injections, and other forced medication that severely damaged his memory and sense of creativity, and threatened with 'electrical catheter treatment', as painfully attested by letters from 1961 pleading for friends' assistance in getting him released from Medfield State Hospital, where he had been forcibly committed by his parents—a forty-day stay that turned into a six-month incarceration (Wieners 2014, 268–69).

174   NEVER BY ITSELF ALONE

Recent work by Raha, Dewhurst, and Stewart has drawn renewed attention to this aspect of Wieners' poetics, which was central to the activist context of *Fag Rag* and Wieners' place within it. In a 1973 interview with Shively published in *Gay Sunshine*, Wieners argues that the asylum violently enforces gender conformity, with patients first institutionalized and then punished within the institution for transgressing behavioural 'norms'.

> I suppose they are in those institutions just because we have created stereotyped roles of what people should look like; what they should wear; how they should converse. Because these individuals fill none of these roles, they're incarcerated. (Wieners 1986, 293)

During Wieners' frequent incarcerations, the very act of writing a poem became something to be wrested from the hands of, or under the noses of, the authorities, and we might (without overstretching the point) read such obscurity as in part a reaction to such censorship. Wieners wrote 'Children of the Working Class' on May Day 1972, 'from incarceration, Taunton State Hospital' (Wieners 1975, 34–35). Wieners sent the poem to *Athanor* magazine editor Douglas Calhoun but was forced to change the original version after reading the poem out loud in group therapy. Wieners wrote the poem on the institution's typewriter so could not prepare the poem to send to Calhoun without making this change—in the end, he managed to keep the original, and crucial, location marker by means of a phone call (Butterick 1981, 129–30). The poem constructs a despairing lineage of the exploited, the downtrodden and the mental costs they suffer. The opening dedication, 'to Somes', puns on mathematical sums, anticipating the later line break on those who are 'crudely numb / ered before the dark of dawn'. Wieners elsewhere writes about the debt his parents incurred from his hospitalization, and 'sums' highlights the economic conditions in which patients are treated as statistics, or as broken parts of sums who must be 'added up' into normative subjects. And, as 'Somes', they are also explicitly 'some' and not 'others'—their situation is particular to their class. Wieners describes the patients 'locked in Taunton State Hospital and other peon work farms'. Institutional peonage was a widespread practice of employing patients to perform productive labour associated with the maintenance of the asylum, such as housekeeping or laundry duties, without adequate compensation. As with the original meaning of peonage—a form of indentured or peasant labour practiced in South America and the Deep South—asylum patients were essentially forced to perform free labour to pay off their debts (Bartlett 1964, 4). As with prison labour, the Thirteenth Amendment could be circumvented in carceral circumstances. Growing outrage over this practice—and the activism of mental patients' groups, or as they began to describe themselves, 'psychiatric survivors'—led to its abolition in some states during this period, but many cases

'A GAY PRESENCE' 175

remained mired in legislation for decades afterwards. Wieners, who knew this condition of indebtedness well, acutely links the ways in which class and labour play into the exploitation of mental health patients.[17] Wieners is not just arguing that conditions of poverty and shame make the children of the working class more likely to suffer from mental illness, but that those same children are also exploited for their labour *within* the asylum, exacerbating conditions of familial debt in a vicious circle, based on the institutions of work and mental health.

As a gender nonconforming, queer 'child of the working class', the poem ends with the speaker forever excluded from Whitman's vision of a democratic America and from a vision of Christian divine love.

> [. . .] I am witness not to Whitman's vision,
> but instead the poorhouses, the mad city asylums and re-
> lief worklines. Yes, I am witness not to
> God's goodness, but his better or less scorn.

This is a critique without resolution. The individual is a victim of both God and state, subject to divine scorn and left out of the vision of a democratic, inclusive America (one which, in Whitman's case, is strongly connected to gay male identity). Yet Wieners refuses the asylum's vicious interpellations.

As Raha notes, Wieners' involvement in 'mental patient liberation meetings' saw him take part in a movement in which patients and ex-patients conceived of themselves as 'psychiatric survivors', as active subjects, rather than passive objects of 'treatment' and punishment, working to organize within and challenge the authoritarian aspects of mental health institutions (Wieners 1986, 293; Raha 2018, 197–237). Particularly influential here was the work of Judi Chamberlin, leader of the Mental Patients' Liberation Front, whose book *On Our Own* posits alternative methods of care (Chamberlin 1978). Influenced by Chamberlin, Erving Goffman, Foucault, Thomas Szasz, and, in particular, the controversial 'anti-psychiatrist' R. D. Laing, the process of de-institutionalization that took place during the 1970s was one way of challenging the oppressive nature of mental health institutions: for instance, institutional peonage was legally abolished the year after Wieners' poem was written, requiring that any work done by patients must be properly remunerated. Yet much of the exploitation that took place in the asylum continued elsewhere. Away from the repressive, disciplinary apparatus of both state and private institutions, patients were still vulnerable. This indicates some of the problems of challenging and dismantling institutions in general: what to replace them with, how to change society when the overall imbalance of power—in whatever institutions it manifests—remains.

* * *

176 NEVER BY ITSELF ALONE

As Geoff Ward has written, *State Capitol* would prove to be in some ways 'both the capstone of Wieners' career and the book that would sink his reputation' (Ward 2002, 192). The book was not well-received. Robert Duncan believed that the Good Gay Poets were trying to destroy Wieners' reputation. Objecting variously to its unconventional typography, embrace of error, visual presentation, and departure from Wieners' previous lyric modes, others saw the book as 'a record of disintegration',[18] and it has since been described, even by its defenders, as 'the epitome of a form of "outsider writing"' (Stefans, 131). Wieners had suffered greatly from his forced incarcerations in mental health institutions and hurt by the negative critical reception of *Behind the State Capitol*. Having published prolifically in the preceding decades, after 1976 he virtually ceased publication of new work, famously claiming, 'I am living out the logical conclusion of my books'; while two full-length books, edited by Raymond Foye, appeared from Black Sparrow Press in the 1980s, these predominantly collected previously written material, including texts that first appeared in *Fag Rag* (Wieners 1988, 17).[19] In his personal life, Wieners continued to be supported by friends such as Shively, Foye, and later, Jim Dunn; John Mitzel of *Fag Rag* would cash Wieners' disability check at the Calamus Bookstore; and Wieners would give occasional readings in Boston and New York before his death in 2002.

Wieners' life lends itself to certain familiar narrative structures which associate queerness with tragic victimhood. Yet, while acknowledging the suffering of Wieners' life, we must resist at all costs reproducing the discourse of the state authorities which condemned him and tortured him in the guise of a queer, as part of a broader tendency of policing gender-deviant, queer behaviour. In the preceding chapter, I hope that I've managed to build on the way such work was understood in the context of Boston Gay Liberation, as well as on the work of Nat Raha, Jim Dunn, and others who have recently returned to the work of this period, and in doing so, to show this poetry as reparative and utopian as much as despairing, opening up a realm of gender performance, political screed, and heartbroken lament to challenge the bases of the economic, gendered, and classed organizations of society as such. Such work forms a place of experimentation and solace, constructing community both within its texts and in the context in which they were produced. Wieners, who had a complex relation to Catholicism throughout his life, conceived of *Behind the State Capitol* as a kind of updated version of the *Inferno* from Dante's *Divine Comedy* (Shively 1985, 80). And such work reads as guide in the *selva oscura* of the present moment, offering commiseration in times of deprivation while holding a mirror up to those times that reflects accurately their distortions and contortions, the weight they make vulnerable lives bear. It is not simply a record of trauma but also of solidarity, improvisation, wit, tenderness, and vital energy, whose victories should be celebrated as much its losses are mourned.

'A GAY PRESENCE' 177

If Wieners had essentially gone silent by the end of the 1970s, *Gay Community News*—formed in 1973, and sharing offices with *Fag Rag*—continued to be, as Christina Hanhardt notes, 'one of the few sources to report on [multi-issue, anti-racist lesbian and gay activism] in Boston, but on leftist lesbian and gay organizations across the country' (Hanhardt, 283, fn. 36).[20] *Fag Rag* itself ultimately published forty-four issues, the last of which, published in 1987, was illustrated with a front-cover photograph of Wieners and Shively kissing at Boston Pride. Into the 1980s, AIDS proved a major stumbling block for *Fag Rag*'s politics of sexual revolution, and for many in the movement, the pandemic put paid to the hopes for a sexual, cultural, and political revolution, as the task became one of survival.[21] I will examine the impact of AIDS later in the book, but in the following chapter, I'll turn to other poets who were published in *Fag Rag* and by the Good Gay Poets—Prince-Eusi Ndugu, Adrian Stanford, Stephania Byrd, and Maurice Kenny—to suggest some other elements of the 'polyvocal chorus' surrounding Wieners' own polyvocal work.

6

'My Real Name'

Racial Framings, Queer Imaginings

'no cosmic ribbon'

From the start, *Fag Rag* sought to link the rejection of normative sex and gender roles with anti-imperialism and an engagement with racial oppression. The first issue proclaimed 'Let there be a Vietnam in each of our hearts / Let Vietnam invade us', in a daring, if mixed metaphor of abdicating imperial power; early issues also printed essays linking Black and queer incarcerated persons as political prisoners and a sixteen-point manifesto for a '3rd World Gay Revolution' modelled on the Black Panthers' famous Ten Point programme (Fag Rag 1971a; Fag Rag 1971b, 1, 8–9, 13–14). Meanwhile, an anonymous piece in the fourth issue criticized the white privilege of many in the gay left:

> I have noticed that most gays connected [. . .] with gay liberation [. . .] the new left would-be heavies, the confused, repressed sons of white middle (or higher) class families who could have had anything they wanted, who spent years learning that they belonged to the master race [come out] because it is politically oppressive to be heterosexual [. . .] These gays came out in a swarm of political hodge podge amidst a circle of gay liberation all walking around looking, sounding, and smelling like the straight men they've been all their lives. So it cannot be surprising that drag queens and other flamboyants are unwelcome, that third world gays don't abound, that the age and beauty standards are the same as they are in straight white Amerika. (Fag Rag 1973, 20)

These pieces were all unsigned. In the twelfth issue, however, a signed piece appeared by Larry Anderson, a former Naval Academy cadet and Black Panther activist who was an important part of the group, subsequently moving to Seattle and working with queer prisoners (Clendinen and Nagourney, 136). Explicitly set up as a dialogue between Black and white gay men on the question of interracial sexuality, the piece was printed opposite an essay on the same topic by Charley Shively called 'Beyond the Binary'. Anderson outlined his thoughts in impressionistic prose, insisting on the ability to distinguish between the complex intersections of class, race, and sexuality rather than generalized statements of

Never By Itself Alone. David Grundy, Oxford University Press. © Oxford University Press 2024.
DOI: 10.1093/oso/9780197654842.003.0007

'Black' or 'White'. 'i think that i feel there is NO COSMIC RIBBON LINKING ME WITH EVERY OTHER HOMOSEXUAL NO COSMIC RIBBON LINKING ME WITH EVERY OTHER BLACK', he writes (Anderson 1975, 6). Detailing the homophobia he had faced from within the Black community, he notes 'the whole trip of political guilt' provoked by the Black Power demand 'that i should relate to all Blacks', yet also the racism with a majority white homosexual community whereby 'there exists a peer pressure (different from identity) to function, appear, respond in a certain way—a way white society expects Africans to perform, dance, sing the blues, almost a stereotype' (7). If both communities expect certain modes of performance of racial and gender roles, based on dividing Black queer people from each other, Anderson suggests that there is nonetheless a potential 'above and beyond that' for 'an ENERGY; an energy of that coming together of Black faggots', one which rejects expectations of 'functioning vis a vis white society'. Such questions of entangled homophobia and racism, of projection, performance, and the possibility of a racialized 'coming together' play out in different ways in the work of all the writers addressed in this chapter, suggesting the ways writers of colour moved within, without, and sometimes against prevailing currents of Gay Liberation thought in order to more accurately diagnose old ways of being and conceptualize new ones in their stead.

In this chapter, I examine works by queer writers of colour published by *Fag Rag* and the Good Gay Poets through four separate case studies. While each of the writers in question appeared in a shared publication context, each lived through very different social intersections. The chapter opens with Canada-based draft-resister Prince-Eusi Ndugu, who in 1974 received his only poetic publication in *Fag Rag* and on whose work this appears to be the first published criticism. My discussion of Ndugu's work is followed by a reading of Adrian Stanford's *Black and Queer*, published by Good Gay Poets in 1977. Briefly discussed in the introduction to this work, this was the first published book of poetry by an out gay Black man in America. Stanford's poems are addressed, in particular, for their framing of gender and the position of feminized persons of colour.

While *Fag Rag* was an admittedly 'gay male newspaper', Good Gay Poets published some books by lesbian writers: self-described 'black lesbian redneck' Stephania (Stephanie) Byrd was a member of the Combahee River Collective, and her debut volume, *25 Years of Malcontent* (1976), is an important piece of writing equally concerned with an explicit, fierce, and unsentimental depiction of lesbian sexuality and with pervasive histories of racialized and gendered violence. In the final section of the chapter, I will turn to a poet whose work is perhaps better known than any of the preceding poets, yet is rarely framed in this context. Famed as a key exponent of the renaissance in Native American literature that paralleled and participated in the American Indian Movement (AIM) of the 1970s, Maurice Kenny is less frequently read as a queer author. Yet, as Lisa

180 NEVER BY ITSELF ALONE

Tatonetti has argued, the work of Kenny's published in *Fag Rag* and in the Good Gay Poets pamphlet *Only as Far as Brooklyn* (1979) reveals new perspectives, not only on his *oeuvre* as a whole and its place within Native American literary history, but also on questions of racialization and identification within the queer imaginings of the period (Tatonetti 2012, 2014). More often framed in terms of Native American literature, Kenny here emerges as a poet in dialogue with queer poetic traditions shared with those of the white writers of the Berkeley and Boston scenes, which he challenges and extends in important ways.

'loving he and him': Prince-Eusi Ndugu

In 1983, Gay Sunshine Press published *Black Men/White Men*, an anthology dedicated to 'the Black and interracial gay experience in America' which promised to be the first publication of its kind. Drawing predominantly on material 'reprinted from gay periodicals', the volume placed well-known predecessors such as Harlem Renaissance writers Bruce Nugent and Langston Hughes alongside more obscure writers: it was edited by Michael J. Smith, the (white) founder of the San Francisco–based anti-racist gay organization Black and White Men Together, an organization which has been both praised for its pioneering challenges to racism within the gay community and critiqued for its politics of racial tourism (Maye n.d., n.p.). Such contradictions are reflected in the volume itself. Reviewing the book for the Black gay male journal *Blackheart* the following year, poet Isaac Jackson argued that *Black Men/White Men* was in many ways problematic in its visual and textual framing of Black male sexuality, noting in particular its perpetuation of sexual stereotypes and the absence of a Black co-editor (Isaac Jackson 1984). Yet, by virtue of its subject and placement, this work is part of a dialogue on sexuality and race more influentially taken up in Essex Hemphill's and Joseph Beam's anthology *Brother to Brother* at the close of the decade. In his introduction, Hemphill deployed work reprinted in Smith's anthology to raise the issue of Black death, obscured lineage, and racism within the gay community—notably, that of Adrian Stanford, to which this chapter will presently turn. Smith's volume also included the only book publication of work by an obscure writer named Prince-Eusi Ndugu (Smith 1983, 198–99). Ndugu's work, however, has not, as far as I have been able to determine, received even a single critical mention in any extant literature.

The twelve short poems printed in *Fag Rag* 11 (Winter 1974) on a single page—of which four were reprinted in *Black Men/White Men*—appear to be Ndugu's sole published poetic record, and biographical information is sparse. Something of Ndugu's biography can, however, be traced through his earlier appearance in the draft-resister press at the turn of the decade. Printing a short

'MY REAL NAME' 181

essay by Ndugu in January 1970, draft-resister newspaper *American Expatriate in Canada (AMEX)* notes: 'The author traded in his slave name. He also traded in countries recently'. Drafted in 1969, Eusi Ndugu—his new name taken from the Swahili words for 'Black brother'—fled Mississippi for Toronto that November and became involved with *AMEX* shortly after his arrival.[1] Ndugu's article equated his flight to Canada with the earlier flight from slavery along the Underground Railroad and was picked up in the nationwide magazine *Jet*: 'I'm a 20th century runaway slave, not a draft dodger. There ain't no way I'd ever go back to the United States—except to destroy it' (Ndugu 1970; *Jet* 1971). No mention is made of Ndugu's sexuality: he is positioned in terms of his race and his political radicalism, as part of a network of flight-as-resistance which deployed an earlier tradition of Black fugitivity as a key motivating trope.

In his 1970 article, Ndugu suggested that he had not encountered the same oppressive forms of racism as in the States and that 'the air of freedom blows a little better in Canada'. Yet while Ndugu was initially positive about the contrast between the United States and Canada, he soon came to realize that Canada's reputation for social tolerance nonetheless manifested its own racism and homophobia. The following spring, he was quoted in an *AMEX* article by John Egerton which asked why so few draft resisters who had made the journey were Black, noting his growing frustrations with the majority white population he encountered and the racist structures which sought, for instance, to limit Black immigration from the States. 'It's like jumping into a pitcher of buttermilk, it's all white—the music on the radio, the pictures in the papers and magazines and on television. There's a race problem here, just like in the Northern cities of the U.S. Whites here are no different. The Canadian Government is putting a quota on blacks immigrating from the States' (Egerton, 14). Likewise, despite Canada's reputation for social liberalism, Fag Rag member John Kyper was banned from Canada for life after attempting to cross the border with copies of *Gay Community News* in 1974, an incident which led to protests that saw the Canadian government repeal the 1969 immigration act ban on gays and lesbians (Kyper 2008). Ndugu's growing discomfort with the racial climate in Canada at the turn of the decade and Kyper's brush with the immigration authorities four years later are not unconnected: the draft-resisters network of the early 1970s and the queer border smuggling later that decade are both networks of clandestine activity, communities shaped and organized, in part, through underground magazine publication, from *AMEX* to *Fag Rag* and *Gay Community News*. While the trope of queer migration from abusive or restrictive family backgrounds and often rural communities rings true for many of the activists and poets addressed here, this also suggests that print formed a network intersecting with such physical roots. Material published in these venues was not restricted to work from the local area. Such papers achieved national distribution through

182 NEVER BY ITSELF ALONE

networks of correspondence and of distribution hand to hand and through queer events and bookstores, and, as Michael Bronski reports, Charley Shively maintained a correspondence with 'almost every gay male (and many lesbian) poets who had published since 1970' (Bronski 2019, n.p.).[2] It's likely that Ndugu encountered *Fag Rag* and thought to send in his work through such networks, suggesting both the transnational reach and ways poetry might serve as a tool of communication and community operating along networks very different from those shaped in standard literary history.

Addressing other African Americans whom it encourages to follow his route and escape the draft into Canada, Ndugu's 1970 *AMEX* article self-frames almost exclusively in terms of his racialized identity. Opening with Muhammad Ali's famous proclamation on Vietnam, Ndugu references his Mississippi upbringing, Swahili, soul food, dashikis, and opposition to American imperialism. The *Fag Rag* publication four years later once more presents Ndugu in opposition to the state's punitive legal apparatus, but specifically within the context of gay identity and activism: his poems are printed next to a statement from chairman of the National Gay Prisoners' Coalition, John Gibbs, detailing the group's struggle to be recognized as a cultural and educational program and the punitive costs of such organization, including solitary confinement, denial of access to a doctor, and the banning of gay publications within prison. The poems themselves are brief, sexually explicit, humorous, and often celebratory: the focus is on sexual experience, yet one which nonetheless intersects with legal prohibition, social stigma, and racial solidarity. 'ummm good' applies Southern vernacular to apply to gay sex, linking racial-regional and sexual identity, and concluding 'down home, we make things ummm good' (Ndugu 1974, 6). Likewise, 'all that is forbidden (is good)' presents the speaker's experience of queer sex in his native Mississippi: 'mississippi boys swimming in forbidden / water holes; / and often stopping to enjoy forbidden sex'. The poem presupposes an in-group address, an open secret, a public knowledge: 'oh you know, the kind of water holes at / gravel pits, / and a kind of sex that's ummm good'. Both revelling in and fearing the possibility of exposure—'Something law can't stop'—in 'the public know', Ndugu writes: 'so secret, so private; your life, my life / entangled in a world / that's all public. / even our love life / is a public secret'. Suggesting both queer gossip—the public revelation of a private affair—and the status of queer sex more generally, these lines ironically suggest state intrusion on and policing of private experience. More often, however, Ndugu celebrates the pleasures of exposure and display, as in the outrageous 'eat it', which reads in its entirety 'walk! / walk! / walk! when do i eat it', or 'imperial queen and the boy', which sardonically depicts a sex work transaction. Likewise, 'have you passed this way' enumerates the pleasures of ephemeral sexual activity—'meeting in baths, hitching a ride, walking beaches . . . and of course, enjoying some man's body for a day or night'—though it ends with a desire for 'a lover for days, and days / and days and nights and nights / and nights and forever'.

This desire for permanence, framed in general, non-racially specific terms, recurs in 'two bodies', which presents its lovers embracing, 'wrapped around, holding / another, holding to life', and 'he and him', in which they form mutually admiring 'mirrors'; 'he and him' in particular suggests a universal, racially non-specific male love in the Whitman tradition: 'wrapped in the arms of mankind, / loving he and him'. But in other poems, Nudgu focuses in more detail on the encounter between racialized bodies. Linking the language of racial pride to that of sexual desire, 'black men (we love each other)' daringly eroticizes the vocabulary of 'brotherhood' familiar from Black Power rhetoric. An ode to a 'beautiful creature like me, / with a badd [sic] afro to compliment your smooth ebony color', the poem ends: 'Loving you black man in brotherhood / and a love that only you and I understand'. This love, as opposed to the potential for universal, homoerotic brotherhood across racial lines, or the non-erotic brotherhood of racial liberation movements, is specific both in terms of personal encounter—the poem as a love poem addressed to a particular person—and in terms of racial solidarity. Ndugu's imaginings of 'past history', meanwhile, depict 'Zulu warriors of old' who 'loved in the coolness of night' emerging into the rising sun: a new dawn at once sexual and racial. The doubly hidden histories of a queer Afrocentricity merge with the pleasures and negotiations of an American present in vignettes that suggest both the fleeting pleasures of sensuality and a broader history of sexual comradeship not in contradiction with, but a part of, a racially affirmative identification.

Black and Queer: Adrian Stanford

In the introduction this book, I addressed the contradictions and difficulties of such reconstituted lineages through a brief close reading of Adrian Stanford's poem 'Sacrifice'. I now turn in more detail to Stanford's work, as printed in *Fag Rag* and in his only volume of poetry, *Black and Queer*, published by Good Gay Poets in 1977. Based in Philadelphia, little can be discovered of Stanford's life. As I noted in the introduction, Stanford was the son of journalist and poet Theodore Stanford—about whom, again, little can be discovered, save for journalism and poetry published in venues such as W. E. B. Du Bois' *The Crisis* in the late 1930s. Adrian Stanford's poetry first appeared in print in the mid-1960s in the pages of *ONE*, the magazine of the Mattachine Society, while a poem in *Black and Queer* is dated to 1961 in New York. Stanford did not publish a wide selection of work: the thirty poems in *Black and Queer*, a pamphlet of thirty-five pages, constitute virtually his entire published legacy. Stanford's work did not appear in

184 NEVER BY ITSELF ALONE

publications associated with the New American Poetry, as did that of Duncan, Spicer, and Wieners, nor the Black Arts Movement, as did the early work of Pat Parker, and it was not until the emergence, post-Stonewall, of queer journals that his work began to find a more regular venue. As well as gay magazines—ONE, *Tangents*, *Fag Rag*, *Mouth of the Dragon*, and Jim Kepner's short-lived, Los Angeles-based homophile magazine *Pursuit and Symposium* (Kepner is a dedicatee of the book)—the poems in *Black and Queer* initially appeared in Philadelphia-based magazines: *Psychedelphia Period*—a 'protest paper' whose fourth issue featured Stanford's work alongside Black Arts writers Larry Neal and Yusuf Rahman in a section entitled 'Black Poetry Revolution'; the *Philadelphia Tribune*—the oldest continuously published African American newspaper in the United States; and the countercultural publication *The Distant Drummer*. Such publications might frame Stanford's work either within (more often) a gay or (less often) a Black poetry context, but rarely in both, caught between the white domination of queer groups and publications and the homophobia that dominated Black Arts publication.

Queer writers were prominent figures within the Black Arts Movement, from Robert Hayden to James Baldwin—who, despite the homophobic attacks exemplified by that of Eldridge Cleaver's *Soul on Ice* (1968), remained an important figure to many in the Movement—and Hoyt Fuller, central to Black Arts publishing with the journal *Negro Digest/Black World*, though Hayden and Fuller, unlike Baldwin, remained essentially closeted.[3] Likewise, Pat Parker and Audre Lorde, the former of whose work will be discussed in Chapter 9, published in Black Arts contexts, even though such work rarely directly addressed lesbian desire, focusing instead on issues of Blackness and gender. Yet heterosexual Black Arts poets, both male and female, frequently used the figure of the 'faggot' as a metaphor for the assimilated, 'white' 'Uncle Tom'. Amiri Baraka, who himself had written with painful frankness about bisexuality in earlier work, is probably the most famous, but others include Larry Neal, Haki Madhubuti, Jayne Cortez, Sonia Sanchez, and Nikki Giovanni. As we saw in the opening chapters, white queer poets used racial analogies in problematic ways, as means of collective self-figuration and as fetishized otherness. For poets like Wieners, Spicer, and Duncan, race more often served as a metaphor for the marginality of queer identity or a locus of sexual fantasy associated with thanatotic dread ('some black man looms in my life'). Such comparative modalities recur in negative form in Black Arts invocations of queerness. One year before Stonewall, Nikki Giovanni used queer sexuality to goad a heterosexual Black subject into action. Giovanni's 'Of Liberation' opens: 'Dykes of the world are united / Faggots got their thing together / (Everyone is organized) / Black people these are facts / Where's your power' (Giovanni 41).[4] Giovanni's formulation erases the possibility of the

Black queer subject, separating 'dykes', 'faggots' and 'Black people' as mutually exclusive categories. Both in such instances, and in the writing of white queer poets, the possibility of the queer Black subject is either erased, fetishized, or circumscribed. Racial others serve as analogies for homosexual organization; Black sexual stereotypes are presented entirely for the illumination of their white subject; queer Black subjects are proscribed as 'wanting to be white', 'Uncle Toms', and a danger to the survival of the race (Cortez 1969, n.p.). It is in this context that the statement of the book's title—Black *and* Queer—is vital. Stanford insists on critiquing *both* white racism (queer and non-queer) and Black homophobia: while his political statements are just as militant in their opposition to anti-Black racism as are statements made by Baraka, Giovanni, and others, they also frame such militancy, and the record of Black suffering, through Stanford's sexual identification. The book's very title renders the connection between militancy, racial pride, and queer sexuality thinkable and graspable.

The title poem itself is a kind of lineated political manifesto which, despite its title, makes little overt reference to sexuality. 'The hate ridden excrement of three hundred and fifty / years of "master race" philosophy is not to be flushed from the American / white mind by a few half-hearted applications from the "integration" eye- / dropper' (Stanford, 22). Race relations in America are likened to the lack of love in 'marriages born of expediency'. Stanford diagnoses the 'western white man's mind today' as characterized above all by fear: 'fear of a racial future founded on a / rotten anti-black past', in which protestations of 'terror haunted friendliness' and 'equalitarian posturings are as false as they are futile'. The text ends with the metaphor of the trojan horse: the promise of equality akin to the 'hollow wooden steed' which brings about the downfall of the city. The marriage metaphor proposes domesticity (heterosexual arrangement) as operative in a similar manner to race relations, with gendered subjugation with such relationships implicitly aligned to that of race. Yet sexuality is such a part of identity that it need not be explicitly stated: against the homophobic readings which elided gay male sexuality with 'Uncle Tomism' and 'whiteness', it's taken as read (yet defiantly stated in the title) that to be queer is entirely commensurate with racial pride and political radicalism.

In a brief biographical entry on Stanford, Damion Clark writes: 'Stanford's work is always conscious of the multiple realities and multitude of challenges facing black queer men in urban spaces, and he frequently writes the black and queer male figure in his poetry as operating in a liminal space' (Clark, 593). In 'yeah baby'—a poem reprinted in both *Black Men/White Men* and *Brother to Brother*—the speaker acerbically reports being caught in the middle of the hypocritical mutual performance of stereotyped sexual-racial identity by both Black and white gay men:

186 NEVER BY ITSELF ALONE

> i've been approached, followed, waited for, hung onto,
> and groped by all those staid white queens that
> don't like *colored boys*.
>
> and certain nigger fags (who don't want nothin but blonde
> hair around the cocks they suck), have more than once pushed
> their fat asses my way!
>
> (Stanford 1977, 9)

Quoting Stanford's poem, Hemphill writes that 'the post-Stonewall white gay community [. . .] was not seriously concerned with the existence of black gay men except as sexual objects ' (Hemphill, xxxix). Poems such as this pull no punches, suggesting, as did the writing of Larry Anderson and the anonymous 'black faggot' in *Fag Rag*, that racialized expectation dogged queer sexual community.

Responding to such framings, Stanford's poems frequently highlight performance, gender, and gender performance, along with the use of existing systems of mythic, artistic, or political discourse, both as tools of sustenance and defiance and as impediments to true understanding. Walter Holland has suggested that Stanford's poems, in 'trying to find a separate voicing for a black gay man [. . .] weave a powerful mythic language around African-American experience' (Holland, 19). Here Holland cites Stanford's 'Remembrances of Rittenhouse Square'—first published in *ONE* in 1965—for its 'invocation of the black drag queen as deity'. Stanford's juxtaposition of queer 'street' life and the language of biblical and classical myth serves as transmutation of that which has been 'despised' into that which will be 'adored', as the book's final poem has it (Stanford, 35). Yet Stanford's 'mythic language'—based, in particular, on the deification of female stars—is far from a simple reversal. The title to 'Remembrances of Rittenhouse Square' already establishes specificity, referring to a well-known queer meeting ground in Philadelphia, and the poem concerns a well-known Philadelphia drag queen named Sarah Vaughan, after the jazz singer (the original printing in *ONE* juxtaposes the poem with an ink drawing of the Philadelphia Vaughan on a facing page).

In an interview with historian Marc Stein, the pseudonymous 'Ray Daniels' recalled the setting. 'Rittenhouse Square was always known for [being a gay neighborhood]. That was the hangout. That was the place you went [. . .] the gays would hang around on the outer part of the Square. And the hippies, or back then they called them the beatniks, their turf was the middle, the center part of the Square' (Stein 1993, n.p.). Daniels recalls that the crowd was 'basically young', 'a mixture of gays', of 'drags', and 'those who weren't in drag'; he also notes the Halloween drag parade which went past the square and queer bars around 13th and Locust Streets, with fifty to a hundred predominantly white

'MY REAL NAME' 187

drag queens marching or driving in open-top convertibles, watched by around a thousand spectators. In Stanford's rendering of this collective environment, a kind of queer kingdom appears to have been established, with 'Black Sarah' at is head. The poem opens: 'black sarah ruled. / and we of lesser divinity paid homage to her / with our pansy smiles' (Stanford, 15). Sarah ushers in a world of queer possibility for her queer followers. 'we breathed magnolia air, dreaming other visions / through the velvet of our mascara lashes'. These visions take on a blasphemous queer religiosity: with Black Sarah as 'divinity', those surrounding her 'blessed ourselves with water from the shallow pond, / and kissed each handsome boy as he passed by [. . .] chattered endlessly, / mingling within, without'. Yet, in this quest for happiness, Sarah's followers ultimately find 'nothing / but the sad green beauty of the trees': they are 'raped, our harpstrings broken' after their 'priestess' moves to 'another temple'. The poem ends as its speakers appeals directly to Sarah: 'ah, good queen sarah, why did you never speak of reality?' This ending appears to render inadequate its preceding visions, sharply breaking the utopia established.

The real-life Philadelphia Sarah Vaughan was herself a survivor. In his interview with Stein, Daniels suggests the racialized undercurrents which rendered Sarah's performances at once more vulnerable and more courageous. Despite the fact that the city's queer bars were 'ninety-nine per cent white':

Sarah Vaughan was very popular and [. . .] went from one bar to another. Bouncers at the door, I don't think they ever hassled her. I don't think anybody would have. I don't know if they'd be afraid to or not. Sarah Vaughan was tough. It was not easy for her. First of all, he was a drag queen and he was a person of color. So he had two things right there. And he had a double battle. He was a strong person. (Stein 1993, n.p.)

Daniels continues: 'Sarah Vaughn is ageless [. . .] It seems like Sarah Vaughan always was and always has been and always will be. She's always, always there'. (Writing on Philadelphia's gay bar scene for *The Advocate* in 1972, seven years after the publication of his poetic tribute to Vaughan, Stanford jokingly reports that Vaughan has gone butch.) But Sarah's real-life ability to move beyond racialized boundaries, to survive and thrive as a femme-identified person of colour, nonetheless relies on the ability of an individual's inner resources to match reality. Admiration for the 'ageless' Sarah might provide a model for others, but Stanford's poem suggests that this model of 'divinity' cannot provide the basis for collective happiness. The poem thus suggests the limits of deification. Its collective voicing—the 'we of lesser divinity' who pay tribute to Sarah and believe in the visions she suggests, and who, at the poem's end, are 'raped, our harpstrings broken', and 'sing no more'—is presumably that of Sarah's

188 NEVER BY ITSELF ALONE

fellow drag queens and queer subjects. The poem suggests too the ambivalence of an identification with female celebrity within a queer iconography: the overlap of glamour and suffering, a more-than-human beauty or power combined with a downfall, melancholy and tragedy presented in a fatalistic manner.

While the incident which scatters Sarah's followers at the conclusion to the poem is unclear, it could refer—literally or metaphorically—to any number of incidents of harassment faced by the queer Rittenhouse Square crowd. Ray Daniels recalls: 'I was harassed with my friends in Rittenhouse Square. [The police] would come through the park and they would chase you out [. . .] They'd say, "Go on, get the hell out. Clear out of here you queers" ' (Stein 1993, n.p.). The sexual assault alluded to also assumes a mythic register, though which precise myth is unclear. One strong possibility is Poseidon's rape of Medusa, related in Ovid's *Metamorphoses*, in which Poseidon violates Medusa while she prays in the temple of Athena while Athena looks away. As the most beautiful woman in the world, Athena had been jealous of Medusa's beauty, and following the assault, turns her hair to writhing snakes and her gaze into one of stone. In both the myth and Stanford's poem, beauty is transformed into ugliness through an act of violence, incapable of resisting the force of that violence, which seeks at once to possess and destroy it. In the Ovidian rendering, Medusa's downfall is framed entirely through Perseus' narration, with Medusa given no voice of her own: she is either the all-ugly or the all-beautiful, 'the object of sight and speech' (Walker, 49). Through the act of violence enacted against the feminized person, that which was considered supremely beautiful, the object of a desiring gaze, becomes that which is too terrible to be looked upon. The returned gaze of the one who has suffered violence invites traumatic memory and shame, both amongst other victims and amongst those who perpetrate or are complicit with such violence.

In 'Rittenhouse Square', Stanford suggests—alluding to the violence myths of the classical world, in which divinity did not protect one from sexual violence— that Sarah's divinity offers only an illusion of redemptive protection, grace, and beauty: a necessary tool against the violence of a queerphobic world, but an inadequate defence against it. In other poems, the use of a feminized Black figure provides access to the violence of a collective racial history, but also an index of survival and strength. 'Psalm of the Visionary', first printed in *Fag Rag* 11, continues the devotional register of the Rittenhouse Square poem: its speaker builds a temple to singer-actor Lena Horne and is granted a vision of Black suffering in America from which he walks home 'wiser' in the night (Stanford, 13–14). Where Stanford's votive poem for Horne differs from the similar address to Black female divas in the work of poets like John Wieners—who claimed 'Billie Holiday was the story / of my whole life and still is' in a poem published in *Behind the State Capitol* (Wieners 1975, 20)—is that Stanford presents himself as a devotee of a cult who has revealed to him, not the suffering of gay men (who are coded as

'MY REAL NAME' 189

white) but a broader history of racialized violence. Rather than passive suffering, the speaker hears in Horne's voice 'gospel songs of vengeance, and sinister / lullabyes [sic] for the redemption of desecrated black skin'. In this visionary experience, the speaker encounters the horrors of slavery through music—gospel songs, plantation songs, and Horne's trademark 'Stormy Weather'—which provide a 'kaleidoscope of suffering' culminating in Horne repeatedly screaming 'NEGRO! N E G R O! N E G R O'.[5] Apparently contemptuous of the Christian vocabulary of the mainstream Civil Rights Movement, emblematized in the figure of Martin Luther King Jr.—a frequent Black Arts trope—the speaker proclaims 'fuck martin luther coon'—parodying such vocabulary while adopting its register in a blasphemous, gynocentric prayer. This deification of the female—whether Black heterosexual entertainers like Horne or Tina Turner, or, in Sarah Vaughan's case, the drag queens named after them—is a key modality of these poems.

Stanford himself was accused of sexism in the penultimate poem in the book, an address to Tina Turner, written in 1961 after hearing a performance in New York at the height of Turner's early popularity (Shively 1978, 11). 'tina turner (after hearing her sing)' frames Turner's performance as an example of assertive female sexuality and racial pride which suggests modalities of collective defiance and possibility that reverse and transcend their framing through the language of misogynist insult. The poem describes Turner as 'a whore in love with life. fucking for the joy of fucking. wild, / abandoned; purely negro' (Stanford, 34). As, in 'Psalm for the Visionary', Horne's songs bring back the long history of slavery, so here, Turner's music attests to collective survival through and from the Middle Passage, bringing alive 'all the fire, hate, and wisdom (silenced / in that long past crossing)'. Such music attests to a collective knowledge that exceeds that of white audiences: 'her asshole murmurings splashing in honkie faces'. Those songs are 'long hurt, sweet / sad rapture [. . .] full of resentment and glories long forgotten; / those yet to come. all black! All proud!' The poem concludes with an address to Turner: 'sing you cunt! Empress of black memories, prophetess of what's comming [sic] [. . .] you are one of us and in your voice we hear the brown nigger nothings / that speak of raising hell (and us all free)'. Through combining conventional terms of insult—Turner as 'whore' and 'cunt'—and terms of praise—Turner as 'empress' and 'prophetess'—the poem seeks to transform the language that conventionally demeans female genitalia and the practice of sex work, repurposing insult as praise. In presenting Turner as nothing but a sexual organ, Stanford's recalls the appropriation of misogynist insult within queer male and drag communities, one which stresses the performative nature of femininity while at the same time deploying the language of biological fact. Appending a mark of location and temporality to the base of the poem—'new york city / January 4, 1961—3 a.m.'—Stanford stresses the materiality of a particular body, a particular performance, and the metaphorical transports of

190 NEVER BY ITSELF ALONE

a collective (re)negotiation of linguistic and bodily meaning, one in which the 'black and queer' subject paradoxically flourishes through a language of insult-as-solidarity. 'as i am hated / so shall i be adored' reads the book's closing poem on the following page.

For Stanford, the example of drag queens such as 'black sarah' and singers such as Horne and Turner counter patriarchal violence and racial fetishization. Yet such usage has its limits. Though written well before the availability of such knowledge, the poem reads quite differently in light of subsequent revelations of Ike Turner's abusive behaviour of Tina Turner and of the ways Tina Turner's image as a sexually assertive Black woman was produced and shaped by the same husband who abused and demeaned her in private. Here, bell hooks' writing on Turner is valuable. In 'Selling Hot Pussy', hooks notes the presence of sexualized black female bodies within popular culture as

> unruly and outrageous. They are not the still bodies of the female slave made to appear as mannequin. They are not a silenced body. Displayed as playful cultural nationalist resistance, they challenge assumptions that the black body, its skin color and shape, is a mark of shame. (hooks, 63)

Such bodies have the 'potential to disrupt and challenge [. . .] dominant ways of thinking about the body [. . .] associated with undesirable and unclean acts'. At the same time, the presentation of such bodies is often mobilized by an imaginary at once misogynist and racist. Thus, for hooks, Turner's image 'has been cultivated and commodified in popular culture [. . .] as 'hot' and highly sexed—the sexually ready and free black woman' (66), a career premised on 'the construction of an image of black female sexuality that is made synonymous with wild animalistic lust' (67). This image came, not from Turner herself, but from her husband Ike, who moulded Tina (born Anna Mae Bullock) into his fantasy of a 'wild woman' drawn from the racial fantasies of 1940s comic books: Tina's very name was chosen to rhyme with the heroine of *Sheena, Queen of the Jungle*. Moreover, Ike's private abuse shapes the contradictory image of self-determining, liberated sexuality. 'Raped and exploited by Ike Turner, the man who made this image and imposed it on her, Turner['s] public persona as singer was shaped by his pornographic misogynist imagination [. . .] She was on one hand in excruciating pain inflicted by a misogynist man who dominated her life and her sexuality, and on the other hand projecting in every performance the image of a wild tough sexually liberated woman' (67).

In Stanford's poem, Turner's image—which, unbeknownst to the poet, had been constructed out of her husband's patriarchal fantasy—provides a mode of identification and a collective repository of hope which can unite both heterosexual and queer Black subjects in a defiant sexuality. Despite such unity, however, the poem's appropriation of the language of misogynist insult reads very differently depending on the real or presumed location of its speaker, its audience, and its general or specific addressee—all the more so in the wake of the revelations of the patriarchal abuse which Turner's public image at once belied and was shaped by—suggesting the complexities of such performative negotiations, and the strengths and drawbacks of Stanford's attempts both to reject and to reclaim racial, gendered, and sexual stereotypes.

Stephania Byrd: 'violence not new / but old'

The year preceding *Black and Queer*, Good Gay Poets published *25 Years of Malcontent*, one of only two books published in her lifetime by Black lesbian feminist poet Stephania Byrd, and it is to Byrd that this chapter now turns.[6] Born in 1950 in Richmond, Indiana, before moving to Lexington, Kentucky, Byrd studied towards a BA in Latin at Ball State University. She came out in 1971, and, as she notes, the book charts her transition towards Black lesbian feminism, fostered by her time in Boston (Byrd 2012, 117). From 1974 onwards, Byrd worked as a gay and lesbian youth advocate at the Charles Street Meeting House and began to give readings as the X Poetry Collective with Normal X and Ken Dudley (the latter a member of Fag Rag)—gay men who preferred to recite their poetry orally than have it published (Enszer 2016, n.p.). Byrd notes that she faced troubled from lesbian separatists for collaborating with gay men, and while she herself later moved closer to a lesbian separatist position, she saw these men as her 'brothers'. As she writes in 'To the Undecided Woman', 'all the men I ever had any truck with / were faggots' (Byrd 1981, 62). Likewise, she writes that the Good Gay Poets collective 'rather liked what I identify as my "black red neck" ways'; for her part, she felt that 'Good Gay Poets were establishing a political beachhead in Boston, Massachusetts', and accepted the offer to publish her first chapbook. *25 Years of Malcontent* came out in 1976; following its publication Byrd became involved with the Combahee River Collective, which at that point held its meetings at the Women's Center in Central Square, Cambridge.

The title to Byrd's 1976 chapbook presents her as Shakespearian malcontent: the one partially excluded from society who acts as its fiercest critic while remaining trapped within its structures, a position which is in some cases, such as that of *Titus Andronicus*' Aaron, racialized. In these poems, everyday events, situations, and circumstances are tied to gendered and racialized trauma, pain, and suffering. From the start, Byrd blurs the distinction between domestic space and racialized violence. What appears to be a scene of bucolic domesticity is soon revealed to be the aftermath of a violence that troublingly and ambiguously

192 NEVER BY ITSELF ALONE

floats between the literal and the metaphorical, with few textual clues provided as to the precise object of that violence.

> The kitchen is inviting
> The summer is epochal
> It's a shame Burley
> died such a way
> Hanging there
> the flesh being plucked
> from his bones

> (Byrd 1976, 1)

Is this victim human or inhuman? Is the corpse an animal hanging up in the kitchen—a chicken to be plucked—or the corpse of a lynch victim? In October 1902, Garfield Burley and Curtis Brown were dragged from the jailhouse, lynched, and hung from a telephone pole by a 500-strong mob in Newbern, Tennessee, after Burley had shot and killed a white farmer. The poem hints at this context as its hidden subject through only a single word. Rendered by his surname alone, Burley's death is presented as if remarked upon by a passer-by, a witness to the act whose understatement indicates the 'normality' of such an act within a system of white supremacist terror. In the book's second poem, an untitled companion piece, the poet is the victim of patriarchal violence, as a hunting victim or subject to sexual assault, whose death is literally covered up.

> Your prey

> I lie now bleeding at your feet

> Draped by caretakers and curtains
> I lie raped yet assured by all
> that such mishaps are quite common

> (2)

These poems question the lens of perception and the distinctions between speaker, poet, and reader. Who is this 'you?' Who this 'I?' Who is it who proclaims the kitchen 'inviting', the summer 'epochal', and Burley's death a euphemistic 'shame'? As these poems suggest, in Byrd's work, experience will not be presented for edification or as confession but in a way that interrogates complicity, silence, and a refusal to name violence for what it is. In 'I Many', a poem from her second book, Byrd produces a kind of detournement of Whitman's declaration 'I am large, I contain multitudes' to reclaim the body

'MY REAL NAME' 193

of the Black female queer both within and against shame, as condition of both victimhood and strength.

> I am a person
> who has large breasts
> a broad flat behind
> and singing knees
> I am a person
> who is a black amerikan
> who takes pride in her tribe

(Byrd 1981, 50)

A poet and an artist, the speaker also

> falls victim to men
> gets beat up by whites and blacks

Byrd was herself an amateur photographer, and at this point racialized reference points transform into the monochrome of a black-and-white photograph developing in a darkroom, the image of the poem's speaker coming into focus:

> now the picture is developed
> tell
> who I am

Rather than establishing the identity of the poem's speaker, these lines in fact present both portrait and person as one 'beat[en] up' by both 'whites and blacks'—assaulted not only by the violence of racial and homophobic discrimination but also by the very forms of representation. At fifteen lines, the poem overspills the traditional duration of the sonnet by a single line: the many-personed subject formally exceeding the frames of both photograph and poetic form within which they might also try to find a means of adequate expression.

The gap between perceiver and perceived, and the ability—or inability—to voice the many I's of oneself is a key question for this work. Byrd's poems often turn on the link between centuries of anti-Black violence, the violence of patriarchal imposition of gender identity, and the (im)possibility of naming oneself when those names are associated with violence. In 'Quarter of a Century', one of Byrd's most important poems, the speaker asks how they can move beyond historical trauma, racist, and homophobic insult, naming their condition in a way that also seeks to transform and move beyond it. Reviewing *25 Years of Malcontent* for *Lesbian Tide*, Terry Wolverton distinguished Byrd's work from

194 NEVER BY ITSELF ALONE

the mytho-poetic focus of better-known contemporaneous feminist texts such as Audre Lorde's 'biomythography' *Zami*. 'Byrd does not call upon theory, matriarchy or the Goddess to deliver her from her anger and pain. Instead she simply, and powerfully, describes her experience of growing up dyke in America' (Wolverton). Byrd's poem begins:

> I'll never know my real name
> Never know its origins [. . .]
> Born into a place where I have no say
> I live with the ghosts of slaves.
>
> (Byrd 1976, 20)

A history of physical violence—the 'scarred and withered' face of an ancestor 'whose head / bore a white man's scalping', 'a field of my brother's / and sister's / bleeding bodies'—parallels the misnaming which blocks a sense of self: 'What would you call me / me whose name is jigaboo / and nigger'. In the poem's second half, the speaker seeks 'naming' in sexual and racial self-definition, turning away from 'the alien ways of / what is white' and towards a symbolic gathering of bones, in echoes of religious devotion to 'heathen gods' and the biblical story of Ezekiel, 'winding serpentine in hieroglyphs and / language' (21). Such naming serves as both reclamation of the past and future prophecy: 'a name long evasive wanderer and prophet / will be written on the stone'. This turn towards a quasi-mystical vocabulary is unusual in Byrd's work, but its mysticism is firmly embedded in physical objects, connecting to the poem's repeated insistence on the fragments of knowledge gleaned from matrilineal descent—the stories of grandmothers and grandmothers' grandmothers, imperfect, distorted, and rumoured, but containing an emotional and experiential truth not present in the official record. In 1977, Adrienne Rich suggested that such a poem might provide methodological guides for contemporary lesbian poets, closing the MLA lecture later reworked as 'Disloyal to Civilization' with a reading of Byrd's poem in order to illustrate her argument that feminist scholars 'listen for the silences [. . .] the gaps in language, the unwritten scenes and absent characters [. . .] rescuing from oblivion, exposing both the limits and the untouched possibilities of literature' (Rich, 23).[7] Byrd herself comments:

I think of 'Quarter of a Century' as my 'drum beating' poem [. . .] You beat the drum when you want people to listen to what it is saying. I was beating out my names, unspoken except by those who cared for me. My drum-beating was a call to women to open their minds and hearts to what I was saying. (Quoted in Enszer 2016, n.p.)

It is the act of speech as well as what is spoken—the raising of the question of the names as much as the finding of the 'real name' which, as the poem proclaims, the speaker may 'never know'. Such performative naming echoes the reclamations of Stanford's poem and anticipates the work of Pat Parker, which will be examined in Chapter 8, and which again links historical trauma, collective suffering, and a collective 'I' which reclaims, renames, and endures.

Poems such as this are more generalized in their political address—and in that sense appropriate for Rich's call to arms. But Byrd's work is equally characterized by poems which focus more explicitly on intimate sexual encounter. Like Ndugu and Stanford, Byrd is open and celebratory about queer sexuality, without sugar-coating or romanticizing it: sex is both antidote to and imbricated with jealousy, suffering, rage, and racialized tension. In 'love poem', queer sex serves to ease the pain of familial trauma: 'My spleen is my mother's / venom drips from fangs / of vicious deceit / poisoning me / leaving me running crazed / and brazen / seeking antidotes / in rosy towers / and greedy women' (Byrd 1976, 19). Thus, 'with painful relief / I move towards you', and the poem moves towards a viscerally rendered sex act, with cunnilingus figured in the language of emotional healing, rendered through reappropriating misogynist ideas of the vagina as disgusting and disease ridden: 'You suck my vagina / draining me / of pus and bile / offering your mouth as antidote'. The final stanza combines a kind of bid for power with erotic and intimate communication, as sex enshrines both death and life— even immortality: 'My immortality is my grand's / she gave up life / to leave me unprotected / she gave up breath / that I might breathe / in threatening waters / my life is immortal / I drape you / in its gauzy cover / thus sharing immortality'. As Byrd told Julie Enszer, the poem was her attempt to counter the stereotyping of lesbian sexuality as 'sick' and 'diseased', encountered in her work with social services for queer youth: 'I crafted imagery associated with power when it sees the act of woman-fucking. Woman-fucking is the antidote for those who would call lesbians sick and diseased' (Enszer 2016, n.p.). This play between the life-giving and deathly energies of sexual interaction recurs in the untitled, penultimate poem of the book a few pages later: 'I can feel breath in my throat / I choke up phlegm / Lick my chest, the lips / Dart in to make me choke again [...] Eat me / Eat me / Eat me / alive' (Byrd 1976, 24). Like the gay male poets of *Fag Rag*, Byrd refused either to censor descriptions of sexuality or to sugar-coat such descriptions in romanticist ideals. Such poems did not present a homogenous depiction of lesbian community, emphasizing both personal and collective fracture as much as moments of shared struggle ('white people / who need so much / from me' [Byrd 1981, 18]). In 'A Peck for a Peck', first published in *Sinister Wisdom* in 1979 and in an edited version in *Sojourner* ten years later, Byrd aligns the process of 'straightened / hair greased and burning flesh / under curling irons and bleaching creams' with the burning crosses of the Ku Klux Klan: 'fire burning

196 NEVER BY ITSELF ALONE

crosses, lawns alight' (Byrd 1989). 'Matriarchy' may be 'present in the gleam of straightened / hair', but this is far from the idealized matriarchal lineage present in certain aspects of a white lesbian feminist imaginary. The original version is even more explicit on this point, its opening lines proclaiming, 'the matriarchy is a racist structure' (Byrd 1979).

In 1981, Byrd self-published a second book, *A Distant Footstep on the Plain*, 'typesetting, designing, and printing the book through a network of women' (Byrd 2012, 5). As in 'Quarter of a Century', the poems of Byrd's second book give witness to a world in which Black queer woman face the ever-present threat of masculinity and whiteness as death; they are insistent reminders of these histories, in which, whether through familial connection or gendered, classed, and racialized collective vulnerability, legacies of violence and suffering are a kind of all-pervasive frame: 'her / grandmother was a slave and / that's all she knew' (Byrd 1981, 16). Such violence both unites and divides. A 'collective suffering [. . .] all those young girls dying [. . .] violence not new / but old / precipitated / against my loved ones' is enacted, not just on racialized subjects but also within racialized communities along gendered lines: 'a violence so rich and good-tasting / it has hooked the black man too' (Byrd 1981, 20). Sharing its argument with poems such as Pat Parker's 'Womanslaughter' and with the murders of women of colour in the Boston area that sparked the Combahee River Collective's activism, 'on black women dying' links misogynist murders and the rise of Klan violence as 'rites of passage': 'in the last 30 odd years / of my life span / there has occurred / a series of events / which have culminated in the death and near dying / of Black women / across the continent of America' ('on black women dying', Byrd 1981, 27–28).

Within this atmosphere, Byrd's poems assume an urgent address and reaches towards collective appeal or denunciation. Byrd's work appeared in well-circulated publications such as *Conditions*, *Sinister Wisdom*, and *The Lesbian Tide* and was occasionally discussed in those venues. Nonetheless, she was suspicious of the ways literary strategy and careerism might leapfrog onto political activism and resisted the pigeonholing of such work. In the spring 1980 issue of *Sinister Wisdom*, Byrd responded to the question 'who do you write for?': 'I write for people who feel they are alone with their feelings. I also write for my friends, lovers, and strangers. Right now I write for myself' (37). Suspicious of what she sardonically calls a 'cultural manumission', she writes:

> I can't really tell
> what is up
> with this movement
> toward ethnicity
>
> ('Distinction', Byrd 1981, 43)

Working as a pest controller, among other jobs, Byrd, like Pat Parker—who she knew and admired—had to combine working with non-writerly paid labour. As she acidly remarks:

> I don't whore for art or money
> and I don't like giving them any more
> than I have to survive
> ('The Earth's Poor Relations', Byrd 1981, 46)

Parker and Audre Lorde served as models: Byrd later called them 'sister soldiers', reviewing Parker's work and introducing her in Boston, and corresponding with Lorde towards the end of Lorde's life (Enszer 2012, n.p.). She never, however, attained their fame. Conducting further studies at Michigan State, Cornell, and Cleveland Universities, she planned a third collection, provisionally entitled *In the House of Coppers*, though this never appeared. Byrd lived with poet and scholar Terri Jewell for a number of years, editing and completing Jewell's book *Our Names Are Many: The Black Woman's Book of Days* after Jewell's suicide in 1995, and teaching at Lakeland Community College, Ohio, until her retirement. Three years before her death in 2015, in the afterword to an ebook edition of her two published chapbooks edited by Julie Enszer, Byrd wrote:

> Black lesbian identity is political and will remain political as long as corrective rape is practiced on black lesbian women who live on the African continent. Therefore it is incumbent upon me to publish my poetry because a poem will find its way to my sister soldiers as they lie quietly waiting for danger to pass. It has the capacity to buoy one when she thinks she may perish; it gives her strength to move on. (2012, 117)

'to strike the spirit of my history': Maurice Kenny's Queered Spaces

Generally attentive to the Black freedom struggle, the radical queer community of the 1970s published comparatively little work on or by queer Native Americans. Nonetheless, writers and activists within this milieu often adopted the image of the 'tribe' and of 'berdache'—an anthropological term for the social role of gay Native Americans now considered offensive—for queer community. It was in the pages of *Gay Sunshine*, *Fag Rag*, and in a 1979 pamphlet published by Good Gay Poets that acclaimed Native poet Maurice Kenny published his most explicitly queer work. As Lisa Tatonetti has argued in her work on Kenny and *Fag Rag*, while existing critical writing on Kenny pays comparatively

198 NEVER BY ITSELF ALONE

little attention to his sexuality, turning to this work gives a new sense, both of Kenny's own oeuvre and of the metaphorical racialized identifications and models of community adopted in the gay counterculture and the gay radical left (Tatonetti 2012; Tatonetti 2014). Such work 'reads' variously depending on how it is framed. Perceived primarily as a gay poet, Kenny's Nativeness might not seem central or even register at all to a reader of *Fag Rag* encountering poems presenting cruising beneath the Brooklyn Bridge or erotic parodies of Housman and Wordsworth. Likewise, those approaching his work from a different context might not be primed for queer content: Kenny's preceding five collections of poetry do not mention same-sex desire at all. Kenny's work thus reads as a kind of doubled interruption—one which problematizes romanticized assumptions concerning Native identity within a broadly white gay movement, and one which problematizes uncritically homophobic and gender-stereotyped attitudes within Native communities.

As Kenny recalls in his memoir, first published in *On Second Thought* and subsequently in expanded form as the posthumous *Angry Rain,* his father had moved from Canada to Watertown, New York, where he worked for the water department, hiring Italian-American and Native American work gangs and finding them housing.[8] Of Mohawk and Irish descent on his father's side and English and Seneca descent on that of his mother's, Kenny's parents spoke little of their ancestry. His father forbade the young Kenny from playing with the children of Native families and would not speak of his heritage directly: nonetheless, without identifying their sources, he sang songs and told stories from the Mohawk tradition, a practice which Kenny retrospectively saw as a mode of transmission and teaching. Following his parents' separation, Kenny travelled around the country, at one point suffering a traumatic sexual assault and a period of suicidal ideation. Moving to New York, Kenny worked as manager of a branch of the Marboro bookshop; studied with Louise Bogan at New York University; and came into contact with numerous authors, musicians, and film stars as an active part of the City's bohemian communities. Nonetheless, having published four early collections in the late 1950s, Kenny would not publish another such collection until 1977, though he later claimed that Donald Allen—whom he met while the latter substituted for Bogan at NYU—told him he would have included his work in the *New American Poetry* had he encountered it earlier.

Inspired by the growth of the American Indian Movement (AIM), and the 1969 Alcatraz Island and 1973 Wounded Knee occupations in particular, Kenny's connections were more and more to the concurrent movement in Native American literature, a small but committed group of writers from varying tribal backgrounds who connected through readings, activism, and publication. Kenny recalls:

'MY REAL NAME' 199

I did some teaching in places like the American Indian Center in San Francisco, things like that. I did a lot of teaching on reservations. I would go out, sort of on tour, for maybe three months, I would go through reservations in the West and I would go and do workshops there and so forth. (Maus 2004, 12)

Likewise, he emphasizes the sense of community and familial closeness found in a circle of Native American writers who offered each other mutual support, most notably, Barbara Cameron, Randy Burns, Sharol Graves, and Paula Gunn Allen.

We were friends and helped each other by suggesting publications and readings. We shared what little was out there [. . .] I had entered a community where I belonged. The feeling of being a real poet was invigorating. Apart from being published, I was in a circle, a sacred circle of life with like kind, my own, native poets. I was no more the loner, the outlaw, not even the delinquent. (Kenny 1995, 89)

Himself a tireless editor, Kenny set up Strawberry Press in the late 1970s to publish Native American writing; from 1976, he co-edited *Contact II*, a long-lived and broad-ranging magazine which published writers from Wieners to Amiri Baraka. Geary Hobson credits Kenny as the writer who 'did the most to bring all these regions and writers and publications together in a true sense of brotherhood and sisterhood', distributing copies of the journals being produced in Albuquerque, the Bay Area, South Dakota, Vancouver, the New York-Quebec region and other areas, 'linking us up then in ways more profound and engaging than we could have imagined at the time' ('Remembering Maurice Kenny', n.p.). Poetically, Kenny pinpoints his turn to Native themes, earlier encouraged by Bogan, to his 1969 poem 'First Rule', but it was with 'I am the Sun'—written after he was unable to attend the 1973 Wounded Knee protests while recovering from a heart attack—that his work turned to an explicitly politicised Native context (Bruchac 1987). During this period, Kenny began to give readings across the country, and his work appeared in developing Native American journals such as the *Greenfield Review* and *Akwesasne Notes*, the latter of which published 'I am the Sun'. The poem adopts a collective voice—'father give us no more graves, father give us back our arrows'—which, for Kenny, marked a newfound sense of identity both poetically and politically.

Yet this sense of collective belonging was fraught: as a person of mixed heritage, Kenny was not universally accepted by the Mohawk tribe with whom he identified himself, and he faced a strain of stereotyped gender roles, homophobia, and machismo within AIM, fostered by the aggressive educational policies of church and state. In a 1980 cover interview with Charley Shively and Clover

200 NEVER BY ITSELF ALONE

Chango for *Gay Community News*, Kenny notes the climate of homophobia that still dominated both reservation life and the 'Red Power' movement:

> You will go to reservations and you will rarely see an overtly gay person there. If there is a limpwristed person, he/she will leave and go off to a center just the way white gays leave Iowa to go to Chicago; leave North Carolina for New York. Reservations are usually small towns. Gays there are the unhappiest around. The only Native people that I know [who don't dislike] gays are probably the Navajo in Arizona [. . .] It's a fact today that most heterosexual Indian males do not like gays. They will go to the point of saying there are no such things among Indian people [. . .] They will go the point of saying poetry is only written by sissies. (Kenny 1980)

As Tatonetti further notes: '[Q]ueer Native people during this period were often represented as products of settler colonialism—Indigenous queerness was therefore crafted not as historical continuity but as a settler incursion into an imagined Indigenous heteronorm' (Tatonetti 2014, 3). By contrast, Kenny and other queer Native American artists and activists argued that it was heteropatriarchy, not queer sexuality, that had been produced by colonialism, and that such attitudes were not the recapturing of a suppressed collective identity but reflections of the very forces they meant to oppose. 1975 saw the formation of the San Francisco-based organization Gay Americans Indians (GAI) by Barbara Cameron and Randy Burns, with Kenny functioning as a New York point of contact. The previous year, Kenny's work had appeared in an issue of *Fag Rag*: these were, according to current scholarship, the first openly queer poems to be published by a writer of Native origin. Another landmark was passed when Kenny's essay 'Tinselled Bucks' became the first piece by a Native writer to offer a historical overview of queerness within Native American culture, previously subject only to the often dismissive and patronizing gaze of white ethnologists. Published in the Winter 1975/76 issue of *Gay Sunshine* alongside the poem 'United', dedicated to Randy Burns, this work would be followed in 1981 by Paula Gunn Allen's essay 'Lesbians in American Indian Culture' and her poem 'some like indians endure' (1982), which, like Stanford's *Black and Queer*, collapsed the metaphorical separation between queerness and Native identity, proclaiming, 'I have it in my mind that / dykes are Indians' (Kenny 1976; Allen 1981; Allen 1982, 75).

Reprinted in Kenny's Good Gay Poets collection *Only as Far as Brooklyn* (1979), 'United' links the suppression of Native queerness to the suppression of Native traditions in general: just as 'old Medicine Men', 'prodded by priest and politician, / no longer wear robes', so 'boys' no longer 'gather holy corn / nor are celebrated on the warpath / and taken in love by strong warriors'. Yet such traditions are maintained 'in lodges and languages', spaces 'where the vision is honoured, / and

'MY REAL NAME' 201

grandfathers know nations will gather'. In 'Winkte', first published in *Manroot* in 1977, Kenny follows through on the historical argument of 'Tinselled Bucks' to argue for the central role of queer people in Sioux, Cheyenne, Ponca, and Crow peoples. Here, the use of the plural voice adopted in Kenny's poems influenced by oral tradition such as 'I am the Sun' itself makes a defiant statement of collective being: not only the I of the tribe, but also the I of the queer members of the tribe. Kenny's note informs readers that the title refers to a 'Sioux word for male homosexual', and the poem begins 'We are special to the Sioux!', going on to outline the roles found for queer people as 'friends or wives of brave warriors', who 'took to the medicine tent, / And in their holiness made power / For the people of the Cheyenne nation', and who 'had power with the people!' (Kenny 1979, 10–11). This 'we' speaks from within the tribe—and the broader Native American, pan-tribal community—in a statement that prioritizes difference over homogeneity, yet nonetheless theorizes a collective belonging.

In both 'Winkte' and 'United', such collectivity is indexed through shared spatial reference: the poems' locations include ancestral lands, mountains, sacred spaces, and lodges, connecting queerness to land, tradition, and to the possibility of Native nationalism based on the remembrance of repressed traditions. Likewise, the book's opening poem, 'Boys', evokes the sacred space outside the community where Native American adolescents engage in a coming-of-age ritual, recasting queerness as a part of cultural survival, spiritual belief, and natural forces. In his glossary to the volume, Kenny notes that such visions take place during 'tribal times', yet the poem's present tense blurs space and time to suggest a living history. The book's glossary, presumably written by Kenny, accompanies the poem with a note:

> *Vision:* During tribal times it was customary for adolescent boys to go to a sacred place . . . usually a high hill or mountain peak. Fasting resulted in dreams or visions that directed the youths [*sic*] name, career and often sexual proclivities. (Kenny 1979, 44)

In the poem itself, the boys of the title appear only in the concluding stanza:

> hawk,
> I must remember this story
> to tell the young boys
> fishing in the creek
>
> (7)

As Tatonetti notes, however, the poem's title and its appearance within a book by a gay-themed press alter potential readings to a significant degree.

202 NEVER BY ITSELF ALONE

Kenny's non-Native queer readers might see the 'young boys' as future members of the gay community to be told about the power and beauty of same-sex desire, whereas Kenny's Native audiences might see this imperative to remember and retell the story of the hawk and the mountain as a classic invocation of the oral tradition. (Tatonetti 2012, 126)

In other words, the poem—in which 'plums grow large and red' and the 'crazy mountain' moves, pleading to the hawk to be caught in its talons—might read according to other more abstract or personal symbolic systems, as a visionary experience not explicitly related to queerness. The poem opens:

> the hawk flew
> to the crazy mountain
> plums grew large and red
> stained hands and mouth
>
> (Kenny 1979, 7)

In his *Gay Community News* interview, Kenny also suggests a personal interpretation which renders the link to queer sexuality all the more explicit. Kenny notes that, in his work, plums tend to refer to testicles, deriving from a personal memory of sexual experimentation with friends at a younger age: 'that was the "Vision"—the visions of plums being testicles—groping for the testicles on the plum tree' (Kenny 1980). Such imaginative re-inscription is, of course, accessible only through Kenny's extra-textual explanation, and the poem reads entirely differently without this autobiographical clue. Nonetheless, it reads as at least partially eroticized within the context of the Good Gay Poets. In this way, it suggests the role of context and imagination within the vision quest: a social initiation and ritual which is also individual and personal, an entry into society which is not simply a reinforcement of heteronormative roles but also of the potential for broader sexual proclivities.

Through such interventions, Kenny figures Native spaces and traditions as venerating, respecting, and accommodating queerness. But while such poems reclaim a relation to land prior to the depredations of settler colonialism, much of the work that appears in *Fag Rag* and in *Only as Far as Brooklyn* occupies the space of the contemporary city which Kenny inhabited for decades. As GAI founder Randy Burns notes, during the 1950s, many Native Americans migrated to San Francisco and other large urban areas as part of the Bureau of Indian Affairs' relocation programme, which encouraged migration from the reservation in search of employment (Burns, 'Preface', in Roscoe 1989). During the 1970s, a similar wave saw a younger generation move in search of higher education and training. For queer people, the move to the city also served as a means to escape reservation homophobia. Kenny's 'Apache' humorously presents a sexual encounter between an Apache 'warrior of the Yamaha / hoteled wild Oakland [. . .] safe from reservation / eyes and rules', the language of warriorhood and pride turned to queer sexual encounter: 'Apache who struck coup on a Mohawk / and left the bed victorious' (Kenny, 1979, 17). Yet if this is a space of solace, of 'gentle hands' and intimate encounter, Kenny was also aware that such urban spaces were spaces of intense alienation and homophobic and racist violence. In 1980, he described the 'torment of the mind, torment of the spirit [. . .] of young gays who are leaving the reservations, who are all messed up, don't know where to turn, how to turn or who to turn to', and noted: 'In large areas like San Francisco, I know a lot of gay people who have had the baloney beaten right out of them. Especially the lesbians have been beaten badly [. . .] This is 1980—not the Dark Ages!' (Kenny 1980). In the poem "Kill Fag's' / Grafitti on the 7th Ave. Subway, N.Y.C., June-1976', printed in *Fag Rag* 18, Kenny registers—and ironically undercuts—the presence of such queerphobic urban violence, presenting those who daub homophobic graffiti as 'threatened / by the fear, dread of revelation / or the joy of male embrace!'

As well as the present threat symbolized by such death-proclaiming graffiti, the poems of *Only as Far as Brooklyn* also reckon with a broader historical erasure. Kenny has written on how his work wrestles with being a 'genuine' Mohawk while embracing a modern urban environment on what is stolen land.

Even the Cheyenne poet Lance Henson said, on visiting me in New York City, that he couldn't understand how any self-respecting Mohawk could live in a place like Brooklyn, not failing to mention that many of Manhattan's structures of high steel and iron were erected by Iroquois men, risking their lives for buildings they would never be allowed to inhabit. (Kenny 2018, 143)

In his other Brooklyn volume, *Last Mornings in Brooklyn* (1991), Kenny responds to Henson's query: 'I burn / Cedar and Sage / and keep / an eye / on the bridge' (Kenny 1991). The bridge here serves to index both the labour of the Native Americans who built it and the cruising ground that unfolds beneath its shadow. In 'Greta Garbo', first published in *Fag Rag* and collected in *Only as Far as Brooklyn*, the shadows of the bridge provide a space of both shame and sexual possibility: the speaker is cruised by an ex-soldier with a disability, who, hiding in shadows, is juxtaposed with Garbo's own famed need for solitude and withdrawal from public life. Centring on figures of the marginal, and the ambiguous realm between exposure and secrecy, Kenny presents those left out of both utopian, sex-positive queer fantasies and the censorious framework of gay respectability politics, making a critical intervention very much of a piece with the sexual politics of *Fag Rag* as a whole.[9]

204 NEVER BY ITSELF ALONE

In another *Fag Rag* poem, 'A Night, a Bridge, a River (Beneath Brooklyn Bridge)', Kenny once more draws attention to the bridge in a parenthetical aside which nods to a shared queer knowledge enabled by the gay publication context (Kenny 1979, 36). As Tatonetti notes, such shared knowledge enables queer readers to construct an alternative geography, a queer counter-public in which one can find fellow queers and counter the homophobic architecture and policing of space (Tatonetti 2014, 36). At the same time, Tatonetti suggests that we read Kenny's Brooklyn Bridge poem as a critical intervention into the body of queer literature which centres on the bridge, suggesting that, for the bridge as a utopian 'geography of queerness'—such as that established in now-canonical works by Whitman and Hart Crane—'to become visible, a concurrent geography of indigeneity must be erased' (Tatonetti 2014, 38). Built on what was traditionally Algonquin land, much of New York's iconic skyline was constructed by ironworkers from Akwesasne Mohawk and Kahnawake communities. And in Crane's *The Bridge*, as Alan Trachtenberg suggests, indigeneity gives a resonance for an Atlantean resurgence which leaves its points of origin behind—much as the Native labourers on the structures that dominate the New York skyline are erased from those structures' histories, unable to access them (Trachtenberg 2005, 279–81). Whiteness—including queer whiteness—both harnesses the power of a Native imaginary and removes it from present actuality. Kenny would later critically address the shortcomings in Crane's and Whitman's imaginings of indigeneity in critical prose, writing that Crane sought to 'climb the Brooklyn Bridge howling for Americans to march west across the continent upon this magnificent bridge a true work of art built in part by Iroquois iron workers and strike out for new conquests', 'show[ing] an immediate lack of concern for American history and no understanding or sympathy with either the earth or the First Peoples' place upon it' (Kenny in Castro 1991). His earlier poem, however, stages its intervention, not through a centralized Native framing, nor direct address to Crane or Whitman, but through implication and brief allusion. Its scene of lovers returning home sees a playful bout figured in terms of counting coup—'Home-way you broke off an elm twig / your charged like a Sioux / striking bare legs with wet kisses of leaves' (36–70). A brief aside in the middle of the poem, this moment functions much like the invocation of the bridge itself for a queer readership: a thread which might be activated by certain groups of readers, leading to further associations that reframe and alter the apparent scene of narrative action. Kenny shows that indigeneity exists within such invocations, even if they have suppressed it. Rather than an *either* queer *or* indigenous reading of the bridge, Kenny's is both.

Gay Appropriations

As suggested by the publication of such work in *Gay Sunshine*, *Fag Rag*, and *Manroot*, in the absence of widespread queer organizations specifically for

Native peoples, the predominantly non-Native queer community offered a measure of solidarity. Randy Burns, for instance, notes the importance of 'reading an article in *Fag Rag* about the place gay people had in the Indian culture before the invasion of the white man's values and education' (Gengel, 40). Likewise, encountering Kenny's work in the pages of gay magazines such as *Gay Sunshine*, *Mouth of the Dragon*, *Manroot*, and *Fag Rag* challenges the assumption that we read Kenny either as a 'Native' or (less often) a 'queer' poet whilst also enriching and challenging the predominantly white milieu of gay publishing venues. Nonetheless, in his 1980 interview with Shively and Clover Chango, Kenny states: 'I don't really think the gay movement gives me very much as a poet' (Kenny 1980). Of an earlier generation, Kenny was both reticent and open about his sexuality: while he here discusses his first sexual experience, along with cruising, he admits that '[q]uite frankly I'm still living back in those dark ages when we had to live in closets and I find it very difficult to talk about things a lot of people can. I'm not really liberated. I'm still back there in those chains' (Kenny 1980). Thus, as a narrative of his coming to being as a poet, even Kenny's later memoir, *Angry Rain* (2018), talks of his earlier consensual heterosexual relationships, but same-sex relations are present only in the form of traumatic incidents of abduction and sexual assault.

The continuing pressures that lead to such anxieties are suggested by an incident which had occurred three years prior to the *Gay Community News* interview. In 1977, *Akwesasne Notes* wrote to the gay journal *RFD* to request removal from the *RFD* mailing list because

> [your publications] encourage a kind of human behavior which our elders consider not normal and a detriment to our way of life. There are so many things that have come from European western society whether it be alcohol, Christianity and its church, educational system and the list goes on, that have had a destructive effect on Indian Culture. And now that list includes the type of behavior your magazine advocates. (RFD Collective)

RFD reprinted the letter, along with a counterstatement, noting that they had copied in a number of organizations and individuals, including Kenny and Buffy Sainte-Marie (RFD Collective). *RFD*, a self-described 'country journal by gay men', arose from the Midwest Gay Pride Conference in 1974 from a small group seeking to establish a 'rural collective life style'; editorship for different issues shifted between similar groups in Iowa, Oregon, North Carolina, Tennessee, and other locations, with the majority of its members white, middle-class men. As such, it echoed the invocations of Indigenous queer tradition and relation to the land explored by other gay organizations such as the Radical Faeries, and in particular advocated by Harry Hay, the original founder of the Mattachine Society (Morgensen, 105). Through a neo-paganist understanding, 'woman-identified men' adopted what Scott Lauria Morgensen calls a 'politicized

206   NEVER BY ITSELF ALONE

effeminacy' which mobilized conceptions of gender running counter to those of normative Christianity and Western thought (106). Such imaginaries linked a countercultural history of Europe with that of the treatment of Native peoples in America: gay identity was linked to historical persecution of witches, figured as 'wise herbal healers, strong women, often lesbians', with 'witches and faggots' as enemies of the church because of their 'rural and communal life styles' opposed to mercantilism (106). In *RFD*, surveys of queer spirituality drew on the popular figure of the Native American shaman, seen in drawings such as Jamal Redwing's 'Faggot Shaman Poet Butterfly Dancer' (107). Noting the middle-class origins of many in such movements and the appropriative logics of countercultural imaginaries they fostered, Morgensen suggests that such invocations served to 'reconcile' gay white settlers 'to their non-Native and normatively white inheritance of settlement' (105). For white gay men to identify with Native Americans served as a means of exculpating collective guilt for prior policies of extermination and for continuing immiseration, with the presence of actually existing Native Americans apparently not a concern. As Lou Cornum notes, 'white gays in settled North America have hung their hopes of liberated sexual futures onto the idea of the tribe. This aspiration for tribalism has only occasionally and with extreme limit supported the ongoing tribal formations of Indigenous peoples, often imagined as roaming around a pre-contact past and disappearing after the catastrophic arrival of heterosexuality' (Cornum, 36).

While the rural commune movement was a specific phenomenon generally removed from the urban focus of *Fag Rag* or *Gay Sunshine*, and more middle class in orientation than *Fag Rag*, white appropriation of Native culture was far-reaching here, too. From 1974, *Fag Rag* serialized Arthur P. Evan's influential series of articles, 'Witchcraft and the Gay Counterculture', subsequently published as a book by the collective in 1978, though these articles were subject to criticism for its historical inaccuracies in the correspondence section of the magazine. Evans' fusion of neo-paganism, studies of witchcraft, ruralism, and anarchist politics incorporated elements of what was perceived to be Native American practice: in particular, he invoked the supposed Native American role of 'berdache' as 'gay shamans', arguing that embracing such histories would create a 'new socialism' in which modern queer groups would *become* those groups that inspired 'a myriad number of autonomous tribes, small in population, growing like plants from the earth', 'tap[ping] into the spiritual powers in nature and ourselves' (Evans, 101–103). Evans' book was of particular influence on the development of the Radical Faeries by Don Kilhefner and Harry Hay, founder of the Mattachine Society, in Los Angeles the following year. Hay had previously held meetings with the Committee for Traditional Indian Land and Life (CTILL), founded in Los Angeles in 1967 by non-Indigenous people to challenge land grabs by the Peabody coal-mining company in Arizona, and the Radical Faeries incorporated elements believed to derive from Native American tradition with gay communalist and ruralist practices. As Cornum notes, Hay saw Native American traditions as a means of understanding the social role of homosexual people in a 'transcultural global history'. This discourse also theorized homosexuality as an alternative gender. In 1970, Hay and anthropologist Sue Ellen Jacobs disputed the role of the 'berdache' within Native societies: for Jacobs, the term—a settler colonial term arising as a slur—collapsed numerous different sexual practices, not all of which were homosexual, into a generalized icon of difference. While Kenny himself used the term in his 1975 essay, and it was not until 1990 that the alternative term 'Two-Spirit' was coined, the result is that understanding of Native sexuality occurs through the framework of what Cornum calls 'colonial knowledge production', then used as the basis for a fantasy return which often overlooks the present of contemporary Native Americans (Cornum, 40).

How might Kenny place himself in relation to such imagined returns? To answer this question, I will end the chapter by considering Kenny's satire on white male appropriations of Native cultural signifiers in the 1980 poem 'Boston Tea Party'. In certain poems from *Only as Far as Brooklyn*, Kenny addresses the sexual encounter between Native and white men: a double taboo, crossing the lines of both race and gender as scene of sexual fantasy and projection onto the bodies of racialized others. 'Santa Fe, New Mexico' presents the obliquely racialized ironies of cruising in a world of Chicano and Navajo tourist stalls and 'Yanqui' sex tourism: the 'underground / toilets / in plush / hotels', places 'for a quick lay', where the sons of 'tourists / from Toledo [. . .] trick', are the 'only place / in town / where an Indian / can touch / an Irishman / with a western / accent / and keep / his Sacred / mountains' (Kenny 1979, 14–15). 'Boston Tea Party', written in 1980 and published in the New Narrative issue of Steve Abbott's *Soup* in 1981, adds a referential framework concerning the founding of America itself, its title referring to the totemic act of 'independence' in which white Americans dressed up as 'Indians' to protest the UK's imperial tax on tea.[10] The poem itself does not address this incident directly, but its ironized presentation of racialized expectations, filtered through 'ritual' erotic encounter are historicized in its appropriative, white supremacist legacy. The actual historical event is presented in the parody of drinking tea together rather than the revolt over taxes. As Cornum writes: 'A common, shared recurring dream for settlers [. . .] of being accepted and absolved by the Native', which, in the work of queer writers, is 'transformed across a desire for sexual and gender freedom'. The poem opens on a nocturnal encounter between the speaker and a white would-be shaman conducting a ritual of his own construction.

208   NEVER BY ITSELF ALONE

> He blew feathers on my ribs,
> danced drums on my naked knees, cheekbones;
> blessed prayers upon my eyelids [. . .]
>
> Mystery shuddered as he knelt before me
> as though asking my hands to bless his life,
> confirm my secret powers.
>
> (Kenny 1981, 32)

At once seeking to take from and to be imparted with the powers of an imagined mystical Native history,

> He conjured buffaloes from my feet, armpits.
> Rattles banged and shook from my teeth.

But these apparent devotions instead serve to humiliate, erase, and trivialize

> [...] those red votive candles lit
> to strike the spirit of my history,
> ancestry, my drums and rattles[.]
> For the white man
> I was savior and warrior, priest and poet,
> fertile and fallow, savage and prophet,
> angel of death and apostle of truth.
> Such projections operate on a masochistic imaginary in which
> His ribs opened for my arrow;
> his head split for the tomahawk, the club[.]

Yet this attitude alternates between dominance and submission, with the white 'shaman' believing he also has much to impart even as the entire 'ritual' effectively acts as a mode of exculpation for white guilt.

> I was to raise the pipe, smoke, allow the puffs
> to bathe his priesthood which he would gladly loan to me,
> naming me the high priest of his foolish
> pagan altar adorn with plastic geraniums and peacock feather
> Pity the unannointed, the damned.
> Absolve the guilty and the hangman

Leaving the apartment, the speaker enters a Boston dawn with its official mementoes of history—including, perhaps, the formative event of the Boston

'MY REAL NAME' 209

'Tea Party' itself another act of appropriation and would-be rebellion predicated on the logic of whiteness.

> I crossed the Charles into the grubby
> Boston Commons to stare at the swan boats,
> consult the aging statues whitened by pigeon dung.
>
> (33)

Sardonic and telling, the poem's encounter is not necessarily sexual—though its language of violence, dominance, and submission certainly has something of the erotic about it—but it does suggest the queer appropriations of Native culture. In his memoir, Kenny recalls early incidents of sexual assault by white men, at once fetishizing and seeking to demean his racialized otherness, and of games of 'cowboys' and 'Indians' as a child when he was tied up and the ground around him set ablaze, as play veered over into the threat of real-life violence.[11] Such appropriations—which are often violent, whether in sadistic attacks on Native Americans or in masochistic fantasies of assault by Native Americans—'his ribs opened for my arrow'—continually replay the traumas of history and the harmful mythologies which enabled them across the private spaces of the bedroom-cum-ritual space, the public spaces of Boston Common, or the alternative lifestyle experiments of the rural commune movement, with its fantasies of exculpatory return to the land and to Native American spiritual traditions.

Against such often violent projections, and the official history written in pigeon dung on Boston's monuments, the collective voicing of 'Boys', 'Winkte', and 'United', as well as Kenny's engagements with a queer and Native Brooklyn, are vital sources of solidarity, sexual fulfilment, and a counter-history which provides cultural, social, and sexual sustenance for the present. Kenny at once reclaims the indigeneity of queer urban space, erased in the history of land dispossession of large American urban spaces such as New York and the invisible Native labour it deployed, and reclaims the queerness of Indigenous space, a productive crossing attentive to the modes of marginalization, violence, and pain that undergird queer modernist imaginings of urban utopia, contemporaneous romanticized projections of queer indigeneity amongst the Gay Liberation Movement, and heteronormative rewritings of Native tradition within AIM, and the erasures performed in all three of these narratives.

Likewise, the work of all four poets addressed in this chapter is still of vital importance for the way we think about gender, race, and sexuality and their relation to linguistic experimentation, naming—the names we call ourselves and others. Such work suggests the vibrancy and militancy of the post-Stonewall generation as it manifested both aesthetically and in activist contexts. In 1977,

210 NEVER BY ITSELF ALONE

the Combahee River Collective drafted its crucial statement on identity politics and intersecting modes of oppression.

Indicating the overlapping nature of queer communities in Boston, members of the Collective worked with *Gay Community News* in the office shared with *Fag Rag* on 22 Bromfield Street (Shively 1984, 29). Queer activism in Boston was not simply a matter of white gay men, however progressive, but of women of colour whose analyses were influential and vital interventions into dominant narratives of political organizing. Having already touched on Stephania Byrd's association with the Collective, the following chapter will address the role of poetry in the Collective's work in more detail.

7

'We cannot live without our lives'

From the Combahee River Collective to *This Bridge Called My Back*

Introduction

In 1977, the Combahee River Collective declared: '[W]e are actively committed to struggling against racial, sexual, heterosexual, and class oppression, and see as our particular task the development of integrated analysis and practice based upon the fact that the major systems of oppression are interlocking. The synthesis of these oppressions creates the conditions of our lives' (Combahee River Collective 1977, 15). Drafted by activists Barbara Smith, Beverly Smith, and Demita Frazier, Combahee's statement was followed by a series of Black feminist retreats in the Boston area, extending this earlier theoretical flowering into a network that, while small, spread across the country. In the spring of 1979, Combahee formed part of a broad coalition drawing attention to a series of murders of Black women in Boston's Roxbury neighbourhood, distributing the pamphlet *Six Black Women: Why Did They Die?* and organizing a series of poetry readings in support of the campaign at which Audre Lorde debuted 'Need: A Chorale for Black Woman Voices', addressing the events of what she called 'this wild and bloody spring' (Lorde 1993, 336).

At the same time, Bay Area lesbian feminists Gloria Anzaldúa and Cherríe Moraga began to co-edit the anthology *This Bridge Called My Back*. In summer 1980, Moraga visited Boston to discuss publishing possibilities, developing a romantic relationship with Barbara Smith and moving to the city the following year. Frustrated by the fact that the feminist publishing networks were still controlled almost exclusively by white women, Lorde, Moraga, Smith, and others founded Kitchen Table Press, the first press run by women of colour in the United States, publishing the second edition of *This Bridge* after the collapse of its initial publisher, Persephone Press. Though Anzaldúa, Moraga, and Smith soon moved to New York, the seeds for this activity were laid in Boston. *This Bridge* and the Combahee River Statement were founding documents of women of colour feminism: they are formative and now-canonical texts whose impact across numerous fields cannot be overstated. This chapter seeks to recover the importance of the Boston context to these texts while further highlighting

Never By Itself Alone. David Grundy, Oxford University Press. © Oxford University Press 2024.
DOI: 10.1093/oso/9780197654842.003.0008

212 NEVER BY ITSELF ALONE

relations between poetry and queer activism in the area. These writers and activists were building a community and laying the ground for a movement. Their legacy lives on.

Conditions: The Combahee River Collective

Combahee first emerged during an economic downturn. Welfare cuts penalized non-normative family arrangements, including queer and single mothers, and the broader impositions of neoliberal policy saw a fresh racialized assault on people of colour, on the poor, and on the queer.[1] The conditions of America's rightward turn were particularly pronounced in Boston, where traditional manufacturing industries were phased out for service industries, where neighbourhoods that had historically been points of refuge for queer communities and for people of colour were destroyed, and where white flight and the emergence of suburban neighbourhoods contrasted with the intense poverty of inner city areas. From the mid-1970s, Boston was at the centre of an escalating racial crisis. In 1974, Judge W. Arthur Garrity ruled that Boston's public schools were unconstitutionally segregated, leading to a new Racial Imbalance Act, requiring that schools be racially balanced. The official desegregation process involved busing students of colour to predominantly white neighbourhoods, triggering over a decade of racist assaults.[2] Combahee co-founder Barbara Smith moved to Boston in 1972, later noting: 'It was absolutely known that as a Black person you did not go to South Boston. You did not go to East Boston. You did not go to Chelsea [. . .] It was really frightening, if one got lost in those neighbourhoods trying to go from one place to another' (Breines, 158). The specifically gendered aspects of such violence were too rarely discussed. Likewise, the city's thriving scene of predominantly white feminist organizing displayed often contradictory attitudes to racial issues.

From the late 1960s onwards, Boston became a 'hub' for New Left and feminist organizing. Separatist group Cell 16 sought to establish a 'female liberation front', publishing the journal *No More Fun and Games*, while the socialist feminist Bread and Roses Collective (1969–1971) advocated the abolition of the nuclear family and the development of alternative childcare arrangements, and joining anti-sterilization and pro-abortion campaigns. In 1970, members of the Collective occupied buildings owned by Harvard, leading to the establishment of the Cambridge Women's Health Center and the publication of the groundbreaking women's health anthology *Our Bodies, Our Selves* (Breines, 98).[3] The same year, former Brandeis University student Susan Saxe—herself a poet—was placed on the FBI's Most Wanted List after a 1970 bank robbery in the Boston area. On her capture in Philadelphia in 1975, Saxe declared herself 'a lesbian, a feminist, and an Amazon'.[4] Activism in support of Saxe was connected to campaigns in support of Joan Little—the African American woman who had killed a jail guard in self-defence in North Carolina in 1974—and Inez García—who had killed her rapist in Soledad, California, the same year.[5] But while coalitions were sought, acts of solidarity declared, and white feminists joined women of colour in struggles around reproductive rights, there were often blocks to coalition building. Largely middle class, white, and college educated, activists within Boston's white feminist milieu sought alliances with Black women but distrusted their commitment to feminism; conversely, Black women distrusted the racial blindness of feminist activists. As Winifred Breines notes, there was still little practical space for women of colour in such settings.[6]

Writing to Boston-based feminist newsletter *Sojourner* in 1979, Barbara Smith cautioned that white women should 'not assume that it means the same thing for us to be feminists and lesbians as it does [for] them', noting 'the still relatively small number of Black women who identify themselves as feminists, and the lack of Black feminist institutions Black women have'.

> The Black feminist movement is in a very different period historically than the white feminist movement, even though the participants in these movements are each other's contemporaries. I have been constantly aware of this 'time-lag'. (Smith 1979)

Given this, as Demita Frazier notes, Combahee's founders were 'refugees' from other movements, from civil rights and Black Power to the largely white anti-war movement (Breines, 122, 124). Frazier had been active in the Chicago Black Panther Party and the Young Socialist Alliance in 1969, and she was part of the Jane Collective, an underground movement providing access to safe abortions. Barbara Smith was involved in the anti-war movement, protested at the 1968 Democratic National Convention in Chicago, and was a fellow traveller of Students for a Democratic Society (SDS); Beverly Smith was active in the Congress on Racial Equality (CORE) in Cleveland before moving to New York and working at *Ms.* magazine. While at *Ms.*, Beverly Smith had met the activists who had formed the National Black Feminist Organization (NBFO) in summer 1973, informing her sister, who attended the NBFO's East Coast Regional Conference that November alongside other women from the Boston area (Breines, 119; Springer, 58). In January the following year, Barbara Smith organized a local chapter meeting in Roxbury, attended by half a dozen women. Influenced by Sharon Bourke, an older Marxist previously involved with the Institute for the Black World in Atlanta, the group disaffiliated from the NBFO, holding meetings at the Cambridge Women's Center and organizing around the Joan Little case and in support of Kenneth Edelin, a Black doctor who had been charged with manslaughter for performing illegal abortions (Springer, 59).

In April 1977, the Smiths and Frazier drafted the Combahee River Collective Statement, named for the location of a raid led by Harriet Tubman in 1863 which succeeded in freeing over 750 slaves and which remains the only military campaign in American history planned by a woman. Though it emerged at a very early stage of their activity, this text remains the group's enduring legacy. Writing in *Sinister Wisdom* in 1983, Cheryl Clarke argues:

> Never before has there been a model of black feminist practice which iridesces all the factors of oppression and attempts to integrate our struggles [. . .] The piece attempts to synthesize all of black women's oppressions, chiefly race, sex, and class, into a dialectic of resistance and liberation. (Clarke 1983, 92–93)

For Robin D. G. Kelley, meanwhile: 'The Combahee River Collective's "Statement" remains one of the most important documents of the black radical movement in the twentieth century' (Kelley, 150).

In July, Combahee held the first in a series of Black feminist retreats in South Hadley, Massachusetts, attended by around thirty women including the Smiths, Frazier, Boston-based activists Margo Okazawa-Rey and Lorraine Bethel and, from outside Boston, poets Cheryl Clarke and Audre Lorde (Duchess Harris 2019, 126). Six more retreats were held through to 1981, providing a space that could not be found elsewhere, and offering ways to share information and creative work; to talk about possibilities for local and national organizing; and to write, to eat, and simply to be together (105). Most, but not all, of the participants were either out lesbians or in the process of coming out: at the third retreat in March 1978, the group discussed the Radicalesbians' 'Woman-Identified Woman' manifesto (127). Yet lesbian sexuality was not the only modality within which Combahee organized, as they sought to establish the importance of 'interlocking' forms of oppression. As Cheryl Clarke put it in minutes from the retreat, they sought to demolish the barriers 'that keep women loving one another whether that love is characterised by sex or not', reconceptualizing gender roles both within and beyond the bounds of sexuality (Springer, 108).

Lorde's example helped push those such as Clarke to write poetry, as members of the group, in Gloria Hull's words, 'tried our creative and critical work on each other' (Breines, 126), arguing that Black women create theory in many forms— from position papers to magazine articles to other forms of poetry and prose (Springer, 104). In 1975, Smith wrote: 'You might find out more about matriarchy by looking at portrayals of Black family life in poetry and fiction than you would in surveying thousands of statistics' (Smith 2014, 100). Editing anthologies and magazine issues and establishing a Black women's salon in Boston to discuss Black women's studies, Smith saw the group as part of a Boston continuum dating back to Maria Stewart—who in 1832 gave the first public speech by an African

'WE CANNOT LIVE WITHOUT OUR LIVES' 215

American woman at Franklin Hall—to activists, writers, and poets Pauline Hopkins, Helene Johnson, and Angelina Weld Grimké (Smith 2014, 10).[7] The task was by no means easy. At the National Conference of Afro-American writers at Howard University in 1978, Smith was denounced by psychologist Frances Cress Welsing, who invoked 'an epidemic in the direction of bisexuality and homosexuality', stating: 'If we endorse homosexuality, then we have endorsed the death of our people' (Smith 2014, 126). One male critic told Smith after the talk that she was lucky not to be 'lynched' (Ross 2003, 65). The Combahee Retreats were a vital space to recuperate from such incidents. But it was the events of 1979 that saw the group begin to affect the conversation on a broader level.

1979

'Why Did They Die?'

In late 1978 and early 1979, a series of sexual assaults occurred in the largely white, middle-class Boston neighbourhood of Brighton. Intense media pressure, combined with witness coercion, led to the wrongful arrest in February of Black house painter Willie Sanders (sands, 16–17). But when, between January and May 1979, twelve Black women and one white woman were murdered in Roxbury and Dorchester, media and police response was almost non-existent. The women, some as young as fifteen, were stigmatized as sex workers. Newspaper reports misnamed or chose not even to name the victims. In response, activists, including veteran South End organizer Marlene Stephens, formed CRISIS, 'an ad hoc organization of Black women that grew in response to the callousness shown by the Boston law enforcement authorities and the mayor's office in their feeble investigations into the murders' (w.s., 17). On March 31, the group organized a memorial service at the Cambridge YMCA at which Stephania Byrd read 'Quarter of a Century' (analyzed in the previous chapter), highlighting the murders as the consequences of a 'racist and misogynist culture' (17). The following day, over 1,500 people, men and women, marched to the city's state house in protest. Though the organizers were largely women, the speakers were largely men: as Barbara Smith noted: 'The speakers talked about race, but no one said a damn thing about [. . .] sexual violence' (Smith 2014, 63). Furthermore, despite the fact that a number of the women were suspected, and later proved, to have been killed through intimate partner violence in the 'safety' of domestic space: 'The message came across loud and clear that [. . .] you stayed in the house and/or found a man to protect you' (Duchess Harris 2019, 132).

In her apartment that night, Smith drafted the text of a pamphlet, *Six Black Women: Why Did They Die?*. Reading the text aloud to others in Combahee

216 NEVER BY ITSELF ALONE

by phone, Smith typeset the text with the assistance of Urban Planning Aid, an organization that offered publishing and advice and resources for activists (Duchess Harris 2019, 132). By the end of the week, Combahee had printed 26,000 copies in both English and Spanish, distributing these as part of the newly formed Coalition for Women's Safety (CWS) which had begun to hold weekly meetings at community centre, Women, Inc., founded in 1972 by Black activist Katie Portis. Involving both Black and white activist groups (Breines, 158), the CWS organized self-defence workshops, trained service workers to deal with assault victims and their families, and set up trust funds for the children of the murdered women, while seeking to 'recognize differences of location and power' (Thuma, 130). Along with white feminists Tia Cross and Freada Klein, the Smiths drafted a series of consciousness-raising guidelines to facilitate conversation on racism,[8] and the route of the 1979 Take Back the Night march was altered to avoid the previous year's spectacle of white women marching through Black neighbourhoods chanting 'stop rape' in unwitting echo of a long history of racist stereotype; likewise, organizers spoke out against Willie Sanders' framing for the Brighton assaults, avoiding divide and rule strategies that offset gender and race (Thuma, 138). For Smith, such activity was 'the culmination of everything I had done, learned, tried to do until then' (Smith 2014, 63).

Combahee organized both separately and within CWS, becoming friends with Marlene Stephens, who in turn defended them against homophobic insults at CRISIS meetings (72–73). In particular, they continued to distribute the pamphlet Smith had drafted the night of April 1. As Terrion Williamson suggests, activists initially found it hard to galvanize support around the murders. Other prominent cases, such as that of Joan Little or the contemporaneous Atlanta child murders, were connected to broader narratives around racial injustice, from the carceral system to suspected Ku Klux Klan activity. But the murders of working-class Black women largely thought to have been killed by Black men from the same communities did not obviously implicate power structures that were the usual target of activism, and even seemed to undermine the community's cohesion (Williamson, 336). Noting that these women 'died because they were women just as surely as they died because they were black', *Six Black Women: Why Did They Die?* both counters racist narratives that suggest these deaths were circumstantial hazards of living within Black communities and emphasizes the role of misogyny in their deaths (Combahee River Collective 1979, n.p.). Though not explicitly focused on lesbian issues, the pamphlet emphasizes the role played by stereotypes surrounding Black women's sexuality in white state responses, noting that the mother of one of the first two victims—a fifteen-year-old girl—was told by the police on reporting her daughter's disappearance that she had 'probably gone off with a pimp'. Noting that 'three of the eleven women were found in their own apartments', the pamphlet also demolishes the argument that 'women should stay in the house': 'If and when they catch the murderers we still won't be safe to leave our houses, because it has never been safe to be a woman alone in the street'. Instead, Combahee stressed action and self-defence, stating, 'WE HAVE TO LEARN TO PROTECT OURSELVES', and providing lists of self-protection tips and resources—healthcare centres, self-defence classes, battered women's shelters—that enacted this slogan in practical terms. Here, they attest, is the community that seems absent. Here is the means of survival.

Deploying 'statistics and hard facts about daily, socially acceptable violence against women', the pamphlet emphasizes the violence's urgent temporality: 'Another way to think about these figures is that while you have been reading this pamphlet a woman somewhere in this city, in this state, in this country has been beaten, raped, and even murdered'. Each new printing corrected by hand the number of victims as more Black women were murdered: within a month, *Six Black Women* had become *Eleven Black Women*.

This urgent temporality is further emphasized in a poem by Ntozake Shange included in some printings as an accompanying pamphlet (Smith 2014, 280). Shange's 'choropoem' *for colored girls who have considered suicide when the rainbow is enuff* (1974-1976), its form influenced by Judy Grahn's 'Common Woman' poems, had been a central and controversial text in the developing articulation of Black feminism—Smith would later call it 'our truth in artistic form' (280).[9] 'with no immediate cause', first published the previous year, likewise takes statistics as its point of departure.[10]

> every 3 minutes a woman is beaten
> every five minutes a
> woman is raped / every ten minutes
> a lil girl is molested
>
> (Shange, 111)

These statistics form the brunt of the poem's shocking reiteration of the everyday nature of gender violence, minute by minute, hour by hour, day by day. Appropriating the language of a newspaper article that worries 'women will murder batterers with no immediate cause', Shange uses these statistics to challenge official narratives which refuse to find a unifying 'cause' in the structural misogyny. But, while white feminist activism often called for increased police presence and other state-based solutions, neither Shange nor Combahee appeal to state authorities as a locus of correction or prevention.[11] Shange instead stages a confrontation with male readers, interrogating the communities into which her words are delivered.

218 NEVER BY ITSELF ALONE

> [. . .] i must know/
> have you hurt a woman today
> did you beat a woman today [. . .]
>
> i have to ask these obscene questions
> the authorities require me to
> establish
> immediate cause
>
> every three minutes
> every five minutes
> every ten minutes
> every day.

(113)

If state and media refuse to see the connections in 'crimes of passion', the speaker presents the horrific possibility that she *cannot* know—and thus must assume—that every man she encounters is capable of lethal gender violence. Shange opens up dialogue with heterosexual men, forcing them to consider their own violence, or their silence on the issue that acts as tacit approval. With desperate urgency, the poem links abstracted, statistical time to the real time experience of reading, refusing to be put off until later. In the context of the Combahee pamphlet, the poem is rendered more urgent yet. In contrast to a book, purchased for later contemplation, the pamphlet emphasizes immediacy: handed out in the street, posted through a letterbox, read on the move. In spring 1979, time was running out, and the particular, performative temporalities of poetry and of the pamphlet were urgent and specific ways of sounding the alarm.

'A Chorale for Black Woman Voices': Audre Lorde's 'Need'

Combahee's use of Shange's poem in *Why Did They Die?* built on existent overlaps with Boston poetry communities. In October 1978, the specially formed 'Bessie Smith Memorial Collective'—involving Barbara Smith, Beverly Smith, and Lorraine Bethel, alongside white feminist photographer Tia Cross (Barbara Smith's then partner) and women's health activist Emily Culpepper—had organized a series of concerts/readings entitled 'The Varied Voices of Black Women', featuring Pat Parker; singers Linda Tillery, Mary Watkins, and Gwen Avery; and popular vocal group Sweet Honey in the Rock, at venues including Framingham Women's Prison (Breines, 164–65). The following summer, Combahee drew on this work to publicize the Campaign for Women's Safety. On

'WE CANNOT LIVE WITHOUT OUR LIVES' 219

the weekend of July 6–July 8, Combahee held its Fifth Black Feminist Retreat at the Boston Women's Center. Coinciding with the retreat, Combahee and the CWS organized two poetry readings: the first on Friday at the Solomon Carter Fuller Mental Health Center in the South End, the second at Harvard University's Fuller Theater on Saturday (Duchess Harris 2019, 4). At the first event, *Off Our Backs* reported, 'an audience of over 200 black and white feminists' heard the work of eight writers: Fahamisha Shariat Brown (later a literary critic), Barbara and Beverly Smith, Kate Rushin, Audre Lorde, activists Faun Wilkerson and Yvonne Flowers, and Dianna Christmas, who later co-ran Sistahs' Bookstore and worked in AIDS-related health services, running a support group for lesbians of colour at the Dimock Community Healthy Center (Dejanikus, 14; Devall, n.p.; Sandy Coleman 1995, 249, 258; Briggs, 10) Following a minute's silence for the murdered women, the event opened with music by feminist percussion and woodwind ensemble La Triba.[12] At Harvard, to another standing-room-only crowd, Lorde read her poems 'The Evening News', addressed to Winnie Mandela, and the newly written 'Need', alongside Adrienne Rich—herself a previous resident of Boston—and Barbara Smith (Devall).[13]

Lorde's Boston reading came soon after her first visit to her mother's birthplace, Grenada, and soon before she delivered famed address, 'The Master's Tools Will Never Dismantle the Master's House', at the Second Sex Conference in New York (Hall 2004, xxxii). Aware of her status as a rising star in the feminist movement, both Lorde, and Adrienne Rich lent weight to the campaign through their celebrity and support. Yet, as Kate Rushin reports, when a journalist sought to interview Lorde for a Boston alternative newspaper, Lorde instead—characteristically— 'encouraged the[m] to talk to women from the area' (the newspaper declined to publish 'a story about unpublished, local Black women writers') (Lorde 1997, 96). Gaps in the available record—the absence of the story Rushin mention or of a recording of the event—make it hard to reconstruct that community in detail. Nonetheless, 'Need', with its explicitly collective in its address to the murders, serves as a vital index of poetry's role within this charged moment of community building. Building on Alexis Pauline Gumbs' exemplary analysis of the poem—thus far its only substantial reading in existing scholarship—it's to 'Need' that I turn now.[14]

Christening Boston 'Raceville' in mordant echo of Sharpeville, Lorde, as Barbara Smith notes, 'really didn't like Boston' (Ross, 74). During her travels, she had, however, been closely following the Boston campaign through news clippings sent to her by Smith (Smith 2014, 280), and in May 1979, drafted a poem which addressed the murders head on.[15] Listed as 'a dramatic reading for three women's voices', 'Need' first appeared in print in the Third World Women's issue of *Heresies*. In these contexts, it built on increasing momentum around the issue of gender violence in the work of Black women poets. A previous issue of

220   NEVER BY ITSELF ALONE

Heresies on women and violence had printed Shange's 'with no immediate cause', Lorde's poem forming part of an already-established dialogue, alongside Shange's poem in the *Why Did They Die?* pamphlet. That same month, Shange addressed these questions further in two poems printed in the 'Black Sexism Debate' issue of *The Black Scholar* alongside Lorde's essay 'The Great American Disease'; following the essay 'Against the Wall' from 1978, their mutual friend June Jordan would publish 'Case in Point'—in which she recounts being assaulted by the head of the local NAACP—'Rape Is Not a Poem' and 'Poem About My Rights' in her 1980 collection *Passion*.[16] In addition, 'Need' builds on Pat Parker's choric 'Movement in Black', first performed in December 1977, and 'Womanslaughter', which addressed the murder of Parker's sister Shirley Jones by her husband, appearing as the title poem to Parker's 1978 Diana Press pamphlet.[17]

'Need' is both dedicated to and partially spoken in the voices of two murdered women: Bobbie Jean Graham, killed in Boston in early May, and, Patricia Cowan, murdered in Michigan two years prior. Graham was kicked to death by her partner, who fled to Seattle and was not convicted until 1989 (*Commonwealth vs. Delrue Lafayette Anderson*); auditioning for a play called *Hammer* in Detroit, Cowan was hammered to death by the playwright ('Actress Is Slain'; Deroze, 1–4). From the start, Lorde's poem confronts its auditors with the violence enshrined in familiar uses of language, its nursery rhyme epigraph enacting a cruel pedagogy of (male) violence and (female) silence:

> *Tattle-tale tit*
> *your tongue will be slit*
> *and every little boy in town*
> *shall have a little bit.*
>
> (Lorde 1979, 112)[18]

In 1978, Frances Cress Welsing's vituperative attack on Barbara Smith had invoked the figure of the Black lesbian as embodiment of the threat of genocide to Black communities; likewise, debate in venues such as the 'Black Sexism Debate' issue of *The Black Scholar* singled out writers such as Shange for drawing attention to gender violence within Black communities, arguing that such critiques participated in racist persecution of Black men by the state. Lorde turns such figures on their head. Rather than 'tattle-tale tit'—snitch, informant, or genocidal threat—it is Black women who are at risk from an epidemic of violence bordering on genocide.

Following the epigraph, the poem begins:

> This woman is black
> so her blood is shed into silence.
>
> (Lorde 1979, 112)

'WE CANNOT LIVE WITHOUT OUR LIVES' 221

If the nursery rhyme is a kind of adaptable, misogynist curse, capable of being hurled at anyone by whom a (male) speaker feels aggrieved, these opening lines add the cause-and-effect of race to the rhyme's generalized violence: *because* this woman is black, her death is ignored. In the following stanzas, Lorde speaks out against such silence in monologues from each of the murdered women, pointing out the disconnect between state discourse on gender violence and the blunt fact of physical death.

> the police call it a crime of passion
> not a crime of hatred
> but you still die
> with a lacerated liver
> and a man's heel imprinted upon your chest.

In the poet's own voice, shocking images of sexual violence are juxtaposed with the repeated word 'blood'— the blood of murdered and raped women, the menstrual blood that traditionally marks out femininity, and the designation 'blood' as affectionate term of (masculinized) racial belonging— presenting such gendered assault, not as unconnected incidents, but as part of a 'bloody war'.

> Dead black women haunt the black maled streets
> paying the cities' secret and familiar tithe of blood
> burn blood beat blood cut blood
> seven year old child rape victim blood blood
> of a sodomized grandmother blood blood
> on the hands of my brother blood
> and his blood clotting in the teeth of a stranger [...]
> is it our blood that keeps these cities fertile? [...]
>
> blood blood of my sisters fallen in this bloody war

The poem's second part turns to address a male second-person figure aligned specifically with the murderers of Graham and Thomas, but also with the more generalized perpetrators of violence against women. In Graham's voice, Lorde asks—

> And what do you need me for, brother
> to move for you, feel for you, die for you?
> You have a grave need for me

—and in Cowan's:

222 NEVER BY ITSELF ALONE

> When you opened my head with your hammer
> did the boogie stop in your brain
> the beat go on
> the   terror run out of you like curdled fury
> a half-smile on your lips?

(113)

Here 'borrowed' discourse covers over the acts of violence from which Black women die daily.

> Borrowed hymns veil a misplaced hatred
> saying you need me you need me you need me
> like a broken drum
> calling me black goddess black hope black strength
> black mother
> you touch me
> and I die in the alleys of Boston[19]

Borrowed from whom? Lorde daringly implies that the Black Nationalist rhetoric posed against white power structures shares their very terms—the 'master's tools' she would speak of in relation to white feminism later that year—of sexual possession, conquest, and violence, those tools literalized in the hammer used to murder Patricia Cowan. Identifying the expression of false need with 'a broken drum', Lorde fuses the 'drumbeat' figurations of Black Power discourse and the gendered trope established by Duke Ellington's and Billy Strayhorn's *A Drum Is a Woman* (1956) with the figure of a 'broken [i.e. stuck] record', repeating the idealized Nationalist discourse of 'queens', 'mothers', and 'goddesses' while covering over the realities of gender violence. Sonically, the poem enacts this very process, the B's of 'blood', 'broken', and 'black' to 'Boston' establishing their own broken beat, linking the very language that purports to celebrate women ('black goddess black hope black strength') to the continuing flow of 'blood' in Boston alleys such language explains away—both broken record and propulsive drumbeat, a series of blows from 'a singing hammer'.[20] 'Need' ventriloquizes the very language it challenges, presenting the flipside to police silence and to the idealized, heteropatriarchal Black family: intimate partner violence, murder, and dismemberment, and the ultimate taboo, the rape of children and the elderly. From such violence flows the sacrificial 'blood that keeps this city fertile', 'shed into silence' that surrounds it on all sides.

Insisting that the poem is of value only if it speaks of real and urgent need to replace the false 'need / that tastes like destruction', a short coda seeks clarity:

'WE CANNOT LIVE WITHOUT OUR LIVES' 223

> The simplest part of this poem
> is the truth in each one of us
> to which it is speaking.

Yet clarity comes at price:

> How much of this truth can I bear to see
> and still live
> unblinded?
> How much of this pain
> can I use?

The poem's final line does not answer these questions directly but instead invokes a slogan which appeared on a banner carried by members of Combahee during the 1979 campaign:

> *"We can not live without our lives."*[21]

Combahee had taken this phrase from the 1974 book of the same name by (white) queer pacifist activist and author Barbara Deming, who had in turn adapted it from Emily Brontë's *Wuthering Heights*, in which it is spoken by Heathcliff following Cathy's death ('I cannot live without my life! I cannot die without my soul!') (Deming, 52). In her essay 'Two Perspectives on Women's Struggle', Deming uses the phrase to analyse the damage caused by the gendered split between 'the so-called masculine and the so-called feminine', in which 'womanliness has been defined as the nurturing of selves other than our own—even if we quite lose our own in the process' (60). For Deming, this split 'has had fatal consequences [. . .] a man is taught violence at his mother's knee, as he watches her left her Self be taken away from her' (61, 63). 'Need' literalizes Deming's metaphor, linking the violence taught at the mother's knee, in nursery rhymes, and in the heteropatriarchal discourses of both white supremacy and its male opponents of whatever race, to the deaths of Black women in Boston and beyond. Yet in proclaiming this phrase, the poem also establishes a performative coalition, however provisional, within the shared space of the Solomon Carter Fuller Center or the Sanders Theatre, marching in the streets, or in the pages of *Heresies* or *The Black Scholar*. This dimension is further emphasized in later revisions: whereas 'Need' originally ends with the poet's voice alone, in the revised version published by Kitchen Table Press in 1990, the final line is spoken twice as a call and response with the audience, the speaker's reflection on communal possibilities echoed back to her by auditors. *Audience* rather than just *reader* is a key modality here. Lorde's 'Need', Shange's *for coloured girls*, and

224 NEVER BY ITSELF ALONE

Parker's 'Movement in Black', are all poems that require more than one voice. Written to be recited in and into social spaces, they urgently address a specific moment, yet exist beyond any one campaign.[22]

The continuing importance of 'Need' is indicated by its multiple reprints: from *Heresies* to *The Black Scholar*, Persephone Press's *Lesbian Poetry: An Anthology* (1981) to Cleis Press's *Fight Back! Feminist Resistance to Male Violence* (1981), Amina and Amiri Baraka's *Confirmation: An Anthology of African American Women* (1983) to Lorde's *Chosen Poems* (1982), and finally, the Kitchen Table pamphlet (1990). The latter was, Lorde notes,

> created for particular use in classes, small community meetings, families, churches, and discussion groups, to open a dialogue between and among black women and black men on the subject of violence against women within our communities. Alterations in the text since the poem was originally published are a result of hearing the poem read aloud several times by groups of women. (Lorde 1990, 3)

Poetry here forms a bridge between activism and literary longevity, reader and audience. The poem is not a singular object or a singular occasion but part of an ongoing dialogue, a dialogue that must exist for as long as women continue to be murdered. 'Need' challenges the deathly histories from which it emerged, the deathly silences into which blood continues to be shed, constructing a community reconstituted in each reading. It's to further articulations of community emerging from the 1979 campaign that I now turn.

From Metaphor to Movement: *This Bridge Called My Back*

This Bridge and Kitchen Table Press

Despite the increasing presence of writers of colour within feminist and lesbian feminist publications, virtually every magazine and every press associated with the movement was controlled by white women, with the notable exception of *Azalea: A Magazine by Third World Lesbians* (1977–1983) formed by the Salsa Soul Sisters, one of the first Black lesbian groups in the country. Plans drawn up for a not-for-profit Black women's publishing network provisionally named Kizzy Enterprises by a group, including Shange, Alice Walker, Toni Morrison, and June Jordan, in 1977 never went beyond the discussion stage. The same year, Lorde was appointed poetry editor of Los Angeles–based magazine *Chrysalis;* frustrated by the journal's treatment of writers of colour, she resigned in 1979, against the backdrop of the Roxbury murders—a time when she was also involved in a dispute with Boston College professor and prominent lesbian feminist Mary Daly over Daly's exclusion of Black women's experiences from her book *Gyn/Ecology* (Gumbs 2010, 385).[23]

Separately but simultaneously, Gloria Anzaldúa, facing similar frustrations on the West Coast, proposed to fellow Chicana lesbian writer Cherríe Moraga that they co-edit an anthology of women of colour writing. Having considered the titles 'Smashing the Myth!' and 'Radical Third World Feminists' Anthology: A Woman-to-Woman Dialogue', the editors eventually settled on *This Bridge Called My Back* (Meredith Benjamin 2021, 53). Both writers had moved to San Francisco in 1977—Anzaldúa from Texas and Moraga from Los Angeles—both were politically active, and both wrote across poetry and prose. Meeting through the Berkeley-based Feminist Writers' Guild (FWG), the two soon grew dissatisfied with the organization's racist and classist belittling of their concerns ('Biographical Sketch, n.d.'; *Feminist Writers' Guild* 1979, 1) As Anzaldúa noted, '[FWG members'] whiteness covered everything they said. However, they wanted me to [. . .] leave my race at the door' (Ikas, 5), while Moraga wryly observed: 'Ironically, here I'm supposed to be dealing with oppression, [. . .] [and] I've never seen so much wealth in my life!' (Anderson 2005, 49). Leaving the FWG to concentrate on the anthology, Anzaldúa and Moraga drew significant inspiration from Combahee, reprinting the 1977 statement following its initial appearance in Zillah Eisenstein's 1978 anthology *Capitalist Patriarchy and the Case for Socialist Feminism* (Moraga 1983, 133). In July 1980, Moraga travelled to Boston to discuss prospects for the anthology, staying with Barbara Smith. Visiting a New England Women's Studies Association (NEWSA) organizational meeting to discuss the proposed anthology, the experiences that had played out in San Francisco were once more repeated, Smith's reaction giving rise to the book's organizing metaphor: 'Barbara said to me, "It's so hard to be a bridge: that's the thing, a bridge gets walked over"' (*This Bridge*, xxxviii). Over the following months, the anthology itself bridged the two cities, Moraga returning to San Francisco that August and briefly moving in with Anzaldúa as the two continued to work on the anthology before departing for Boston to be with Smith, with whom she was now romantically involved.

Anzaldúa and Moraga had placed the book with the Massachusetts-based lesbian feminist Persephone Press, run by white publishers Pat McGloin and Gloria Z. Greenfield. Yet tensions soon emerged. A Boston launch for the Press's *Lesbian Poetry* anthology, edited by Ellly Bulkin and Joan Larkin in May 1981, was attended by 900 people (Dearborn); the following month, the launch for *This Bridge*, the audience had dwindled by half (Tilchen; Lovelock; Fiorenza, 15).[24] Though the event was still attended by 500 people—indicating the strong climate for lesbian feminist poetry in Boston at the time—as Veneita Porter observed in her *Gay Community News* report: 'It [is] clear that Third World Women's events are

226 NEVER BY ITSELF ALONE

not a priority in *any* community' (Porter, 8). Meanwhile, following Persephone's rejection of a manuscript by Hattie Gossett and their abrupt termination of a contract held by Jan Clausen, authors of colour were intensely aware of the power imbalance between themselves and white publishers.[25] Smith and Moraga wrote to McGloin and Greenfield: 'You hold the purse strings. That's a fact . . . We can't change the fact that you have the resources and financial power that, if shared, are indeed beneficial to us' (Enszer 2013, 177). The issue was exacerbated by precarious employment: for writers of colour with no regular source of income, royalty payments were vital. Barbara Smith inaugurated a conflict-resolution meeting with Persephone in 1982; the following year, themselves affected by the economic downturn, Persephone declared bankruptcy, selling their catalogue to Beacon Books.[26]

But Lorde, Moraga, Smith, and others had themselves been taking concrete steps toward self-determination in publishing. Following a prepublication reading for *This Bridge* co-organized in Roxbury by Combahee and the Bessie Smith Memorial Collective on Halloween 1980, Lorde initiated a meeting at Smith's house to discuss the possibility of forming a press controlled entirely by women of colour. The meeting was attended by Lorde, Smith, Moraga, Kate Rushin, and Myrna Bain (Smith 2014, 149).[27] Kitchen Table: Women of Color Press (KTP) was announced at the Women in Print Conference at Washington, DC the following year, initially distributing Cheryl Clarke's self-published *Narratives: Poems in the Tradition of Black Women* (1982) (Enszer 2013, 208). Negotiating back the rights to *This Bridge*, Kitchen Table published a second edition, now 'conceived of and produced entirely by women of colour', in 1983. Highlighting writing by 'Third World Women of all racial/cultural heritages, sexualities, and classes' (Smith 2014, 246), KTP furthered the Black feminist networks of the Combahee retreats and the 1979 campaign, publishing work by Merle Woo, Mitsuye Yamada, and Filipina dissident poet Mila D. Aguilar alongside anthologies like *This Bridge, Home Girls*, and *Cuentos: Stories for Latinas*. At conferences, KTP's book table would become what Smith called 'a political gathering point' (Enszer 2013, 214).

This Bridge in many ways emblematized KTP's project. Emerging out of frustration at being a 'bridge' between white feminists and communities of colour, the book also manifests a more positive sense of bridge building: a work-in progress, an opening, a home-in-motion, rather than temporary tokenism. Its genre-crossing, communal, dialogic form extended beyond the page. In 1981, Anzaldúa and Moraga curated a series of readings from the anthology on the East Coast, seeking to 'make it into a 'performance' rather than just a reading'. Writing to participants ahead of the June 5 Boston launch, Moraga explained:

Since the evening involves a dramatic presentation of the book, each person will receive a script when she arrives, indicating her part [. . .] Everyone will read a short excerpt from their own work & then read a piece from someone else's & then participate in one-liners & chorus parts. Barbara Smith, Kate Rushin, & I have put this thing together to cover the book thematically. (Benjamin 2021, 57)

Arranged into four acts corresponding to sections in the book, these collective performances were tools of coalition building with other women of colour, in which frustrations with white feminism could be openly expressed. At the Boston event, participants performed in front of the banner from the 1979 campaign that proclaimed, 'WE CANNOT LIVE WITHOUT OUR LIVES', extending the work begun two years before. In *Gay Community News*, Veneita Porter describes 'this whole rainbowed group of women spit out every clichéd piece of white liberal rhetoric that you, as a woman of color, have ever heard, even in your most well-meaning women's group' (Porter, 9).[28] Titled 'Chile Let Me Tell You: Racism Movement Style' and attributed to Kate Rushin, the section to which Porter refers was made up entirely of lines paraphrased or quoted from elsewhere (Benjamin 2021, 58). Borrowing the anecdotal structure of consciousness-raising groups, the performance turns racial microaggressions that otherwise pass unnoticed into staged, dramatic dialogue, forcing a confrontation with white women's racism as Shange and Lorde forced conformation with gender violence, and provoking recognition and realization for both women of colour and white women in the audience. Meanwhile, the final act, structured around the refrain from Rushin's 'Bridge Poem', turned the statement of being used—of being the bridge that is 'walked over' by white women—into choric affirmation of power. Porter reports:

Taking the stage together, dressed in reds, blacks, and whites, the ten women chanted, singly then in unison, from a whisper to a shout . . . This Bridge Called My Back . . . This *Bridge* Called My Back . . . *This Bridge Called My Back. Our work is to make revolution irresistible.* (Porter, 9)

Repeating the singular possessive together, this chorus defiantly turns from individual silencing to collective speaking out. Yet, as Meredith Benjamin notes, 'the refrain does not explain what the bridge is, critique or celebrate it, only emphasizes its existence' (Benjamin 2021, 59–60). In the following section, I'll now turn more specifically to the ambiguities inherent in the bridge metaphor as they manifest in texts by Moraga and Rushin.

228   NEVER BY ITSELF ALONE

'Making some sense of the trip'

As Lizzy LeRud notes, metaphors of bridges and backs 'circled widely among social and political groups of this era', from the feminist newspaper *Off Our Backs* to the journal *Bridges: An Asian American Perspective*, and the anthology of Black women in literature, *Sturdy Black Bridges* (1979) (Le Rud 2017, 206, fn. 7). But importantly, *This Bridge* also plays on notions of movement in time and place: the connections, as well as the blocks, between women, between cities, in the process of building women-of-colour feminism from local instantiation to political movement. Such concerns are exemplified in Moraga's preface, later retitled 'La Jornada'. Writing in journal form, Moraga recounts her experiences seeking a publisher for *This Bridge* in Boston in summer 1980 and her subsequent return to San Francisco, movements which metaphorically and literally hinge her analysis. Moving, in the opening section, from the comfortable suburbs of Watertown, Massachusetts, where Persephone was based, to Barbara Smith's home in Roxbury, Moraga takes Boston's class and race segregation as metaphor for wider problematics.

> Take Boston alone, I think to myself, and the feminism my so-called sisters have constructed does nothing to help me make the trip from one end of town to another. Leaving Watertown, I board a bus and ride it quietly in my light flesh to Harvard Square, protected by the gold highlights my hair dares to take on, like an insult, in this miserable heat.
> *I transfer, and go underground.* (*This Bridge*, xxxvi)

Moraga recalls Julie, a friend stopped for walking through the suburbs, subject to gender and racial policing—'Can't tell if it's a man or a woman, only know that it's Black moving through that part of town'; witnesses undercover police arresting a 'black kid' on the subway; and recalls the murder of a fourteen-year-old Black boy the previous day. 'I hear there are some women in this town plotting a *lesbian revolution*', she writes. 'What does this mean about the boy shot in the head is what I want to know'. 'Lesbianism is supposed to be about connection', Moraga argues, yet white lesbian separatism has instead fostered division and exclusivity, constituting 'the deepest political tragedy I have experienced [. . .] I call white women on this' (*This Bridge* xxxvii). Instead, 'I want a movement that helps me make some sense of the trip from Watertown to Roxbury, from white to Black. I love women the entire way, beyond a doubt' (*This Bridge* xxxvi).

Mapping the question of a political movement onto bus and train transfers shaped by knowledge of the busing crisis, Moraga's method is at once metonymic and specific, the details she observes in turn haunted by Boston's

'WE CANNOT LIVE WITHOUT OUR LIVES' 229

shift from industrial town to service economy—itself part of broader processes of globalization—and the conditions of white flight, suburbanization, and the destruction and scapegoating of racialized communities—of which the destruction of queer enclaves such as Scollay Square and the West End in the 1950s, earlier noted by John Wieners and Stephen Jonas, were the first premonitions.[29] On the one hand, 'going underground' provides an analogy for movement building. On arriving in Roxbury, Barbara Smith greets Moraga with a proclamation of sisterhood, sealed by a kiss and embrace. Such loving solidarity, Moraga writes, is 'earned' rather than 'a given', offsetting the 'pain and shock of difference' with 'the joy of commonness, the exhilaration of meeting through incredible odds against it' (*This Bridge*, xxxvi). On the other hand, the movement across the city and across raced and classed lines it maps—itself a kind of 'bridging'—creates a feeling of exhaustion, as Moraga struggles to contain within herself the distance between the white women, Moraga's temporarily ungendered friend Julie, and the teenager shot by a cop.

Preparing to return to San Francisco five days later, Moraga laments the feeling that white feminists use 'my body to be walked over to make a connection', asking:

> *How can we—this time—not use our bodies to be thrown over a river of tormented history to bridge the gap?* Barbara says last night: 'A bridge gets walked over'. Yes, over and over and over again. (xxxvii)

Back in San Francisco the following month, the bridge metaphor stands in for the collapse of usable connections between women—friends, family, and lovers. Moraga names the 'calculated system of damage, intended to ensure our separation from other women [. . .] The failure between lovers, sisters, mother and daughter—the betrayal. How have we turned our backs on each other— the bridge collapsing' (xxxix). Nonetheless, Moraga finds a renewed sense of community in gathering with 'Five avowed Latina Feminists'—Anzaldúa, Jo Carillio, Aurora Levin Morales, Chabela (Isabel Yrigoyen), and Mirtha Quintanales—all of whom but Chabela appear in the anthology.

> [We] walk down Valencia Street singing songs in Spanish [. . .] buy burritos y cerveza from 'La Cumbre' and talk our heads off into the night, crying from the impact of such a reunion.
> *Si, son mis comadres.* Something my mother had with her women friends and sisters. Coming home. (xxxix)

Echoing the book's jointly authored introduction, which ends '[t]he revolution begins at home', and anticipating Smith's *Home Girls*, the metaphor of

230 NEVER BY ITSELF ALONE

homecoming joins that of the bridge in sisterhood's alternative 'family': the sense of togetherness with other women, both geographical and metaphorical; the occupation of space as racialized subjects without fear.

In the final section, Moraga refigures the bridge metaphor in a more hopeful light—not the experience of being walked over, or of women 'turn[ing] our backs on each other', but of those who band together as 'women without a line [. . .] who contradict each other' (xli), who voluntarily assume the bridge functions *together*, rather than as solitary bridges for white women to step over. Moraga concludes:

> For the women in this book, I will lay my body down for that vision. *This Bridge Called My Back*.
> In my dream, I am always met at this river. (xli)

'The Bridge Poem': Kate Rushin

Boston poet Kate Rushin had played an important role in the 1979 campaign, reading at the Solomon Carter Fuller Center and again at the prepublication reading for *This Bridge* in 1980. Overhearing Barbara and Beverly Smith discuss the title to the anthology at the latter event, Rushin had debuted her 'Bridge Poem', prompting Moraga to request its inclusion. (Hogan 2016, 75–76), As Catherine London wrote of Rushin's recitation at the Boston launch the following year, 'The Bridge Poem' was 'the focal point [. . .] cause to hold one's breath to avoid missing a syllable' (London 1981, 32), and its subsequent importance to the book is indicated by its placement immediately before Moraga's preface as the only work of poetry in the frontmatter.[30] Like 'La Jornada', the poem embraces (and rejects) contradictory definitions of the bridge in a manner that still speaks to the complexities and contradictions of identity politics today.

Moving from New Jersey to Boston in 1976 to take up a three-year position as poet in residence in the schools, Rushin was thrown into the ongoing violence of the city's busing crisis (Hogan 2016, 77). Travelling to work in South Boston, she was advised not to ride the bus and instead picked up in a van by school workers. One day, Rushin decided to take the bus and walk to the school: following a bus ride on which she and the driver were the only people of colour, Rushin encountered racist abuse from pupils outside the school gates. As she recounts:

> I walked up the steps, I just kept going. I put my hand just like this, put my hand on the door to go into the school; a bottle shattered next to me, right in the

corner, and then I went in. And I went right to class, because I had my workshop to teach. On my way to class I saw the headmaster, and I told him what had happened, and his response was, 'Well, you know, we can't be responsible for you outside of the school'. (Hogan 2016, 77)

As such stories indicate, Rushin functioned in her job as a 'bridge' between communities, in tandem with the desegregation process in Boston's public school system, a position not merely exhausting but also dangerous. No wonder the speaker of 'The Bridge Poem' begins by rejecting the bridge function:

> I've had enough
> I'm sick of seeing and touching
> Both Sides of things
> I'm sick of being the damn bridge for everybody.
> (*This Bridge*, xxxiii)[31]

The poem's third stanza lists those the speaker must 'explain' to each other: all the various groups in which she moves—family members, members of different class brackets, race brackets, sex brackets—'I explain my mother to my father [...] The white feminist to the Black Church folks'—ending with a mordant joke: 'I do more translating / than the Gawdamn UN'. Reiterating such frustration— 'Forget it / I'm sick of it'—a new set of repetitions enumerate all the tasks of which the speaker is 'sick', ending: '[I'm] Sick of being the sole black friend to 34 individual white people' (xxxiv). Addressing a second-person subject aligned with these 'white people', Rushin writes: 'Find another connection to the rest of the world / Find something else to make you legitimate'. Refusing to be 'the bridge to your womanhood', she metaphorically demolishes the bridge, proclaiming, 'Stretch or drown / Evolve or die', and proposing, 'I must be the bridge to nowhere / but my true self'. This is not, however, an individualist rejection of community. As the bridge to their true self, the speaker proclaims: 'And then / I will be useful'. The poem does not specify to whom the speaker will be useful: this open-endedness is precisely the point, for the community which takes into account all the facets of Rushin's identity as Black lesbian feminist does not yet exist in socially sanctioned form.

As Julie Enszer argues, while both poem and anthology 'embrace the metaphor of a bridge to build a new world, they also decline the role of a bridge for individual women of color', thus creating a 'dynamic tension between how organizations could operate in making new worlds through coalition work and how individual bodies were situated, often forced to do bridging work to the exclusion of their own self interest—of discovering their "true selves"' (Enszer 2013, 221–22). Such tensions were not easily resolved. Given Boston's racism,

232 NEVER BY ITSELF ALONE

many of the writers addressed in this chapter chose to move away, even as the energies of 1979 fed into the 'rainbow coalition' of Mel King's 1984 mayoral campaign (Dejanikus and Kelly 1979, 26; Smith 2014, 74).

Yet Rushin remained a key presence. In the early 1980s, she began to work at the New Words Bookstore in Cambridge. As Laura Zimmerman would write on Rushin's retirement from the bookstore in 1992:

> It wasn't clear if the customers came to buy books or to catch a glimpse of Kate Rushin, Boston's best-loved poet [. . .] Kate comes closer than any of us to keeping that perennial finger on the pulse of the community. Someone is always asking for her name [. . .] all our guidebooks and journals together don't begin to offer the knowledge Kate carries in her head of what's going on locally, nationally, and internationally. If she's not directly involved in a project or event, she knows who is, and links the stories with each of them [. . .] though she only recently began teaching African American Women's Literature at MIT, she's been educating us and many of our customers on this subject since she first came to the store. (Zimmerman, 41)

Rushin's largely unremarked presence at New Words represents a long-term commitment to community building that parallels Smith's dedication to Kitchen Table Press, and the ongoing coalitions and conversations fostered by Combahee and *This Bridge*, and her public reputation as a poet in the local area belies her virtual absence from scholarship.[32] Likewise, her first and only collection, *The Black Back-Ups*, published by Ithaca-based lesbian feminist press Firebrand Books in 1993 consistently locates the individual voice in the context of community. Dedicating the book to the memory of her grandparents, her mother, and the recently departed Lorde, the acknowledgement page in addition forms a virtual community, listing friends and supporters from New Words Collective to Stone Soup founder Jack Powers; Moraga and Anzaldúa to members of Combahee; Cheryl Clarke, Jewelle Gomez, and other important Black lesbian writers to Umbra Workshop co-founder Calvin Hernton, who taught Rushin at Oberlin College (Rushin 1993, 5–6). Taking the figure of Black female backing singers—notably those interpellated as 'coloured girls' as part of the racial tourism in Lou Reed's hit 'Walk on the Wild Side'—the title poem brings them, finally, to centre stage. Interweaving dedications in the body of the poem itself, Rushin lists singers from Fontella Bass and Gwen Guthrie to 'all of the Black women who sang back-up for / Elvis Presley, John Denver, James Taylor, Lou Reed. / Etc. Etc. Etc.' (18). Following the quoted chorus from Reed's song, the dedications continue—family members, 'Black women riding on buses and subways', and mothers and domestic servants—continuing through the poem from Hattie McDaniel and Aunt Jemima to 'mama', and ending with another dedication: 'This is for the thousand thousand Black Back-Ups' (20–21). Such dedications, at once loving and ironic, recall the lists of 'The Bridge Poem', but here they are amassed as a chorus for and through whom the poet speaks, rather than as an unbearable burden on the self as bridge.

In 'The Black Back-Ups' (as individual poem), self and community sing together, displacing white male narratives through reappropriating the very form—the Black back-up singer—that these singers in turn appropriated from Black music and its gendered labour. *The Black Back-Ups* (as book) further suggests a community in miniature, traversing Montgomery, Alabama, to West Africa, Boston to Syracuse to Camden, New Jersey, in poems assembled over many years, from newer work to those familiar to local communities, lightly revised and altered over time.[33] Rushin reprints 'The Bridge Poem' a third of the way through (33–35), and the book reads as an extended exploration of the bridging metaphor, as sections of prose, reminiscing over her upbringing in New Jersey, alternate with poems—themselves often dedicated to figures from Rosa Parks to Bessie, the fictional girlfriend murdered by Bigger Thomas in Richard Wright's *Native Son*.[34] Paying attention to 'unpoetic' lives—to those of aunts, uncles, gender rebels, lesbian lovers—and setting them alongside a history of Black literature and culture, Rushin also refuses easy divisions of poetry and prose, lyric and narrative, presenting queer sexuality and gender nonconformity as part of a wider canvas of Black life. This is an expanded notion of literary, personal, and political community that does not shun trauma, pain, prejudice, and difficulty—what Anzaldúa called 'the enormous contradiction in being a bridge' (*This Bridge*, 206)—but harnesses them to build and rebuild that bridge, step by step: a task that is still ongoing.

Conclusion: Bridges to the Future, Survivals of the Past

Toni Cade Bambara's foreword to *This Bridge Called My Back* famously notes: 'Quite frankly, *This Bridge* needs no foreword. It is the Afterward that'll count' (xxxi). And while the metaphor of the bridge soon spilled out into academic and activist contexts, these bridges, coalitions, publications, recitations are bridges to a future that has not yet come. The following years saw both the consolidation of the work begun in 1979 and its vulnerability in the wake of economic depression, conservative backlash, and the increasing academic and institutional incorporation to which the movement was subject.[35] Often, the process of liberation was interrupted, as energies dissipated and moved elsewhere, class and race binaries remaining firmly intact, despite institutional gestures to 'diversity'.[36] At the time of writing, few of the feminist and lesbian periodicals that flourished in the 1970s and 1980s survive—though *Sinister*

234 NEVER BY ITSELF ALONE

Wisdom and *Lesbian Connection* are importantly still publishing. Kitchen Table Press, meanwhile, eventually folded in 1997. Despite the fame of Lorde, Combahee, and *This Bridge,* literary scholarship has been slow to pick up on this work: few scholars address 'Need' or 'The Bridge Poem', while the Combahee Statement is too often treated as a generalized signifier for Third Wave politics (often in tandem with Kimberlé Crenshaw's later coinage 'intersectionality'; Crenshaw, 139–76), its originating context in the working-class, coalitional, anti-racist activity of lesbian feminists in and around Boston overlooked.[37]

In turn, such neglect relates to the very real question of death and survival— not simply literary posterity, inclusion in the canon, or undying fame, but of simply being able to live. As Terrion Williamson observes in his article on the Roxbury campaign, 'the serial murders of Black women have continued unabated since 1979' (Williamson, 328). The term adds a terrible, deathly alternate dimension to the 'serial poem' discussed in earlier chapters, and Williamson's concept resonates more than ever in the wake of the continuing police murders of 2020, of 2021, of each succeeding year. As Lorde puts it, Black women's blood continues to be 'shed into silence', or, alternately, into grotesque hyper-visibility. A year before I first drafted this chapter in London, the bodies of the murdered sisters Bibaa Smallman and Nichole Henry were discovered by their families after police neglected to investigate their disappearance. Photographs of the bodies then circulated among a police WhatsApp group in what the victims' mother likened to a lynching (Quinn, n.p.; Dash, n.p.; 'Wembley Park Murders', n.p.). As James Baldwin argued of the Atlanta child murders in 1980, 'the publicity given to the slaughter becomes, itself, one more aspect of an unforgivable violation' (Baldwin 1985, 10). In a November 1979 journal entry, Lorde contended: 'I am not supposed to exist. I carry death around in my body like a condemnation. But I do live [. . .] There must be some way to integrate death into living, neither ignoring it nor giving in to it' (Lorde 1997, 11). During this period, both Lorde and Anzaldúa underwent major surgery for conditions of which both would pass away: Lorde, of breast cancer in November 1992, Anzaldúa of diabetes in May 2004.

Poetry can't bring back to life Lorde or Anzaldúa; it can't bring back to life Bibaa Smallman and Nicole Henry, Breonna Taylor, and Sandra Bland or the women murdered in Roxbury in the spring of 1979: Christine (Chris) Ricketts, fifteen years old; Andrea Foye, seventeen years old; Gwendolyn Yvette Stinson, fifteen years old; Caren Prater, twenty-five years old; Daryal Ann Hargett, twenty-nine years old; Desiree Denise Etheridge, seventeen years old; Darlene Rogers, twenty-two years old; Lois Hood Nesbitt, thirty-one years old; Valyric Holland, nineteen years old; Sandra Boulware, thirty years old; Bobbie Jean Graham, thirty-four years old. But it could and does survive them, and in it, part of them survives. Poetry's open temporality—its urgent questions, interrogative address, gesture of solidarity, and shifting metaphors—attests to the gaps that cannot be bridged, the silences that cannot speak, while paradoxically reaching across those gaps and speaking out of those silences. At least, that is what poets must believe.

In the following chapter, I examine these questions from a different location, turning to San Francisco at the beginning of the previous decade, and the means by which Bay Area poets set out to create a new lesbian poetic tradition that grew out of, but also outgrew, the canonical reclamations and innovations of the Women's Movement, giving voice to experience in common, standing up to death, and giving fresh hope.

PART III

BAY AREA COMMUNITIES

Lesbian Feminism to the AIDS Era (1969–Present)

Part III turns to the development of lesbian poetics in San Francisco, examining the work of Pat Parker and Judy Grahn, and of the socialist feminist poets Karen Brodine, Merle Woo, and Nellie Wong. The final chapter turns to New Narrative writing and questions of community building and the response to AIDS in the 1980s. A coda addresses subsequent legacies into the twenty-first century.

8
'She Who'

Judy Grahn and Bay Area Gay Women's Liberation

Formed in late 1969, the loose network initially known as Bay Area Gay Women's Liberation (GWL) soon came to form part of a local and national community, including the establishment of a 'knowledge economy' of women's households, presses, and bookstores, and the provision of resources for those who fell outside the support networks of family or state (*ASR*, 169). It was in response to the indifference with which Judy Grahn's position paper 'On the Development of a Purple Fist' had been received by a group of gay male activists that she and other women began separatist organizing, and this speech served as an important early articulation of a lesbian feminist politics. But it was Grahn's poetry that would give the movement its voice. 'Poetry', Grahn proclaimed at the inaugural Outwrite conference, held in San Francisco, in 1990, 'is the mapmaking of our movement [. . .] Poetry predicts us, tells us where we are going next [. . .] Poetry sets the rhythm for what we are doing as a group' (Enszer and Gross, 24). Yet she continues, 'if there is a gay or lesbian writer who has never done any organizing, that person is taking a free ride'. From 'going into the streets and public halls in action, shouting, risk-taking, demonstrating at top volume', to 'holding and attending endless dull meetings, or voter registering, or paper pushing of one kind or another', to the development of independent bookstores, distributors, and supply chains, and the work of care—'keeping [others] from suiciding or OD'ing or dying of poverty and despair and neglect'—the lesbian feminist poetry of the 1970s and beyond was produced in a community context and cannot be understood outside it (22–23). In the two chapters that follow, I read Grahn's poetry of the late 1960s and early 1970s and Pat Parker's up to her death in 1989 to examine the growth of Bay Area lesbian feminism, the embrace of separatism, and the (re)turn to coalitional organization during the Reagan era. 'As a feminist', Grahn states in her Outwrite keynote, 'I am not so much interested in taking back the night as I am in taking back the world' (26). As I go on to argue, the efforts of lesbian feminists to take back the world, in poetry and in activism, have lessons for us today.

Never By Itself Alone. David Grundy, Oxford University Press. © Oxford University Press 2024.
DOI: 10.1093/oso/9780197654842.003.0009

240　NEVER BY ITSELF ALONE

'A very dangerous box to fall out of'

Judy Grahn was born to working-class parents in Chicago in 1940. At the age of eight, her father, a Swedish-born labour organizer, was laid off from his job at Ingersoll's steel factory, so the family moved to Las Cruces, New Mexico, a town marked by 'colonial separation and injustice', near to which stood the White Sands Missile Range (*ASR*, 7, 26, 41). As Grahn suggests in her 2012 autobiography, *A Simple Revolution*, the traumatizing effects of factory labour and unemployment alike manifested in her family through addiction and mental illness. Nonetheless, she strikes a note of class pride: her parents, she recalls, were 'completely themselves, honest and true' (3, 26).

But if class was one thing, gender was another. 'As puberty set in,' Grahn writes, 'I was beginning to manifest a transgender sensibility and a lesbian sexual orientation that went beyond being a tomboy', conceiving of the 'luminous [. . .] in-between space of masculine and feminine' through Joan of Arc and 'that perfectly balanced, androgynous character of Puck' in *A Midsummer Night's Dream* (27, 31–32). 'At age sixteen', Grahn continues, 'I looked up the word 'lesbian' in the dictionary. No one I knew used that word [. . .] the gender box felt to be a very dangerous one to fall out of' (38).

Grahn left home at seventeen to attend New Mexico State University; at the age of eighteen, she met her first partner, schoolteacher Yvonne Robinson ('Von'), living with her in Portales, New Mexico (50–53). A year later, she followed her brother's lead and joined the military to pay her way through college, assigned to a base in Washington, DC (55). Though lesbian-baiting was not central to the logics of the Red and Lavender Scares, it served an important function at a time when female military service, previously necessitated by wartime mobilization, threatened existent gender boundaries (Del Rio, 60). And when Grahn revealed her sexuality to her commanding officer, she was interrogated, placed under barracks arrest, and subsequently discharged. As she notes: 'My country [. . .] wouldn't spend five thousand dollars to educate me, yet could spend tens of thousands of dollars to harass me, my friends, my lovers, and my family [. . .] Perhaps seventy-five to a hundred thousand national dollars was invested in criminalizing me' (*ASR*, 67).

As a result of this harassment, Yvonne Robinson was nearly fired from her job, and both she and Grahn's father temporarily broke off relations with Grahn (57, 68). Upon release, Grahn underwent psychoanalysis in Washington with Frank Caprio, author of the study *Female Homosexuality*, an experience satirized in her first major creative text, 'The Psychoanalysis of Edward the Dyke' (1965/71) (62). Reconciling with Robinson and entering the city's nascent lesbian bar scene, in 1964 Grahn was accepted as one of the few white students at the HBCU Howard University. Here, Grahn's teacher, sociologist

Nathan Hare—a few years later to play a key role in the Third World Students Strike in San Francisco—showed his class a copy of Daughters of Bilitis (D.O.B.) magazine *The Ladder* as a comparative example of 'minority' activism (69–70, 76–77). 'This', Grahn recalls, 'was the first openly positive response to Gay culture I had ever heard from a straight person, and I was singularly impressed' (*AMT*, xix). While in Washington, Grahn and Robinson became involved with the D.O.B.'s sister organization, the Mattachine Society, in April 1965 picketing the White House alongside a dozen other activists, including *Ladder* editor Barbara Gittings. Meanwhile, under a pseudonym, Grahn's essay 'A Lesbian Speaks Her Mind' appeared in long-running 'sex science' magazine *Sexology* (*ASR*, 78). There was, however, little organized outlet for a queer politic. It was in poetry, Grahn's 'first love', that these nascent concerns would find their first extended expression (81).

Edward the Dyke as Gender Outlaw

Dropping out of Howard, in late 1965 Grahn wrote 'The Psychoanalysis of Edward the Dyke', a satirical prose text inspired by her experience with Frank Caprio, here parodied as the money-obsessed psychoanalyst 'Doctor Merlin Knox'.[1] Challenging the respectability politics of the current homophile movement, along with existent medical frameworks for understanding queer sexuality, the piece could not be published until 1971, when, lending its title to Grahn's *Edward the Dyke and Other Poems*, it served as a founding text of Gay Women's Liberation. As well as reinforcing Grahn's later claim that poetry is frequently *in advance* of social movements, 'Edward' exists on multiple temporal levels: as a text written in the mid-'60s, that could not be published within this context; as a founding text of GWL; and, today, amidst often fractious debates about the relation between sexuality and gender identity.

The word 'dyke', Grahn suggests, was, at the time,

> more taboo to say out loud than lesbian or queer [. . .] It is a lower-class word, not written into literature or the dictionary [. . .] used, especially by lower-class, 'straight' people, to describe a tough, brave, bold Lesbian who is considered 'mannish' or 'butchy' in her characteristics or mannerisms [. . .] Dyke was one way of being a lesbian [. . .] [but] the word does not apply as much to her Lesbianism [. . .] as it does to her toughness. (*AMT*, 135)

As Catherine Irwin (2019) has suggested in an important recent article, Edward's is a challenge, not just to sexual but also to gender identity, as well as to the history of clinical attempts both to separate and blur the two.

242 NEVER BY ITSELF ALONE

'Dr. Knox', Edward began, 'my problem this week is chiefly concerning restrooms [...] Naturally I can't go into men's restrooms without feeling like an interloper, but on the other hand every time I try to use the ladies room I get into trouble'. (Grahn 1985, 26)

Edward goes on to recount being attacked in a female restroom by 'three middle-aged housewives [who] came in and thought I was a man', calling for help from a male cop who, in turn, opens fire on Edward. Here is a classic case of what Jack Halberstam famously identifies as 'the bathroom problem' affecting butch lesbian and trans subjects alike, in which the gender policing experienced in female restrooms reveals a deep-rooted anxiety about the extent to which gender boundaries are biologically signified and the extent to which they are culturally signified (Halberstam, 20). In Grahn's text, the housewives' attack is both cultural and biological: in 'screaming about how well did I know Gertrude Stein', they seek to read Edward through language as culturally a butch lesbian; in ripping off Edward's clothes, they seek to remove any traces of sartorial ambiguity by discovering the biologically signifying body beneath, thus, through physical violence, insisting that gender is bodily essence rather than a socially produced set of meanings. While the housewives identify Edward as 'biologically' female within a public space, Irwin suggests that, within the clinical setting, Dr. Knox instead misreads Edward as 'a gay man seeking sex reassignment surgery (SRS) who enters bathrooms not only to "compulsively attack" and "accost girls in restrooms," but also for other criminal "sexual escapades" '—that is, according to stereotypes of gay male public promiscuity—urging them instead 'to be the little girl you've always wanted to be' by amputating eight inches off their six-foot frame and increasing their breast size: 'nothing a few hormones can't accomplish in these advanced times' (Irwin 2019, 79; Grahn 1985, 27). For today's reader, Edward's gender may signify variously as butch lesbian, transmasculine, or transfeminine. What is clear is that, in refusing the category of either the 'well-adjusted lesbian' living within a conventional gender identity—Linda Garber's interpretation (Garber, 35)—or of the 'well-adjusted' transfeminine gay man—Irwin's— Edward has fallen out of what Grahn terms 'the gender box'.

Over the course of the piece, Edward's gender is constantly 'read' by others, through verbal questioning and physical violence, and the violence of the verbal questioning. And this 'reading' of Edward likewise extends to the genre of the text itself. 'By insisting that "Edward" was a poem', Grahn writes, 'I was telling myself that women must define what our poetry is. I believe this about every other aspect of our lives also' (ASR, 81). Likewise, as Sandy Stone has argued:

In the transsexual as text we may find the potential to map the refigured body onto conventional gender discourse and thereby disrupt it, to take advantage of the dissonances created by such a juxtaposition to fragment and reconstitute the elements of gender in new and unexpected geometries [. . .] I suggest constituting transsexuals not as a class or problematic 'third gender', but rather as a *genre*—a set of embodied texts whose potential for *productive* disruption of structured sexualities and spectra of desire has yet to be explored. (Stryker and Whittle, 231)

Within what is predominantly a prose dialogue, Edward also speaks in 'poetic' utterances that hint at such 'dissonances created by [. . .] juxtaposition', indicating the attempt to break through to a new language outside existing, pathologized frameworks for gender and sexuality. Having related the bathroom incident, Edward is asked by Dr. Knox, 'tell me briefly, what "homosexuality" means to you, in your own words', to which they reply:

Love flowers pearl, of delighted arms. Warm and water. Melting of vanilla wafer in the pants. Pink petal roses trembling overdew on the lips, soft and juicy fruit. No teeth. No nasty spit. Lips chewing oysters without grimy sand or whiskers. Pastry. Gingerbread. Warm, sweet bread. Cinnamon toast poetry. Justice equality higher wages. Independent angel song. It means I can do what I want. (Grahn 1985, 27)

At this stage, however, any nascent poetry is largely constrained by the piece's dialogic prose structure, in which Edward's dialogue is constantly policed, evaluated, and punished. ' "Now my dear", Dr. Knox said, "your disease has gotten completely out of control'" (27). Edward's poetic definition can, on the one hand, be read as an attempt to prove 'how well did I know Gertrude Stein', thus fitting an existing, if poorly understood, cultural template for lesbian identity. Equally, however, in combining conventionally feminine signifiers with vaguely political slogans, it suggests the compromised discourse of the homophile movement, whose liberal respectability politics tones down the more radical implications of gender and sexual non-conformity. As Stone suggests: 'To attempt to occupy a place as speaking subject within the traditional gender frame is to become complicit in the discourse which one wishes to deconstruct' (Stryker and Whittle, 231). Against stereotypes of queer promiscuity, Edward idealizes monogamy; defining experiences of queer sexual pleasure, they resort to a language of euphemisms ('melting of vanilla wafer in the pants') and bodily disgust ('no teeth, no nasty spit'). Despite Edward's claim that homosexuality means 'I can do what I want', they have not yet found a language that can evade the frames of informal gender policy and psychiatric scrutiny—or, more importantly, a *context* in which that language can be heard. For Stone, the 'culturally intelligible gendered body [. . .] *is itself a medically constituted textual violence*' (231). Defined by external

244 NEVER BY ITSELF ALONE

violence and internal self-hatred, as the text ends, Edward is subjected to electroshock therapy, screaming 'I am vile! I am vile!' (Grahn 1985, 30).

As Linda Garber writes: 'no role models or community exist in the world of the poem to support [Edward's] identity' (Garber, 35). And in many ways, we *still* do not have a widely accepted identity for Edward: as working-class 'dyke' or lesbian, as butch—similar, but not identical to trans identity (Bettcher, 287–88)—and as a subject interpellated both as a FTM and a MTF trans person who must be disciplined into the 'correct' gender. As Joan Nestle recalled in her 1981 essay 'Butch-Femme Relationships': 'When we broke gender lines in the 1950s, we fell off the biologically charted maps' (Nestle, 106). Yet, as Nestle notes, elements of gender outlaw identity found in earlier butch and femme roles— roles which emphasized the performativity of gender—were being shut out both by the often classed and raced emergence of queer assimilationism and by the biological essentialism advanced in certain sectors of radical feminism.

In the late 1960s, a developing lesbian politics rejected the pathologizing medical discourses which conflated gender variance and homosexuality, reading homosexual men as 'effeminate' and homosexual women as 'masculine' (Stryker and Whittle 415). Consequently, early lesbian feminist attempts to de-pathologize lesbianism not only included *embracing* gender nonconformity but also its opposite: emphasizing lesbians' biological position within the category of 'woman' (441). *Edward* was first published in 1971. By 1973, what Susan Stryker calls a 'rising tide' of anti-trans hostility began to surface amidst the lesbian feminist movement (Stryker 2008, 102). In San Francisco, two separate Pride parades were organized, one of which excluded those in drag or those who were transgender; Sylvia Rivera was booed and heckled at the annual Christopher Street Liberation Day in New York while delivering her 'Y'all Better Quiet Down' speech; and, at the West Coast Lesbian Feminist Conference, the presence of folk singer Beth Elliott was opposed by a vocal anti-trans minority, their position amplified by (heterosexual) keynote speaker Robin Morgan, both in her speech at the conference and its later revision in her book *Going Too Far* (1977; 101–104). While these were minority positions, they were retrospectively popularized in the work of prominent feminist authors, published by widely circulated trade presses, from Morgan's *Going Too Far* to Janice Raymond's *The Transsexual Empire* (1979).

In 1976, Grahn recorded a successful album with Pat Parker for the lesbian record label Olivia Records. As she recounts in her autobiography:

The Olivia Records women had just hired a recording engineer, and I found her very attractive. On being told that Sandy Stone was a transgender person I was dismayed, which hurt her feelings. I examined my response carefully and then wrote her a letter of apology. 'My attraction to you threatened my lesbian identity,' I said. I was shocked to think I might just be locked into something as simple as an 'identity' (*ASR*, 237).[2]

Ten years earlier, 'The Psychoanalysis of Edward the Dyke' had given excoriating expression to the medicalized double-binds of sexuality and gender. Yet, despite her teenage sense of her 'genderlessness', her identification with Joan of Arc and Puck, Grahn had briefly allowed herself to express some initial discomfort with trans identity. Today, so-called gender-critical positions are increasingly promulgated—particularly in the UK, from where I write this manuscript, but also in the United States—and are used to create fault-lines that are increasingly exploited by the right in manufactured 'culture wars' (Edie Miller 2018; Lewis 2019; Vincent, Erikainen, and Pearce 2020). But Grahn's correction of her initial discomfort, as well as her embrace today of a gender-bending sensibility, suggests that this process was by no means a given, and trans inclusiveness has been the norm of her poetics and politics.

From Pauli Murray's 'Peter Panic' to Sylvia Rivera and Marsha P. Johnson, the drag queens of the 1966 Compton's Cafeteria Riot, or, indeed, Edward themselves, gender outlaws have always been at the forefront of US queer activism. And this interrogation of gender was by no means abandoned with the advent of lesbian feminist poetics. In her collections *The Female Freeway* (1970) and *A Lesbian Estate* (1977), musician and poet Lynn Lonidier, cousin of Karen Brodine, friend to Robert Duncan and Jess, and former lover of Pauline Oliveros, focused on the figure of the hermaphrodite throughout history. In the poem 'The wish to be both sexes', for instance, Lonidier joins the two-gendered figures of Tiresias and Joan of Arc to the entwined rainbow serpents of Haitian *vodou*. Rather than 'abandoning Joan to the / psychiatrists', Lonidier instead embraces the 'crackling power' of hermaphroditism (Lonidier 1977, 12). Likewise, Pat Parker's 'my lady ain't no lady' (1978), wittily capped off with the line, 'my lady is definitely no lady / which is fine with me, // cause i ain't no gentleman', teases at the gap between gender performance and sexual orientation, with gender a (sexually inflected) trading of roles, in which pleasure can be obtained from subverting existent social codes (Parker 2016, 120). 'Gender-bending', Grahn argued in her Outwrite speech, 'is one of the tasks of gay artists' (Enszer and Gross, 27). And today, returning to such texts, which refuse divisions between lesbians, feminists, and trans subjects, not only provides a more accurate portrayal of the origins of lesbian feminism but also suggests the basis for a solidarity that is more necessary than ever.

'On the Development of a Purple Fist'

Following the composition of 'Edward the Dyke', Grahn's developing articulation of a gender and a sexual identity also saw her more readily embrace another

246   NEVER BY ITSELF ALONE

sometimes-stigmatized identity: that of the poet. In 1967, Grahn and artist Karla Tonella rented poet Robert Creeley's house in Placitas, New Mexico, associating with a scene of poets including Larry Goddell, Stephen Rodefer, and Gene Frumkin. Here, Grahn wrote her first published poems; the following year, she moved with her new partner, artist Wendy Cadden, to a radical collective household in Antioch, Ohio, working on a theatrical happening, 'The Cell' (*ASR* 94–96, 100–103).

Though never published, a script for the piece exists in the Paul Mariah papers at SUNY Buffalo, reading as at once a poem and a set of performance instructions, which allegorizes Grahn's own ambivalent position as a queer woman at the intersection of the New Left, Black Power, and homophile movements, for whom there was as yet no satisfactory political identity. The titular cell is not only the space of a prison, but a separate 'cell, a transparent and fragile sac / with a woman in it [...] located [...] so that everyone can see it', surrounded by prison guards and prisoners: 'they are to bring [it] to life / they stroke it / they poke it / they curse it' (Grahn n.d., 6–7). From the sac, the woman is 'born [...] gradually and with great effort [...] she is a pod bursting / brimstone / if she had been arrested the charges would be / prostitution / and biting an officer in the course of his duty' (11). Surrounding the woman, the other participants 'cannot find a use for [...] what the cell brought them / it's no good for fucking / it doesn't make them rich [...] they use it as a decoration / but the cell provokes them and [...] they step over the line' (12). Stepping over the line suggests at once the possibility of the woman's actions to provoke the others to action and to act with renewed misogynist violence and incomprehension, and the piece sketches out three alternative endings, based on the decisions of guards and prisoners to challenge or to reinforce the hierarchical norms in which they are placed. In leaving the choice up to the participants, Grahn intended the central figure to make 'pro-lesbian statements'. In the end, however, the part was taken by an African American activist and the performance was dominated by conflicts between male Black and white students, in which white radical students invaded the stage, replaced the guards, and began barking out orders, proving unable to see beyond their own prejudice and privilege. As Grahn recalls in correspondence, 'I directed the play but then had no seat in it, no place'. 'The play experience had taught me a great deal', Grahn writes in her autobiography, 'about my own sense of being literally nowhere [...] The black men wanted to claim their own and go somewhere else together. The white men wanted to replace the white guard authoritarian structure with themselves. The white women, meantime, were off in another world, almost unrelated to this one, waiting to be born' (*ASR*, 103).

The following day, Grahn and Cadden set off for San Francisco. Arriving in late spring 1968, Grahn worked as a typesetter for the *San Francisco Express Times*: she and Cadden became intensively involved in activism, working as 'nonstudent organizers' as part the Third World Students Strike, which was in part organized around Grahn's former mentor Nathan Hare at San Francisco State University; doing publicity work for the Black Panther Party (BPP); participating in the People's Park protests in Berkeley; and working with radical film collective Newsreel (108–109). With the emergence of the BPP in Oakland in 1966, the Bay Area had become a centre for Black liberation activity. On one occasion, Grahn and poet Marilyn Buck—a former Students for a Democratic Society (SDS) member later arrested as part of the Black Liberation Army for her participation in the 1979 prison escape of Assata Shakur—were arrested for flyposting posters of Eldridge Cleaver (109–10). And in her essay 'Ground Zero: The Rise of Lesbian Feminism', Grahn traces the genesis of Bay Area Gay Women's Liberation at a solidarity action for the Panthers, when, in December 1969 she, Cadden, Louise Merrill, and Cynth Fitzpatrick joined a 'living wall of defense' or 'white buffer' called by the San Francisco BPP following the assassination of Fred Hampton in Chicago and a police assault on the Panthers' Los Angeles office (Grahn 2009, 312). Following Huey P. Newton's August 1970 speech in favour of women and gay liberation, Grahn was involved in the short-lived Revolutionary People's Constitutional Conventional (RPCC), an attempted linkage between gay liberation, feminist and other activist groups spearheaded by the BPP (Hobson, 52).[3] Though the RPCC was short-lived, GWL members drew on the Panthers' emphasis on self-defence to leaflet, organize vigils, and intimidate perpetrators of gender violence, with Red Jordan Arobateau teaching GWL members self-defence skills; such activity led to the formation of San Francisco Women Against Rape (SFWAR), one of the first crisis centres in the US (52).

San Francisco also had an important recent history of specifically lesbian organizing. San Francisco D.O.B. had continued to grow since its establishment in the 1950s, paving the way for the lesbian feminist communities to follow, from the presence of longstanding D.O.B. members Alice Molloy and Carol Wilson in GWL to the presence in print and in readings of the older lesbian anarchist poet Elsa Gidlow alongside Grahn and others of the new poets of Gay Women's Liberation.[4] As Barbara Love and Sidney Abbott argued in *Sappho Was a Right-On Woman* (1972): 'Feminists arrived at a turning point in the history of women only to find that Lesbians were already there' (Love and Abbott, 136). Between 1968 and 1970, at least sixty feminist consciousness-raising (CR) groups appeared in the Bay Area, their activities presaged by the 'gab 'n java' social activities organised by the D.O.B. as far back as 1957, and open to interested heterosexuals (Del Rio, 4, 72). While continuing to publish in *The Ladder*, Grahn also attended a Gay Men's Poetry Group facilitated by Paul Mariah—prison activist, former student of Robert Duncan's, and an extremely active presence in the Bay Area's emergent gay poetry scene—out of which grew the magazine and

248 NEVER BY ITSELF ALONE

press *Manroot* (*Manroot*, 3; *ASR*, 113–14). Yet, as she comments: '[M]y attention was going elsewhere, toward women' (114).

Historically, if emergent feminist consciousness raising groups too often failed to draw both the economic connections between women, regardless of sexuality, and the specific conditions faced by lesbians, gay male activists too often downplayed the importance of a feminist analysis. At Mattachine's first conference in 1959, D.O.B. president Del Martin denounced the organization for failing to recognize 'that Lesbians are women and this twentieth century is the era of emancipation of women. Lesbians are not satisfied to be auxiliary members or second-class homosexuals' ('Mattachine Breaks'). Ten years later, such tensions coalesced at the North American Conference of Homophile Organizations (NACHO), held in Berkeley in November 1969, at which Grahn delivered a speech entitled 'On the Development of a Purple Fist'. Later retitled 'Lesbians as Women', Grahn's speech was printed across the Bay Area underground and gay press, and included in *Lesbians Speak Out*, an anthology of early movement writings published by the Women's Press Collective under Carol Wilson's editorship the following year. Significantly, this formative text of lesbian separatism is, in fact, an appeal to coalition building which emphasizes the interconnectedness of multiple struggles. Linking the lesbian cause to Black Power, poverty, student activism, homelessness, and environmentalism, Grahn provides an overview of interlinked structural inequalities: expensive transportation; debt cycles; environmental despoliation; unequal schooling systems; 'welfare ruts'; 'marriage [. . .] as a life-long labour and child support contract signed by heterosexual men'; 'white supremacy [. . .] as a compensation for badly paid white workers'; 'antihomosexualism [. . .] as a compensation for heterosexuals' (Grahn 1971, 3–4). 'Antihomosexualism', she asserts, is 'one stick in the whole structure of the society. To find out how to fix it, we have to examine the entire house and all its fences; otherwise we are going to be stuck with a bunch of splinters' (1). Yet while Grahn's speech called for a recognition of the shared political aims of the Women's, Gay Liberation, and Black Power Movements and demanded a strategy to match, her words were received with indifference by the largely male, more politically moderate audience. A few days later, she and Cadden hosted the inaugural meeting of what would become Gay Women's Liberation at their Mission District apartment (*ASR*, 116–17, 119, 122).

GWL participants' backgrounds suggested the group's emergence from a prior decade's activism. Carol Wilson and Allice Molloy, both members of the D.O.B., co-parented Wilson's child; Linda Wilson self-identified as a 'black activist dyke'; Louise Merrill had grown up in South America, working in the labour movement, running as a socialist for the New York Senate and helping found the Workers World Party; painter, writer, and pioneer of 'street lit', Red Jordan

Arobateau subsequently identified as a trans man, and for decades wrote with passion and verve, in often self-published works, of conditions 'down on the abject bottom of society' (*ASR*, 154; Del Rio, 102–104; Arobateau, 4).

Coalescing from these diverse backgrounds, GWL was initially, as Chelsea Del Rio observes, 'movement building at its most intimate' (Del Rio, 108). With the group core of Grahn, Cadden, Alice Molloy, and Carol Wilson, GWL functioned as 'a loose confederation of small groups and individuals' in what was intended as an organization 'more activist and political than established lesbian organizations like Nova and the Daughters of Bilitis' ('What's Happening'; 'Gay Fem'). Importantly, the group also sought to bridge the class and race divisions between San Francisco, Berkeley, and Oakland; its weekly meetings alternated between San Francisco and the East Bay. Initial GWL meetings soon attracted up to eighty members. Early on, they organized women-only dances and poetry readings, a mixed-gender CR group that met through 1970, attending 'marches, rallies, speeches' (126), the interruption of a lecture by a psychiatrist 'expert' on female homosexuality (130), and intervention in cases of sexual assault, including vigils inside battered women's houses (147–49).

For Grahn, GWL activities went beyond the small CR groups held in middle-class, heterosexual women's living rooms in part because, as working-class lesbians, most GWL members were already 'conscious', having left violent relationships, been criminalized and demonized by mental health services for their sexual orientation, raised children on their own, and gathered to discuss these issues for years in gay bars and living rooms (Grahn 2009, 315). As she notes: 'Many gay people of whatever gender were deeply estranged from, and sometimes in danger from their families of origin [. . .] forming chosen community relationships that would protect them if necessary *from* their families of origin'—the quest 'for any kind of family structure that would work for them' (*ASR*, 140–41).

In May 1971, Grahn and Cadden moved into an all-women's household at Terrace Street in Oakland, established by Carl Wilson, Alice Molloy, and Natalie Lando after the landlord had evicted the Bay Area's first collective lesbian household (151). Grahn would live here for five years: during this time, she remembers at least forty other queer women living in the space. In this and other collective households, resources were shared and political activities collectively organized. From collective households emerged the newspaper *It Ain't Me Babe*, the Women's Press Collective, A Woman's Place Bookstore in Oakland, Old Wives' Tales Bookstore in San Francisco, the Oakland Feminist Women's Health Centre, located in Laura K. Brown's household, and the Lesbian Mothers' Union, founded by Pat Norman and by D.O.B. founders Del Martin and Phyllis Lyon (*ASR*, 314; Del Rio, 126–30, 153). Within the next few years, Grahn suggests, 'the movement took on the feeling of being "our own college" [. . .] the college we

250 NEVER BY ITSELF ALONE

always wanted, the college that would let us center on ourselves as subject' (*ASR*, 169; Grahn 2009, 315). A community was being built from the ground up.

The Common Woman and a Common Poetics

Rather than political leaders, Grahn suggests, the early lesbian feminist movement had 'poets and artists' (*AMT*, 183). Grahn had early on observed that attendees at early GWL meetings were starved of written material. Without distinguishing between 'creative', critical, and political writings, she and Cadden began operating a mimeograph machine in their kitchen, distributing 'The Psychoanalysis of Edward the Dyke' alongside 'Lesbians as Bogeywoman' and reprints from New York's *RAT* magazine of articles by Radicalesbians Rita Mae Brown and Martha Shelley, along with an early mimeograph edition of Grahn's sequence *The Common Woman*. Building on this momentum, Grahn and Cadden assembled the anthology *Woman to Woman*, an assemblage of work by twenty-eight poets, including Grahn, Parker, Gertrude Stein, Diane di Prima, and Sonia Sanchez, chosen by Grahn in collective consultation with sixty other women, which placed 'grassroots' poems by unknown poets alongside established writers (132). As with Boston's *Fag Rag*, the anthology evinced an anarchist approach to artistic standards, in which the emergent community itself defined what counted as literary value and in which the claims of individual authorship took second place to a cumulative, collective vision. The unsigned introduction claims: 'We know that "famous" women are used as tokens in the publishing world, and our attempt in Woman to Woman is to reject the exploitative standards of that world and at the same time reject the divisions which fame creates among women' (*Woman to Woman* 1971, n.p.). As a one-off experiment—'an odd structure, which will probably never be repeated'—authors' names were listed only in a back-page index: poem followed on poem without immediate attribution. Likewise, the book's production methods were conceived as a political structure, bringing

> the women who worked on this book together in a concrete bond—not as rivals, not as wives, secretaries, mistresses or 'girl' Fridays—but as sisters [. . .] We produced a small book by pooling our lives as much as we knew how. One watched the kids while two ran the machine and one fixed supper. With real child care centers and real equality we could all build bridges. (*Woman to Woman* 1971, n.p.)

From such bonds emerged the Women's Press Collective. In the fall of 1970, Grahn travelled to Boston to learn printing at the New England Free Press, later joined by other GWL members who had driven across the country, distributing *Woman to Woman*, along with the first publications of Alta's Shameless Hussy press, formed the previous year (*ASR*, 133). In December, Ruth Gottstein of the Glide Memorial Church provided a grant, enabling the Collective to buy a printer, reprint *Woman to Woman*, and assemble Grahn's first collection, *Edward the Dyke*, mimeographing 2,000 copies in March 1971 (142–43). Operated by Grahn, Pat Parker, Wendy Cadden, and Willyce Kim out of ICI (Information Center Incorporate): A Woman's Place Bookstore, three blocks away from the Terrace Street House, the collective aimed to make 'women's writings and graphics [. . .] accessible at minimum cost' (*Woman to Woman*, n.d, n.p.). In succeeding years, as Bertha Harris wrote, the press 'devoted itself exclusively to work by lesbians disenfranchised by race or class', printing work by Grahn, Parker, and Kim, along with a pamphlet in defence of Joann Little, a book of poetry by women in the Weather Underground, and 'a primer on handguns', *The Women's Gun Pamphlet* (Bertha Harris 1993, xxxi),

While print expanded the reach of local collective households to national and even international levels, poetry readings offered an affirmation, and sometimes a challenge, to the developing values of communities of women. Some of the earliest GWL events involved women-only poetry readings and dances which, as photographer Cathy Cade remarked, 'somehow united us a community' (123). 'San Francisco', Ntozake Shange observed, 'was inundated with women poets, women's readings, and a multilingual presence, new to all of us and desperately appreciated [. . .] as we directed our energies towards clarifying our lives [. . .] as women [. . .] Shameless Hussy Press and the Oakland Women's Press Collective were [. . .] reading anywhere and everywhere they could' (Elliott, 797–99).

As Grahn recalled: 'Our readings drew large, loud, engaged audiences, all women, who went wild—sometimes screaming and standing on chairs—six hundred, twelve hundred a time. These gatherings helped tell us that we had a movement, and that it had collective power' (Grahn 2009, 315). From 1970 onwards, Grahn and Parker often read together, 'joined frequently by our friend [Willyce] Kim, a Korean-American, in a fortuitous public effect of dyke multiculturalism'. Grahn recalls a pivotal reading with Parker at the Addison Street lesbian household in Berkeley. Stripping to the waist 'to display the nakedness one needs to tell new truths'—a lesbian echo of earlier gestures by Robert Duncan and Allen Ginsberg in the mid-'50s San Francisco scene—she set fire to her poems 'in memory of Sappho and the historic burning of her work', and 'read virtually every poem I had every written in my life [. . .] sealing a partnership between Parker and me, a ritual that felt like setting lesbian poetry into a path of social change' (Jarnot, 135; *ASR*, 134).

In October 1969, following a homophobic incident at a women's liberation group meeting, Grahn 'formed my own fantasy CR group, writing it into a

252 NEVER BY ITSELF ALONE

set of poems' (115). Influenced by Nina Simone's cover of Leonard Cohen's 'Suzanne', which Grahn played on repeat during its composition, by the 'heroic, oracular voice' of Carl Sandburg's Chicago poems—'workers' voices speaking to ordinary people', to which Grahn's father had introduced her as a child—and the work of 'Bard of labour' Edwin Markham, the resulting sequence, *The Common Woman*—described 'women who had no voice, not even in the literature I read' (Yalom 1983, 94; *ASR*, 5, 115; Lisa L. Moore 2013, n.p.; Grahn 1985, 60). As Sandburg and Markham had done in their earlier socialist poetics, with its reclamation of working-class lives, so Grahn's poetry makes claim to the existence of lives hitherto excluded from literary realms. The sequence is a series of portraits—termed by Grahn 'self-defining, flexible sonnets'—of seven women, identified by first name—Helen, Ella, Nadine, Carol, Detroit Annie, Margaret, and Vera—either working or refusing work in the official or unofficial economy. 'The common woman is as common / as the common crow' reads the first iteration of a refrain recurring at the end of each individual poem (Grahn 1985, 60). By the sequence's end, 'common' has been reclaimed from term of denigration to one of triumphant assertion:

> the common woman is as common as the best of bread
> and will rise
> and will become strong[.]
>
> (73)

The Common Woman sketches a world of negative circumstance—the self-administered abortion, the woman whose child is taken away from her after she shoots a lover in self-defence—alongside moments of defiance, the determination to survive at whatever cost. Only the fourth poem explicitly presents a lesbian subject:

> She has taken a woman lover
> whatever shall we do [...]
> She walks around all day
> quietly, but underneath it
> she's electric;
> angry energy inside a passive form.
> The common woman is as common
> as a thunderstorm.
>
> (67)

Yet, regardless of sexual orientation, the connections between all seven women—'all the world we didn't know we held in common / all along'— serve as the political basis for Grahn's vision of lesbianism and, in turn, of a transformed society.

Grahn's 1970 poem 'A History of Lesbianism', first printed in *Edward the Dyke and Other Poems*, ends with a firm prosaic statement.

> The subject of lesbianism
> is very ordinary: it's the question
> of male domination that makes everybody
> angry.
>
> (55)

Rhythmically and syntactically unadorned, the statement both interrupts and flows out of the poetic line, emphasizing its bold clarity, its 'common' sense. Lesbianism names day-to-day relation between women that *already exists*, against which heteropatriarchy itself is, in fact, the social aberration. Likewise, in *The Common Woman*, Grahn reclaims a term of classed insult, turning it into one of praise. The word 'common', she later remarked, 'reminded me of 'common whore', 'common slut' or something that's sexual property [...] [It] also reminded me of [. . .] what we have in common, which is a cross-connection between us all' (Yolam 1983, 94). 'Common' suggests shared experience, its heritage lying in the older idea of the commons, of collective life.

This life was not only named by the poems but also facilitated by them, as GWL, in Grahn's words, moved from the recognition of '*commonality*' to the building of '*community*'—'the attempt to concretize the bonding of women into a group identity' (*THA*, 75, 76–77). First published in a stand-alone pamphlet, with illustrations by Cadden, *The Common Woman* was distributed at the radical Maoist bookstore China Books by Henry Noyes, a participant in the Gay Men's poetry group in which Grahn had been involved. Grahn soon found the poems, within women's communities, 'quoted orally [and] suddenly plastered on refrigerators all over town' (*ASR*, 203; Grahn 2009, 313). The sequence would be reprinted in *Woman to Woman*, before serving as the culmination of Grahn's first pamphlet, *Edward the Dyke and Other Poems*, and, later lending its title to her 1978 collected poems, *The Work of a Common Woman*, its words also 'quoted and sloganized over a million times in media that ranged from television to T-Shirts', with each new appearance charting a new stage in the articulation of common identity and lesbian community (Grahn 2009, 272).

Poetry, in other words, served to actively build Gay Women's Liberation as both a local and national force, with 'commonality' and 'community' manifesting in a mutual circuit of dialogue and influence between poems by different women. Pat Parker's 'Goat Child' inspired Grahn's 'A Woman Is Talking to Death', which in turn inspired Parker's 'Womanslaughter'; Grahn's 'The Common Woman'

254   NEVER BY ITSELF ALONE

inspired Ntozake Shange's *for colored girls who have considered suicide when the rainbow is enough,* which in turn inspired Grahn's 'Confrontations with the Devil in the Form of Love' (Grahn 1985, 134; Elliott, 799). The *form* of these poems, too, was insistently collective, adopting multiple voices, perspectives, and narrative sketches to build a picture of collective life. Community existed at every stage, from inspiration to poetic form, from reading to printing, and distribution. In such writing, individuality cannot be understood apart from the totality of the community the poem calls into being. As Grahn writes in her 1972 sequence *She Who:*

> Singing: I am the woman, the woman
>   the woman—I am the first person
>   and the first person is She Who is the first person to
>   She Who is the first person to no other. There is no
>   other first person. (Grahn 1985, 78)

Such poems often, of necessity, offered positive images: images of togetherness, anthems, chants, and calls to arms, which affirmed a community in formation. Grahn's next sequence, however, would focus on the racial, gendered, and sexual splits that divide and foreclose the possibility of community.

A Woman Is Talking to Death

Entitled 'testimony in trials that never got heard', the first section of 'A Woman Is Talking to Death' (1973) narrates an incident on 'the long Bay Bridge' between San Francisco and the East Bay, in which the a middle-aged African American driver accidentally knocks down and kills a reckless young white motorcyclist ('the arrogant young man who thought he / owned the bridge', 118). Out of fear of harassment as an unemployed, unmarried queer woman ('an unemployed queer woman / makes no witness at all [...] what does / she do, and who is she married to?', Grahn 1985, 117), Grahn refuses the driver's request to stay behind as a witness, later learning that 'six big policemen [...] put the driver up against his car / and beat the hell out of him [...] held him five days in jail / without a phone call', his lawyer encouraging him to 'cop a plea' and accept a lengthy jail sentence (Grahn 1985, 113–17).

As in Cherríe Moraga's 'La Jornada', analyzed in the previous chapter, the route across the city prompts reflections on the intersections of race, gender, and class, grounded in the specific dynamics of a particular city, which extends to the conditions of the nation as a whole. The sequence emerges out of the specific geography of San Francisco—in particular, 'the long Bay Bridge', the raced and class dividing line between San Francisco and Oakland—sparking memories of Grahn's earlier encounters with police, the military, and psychiatrists, along with incidents from the early days of lesbian feminism. Alongside these spaces—spaces of domestic safety and domestic harm, of institutional power, of public and private violence alike—exists a realm of poetic apostrophe, of queer love lyric and the defiance of death, which locates itself in the relation between addressee and addressed rather than in a particular location, and first manifests in in the brief lyric couplet that opens the poem—'my lovers teeth are white geese flying above me / my lovers muscles are rope ladders under my hand'—lines which will recur throughout as one of a number of refrains (Grahn 1985, 113).

Subsequent sections are organized around refrains and recurring of anecdote, narration, and historical analysis, from 'the European witch trials' in the period of primitive accumulation, to the present, when 'death tells the woman to stay home / and then breaks in the window' (126). In the fourth section, 'a mock interrogation', Grahn returns to the dialogic form of 'Edward the Dyke': now, however, patriarchal accusation is repurposed, as the speaker self-accuses for having abandoned woman-to-woman connection out of fear, as she abandoned the driver on the bridge: 'Yes I have committed acts of indecency with women / and most of them were acts of omission. I regret them / bitterly' (125). In turn, these 'acts of omission' contrast to acts of love found in the recurring love lyric, Grahn's nursing women in the military hospital or cradling the head of a middle-aged South East Asian woman found assaulted and abandoned by a taxi driver in the Boston snow by members of the Women's Press Collective (*ASR*, 137).

In each case, individual incidents are connected to structural analysis: an analysis that does not precede, but emerges out of this panoply of narration, reminiscence, and testimony. As an 'unemployed queer woman', Grahn's decision not to come forward as a witness on the bridge is a result both of her social stigmatization—the fear of police harassment and of not being believed—and of her ability, as a white woman, to avoid the same level of police scrutiny as the African American driver on the 'long Bay Bridge'. Later in the poem, she both suffers from police indifference when she herself is physically attacked and witnesses police indifference to other assaults. A thanatotic attachment to death, Grahn suggests, undergirds all existing institutions, from the police in Boston and San Francisco to military interrogation and the cultivation of social indifference among men and women alike. Yet an alternative vision of community emerges in acts of care and connection, breaking through the barriers of fear. Kissing the head of the beaten woman in Boston, Grahn writes:

> [...] I wanted her and me to own and control and run the
> city we lived in, to staff the hospital I knew would mistreat
> her, to drive the transportation system that had betrayed

256 NEVER BY ITSELF ALONE

> her, to patrol the streets controlling the men who would
> murder or disfigure or disrupt us, not accidently with
> machines, but on purpose, because we are not allowed out
> on the street alone.
>
> (Grahn 1985, 124)

For Grahn, the poem was 'a redefinition for myself of the subject of love', writing 'from the context of a woman's community into the context of the society at large' (*THA*, 50): callousness in love is parallel to the callousness with which marginalized groups ignore each other—'we left, as we have left all of our lovers / as all lovers leave all lovers / much too soon to get the real loving done' (Grahn 2009, 129). The individual abandonment of those in need—from the driver on the bridge to lovers left behind—is figured at once as a personal failing and as symptom of broader social inequalities in which even the most intimate relationships and feelings have their being.

In the ninth and final section, Grahn confronts the force of death with defiant bravado, the first-person lyric couplet which opened the poem now turned to collective phrasing—'hey you death // ho and ho poor death / our lovers teeth are white geese flying above us'—alongside images of flight by air and sea, and of rooted defiance, détourning the Homeric opening to Pound's *The Cantos*: 'even though no women yet go down to the sea in ships / except in their dreams' (130). 'To my lovers I bequeath / the rest of my life', writes Grahn in a closing benediction, conceiving of a collective, anti-capitalist subject who organize their lives 'for our own use'. By this final 'redefinition [. . .] of the subject of love', the term 'lover' extends to Wendy, the speaker's own lover, to Josie, the high school classmate made pregnant as a teenager, to the driver beaten by the police, to the woman found beaten in Boston, to soldiers sent to drown in malfunctioning amphibian tanks during the Second World War, and to lesbian friends and comrades at a bar. Love becomes an identity at once erotic and social, a designation of the ties that create a social community. For now, the space in which this socialized understanding of love might be glimpsed is the apostrophic space of the poem itself—a space which, Grahn insists, must urgently manifest in the material world. As Grahn would write in 'Confrontations with the Devil in the Form of Love' (1977):

> not until we have ground we call our own
> to stand on
> & weapons of our own in hand
> & some kind of friends around us
> will anyone ever call our name Love.
>
> (158)

'SHE WHO' 257

'all the sides of it'

By the second half of the decade, Grahn's reputation was at its height. In 1976, Olivia Records had put out the record *Where Would I Be with You*, on which Grahn and Pat Parker read their poetry; in 1978, Diana Press, newly merged with the Women's Press Collective, published hardback editions of Grahn's and Parker's respective collected poems, with introductions by Adrienne Rich and Audre Lorde. Yet Grahn was increasingly suffering from burnout: the implosion of grassroots projects from 'forces, interior and exterior'; the traumatic effects of a printing accident in which she almost lost her eye; and a 1977 attack on the headquarters of the Women's Press Collective, which caused severe damage to books and equipment and saw her stand armed guard outside the Press overnight. Never solved, the crime resonates with the arson attack on the Fag Rag headquarters five years later, detailed earlier in this book (*ASR*, 239–40, 248–49). Gradually stepping back from the movement, Grahn evaluated its achievements. Separatism, she suggested, had been a necessary tactic in response to a particular historical conjuncture, enabling the movement in general to learn from both its advances and mistakes (254). Yet the conditions of the 1980s, with 'the national sharp turn to the right, [and] an intentional, pervasive move to increase the wealth and power of the upper classes', increasingly necessitated a coalitional politics. Corresponding with female prisoners and gay men with AIDS alike, Grahn was a pivotal figure for the predominantly gay male New Narrative writers for whom her work provided a way out of the impasse created by other experimentalist literary traditions. Such affinities manifested in particular in the Left/Write Conference organized in 1981 by three gay men—Robert Glück, Steve Abbott, and Bruce Boone—among many others of various genders and sexualities, including Jack Hirschman and Denise Kastan, at San Francisco's Small Press Traffic bookstore. Recalling the coalitional efforts of Grahn's first years in San Francisco, this conference, at which Grahn spoke, is examined in this book's eleventh chapter.

Over the following decades, Grahn authored a series of historical, biographical, and mythological studies, including the poetic sequence *The Queen of Wands* (1982) and *The Queen of Swords* (1987), the novel *Mundane's World* (1988), and the prose studies *Another Mother Tongue: Gay Words Gay Worlds* (1984), *The Highest Apple: Sappho and the Lesbian Poetic Tradition* (1985), *Really Reading Gertrude Stein* (1990), and *Blood, Bread, and Roses: How Menstruation Created the World* (1993): at once reckonings with a longer history of queer art and culture and autobiographical refractions of what she had experienced during the birth of lesbian feminist activism. Most recently, she has authored an autobiography, *A Simple Revolution* (2012), a vital reckoning with the legacies of early US lesbian feminism, and the cross-genre *Eruptions of Inanna: Justice, Gender, and Erotic*

258 NEVER BY ITSELF ALONE

Power, published in 2021 as I was writing this book. This work, which came out almost exclusively with non-academic, activist presses, has been largely ignored in existing literary histories, and it's to be hoped that more work is to emerge on the last four decades of Grahn's work.

Throughout her career, Grahn's writing has never been simply the adjunct of political organization. Rather, it has had a specific function within the building of the movement and the living of life within it—building up a mythos for that community in 'The Common Woman' and 'She Who', and questioning the limits of existing frameworks in 'Edward the Dyke' and 'A Woman Is Talking to Death'. In the following chapter, I further explore poetry's relation to lesbian feminist community, extending the analysis to the politics of the Reagan era in the work of Grahn's comrade Pat Parker.

9
'The first everything'
Pat Parker

As Jewelle Gomez put it in *Gay Community News* (*GCN*) following Pat Parker's death from cancer in 1989, Parker 'had the courage to be the "first black," the "first lesbian," the first everything. [...] [She] made[e] it clear we didn't ever have to be alone' (*GCN* 1989: 7) Though Parker is almost completely ignored in academic accounts of American poetry, her influence in fact extends well beyond that of many canonized writers. Parker's work, suggested Angela Davis, 'foreshadowed and helped to forge the cultural and political values that continue to inspire so many of us', its impact reaching even those who may not even know her name (Parker 1999, 28). (In 2019, for instance, Parker's poetry was sampled on fellow Texan Solange Knowle's top-ten charting album *When I Get Home*.[1]) Poetry was never Parker's only sphere of activity. A health worker and activist, 'Parker understood', recalls Barbara Smith, 'that a part of [her] work on earth was to join with others to fight oppression on many fronts, that writing was not enough' (Parker 1999, 38). Yet Parker's poetry was also a part of her activism, and her activism part of her poetry. Though many of these poems deploy the first person, the model Parker adopts is not the musing aloud of lyric poetry 'confessing itself to itself, in moments of solitude' but an insistent position-taking in which Parker claims a place for *all* the aspects of her identity—as Black, female, and lesbian alike (Mill 1859, 64). Its meaning emerging within and against a social context, Parker's poetry attempts to re-envision community from the ground up.

'& a woman was born': Parker's Early Years

There are relatively few published sources on Parker's life and work, though Julie Enszer is currently working on a much-needed biography. In this chapter, I draw on five interviews published in Parker's lifetime, along with Grahn's autobiography and Parker's archival correspondence (Jane; Cornwell; Woodwoman; Douglas; Rushin 1985; *ASR*).[2] Born Patricia Cooks, Parker grew up 'barely working class' in Houston's Third Ward (*GCN* 1989, 12). The house was isolated and cramped, fitting two adults and four children: Parker recalled that her mother 'knocked all the walls out and transformed the house into this

Never By Itself Alone. David Grundy, Oxford University Press. © Oxford University Press 2024.
DOI: 10.1093/oso/9780197654842.003.0010

260 NEVER BY ITSELF ALONE

one big room [. . .] like living in a cabin' (Cornwell, 40). As a teenager, Parker was in a lesbian relationship lasting for several years. 'I had had this thing with a girl when I was about eleven—from about eleven to seventeen—and my parents found out about it. Their reaction was highly negative. *Very negative.* I was told, "Don't *ever* do that again"' (Cornwell, 41). As Parker writes in the posthumously published autobiographical short story, 'Funny': 'We didn't know the name for what we were and what we were doing, but we did know it had to be a secret. We had received our first closet keys' (Parker 2016, 185). The same year, Parker recalled, 'Claude, the local newspaper boy was killed by other kids in the community. They beat him up one night and threw him in front of a car. And everybody shook their heads and said how sad it was, but before then everybody had talked about how *strange* he was. So those kids were able to get away with killing him because the community just felt that it was sad, but he *was* a faggot, right?' (Cornwell, n.p.).

Parker again recollects the incident in the poem 'My Brother', written for her friend and performing partner, singer-songwriter Blackberri, perhaps best known for the songs he provided for Isaac Julien's *Looking for Langston*. Claude was, she notes, a model child—'works hard / goes to church / gives his money to his mother', yet

> some young men howled at him
> ran in a pack
> reverted to some ancient form [. . .]
> yelled faggot
> as they cast his body
> in front of a car
>
> (Parker 2016, 197)

'How many cars have you dodged, Berri?', asks Parker, recalling the 'simple ritual' of their own friendship. 'What is this world we have? / Is my house the only safe place / for us?' (199).

School was, Parker recalled, 'my freedom', giving her the opportunity to develop public speaking skills, while writing—poems and limericks for friends, along with school journalism—served as a way to communicate for the youngest child in the family (Cornwell, 40; Douglas, 5). Parker left home at seventeen, following her sisters to Los Angeles and studying at City College from 1961 to 1963. Here, she met the writer Ed Bullins, then editor of the college's literary magazine, *Citadel*, for which Parker served as poetry editor: the two married when Parker was eighteen, moving to San Francisco. Bullins, soon to be a major figure in the Black Arts Movement, would be briefly appointed the Black Panther Party's minister of culture in 1966, associating with San Francisco's Black House

'THE FIRST EVERYTHING' 261

and Black Arts/West Theatre group. During their marriage, he introduced Parker to radical political and artistic scenes, but he relentlessly criticized her writing and was physically abusive (Jane, 10; Woodwoman, 60; Bullins 1967, n.p.). As Parker recalled: 'I think I left my husband about eight times, but people would always tell him where I was [. . .] I was terrified of him [. . .] I was scared to death [. . .] I know that I was a very frightened child. And my growing into womanhood happened during the course of my getting out of that' (Cornwell, 41).

Parker published a handful of poems and prose pieces in journals such as *Black Dialogue, Black World/Negro Digest, Perspectives,* and *Soulbook* while married to Bullins, her 'primary goal [. . .] to be accepted as a "good poet", not just a "good woman poet"' (Parker 2016, 464).[3]

> The first reading I ever did in public [. . .] was in 1963 at the Blue Unicorn Coffeehouse, when I was still married. Back then I was competing in a male poetry scene [. . .] I was very determined not to write about birds and flowers. Most of the women were writing about those things, but I was saying, 'No! Why are they writing this crap? Guys are writing about civil rights, and Vietnam. I have feelings about this—I can write about this, too.' (Rushin 1985, 28)

In these early poems, Parker oscillates between dreams of power, statements of love, and defiance of the conditions in which she finds herself, often obliquely relating to her marriage. An untitled poem published in *Black Dialogue* in 1966 presages the themes of Grahn's 'A Woman Is Talking To Death' by some seven years. The poem opens 'I have seen death / Burst into a live body / & strangle out life / Like an irate husband', ending with the thrice-repeated 'I do not fear death. / I do not fear death. / I do not fear death' (Parker 2016, 335). A portrait of Bullins as 'the Buddha' appears in Parker's first major long poem, the 'emboldened bildungsroman in verse' 'Goat Child', printed in *Child of Myself* in 1973, which charts a rejection both of oppressive familial circumstance and, in the final section, '1962–1966' the domestic situation with Bullins (Wade, n.p.). From being 'a frightened child / capable only of giving birth', Parker writes, 'the goat-child died / & a woman was born' (Parker 2016, 40, 39). Likewise, in the poem 'Exodus', subtitled '(To my husband, lovers) / *a going out or going forth;/ departure*', Parker turns on the trope of the biblical liberation from Egyptian slavery so resonant in Black political struggles to the context of gender relations. 'Trust me no more / Our bed is unsafe / Hidden within folds of cloth / A desperate slave' (46). While Parker's feminism emerges before her explicit lesbianism, it deeply informs and lays the ground for it. And, along with her racial identity, Parker's lesbianism and her feminism would form the bedrock for all her subsequent work, even as different audiences were often unprepared to fully acknowledge all three aspects.

262   NEVER BY ITSELF ALONE

Following her separation from Bullins, Parker married again, to a white bohemian accountant, poet, and 'classical music buff', Robert F. Parker, but the marriage, while not abusive, was short-lived (Parker 1967, 1). As Parker told Cornwell: 'I [got married] a second time, which was totally absurd, you know? [. . .] I think there was this hidden thing in me fighting off my lesbianism' (Cornwell, 411). Within the countercultural milieu of San Francisco, Parker was coming into her own as a poet. In 1970, for instance, she appeared as one of only three female writers in Adam David Miller's anthology *Dices or Black Bones: Black Voices of the Seventies* (1970), oriented toward lesser-known and more experimental writers of the Black Arts Movement, while, in Umbra poet David Henderson's poem 'wolfbane', she appears alongside writers and artists of the New York and California 'multiculture', including Bob Kaufman, Allen Ginsberg, Diane di Prima, and Maya Angelou (Henderson, 10). Soon, Parker would make the courageous decision to read and write as an out lesbian.

Coming Out and Coming to Poetry

Following her split from Bob Parker, Parker returned to Houston to work on a novel, entitled, ironically enough, *You're Damn Sure You Can't Go Home Again* (Jane, 10).[4] As she recalled, she was only able to stay ten days. 'That was all I could take. I realized that in my parents' house I would still be the child. And by that time I was a woman, and I was used to doing my own thing and controlling my own life' (Cornwell, n.p.). In Houston, however, she reconnected with her teenage lover, who had now come out, and, against her parents' protests, took her to a queer bar. Returning to San Francisco, Parker entered the lesbian bar scene and embarked on a new queer relationship. 'I felt that this was where I should be', she recalled. 'After my first relationship with a woman, I knew where I was going' (Cornwell, n.p.).

It would not, however, be until the end of the decade that anything like the momentum found amongst heterosexual poets in the Black Arts Movement would be achieved by queer writers of colour, and, even after she had come out within a lesbian community, Parker's readings in other settings saw her playing down or omitting queer material. In 1957, Lorraine Hansberry had written several letters under a pseudonym to D.O.B. magazine *The Ladder* and was invited to join the organization the following year, though she declined. Hansberry's letters to *The Ladder* had been published only under the initials 'L.N.' and were only revealed as hers by Barbara Grier in 1970, though at this stage they were hardly widely known. Even today, her articles on feminism and queer sexuality have only recently been unearthed, while her play 'Andromeda the Thief' (1958–1961), a historical materialist take on Sappho concerning the attempted abolition of Greek slavery, remains unpublished to this day (Stein 2017, n.p.; Higashida 2011; Perry 2018; Rich 1979; Mumford 2014, n.p.). Besides Hansberry, other lesbian black writers of an earlier generation included Philadelphia-based Anita Cornwell, a contributor to *Soulbook, The Ladder, and Negro Digest*, who in 1983 wrote the first collection of essays by an African American lesbian, *Black Lesbian in White America*, and who would interview Parker in 1975; and journalist, novelist, and librarian Ann Ellen Shockley, who in 1974 would publish *Loving Her*, likely the first novel published in the US to feature a Black lesbian protagonist (Shockley 1997, 285). When Parker came out in writing, however, Shockley had not yet published her novel; the queerness of the Harlem Renaissance, later excavated by Gloria Hull, Maureen Honey, and others, remained underexplored or unknown (Hull; Honey, 24; Johnson, xviii). As Barbara Smith wrote in her 1978 essay 'Towards a Black Feminist Criticism', Parker was breaking ground 'in the vast wilderness of works that do not exist' (Smith 1978b, 26).

In the absence of Black queer predecessors, it was through her developing friendship with Judy Grahn that Parker found validation for her voice as a lesbian poet. As she later told Kate Rushin: 'There was me and Judy. We could decide to be enemies and compete, or we could decide to support each other. We took the route of supporting each other' (Rushin 1985, 28). Another key friendship would be that with Audre Lorde, whom Parker first met in 1969 on Lorde's 'first trip to the West coast', and whom, a few years later, she persuaded to 'come out with her poetry' (Parker 2016, 25; *ASR*, 188).[5] The two would correspond until Parker's death, and though the relationship could be fractious—in part due to classed differences of attitudes to literature—it remained deeply sustaining for both.[6]

From 1970 onwards, as Grahn notes, Parker had, in effect been 'straight to the black community and gay to the white community [. . .] [she] would arrive at the Black Cat in North Beach for readings to her straight audience in skirts, and show up to her lesbian readings as a dyke in cowboy boots and pants. She must have done this from 1969 at least through 1971' (*ASR*, 186). Increasingly, however, Parker began to bridge these worlds. Four of Parker's poems had appeared in *Woman to Woman*; her first book, *Child of Myself*, appeared from Alta's Shameless Hussy Press in 1971 and the Women's Press Collective the following year. Reprinting poems from previous publications and poems concerning her first marriage, her relationship to her mother, beauty standards, love, and the self, the collection ends with a tentative series of lesbian love poems: the first, which begins, 'move in darkness / know the touch of a woman', ends on self-hatred— 'wrinkled ugliness / sin / fear / admission // two days later / you shutter [*sic*] / & take 2 aspirins'—but the subsequent poems move to self-acceptance—'with the sun - / fear leaves me'—and a newfound note of queer eroticism: 'A woman's flesh learns slow by fire and pestle, / Like succulent meats, it must be sucked and eaten' (Parker 1972, n.p.). The final poem resolves:

> Let me come to you naked
> come without my masks
> come dark
> and lay beside you [...]
> Let me come to you strong
> come sure and free
> come powerful
> and lay with you.
>
> (Parker 1972, n.p.)

'I was making [my early love poems] sound like they could be for a man', Parker later observed. 'Finally I stopped trying to be so damned universal. I write out of where I'm at' (Woodwoman, 61). 'By 1972, when we published the revised edition of *Child of Myself*, wrote Grahn, Parker 'allow[ed] herself a completely dyke public identification to all her communities' (*ASR*, 186). Parker's second collection, *Pit Stop* (1973), opens with a more affirmative and explicit poem of queer love: 'My lover is a woman / & when i hold her - / feel her warmth - / i feel good - feel safe' (Parker 1973, n.p.). By 1975, Parker could assert: 'I'm a lesbian, a feminist, and I'm Black. I know there are problems splitting within those groups but to survive I cannot separate myself from any of them even though at times I'm isolated from all three' (Jane, 10). Likewise, asked to define 'revolution', she would remark:

> If I could take all my parts with me when I go somewhere, and not have to say to one of the, 'No, you stay home tonight, you won't be welcome', because I'm going to an all-white party where I can be gay, but not Black, or I'm going to a Black poetry reading, and half the poets are antihomosexual, or thousands of situations where something of what I am cannot come with me. The day all the different parts of me can come along, we would have what I would call a revolution. (Parker 1978, 11)

Parker's poetry frequently turned on the conscious and unconscious exclusions that prevented the formation of a community in which 'all the different parts of me' would fit. Such concerns were of particular import for the concerns that, as we saw in the previous chapter, had led to the emergence of lesbian separatist organizing out of the confluences of the Black Power, New Left, and Women's Liberation movements, and Parker remained particularly attuned to the blind spots, as well as the new possibilities, that remained within emergent lesbian feminist communities. Her poem 'I have a dream too', first published at the conclusion to *Pit Stop*, provides a concise summary of the politics that drove such a position, for which poetry often remained the first place of articulation.

'THE FIRST EVERYTHING' 265

Suggesting at once Martin Luther King's famed March on Washington speech, Langston Hughes' 'I, too, sing America', and Hughes' famous 'dream deferred', referenced in Parker's later 'Jonestown'—Parker enters a tradition of African American oratory and poetics, in dialogue with both white supremacy and with the gendered oversights within the movement itself. The speaker insists, in the opening stanzas, that their 'dream' is

> not Martin's [...]
> not the dream of the vanguard
> not to turn this world—all over
> not the dream of the masses
> not the dream of women
>
> (Parker 2016, 90)

Parker's dream is instead more local: that of being able to walk down the street, into bars and bathrooms, without fear of harassment from the police, bikers, and homophobes of all kinds. In its analysis of the meanings of the word 'revolution'—a term with much contemporaneous currency—the poem might appear to criticize or step back from the goal of large-scale revolutionary transformation. Yet, by placing the analysis at the level of movement through daily life—the street, the hamburger stand, the bathroom, the queer bar, 'ghetto streets'—the poem aims to return to the specific reasons for struggle, moving abstractions, and beyond the condemnation and sidelining of queer women's desires, particularly those of queer women of colour, historically felt within movements claiming revolutionary goals. What is at stake above all is the body: Parker's body, the bodies of her friends, raced, gendered, sexualized; the body placed on the gears for a number of social movements from Women's Liberation to the New Left yet excluded and abused whenever it trespasses its assigned place.

In *Pit Stop*, Parker castigates the misogynist violence covered over by male activists with talk of 'the system'—'Brother [. . .] that system / you hit me with / is called / a fist'; likewise, she calls out white women for unacknowledged racism: 'SISTER! your foot's smaller / but it's still on my neck' (Parker 1972, n.p.). But 'I have a dream' does not reject the dreams found in anti-imperialist dreams: 'malcolm's and martin's / [. . .] mao's and huey's [. . .] george's and angela's / in the north & south / of Vietnam & America / & Africa' (Parker 2016, 91). Punningly joining struggles in the American South to those against American imperialism in South Vietnam and South America and against apartheid in South Africa, Parker identifies Global North and Global South as linked spheres of struggle, of which the local locations where she experiences harassment—hamburger stand, bar, street, bathroom—are also fronts. And while the poem privileges these local experiences over broader geographies that may

266 NEVER BY ITSELF ALONE

be experienced as abstractions, it also allows for the possibility that they might mirror each other, that both locations might form the basis of revolutionary social transformation. 'now I'm tired / you listen!' Parker insists in the poem's final lines. 'i have a dream too / it's a simple dream'.

Movements in Black

Involved in collective households since 1971 and closely involved with the multi-racial Women's Press Collective, Parker nonetheless felt a social gap within the developing Bay Area lesbian feminist scene, and it was during this time that she formed the group Gente as a support group for lesbians of colour. As she explained to Libby Woodwoman:

> Gente grew out of the bar scene in San Francisco [. . .] The bars are run by white women, and they're just trying to make money [. . .] Black people feel unwelcome in the bars—they don't cater to us, even the music on the jukeboxes is white music. When we come into a bar together, a group of black and 3rd World women, they assume we're going to make trouble [. . .] We formed our own 3rd World [basketball and softball] team, and then the shit hit the fan. (Woodwoman, 60–61)

In part a consciousness-raising group, meeting in Parker's living room, in part a softball team and singing group, Gente expanded to nearly forty members, including novelist and professor Dodici Azpadu, musician Linda Tillery—a key member of the Olivia Records Collective and producer of the 'Varied Voices of Black Women' tour on which Parker performed in 1978—and Linda Wilson, earlier a member of GWL (Hobson; *ASR*, 161; 'We have to be our own spark', 25). The group also raised money for women in prison and were active in the campaigns to free Inez García and Joann Little. Though Gente disbanded in 1976, its bonds continued: Gente member Joanne Garrett was nursed through end-of-life care by another member of the group, while Linda Tillery and a group of other African American lesbians lived on the same block in Emeryville, offering each other camaraderie and support (*ASR*, 227).

Parker attests to the renewed experience of community found in Gente; the two poems that open her third pamphlet, *Womanslaughter*. 'Gente' charts an experience of finally being able to speak out:

> [. . .] to say
> my sisters
> and not have

'THE FIRST EVERYTHING' 267

> *any* reservations.
> [. . .] to sit in a room
>
> and say
> 'Have you ever felt like . . . ?'
> and somebody has.
>
> (Parker 2016, 141)

'Group' opens with an unattributed epigraph: 'The primary lessons learned by any / minority is self-hatred'. 'I do not know / when my lessons began', Parker writes, before outlining incidents of racial hatred and internalized self-hatred—whether through schooling, playground chants, make-up products used to enforce white female beauty standards—such 'teaching' is both institutional and extra-institutional. It goes all the way down, and naming it defies the existing modes of knowledge by which we are taught to apprehend the world and navigate it as social beings. The poem ends by contrasting these 'lessons' to the new paradigm found in Gente. For Parker, the 'Beautiful Black Women' in the group function as 'new teachers' offering 'news lessons', their presence facilitating a process of self-discovery predicated on a love at once erotic, sisterly, and social:

> [. . .] I am in love
> with each of them
> & [. . .] in the act of loving
> each woman
> I have learned a new lesson
> I have learned
> to love myself.
>
> (Parker 2016, 144)

In Parker's collected poems, *Movement in Black*, 'Group' and 'Gente' both appear in a section entitled 'Love Poems'. As in Grahn's 'redefinition [. . .] of love' in 'A Woman Is Talking To Death', love offers not just erotic companionship but also a paradigm shift, countering the internalized, everyday lessons of racial and gendered violence and belittlement. Such poems sketch out a counter-education and a new way of being. This collective dimension, predicated on a reckoning with self, manifested in particular in the sphere of poetry readings and performance. As we saw in the seventh chapter, the collective readings around Audre Lorde's 'Need' and the launch events for *This Bridge Called My Back* coalesced around communities at once poetic and political. And perhaps no poem of the '70s exemplifies this tendency more than Parker's 1977 poem 'Movement in Black'.

268 NEVER BY ITSELF ALONE

As Cheryl Clarke notes, at readings, 'Parker was known to read new work, ask for feedback from her audiences *in medias res*, and write in the changes right there on the spot' (Parker 1999, 15). For 'Movement in Black', Parker would always read the poem with other women in attendance. 'She was lead voice and caller. Black women from the community of her audience and those sharing the stage with Parker would be volunteered to be back-ups and response chorus' (Parker 1999, 19). The poem's performance history establishes multiple, shifting communities around the presence of Parker herself—and, indeed, in the tribute readings that took place after her death: from its debut in Oakland in December 1977, to its appearance on the 1978 'Varied Voices of Black Women' tour, which began in San Francisco and ended, in conjunction with the Combahee River Collective and the Bessie Smith Memorial Collective, in Massachusetts, with musicians Vicki Randle, Alberta Jackson, and Gente member Linda Tillery; with fellow queer writers Cheryl Clarke, Jewelle Gomez, and Barbara Smith at the National Conference of Black Lesbians and Gays in St Louis in 1985; and with family members at Cal State the year of her death in 1989 (Parker 2016, 93; 'Varied Voices', n.d., n.p.; *GCN* 1989:7).

'Movement' adopts the collective, multi-sectional form also found in Grahn's 'The Common Woman' and 'A Woman Is Talking To Death', Ntozake Shange's *for colored girls who have considered suicide when the rainbow is enuff*, and in Lorde's 'Need', on which, as I've argued, it was likely a direct influence. The poem's three sections perform variants on individual and collective identity and historical progress, offering a kind of extremely condensed potted history of Black women in America. The first addresses slavery and the acts of defiance and sacrifice that have gone unnoticed and unrecorded— 'I am the slave / that chose to die / I jumped overboard / & no one cried'; in the second, the refrain 'I am the black woman / & I have been all over', anchors a series of events and actions set during the War of Independence, through the Civil War and to 'San Francisco / with gay liberation [...] / D.C. with / the radical dykes' (Parker 2016, 95–96, 98). The third focuses on contemporary lives, while the fourth offers a 'rollcall' of notable Black women through US history as a kind of concluding litany or blessing.

Adopting the first person as inherently multi-voiced, Parker lays claim to multiple lives, supported by the collective refrains provided by a kind of Black women's backing chorus, akin to that in Kate Rushin's Black Back-Ups, but her placed centre stage. The multiple resonances of 'movement' in the poem's title suggest at once: political movements; the sectional form of the poem, akin to movements in a musical work; the kinetic insistence of dance, of work song, of church service or protest march; and historical movement in time—not only the charting of past sufferings but also the process of revolution and the establishment of a more just world. As in the chorus to a song, the repetitions of the poem's title-refrain—'movement in black / can't

'THE FIRST EVERYTHING' 269

keep 'em back'—are each time the same, yet each time transformed by the verses they surrounds: each verse builds up a fuller picture of the movement named and enacted by the refrain and of the multiple lives encompassed by the category of 'the black woman'.

Cheryl Clarke compares the poem's opening to Sterling Brown's 1931 poem 'Strong Men'—'Strong men just keep a-comin' on / The strong men git stronger', as a bold adaptation of Brown's collective, masculine vision of race pride and the movement from slavery to freedom which serves as both homage to and partial corrective of a spirit of collective pride which explicitly or implicitly overlooks 'half the human race' (Parker 1999, 17). Likewise, in the second section, the refrain—'I have been all over [. . .] I was there'— suggests its own variant on Section 33 of Whitman's 'Song of Myself': 'I am the man, I suffer'd, I was there' (Whitman, 59). As Rachael L. Nichols notes these lines—also adopted as the epigraphs to James Baldwin's *Giovanni's Room*—'evoke the complicated politics of inclusion in Whitman's work: the push-pull between sympathetic embrace and forced appropriation that is intimately bound up with Whitman's thought about race [. . .] appear[ing] shortly before one of the most well-known stanzas, "I am the hounded slave, I wince at the bite of dogs" ' (Nichols 2015, 503; Wilson 2014, 12). 'All these I feel or am', Whitman argues in a catalogue of suffering: 'Agonies are one of my changes of garments, / I do not ask the wounded person how he feels, I myself become the wounded person' (Whitman, 60). In the foreword to her 1981 collection *Passion*, June Jordan would famously argue that Whitman's act of radical sympathy afforded formidable inspiration for a contemporary 'people's poetry' (Jordan 1980, ix–xxvi). But whereas Whitman claims presence as *witness*—including to the injustices of slavery and genocide against Native Americans—Parker's 'I' claims present as *participant* and 'survivor' (Parker 2016, 101).

If the second part of Parker's poem glances at a foundational statement of democratic aspiration within queer male American poetics, its third part suggests a more laconic variant on Grahn's 'She Who'. Grahn's 'I am the dyke in the matter, the other / I am the wall with the womanly swagger / I am the dragon, the dangerous dagger / I am the bulldyke, the bulldagger' becomes in Parker's poem: 'I'm a junkie with jones / I'm the dyke in a bar/ I'm the matron at a county jail / I'm the defendant with nothin' to say' (96). Here are found the voices of suffering and silence as much as of defiance. The identity the poem so insistently claims—that of 'the Black woman', the 'survivor', contains Whitmanesque multitudes—the voices of the defeated, the silenced, the suicided, and of slave-era collaborator—acknowledging that this selfhood cannot simply be affirmed without acknowledging the contradictions that have formed and continued to shape it. Hence the present tense imperative: 'I am the slave / that chose to die', 'I am a survivor'.

270   NEVER BY ITSELF ALONE

History is a process of continual movement; it is also contested territory, and Parker's call to community seeks to intervene against centuries of silencing. Textually and in its performative dimension, Parker's is a literal call to presence, a reminder of continuing existence, a position from which to build. The poem's fourth section offers a 'rollcall' of the names of Black women, from Phillis Wheatley and Sojourner Truth through to Nikki Giovanni, Jordan, Lorde, and 'all the names we don't know yet' (97). As I suggest in this book's introduction, these are the names, not just for notable individuals but also for the nameless and unnamed, for collective movements and identities, and, ultimately, for a transfigured and transformed world. Lines of mourning and reckoning, they also serve as a utopian placeholder for what's to come.

'I have gained many sisters': 'Womanslaughter'

In March 1989, Parker performed 'Movement in Black' at Cal State, Los Angeles, with her niece, two sisters, Ethel and Diane, and writer Ayofemi Stowe Folyan in what would be her final reading, given just four months before her own death (Parker 2016, 93, 457; *GCN* 1989:7). In this reading, Parker came full circle. From her earliest poems, she had addressed the structures, at once offering the possibility of love and the reality of violence and exclusion, of the family: her abusive relationship to Ed Bullins, her difficult relationship to her parents. Parker was acutely aware of the unacknowledged trauma, repression, and violence that can be passed down through and within family. In the second poem from *Pit Stop*, Parker writes:

> my self is
> my big hands -
> like my father's
> & torn innards
> like my mother's
> & they both felt
> & were -
> & i am a product of that -
> & not a political consciousness
>   (Parker 2016, 51)

In Parker's work, the family both protects against and reinforces the psychic hurt perpetuated within existing social structures. As Grahn suggests, Parker often figures this complex, conflicted web of 'tightly held feelings' through the metaphor of 'innards': 'My innards are twisted / and torn and sectioned - / like

'THE FIRST EVERYTHING' 271

my father's' (18, 52). In 1971, five months after the death of their father, Parker's sister, Shirley Jones, was murdered by her husband, who was then acquitted of the charge of murder. 'Innards' recur at the beginning and the climax of 'Womanslaughter', the poem in which Parker reckons with this horrific event. 'It doesn't hurt as much now - / the thought of you dead / doesn't rip at my innards', the poem begins (149). The poem ends with a warning of revenge against perpetrators of femicide: 'I will come with my many sisters / and decorate the streets / with the innards of those / brothers in womenslaughter' (156).

'Womanslaughter' opens with Parker and her sisters coming together for the funeral of their father, five months before Shirley's death—'children, survivors / of Texas Hell, survivors / of soul-searing poverty, / survivors of small town / mentality'—and it ends with a claim to sisterhood that both includes and expands beyond that of the bonds of the biological family (149). The poem stages a coming together, based on the real-life coming together at family occasions— weddings and funerals—and the difficulties and contradictions of speaking about the issues of gender violence within the family, but this coming together also insistently moves outside the poem. 'I worked on that poem for three years', Parker later recalled. 'I couldn't do anything else until I got that one out' (Woodwoman, 61).[7] Reading Grahn's 'A Woman Is Talking To Death' provided the key: 'I read it over and over. Then it hit me how to get *Womanslaughter* out' (61). As Grahn observed, 'A Woman Is Talking To Death' had itself been modelled on Parker's 'Goat Child', 'the first deliberately autobiographical poem by a woman that I had ever heard' (Parker 1978, 13–14). This community in writing enables Parker to bear witness to the heteropatriarchal violence which so often structures the bonds of intimate community, unacknowledged, but ever present in courts of law and in the daily cultural imaginary, and in so doing, to build community once again.

As in Grahn's poem, a death is central: but whereas that poem turns on the state's punitive, racist sentencing of a Black man for an accidental death, here, the courts *refuse* to fully punish the femicide of a Black woman, Parker's title a bitter pun on the lesser charge by which her sister's murderer is sentenced. Grahn's defiant apostrophe, 'ho death', is instead literalized as 'Hello, Hello Death', in response to the phone calls informing Parker of the murder, and her sister's desperate calls to disbelieving police: 'Hello, Hello Police [. . .] my husband means to kill me' (Parker 2016, 149, 52). In the seventh chapter, I suggested that the nursery rhyme epigraph to Audre Lorde's 'Need'—a poem likely inspired by 'Womanslaughter'—alludes to the informal linguistic pedagogies which establish male violence as cultural norm. Likewise, the third section of Parker's poem opens with an ironic variant on the nursery rhyme 'There Was a Crooked Man':

272 NEVER BY ITSELF ALONE

> There was a quiet man
> He married a quiet wife
> Together, they lived
> a quiet life.
>
> Not so, not so
> her sisters said
> the truth comes out
> as she lies dead.
> He beat her.
>
> (151)

In its dialogic structure, the poem offers a riposte to the silence that hides away domestic violence. Yet in the following lines, the court of law only serves to reinforce such silence, as Parker goes on to relate the trial in which her sister is subjected to posthumous slander, accused by the courts of lesbian affairs that 'justified' her husband's jealous rage, an angle leading to his ultimate acquittal.

> What shall be done with this man?
> Is it a murder of the first degree?
> No, said the men,
> It is a crime of passion.
> He was angry.
>
> (154)

As Parker ironically summarizes, in the eyes of the law: 'Men cannot rape their wives / Men cannot kill their wives / They passion them to death' (156). In its final section, the poem challenges this crime of acquittal—and the state's leveraging of harsh sentences against poor and Black subjects—ending in a passionate claim of sisterhood that extends to and beyond Parker's murdered biological sister.

> I have gained many sisters.
> And if one is beaten,
> or raped, or killed,
> I will not come in mourning black [. . .]
> I will come with my many sisters
> and decorate the streets
> with the innards of those
> brothers in womenslaughter [. . .]
> I will come to my sisters,
> not dutiful,
> I will come strong.
>
> (156)

'THE FIRST EVERYTHING' 273

In its composition and subsequent circulation, 'Womanslaughter' moved from the local to the global, travelling the paths of violence—particularly gendered violence—that have characterized the movements of racial capitalism. In 1976, Parker presented the as-yet unpublished poem at a panel on femicide at the International Tribunal on Crimes against Women, a people's tribunal indirectly inspired by Bertrand Russell's International War Crimes Tribune concerning the war in Vietnam, and organized by Diana E. H. Russell, a Berkeley-based activist formerly involved in armed struggle against the South African state, and Belgian journalist Nicole Van de Ven. Taking place from March 4–8, 1976, in Brussels, the conference was attended by 2,000 women from forty countries (Russell 1976, xiii, xvi–xvii, 145–50, 219). On this global stage, Parker's poem offered a testimony as telling and stark as the witness statements offered in more conventional formats. Ten years later, Parker once more presented the poem, travelling to Nairobi, Kenya and Ghana with a UN women's delegation raising awareness about gender violence (Parker and Lorde, fn. 64, 65).

Parker's *Movement in Black* is dedicated 'To my families, the one I was born into & the one I've chosen'. Below are Adinkra symbols for 'AYA, the fern, a symbol of defiance' and 'NKYIMKYIM, twisted pattern, changing one's self or playing many parts' (Parker 1999, 12). And, in the 1980s, Parker ended up playing an unforeseen role, co-parenting a child with ex-partner Laura Brown and adopting and raising another with her partner Marty Dunham (Rushin 1985, 29; Parker and Lorde, 50–51). Speaking out against Anita Bryant's 'Save Our Children' campaign and the Briggs Initiative in California, specifically targeted at gay and lesbian school workers and based around homophobic fears and stereotypes of queer people as predating on children, Parker's poem 'For The Straight Folks Who Don't Mind Gays But Wish They Weren't So Blatant' was recorded for *Lesbian Concentrate,* a 1977 album responding to Bryant's campaign. Sardonically responding to Bryant's comments about 'blatant' homosexuals, the poem was advertised the following year in a Diana Press blurb as 'the poem that Anita Bryant made famous' (Garber, 66). 'The nuclear family is the basic unit of capitalism and in order for us to move to revolution it has to be destroyed', Parker argued in 1980 (Parker 2016, 258; Lewis 2022, 31–35). But, as Parker notes in her 1987 essay 'Gay Parenting, Or, Look Out, Anita', first published in *Politics of the Heart: A Lesbian Parenting Anthology*, her own decision to become a queer parent drew on non-normative traditions also found with the Black family. 'The family structure we utilized is not new. Extended families have always existed in Black culture. We simply modified it slightly' (Parker 2016, 269).

From 'innards'—the 'torn', 'twisted', and 'calloused' connections that bind families together—to creatively 'twisted patterns' and the 'many parts' of her life as poet, activist, and lesbian mother, Parker's project was a constant interrogation of the limits and interconnections of existing patterns of behaviour and being for community and for self. 'once upon a time,' writes Parker in the final poem in *Movement in Black*, 'there was a dream / a dream of women. A dream of women /

274 NEVER BY ITSELF ALONE

coming together and turning the world / around [...] all women being sisters. / a dream of caring; a dream of protection, a dream / of peace'. Yet, 'for the / women who believed the dream - there is dying, women, / sisters dying' (Parker 2016, 162). Nonetheless, that dream, Parker concludes 'lives for those who need a sister / it lives for those who once upon a time had a dream'. Whether in poetry or activism and community work, Parker's work through the late '70s and '80s would endeavour to keep that dream alive.

'Where do you go to become a non-citizen?'

In 1978, Parker began a full-time job at the Oakland Feminist Women's Health Center, one of the first women's abortion clinics in the country. 'Evolv[ing]', as Parker noted, 'out of the self-help movement which began in Los Angeles back in the early '60's', the Center had been established in 1972 from an Oakland household by then-teenaged Laura Kay Brown, later Parker's partner for a number of years: Parker served as board member and medical coordinator until 1987, overseeing its growth from one to six sites (ASR, 157–59; Parker and Lorde, 50–51; Douglas, 3; GCN 1989: 12). This expansion was, however, met with the very real threat of violence. As Parker observed in 1984: 'The right to abortion is dangerously in jeopardy now. Clinics are being bombed, doctors are being kidnapped, people who work in the clinics are having pickets outside their homes. One never knows from one day to the next when they go to work, whether or not they're going to walk into a building or if they're going to walk into a burned-out shell' (Douglas, 3). The following year, the Center's Los Angeles clinic was indeed firebombed. Co-worker Debbie Gregg recalled: 'Except for what Pat believed was an act of the goddess, she would have lost her life in that firebombing: she had intended to sleep at the clinic the night that it was attacked but changed her mind at the last minute and went to stay with family' (GCN 1989, 7).

As such incidents indicate, the 1980s were a time of increasing right-wing hostility on almost every front. Such conditions necessitated coalitional organizing. As Emily Hobson notes, the struggle against the Briggs Initiative in 1978 drew multiple groups together because it was at once an attack on sexuality and workers' rights; meanwhile, queer activists organized in solidarity with the Chilean left against Pinochet, and in the 1980s, against further US intervention in Nicaragua, and in tandem with anti-nuclear activism, while the 'White Night Riots', sparked by the acquittal of Harvey Milk's murderer, supervisor Dan White, indicated a continuing militancy on the part of significant sectors of the Bay's queer community (Hobson, 88–90). In turn, such activism coalesced with some of the earliest direct activism against AIDS, as explored in relation to the protest at the Livermore Labs in this book's eleventh chapter. As suggested by the

'THE FIRST EVERYTHING' 275

present chapter's readings of 'I have a dream, too', as well as by her participation in international initiatives concerning violence against women, Parker had always maintained an international consciousness. In September 1975, for example, she had read alongside Tede Matthews at a march held by Gays in Solidarity with the Chilean Resistance (GSCR) and the sex worker's organization COYOTE (Call Off Your Old Tired Ethics) to mark the second anniversary of the fascist coup in Chile (Hobson, 75–76). And, in April 1980, spurred by the hostage crisis in Iran, increased talk of nuclear escalation with the Soviet Union, US intervention in South America, and the rise of right-wing violence and state homophobia domestically, she wrote to Audre Lorde to propose the creation of a group she called the Revolutionary Black Women's Council.

'I feel', Parker writes, 'that now is the time for people to understand and implement coalition politics; that now is the time for an organization that addresses itself not only to the needs of Black people in this country but to have a global perspective and understand our connection with other third world countries' (Parker and Lorde, 52). The following August, Parker gave a speech under the auspices of the Council at ¡BASTA! Women's Conference on Imperialism and Third World War in Oakland: entitled 'Revolution: It's Not Neat or Pretty or Quick', it would be published in *This Bridge Called My Back* the following year.[8] 'In order to leave here prepared to be a strong force in the fight against imperialism', Parker argues, 'we must have a clear understanding of what imperialism is and how it manifests in our lives'. Behind the hostage crisis in Iran lies a longer history of oil and power: under the Shah, 'the people of Iran were exploited in order for Americans to drive gas-guzzling monsters' (Parker 2016, 254). Domestically, the alarming resurgence of the KKK and neo-Nazis cannot be disentangled from the racism of the state. '[These] are functionaries, tools of this governmental system', Parker argues, '[who] serve in the same ways as our armed forces and police [. . .] [They] are the arms and legs of the congressmen, the businessmen, the Tri-lateral Commission' (255–56). 'I am not a good American', Parker continues. 'I do not wish to have the world colonized, bombarded and plundered in order to eat steak' (256).

Arguing that 'the women's movement has allowed itself to be co-opted and mis-directed'—as, for instance, in in the argument that 'women should be drafted in exchange for passage of the ERA [Equal Rights Act]' (256)—Parker diagnoses the co-option of both feminist and queer movements through what is today known as 'pinkwashing'. Single-issue politics, Parker insists, will never accomplish widespread change. Without giving up her commitment to the Black struggle, Parker insists on coalitional politics; without giving up her commitment to lesbian feminism, she insists that women cannot act alone. Concluding her speech by quoting Grahn's 'She Who', Parker insists that, while the conjuncture of the late '60s may have necessitated separatist organizing, it is the task of the '80s

276 NEVER BY ITSELF ALONE

to build a new coalition that corrects the errors of previous tendencies, separatist and integrationist alike, along anti-imperialist lines.

> In order to survive in this world we must make a commitment to change it; not reform it [. . .] Here is where we should air our differences but here is also where we should build [. . .] Here is where we begin to build a new women's movement, not one easily co-opted and mis-directed by media pigs and agents of this insidious imperialist system. (259)

In the years following Parker's speech, conditions worsened. In August 1985, she wrote to Lorde:

> Sister love, the shit is scaring me. The fascists are getting bolder and bolder and the people are eating up this patriotic, nationalistic madness. I listen to the call in radio shows and it makes me want to go out and buy a machine gun [. . .] [c]ompared to the madness that I think is coming, Hitler was a choir boy. We are not going to have to deal with one maniac, but with a whole nation of maniacs. (Parker and Lorde, 75–76)

Parker's work would speak strongly and powerfully to the specific historical conjuncture in what would be the last book of new work published in her lifetime, *Jonestown and Other Madness* (1985), focusing on incidents such as the mass suicide of nearly a thousand of Jim Jones' primarily African American followers in Jonestown, Guyana in November 1978 and the Atlanta child murders of 1979–1981. At the time, the so-called 'Jonestown massacre' was 'the largest single incident of intentional civilian death in American history' (Conroy, n.p.). Jones' Peoples Temple had originated in California with a nominally socialist politics, and, shortly before its horrific *dénouement*, had received messages of support from Angela Davis and Huey P. Newton, unaware of the cultish conditions in the settlement. The title poem juxtaposes a narrative of the Jonestown massacre with a message drummed into Parker's head as a child: 'Black folks do not commit suicide' (Parker 2016, 221). Quoting an interview from a former member of Jones's People's Temple who remembers that, before Jones, 'no one had ever cared / that much about me before', Parker insists that 'Jim Jones was not the cause / he was the result / of 400 years / of not caring' (225, 227). It was the indifference or hostility of white Americans—from 'teachers' to 'policemen', 'welfare workers', 'shopkeepers', 'church people', and 'politicians'—which, Parker suggests, drove Jones's followers to their deaths.

> the Black people
> in Jonestown

> did not commit suicide
> they were murdered in
> small southern towns
> they were murdered in
> big northern cities [. . .]
> they didn't die at Jonestown
> they went to Jonestown dead
>
> (226)

In 'Georgia, Georgia, Georgia On My Mind', concerning the Atlanta child murders, Parker contrasts suppositions on the part of the police that the killers are Black and fears within her own community that the perpetrators are a Klan or a Neo-Nazi group, insisting that the question of whether the murders were collectively planned or the actions of 'one insane fool' is not the key issue. Those ultimately responsible for the systematic, structurally enforced social murder of Black children 'wear the suits of / businessman / buy ghetto apartments / and overcharge the rent [. . .] scream about / juvenile crime / and refuse to build childcare centers' (202). They may even masquerade as saviours.

In these poems, as in 'Womanslaughter', Parker's systemic analysis is predicated on a bitterly ironic verbal turn of phrase, from everyday speech or from legal judgements or newspaper reports. Pivoting on such phrases, the poem contextualizes the common sense that attempts and fails to make sense of apparently inexplicable acts of violence directed outwards or of self-harm. As she writes in the foreword: 'The tragedy of Jonestown occurred in 1978. It is amazing to me that we have not demanded better explanations of what happened' (189). 'Explanation' here does not mean simply an investigation into the particular circumstances of Jonestown—an investigation that might, for instance, allege state involvement. Rather, it suggests a much broader social diagnosis of the conditions that produced an incident which appears, at first sight, to be a horrific aberration. No incident is 'isolated', to be explained away by labels like 'crime of passion', 'suicide', or 'insane fool': instead, this work relentlessly disentangles the 'innards' that string together life in Reagan's America—an America whose legacy persists to this day.

'Where do you go to become a non-citizen?', asks a poem of Parker's first published in *Womanslaughter*. 'I wanna resign; I want out' (Parker 2016, 69). Growing up in the apartheid South in the '40s and '50s, and coming to poetic and political maturity within the Bay Area radicalism of the '60s and '70s, Parker knew what it was like to be 'a child of America / a step child / raised in the back room / yet taught / taught how to act / in her front room' (71). Refusing to be a 'good American', she remained a vociferous critic of that nation until her death.

278 NEVER BY ITSELF ALONE

Conclusion: On Simplicity, Class, and Literary Judgement

In a late essay, 'The 1987 March on Washington', Parker emphasized the need for struggles specific to women's communities—notably, the cancer from which she, Audre Lorde, and Karen Brodine would pass away—with the cross-community effects of AIDS and demands for universal healthcare. Radicals must, she emphasized, 'organize and march for a national health care system so that any person needing medical care can get it in this country' (Parker 2016, 276). Such issues were close to home. Diagnosed with breast cancer in 1987, the very year she had left the Oakland Feminist Women's Health Center to concentrate on her writing, she passed away in June 1989 at the age of forty-five (White, 214). Parker's was a life and an oeuvre that remains incomplete. And this extends to the absence of subsequent critical evaluations of her work. Given this, I'd like to end this chapter with some brief comments on her place in literary history and the classed standards by which her work has been judged—or ignored—to date.

As her correspondence with Audre Lorde suggests, Parker frequently found that she did not have time to write due to the need to earn a wage—including working full time with the Oakland Feminist Women's Health Center from 1978 to 1987, a situation she dramatizes with characteristic wit in the poem 'maybe i should have been a teacher': 'The next person who asks / "have you written anything new?" / just might get hit' (Parker 2016, 211; Rushin 1985, 29; Parker and Lorde, 62; White, 214) In a memorial piece published in *Gay Community News*, co-worker Debbie Gregg comments: 'I continue to be amazed at how productive Pat was as a poet, while she was putting in 60-plus hours per week at the Center' (*GCN* 1989: 7). Yet Parker's ability, attested by Gregg, to speak to women of all backgrounds as part of her work at the Center, in women's prisons, and in many other situations, suggests that the reach of her poetry far outstrips the time she was able to devote to it.

Throughout her career, Parker's work reached those not normally touched by poetry. In 1985, for instance, after a reading in Boston, she observed to Kate Rushin: 'A lot of women came up afterwards to say—and I still hear this to some extent—that they didn't like poetry, were never interested in it, but that they heard things expressed in the poems they never knew anybody else was thinking or feeling' (Rushin 1985, 28). In her poems, Emily Erwin Culpepper argues, Parker 'crafts regular speech into a vehicle for complex meanings' (*GCN* 1989: 6). As Parker suggested to Rushin: 'My poetry is understandable, and that confuses a lot of people. It seems very simple, and people don't realize how much work that is [. . .] Unfortunately, many people assume this is an easy thing to do, and that's hurt my credibility as a poet—I'm not "academic" enough' (Rushin 1985, 28). The apparent simplicity of Parker's work is invariably complex because it speaks of social facts excluded from the raced, classed, and gendered world of what had

'THE FIRST EVERYTHING' 279

hitherto been accepted as literature, of what enters the marketplace of literary, philosophical, and political value.

Judy Grahn has insisted that the levels of skill and craft—that's to say, labour—involved in her own and in Parker's poetry were often bypassed because she and Parker 'carefully advertised ourselves as working class', reinforcing assumptions about the relation between 'expressive' and 'skilled' poetry, and thus of the relation in general between expression, skill, and labour (*ASR*, 183). Grahn notes key facets of Parker's work as 'irony and suspense': the poem building toward the punch line that reinforces a point, opens up a new question, or suggests an answer, either leading towards affirmative recognition, and thus group building, on the part of the audience, or reinforcing the inequalities, imbalances, and separations within that audience (184). Humour, whether warm or mordant, speaks to issues from gender violence to white supremacy, and the ironies of social relations of all kinds: 'your sounds drift down / oh god! / oh jesus! / and i think— / here it is, some dude's / getting credit for what / a woman / has done, / again'; 'brother [. . .] that system / you hit me with / is called / a fist'; 'Tour America! / perhaps, / it would be better // to blow it up'; the final line of 'Group', 'i have learned / to love myself'; the final line of 'my lady ain't no lady', 'cause i ain't no gentleman' (Parker 2016, 110, 54, 77, 144, 120).

Because Parker's work had such directness, and because her reading style was so persuasive, the careful placement of line, phrase, and image in her work was de-emphasized, even by friends and supporters, who criticized Parker's supposed temporal limitations, arguing that the work was primarily 'oral' rather than page-based (Parker 2016, 25; Smith 1978a, 99). Yet, as Grahn notes, in selecting material from Parker's notebooks for her first book, 'we discussed everything about the structure of her poems, every line and punctuation' (*ASR*, 185). Parker's poems were carefully honed interventions, designed, as Grahn puts it, to be 'accessible, political, and effective' (184). And their effectiveness is perhaps, paradoxically, indexed in the fact that they are so often ignored by a literary criticism that bases its criteria of value on precisely those qualities—ambiguity, complication, density—which Parker strenuously condenses into the complex simplicity of her work.

Parker, as Cheryl Clarke argues, drew on the poets of the Black Arts Movement: work which likewise emphasized, in Clarke's words 'a hard literacy of blackness', in which 'her family and the working-class roots of her black consciousness were subtexts' (Parker 1999, 17). In this, the insistence on drawing on vernacular speech—the varied forms, from the dozens to the church, to the elaborate verbal structures, full of signifying, irony, metaphor, exaggeration, understatement, and wit, that form a part of daily life—also harks back to the poets of the blues, of the oral tradition, and its influence on the work of Sterling Brown and Langston Hughes decades prior. Parker's was a *classed* voice: a voice

280 NEVER BY ITSELF ALONE

she refused to compromise; and, like the Black Arts Movement poets on whom she modelled her work, her work has often been dismissed as 'un-poetic', when in fact what their work accomplishes is precisely to draw on the poetic qualities—wit, telling irony, substitution, the play between speaker and auditor—that characterize the give-and-take of classed and social speech (Douglas, 5; Rushin 1985, 28).

'To hear [Parker] read', writes Grahn in her 1978 introduction to the first edition of *Movement in Black*, 'is to take the various roles which compound her life—*to be them*. And because one of the parts which Parker plays is like a lawyer, it is in her poetry, the sensation of suddenly having a case formally presented to a court, and you will sometimes feel like the defendant, sometimes the jury or the judge' (Parker 1978, 12). As Grahn suggests, Parker's work aimed not just to speak from the perspective of the individual about concerns specific only to that individual, but also to speak about broader social dynamics within lesbian communities that tended to be airbrushed or pushed aside, whether in official declarations or in the dynamics of everyday social interaction.

> Parker's way of working has always been to keep her ears open among a community of people, and take on the personal responsibility for saying [...] what was not being said other places [...] What white women could not hear at a meeting, we just might hear on a stage, boomed through a microphone. What men would not hold still for on the street, they might listen to in a more formal situation. (Parker 1978, 12)

This is not only an intervention in a literary lineage but also an example of how Parker's work operated, specifically as poetry within activist contexts. The very qualities in her writing that made Parker such an important figure in the grassroots lesbian feminist movement may have ensured her absence from most scholarly accounts. Yet, of any of the poetries examined in this book, it's perhaps that of Parker and of Grahn that played the largest role in community life and the building of a movement at every stage: from the local to the national and international. That their work is neither cemented in academic studies of twentieth-century US poetry, nor widely available in mass-distributed public fora, indicates how far we still have to go to find a history in any way adequate to what happened on the ground throughout the twentieth century: a history that would put into practice the idea of a literature from below.

For now, in this book's two final chapters, I will turn to the socialist lesbian feminism of Karen Brodine, Merle Woo, and Nellie Wong and then to New Narrative writing to further explore the challenges facing the establishment of queer poetic and political communities in the Reagan years and to take the story up to the present day.

10

'Blasting the true story into breath'

Writing, Work, and Socialist Feminism

This chapter opens by addressing the emergence of Asian-American lesbian writing in the 1970s and '80s, alongside the multicultural feminist scenes fostered by the Third World Student strike and the beginning of ethnic studies at San Francisco State University (SFSU) and UC Berkeley. I then turn to the work of poet-activists Merle Woo, Nellie Wong, and Karen Brodine, nurtured within the SFSU-based Women Writers Union (WWU) and the socialist-feminist groups Radical Women (RW) and the Freedom Socialist Party (FSP). Woo, Wong, and Brodine focus on women as workers and on work as a space reinforcing raced and gendered norms, including sexuality, but also, in Brodine's words, 'the resistance of [. . .] workers, on the job' (Brodine and Le Sueur, video recording). I end with Brodine's late poems, written in the era of AIDS and her cancer diagnosis in 1986: work that forms a moving testament to the work of resistance and survival that poetry can accomplish even after death.

The Third World Student Strike, the WWU, and Asian-American Lesbian Writing

As noted in previous chapters, the 1968–1969 Third World Student Strike was inspirational for a number of writers addressed in this study and a key galvanizing point for various strains of radicalism into the 1970s. In the following years, students continued to agitate for change within often conservative and exclusionary programmes. In 1975, after SFSU graduate student Sukey Durham (today known under the name Sukey Wolf) was prevented from studying the work of Tillie Olsen, a group of fellow students came together as the Woman's Caucus in Creative Writing and Literature, campaigning for representation of women on the faculty and in curricula. By the following year, the founders of the renamed Women Writers Union (WWU) 'were gradually loosening our ties to academia and expanding into the community [. . .] hold[ing] regular poetry and prose workshops and sponsor[ing] public readings and forums' (*Our Vision*, n.p.). In November 1976, WWU members read at an event held at Glide Memorial Church and organized by the San Francisco Women's Center in

Never By Itself Alone. David Grundy, Oxford University Press. © Oxford University Press 2024.
DOI: 10.1093/oso/9780197654842.003.0011

282 NEVER BY ITSELF ALONE

conjunction with the San Francisco Conference on Violence Against Women; an associated anthology appeared that summer, which saw the first publication of Pat Parker's 'Womanslaughter' (*Poetry from Violence*). Meanwhile, the WWU expanded its activism from the struggle within the academy to the broader poetry community, engaging in a public controversy over Carol Bergé's poem 'Chant for Half the West Coast', published in the magazine *Beatitutde*, which, as Brodine, Wong, and Woo noted, traded in Sinophobic stereotypes (*Our Vision*, n.p.). The group was active in benefits for the Cassandra Peten Defense Fund and the Wendy Yoshimura Defense Fund, as well as the 'CAN Charlie Chan Coalition', a campaign against Hollywood's revival of the 'benevolently' racist 1930s serial, and participated in the Gay Freedom Day March, abortion rights demonstrations, forums, workshops, readings, and classes (Women Writers Union, n.d., n.p.).

Particularly active within the WWU, which also included Gloria Anzaldúa and Gabrielle Daniels, were writers Merle Woo and Nellie Wong (Anzaldúa 2009, 230). Born to a Korean mother and Chinese father, Woo grew up in San Francisco's Chinatown in the 1940s and '50s. Though, as Malinda Lo notes, 'Chinese American lesbian[s] were nearly invisible in the historical record [...] mentioned in passing or relegated to footnotes', Filipina-American women Rose Bamberger attended the first meeting of the Daughters of Bilitis, with the idea of setting up a queer social club, and Woo remembers the club Forbidden City, a nightclub on the outskirts of Chinatown owned by Chinese-American entertainer Charlie Low, and frequented not only by Chinese tourists but also by Asian-American lesbians, whose orientation was clear even if they were not publicly out. Though she would not come until the 1970s, Woo had a gig as a jazz singer at the club after graduating from high school in 1959 (Lo, n.p.).

Subsequently married and with two children, Woo studied for a BA and MA at SFSU; in 1969, she was hired in the new ethnic studies programmes resulting from the Third World Students' Strike, moving to UC Berkeley in 1978. 'Teaching', she remarked in 1981, 'made me politically aware fast': Woo observed how students were excluded for reasons of class and race, 'how students are put down, how propaganda moulds our experience' (Brodine 1981, 5). More than teaching, however, 'going to the Women Writers Union was the beginning of self-affirmation. I saw that my experience was necessary to others [...] the images flow back and forth' (5). During the late 1970s, Woo came out as queer, divorcing her husband, meeting Nellie Wong, then taking classes at SFSU, and becoming increasingly involved in the WWU.

Several years older than Woo and Brodine, Wong had grown up in Oakland's Chinatown during the 1930s and '40s to immigrant Chinese parents, the first in her family born in the United States. Discouraged from continuing her education by her parents after graduating from high school at age seventeen, Wong began her secretarial career in the same school, where she worked for seven years, before moving to United Grocers for a further five, and then to the Bethlehem Steel corporation (Wong 1982, 1). In the 1970s, married and already in her mid-thirties, Wong attended night classes at SFSU as a mature student under Bethlehem Steel's Educational Assistance programme. Encouraged by Brodine and Brodine's then-partner, WWU co-founder Sukey Durham, she began 'writing feverishly as a new-born student and organizing for the inclusion of women and people of colour in the English and Creative Writing Departments [and] [. . .] organizing a full-day conference for International Women's Day' (Wong 2019, n.p.). For Wong, a clerical worker since her teens, it was poetry that served as the beginning of political education: 'When I began writing poems, I realized I had definite ideas' (Brodine 1981, 5). Her first book, *Dreams in Harrison Railroad Park*, appeared from Kelsey Street Press in 1977, and she became a central member of both RW and the FSP, appearing frequently, often alongside Woo and Woo's new partner, Karen Brodine, in contexts from the Left Write conference to Gay Pride parades.

Woo's and Wong's writing and politics were shaped not only by the 'multi-issue' feminist politics they encountered at SFSU (Women Writers Union, n.d., n.p.) but also by the developing Asian-American movement which had likewise developed in the atmosphere of the Third World Student Strike. During the 1970s and 1980s, the line that homosexuality was a 'bourgeois deviation' was held, for example, by the (Maoist) Revolutionary Union (later Revolutionary Communist Party, USA [RCP]) and the Asian-American Maoist groups I Wor Kuen and Wei Min She; the (Trotskyist) American Socialist Workers Party offered 'unconditional support' to gay rights as a democratic necessity, but it held that the gay struggle was also 'narrow', 'limited', and 'peripheral to the class struggle' (Ordona, 94; Elbaum, 138–39; 'Memorandum'). Such sexism and homophobia extended to the Asian-American movement, extended by an often-misogynist counter-reaction to stereotypes of Asian-American men as feminized (*This Bridge*, 160–61). Given this, while many were active in the Asian-American movement—for instance, Janice Mirikitani and Kitty Tsui's involvement in campaigns against the eviction of the largely Filipino inhabitants of the International Hotel in Manilatown—organizing by Asian-American women specifically as feminists and lesbians initially took place in private.

In 1977, performance artist and activist Canyon Sam and activist Doreena Wang, who had met on a women's commune in Oregon, formed Asian American Feminists (AAF) (Ordona, 124–28). Meeting in Sam's apartment, a group of around fifteen women, including Woo, Wong, and Willyce Kim met for the next four years, sharing stories and offering support. Though Wong was heterosexual, she and her sister, Leslie Jow, were central members of the group. Wong's politics was shaped by her queer comrades; as she suggests in 'In Search of the Self as Hero', a prose text published in *This Bridge Called My Back*, writing took her

284 NEVER BY ITSELF ALONE

away from the expectations of a heterosexual marriage, towards activism and towards poetry: a rejection of the socio-heterosexual contract, whatever Wong's orientation (Ordona, 132–33).

In October 1979, AAF members Sam, Woo, Wong, Tsui, Genny Lim, and Nancy Hom formed the poetry-performance collective Unbound Feet for a reading at the James Moore Oakland Museum Theater (Ordona, 134). Taking its name from the traditional Chinese foot-binding practice—one which deformed and literally immobilized women's feet in the service of a distorted idea of female beauty—the group's title poem, co-composed by Wong and Lim, describing a foot-binding ritual in which a mother 'beg[ins] to shape her daughter's destiny', countered by a defiant chorus: 'I am unbinding my feet. / I am a woman who writes. / I am a woman who works. / I am a woman who makes her presence in the world' (Hogan 1980, quoted in Ordona, 135). Though performances focused on issues of 'family, immigration and sexism' rather than sexuality, Unbound Feet drew both a largely heterosexual Asian-American and a multiracial lesbian and gay audience, their performances attended, as Sam recalled, by 'radical gay fairies, like Tede Matthews [. . .] We got a lot of the progressive lesbian and gay people and everyone in between, then this very straight, Asian American mainstream community' (Ordona, 134–36). As many as 600 people attended their final reading (Ordona, 134). However, in late 1981, Unbound Feet split after Sam, Lim, and Hom objected to Woo's criticism, at a reading hosted by UC Berkeley, of the university's failure to renew her teaching contract. When Woo, Tsui, and Wong continued performing as Unbound Feet Three, the other members threatened to sue, picketing their readings and leading to public dispute in the pages of the feminist press which lasted for nearly a year.

As Filipina-American activist and historian Trinity Ordona has noted in her history of Asian-Pacific queer activism in the Bay, accounts that see the post-Stonewall period as unequivocally characterized by movement towards visibility and liberation downplay the culturally differentiated difficulties faced by Asian-Pacific women within a family-focused cultural community: difficulties that arose as much from the internalization of American homophobia and conservatism as from the residual patriarchal structures of Asian cultural inheritance. (Ordona herself did not come out until 1986, after over twenty years of activism; Ordona, 206.) And, while Unbound Feet's poetry served as a galvanizing force in the formation of Asian-American lesbian community, such poetry was not always explicitly framed as lesbian feminist in the way that, for instance, the Women's Press Collective had been. As Merle Woo put it: 'Asian American lesbians [. . .] are invisible within an already invisible American minority' (Woo 1983).

In 1972, the Women's Press Collective had published Hawaiian-born, Korean-American Willyce Kim's *Eating Artichokes,* one of the first books of poetry by an out lesbian Asian-American to appear in the United States. After the manuscript was accepted, Kim joined the Press, working with them for the next five years; Kim, Grahn, and Pat Parker forming a reading triumvirate in the Collective's early days at venues from A Woman's Place bookstore to the lesbian biker bar Scott's (Brandt, 218). Kim's poetry in *Eating Artichokes* startles with its unabashed presentation of lesbian eroticism: 'I feel fire in my cunt. / If I were in the country / I'd take a long walk / and howl / like a wolf'; 'I take my tongue / swallow your womb / drink the whole / earth down / and drown / in the eye of / your cave' (Kim 1972, n.p.). Though the poems are rarely *specifically* centred on Kim's ethnicity—which is instead part of more generalized Third Worldism—in 'Poem for Zahava', Kim imagines responding to a racist male catcaller who says 'you smell like Telegraph avenue'—a street in downtown Oakland associated with Korean-American communities and protests against the Vietnam war: 'in my dream I nailed / his balls with my right boot. / All things are quite possible'.[1] As Hyo Kyung Woo notes, through this moment of violence, even in fantasy, 'the narrator resurrects Telegraph Avenue's legacy of countercultural resistance' (Hyo Kyung Woo, 185).

Yet, following *Eating Artichokes*, it would be over a decade until another book of poems by an Asian-American lesbian writer would appear, when *Words of a Woman Who Breathes Fire* by Kitty Tsui—who was for a number of years' Kim's partner—came out from Spinsters Ink in 1983.[2] Facing widespread homophobia, attempts at Asian-American queer organizing had a delayed effect. As Ordona suggests: 'only Asian lesbians from RW/FSP, which did not maintain continuous work in the Asian American community and movement, were open in the political movements of the late 1970s' (Ordona, 78). For Kim, Tsui, Woo, and Wong alike, ties of solidarity and community existed across racial, sexual, and gender lines. Separatism was not an option. And for Woo and Wong, this was in turn connected to a socialist feminist analysis, concentrated within the orbit of the Trotskyist organizations RW and the FSP.

In these contexts, Woo's and Wong's closest comrade was the (white) lesbian poet Karen Brodine, Woo's romantic partner. Brodine had been raised in Seattle by radical parents, her grandmother, Harriett Pierce was a former indentured servant from Sweden, and in the 1940 and '50s, an organizer in Detroit and Seattle. 'I remember one time she got so furious she sent the governor a jarful of maggots that was in the prisoners' bread in the jail . . . so they hauled her up before HUAC', Brodine recalled (Reyes). In the early 1970s, Brodine moved to San Francisco to study dance, marrying fellow dancer John Daley. After an injury ended her career, she took an MA in creative writing at SFSU, working as a sessional teacher and becoming involved in the Berkeley Poets' Co-Operative, who published her first book in 1975; the previous year, she had co-founded the feminist Kelsey Street Press, which published her second book, *Work Week*, in 1977.[3] For Brodine,

286 NEVER BY ITSELF ALONE

teaching, writing, coming out, and becoming involved in political organizing were interrelated experiences, facilitated by her growing friendship with Wong and Woo and her relationship with WWU co-founder, poet, and activist Sukey Durham, who had recently founded San Francisco chapters of RW and the FSP.

Radical Women had first emerged from classes led by veteran socialist activist Gloria Martin at the Seattle Free University in 1967. Martin and co-founder Clara Fraser were members of the FSP, a Trotskyist organization formed after the Seattle branch of the American Socialist Workers Party (SWP) split over issues of feminism, and RW formally affiliated with the FSP in 1973 (Slater, n.p.). In the late '70s a number of the WWU's members joined RW. Within the WWU, meanwhile, divisions increasingly emerged between those members of the group drawn to socialist feminism, such as Brodine, Wong, and Woo, and to their involvement in writing in activist contexts, and those suspicious of what they saw as a subordination of writing to politics (Brodine, Notebook June–December 1977, KBP, n.p.). For these writers, RW and the FSP offered an alternative, both to Stalinist-Maoist condemnations of feminism and queer sexuality as 'bourgeois deviations', and to feminist anti-Marxism, insisting that sexuality, gender, race, and class were all equal vectors of struggle, and adding a materialist analysis sometimes lost in feminist and queer contexts. The increasing split along class and race lines within the queer community is, for instance, suggested by a poem read by Merle Woo at the Gay Freedom Day Parade in 1981, 'And Who Will Be With Me On The Front Line Of Freedom?': 'I march with the poor lesbians and gays who have no legal aid', writes Woo, 'who don't know what it's like to eat Veal Piccata'.

Brodine joined RW in 1978; Woo and Wong joined around the same time, Brodine and Woo beginning a romantic relationship (Brodine, Notebook January–December 1978, n.p.; Brodine, Notebook October 28, 1981–October 1983, KBP, n.p.). In a 1977 notebook, Brodine writes: 'Does socialism [. . .] seem like some alternative? Look—once you don't believe in reform, there is no other choice. Not for a dyke. Except dishonesty [. . .] Anything else is long skirts and secrecy and foolishness' (Notebook, June–December 1977, KBP, n.p.). Within the FSP and RW, Brodine as a typesetter, Woo, as a teacher, and Wong as a secretary, found ways to sharpen their analysis of the intersections of gender, sexuality, labour conditions, and workplace organizing, while their writing afforded them the dialogic structure and clarity of images to hone this analysis. It's to this work that I now turn.

'we are the clatter of type / in your dreams': Poetry and Work

'Sitting at the Machine, Thinking'

'I learned about politics first from poetry', Brodine recalled in 1980, 'the actual nerves and bone of feminism in those roughly printed pamphlets. [. . .] The process begins with confusion, anger, a vague sense of disturbance, isolated incidents of oppression, and ends with connection—a wire strings together everything, and burns red-hot, and I jump to the typewriter and through the actual writing, see clearly, get at what needs to be done' ('Mainstream Exiles', n.p.).

'To edge into a powerful growing sense of your own sexuality [is] a terrifying thing', Brodine wrote in a notebook seven years earlier ('Woman and Machines', n.p.) In her first book, *Slow Juggling*, poetry offered clarity and direction connected to her divorce and her queer sexual awakening. Moving away from compulsory heterosexuality and into supporting herself through work, in 1975, Brodine began part-time work as a typesetter and teaching night classes at SFSU, writing in her journal: 'I fantasize coming home that I come home to a woman, strong + a working person I come home + we are warm in a warm house + perhaps she has just walked in the door' (Notebook 1975, KBP, n.p.). In *Illegal Assembly* (1980), Brodine recalls: 'My mother always said, "A woman has to have some independent means of income, independent of marriage, I mean, Karen . . ." In the back of my mind, a practical little hand taps out, "she can type, she can type, and fast too" ' (37–38).

Brodine was intensely aware of conditions of feminized labour passed down through her family: 'grandma, indentured servant / at 16, sailed from Sweden and worked / first for an owner, then a husband, / and 8 children. work and work' (Untitled poem, 1985, n.p.). 'I know I'll always have to work', Brodine writes in 1977 (Notebook, December 1976–77, n.p.). During this time, as Marina La Palma notes, Brodine sent part of her wages to her mother, who was unable to afford medical and care expenses after suffering a stroke (LaPalma, 1). In turn, these classed and gendered conditions carried through to Brodine's own death, aged just forty, from a belatedly diagnosed cancer that may have been caused by inhaling noxious fumes while working as a typesetter (Notebook, June 1980—February 1981, n.p.).

For Brodine, however, work was not simply a place of misery. As she explains in a 1981 reading given with Meridel Le Sueur—herself a pioneering writer of women and work several decades before: 'I think too often we think of work as dreary [. . .] but it's a tremendous source and place of resistance and humor' (Brodine and Le Sueur, video recording). From her second book, *Work Week* (1977), Brodine's work increasingly focused on these experiences of labour, experiences that, in her third book, *Illegal Assembly* (1980), occur within an increased sense of community, workshopped as they were within RW and the WWU, alongside ultimately successful struggles to unionize the workers at the magazine Communication Arts, Inc. (Solomon, 247).

'They accuse you of talking or eating or thinking / on the job', Brodine writes in 'Quota' from *Work Week*, also published as a centrespread for Vancouver magazine *Gay Tide* in May 1978. Against this, Brodine insists on other modes

288   NEVER BY ITSELF ALONE

of communication—'we watch / the faces of the other women / for clues, to discover which tribe, / we watch their soft faces / for the quick glance, the laugh / of recognition, what we call / the understanding' (Notebook, June–December, 1977, 9). In the sequence 'Woman Sitting at the Machine, Thinking' (1981), Brodine turns to the paradox by which typesetters consistently process others' written words, while they themselves are denied access to written or spoken language: 'my day so silent yet taken up with words [. . .] / all this language handled yet the room is so silent. / everyone absorbed in feeding words through the machines (Brodine 1990, 5). Such isolation was heightened when, working at Howard Quinn, Co., Brodine was physically partitioned from other workers after attempting to join the union (Solomon, 254). In 'Woman Sitting', she finds ways to turn this situation to her advantage, suggesting the socialized sphere of an apparently solitary act: that of thinking.

Brodine's work had already been concerned with using language that moved beyond the everyday, particularly the world of dreams, which provided images and language for her work. 'My dreams', Brodine wrote in 1976, 'move me out into the body of a woman I never knew [. . .] What do my dreams tell me about resistance?' (Notebook, December 1976–1977, KBP, n.p.) Night dreams occur when one is not working, suggesting a world in which the constraints of exploitative labour can be refigured, and perhaps challenged; the unconscious revealing more than the dreamer's conscious mind might allow. So too, as Kathi Weeks suggests, daydreams can serve as utopian, collectively oriented desires for a better world, despite—or because of the fact—that they are 'a notoriously unproductive use of time' (Weeks, 190).

At work, Brodine's daydreams turn erotic: 'thinking about lovemaking last night, how it's another land [. . .] the delicate fabric of motion and touch / knit with listening and humming and soaring' (Brodine 1990, 5). In a contemporaneous notebook, Brodine observes: 'I want to write something about the lyrical power of our love making. Why doesn't it work to write about this? Everything goes into words. Why not this. Because it's so felt in the hands and nerves. I can't translate this' (Notebook June 1980–February, 1981, n.p.). But in the poem itself, Brodine suggests that sex provides an extra-linguistic mode of communication which in turn gives rise to speech:

> never a clear separation of power because it is both our power
> at once. hers to speak deep in her body and voice [. . .]
> mine to ride those rhythms out and my own, [. . .]
>   a speaking together from body
> to mouth to voice.

(Brodine 1990, 5)

Such writing, as Brodine's notebooks suggest, emerges from her relationship to Merle Woo, as lover and comrade.

This intimacy of talking and images - with Merle today [. . .] the desire to push conversing to its very limits: the whole urge and desire of my life has been intertwined with a struggle with silence [. . .] feeling, wanting [. . .] always crying for another body to speak with [. . .] And now we have come more than ever to share the struggle. That deepens also the feeling. Because we are loyal to one another and to the fight [. . .] She knows I love her words. (Brodine, 'Merle Journal Notes' 1983, n.p.)

Sexual and romantic love here is comradeship of another kind. Brodine refuses the partition between resistance on the job and queer lovemaking outside the workplace. Whether in lovemaking or on the job, work, sex, and gender are all expressed and encountered first in the body, and poetry expresses and clarifies the ways conditions of domination and resistance are embodied and communicated. 'my life and dreams are filled with the people I work with', Brodine wrote, 'we are an assembly—an illegal assembly—because everything we fight for—as women, as workers, as people of color, as lesbians, as radicals challenges the exploitation this country is built on and feeds on' (Brodine, *Illegal Assembly* Bookparty', 1980, n.p.). In 'Woman Sitting', Brodine seeks to collectivize individual (day)dreams of queer lovemaking, as they merge with the silent communication between women in the workplace, both facets of the struggle for a non-alienated totality.

how can they know the quirk of an eyebrow behind their backs? [. . .]

they try to control us, building partitions [. . .]
we say—even if they stretched tape
across our mouths
we could still speak to one another
with our eyebrows

(Brodine 1990, 7–8)

In Adrienne Weller's words, Brodine 'shows how abstract thought becomes concrete'. Translated to writing and 'collective work', the process of thought—including daydreams—provides what Brodine calls 'images [which] leap / out of contradiction, blasting the true story into breath' (Weller, 5; Brodine 1990, 36).

'Do You Read What You're Typing?'

As Sam Solomon notes, in addressing her work as a typesetter, Brodine wrote of an increasingly feminized, 'pink-collar' job. So too Nellie Wong's contemporaneous writing focuses on traditionally feminized secretarial work. Like Brodine's, Wong's job involved working with language—literally writing, while symbolically removed from the position of the 'writer'. But whereas

290 NEVER BY ITSELF ALONE

Brodine came to typesetting with an already developed sense of herself as a poet, Wong's writing, as a secretary since her teens but only a relatively recent writer, suggests her coming to awareness of herself as a writer, rather than simply one who types. In 1986, Wong writes: 'I do not separate the joy of typing from the necessity of walking, the euphoria of plotting from the attraction of fighting. I want to write stories, poems, plays, to write and write and stand by them, tall, no twins or copies, but firsts, until my last breath' (Wong 1986, 55).

In the prose text, 'In Search of the Self as Hero', from *This Bridge Called My Back*, the typewriter is the scene of liberation: '[Y]ou tiptoe down the stairs to write, to face your typewriter like a long, lost friend, welcoming her this New Year's Night' (*This Bridge*, 177–78). Meanwhile, in the satirical boss-worker dialogue 'When You Type, Do You Read What You're Typing?' (1980), it becomes the site of struggle. 'ANYONE CAN TYPE, YOU KNOW', the male boss declares. 'ANYONE CAN SIMPLY COPY FROM TEXT AND TYPE. I WAS JUST WONDERING. DO YOU READ WHEN YOU'RE TYPING?' The secretary replies:

> No I don't always read because my fingers type too fast. They've got their own fingernaility. They're kind of independent, feisty, uppity if you will! [. . .] I'm dreaming of a new world where we work equally, where everyone knows how to do everything well, where you don't spat [*sic*] on me, assuming I don't read when I'm typing. (Wong 1980, 1)

Wong's (typed) text draws attention to the gendered labour on which the boss both relies and dismisses, without which the boss's work could not be done, yet which he must insistently demean in order to lessen his sense of his dependency. In developing an independent, critical relation to her work—having her own opinion, reading, and thinking about what she types—Wong threatens the gendered hierarchies of skill on which the boss's role relies. Reflecting contemporaneous anxieties about 'pink-collar' jobs for women and gay men, the boss asks, 'what do you think about men working for a manager who is . . . homosexual?' (2), to which the speaker replies: 'people can love whomever they want' (2). The piece ends by reversing the boss's opening question: 'I've my sword ready. Whoops, I mean pen! Just hurry it up so I can get back to my thinking. Say, I was just wondering, sir, Can you type?' (3).

Inherently gendered, such questions also relate to the racialized circumstances of Asian-American workers as 'buffer' and 'model minority'. Labour was at the root of the East Asian presence in America. During the California Gold Rush of 1848–1855 and the building of the first transcontinental railroad, Chinese immigration to San Francisco—known as 'Gold Mountain'—resulted in what Kitty Tsui claimed was the largest concentration of Chinese people outside

China (Tsui 1990, 55). Migrating to cover labour shortages in the building of the railway, Chinese workers were also played off against newly freed African American workers, serving, in Lisa Lowe's words, as an ideal of a 'free, yet racialized and coerced' labour force, a 'buffer' between Black and white workers (Lowe 1996, 2021; Manura). As Merle Woo puts it in a 1981 conversation with Wong published in the *Freedom Socialist* newspaper: 'The Chinese were brought in right after the Civil War because cheap labor was needed. Coolie labor versus slave labor! It's still the same' (Brodine 1981, 5).

Woo further notes the gendering of East Asian immigrants in San Francisco of the pre-and postwar eras. 'Any work white men didn't want to do—low-paid labour such as laundry and cooking—Asian immigrants did. The men were consequently stereotyped as "women", supposedly obsequious, passive, and obliging. They were victims of racism and sexism' (Brodine 1981, 5). In the late nineteenth century, immigration panics and fear of miscegenation limited female immigration, leading to the perception of Asian men as feminized, both in the labour they performed and their cultural mannerisms. In *This Bridge Called My Back*, Woo writes:

> I understand all too clearly how dehumanized Dad was in this country. To be a Chinese man in America is to be a victim of both racism and sexism [. . .] He was made to feel soft and weak, whose only job was to serve whites. [. . .] [A]t one time I was ashamed of him because I thought he was 'womanly'. When those two white cops said, 'Hey, fat boy, where's our meat?' he left me standing there on Grant Avenue while he hurried over to his store to get it [. . .] I was so ashamed after that experience when I was only six years old that I never held his hand again. (*This Bridge*, 145)

Conversely, as Wong suggests in the same conversation, families themselves remained patriarchal in their expectations, with education and the chance for upward mobility afforded to male children and women funnelled into less prestigious, gendered labour such as secretarial work. 'My parents couldn't afford an education for us all. My sisters had to work as waitresses and fight to go to school. It was assumed that my brother would go' (Brodine 1981, 5). Against this background of externalized and internalized stereotypes which keep Asian-American men and women in traditionally women's work, for the secretary in Wong's 'When You Type', writing, thinking, and dreaming provide new ways to conceive of self as worker, moving away from gender roles that at root are economic, which are in turn connected to the regime of compulsory heterosexuality (*This Bridge*, 145–47): As Wong writes in *This Bridge Called My Back*: 'What is this adventure, this hunger, that roars in you now, as a woman, a writer, an Asian American, a feminist? [. . .] You have the love of your husband

292 NEVER BY ITSELF ALONE

and your siblings, and yet you turn from them, run with this force, this necessity, this light toward art, toward politics and writing' (*This Bridge*, 177–78).

'Polymorphously Perverse'

Employed in a more traditionally prestigious position than Wong, Merle Woo's work was nonetheless also deeply invested in the workplace investigations of her FSP comrades, particularly as she embarked on her own workplace suit against UC Berkeley for refusing to renew her teaching contract due to her being outspoken as a lesbian and political radical. As she writes in the poem 'For International Women's Day, 1981': 'New forms / from new content / a secretary's chair / is a fire escape / holding us high to / Leap out / Breaking out of marriage / —the security— / into the unknown and / Unacceptable' (Woo 1981, n.p.).

As we saw in Brodine's 'Woman Sitting', the relations between *thinking*, *typing*, and *reading* as forms of gendered embodiment connect to the valences of queer sexuality. In turn, both Brodine's and Merle Woo's work sought to develop a vocabulary for describing queer desire. Building on the erotic frankness of Willyce Kim's earlier *Eating Artichokes* and Kitty Tsui's *Words of a Woman Who Breathes Fire*, in a number of poems from her 1986 collection *Yellow Woman Speaks*, Woo seeks a language for sexuality that is neither pornographic nor, as was often charged of poetry of the Women's Movement, overly sentimental, romantic, or detached from bodily experience.

'Aggressive. Oh you'll see', begins 'Polymorphously Perverse'. 'You won't know from where or to what—' (Woo 2003, 44) .Woo's title gestures at the radical conception of sexuality advanced in the late '60s and early '70s—one which moved beyond the division between heterosexual and homosexual towards a fluidity we'd now term 'queer'. During this period, such discourse had a key historical context. As John D'Emilio recalled:

> Early gay liberationists had argued that sexuality was malleable and fluid ('polymorphously perverse') and that homosexuality and heterosexuality were both oppressive social categories designed to contain the erotic potential of human beings. By the late 1970s this was fading. In its place, gay activists laid claim to the concept of 'sexual orientation', a fixed condition [. . .] useful in a political environment that sought 'rights' [but which] also fudged some troubling issues. (D'Emilio 1992, 3)

In using what was by this stage a relatively old-fashioned phrase, Woo harks back to a discourse in which sexual orientation was not conceived of as a set of entirely separate identities—heterosexual, homosexual, bisexual—but

'BLASTING THE TRUE STORY INTO BREATH' 293

as a fluid formation negating the social prohibitions and roles attendant on sexuality, deeply connected as they were to issues of reproductive labour, to the patriarchal constructions of marriage, the family, and the state. In turn, by centring the discourse of the body in all its variety, Woo imparts a sexually liberationist discourse within the context of a US Marxist-Leninist politics that had, historically, remained either relatively squeamish or puritanical about issues of sexuality or actively hostile to queer and feminist issues as 'bourgeois' distractions from the class struggle.

Writing to Brodine in 1985, Woo observes:

> I read in different places these days how sex is not central in a lesbian relationship, like [singer-songwriter and activist] Holly Near who said 'lesbianism has less to do with questions of sex and more to do with commitment, loving women, caring for one another. And that can happen with or without sex'. Puh-leeze, give me a break [. . .] I think that sex is muy importante [. . .] Of course, I'd never say that publicly, because so many people, that's all they want to see us as—a problem with deviant sexuality. (Woo to Brodine 1985)

Woo's erotic poems voice a sexuality that is linked, not so much to 'identity'— understood as a fixed, rights-based category—but to experience, to the ways that social relations are enacted at every level, from the erotic to the care-based support networks available for those on the margins. Woo's erotic poems refuse to present sex as separate from the social and political. In 'You are Special', the language of queer lovemaking merges with the language of revolution via a slyly transformed image of traditionally feminized domestic labour:

> You are [. . .]
> Soft Strong
> pliant like good silver
> as hard as revolution makes.
> I want to polish you
> with my tongue
> until you're shining
> > ecstatic [. . .]

> (Woo 2003, 47)

Sex accords to the principle of dialectics:

> We are not one
> but one as two
> Double the pleasure

double the fight.

(47)

Is sex here a metaphor for revolutionary struggle, or is revolutionary struggle a metaphor for sex? Within the poem, at least, such divisions, Woo suggests, are meaningless.

At the end of her poem *Yellow Woman Speaks*, speaking in the archetypal figure of 'yellow woman, a revolutionary', Woo writes:

> They have mutilated our genitals, but I will restore them;
> I will render our shames and praise them [...]
> Those young Chinese whores on display in barracoons;
> the domestics in soiled aprons [...]
>
> Painted lady, dark domestic—
> Sweep minds' attics; burnish our senses;
> keep house, make love, wreak vengeance.

(52)

As it is for Brodine and for Wong, writing is here both a source of metaphorical power and a material force, a worker's tool. Poetry is expression of sex and solidarity, discovery of worker's power or of histories of despised sexuality reclaimed from shame: the fight dialectically doubled at every turn, providing conditions from which to build.

'No One Immune'

In May 1980, Brodine wrote to Judy Grahn: 'We seem to be edging toward another McCarthy period. Every day attacks against, radicals, gays, people of color, working people, intensify [...] And writers on the line—feminist, or socialist writers—women of color writing—lesbians writing—we are all out on that limb together' (Brodine, Letter to Judy Grahn May 2, 1980, KBP, 2). By this time, Brodine felt that the 'tremendous unity' she had experienced in the feminist poetry scene of the 1970s, exemplified in Grahn's and Parker's reading to 2,000 people at Glide Memorial Church, had fractured (Brodine, 'Women Writers' 1986, n.p.). The challenges of the new decade meant that the lesbian separatism to which ingrained misogyny had given rise was not enough.

Later that year, speaking at *Mainstream Exiles: A Lesbian and Gay Men's Cultural Festival* organized by Canyon Sam, Brodine called for a writers' organization akin to the Anti-Fascist Writers League in the 1930s, the

'BLASTING THE TRUE STORY INTO BREATH' 295

International Writers Union; likening this to the recent activities of Unbound Feet, the WWU, and the Combahee River Collective (Brodine, 'Mainstream Exiles' 1980, n.p.). In this, she drew inspiration from the writers of the 1930s: a lost tradition of feminist writing ignored by a patriarchal literary establishment—a continuum symbolized when Brodine and Le Sueur read alternating poems, rather than separate sets, in a joint reading at the Poetry Center in 1981. As Le Sueur quipped before her reading: 'This makes it more like the continuous woman, not separated' (Brodine and Le Sueur, video recording). Brodine also drew inspiration from an internationalist tradition, from Bertolt Brecht to Roque Dalton and Nâzım Hikmet. So too, in her poem 'China: For Nellie Wong', Merle Woo cites the feminist writer Ding Ling, 'the courageous writer and worker being censored for decades—/ a victim of both the Kuomingdong and the Chinese Communist Party', while Wong in turn quotes Li Chu, whose poem 'Harvesting Wheat for the Public Share' Wong quotes in a speech for International Women's Day (Woo 2003, 10; Wong 'Opening Remarks', n.p.; *This Bridge*, 197). Other poets mentioned by Wong, Woo, and in FSP material include the Chinese-Malaysian Bee Bee Tan, the Japanese Yosana Akiko, Vietnamese Hien Luong, and the Chinese Chi'u Chin.

The majority of Brodine's, Woo's, and Wong's political work in the new decade involved organizing with RW and the FSP: notably, the Merle Woo Defense Campaign, successfully contesting UC Berkeley's refusal to renew Woo's teaching contract, and a lengthy legal battle against a disgruntled former FSP member demanding the return of a donation he had earlier given the party, work often taken up with fierce external and internal polemics (Ordona, 247; Hoddersen).

In 1986, Brodine was diagnosed with cancer; she would pass away the following year. Rejected by various publishers, the book she increasingly knew would be her last, *Woman Sitting at the Machine, Thinking*, was published posthumously by the FSP's Red Letter Press in 1990. *Woman Sitting* drew together poems on Brodine's workplace organizing, the struggles against a resurgent right wing during the '80s, and her family history; the latter through reflections on and found documents from her mother's and grandmother's radical pasts, revisited in the wake of their deaths. Between 1984 and 1985, Brodine worked on the four-part poem 'No One Immune', in which the conjunctures of the decade are laid out in sections concerning the rise of Reaganomics, the right-wing handling of the AIDS crisis, and the presence of Neo-Nazism. In 'Bones', the final poem, Brodine addresses the serial gender violence of the 'Green River Killer' case—the murder of forty-eight women and girls, many of them sex workers, in Seattle. Like the Combahee River Collective before her, Brodine refuses to see such violence as exceptional or pathological but instead as 'terrorism', metaphorically linking the murdered women to the *desaparecidos* of the US-backed coup in Chile and imagining them rising again to call out their murderer's name (Brodine 1990,

296 NEVER BY ITSELF ALONE

71–74).[4] In the second poem, 'Sickness Slept in Us', Brodine quotes a report from the *Seattle Times* in which the West German government considers prison terms for those who know they have AIDS and 'continue having sex', reckoning with the representational crisis fostered by what Paula Treichler in 1987 called 'an epidemic of signification' (Treichler). Echoing the question posed to suspected communists—such as her grandmother—by the House Un-American Activities Committee—'are you now / or have you ever been / a member of [. . .]', Brodine identifies people with AIDS as social scapegoats—'the new lepers / under wrath of god'—a long lineage of outsiders victimized in periods of political and economic crisis. In response to this imagined question, Brodine defiantly responds with one of her own: 'Can they lock us all up?' (Brodine 1990, 72).

In her journals, Brodine continued to reflect on what she saw as a *political* epidemic of violence and reaction, from gender violence to AIDS to cancer. 'my brothers are dying // in general / hospital / in particular / each week / new obits / all these young ones / my brothers are dying' (Brodine, Untitled poem, KBP, 1985, n.p.). 'Too many of us dying, too many—1 in 5—of cancer, and this is not an epidemic? Not? Too many of us dying, too young, too old, too middleaged to die of this terrible disease. [. . .] I want to combat it, never let it sneak up on me as it did before, warn others too' (Brodine, Untitled poem, 1985, n.p). Shortly after her own cancer diagnosis, Brodine wrote a letter to the *San Francisco Chronicle,* asserting: 'No fight is an individual problem only. Cancer is political [. . .] We must see cancer not as an individual, mysterious fate, but as an increasing danger which the whole society faces and which the whole society must solve—scientifically, politically, and soon' (Brodine, 'Cancer', 1986). She continued to agitate across a range of issues until just before her death. In early 1987, Merle Woo's daughter, actor-activist Emily Woo Yamasaki, represented RW on an Oprah Winfrey episode with the theme 'Does Male Chauvinism Exist?' The producers had lined up 'four sexist men and Susan Brownmiller' alongside Yamasaki. Incensed at the misogynist array, Brodine spoke up from the audience, a move emblematic of her fighting spirit (Abbott 1987).

'Poetry always saved me', Brodine wrote in an unpublished poem shortly before her own death. '[I]t saved me because I / used it to understand / and to act. / I used it to muddle through— / and in the midst of / understanding how to say it, / I often gained clarity / on what to do' (Hill 1987, 4). Realizing that, given her terminal diagnosis, 'this time / poetry can't save me', Brodine mourns, not only for the loss of her own life but also for 'the new poets / I will never hear'. In this devastating act of leave-taking, Brodine nonetheless maintains an ear to the future. Writing was always the place in which Brodine came to analysis and clarity—an analysis which by no means disavowed the flux of feelings and the painful experiences of real contradiction: sexual, gendered, political, social,

'BLASTING THE TRUE STORY INTO BREATH' 297

aesthetic. Poetry may not be literally have been able to save Karen Brodine's life, but today, her work, like that of her living comrades, Woo and Wong, provides a through line, a bequest, a queer, clear, singing wire, 'the lively humming thread of the struggle' stretching out into the future (Brodine, Notebook, October 28, 1981–October 1983, KBP, n.p.).

11

New Narrative, New Communities
from Left Write to AIDS

'New narrative? What a stupid name', Bruce Boone remarked in the very process of coining the term (Jackson 1993, 26). The writing grouped under this label resulted, in the first instance, from a set of friendships—most notably, that of Boone and Robert Glück, who'd met in San Francisco's gay counterculture in 1972—along with series of overlapping attempts to build community during a time of political retrenchment, from the murder of Harvey Milk to the emergence of AIDS. Poets who, in the late '70s, began to write prose, Boone and Glück attempted to map gay community in new ways through a fusion of Marxism, porn and gossip. In 1981, they joined Steve Abbott—a former member of Students for a Democratic Society (SDS), single gay father, editor of the *Poetry Flash* newsletter, and, in Glück's words, 'a tireless community-builder'—to host the Left Write conference, at which members of multiple communities debated the possibilities for organizing together, as poets, against the challenges of the new decade (Glück 2016, 23). Though such efforts were short-lived, throughout the 1980s, New Narrative flourished through Glück's writing workshops at Small Press Traffic bookstore and magazines such as Abbott's *Soup*, Bryan Monte's *No Apologies*, and Kevin Killian and Dodie Bellamy's *Mirage/Period[ical]*: writing that continues to influence younger writers both in San Francisco and worldwide to this day.

This chapter begins by examining New Narrative's origins in San Francisco's gay counterculture before turning to Boone's attempt to theorize a Gay Marxism in *Century of Clouds*, a text drawing on his experience at the Marxist Literary Group (MLG) Summer Institute, and the resulting essay 'Toward a Gay Theory for the 1980s'. I then turn to Left Write, noting the way homophobia stymied its coalitional efforts, before outlining New Narrative's development after the conference: in particular, its attempt to rearticulate gendered expectations. The chapter's final third turns to AIDS: outlining Glück's participation in the first public civil disobedience against government handling of AIDS with 'faggot affinity group' Enola Gay, I then address the ways in which AIDS figures in in Glück's novel *Jack the Modernist* and in unpublished writing by Bruce Boone. Finally, I turn to work published in the 1990s by 'second-generation' New Narrative writers Dodie Bellamy and Kevin Killian. Negotiating the aesthetics of

Never By Itself Alone. David Grundy, Oxford University Press. © Oxford University Press 2024.
DOI: 10.1093/oso/9780197654842.003.0012

elegy and the demands of representation, Bellamy's *Letters of Mina Harker* and Killian's *Argento Series* interrogate the popular idea that AIDS was 'over' by the late 1990s, refusing closure in the interests of moving towards a future.

New Narrative and the Possibility of a Gay Left

'Gay Sunrise'

Shortly after their first meeting, Robert Glück sent Bruce Boone a postcard from New Mexico: 'Dear Bruce, I like your manifesto, and I like you too. This is actually a love letter' (Glück 1972, n.p.). It was from this friendship that what would become New Narrative emerged. Boone had initially come to California from Oregon to attend Saint Mary's College, Moraga, subsequently alternating between graduate study and theological training, living on a Radical Faerie commune in Wolf Creek, Divisadero, Washington, before studying for a PhD on Frank O'Hara at UC Berkeley (Sneathen 2018b, n.p.). Glück led a similarly peripatetic existence, studying ceramics at the Edinburgh College of Art, literature at the University of Edinburgh, and subsequently English at Berkeley, in 'the days of People's Park' (Sneathen 2018a, n.p.). Like Boone, he had briefly lived on a commune before moving to New York where he came out and attended poetry workshops held by Ted Berrigan while working night shifts at the Post Office. He then relocated to San Francisco in 1970, where, along with his lover artist Ed Aulerich-Sugai, he was involved in activism, 'picketing racist gay bars and isolating preachers who sent us to camps to straighten us out' (Sneathen 2018a, n.p.).

Boone's and Glück's early work appeared in Gay Liberation journals such as *RFD* and *Sebastian Quill*, run by poet, publisher, and early music specialist James Mitchell, from 1967 on an important member and later chronicler of San Francisco's gay counterculture, a moment he terms 'Gay Sunrise' (Mitchell 2018, Mitchell 2019). Alongside *Sebastian Quill*, Glück emphasizes the importance of Winston Leyland's *Gay Sunshine*, begun as a Berkeley collective in 1970 before Winston Leyland assumed control and moved it to San Francisco. 'Boston had *Fag Rag* [. . .] and we had *Gay Sunshine*', Glück remarks. '*Gay Sunshine* was mother church, and Winston her bishop' (Sneathen 2018a, n.p.). Glück, he recalls, transcribed some of the interviews that appeared in *Gay Sunshine* and was 'once [. . .] on the cover—my torso, drawn by [Aulerich-Sugai]. The German filmmaker Rosa Von Praunheim, during his trip to California, cited my image as an example of the headlessness of the gay community. We were a community without a head' (Sneathen 2018a, n.p.). Challenging this view, Glück remarks: 'Basically, gay hippie culture saved my life. People look back at [the

300 NEVER BY ITSELF ALONE

1970s] as a heedless time, but there was actually the tremendous achievement of creating a gay community, a gay readership, a gay voting bloc' (Sneathen 2018a, n.p.). Nonetheless Von Praunheim's critique, Glück suggests, also points to the limitations of the gay counterculture. In particular, 'feminists shook up everything by showing how power dynamics happen at home in intimate relationships, not just between states and armies [. . .] an understanding of power relations that hippies didn't have' (Sneathen 2018a, n.p.). As Boone and Glück developed a literary friendship, Marxism would become an equally important consideration.

The work of the 'gay sunrise' and the 'gay hippies', like that of *Fag Rag* in Boston, was radical, often anarchist in its slant. Yet these radical energies were increasingly displaced by a commodified vision of gay community, the emergence of a gay middle class—consumerist, apolitical, and largely white and male—in turn playing into the ongoing disparities of race and class involving gentrification and the first ominous stirrings of the far right with the Briggs Initiative and the murder of Harvey Milk, cemented in 1981 by the presidential election of former state Governor Ronald Reagan (Lauria and Knopp; Castells). In his 1969 play 'Fucked Up', published in *Sebastian Quill*, Boone had satirized the apolitical, self-consciously outrageous behaviour of the gay men on the commune in which he lived at the turn of the decade. And in the unpublished 1977 poem 'Castro and Market Dialectics (or, Discussing our Growing Consumerism)', Boone takes aim at a gay community which ignores the continuing violence done to queers by insulating itself in an apparently self-contained gay consumer culture—a position he likens to that of the Southern belle Scarlett O'Hara in *Gone with the Wind*. 'I used to think I was a gay man', Boone sardonically remarks. 'I did. / I ate it up. It was fun'.

> You go up to Castro St. and zing! Presto change! Just
> by going to some rip-off boutique [. . .]
> you're legit and nothing
> can hurt you again.
>   [. . .] And if gangs of kids go by
> shouting unspeakable things at you, put
> your hands over your ears and you won't hear
> a thing.
>   (Boone, 'Castro and Market Dialectics' 1997, n.p.)

'I wonder what we faggots think of / when we keep stumbling over faggot corpses', Boone asks with bitter sarcasm. 'it's so embarrassing. It's unchic'. Rejecting this position, the poem ends: 'We're not mindless after all and we're not / stupid. You can't help but notice a corpse'.

'A Community of the Future': *Century of Clouds*

But how would this consciousness come about? Boone insists that queers—often wary of Marxism for the vitriolic homophobia amongst Bay Area Stalinist and Maoist groups—look once again to the left. In 1973, Boone had attended meetings of the anti-revisionist (formerly Maoist) Marxist-Leninist Progressive Labor Party while working on the poems published in the pamphlet *Karate Flower* (Boone 2020, v).[1] In the preface to an unpublished collection from 1977, he decries the gay movement's 'almost complete lack of relations with the organized militant Left groups and Left movement intellectuals', insisting that 'we have two simple choices: either we resolve our disputes with the Left [. . .] or else resign ourselves to the inevitable pogroms, rehabilitation programs and concentration camps of the socialist future that past history and present Left programs seem to envisage for us' (Boone, 'Note to the Reader' 1977, n.p.).

To an extent, that which Boone called for was already in existence. Emily Hobson, for examples, has argued that 'the early 1970s marked the start of a new political current: a gay left [. . .] by the end of the decade, activists built a gay and lesbian left that pursued multiracial and anti-imperialist solidarity' (Hobson, 40). Hobson notes here both organized campaigns such as that against California's Proposition 6 (the so-called Briggs Initiative), which, in 1977, successfully linked concerns around 'sexual freedom, workers' rights and unions', and the 'White Night Riots' of May 1979, in which gays and lesbians fought back against the police after former cop Dan White was acquitted for the murders of Harvey Milk and Mayor George Moscone the previous year (88). Serving as inspiration for future activists, the riots were commemorated in an anonymous flier of a burning police car alongside the words 'No Apologies!'—a slogan borrowed both by ACT UP and for the title of a New Narrative magazine edited by poet Bryan Monte—and would be invoked in Boone's essay 'Toward a Gay Theory for the 1980s' (Monte, n.p.). Boone was also inspired by the attempt of the Marxist Literary Group (MLG), founded in 1969 by Fredric Jameson and graduate students at UC San Diego, to establish what Jameson called 'a Marxist intelligentsia and a Marxist culture', filling in what he saw as the lack of solid theoretical foundations for the New Left (Homer, n.p.). During the period of Briggs and the White Night Riots, Boone attended the first two meetings of the MLG's summer institute at St Cloud, Minnesota, and this experience is central to Boone's book-length prose text *Century of Clouds*, written in 1979 and published the following year.

Neither quite a prose poem, a novel, nor an autobiography, *Century of Clouds* charts 'expanding visions of community' in what Boone describes as 'three concentric circles': the religious community of his youth, San Francisco's gay hippies, and, finally, a desired future synthesis of queer and Marxist communities (Boone 2020, 245). 'The religious communities of my past stand for political

302 NEVER BY ITSELF ALONE

communities in my present, and these in turn for a community of the future that exists only in dreams,' Boone writes mid-way through the text (Boone 1980, 31). The original manuscript begins with an epigraph from the well-known labour movement song, 'yes it is bread we fight for but we / fight for roses too', thus inserting its queer endeavour into a socialist tradition of struggling for survival and more than survival with its roots in the feminist struggles (the phrase has its origin in a 1910 speech by women' suffrage activist Helen Todd). The book's title, meanwhile, is both a joking reference to the MLG Summer Institute's location in St Cloud, and an allusion to Guillaume Apollinaire's 1913 poem '*Un fantôme de nuées*': as Boone notes in a later afterword, 'an image for the transient, for what passes' (Boone 1980, 87). *Century of Clouds* begins with a dream of flight above an 'enchanted forest', 'catalogs of flora [. . .] moving toward a brilliant future. Wave upon wave of collective life displaying ever new patterns', an image recurring at book's end: 'Taking a step, I wade in. They're waist high. Don't slow down now! They're glorious—but go on!' (3, 86).

The utopian vision is, however, soon interrupted by a list of contemporaneous political calamities.

> There's an explosion when I think these thoughts. Letelier is being blown up in his car by the agents of Chilean reaction.[2] The sound of nearly silent bullets— and 9 black men are dead in Oakland from police assassination. Racism; poverty. Lives of women and gays oppressed in patriarchy. Daily violence done to workers. A workers movement now bloody and sundered with wounds.
>
> These thoughts large and public, how to relate them to my life? (4)

Boone's earlier *Karate Flower,* he explained to Rob Halpern, 'aim[ed] to catch every possible "enemy" in its grasp by way of its capacious "you"—a commodious direct address capable of embracing 'everything and everybody'—so that were the poem to succeed in its rebarbative attack, it would succeed in destroying every adversary standing in the way of social justice!' (Boone 2020, v). Here, however, 'you' opens out onto a community of writer and reader. Addressing the reader directly, Boone suggests a potential way to answer the questions he's raised: 'Perhaps beginning to tell you stories. Some important friendships, in between spaces as my life moves outward. Problems. Questions' (4).

The book that follows unfolds as a series of self-interrupting stories, a method Glück would term 'text-metatext'. 'A story', Glück writes, 'keeps a running commentary on itself from the present [. . .] asks questions, asks for critical response, makes claims on the reader, elicits comments [. . .] text-metatext takes its form from the dialectical cleft between real life and life as it wants to be' (Glück 2016, 17). Interrupting the narrative, Boone addresses the reader, reflecting on the writing as it's being composed and arguing that his desire is for the reader not just to 'think about certain political matters' but 'to feel pleasure, even joy': an erotics of connection (Boone 1980, 16). Bodily experience affords a verifiable connection and grounding for theory: 'telling you stories' provides a way to link the experience of desire to other experiences felt as abstractions, while also suggesting the way in which abstractions determine experiences of desire. This poetics of address develops the direct address of Frank O'Hara's coterie-based poetry, but it also draws on the dynamics of grassroots, community readings in the Women's Movement. (Indicative of such dynamics are occasions such as that recalled by Cheryl Clarke, in which Pat Parker asked for audience feedback in the middle of a reading, rewriting lines on the spot (Parker 1999, 15)). Rather than a closed object, the text is a process, something in negotiation and dialogue between writer, reader, and listener.

At St Cloud, Boone presented a draft of his essay on O'Hara subsequently published in *Social Text*, reactions to which tensions between theory espoused predominantly by white male leftists and their apparent undervaluing of queer and feminist arguments came to a head. In *Century of Clouds*, the failure of the MLG to practice what it theorizes comes to a head in a climactic volleyball game. 'Volleyball brought out hidden conflicts that had never been resolved, and often were not even discussed. Volleyball turned out to extend certain power realities based on sex' (Boone 1980, 67–68, 77–79). In the climax to the book, some sort of rapprochement is reached when, having 'feuded semi-publicly over feminism and the gay movement', Fredric Jameson visits the apartment in which Boone lives, creating a moment of potential erotic frisson as he speculates on Jameson's sexuality, previously an apparent heterosexual closed book (79).

> Fred is starting to look so *nice*! [. . .] He's looking quite attractive. I feel I'm in the middle of a poem about the future or the sun, or something glowing and tender or maybe all of these things mixed together. I feel I am growing more reddish myself with every moment. What strange feelings! (82)

Jameson's own writings contain little on sexuality; in deliberately gossipy fashion, placing him in relation to queer desire questions the separation of the issue of queerness from much contemporaneous Marxist analysis. *Century of Clouds* seeks to reveal the too often unremarked sexual and gendered power dynamics that manifest within *all* communities—whether or not those communities are explicitly organized around sexuality or sexual orientation—removing theory from its implicit heterosexuality, and suggesting the political role of gossip, which will go on to play a key role in New Narrative conceptions of community.

'You want what you write to actually cause these things to exist, you don't just want to describe them,' Boone writes (47). Practical attempts to organize within and across communities marked New Narrative's next phase.

304 NEVER BY ITSELF ALONE

Organizing for Unity: Left Write

In summer 1979, Boone drafted the essay 'Toward a Gay Theory for the '80s' as a result of discussions amongst the MLG's ' "semi-official" gay caucus of Alex [Wilson], Robbie [Schwartzwald, queer academic and then Boone's partner] and myself'. As he wrote to Jameson that August, the essay was intended as an 'analysis of the state of the gay movement at present, as well, I hope, as a program for action' (Boone 1979, 1). Completed in October, the essay was published in Vancouver as a mimeographed pamphlet the following year.

Within San Francisco, gay identity, Boone suggests, was becoming increasingly commodified, losing its radical edge. While the gay community was created as a defensive bloc—one which was and continues to be literally lifesaving for many gay men—it also reproduces raced and classed inequalities. Nonetheless, Boone goes on to argue, given that the commodification around which the 'gay ghetto' is organized must be treated as dialectical site of analysis, rather than merely condemned or explained away. Historically, Boone argues, 'institutions like the bars' have served as 'critical locations for the development of a new politics', here citing the work of the San Francisco Lesbian and Gay Men's History Project on the militant role of bar clientele in pre-Stonewall activism and its more recent manifestation in the White Night Riots (Boone 2020, 85–86). Given this, he calls for three principal strategies: unionization for gay employees subject to workplace discrimination within the gay community—for example, in bars; the development of city-funded community centres and gay health clinics; and the development of 'educational and agitational' strategies to combat homophobic violence, inspired by feminist and Black Power self-defense strategies (83, 87–89). These strategies, Boone argued, might be facilitated by a 'socialist-oriented' though non-sectarian organization of gay men within San Francisco, in turn linking up to other such organizations elsewhere (90–91).

By the time the pamphlet appeared in February 1981, over a year after the essay's original composition, Boone was in the midst of organizing meetings for the Left Write conference, an event exemplifying the coalitional activity he calls for in the essay's postscript. Bringing together various left-wing poetry scenes in San Francisco and the Bay Area in the interests of resisting the New Right, Left Write was conceived by Steve Abbott, with Boone and Glück enthusiastic recruits. (The steering committee also included Denise Kastan, finance, and John Mueller, publicity, with John Curl as conference coordinator; many others, including Merle Woo, helped coordinate workshops; *Left Write*, n.p.) Though the committee did the majority of the work, the conference was organized through a series of opening planning meetings: as Abbott notes in a volume of edited transcripts published later that year, it 'was sponsored by no one political or

NEW NARRATIVE, NEW COMMUNITIES FROM LEFT WRITE TO AIDS   305

aesthetic group but arose democratically from the interest and energy of many independent groups and individuals' (*Left Write*, 1).

Held in February 1981 at the Noe Valley Ministry, and attended by an audience of around 300, the two-day Left Write conference involved speakers such as Woo, Nellie Wong, Judy Grahn, Maurice Kenny, Diane di Prima, Gabrielle Daniels, Amber Hollibaugh, Ron Silliman, Jeffrey Escoffier, and Mirtha Quintanales. Disagreements soon emerged, however, between the 'class-first' analysis of the Old Left and the concerns of feminists, gays, and writers of colour.

Replacing an indisposed Tillie Olsen on a panel with Silliman, di Prima and veteran activist and Sovietologist William Mandell was Amber Hollibaugh, whose work Boone had cited in 'Toward a Gay Theory'. A self-described 'lesbian sex radical, ex-hooker, incest survivor, Gypsy child, poor-white trash, high femme dyke', Hollibaugh had co-founded the San Francisco Gay and Lesbian History Project and would later found the Lesbian AIDS Project (LAP) (Day 202–, 140–42, 145). At Left Write, she recounted her experience of travelling across California agitating against the Briggs Initiative: addressing the question of building queer community outside the San Francisco bubble, she observed: 'People would call up (on a radio talk show) and say, 'I've heard all gay people are communists'. Well, it would be hard to be gay in this society and not be. I took the Communist Manifesto with me and handed it out like I handed out the gay stuff' (*Left Write*, 45).

Hollibaugh's specific example of the links between queerness, organizing, and the left appeared to fall on deaf ears, as Mandell critiqued Judy Grahn's and Nellie Wong's focus on gender and race in a previous panel, despite the fact that both extensively discussed their class background, while di Prima argued that 'the gay movement is [...] to some extent at fault for not aligning itself with other op-pressed peoples' (*Left Write*, 42).[3] The following day, Hollibaugh pointed out that, despite nostalgic invocations of left unity and the Popular Front in the 1930s, neither she, Grahn, nor Wong would have been heard on a panel (*Left Write*, 61). In turn, Boone noted that, while much of the organizing for the conference had been done by women and gay men, others involved had been 'outright sexist and homophobic'. As Tede Matthews remarked from the floor in response to di Prima's comments: 'Gay people had the idea for this whole conference. It's been built on our labour. When has the straight Left ever called us up to do benefits for gay struggles?' (*Left Write*, 56).

A key point of the conference was that, though organized primarily by gay men and women, it was intended as a fulcrum for the broader community. That community however, appeared unable to accept such overtures, as the conference foundered on the familiar obstacles of Old Left sexism, homophobia, and racism. Subsequent meetings of a Left Writers Union soon fell apart, and the original organizers—Boone, Glück, and Abbott—ultimately walked out at disgust in continuing homophobia (*Left Write*, 2). If, then, Left Write served as an important symbolic manifestation of what Emily Hobson has termed a 'Gay Left', it also served to illustrate the pitfalls of left homophobia which radical queers still faced, and the tendency of attempts at unity to fall into fracture, internal strife, and splits (Hobson 2016). Left Write was, however, but one manifestation of a drive towards community that was already in motion and would continue after the initial efforts that went into the conference had ground to a halt. And it's to those continuing efforts that I now turn.

'A village common producing images': New Narrative After Left Write

In 1974, James Mitchell and Denise Kastan set up Small Press Traffic (SPT), a non-profit distribution point for small press publications. SPT would be a key venue for New Narrative writing. Taking over as co-director with Kastan in 1977, Glück began hosting numerous events by 'leftist and queer poets' and poets of colour, including Gloria Anzaldúa's El Mundo Zurdo workshop and reading series, where Dodie Bellamy gave her first public poetry reading in San Francisco. Such events established the venue, in Anzaldúa's words, as 'a little center of the literary movement in San Francisco, the radical alternative literary movement' (Glück 2016, 22; Espinoza et al. 2018, 116). In a 1980 diary entry, Karen Brodine writes: 'I'm going to pursue a friendship with Bob [Glück] because he loves to talk', and Brodine and members of the WWU often participated in events at SPT (Brodine, Notebook, June 1980, n.p.).

Glück himself led three workshops, each with equal amounts of prose and poetry, all free to attend. One workshop was open to all; another, for gay male writers, served as an important venue for the developing scene of 'New Narrative'; and the Older Writers Workshop gathered '50s-generation radicals, some of them previously called before the House Un-American Activities Committee. Among the older writers, Peggy Roche, Mildred Weitz, and Edith Jenkins were former activists; other attendees included John Norton, Phyllis Taylor, Richard Schwarzenberger, Tom Tolfa, and Clara Sneed, and the workshop produced the anthology *Saturday Afternoon, an Anthology of Older Writers* in 1986 (Rosa 2009, n.p.; Glück, personal communication, 2023).

Over the next decade, these workshops, their membership often overlapping, would be New Narrative's principal incubator, bringing together Boone, Glück, and Abbott with former members of the Spicer circle, older radicals, and a 'second generation' of New Narrative writers, including Dodie Bellamy, Kevin Killian, Camille Roy, and the heterosexual working-class writer Mike Amnasan, with Boone and Abbott informally mentoring writers such as Gabrielle Daniels outside the official workshops.[4] The new writing was frequently disseminated through magazines. In 1983, Bryan Monte began the magazine *No Apologies: A Magazine of Gay Writing* with assistance from Bellamy, then working as a graphic designer, and Killian, who typeset it on a workplace word-processing machine, and a cover designed by gay graphic artist Mike Belt, who would, Bellamy recalls, be the first person she knew to die of AIDS (Bellamy 2010, n.p.). When Monte left for an MFA at Brown, Killian began *Mirage*, named after a neighbourhood bar in the Mission District; with Bellamy joining as co-editor of the renamed *Mirage/Period[ical]*, they went on to produce over one hundred Xerox issues well into the new century.

In 1980, Steve Abbott published the first of four issues of *Soup*, its first issue a kind of 'mini-anthology [. . .] a cross section of current work emphasizing new directions', including work by Brodine and Maurice Kenny, and a lengthy interview of Robert Duncan by Abbott and Aaron Shurin, with Duncan, Jack Kerouac, and Anne Waldman prominently featured on the cover. By the second issue, Abbott wrote, 'gradually I realized my main interest was towards "New Narrative" writing' (Abbott 1981). In some ways, *Soup* maps the trajectory of New Narrative as a whole: on the one hand, the coalition building across multiple communities of endeavours such as Left Write; on the other hand, the turn to smaller communities, to intimate details and direct address and gossip.

Published in the fourth issue, Abbott's essay 'Notes on Boundaries / New Narrative' offered the first major theoretical definition of New Narrative, discussing the work of Boone, Glück, Dennis Cooper, and Kathy Acker, alongside Judy Grahn, New York graffiti artists, and Georges Bataille, to suggest that the possibility of a political future be construed primarily on an acknowledgment of that which has been scapegoated or cast out—including within gay community itself. 'What's cast out as "marginal" has to be first within [. . .] The self has been erased only to return with the sacred vengeance of a cry' (Abbott 2019, 182). Community was not to be built through statements of affirmation but through an aesthetic negativity which strenuously resisted idealism.

New Narrative shatters linearity, proceeds by flashes, enigmas, and yields to a florid crying-out theme of suffering horror. Unlike the abject, however, which can't go 'out' because it has no real self to go out from, New Narrative bridges out, in its suffering-horror feature, to a future [. . .] New Narrative explodes, speaking to and creating community. (Abbott 2019, 182)

New Narrative centred intimacy and shame—the capacity to feel (gay) shame and to move beyond it—by putting it in print. As Glück writes in his own later essay 'Long Note on New Narrative': 'We were attracted to scandal and shame, where there is so much information. Shame is a kind of fear, and fears are what

308 NEVER BY ITSELF ALONE

organize us from above, so displaying them is political' (Glück 2016, 20).[5] Novels such as Glück's *Jack the Modernist,* Bellamy's *Letters of Mina Harker,* and Abbott's *Holy Terror* foreground community gossip as one of the means by which the community tells stories to and about itself. 'We brought gossip and anecdote to our writing', Glück continues, 'because they contain speaker and audience, establish the parameters of community, and trumpet their "unfair" points of view' (23). In *Jack the Modernist,* to the character Jack's assertion that 'Gossip is crude', Bob replies: 'Gossip registers the difference between a story one person knows and everyone knows, between one person's story and everyone's. Or it's a mythology, gods and goddesses, a community and a future' (Glück 1995, 9).

Between 1975 and 1985, Glück writes, he and Boone 'carried on what amounted to one long gabby phone conversation': a near-constant exchange of ideas, plans, and gossip that informs texts such as the Boone-Glück collaboration *La Fontaine,* Glück's 'When Bruce was 36 (Gossip and Scandal)', and Boone's *My Walk with Bob,* and 'The Truth About Ted' (Glück 2016, 23). Boone and Glück's private conversations and walks would be interpolated directly into the text through 'text-metatext'—gossip, direct address, asides, self-reflexive commentary—in which the community—even if just a community of two— narrated itself to itself. When, in 1979, they co-founded a small press, Black Star Series, its first two publications were Boone's *My Walk with Bob* and Glück's *Family Poems,* with an afterword by Boone, to be followed in 1981 by their collaboration, *La Fontaine,* which Glück termed a 'valentine to our friendship' (Glück 2016, 23). Glück later wrote: 'I write for gay men the same as La Fontaine wrote for the court of Louis XIV' (Glück 1995, 221). But, as La Fontaine himself had done, he also sought to problematize what that community might mean. What shared experiences held it together? In what directions was it heading?

In 1982, Glück's book of short stories, *Elements of a Coffee Service,* was published by Donald Allen's Four Seasons Foundation, a venue which suggested continuities with earlier scenes of queer writing. Himself a gay man based in San Francisco, Allen's anthology *The New American Poetry* had effectively canonized numerous currents within the poetry of the 1950s. *Elements* is blurbed by Robert Duncan, and excerpts had appeared in *Gay Sunshine, Soup,* and *Social Text.* But it is also a text very much of its historical conjuncture. The book opens with 'Sanchez and Day', one of Glück's first prose pieces. Discussing this work with Kasia Boddy some years later, Glück recalled a conversation with friend and fellow poet Kathleen Fraser, in which Fraser was appalled to hear of a queer-bashing incident in a way that Glück's gay friends—accustomed to such violence—were not. Realizing that such violence was largely invisible to those who were not its recipients—or perpetrators—'the newspapers didn't ever report it and in fact you wouldn't want to call the police because they could bash you worse than the queerbashers'—Glück 'decided to make a story of [it] [. . .] out

NEW NARRATIVE, NEW COMMUNITIES FROM LEFT WRITE TO AIDS 309

of an impulse to let straight people know what was happening, like a newspaper'
(Boddy, 1261).

The story's penultimate paragraph finds Glück back in his room, having outrun his queer-bashing pursuers, looking toward the future from the retrospection of the past tense. 'I stood a minute,' he writes, 'enjoying the sheer pleasure of breathing in and out. I resolved to make my bed, throw away papers, read Gramsci's *Prison Notebooks*, have an active, no, a famous social life' (Glück 1982, 5). Both utopian and ironic, these resolutions are also connected to Glück's literal survival, standing in his room rather than bleeding on the pavement. Throughout, the text emphasizes the violence which still menaces the city's gay community: 'Kevin's bashed-in teeth and Bruce getting rousted and then rousted again by the police and the Halloween when a man yelling "queer" charged Ed and me with a metal pipe', an acquaintance 'murdered by someone he brought home' (2). In the story's final paragraph, Glück moves from a specific time and location—his return to his room after escaping the would-be queer-bashers—towards a passage, addressed to a second-person reader, which is more generalized in its spatial and temporal location: which is located, one might say, within the space of writing itself. 'I resolved', he writes, 'that I would gear my writing to tell you about incidents like the one at Sanchez and Day, to put them to you as real questions that need answers, and that these questions, along with my understanding and my practice, would grow more energetic and precise' (4). Here we see a movement from the particular to the general, with literature as a space of reckoning, summation, and provocation: the second-person plural addresses both confronts heterosexual readers with a violence of which they may be unaware, implicitly demanding their solidarity, and gestures towards a shared experience that cements bonds within the gay community.

There is here an activist impulse, dovetailing with Glück's work in the campaign against William Friedkin's film *Cruising*, for its association of gay life with murder and self-hatred. Gay men, Glück later wrote, 'had been disastrously described by the mainstream—a naming whose most extreme (though not uncommon) expression was physical violence. Combating this injustice required at least a provisionally stable identity' (Glück 2016, 14–15). Yet New Narrative also refused to provide model images to counter such descriptions; rather, such writing sought to acknowledge the ways in which notions of gay identity were negotiated and constructed, whether from without (Hollywood cinema) or from within (the emerging trend of mass-market gay fiction).

Writing to Fredric Jameson in 1979, Bruce Boone insisted that, of the literary forms, poetry was currently the main site of community praxis in the United States (Boone 1979, 2). Naming Amiri Baraka's *Hard Facts* and Judy Grahn's *The Work of a Common Woman*, among others, Boone insisted that 'the form of [such] poetry [. . .] is not that of the guardians of the community, those who

310 NEVER BY ITSELF ALONE

speak on behalf of the community [. . .] but in the <u>form</u> [. . .] it is actually the community' (6).[6] Yet, as Glück noted, 'many of my experiences as a gay man had yet to reach the stage of literary production except in pornography [. . .] there was nothing else to put those kinds of experiences in' (Boddy, 1260). Despite the upsurge of Gay Liberation poetry charted throughout this book, in Gay Liberation's second decade, prose remained a more familiar zone of gay self-representation, in the form of popular mass-market paperbacks or the novels of writers such as Armistead Maupin, of which Steve Abbott advanced a critique in the pages of the *San Francisco Sentinel* (Abbott 2019, 238–42). Given this, though New Narrative writers remained deeply invested in poetry, consistently referring to poets, poetry readings, and poetry communities in their work, much of the writing itself is in prose, drawing on techniques of fragmentation, pastiche, and distancing present both in (prose) pornography and in avant-garde poetry, seeking, in Glück's words, to reflect a 'fledgling gay identity which was so new that its parts were clearly visible [. . .] to devise a kind of writing that looked like the world to me' (Boddy, 1260; Gardner, 78–81).

Gay identity, Glück argued, was 'new enough to know its own constructedness' (Glück 2016, 15). Such identity was both constructed and contested. Seeking to avoid the trap of reified descriptions—whether external, homophobic descriptors or idealized, internal self-images—this vision of community centred negativity as well as affirmation, destructiveness as well as love, death as well as sex. This community, with disorder and otherness built into its core, functions to challenge the restrictions of conservative family life and the acts of violence concealed within the relations of family and state. At the same time, it involved practical efforts to organize alternative futures: Steve Abbott's queer parenting, for example, saw him organize a group for gay fathers, echoing other queer activists' attempts to build alternative models of community and family structures, from the Boston-based Men's Child Care Collective to Street Transvestite Action Revolutionaries (STAR) shelters in Manhattan for homeless trans youth.

As New Narrative moved from a grouping of predominantly gay men to a more capacious tendency amongst participants in Glück's workshop, alongside affiliates such as Kathy Acker, Dennis Cooper, Ishmael Houston-Jones, and Gail Scott, its founders' emphasis on gay community and gay self-representation was adapted to fresh concerns, particular those associated with feminism and the politics of gender in the work of writers such as Dodie Bellamy, Gabrielle Daniels, and Camille Roy. A friend of Karen Brodine and Merle Woo, Daniels spoke at Left Write as a representative of the WWU, in turn developing close friendships with Boone and Abbott, whose advice she credits with giving her a model for writing about (heterosexual) 'interracial sex and love' beyond 'fetishised and dehumanised' stereotype (Daniels 2021; Townsend 2022b).[7] The daughter of former Communist Party USA (CPUSA) radicals from Chicago,

NEW NARRATIVE, NEW COMMUNITIES FROM LEFT WRITE TO AIDS   311

Camille Roy found that New Narrative offered a frame to speak of her formative experience of a queer community involving lesbians, drag queens, sex workers, former Weather Underground radicals, and union activists: one increasingly at risk of disappearance (Tremblay-McGaw 2008; Townsend 2022a). Combining narrative clarity and poetic disjunction, New Narrative spoke at once of a queerness unarticulated within current systems of discourse—thus anticipating queer theory—and of the need to articulate terms for shared identity. Prose afforded the necessary clarity to articulate an 'exhilarating social life that I could not describe'; poetry offered a queered opacity, 'a space of privacy', moving away from a focus on 'meaning', which reflected the 'disjointed, dissonant, dissatisfied' aspects of Roy's experience—those which chafed at the edges of identity (Halpern and McGaw, 300; Townsend 2022a). As Roy puts it in the afterword to her collected stories, *Honey Mine*: 'We played with butch and femme with more expressive freedom because we got to be meaningless: a freedom which can't be bought. We were at the intersection of nothing and gender' (Roy 2021, 321).

'To me,' Dodie Bellamy writes, 'being queer means doing without the false solace of categories' (Bellamy 2000, n.p.). In the early 1980s, the marriage of Bellamy—emerging from a long lesbian relationship that had lasted since her teens—and Kevin Killian—a flamboyantly gay man—paradoxically served as social glue within a group of largely gay male poets. As Glück remarks: 'I think the meeting of Dodie Bellamy and Kevin Killian will secure my workshop a place in legend' (Bellamy and D'Allesandro, i). 'Female sexuality has been my primary subject', Bellamy writes. 'But in my formative years, it was hard to find models that moved beyond objectification. Gay writing, on the other hand, gave me a sexual vocabulary, as well as techniques for turning the tables and objectifying men' (Bellamy 2000, n.p.). Within New Narrative's predominantly gay male frame, Bellamy found new ways to write of female sexuality. Such work expands a sense of what queer community might be; not as the subsumption of gay identity to heterosexuality—the tension that had derailed Left Write—but the opposite process, in which heterosexuality refuses to fence itself off from queer sexuality: an expanded and generative vision rejecting falsely naturalized sexual boundaries.

During this period, Bellamy embarked on *The Letters of Mina Harker*, writing to others within the New Narrative community under the nom de plume of Bram Stoker's heroine, in a text liberally laced with relentless, uncited italicized quotations that interrupt and flow through it like electric currents. Simultaneously, Bruce Boone's ultimately unfinished novel *Carmen* likewise incorporated text from writers within the community, including letters to and from Bellamy that in turn fed into *The Letters of Mina Harker*. In *Carmen*, he recalls, Boone aimed 'to take the work of *Century of Clouds* to a "higher level"', following up on community lessons by way of a drag-queen narrator named

312 NEVER BY ITSELF ALONE

Orlando (thank you Virginia Woolf) [. . .] gender fluid, emotive, gushy, and paranoid' (Boone 2020, 208). Continuing the project of 'text-metatext', of breaking down boundaries between reader and writer, Boone conceived of a text that moves beyond any one author or body. As he writes in an unpublished note: '[T]hese stories of future events and [. . .] dreams [. . .] might gradually become indistinct from each other just as the reader becomes indistinguishable from me. Just as [. . .] my work is in key aspects (certain elements of style, philosophic or political viewpoint, etc.) indistinguishable from Kathy Acker's, Bob Glück's, Dennis Cooper's . . .' (Boone, 'Writing Projects', n.d., n.p.).

Meanwhile, Glück's novel *Margery Kempe* sets the narrative of the medieval female mystic and her eroticized desire for Christ alongside his own affair with a handsome member of the ruling class in ways that frequently challenge gender norms. 'I want to be a woman and a man penetrating him, his inner walls rolling around me like satin drenched in hot oil, and I want to be the woman and man he continually fucks', writes Glück. 'I want to be where total freedom is' (Glück 1994, 49). Creating community through collage, *Margery Kempe* includes uncited descriptions Glück had solicited from forty friends and acquaintances, a process he likens to 'a village common producing images' (92). In such work, as in *Carmen* and *The Letters of Mina Harker*, challenges to gender are also challenges to conventional notions of individual authorship. Bellamy, Boone, and Glück conceive of a community at once sexual and textual, based around often-scandalous revelations of details of personal life, in which the boundaries of the individual are transgressed and refused. As we'll see, such writing assumed even greater resonance in the era of AIDS, as moral norms were reasserted and the fragile gains of Gay Liberation faced their most significant threat to date.

New Narrative in the Era of AIDS

Enola Gay

The first news story on AIDS had appeared in the gay newspaper *New York Native* in May 1981, a matter of months after the Left Write conference: the term AIDS itself was coined the following year.[8] New Narrative writers were among the first to pay attention. In 1984, Robert Glück was involved in one of the first recorded instances of AIDS activism in the US with the 'faggot affinity group' Enola Gay. Founded in July 1982, Enola Gay was 'named after the airplane that dropped the bomb over Hiroshima (which was in turn the pilot's mother's name)', and their actions linked subversive gender performance, ritual, and the tactics of non-violent civil disobedience (Jack Davis 2017, n.p.). In June 1983, Glück and other members of Enola Gay joined the Livermore Action Group for a protest

NEW NARRATIVE, NEW COMMUNITIES FROM LEFT WRITE TO AIDS 313

at the California-based Lawrence Livermore National Laboratory, a nuclear research centre fifty miles south of San Francisco established by the University of California in 1952 ('Our History', n.p.). The following September, Enola Gay staged what would be the first public action to draw attention to the AIDS crisis at Livermore, under the slogan 'money for AIDS, not for war' ('Enola Gay', 2020, n.p.). Conceived of as a 'blood and money ritual', the event began with Jack Davis reciting a chant and a 'litany of the needs of people with AIDS' (Brookie, n.p.). Blocking traffic and forming a circle, Enola Gay members poured vials of their own blood over the road while chanting 'blood is holy / blood is sacred / workers that come this way / will cross the blood of gay men every day', before pricking their fingers and smearing the blood on dollar bills on which they'd printed the slogan 'Gomorrah for tomorrah' (Bieschke, n.p.).

In 'Sanchez and Day' and *Century of Clouds,* Glück and Boone had juxtaposed their daily lives in San Francisco with the spectre of mass death internationally: US intervention in South America, police violence, political assassination. Enola Gay's action was another way of making such connections. Intervening on the site of a laboratory separated from the spaces of urban life where AIDS took effect, as well as the locations outside the United States where US weaponry slaughtered—and continues to slaughter—others, the protest made specific geographical connections through ritual. 'Every contract this lab gets has blood on it', argued protester John Lindsay-Poland in *Gay Community News.* 'When we put blood on money [...] we're making the blood visible' (Brookie, n.p.).

In a diary of the 1983 Livermore protest commissioned for—and rejected by—the *Village Voice,* Glück writes: 'Civil disobedience is elegant. Like sex, you do it with your body' (Glück 2016, 210). Arrested and interned in a giant circus tents at the 1983 action, Enola Gay staged a cross-dressing talent show for Gay Freedom Day, to support and cheers from the predominantly heterosexual inmates (209–10, 213). When the Livermore Action Group staged a mock invasion of Angel Island following the United States' invasion of Grenada, Enola Gay attended dressed as cheerleaders; and in early 1985 they staged a fashion show in downtown San Francisco, in which clothes were described in terms of geopolitical conflicts and causes ('Enola Gay', n.p.). 'If you're trying to build the left', Glück argues, 'you have to make it a place where people go to live, not just a place where people do actions or where people you know it has to be cultural and it has to be artistic' ('Enola Gay'). In this light, New Narrative emerges as part of a broader picture: not simply as a literary movement, a coterie, or a series of friendships, but as part of a mosaic of activities out of which a gay left might emerge, one which actively sought to challenge existing conditions, not least among them the threat of AIDS.

As the decade wore on, for Enola Gay, acts of care replaced acts of civil disobedience. As Richard Bell observes: 'A lot of us were being diagnosed [...]

314 NEVER BY ITSELF ALONE

a lot of time [was] spent just taking care of each other physically' ('Enola Gay', n.p.). Nonetheless, the activity of Enola Gay both predates and feeds into the better-known work of ACT UP, which in turn develops from the gay left and its ties to anti-war, anti-nuclear, and anti-imperialist activism. But how did responses to AIDS manifest in New Narrative writing? In the remainder of this chapter, I'll attempt an answer to this question by focusing on work by Glück, Dodie Bellamy, and Kevin Killian.

The Bathhouse in the Era of AIDS

In 1985, Glück published a novel he later described as 'a sort of love letter to the Gay Community' (Boddy, 1262). Amidst its narrative of love affairs, gossip, and aesthetic debate, AIDS is rarely addressed. Yet AIDS cast a long shadow over 'The Sky Looked Bruised, and That's the Way the Air Felt, Achey', a chapter which first appeared as a standalone piece in Bryan Monte's No Apologies in spring 1984. As Bellamy and Killian later put it, the piece is 'a scandal on purpose':

> [T]he bathhouses, which dotted San Francisco like the jacaranda trees once, had been closed down by an avaricious public health system looking to limit public exposure to HIV. Thus accounts of multiple sex partners in a single night [...] could never be neutral events [...] Fraught with trails of warning, blame, guilt, and sorrow, [Glück's text] stood as a majestic monolith, like Stonehenge, of an occluded sexual past. (Bellamy and Killian, 481)

As Stephan Ferris notes: 'In 1984, San Francisco effectively shut down gay bathhouses in a desperate attempt to curb HIV transmission, assuming that these venues create what is presently referred to as "super spreader events". Despite changes in the global understanding of HIV and scientific advances in medication, these cultural centers remained effectively banned for over 36 years' (Ferris, n.p.). The bathhouses were not utopia. Glück notes that his partner, Ed Aulerich-Sugai, was turned away from bathhouses and bars because 'he couldn't equal our racist community's self-description', leading Glück and others to organize a picket line (Glück 2020, n.p.). Nonetheless, since the turn of the century, bathhouses had been crucial venues for gay community self-formation (Bérubé 2011, 64; Bérubé 1984; Bérubé 2003). As activist Cleve Jones, co-founder of the Names Project, observed: 'On a good night I would have sex, but on any night, I would run into friends, we could sit in the Jacuzzi and gossip or plan our next political actions [...] It really was, for many of us, an important community experience that went beyond the sexual behavior that might occur on any given night' (Kost, n.p.).

NEW NARRATIVE, NEW COMMUNITIES FROM LEFT WRITE TO AIDS   315

As Allen Bérubé observed: 'Gay bathhouses and sex clubs aren't the first institutions to be scapegoated for the city's inability to stop an epidemic. In 1903, amidst an outbreak of bubonic plague, "the state Board of Health recommended that Chinatown be razed to the ground and saturated with chloride of lime and carbolic acid"' (Bérubé 2011, 62, 64). And the bathhouse panic, he argued, confused sociality with cause: rather than focusing on sexual practices, it focused on 'sites of sexual activity', thus 'promot[ing] the illusion that romantic sex with one person in private is safe' (65). For Bérubé, however, acknowledging the scapegoating function of public health authorities and the vital community function of the bathhouses should not blind the gay community to the fact that 'bathhouse owners have been living in a never-never land, pretending that AIDS and safe sex don't exist' (65). Advocating that bathhouses remain open with safe sex mandated, Bérubé noted that their closure would 'force casual sex underground, may help spread AIDS, and will invite a wave of political repression' (65).

Following undercover police surveillance of bathhouses, in October 1984, the Health Department ordered the closure of fourteen gay establishments, mainly bathhouses: while their legal closure was overturned the following month, monitoring requirements on sex practices and prohibitions on private rooms with locking doors effectively led to their collapse. The fear continued: in 1996, the Health Department refused to countenance 're-opening' the baths due to continued high infection rates (Ferris, n.p.). Not until 2020 was the symbolic ban lifted (Kost, n.p.).

Though such debate is not directly mentioned, Glück's 'The Sky Looked Bruised' foregrounds the bathhouses at a time when they appeared as a site of intense political debate, from those in the gay community urging caution to those comparing the closure to Nazi repression ('Out of the baths into the ovens?' read one slogan) (Kost). The chapter begins as Bob picks a quarrel with his lover, the insular 'modernist' aesthete Jack and goes to the city's Club Baths in search of compensatory sexual community.

> One man eased his cock into my ass [. . .] while another blew me [. . .] while still another tongued my nipples and kissed me and many others touched my body lightly as though they were sensual Greek breezes [. . .] I relinquished the firm barrier that separated us—no, that separated me from nothing. (Glück 1995, 53, 54)

'Embrac[ing] body after body', Bob seeks to '[g]o where no meaning is to create meaning. Take pleasure with the abruptness of deities' (55, 57). Initially, the 'potential interchangeability' of lovers enables him to break out from the limits of individuality, and by extension, the individual possessiveness and jealousies of his relationship with Jack, in a kind of Fourierist sexual communism, a

316 NEVER BY ITSELF ALONE

'*dreamtime logic [. . .] a unity that can't be dismissed or [. . .] broken into parts*'
(56). Yet the poetic descriptions of group sex are gradually interspersed with
a more quizzical voice in italics: '*sex is a consciousness-altering state—yet the
[. . .] experience is limited to so few*' (57). Text-metatext here introduces, not the
reaching towards community found in *Century of Clouds* or 'Sanchez and Day',
but an element of doubt.

Imagining himself 'a machine whose quirks and eccentricities are appraised
in a cheerfully businesslike way', Bob likens the process to the vicissitudes of
the stock market: 'I haunted the halls and dark places of the Club Baths feeling
less and less physically present. [. . .] My stock was plummeting' (60). 'Glück's
bathhouse patrons', writes Diane Chisholm, 'appraise each other's erotic capital
while accumulating orgasms', in a world that, while it offers community, can
also be unforgiving, competitive, and, as Glück's memories of Ed suggest, racist
(Chisholm, 41). In his final sexual encounter, Bob 'recoil[s]' from a man whose
'cock [. . .] had warts', imagining, while fucking him, that 'his ass [. . .] lubricated
with the sperm of untold others [. . .] was a crock pot for every disease known
to man [. . .] When I finished he didn't even bother turning around to his past
to reminisce, he just went forward looking for his next cock' (Glück 1995, 60).
Returning home to his equally unsatisfying domestic relationship, Bob 'mentally
start[s] a bitter quarrel with Jack that continued for a year' (60). The movement
from home to bathhouse back to home becomes a closed circle, the orgy offering
only brief compensation for the jealousies of the couple to which Bob ultimately
returns.

As Glück comments: 'After knowing about HIV, the meaning of sex in a
bathhouse changed, and the novel appeared right at that transition' (Wintz, n.p.).
Jack the Modernist is set during the pre-AIDS moment of 1981: almost as soon as
it appeared in print, the experience offered by the bathhouse would be foreclosed
by the city's legal measures in response to AIDS, rendering the community it
describes in effect unavailable. Later, Glück would write in more detail about
AIDS, notably in the story 'The Purple Men', from the 2003 collection *Denny
Smith* (his memoir *About Ed*, years in the making, had not been published when
the present manuscript was completed). As it stands, *Jack* catches a community
on a historical cusp, catching glimpses of a future that can as yet only be intuited,
and offering a portrayal of gay community at once nostalgic and tinged with
dread. 'In the wake of the gay bathhouse,' writes Diana Chisholm, 'we see the
catastrophe of urban (post)industrialism. At the same time, we glimpse the first
and last metropolitan site where citizens could make erotic connection across
power lines that divide class and race, the basis for a new body politic and
communal praxis' (Chisholm, 98). And, despite its 'trails of warning [and] blame',
ultimately, writing such as Glück's offered—and still offers—a space within
which to maintain the memory of a sexual community destroyed by AIDS: in

NEW NARRATIVE, NEW COMMUNITIES FROM LEFT WRITE TO AIDS 317

Chisholm's words, to 'knit community together in the face of ruin' (Bellamy and Killian, 481; Chisholm, 53).

Of AIDS and the Undead: *Real* and *The Letters of Mina Harker*

Begun in 1985, but not published in full until 1998, Dodie Bellamy's *The Letters of Mina Harker* registers a historical crisis in progress. As one of five fellow writers in correspondence with whom Bellamy built the text, Bellamy and Sam D'Allesandro began corresponding, in character as 'Mina' and 'SX', in 1985. D'Allesandro would die of AIDS-related complications three years later: the resulting text, particularly in what Bellamy calls its 'spin off', *Real: The Letters of Mina Harker and Sam D'Allesandro* (1994), elegizes D'Allesandro while pondering the limits to a narrative of witness: concerns that are shared with D'Allesandro's own writing. His attitude deeply shaped by punk and performance art, D'Allesandro—born Richard Anderson—came into New Narrative circles around 1983, publishing in venues such as *No Apologies* and *Mirage*. In a letter to Kevin Killian, D'Allesandro challenged the increasing pathos of AIDS narratives.

> I keep seeing obituaries in which the deceased AIDS person is characterized as 'a fighter who fought to the very end' and who somehow provided an incredibly positive experience of strength for those left behind. What macho bullshit. I don't believe such descriptions will help anyone facing the loss of his lover/ best friend when there are so many other hard emotions to encounter at such a time. (D'Allesandro, 114)

Following his own diagnosis, D'Allesandro writes a letter to Bellamy signed—as will be the rest of the published letters from this point on—'Sam' rather than the alter ego 'SX'. At first sight, it appears that D'Allesandro is finally writing in his 'real' voice, dispensing with the need for a fictional entity: 'God, I think we could be so real if we could only find the way' (Bellamy and D'Allesandro, 38). Focusing on the 'real' of the body, much of the letter is taken up with a detailed description of wetting the bed, overlaid with 'sickening visions [from the film *Rosemary's Baby*] of Mia Farrow's enormous, Satanically impregnated belly', as D'Allesandro contemplates the possibility of suicide and accidental overdose (49–50). Such writing is both overshare—the infantile humiliation of bedwetting—and determined refusal to confess or divulge. 'I have a disease', D'Allesandro writes. 'And I will have it forever but hardly anyone will know. Now I've told you one of my secrets. Again. But I'll never tell them all' (51). As a person with AIDS, Sam claims a right to opacity in the face of either the punitive and prurient gaze which

318   NEVER BY ITSELF ALONE

exposes the dying person to homophobic, judgmental scrutiny or the denial of his existence which ushers him out of sight.

But what happens after D'Allesandro's death? In its final third, *Real* becomes a kind of poetic tomb for D'Allesandro, incorporating a transcription of his final, unfinished short story, a copy of the programme for his memorial service, and a final letter from Mina to 'SX', written six years after his death. Incorporating D'Allesandro's words, the text renders him alive; or rather, given the vampiric framing of the text, *undead*. 'By addressing you and others like you these letters circumvent the anonymous reader', Bellamy writes (180). Community is established by direct address—a community that now has, of necessity, to include the dead.

As Glück writes: 'Dodie's plan broke the form of the epistolary novel by making it real; in doing so she allowed her correspondents to display the fiction of their personalities' (i). Throughout the project, Bellamy has created a public intimacy aware of its own fiction, that even in the wake of D'Allesandro's death, seeks to avoid the pathos of traditional elegy. In the final letter, still writing in character, 'Mina' recounts an encounter with a person with AIDS in a neighbouring apartment alongside reminiscences of her wedding to Killian, an affair with a man referred to as 'Death', and a performance by D'Allesandro at a Halloween party in which he hurls plastic skeletons at the audience, before interpolating a series of graphic descriptions of physical trauma: a woman's dismembered body, her corpse torn apart by villagers who cut out her heart—apparently a scene from a real or imagined horror movie—an unspecified medical procedure undergone by Mina herself, and a visit to a hospital ward of AIDS patients, all presented without narrative connection (Bellamy 1998, 176, 202, 188–89). As Christopher Breu suggests, in 'imagining a connection and a shared relationship between bodies differently situated', Bellamy resists the symbolic cordoning off people with AIDS as social scapegoats (Breu, 283).[9] Yet, viewing the ward, Mina exclaims: 'I have no right to see this' (Bellamy 1998, 189). Caught between her awareness of the limits of representation and the immorality of a voyeurism disguised as witnessing and her guilt at *not* witnessing, *not* being present, a few pages later, Mina writes to the now-dead Sam: 'I never saw you when you were sick' (194).

Is there a way out of this impasse? Should one even attempt to find one? Bellamy's letter ends with a moment of direct address that fulfils the painful function of elegy—to recognize the impossible distance from the other with a pathos that impossibly calls across it—while rejecting the redemptive pathos often associated with elegy. Looking at a set of photographs of D'Allesandro taken by Robert Girard a month before his death, Bellamy/Mina writes:

[Y]our eyes will remain unreadable to me, will never 'reveal'—but that's not the point is it—the point is to look, not in horror not in pity or even in compassion, but to look as precisely as possible at the ever-wavering presence right in front of one—this is the closest beings as imperfect as we can come to love. (195)

'The letter form appeals to me', Bellamy wrote in 1986, 'because of its potential to blur the boundaries between private and public: information is exchanged between correspondents—the reader is both inside and outside this intimacy, conspirator as well as voyeur' (Bellamy 1986, n.p.). In moving from 'you' to 'we', Bellamy writes in the voice of community—not just that of the living, of the survivors, but of the living and the dead, of writer and reader alike. Having reached the abstraction of a general philosophical truth—a definition of love, no less—Mina breaks off into a moment of painful, intimate direct address, quoting a poem printed in the programme for D'Allesandro's memorial service, the pathos of rhyming poetry following the moment of prose summary: '*Goodbye / my dream of me / goodbye / my mystery / goodbye*' (Bellamy 1998, 195). As Bellamy suggested to Christopher Breu, the passage manifests 'a politics of recording or even just looking'.

I really have problems with the whole notion of understanding. And, for me, it's part of a critique of liberalism. As soon as you understand, you're just projecting. How can you possibly understand? There's something amoral about taking the stance of understanding. What's moral is to say no, I'm never going to understand you, but I'll look at what's there. (Breu, 283)

In such writing, as D'Allesandro is, as he'd earlier put it, allowed to 'face death with some of the same ambiguity he has always felt towards life': an act of love, an elegy worth its name (D'Allesandro, 114).

'I saw something I can't remember': Kevin Killian's *Argento Series*

Throughout *The Letters of Mina Harker*, Bellamy uses horror cinema to suggest the monstrousness of a society which condemned and ostracized people with AIDS, while refusing to relinquish the force of the negative, of deviant eroticism, and of a fascination with Thanatos, in favour of what Dennis Altman called a 'new puritanism' (Altman 1986). In the final letter, she recounts sitting with Kevin Killian to watch Dario Argento's *giallo* movie *The Bird with the Crystal Plumage* (*L'uccello dalle piume di cristallo*) (Bellamy 1998, 198). Argento's cinema would likewise serve as the central pivot for Kevin Killian's own reckoning with AIDS, the book-length poem *Argento Series*.

'Throughout the eighties', Killian suggests in his essay 'Activism, Gay Poetry and AIDS', 'we in the New Narrative saw ourselves as the last bastion of sexuality'

320 NEVER BY ITSELF ALONE

(Killian 2011, 14). Yet, in his own writing, Killian struggled to find a means to write adequately of AIDS. Killian's *Argento Series* would not appear until 1997, when half of the sequence appeared as a chapbook from Meow Press, and not until 2001 in the full edition from Krupskaya. By 1991, Killian noted, 'the number of those dead with AIDS surpasse[d] the total of American dead in Vietnam' (Harris 2011b, 642). As he later wrote, Killian was himself 'frozen, unable to think of a way to write about AIDS crisis' (Killian 2001, n.p.). The following year, Kathy Acker suggested he might deploy Argento's *giallo* cinema as allegory for the effects of AIDS. A 'fellow traveller' of New Narrative, Acker would herself pass away from advanced breast cancer in 1997, the year in which an initial version of *Argento Series* first appeared in print. The back cover to the full, 2001 printing presents a chronology of the AIDS crisis, beginning with Killian's meeting with poets Tim Dlugos and Eileen Myles in New York in 1979 and proceeding to a list of deaths, mainly from AIDS—D'Allesandro, Steve Abbott, Rock Hudson—but also including victims of gay-bashing (Matthew Shepard) and long-term health conditions (Bob Flanagan), ending with Acker's death in 1997 (Roy 2021, 334; Killian 2001, n.p.). For Kaplan Harris, 'the entire statement can be read as a miniature autobiography, even a poem in itself' (Harris 2011b, 646). As chronology, it removes precisely the element of narrative on which New Narrative had been constructed—the allusive, winding, text-metatext nature of anecdote and gossip, in which community unfolds with the luxuriousness of storytelling. Instead, the list 'ascribes no cause and effect, no justification for events, and no morality to the tale' (646).

The same year that Acker suggested the book's conceit, Francis Ford Coppola announced plans to make a film on the scientists finding a cure for AIDS entitled *Cure*. No cure, however, was forthcoming, and the film was never made. AIDS did not—and has not—proceeded according to Hollywood storylines ('Francis Coppola' 1992). Turning to another mode of cinema, *Argento Series* uses the tropes of horror cinema to undercut the tropes of direct experience, the pathos of witnessing, and the appeal to truth present in survivor's memoirs. In *giallo* films, the perpetrators of numerous, elaborately staged killings are revealed in the final reel. For the majority of their running time, however, these films defy narrative logic, attaining a dream-like, even improvisatory quality, in which violence comes from unknown sources, the disorientation created in the viewer mirrored in the film's narrative, turning as it does on the figure of the unreliable witness (Koven, 38). 'Conventions of horror', Killian writes, 'demand a nut, / eyewitness, whose eyes can't be trusted, / but the life I've lived—gross [. . .] I saw something / important that I can't remember' (Killian 2001, 47). This final phrase, a line from Argento's *Suspiria,* also serves as the book's epigraph. Adopting this untrustworthy role, the poems interrupt themselves with deliberate flippancy— 'I don't have / many T cells left, but I used to have 8 [. . .] this is the curve that

NEW NARRATIVE, NEW COMMUNITIES FROM LEFT WRITE TO AIDS   321

/ will kill you • pal' (16); 'Larry Eigner, Bob Flanagan, you guys / were kind of sick before you died, huh?' (57)—or transgressive fantasy, including a sex act with a hospitalized AIDS patient—'Rip that tube from the wall and feel me up / loving you and forcing you to wriggle a bit / a sausage on griddle, hot' (51). In 'Giallo', Killian combines a visit to the terminally ill Steve Abbott with stylized invocations of horror film soundtracks, grotesquely *détourned* song lyrics—'*your breath makes me love you, / in AIDS is pleasure*'—and the transgressive, cinematic juxtaposition of sex and death: 'he gives her a blowjob [. . .] the camera pulls back [. . .] it's a football field of dead men in trenches' (14).

Like Bellamy, Killian suggests that the need for the exemplary victim is the flipside to the social scapegoating of the person with AIDS onto whom societal fears are projected. The *Argento Series'* penultimate poem, 'The Phantom of the Opera', is an elegy for the murdered gay teenager Matthew Shepard, first published in the anthology *Blood and Tears: Poems for Matthew Shepard* (1999), which, its blurb claims, includes contributions from 'almost every major gay American poet of the late 20th century' (Gibson, n.p.). Though deliberately odd in their phrasing, the opening lines suggest the poem will fulfil traditional functions of elegy, to mourn and praise the dead. 'His little feet are green', Killian writes. 'Take the barrel off the wright / for his green feet' (Killian 2001, 82). But this tone is soon undercut. Comparing the corpse to a scarecrow—'the beautiful birds this dead boy scared away / the welts forensics took for burns' (82)— Shepard's corpse appears throughout the poem as a kind of intrusive physical fact—'Mathew Shepard, 105 pounds, five foot two' (83), 'his neck burnt black' (84)—amidst a welter of other detail: queer-bashing in Killian and Bellamy's neighbourhood on Minna Street, celebrity spotting, a parodic alphabet game ('A is for Kevin / B is for missed the bus'). The poem ends with bitter irony: 'the corpses change but the party goes on forever' (85).

'AIDS deaths dropped in half in 1997, now only the 15th killer / in America', Killian writes, yet 'other causes leap out of the pack / accident, suicide, murder, sign of the cross / as AIDS drop down to 15 / after 15 years / and murder in Laramie' (83). For Kaplan Harris, the poem's ultimate message is that America would prefer gay men to be killed than to be visible (Harris 2011b, 648). But the poem also questions what such visibility means: a parade of the dead, from the victims of AIDS to the homophobic violence of which Shepard's death is only the tip of the iceberg—as AIDS deaths in the US go down, incidents of queer-bashing rise—and which continues to disproportionately affect trans people, people of colour, those who are marginalized for reasons of racialized, economic, and gender identity.

'The nineties were spent largely in hoping for a cure for AIDS', Killian commented in 2019, a few months before his own passing. 'We didn't get a cure, exactly, but we got enough' (Branton, n.p.). This concluding 'enough' contains

322 NEVER BY ITSELF ALONE

a characteristically elusive yet telling irony. What *would* be enough? Of what social systems does AIDS become a symptom? In what global context is AIDS understood? Without in any way minimizing the horror of his death, it has been argued, for example, that, as white and middle class, Matthew Shepard's was a *grievable* queer life—a grievability evidenced, for instance, by the *Blood and Tears* anthology. As such, his death was only the tip of an iceberg of queerphobic violence elided, in particular, with anti-Blackness, and rendered invisible within the existing grammar of suffering (Eric Stanley 2011, 18; Glave 2005, 200–204; Warren 2015, 1-17). Likewise, as poet-critic Cam Scott suggests:

> [O]ne cannot speak of an end to the AIDS crisis, in spite of its increased management within affluent and largely white enclaves of the imperial core, where the economic vectors of infection persist. Much as HIV and AIDS chiefly afflicted gay men during a period of cultural persecution, it continues to impact marginalized populations today [. . .] Official strategies of recognition simply outsource privation to the nearest periphery. (Scott 2020, n.p.).

In its citational, gossipy, and disjunctive surface, its foregrounding of sex and death and its address to community, *Argento Series* is a New Narrative text, but, in contrast to the fluent and fluid prose of early New Narrative—the gossipy analysis of Glück's *Elements,* the utopian hopes of *Century of Clouds*—a New Narrative newly fragmented by the experience of collective trauma. A poetry of mourning that doesn't explain away, whitewash, or romanticize, Killian's *Argento Series* throws up its mangled voices and its mangled facts in ways that provoke, preserving the gaps, the paradoxes, and the double-binds of an era—that of AIDS—that we too easily disavow as past. Even as the poem's speaker claims that 'I saw something important that I can't remember', such writing accomplishes the task of historical memory against wilful forgetting. In this, it is another way of building community: a community that encompasses the dead as well as the living, that refuses the boundaries of morality or mortality, that refuses to move on or to forget. Here, even with deliberately mangled, damaged, disjunctive vision, community survives, in all its contradiction and damage: its rumours, its gossip, its legends, its secrets, its hopes. And here, still, is where the utopianism of early New Narrative still lies—'flashes, enigmas [. . .] a florid crying out theme of suffering-horror [. . .] a future' (Abbott 2019, 182).

Coda

'When politics show'

'Inaudible substance of catastrophe'

The AIDS crisis is often portrayed as the end of an era, a truly devastating generational rift which means that even today those in the West who, like myself, did not live through that moment as adults, can access it only as if through a veil, the other side of the glass. As Kevin Killian remarked of the shift from Gay Liberation to AIDS: 'There was a social formation [. . .] a leap into consciousness, then a disaster' (Killian 2014, 18). Yet this sense of cataclysm or ending should not blind us to the community strengths that enabled so many to survive it. As Michael Bronski argues, while the sexual communities of gay men and queer people in general were blamed for the spread of the disease, in fact, it was precisely the queer community's generous remodelling of social life that enabled queer people to live through this period, forming support networks in the criminal absence of the state and in the face of mass public indifference and hostility. Not least amongst these were communities of writers and poets for whom writing, too, served as a place to figure and refigure future directions. 'AIDS', Bronski writes,

> touched all queer lives, and disproportionately those who had been excluded from queer literature by myopic publishers—people of colour, the poor, transgender people, and others [. . .] [T]his new demographic of AIDS writers was more open and inclusive than published 'gay writing' had been. This sea-change would bear fruit in the 1990s, when queer writers who gathered at the community-run OutWrite Conferences (beyond the gatekeeping of mainstream publishers) claimed their places in the queer polity of literature, and fought about it. (Bronski 2021, n.p.)

Initially organized by *OUT/LOOK* in San Francisco, and from 1992 by *Gay Community News* in Boston, the OutWrite conferences were held for nearly a decade, ending on the brink of the millennium. At the inaugural OutWrite conference, held in 1990 in San Francisco, the keynotes were given by Allen Ginsberg and Judy Grahn, signifying continuities with the visions of gay and lesbian poetry communities of the previous era. Bronski, who was on the

Never By Itself Alone. David Grundy, Oxford University Press. © Oxford University Press 2024.
DOI: 10.1093/oso/9780197654842.003.0013

324 NEVER BY ITSELF ALONE

organizing committee, describes the ritual of the calling out of names of the dead at each conference, a toll which also served to counteract what was perceived as the creeping mainstreamization of the queer movement, with each conference debating where to go next in regard to topics from AIDS to the role of the grassroots, figurations of gender and race, and the role of literature within all of these different understandings of community.

Looking to the future, such communities also harked back to the examples of the past, as each successive generation had done before them. From Charley Shively's championing of John Wieners and Stephen Jonas, to Jack Spicer's fascination with the *George-Kreis* or the Wobblies, Bruce Boone writing of Spicer, or Judy Grahn investigating Gertrude Stein, examining early instantiations of community—instantiations so often shaped by and in poetry and in other forms of literature—not only served to show how far the queer community had come but also revealed radical moments of potential; moments that could prove instructive in the continuing struggle between incorporation into a violently imperial nation-state and the desire for its total transformation and overthrow from within on every axis: those of race, class, gender, and sexuality alike.

In particular, the lesson for such work today lies in the global, international dimension of movements that often operated in the interstices of the local. As Dennis Altman notes, AIDS has long since been a global epidemic, yet today, the continuing focus on the era of the '80s and of what Altman calls 'the Atlantic world' blinds us to this fact (Altman 2001, 52–67). While treatment in the Western world, particularly for gay white men, has rendered the situation at the time of writing tolerable, AIDS has become yet another problem outside the borders, affecting queer and heterosexual men and women not racialized as white, affecting those who fall outside the economic safety net of white bourgeois subjects. At the time of writing, the highest concentration of people with AIDS are in the American South and on the African continent. As Sarah Schulman commented in 2021:

> For everything that was won for people with AIDS, the issue of access was not won [. . .] We have drugs, not just for HIV, but for all kinds of things, but plenty of people can't get them [. . .] Black gay men in the U.S. South have a higher rate of HIV infection than any population in the world. In 2017, even though these drugs have been around since 1996. Because we [still] don't have a functional healthcare system. (Cohen 2021, n.p.)

As Schulman suggests, such issues are ones that had been raised by community organizations, by activists, by writers, and by poets for at least thirty years.

From the beginning, feminist activists, particularly feminist activists of colour, had linked the fight against AIDS to the fight against cancer, and the more widespread effects of US healthcare inequality in general. And writers and activists have continued to testify to the way that AIDS has continued to decimate communities, challenging dominant narratives that present AIDS as an exclusively white male disease. Valuable testimony of such work in Boston and San Francisco is provided in Pamela Sneed's recent *Funeral Diva*—so named for Sneed's capacity for poetry and oratory at the many AIDS funerals she had to attend—and in Imani Harrington's beautifully fierce poem 'The AIDS of America'. Harrington's poem appears in 1994 in *The Black Women's Health Book*, edited by Evelyn C. White, alongside contributions from Evelyn Hammonds, Angela Davis, Beverly Smith, and—posthumously—Pat Parker, that speak to such connections, linking the experience of Black women with AIDS to the Tuskegee experiment, the policing of Black women's bodies, queer and straight alike, through stereotypes of sexual promiscuity, and what Smith calls 'the systems of inequality which AIDS highlights' (Sneed 2020; White 1994; Briggs 1990). Today, in the era of PEP (Post-Exposure Prophylaxis) and PrEP (Pre-Exposure Prophylaxis), we should bear these truths in mind.

In drawing to a close this study of poetic communities in San Francisco and Boston, it is vital that this closing chapter is not conclusion: that it be linked to an ongoing political analysis, and an ongoing analysis of the role that poetry can play alongside this analysis. Following the urgings of Altman and Schulman, what's key is that this legacy is a *global* legacy. The work of Emily Hobson on the 'Gay Left' in San Francisco, the radical internationalist demands of *Fag Rag*, of Pat Parker or the Combahee River Collective: all these serve to index how queer life in North America can never be adequately understood solely within North America's shores. The writers addressed in this study were always aware of this, whether Enola Gay protesting Livermore Labs, Bay Area Gay Liberation staging solidarity with the South American fight against US imperialism, Robert Duncan and Jack Spicer propounding internationalist analyses, *Fag Rag* unveiling its ten-point plan at the 1972 Democratic Convention, or Pat Parker speaking at the 1987 March on Washington the following decade. And today, a queer writing worthy of its name will be one that continues the queer lineages of community, of internationalist politics, and of an analysis that links sexuality and gender to the world system of capitalism in which its dynamics are produced and contested.

To pay full attention to such work as it has developed in the twenty-first century, after the ending of this study, would require another book in itself. But, for this coda, some pointers. Merle Woo continues to write, as do Judy Grahn, Kitty Tsui, and the older New Narrative writers. Likewise of vital importance, is the gender-defiant work of the late kari edwards—in turn mentor of younger writers such as Rob Halpern, Taylor Brady, and Julian Talumez Brolaski—in which a dismantling of conventional understandings of gender is seen as inseparable from a dismantling of other systems of power, including the power residing in

326   NEVER BY ITSELF ALONE

language. In 2020, Andrea Abi-Karam and Kay Gabriel's anthology *We Want It All* presented a range of trans writers, a number from the Bay Area, whose work insistently interrogates the boundaries of gender, race, and class from a left perspective. Abi-Karam's own work in their books *Extratransmission* (2019) and *Villainy* (2021) chart the costs of the War on Terror and Donald Trump's more recent 'Muslim Ban' in furious, splintered queer narratives of trauma, while Gabriel forms part of a younger generation of Marxist scholars engaged with New Narrative, alongside Cam Scott, David W. Pritchard, Jamie Townsend, and Eric Sneathen, and before them, Rob Halpern, Kaplan Harris, Robin Tremblay-McGaw, and others. In the UK, younger poets like Nat Raha, Laurel Uziell, Sophie Robinson, Sam Solomon, Francesca Lisette, and the late Callie Gardner have written poetry and produced scholarship under the influence of John Wieners and New Narrative, championing this work as a living tradition. In the Bay Area, meanwhile, we might also invoke the work of Cedar Sigo, a devotee of John Wieners and Stephen Jonas, of the Black Radical Tradition, of Audre Lorde and Diane di Prima and Joanne Kyger and Kevin Killian, whose work, in books such as *Royals* (2017), negotiates between his position as a gay man within San Francisco's artistic communities and an Indigenous person who grew up on the Suquamish reservation near Seattle, Washington, negotiating a memory 'more fragmented than Sappho' while consistently paying tribute to poetic peers in dedications and tribute (Foerster, n.p.).

Sigo's work has a generous expansiveness. Yet as his comments on fragmented memory suggests, queer community—and the multiple other communities with which it is in complex relation—is not simply a utopian place of refuge. Vital to many of the writers I name above is a sense of using queerness itself as a mode of critique. In their 2016 study *The Estrangement Principle,* for instance, Ariel Goldberg argues that to build a writerly community around sexuality does not necessarily imply a shared politics or even aesthetic. Instead, Goldberg builds on an argument made in Renee Gladman's important late '90s Bay Area journal *Clamour: A Dyke Zine* to suggest that a radical queer community today might gather around feelings, not so much of belonging to but of estrangement from mainstream definitions of queerness, particularly in the face of the uneasy alliance between queerness, whiteness, gentrification, police brutality, and wealth disparity in the San Francisco dot-com boom of the 1990s onwards, a sudden and rapid transformation in the city's economic life (Goldberg, 128–40).

Such estrangement is, perhaps, taken to an extreme in the work of Rob Halpern, a latter-day New Narrative writer nurtured in the writing workshops of Dodie Bellamy and Robert Glück and in close friendship with Bruce Boone, whose selected writings Halpern has edited over a number of years. The relation between a politics of gay male desire and the workings of American imperialism is often shockingly dramatized in the books *Music for Porn* (2012) and *Common*

Place (2015), a project which stages masturbatory fantasies around the figures of US soldiers and Afghani and Iraqi detainees killed during the so-called War on Terror. Halpern's work in these poems, poised on a knowing knife-edge of appropriation and violence, has received sustained critical attention from an international range of poet-critics, among them Lisa Jeschke, Sam Ladkin, Tom Bamford-Blake, Lukas Moe, and Tyrone Williams: what I offer below is a thumbnail sketch.

In Halpern's words: 'Coming of age in the shadow of AIDS, struggling to understand a form of desire that seemed to be in the process of being negated for me before I could assume it as a bequest [...] A historical moment when the idea of a Love could no longer harbor any illusion of beneficent inclusion' (Halpern 2020, n.p.). In a recent essay, Halpern locates such questioning in the lineage of Robert Duncan's essay 'The Homosexual in Society', with which the present book began. As we saw, for Duncan, the struggle for Gay Liberation must not particularize gay identity separate to or above and beyond other struggles, instead seeking a realization of the struggle for gay freedom that would reach its full expression only within the wider transformation of society as a whole. Writing during the instantiation of the military-industrial complex, exactly what Duncan has predicted has come to pass: with the national military mobilization of the Second World war enshrined as the new norm, and the Cold War subsequently extended to every facet of domestic life, queer politics has been demonized, scapegoated but also incorporated into what Jasbir Puar has termed US 'homonationalism' (Puar).

For Halpern, the music of Duncan's poetry—along with the 'Drum-Taps' of Whitman's Civil War poems—serve to index a failure in the gay American poetic tradition which believes itself to have transcended the identification of gay eros with American state power, and poetry must bear the mark of this exclusionary and violently formed community, in which, while queer subjects— generally white gay men—have achieved a certain incorporation within the body politic (freer, for instance, to serve in the army), this freedom is bought at the price of the detainee those soldiers torture and kill. Halpern's own poetic work engages with the long tradition of connection between eroticized militarism, male camaraderie. and US national identity, from the poems of Whitman's *Drum Taps* (especially 'The Wound-Dresser') (1865) through to the work of Robert Duncan a century later, and back to the work of European writers and filmmakers such as Pier Paolo Pasolini, Christopher Marlowe, and the Marquis de Sade. In his final film, *Salò* (1975), for example, Pasolini adapted de Sade to the context of 1930s fascism—viewed from the historical lens of the 1970s. Here, the excess of perversions practiced by the trilogy of church, state, and military are relations of domination, challenging the argument that sexual liberation, or liberalization, is inherently progressive. Such critiques, made at a nascent point

328 NEVER BY ITSELF ALONE

of gay liberation—along with those of Rainer Werner Fassbinder and Rosa von Praunheim, who construct their analysis of gay male sexuality through the lenses of class exclusion—inform Halpern's own sense that the gay community (or, indeed, the idea that there is any one such singular community) is by no means inherently liberatory.*

For Halpern, borrowing from Anahid Nersessian's recent work on Romanticism, poetry, in its ability to maintain multiple dimensions simultaneously, through the conceit, wordplay, wit, simile, metaphor, rhyme, and other forms of linguistic metonymy, creates a modern 'calamity form' (Nersessian 2020). As Halpern writes in a poem for the late UK poet Sean Bonney: 'rhyme for what I can't even hear / Inaudible substance of catastrophe a heavy-handed conceit [. . .] like the soul' (Halpern 2021, 36). Ultimately, Halpern suggests, 'the poem's competence is [. . .] as a point of departure [. . .] a move beyond the poem, out of poetry, headlong & recklessly into the world' (57).

The End of Gender, Coast to Coast

In 2016, Eileen Myles moved from female to gender-neutral pronouns, thus making public a trans identity that was both contained within and exceeded their previous identification as a 'dyke'. But queer writers, Myles notes, have been telling us these things for years. As poet Erica Kaufman notes in a piece on Myles for *Boston Review* entitled 'The End of Gender', Myles in the 1980s and '90s was able to write, as a lesbian, of the embodied experiences of sexuality or menstruation typically gendered as female in a way that established perspective from neither a male nor female angle (Kaufman, n.p.). 'It is much easier to label a text as concerned with "sexuality"', Kaufman writes, 'than to examine rigorously the ways the poetry requires a reader to think about experiencing the world as both female and lesbian while rejecting easy definitions of either term'. Quoting Myles' poem 'Snowflake', which begins 'There's no female / in my position // There's no man', Kaufman argues 'Myles makes a new queer "norm" possible, visible'.

The gendered and non-gendered 'position' Myles' work comes from is also one of place and one of class. 'I'd like to thank the State of Massachusetts and the bowl of language that surrounds and survives me', they write in *Cool for You* (Myles 2000, 196). Though much of their career was conducted in New York, a city to which they moved in their early twenties in 1971, Myles' use of language is still heavily shaped by Boston, as they attested in a recent lecture-reading hosted by Harvard's Woodberry Poetry Room, at which they discussed their research into the work of writers from the Boston area: John Wieners, Stephen Jonas, Margo Lockwood, and the African American poet Helene Johnson (Myles 2016, n.p.). In turn, growing up in the city during the 1950s and 1960s, the classed and performative elements of accent that Myles discusses cross over with the interrelated performances of gender and of whiteness within a de facto segregated city. Of their Boston accent, Myles writes: 'in a way everybody is doing drag [. . .] everybody is doing their accent really consciously, you know'.

Myles' short story 'Gay Sunshine, 1971' was written in 2009 for an event organized in San Francisco by poet Michelle Tea, a former colleague in the lesbian poetry performance collective Sister Spit, in which Tea commissioned artists to focus on material from the archive at the city's GLBT Historical Society. As Myles notes in a blog post from the time, they felt uncomfortable being a 'woman' poet so decided to write as a gay male poet, inspired by the acts of 'hero worshipping' devotion between gay men in John Wieners' *Hotel Wentley Poems*. 'I'm thinking hmm not particularly "a woman"', Eileen [. . .] I can only conclude I'm functioning more as a queer poet more than anything else [. . .] I decided to be a male homosexual poet in the piece I wrote' (Myles 2009, n.p.).

Myles' story is a genre pastiche of the coming-out stories found in the gay press of the early 1970s—the time of Myles' own coming out and move to New York. The narrator goes through the motions of heterosexuality before discovering copies of *Fag Rag* and *Gay Sunshine* at their place of work, reading in their pages Wieners' poem, which readers may remember from earlier in the present book (Myles 2012). In Myles' story, the encounter with the poem prompts the narrator to depart Boston for San Francisco, where they encounter—and turn down—none other than the editor of *Gay Sunshine*, textuality and sexuality enmeshing in deliriously self-conscious fashion. Myles' text literalizes the move from coast to coast that this study has enacted. And in its act of homage to the gay male press of an earlier era, Myles' story reveals these earlier moments to have been *already queer*. At the climax to Myles' story, the speaker neglects to attend a Gay Pride Rally, instead fucking another man to its sounds from outside the window. This is not, however, a rejection of politics. As Myles writes of the project that gave rise to the story:

> [W]hat was remarkable was that as a group of writers we were performing a sort [of] public service. We were herding the community towards their archive. They need to know about it. And not only did we have to find something in the archive that moved us—it had to move us toward a contemplation of activism, and acts of political outrage. When politics show. (Myles 2009, n.p.)

330   NEVER BY ITSELF ALONE

'To tell you stories'

Politics show throughout the history of queer San Francisco: the 1940s scene of the intelligentsia, of conscientious objectors, and of Trotskyist and anarchist groupings glanced at the beginning of this study; the counterculture in the 1960s, with the New Left symbolized in the popular imagination by Berkeley and the working-class Black insurrection symbolized by the Panthers across the Bay in Oakland; the 'gay mecca' of the 1970s—the bathhouses and bars and explosions of possibility on the Castro, the emergence of lesbian feminism, and of experiments in alternative living on the one hand and the corporatization of the gay movement, and the rise of the New Right on the other; and then the crisis of AIDS in the 1980s both as an attack on and a drawing together of the currents of solidarity and community established in preceding years; and finally, as AIDS itself became a kind of outsourced spread into the Global South, its memories fading in a new generation, the rise of homonationalism, the forgetting of queer radicalism, and the San Francisco tech boom which has transformed the city almost beyond recognition.

As of 2024, San Francisco is a city of immense wealth with a crisis at its margins, starkly demonstrated by the ways the humanly visible effects of the opioid crisis play out beneath its vast edifices. The manufacturing sector having left for cheaper locations by the end of the '80s, the tech boom—with networked cafes, social media headquarters, tech gurus etc., that in fact govern much of the world's communication platforms—Apple, Google, Facebook, Twitter— at once abstracts and builds on the city's financialized history: the legacy of the California Gold Rush as the West Coast's principal banking and financial centre, of Wells Fargo and Bank of America, into the 1990s dot-com bubble and the late 2000s social media boom, tech employment rising by 90 percent between 2010 and 2014, with payroll tax exemptions for biotech companies (Federal Writers' Project 2011, 114; Stehlin 2016; Heller 2013; Holliday 1999).

So too, Boston has gentrified, housing prices rising in the 1990s, Boston's living costs rising to amongst the highest in the United States: a region of new companies and new technologies, alongside the back alleys and highways of government in a region soaked in violence and history—from abolitionist heritage to segregation and the busing crisis, the queer bohemia of Beacon Hill in the '50s and its destruction to pave the way for today's city of Boston Dynamics, with its police robodogs, its delivery 'dark sites', its megalopolis highways towering over forgotten alleys, its giant edifices of glass and steel ('Cost of Living Index' 2007, n.p.). John Wieners wrote with poetic clarity of the beginnings of this process in the 1960s. As he once asked: 'How can a poor person matter in this world?' (Wieners 1975, 125).

Forty years since Wieners' poem for Alice O'Brien, and sixteen after the Roxbury campaign of 1979, Chanelle Pickett, an African-American trans woman, was picked up at the long-running gay bar Playland (in whose honor Wieners wrote the poems 'Exchange of the Lady's Handmaids' and 'Playland's Aftermath'), and murdered by white computer programmer William Palmer. Palmer was ultimately sentenced to two years in prison for assault and battery but acquitted of murder. (Nangeroni 1997, n.p.) Pickett's murder, along with the murders of other trans women of color in the Boston area, among them Rita Hester and Monique Thomas, became one of the incidents sparking the instantiation of the Trans Day of Remembrance (TDoR) at the turn of the Millennium. (Walters 2019, n.p.) A public display of memory and mourning against the prejudice, hostility and willed forgetting surrounding such deaths, TDoR shares its impulse with Wieners' poem, with the Combahee River Collective's campaign against gender violence, and with the refusal to forget found in all the work addressed in this book.

'In different ways and with different consequences,' writes scholar Ann DuCille, 'we all experience the pain and disappointment of failed community'. DuCille (2003) writes of the disconnects between (white) feminist and (male) Black scholars, of those whose work bridges communities or exists outside those communities, making the links for a community not yet in existence: one that is to come. Likewise, speaking of a lineage of Boston poetry, from the white working-class Catholic background of Wieners to the African American Helene Johnson and the mixed-heritage Stephen Jonas, Eileen Myles suggests: 'There's this kind of erasure that is so increasingly the condition of how we live' (Myles 2016, n.p.). This erasure—of individuals, of communities, and of the poems that emerge from those individual and community lives—is the condition of much of the writing addressed in this book, and challenging it is a long but urgent process. One way to start is simply to tell the story of those outsiders, those writers, those who made the links yet whose work was ignored and excluded, and continues to be ignored and excluded, from standard accounts. As Bruce Boone puts it in *Century of Clouds*: 'Perhaps beginning to tell you stories. Some important friendships, in between spaces [. . .] Problems. Questions' (Boone 1980, 4). Any account will be a beginning, a new beginning, but of beginnings a movement emerges. History, and the stories of which it consists, is not set in stone, but is a space of contestation.

How to go about this? Examples—themselves too often neglected—abound. Kevin Killian and Lew Ellingham first met as part of Robert Glück's SPT writing workshop in the early 1980s. In 1990, Killian took over a project begun by Ellingham on the Spicer circle, conducting new research of his own, organizing the Spicer archives, and ultimately shepherding this research into their co-authored biography of Spicer, *Poet Be Like God*, in the process becoming an irreplaceable fount of knowledge on Spicer's life and work (Bradshaw 2009, n.p.). 'Over the past fifteen years', write Killian and Ellingham in their introduction, 'hundreds of men and women have helped us make this book what it is: a social history, a biography, a literary account' (Killian and Ellingham, xv). Yet Killian's and Ellingham's work on Spicer was dismissed by one academic peer reviewer because Spicer was supposedly 'a coterie poet', whose work had appeal only to a 'handful of California homosexuals' (Bradshaw 2009, n.p.). What Killian's work,

332 NEVER BY ITSELF ALONE

along with that of Peter Gizzi and others, did, was to show, both that this was absolutely true, and that it is through the local that we might access the general, the coalitional, and the transnational.

Poetry begins in the individual and collective alike. A poem is never by itself alone. Poetry communities are not simply self-contained entities, literary movements to be historicized in boxes, but living and flowing spheres of influence, charges flowing from the dead to living, legacies and bequests in language. Killian passed so much information down, much which died with him. But he was always seeking to transmit, to transform. His research on Spicer defied the model of the scholar as a self-enclosed entity defining their own pool of knowledge and jealously guarding it against intruders: the model of knowledge as private property.

Killian died just as I began writing this book; the last email I received from him included a scan of an issue of *No Apologies* with some thoughts on the symposium conducted amongst New Narrative writers therein—an obscure neorealist-meets-Hollywood film from 1954 released in two versions as *Stazione Termine* (*Terminal Station*) and *Indiscretion of an American Wife*, directed by Vittorio De Sica in the Roma Termini railway station and starring Jennifer Jones and Montgomery Clift (Killian 2019, n.p.; Killian 1984). Killian reflected on how this film's awkward blend of neo-realism and Hollywood melodrama might have figured into very early attempts by New Narrative writers to work out how they were going to write about AIDS. 'What I now take away from this sort of party investigation', Killian wrote, 'is that it took place on the very edge of AIDS and that what was happening underneath was our preliminary investigation of Italian neorealism as perhaps one way to begin making art of aids, not AIDS precisely, but that may be the postwar neorealism movement of Italy, with its deliberately anti-art gestures—including documentary and leftist politics, mixing acting of non-actors with Hollywood flirtation—was going to be one way to proceed in the nightmare that AIDS was going to become [. . .] We were all reflecting [. . .] on how neo-realistic was the coming war against AIDS going to turn out to be' (Killian 2019, n.p.).[1] Throwing crumbs to the younger scholar, this was typical of the way Killian interacted with almost anyone with whom he came into contact. And throughout this project, begun in the immediate wake of his death, his example and generosity has been a model.

As it turned, out the *Stazione Termine* symposium was one of many potential directions that fell by the wayside during the writing of this book. While the earlier chapters present nascent activity at a time when specifically queer poetry scenes were not often existent, its final chapters can only hope to provide a capsule vision of San Francisco's varied and thriving queer poetry scenes in the area in the era of Gay Liberation and beyond. The book's final third selects particular writers and groupings as representative of particular trends: the lesbian publishing scenes surrounding Judy Grahn and Pat Parker, the socialist feminist work of Karen Brodine, Merle Woo, and Nellie Wong, and finally the work of New Narrative writers, which both emerges from and challenges some of the emphases of the previous decade's Gay Liberation work. In selecting these focal points, I have not pretended towards a comprehensive survey but have sought to balance the local and the detailed while hinting at a broader overview.

I regret that space has precluded further work on the following writers: Aaron Shurin, whose poetic and personal relation with Robert Duncan provides a link to the earliest generations examined here, whose poem 'Exorcism of the Straight Man/Demon' was the first (broadside) publication by Good Gay Poets Press, and who was later in dialogue with writers such as Steve Abbott and Karen Brodine;[2] Paul Mariah, editor of the magazine *Manroot* and a tireless publisher, poet, and prison activist; Winston Leyland, prolific editor of *Gay Sunshine*; genderqueer poet and activist Tede Matthews; British exile Thom Gunn, whose work likewise engaged with the queer milieu through more traditional verse forms; Alta's work with Shameless Hussy Press; the sui generis experimental work of Lynn Lonidier, a cousin of Karen Brodine's, and the former partner of musician Pauline Oliveros, whose books, including the books *A Lesbian Estate* (1973), *Clitoris Lost: A Woman's Version of the Creation Myth* (1989), and the posthumous *The Rhyme of the Ag-ed Mariness* (2001) explore the boundaries of textual, sexual, and gender identity[3]; the 1975 formation by Boston-based activist Merissa Sherrill of the long-running newsletter and magazine *The T-V Tapestry* (later *Transgender Tapestry*); the scintillatingly queer work in poetry and collage of Helen Adam within the Duncan and Spicer circles, with its delirious fairytale deconstructions of myths of heterosexual domesticity; the work of Lani Ka'ahumanu, founder of the San Francisco Bay Area Bisexual Network, of Menominee writer and two spirit activist Chrystos, a key figure in *This Bridge Called My Back*, and, in Boston, of George-Thérèse Dickenson, a one-time stripper in Boston's 'Combat Zone', and of Pat M. Kuras, whose respective books *Striations* (1976) and *The Pinball Player* (1982) were published by Good Gay Poets; the vital contributions of Kitty Tsui, Willyce Kim, and Martha Shelley; and the work of writers themselves not gay but associated with and inspired by the writers I do address, including Ntozake Shange, Gabrielle Daniels, Francesca Rosa, Edith Jenkins, Ruth Weiss, and Michael Amnasan. And always, alongside the known names, there are, to return to those words of Pat Parker's invoked in this book's introduction,

> all the names we forgot to say
> & all the names we didn't know
> & all the names we don't know, yet.

'We cannot live in the past, nor can we re-create it', writes Judy Grahn. 'Yet, as we unravel the past, the future also unfolds before us, as though they are mirrors without which neither can be seen or happen' (*AMT*, 282). In 1988, Samuel Delany invoked the possibility, 'once the AIDS crisis is brought under control', of 'a sexual revolution to make a laughing-stock of any social movement that

334 NEVER BY ITSELF ALONE

till now has borne the name', in which 'clear and articulate language' enters into 'the marginal areas of human sexual exploration' (Delany 1988, 175). Grahn, Delany, Parker, and all their queer aesthetic kin, present a queerness that is always political, and one in which poetry can play a role in articulating community: critiquing it, supporting it, expanding our sense of what's possible. In their writing, a poem is never by itself alone. Rather, it makes and remakes itself and language in community, in common; life, in all its contradiction and terror, its sights on a queered horizon and a transformed world.

A poem is never by itself alone.

NOTES

Introduction

1. For a more exhaustive treatment of the role of translation in the book, see Eshleman. For 'comrade', see Whitman, 99–100.
2. For a further elucidation of the serial poem concept, see the second of Spicer's 1965 Vancouver lectures (Spicer 1998, 49–56).
3. The original letter—which differs only in a few instances of italicization—was reprinted in Spicer 1987, 53–54.
4. For mirrors, see Spicer 1998, 220–21.
5. For such a distinction, see, e.g., Bredbeck. 'The preference for queer represents, among other things, an aggressive impulse of generalization; it rejects a minoritizing logic of toleration or simple political interest representation in favour of a more thorough resistance to regimes of the normal' (Warner, xxvi).
6. For a similar reclamation of lesbian feminism as presaging queer theory, see Garber.
7. Wittman's text was first completed in March 1969 and distributed in San Francisco in May that year.
8. I have unfortunately not had space to fully examine the relation between queer writers and the left, in its sometimes fractiously competing instantiations, during the period of this study. Important recent scholarship has been done in this regard by Aaron Lecklider (Lecklider 2021). In the present study, however, such diverse affiliations will emerge as the result of local detail—the ways they were often experienced by the poets themselves—rather than as part of a theoretical argument. To take some examples, in the 1940s and 1950s, Duncan and Spicer were associated with the anti-Stalinist left, both Trotskyist and anarchist; in the 1970s, *Fag Rag* were unabashedly anarchist, while Karen Brodine, Merle Woo, and Nellie Wong, examined in the tenth chapter, were aligned with Trotskyism. Other currents, from the CPUSA (Communist Party USA) to Maoism, Marxism-Leninism, anarchism, women's liberation, and Black feminism, are traced throughout the book. Thanks to the anonymous peer reviewer for suggesting that I clarify this point.
9. See, for instance, John Shoptaw's influential reading of 'encryption' in John Ashbery's poetry (Shoptaw 1994).
10. *Evergreen Review*, Vol. 1, No. 2, 'San Francisco Scene', March 1957. The issue was introduced by Kenneth Rexroth, and contained work by Spicer and Duncan, including Duncan's important poem 'This place, rumord to have been Sodom' and Spicer's sardonic 'Berkeley in Time of Plague'.
11. For a discussion of the Beats as model for queer lifestyle, see D'Emilio 2012, 181–82.

336 NOTES

12. See, for example, the collapse of the Berkeley Writers' Conference, a creative writing workshop taught by Spicer, Duncan, and Blaser among others, in large part due to faculty homophobia. See Killian and Ellingham, 24–25. See also Michael Davidson 1989, 40.

13. See Hartman's trilogy *Scenes of Subjection, Lose Your Mother,* and *Wayward Lives, Beautiful Experiments.* Equally informed by detailed archival investigation, the style of these books departs further and further from standard academic-historical practice and towards a style informed by imaginative recreations and re-inscriptions more akin to what might be termed 'creative non-fiction' (Hartman 1997, 2007, 2019).

14. For Killian, see John Emil Vincent 2011, 16–35. Raha's 2015 review-essay of the most recent Wieners Selected Poems, *Supplication,* in Boston online quarterly *The Critical Flame,* was a key point in recent Wieners criticism; it was followed by a PhD and related book chapter in 2018 and 2019 (Raha 2015, 2018, 2019). These, along with the work of Robbie Dewhurst and Michael Seth Stewart, remain high points of Wieners scholarship to which my work here is indebted. For recent articles on Gay Liberation in Boston by Michael Bronski see Bronski 2016, 2017, 2019. See also Amy Hoffman (for Boston) and Emily Hobson (for San Francisco). Julie Enszer's book manuscript *A Fine Bind: Lesbian-Feminist Publishing from 1969 through 2009,* is forthcoming; her articles appear at *LAMBDA Literary, The Poetry Foundation,* and she runs the online *Lesbian Poetry Archive,* as well as editing the still-running *Sinister Wisdom.*

15. For Parker's involvement with the softball team Gente: see Parker 2019, 384, and Hobson, 12–13, 53–54, 82–83. For Grahn and the Weather Underground, see Grahn 2012 and Hobson, 56–577.

16. For the use of the term 'gay women' and the formation of the San Francisco's Gay Women's Liberation collective by Grahn, Wendy Cadden, and others, see Grahn 2012, 122. See also Garber, 17–18 for a discussion of debates between those who self-defined as 'gay women' and those who self-defined as lesbians.

17. Description taken from Collection Overview, 'Black Lesbian Newsletter / Onyx Collection, 1979–1989', James C. Hormel LGBTQUIA Center, San Francisco Public Library.

18. Bulkin 1981. This essay is a revised version of Bulkin 1978. *Lesbian Poetry: An Anthology* is likewise a revised and expanded version of Bulkin and Larkin, *Amazon Poetry: An Anthology* (New York: Out & Out Books, 1975).

19. Bulkin here quotes Allen's poem 'Beloved Women', first published in *Conditions 7* (1981) and refers to a personal letter from Barbara Noda, quoted in the 1978 version of the article: 'My point is that the words "Asian-American", "lesbian", "historical" and even "poet" need to be re-examined if one is to write a history from which lesbians, especially Third World or working class lesbians, could draw strength' (Bulkin 1978, 15, fn. 4).

20. It should be noted that, while the idea for *ONE* was reportedly first discussed at a Mattachine discussion group, it was never formally associated with the Mattachine Society.

Chapter 1

1. For an overview of 'treatments' for queer sexuality, including sterilization, in the United States, see Chapter 2, 'Treatment: 1884–1974', in Katz 1992, 129–207. See also the work of Alexandra Minna Stern on sterilization and eugenics in California. 'Sterilizations in California's homes and hospitals were made possible in legal and administrative terms by state laws, which, from 1909 until full-fledged repeal in 1979, were firmly rooted in eugenic theories of hereditary improvement. Moreover, as a growing body of scholarship suggests, eugenics encompassed more than strict hereditary control, extending into strategies of reproductive regulation such as institutional segregation (as in Illinois or New York, which had no sterilization statutes), patriarchal containment of women who transgressed gender and sexual norms, or remedial vasectomies on men classed as homosexual who posed little threat of unrestrained procreation' (Stern 2016, 198). See also Chapter 4, 'California's Eugenic Landscapes', in Stern 2005, 115–49.
2. Biographical information in this section draws on Faas 1983 and Jarnot 2012.
3. See, for instance, the piece on 'The Destruction of the World' by French surrealist Pierre Mabille which leads off the magazine's very first issue.
4. References to Duncan's essay will be to its reprinting in Faas. Originally printed in *Politics* in 1944, the essay was reprinted in *Fag Rag* and *Out Look* and, in its expanded form from 1959, in *Jimmy and Lucy's House of K* and in Duncan's *Collected Essays and Other Prose*.
5. See here David Bergman's incisive reading of M. L. Rosenthal's homophobic response to Duncan's work. Bergman 1993, 95–96.
6. The poem was eventually published as 'Toward an African Elegy' in *Circle* in Summer 1948, and it is under this title that it appears in Duncan's *Collected Early Poems and Plays*.
7. See also Duncan 1976, 105, for a slightly different telling of the same anecdote.
8. Lisa Jarnot makes the same comparison in relation to passages of Duncan's 'The Venice Poem' (Jarnot, 114).
9. Blaser was an important part of the poetic scenes in both Boston and San Francisco that I trace in the following chapters, as friend, confidante, and poet. Following Spicer's death and a falling out with Duncan, he departed for Canada, where he spent the rest of his career at Simon Fraser university. I regret that this study has not found space for a more detailed study of Blaser's work. For a more detailed examination, see Miriam Nichols' incisive recent biography (Miriam Nichols 2019).
10. The definitive work on George in English is Robert E. Norton's *Secret Nation* (Norton). George's poetic work is addressed in more depth in Rieckmann. George is satirized in the queer German leftist filmmaker Rainer Werner Fassbinder's *Satansbraten* (*Satan's Brew*) (1976), a coruscating examination of what Fassbinder called George's 'special breed of fascism' (Peucker, 63–64).
11. On Kantorowicz and the Berkeley Renaissance, see Holt and Damon, 153.
12. On '*dignitas*', see Blaser 2006, 74.

338 NOTES

13. See also Hamilton and Mary Tyler's essay in the same volume on Duncan's interest in the figures of Christ and Apollo during the period in which he began working on the poem (Bertholf, 1–13).
14. Note: Duncan's removal of the 'e' in 'reveald' is a characteristic idiosyncrasy.
15. On 'manifest domesticity', see Kaplan.
16. For more on this aspect, see McDowell.
17. For a Gay Liberation era reading of Dante's attitude to the 'sodomites' in hell, as part of an argument about the queerness latent and denied within the construct of heterosexuality, see Mieli, 134–38. See also Blaser 2015, 119.

Chapter 2

1. The poems were published in the pamphlet *An Ode and Arcadia* in 1974 (Spicer and Duncan, 1974).
2. Jonas writes to Gerrit Lansing: 'my place in an up-roar today. the Police were here and searched the place for hypodermic needles, pot and heroin—none of which I need but Joe Dunn has been staying over and they watch him [...] They found all of my sex (boys) pictures—some of which were nude—completely [...] I knew that they had no search warrant and the evidence would be valueless in court. I took the detectives [*sic*] advice and destroyed same [...] somhow [*sic*] it seems all wrong' (Jonas 1961, n.p.).
3. Other instances from the period include the prosecution of Amiri Baraka and Diane di Prima's *The Floating Bear* for 'obscene content'—queer references in texts by Baraka '('The Eighth Ditch (is Drama')', and William Burroughs '('ROUTINE: Roosevelt after the Inauguration')'.—in October 1961. The issue in question, published in June that year, appeared the same month as the issue that reprinted Wieners' poems from the *Boston Newsletter*.
4. While Robin Blaser reprints 'What to Do with the Boston Newsletter' as an appendix to the 1975 edition of Spicer's *Collected Books*, the document itself has only recently been unearthed in archives, in a carbon copy from the Jack Spicer papers (1938–1975), Rare Book Library, Emory University, Atlanta. My thanks to Kevin Killian and Nick Sturm for providing me with the material in 2016. The *Newsletter* contains the following poems: Jack Spicer, 'Song for the Great Mother', 'Central Park West', 'A Prayer for Pvt. Graham Mackintosh on Halloween', 'Midnight at Bareass Beach', 'Five Words for Joe Dunn on his 22nd Birthday', 'A Dialogue Between Intellect and Passion', 'Hibernation'; Robin Blaser—'R', 'A 4 Part Geometry Lesson (for Sylvia Townsend Warner)', 'For Charles Who is a River', 'Two Astronomers with Notebooks', 'Letter to Freud'; Joe Dunn, 'The Head', 'September 15th'; Steve Jonas, 'Michael Poem' [aka 'Love, The Poem, The Sea']; John Wieners, 'Ballade', 'YOU CAN'T KILL THESE MACHINES', 'THAT OLD GANG OF MINE' [aka 'Hart Crane, Harry Crosby . . .']; [Collective], 'Letter to Ford Foundation'. Spicer's poems appear in Spicer 1980; Blaser's in *The Holy Forest*; Dunn's are uncollected; Jonas' 'Michael Poem' was first republished in the pamphlet *Love, The Poem, The Sea and Other Pieces Examined by Steven Jonas* (Jonas 1957) and

NOTES   339

subsequently in Jonas 1994; Wieners' poems later appeared across *The Floating Bear*, *Angels of the Lyre*, and *Cultural Affairs in Boston* (Wieners 1961; Leyland 1975; Wieners 1988). Material relating to the *Boston Newsletter*, including poems that were ultimately not included, is available in the Jack Spicer archives at UC Berkeley.

5. This association would be maintained through the following decades: Mackintosh wryly noted that their relationship 'survived such intimacy' (Killian and Ellingham, 56) and would later serve as an important champion of Spicer's work, reviving White Rabbit Press after the original imprint had been abandoned due to original publisher Joe Dunn's drug addiction, and typesetting and printing Spicer's *Collected Books* and other volumes following Spicer's death.

6. The figure of the Pepsi Cola bottle also resonates with the following from the Oliver Charming manuscript, which describes the opinion expressed by Charming's psychiatrist 'that to try to force the truly Mertzian act upon reality is like trying to make a collage out of a sheep's belly or forcing a penis into an empty Pepsi Cola bottle' (Spicer 2008, 82). Barton Barber's auto-erotic act—albeit one which refigures the penetrative for the penetrated—might similarly be read as a degraded substitute for the 'cosmic nonsense' that, as we'll see, forms the basis for an 'unvert's' view of sexuality.

7. 'My soldier' likely here refers to Graham Mackintosh.

8. Here I paraphrase Radcylffe Hall's definition in *The Well of Loneliness* (1928).

9. As Kilian notes, while in Mattachine, Spicer questioned Hay's dubious etymological speculations, as filtered through to Gerald Brissette (Killian 2011, 28–29).

10. In this regard, as Snediker suggests, Spicer's work should also be read through later, more positive assessments of the possibilities of non-monogamous, serial relationality by later writers such as Leo Bersani: here I would add French gay activist Guy Hocquenghem and novelist Samuel Delany (Snediker in Vincent 2011, 182; Bersani; Hocquenghem, 131–32; Delany, 129–30).

11. For biographical material and memoirs on the Spicer circle, see Killian and Ellingham; the reminiscences by Harold Dull, Lew Ellingham, Gerald Fabian, James Herndon, Richard Taggett, Hunce Voelcker, and others in the Spicer issue of *Manroot* (No.10, Fall 1974); and the recent book-length memoir by Larry Kearney (Kearney 2019).

12. As Spicer explained in his 1965 Vancouver lectures, as well as 'Martians', other 'sources' include W. B. Yeats' use of spiritualism and the radio messages from the underworld in Jean Cocteau's *Orphée*. See Spicer, 'Dictation and 'A Textbook of Poetry" (Spicer 1998, 1–49). On the figure of the 'Outside' in Spicer's poetry, see further Robin Blaser's influential essay 'The Practice of Outside', printed as the introduction to Spicer's *Collected Books* in 1975 and reprinted in Blaser 2006.

13. The *Boston Newsletter* alone contains poems for Ryan ('Midnight on Bareass Beach') (Killian and Ellingham, 57); Dunn ('Words for Joe Dunn's 22nd Birthday') and Mackintosh ('A Prayer for Pvt. Graham Mackintosh'); and Spicer dedicated two separate sequences to Alexander (Spicer 2008, 203–30).

14. I allude here to Giorgio Agamben's work on the 'coming community'—whose terms of love, singularity, and the refusal of identity resonate with those of Spicer, and whose work was later important to Spicer's close companion Robin Blaser (Agamben 1993; Blaser 2006, 98–110). See also Jean-Luc Nancy's work on the 'inoperative

340 NOTES

community'—one which is defined in large part by writing, as well as finitude and the fact of death (Nancy, 16, 64).

15. Other, shorter-lived magazines included Lewis Ellingham's *M*, George Stanley's *Capitalist Bloodsucker—N*, Dale Landers' *Mithrander*, and Luther T. Cupp [Link Martin]'s *COW*.

16. Actor Mary Murphy had portrayed the policeman's daughter rejected by Marlon Brando in the recently released movie *The Wild One* (1953), thus manifesting both an identification with and scepticism towards the rebellious youth culture epitomized by Brando's performance typical of Spicer's attitude towards first the Beatniks and, subsequently, the early stages of the counterculture.

17. Maps would form a key trope for Spicer, as in the unfinished 'Map Poems' sequence of 1964 (Spicer 2008, 452).

18. It should be noted, however, that, whatever its opposition to the state as currently constituted, the concept of the Pacific Nation still depends on the geographies established by settler colonialism and its dispossession of indigenous inhabitants in both the United States and Canada.

19. For accounts of the poem and its background, see Blažek and Rauvolf. The poem is collected in Ginsberg 1968.

Chapter 3

1. I am indebted for biographical information and resources on Marshall to poet and bookseller David Abel, who has researched and gathered Marshall's work in a dedicated act of independent scholarship. See also Butterick 1983.

2. Manuscripts for *Pole Vault* and two versions of an alternative selected poem overseen by R'Lene Dahlberg in New York are available in the Rosenthal papers at Stanford University.

3. 'Yohenbine' is presumably an alternative spelling of yohimbine, a drug sold as an aphrodisiac.

4. Wieners here names long or book-length poems by Charles Olson, T. S. Eliot, Robert Duncan, Ed Dorn, Allen Ginsberg, and David Jones.

5. See the poems 'Toxactl' and 'Play'; the latter first published in *Measure* as 'One' (Marshall 1960b, n.p.).

6. Unamuno suffered at the hands of the Francoist regime, his encounter with the fascist Millán Astray at the University of Salamanca in 1936 often read as confrontation between the forces of fascism and of Spanish democratic liberalism (Thomas 1961, 352–55).

7. Much is still uncertain here. For biographical information on Jonas, see Rich in Jonas 2019, 249–60; Torra in Jonas 1994, 1–12; de Gruttola, 30–31. I am also indebted to personal conversation and correspondence with Torra and Rich.

8. On Jonas and Townsend, see further Jonas 2019, 253; Shand-Tucci, 226–57; Shively 2002.

NOTES 341

9. The poems in question are by Spicer, 'Ode to Walt Whitman' (from *After Lorca*), 'For Steve Jonas who is in Jail for Defrauding a Book Club', and the unpublished 'A Gentle Word from One Martian to Another'; by Jonas, 'Cante Jondo for Soul Brother Jack Spicer, His Beloved California and Andalusia of Lorca', 'A Long Poem for Jack Spicer Because He Needs It' (also printed as 'A Long Poem for Jack Spicer Who Needs It'), and 'Morphogenesis' (Spicer 2008, 126–30, 192; Killian and Ellingham, 72; Jonas 1994, 156, 160; Jonas 1958; Jonas 1974).

10. A letter to Lansing from May 1967 suggests the latter: '[T]here can be no laying down with the 'coons' to dirt level equality. they lost their Kulture & want you to give over & for what? Martin Luther King // oughtta be horsewhipped & if John Randolph alive he'd see to it that he got it' (Jonas to Lansing, May 1967).

Chapter 4

1. This work relates to my previous writing on Wieners (Grundy 2021 and forthcoming).

2. For detailed biographical information on Wieners, I am indebted to the work of Robert Dewhurst, whose doctoral thesis presents Wieners' complete poems alongside a career biography, the latter currently in development as a full-length book (Dewhurst 2014). I am also indebted, for personal discussions of Wieners and for their critical work, to Nat Raha, Francesca Lisette, Luke Roberts, Robbie Dewhurst, Michael Seth Stewart, and Raymond Foye (Raha 2018; Lisette 2010; Roberts 2018; Dewhurst 2014; Wieners 2020).

3. The venue was later to be a focal point for the thriving scene of gay activism surrounding groups like *Fag Rag* and *Gay Community News*, in which Wieners would be involved in the 1970s, a context explored later in this book.

4. All three poems—'Ballade', 'You Can't Kill These Machines', and 'Hart Crane, Harry Crosby'—were subsequently published in lightly revised form (Wieners 1965; Leyland 1975, 216–17; Wieners 1961; Wieners 1988). My source texts here are the original printings in the *Boston Newsletter*.

5. There is likewise some ambiguity as to the authorship of this poem. Writing to Charles Olson in 1957, Wieners refers to a 'Ballad of Alice O'Brien, by Marshall' (Wieners 2014, 135). However, the style, while not typical of Wieners' mature work, is far more similar to his early poems than to those of Marshall. Given that Wieners separately sent the poem to Fred Wah for publication in the *Magazine of Further Studies* in 1965, referring to the poem in a separate letter to Donald Allen (Wieners 2014, 393–94), and authorized a further reprint (Leyland 1975), the evidence suggests that he is, in fact, the poem's author. My thanks to Raymond Foye and Robert Dewhurst for correspondence on this issue.

6. Wieners refers here to Frederick Lewis Allen, *Only Yesterday: An Informal History of the 1920s* (1931), its title borrowed for a 1933 Hollywood film, and Mark Sullivan's multivolume history *Our Times*.

342 NOTES

7. Wieners refers here to the closing line of Rimbaud's poem 'Parade' from *Illuminations*—"*J'ai seul la clef de cette parade sauvage*"—in Varèse's translation (Rimbaud 1957, 23).

8. Otherwise uncollected, the poem was printed in *Floating Bear* (Wieners 1961) as part of a selection of Wieners' early work.

9. Portions of the following section are revised from my essay 'John Wieners and "the only one who ever mattered" ' (Grundy forthcoming).

10. Mindful of censorship—the 'Howl' trial had happened the previous summer—publisher Dave Haslewood and Wieners removed the word 'cock' from initial editions, leaving only a blank space. Criticized for this decision by Charles Olson, Wieners wrote the word 'cock' in red pencil in all the remaining copies; an image suggestive of the combination of secrecy and boldness in this work (Dewhurst 2014, 68).

11. For further biographical information on Lansing, see Lepson; Lansing 2012; Lansing 2015. I am also indebted to personal correspondence with David Rich.

12. From the undated draft poem 'On Praxis' in Lansing's papers. I am indebted to David Rich for providing this quotation.

13. Thanks to Mitch Manning for providing me with a copy of this piece.

14. A murky affair in which La Touche's family accused Martin of his murder is recounted in further detail in Kinross 1961, 189–91 and in Pollack 2017, 348–50, 463–72.

15. On the development of the concept, see the work of Constantin de Volney 1795, Charles Dupuis 1781, and Francois Delaunaye 1791; Max Heindel's *The Message of the Stars* (1900); Levi Dowling's *The Aquarian Gospel of Jesus the Christ* (1907); and in particular the writings of Rudolf Steiner, Aleister Crowley's sense of an approaching 'Aeon' of love and self-realization, and Jung's *Aion*, the latter cited in Lansing 2015, n.p. On the Age of Aquarius and the New Age movement, see Campion 1990, 2004, 2012 and Hanegraaf 1998.

16. Notably, the figure of the hermaphrodite anticipates the later development in the work of Bay Area writer Lyn Lonider, whose book *A Lesbian Estate* was illustrated by Robert Duncan's partner Jess, and in which the hermaphrodite serves as a challenge both to patriarchal gender norms and to elements of gender essentialism within the lesbian feminist community.

17. Drawing on Yoruba writer Adebayo Adesenya and Rwandan philosopher Alexis Kagame's *Philosophie Bantu-Rwandaise de l'Être* (1956), which describes 'ntu' as equivalent to 'being' or 'essence' in Western philosophical systems, Jahn's work was highly influential, being praised, for instance, by the likes of C. L. R. James (Hernton 1990, xi). Nonetheless, critiques of its presumptions and scholarly methods have been advanced by African writers and scholars, including Wole Soyinka (Songolo 1981; Greene 2012, 72; Nielsen 2017, 12).

18. For an important reading of Wieners' experience with the mental health apparatus, see Raha 2018, Chapter 4: 197–237.

Chapter 5

1. The quotation in the chapter title is the subtitle to Wieners 1972.

2. These early essays on Wieners offered intelligent and passionate readings that situated the poetry's textual experimentation firmly within the context of Gay Liberation, with

NOTES 343

its liberatory sexual and gender politics. Yet because they appeared well outside the sphere of 'mainstream' or even (predominantly heterosexual) 'underground' critical circuits, they were virtually ignored, and much Wieners criticism has focused on his earlier and better-known work. Both during his lifetime and after his death, the memory of Wieners' post-1969/70 work was kept alive by his friends and comrades amongst local scenes, among them Shively, Jim Dunn, John Mitzel, and Raymond Foye; by those profoundly influenced by this work, including the New Narrative writers; by British writers John Wilkinson and Geoff Ward; and by younger poets such as Cedar Sigo, who wrote an appreciation of Wieners' *Behind the State Capitol* for *The Poetry Foundation* in 2010. (See *Mirage: The John Wieners Issue* [1985]; Wilkinson; Ward 1993; Ward 2002; Sigo 2010.) In 2014, Robbie Dewhurst and Seth Stewart produced as PhD dissertations critical editions, respectively, of Wieners' letters and poems, elucidating Wieners' career in unprecedented detail; and in 2017, Wieners' close friend Jim Dunn wrote a master's thesis on Wieners' late work at the Harvard Extension School (Wieners 2014, 2015A, 2020; Dewhurst 2014; James C. Dunn). Outside academia, Wieners' work of the 1970s came to fresh public attention with the publication of a new selected poems, *Supplication*, co-edited by Dewhurst, Joshua Beckman, and CAConrad in 2015, containing facsimile reprints from the long out-of-print *Behind the State Capitol* (Wieners 2015b), Nat Raha's important review-essay of *Supplication*, extended in her subsequent academic writing, while further unpublished work by Francesca Lisette also provides close readings of *State Capitol* (Lisette 2010).

3. An unpublished essay by Shively provides more details on the split. Following the publication of the first joint issue, the gay community centre associated with *Lavender Vision* had closed down after 'a police agent made off with $700' and 'those males most involved in the *Lavender Vision* left for San Francisco'. As part of the Boston Gay May Day Group, Shively approached the remaining lesbian contingent in April 1971 with the suggestion that the group be revived with new membership, but Katz suggested that they organize separately as a gay male collective given that 'a lot of women's energy had been trained by males in *Lavender Vision*'. Shively, 'A View of Fag Rag' [unpublished essay draft], 1–2. Charley Shively Papers, General Collection, Beinecke Rare Book and Manuscript Library, Yale University. My thanks to Raymond Foye for drawing this essay to my attention.

4. Exceptions are Bronski 2017 and Patrick Moore 2004, 3–15.

5. The biographical summary here draws on Bronski 2017 and on Shively's own writings in *Fag Rag*.

6. *Calamus Lovers: Walt Whitman's Working Class Camerados* (1987) and *Drum Beats: Walt Whitman's Civil War Soldier Boy Lovers* (1989).

7. See for a sample of responses, with Shively's comments, 'dear cocksucker' (Shively 1972).

8. Facsimile copies of the Wieners-Shively correspondence (predominantly typed on Shively's part, and handwritten on Wieners'), were distributed by John Mitzel, and I have consulted these in my research. 'Fenway' refers to a well-known Boston cruising spot.

9. *Fag Rag* texts not collected in *Behind the State Capitol* are as follows: '1972-3' (*Fag Rag* 5, Summer 1973,13); 'Gay American's Day in Rose Kennedy's Estate' (*Fag Rag*

344 NOTES

6, Fall-Winter 1973: 10, 28, 29); 'Quart' (*Fag Rag* 7/8, Winter-Spring 1974: 10), subsequently reprinted as a chapbook by Raymond Foye's Hanuman Books); 'As the most beautiful woman in the world' (*Fag Rag* No. 9 / *Gay Sunshine* No.22: Stonewall 5th Anniversary Issue, Summer 1974: 2, 25); 'Upon Mata Hari Paul Mall' (*Fag Rag* 10, Fall 1974: 5); 'A Comparative Study of *Studies for an Actress and Other Poems*; Women's Newspapers; Homophile Bulletins; and The Underground' (*Fag Rag*, 10 Fall 1974: 22–23); 'Conjugal Contraries' (*Fag Rag* 11, Winter 1974: 11, subsequently reprinted as a chapbook by Raymond Foye's Hanuman Books); 'Harlem Bodyguard' (*Fag Rag* 13, Summer 1975); 'MIDAS, METHUSALA, SOLOMON: AN ESSAY ON STEPHEN JONAS' (*Fag Rag* 28, Spring 1976). With the exception of 'As the most beautiful woman' and 'Upon Mata Hari', these are all prose texts; 'Harlem Bodyguard' is a play.

10. For an in-depth discussion of Wieners' work with/in *Fag Rag* as manifesting practices of collective 'queer labour', see Raha 2019. In an earlier version of the current chapter, I framed such practices through the lens of publication and revision (Grundy 2021).

11. The book had been printed in an edition of 1,564 (paperback) and 110 (hardcover). (Shively 1984, 29).

12. For more on Matthews, see Emily Hobson. For writing on femme identification in *Fag Rag*, see also Cummings and Shively 1977.

13. 'Memories of You' was first published in *Fuck You*; 'Yours to Take' in *The Transatlantic Review*, No. 52 (Autumn 1975): 8.

14. In conversation, November 2019.

15. The quotation that heads this section is the title to an essay by Wieners published in *A Book of PROPHECIES* (Wieners 2007, 37–39).

16. On such techniques, see Jackson 1970.

17. On debt, see Wieners 1975, 98 and Wieners 1986, 226.

18. William Corbett, quoted in James C. Dunn, 43. Corbett later revised his opinion: see 'William Corbett: "Charity Balls" by John Wieners'. Video footage from *A Legacy Celebration of John Wieners*, St. Mark's Poetry Project, April 6, 2016, online, https://www.youtube.com/watch?v=q3-UOrQiIM0.

19. As far as I have been able to determine, the full list of Wieners' published writing post-1976 is as follows. Wieners published new poems in the first and fourth issues of Alan Davies' *A Hundred Posters* (January and April 1976), some of which can be heard in a reading given at the Allentown Community Center, February 19, 1976, along with much material which appears to have remained unpublished. (*Penn Sound*, https://media.sas.upenn.edu/pennsound/authors/Wieners/Buffalo/Wieners-John_Allentown-Community-Center_Buffalo-NY_2-19-1976.mp3.) Besides earlier work which appeared in Dennis Cooper's *Little Caesar* (1979), Maurice Kenny's *Contact II* (1985), and Kevin Killian's *Mirage* (1985), the major publishing events of the 1980s were the two volumes edited by Raymond Foye for Black Sparrow Books: *Selected Poems 1956–1984* (1986) and *Cultural Affairs in Boston* (1988). The only new work to appear in these volumes was *She'd Turn on a Dime*, poems written between 1983 and 1984 (Wieners 1986, 363–86); in his preface, Foye claims that Wieners wrote 'fewer than a dozen poems' between 1976 and 1983 (these, along with three poems from 1985, appear in *Cultural Affairs*). Shively notes that '*Behind the State Capitol*

had been projected as the first part of a work which included two additional books, *Under Bismarck Bridges* and *Marble Harbor*. Most of John's *Purgatorio* had been assembled before he simply threw it away and abandoned the whole project' (Shively 1985, 80). Though a number of other publications have appeared in subsequent periods—the republication of journals from the 1950s through to the 1970s as *A New Book from Rome, Stars Seen in Person, A Book of Prophecies*, and *The Journal of Scott Street*, and texts from *Fag Rag* published by Foye's Hanuman Books as *Conjugal Contraries* and *Quart*—the only new material from Wieners' last decades appeared in *o·blēk* (1991), *The East Village* (1999), and *Big Bridge* (2000), along with the journal *Kidnap Notes Next*, published posthumously (2002). Unpublished poems also appear in correspondence with Gerrit Lansing (Gerrit Lansing Papers. General Collection, Beinecke Rare Book and Manuscript Library, Yale University.)

20. An excellent account of *Gay Community News* is provided in Amy Hoffman's book *An Army of Ex-Lovers: My Life at the Gay Community News.* (2007)

21. See here Michael Bronski's essay 'The Last Gay Liberationist', which outlines Shively's failure to come to term with AIDS (Bronski 2017).

Chapter 6

1. In Swahili, '-eusi' translates as 'black, dark'; 'ndugu' translates as 'brother, comrade', though the word is not always gendered, and can also mean 'sister, cousin, relation' (Madan 1903, 63, 277). There are variations in the spelling of the poet's name in his few appearances in print: as 'Prince-Eusi Ndugu' in *Fag Rag*, as 'Prince Eusi-Ndugu' in the anthology *Black Men/White Men*, and as 'Eusi Ndugu' in an article in the Canadian draft-resister press (Ndugu 1970, Ndugu 1974, Smith 1983). Variations may arise from the fact that, in Swahili, the adjective '-eusi' is rendered with a preceding dash, as the word is normally modified with a prefix agreeing with the noun that the adjective modifies (Madan 1903, ix–xi).

2. For more on the Fag Rag collective's work with prisoners, see Mumford 2016, 92–97.

3. For a discussion of homophobia and misogyny within the Black Arts Movement, see Clarke 2005. For Hoyt Fuller, see Fenderson.

4. For a more detailed reading of these lines, see Reid-Pharr 2007, 140 and Clarke 2005, 83–85, 127. Giovanni has subsequently herself been described as queer; her work appears in the recent *Nepantla: An Anthology Dedicated to Queer Poets of Color*, edited by Christopher Soto (New York: Nightboat Books, 2018).

5. Though this interpretation is speculative, it's possible that Stanford's use of the repeated phrase echoes Horne's repetition of the word 'Now!' in her 1963 protest song of the same name (where it is sung to the tune of the Ukrainian Jewish *nigun* collected and popularized by A.Z. Idelsohn as 'Hava nagila').

6. Byrd's name is rendered as 'Stephanie' in much of her published work, but as she notes in an interview with Julie Enszer, the name as rendered on her birth certificate, as well as her preferred spelling, was 'Stephania' (Enszer 2012, n.p.).

346 NOTES

7. Rich's text, as printed in *Sinister Wisdom*, is a transcript of panel at the Annual Modern Language Association Convention, Chicago, December 1977. Other talks were by Mary Daly, Audre Lorde, and Judith McDaniel. Rich's talk was printed in revised and expanded form, without the citation of Byrd's poem, as 'Disloyal to Civilization: Feminism, Racism, Gynephobia' in Rich, *On Lies, Secrets, and Silence: Selected Prose* (New York: W. W. Norton, 1979).

8. The following account draws on both versions of this memoir (Kenny 1995; Kenny 2018).

9. For a detailed and incisive reading of this poem, particularly as regards the politics of disability, see Tatonetti, 40–45.

10. For brief readings of the poem, see Bruchac 1985, 475; Castro 1991.

11. See Kenny 1995; Kenny 2018.

Chapter 7

1. See, for instance, the account provided by Duchess Harris 2019 (13–18, 30).

2. For detailed accounts of the busing crisis, see Delmont and Formisano2012.

3. On the controversies and legacy surrounding *Our Bodies, Our Selves*, see Kathy Davis 2007.

4. The following year, a book of Saxe's poetry, entitled *Talk Among the Womenfolk* and dedicated to Assata Shakur, was published in support of her defense fund by Common Woman Press, Milwaukee, Wisconsin (Saxe 1976).

5. Though the legal spelling of Little's forename was Joan, her name was pronounced, and occasionally spelt, Joanne. See, e.g., Jayne Cortez's poem for Little and García, 'Rape' (Cortez 1984, 63–64).

6. Winifred Breines provides important context on Bread and Roses and on white anti-racist activism in Boston more generally, reflecting on the contradictions and difficulties of the movement and the tensions that developed between white women and women of colour (Breines). See also Kimberly Springer's work on predecessors to Combahee such as the Third World Women's Alliance (TWWA) and on early problems with homophobia within such groups (Springer, 130–37).

7. Attendees at the salons included Claudia Tate, Nellie McKay, Andrea Rushing, Hortense Spillers, and Cheryl Gilkes.

8. These guidelines, later incorporated into the 1981 NWSA conference 'Women Respond to Racism', were published as 'Face to Face, Day to Day: Racism CR' in *Sojourner* (May 1979): 11, and in *But Some of Us Are Brave* (Hull, Bell-Scott, and Smith, 52–60).

9. Robert Staples' essay attacking Shange's choropoem and Michelle Wallace's *Black Macho* in *The Black Scholar*'s March/April 1979 issue (Staples). The following issue, entitled 'The Black Sexism Debate', featured response to Staples' essay from Lorde, Shange, June Jordan, Maulana Ron Karenga, Kalamu ya Salaam, and others. As indicated by a letter published in the back of the issue, Smith was asked to contribute but declined (*Black Scholar*, 89).

NOTES 347

10. By the time a similar survey was conducted in 1992, the number had changed to once every 1.3 minutes. ('Research Fact Sheet', n.p.)
11. See Hong, xxxiii, and Hanhardt, 126–27, for a more detailed version of this argument.
12. On La Triba, see Leila Peters, 49.
13. As Devall reports, Smith read from her journals: most likely, those excerpts published in 1985 in Culley, 305–309, which address Smith's feelings during the 1979 campaign and their relation to her writing.
14. See Gumbs 2010, chap. 4, esp. 411–19. A shorter reading is offered by McRurer, 276–97.
15. For this date, see Spencer, Banks, and Williams, 37.
16. Shange, 'is not so gd to be born a girl' and 'otherwise i would think it odd to have rape prevention month' (The Black Scholar, 28–30); Lorde (17–20). Jordan 1995, 147–50; Jordan 2007, 256–58, 304–306, 309–12. See also Jayne Cortez's 'Rape', on the Joan Little and Inez García case (Cortez 1984, 63–64). For an overview of writing on Black women's writing on sexual violence during this period, see Adisa.
17. Parker read 'Movement in Black' at the 1978 Boston readings organized by the Bessie Smith Memorial Collective, having debuted the poem in Oakland the previous December (Breines, 164–65; Varied Voices).
18. Revisions occur across the different reprintings of the poem, which, following printings in Heresies (1979) and The Black Scholar (1981) first appeared in book form in Lorde's Chosen Poems: Old and New (New York: W. W. Norton, 1982), with the new subtitle 'A Choral of Black Women's Voices' (111–115). A final revised version appeared as a pamphlet in 1990 from Kitchen Table Press as Need: A Chorale for Black Woman Voices and should be considered the text's definitive final form (Lorde 1990). Here, however, I cite the earliest printed version of the poem, in Heresies, as the closest to that which Lorde would have read in Boston.
19. For a similar engagement with the gendered trope of the drum, see Jayne Cortez's 'If the Drum Is a Woman', recorded on her LP There It Is (1982) and published in Coagulations (New York: Thunder's Mouth Press, 1984), 59–59. Kate Rushin would provide a further critique of the 'black goddess' trope in the poem 'Black Goddess', published in Barbara Smith's anthology Home Girls in 1983.
20. For more on the trope of the drumbeat and blood as 'the unacceptable rhythm that holds the passage together', see Gumbs, 412.
21. As Michelle Moravec notes, the banner continued to be used at feminist events in Boston: it was, for example, present onstage in the launch of This Bridge Called My Back at the Arlington Street Church in May 1981 (Moravec, n.p.).
22. Cheryl Clarke's discussion of the role of community in women's poetry of the Black Arts Movement, particularly that of Shange, provides a useful extension of such arguments. See Clarke 2005. See also Barbara Smith and Gloria Hull's work on accountability in Black women's studies (Barbara Smith and Gloria Hull, 'The Politics of Black Women's Studies' [1982], originally printed in But Some of Us Are Brave [1982]; Smith 2014, 105) and Alexis Pauline Gumbs' work on the community-accountable activist/intellectual (Gumbs 2010, 456–57; specifically in relation to Lorde, 306–308, 409, 426–47).

348 NOTES

23. On Lorde's appointment to *Chrysalis*, see De Veaux, 177–78; on the tensions leading to her resignation, see 211–12, 225–27, 232, 245–46, 258–59. Following the failure of attempts to broker the dispute by Adrienne Rich, Lorde's 'Open Letter to Mary Daly' was ultimately published in *This Bridge*, minus its opening paragraphs, and in full in *Sister Outsider* (1983). In print and in interviews, Lorde claimed that Daly had not responded at all, though a copy of Daly's reply exists in her archives. For more on the incident, see Alexis De Veaux's biography of Lorde (De Veaux, 233–39, 246–53).

24. *Lesbian Poetry: An Anthology* contained Parker's 'Movement in Black', with its dedication to 'all the names we don't know, yet', along with Lorde's 'Need'. Readers at the launch were Bulkin, Larkin, Parker, Lorde, Moraga, Jan Clausen, Marcie Hershman, Adrienne Rich, Paula Gunn Allen, Robin Becker, Michelle Cliff, and Judy Grahn (Deaborn).

25. To complicate matters, Clausen's novel was rejected for perceived anti-Semitic content. For more details on these incidents, see Enszer 2013, 180–84.

26. For a detailed account of Persephone's collapse, see Enszer 2013, 180–88, and Greenfield and McGloin's own account in Fiorenza. Greenfield and McGloin note, e.g., that they ran large-scale events such as the *This Bridge* launch at a loss of several thousand dollars.

27. The collective later came to include Rosío Alvarez, Sonia Alvarez, Helena Byard, Alma Gómez, Brenda Joyce, Leota Lone Dog, Mariana Roma-Carmona, Rosario Morales, Ana Oliveira, and Susan Yung (De Veaux, 276; Smith 2014, 158).

28. I am indebted for this account of the *Bridge* readings to Porter's report and to the archival work conducted by Meredith Benjamin in Moraga's and Anzaldúa's papers (Benjamin 2021).

29. See Grace Kyungwong Hong's reading, viii–x.

30. The most recent (2015) edition switches the order, printing 'The Bridge Poem' after 'La Jornada'.

31. On variations between the poem, see LeRud 2020. I refer here to the most readily available text of the poem in the 2015 edition of *This Bridge*, which in turn follows the 1983 printing.

32. For exceptions, see Hogan's account of feminist bookstores, which draws on interviews with Rushin (Hogan, 76–78, 108, 114–15, 123–24) and LeRud's reading of 'The Bridge Poem' (LeRud 2017, chap. 5 and LeRud 2020).

33. For more detail on Rushin's revisions, see LeRud 2020.

34. I draw on LeRud 2020 for this insight. Note too that, just as *The Black Back-Ups* reprints 'The Bridge Poem', later editions of *This Bridge* include 'The Black Back-Ups', which had not been written at the time of the original anthology.

35. Combahee member Chirlane McCray, for example, went from authoring the pioneering 'I Am a Lesbian' in *Essence* to marrying former New York City mayor Bill di Blasio, with whom she shares a net worth of $2.5 million (Alexander, Dan, Peterson-Withorn, and Tindera, n.p.).

36. In this regard, Anzaldúa's and Moraga's prefaces to newer editions of *This Bridge* note the recuperation of radical queer politics, academic feminism, and the continuing wave of repression and resistance globally, while Norma Alarcón dissects white

appropriations of the anthology in her 1991 essay 'The Theoretical Subject(s) of *This Bridge Called My Back* and Anglo-American Feminism' (Alarcón 1991).

37. Patricia Hill Collins and Sirma Bilge (2020) provide a more comprehensive account of popular usages of the term. For an overview of academic development of intersectionality, see Bilge 2010; Bilge 2013; and Carastathis 2016.

The work by female scholars cited in the present chapter forms a notable exception to generalized conflations of Combahee and Crenshaw. Such scholarship includes but is not limited to the work of Meredith Benjamin (on *This Bridge*), Winifred Breines (on inter-racial relationships in the women's movement), Julie Enszer (on Kitchen Table Press), Alexis Pauline Gumbs (on Lorde and Black feminist publishing), Duchess Harris (on Combahee and the development of Black feminism), and Kristen Hogan (on women's bookstores and the feminist movement), all of which I have drawn on in this chapter.

Chapter 8

1. I borrow the term 'gender outlaw' in the section title from Bornstein 1994.
2. A few years later, anti-trans backlash against Stone's position with Olivia Records would lead to Stone's resignation, despite the label's support (Enke, 22–23).
3. Newton's speech, delivered on August 15th, 1970, appears in print as 'The Women's Liberation and the Gay Liberation Movements'. (*The Huey P. Newton Reader*. Eds by David Hilliard and Donald Weise. (New York: Seven Stories, 2002), 157–59).
4. A Bay Area fixture for decades, Gidlow had authored the first collection of out lesbian poetry published in North America, *On a Grey Thread* (1923). Grahn read with Gidlow at a 1973 Glide Memorial Church benefit for the Council on Religion and the Homosexual; like Grahn's, her poetry appeared in *The Ladder* in the late '60s.

Chapter 9

1. Parker's 'Poem to Ann no. 2' appears on the skit 'Exit Scott (Interlude)' (Solange, track 16).
2. I am grateful to Julie Enszer for discussions of Parker's life and work and for providing me with access to correspondence from Parker's papers at a time when Covid restrictions made it impossible to consult these in person. Errors remain my own.
3. As Patricia Bullins, Parker published the poems 'The Mirror' and 'Of Life', in *Citadel*, Fall 1964; 'A Woman's Love', *Black Dialogue* Vol.1.2. August 1965; 'Aftermath' and 'Two Faces of Black' (*Free Poems among Friends*, 1965); and an untitled poem ('I have seen death'), *Black Dialogue* Vol 1.3-4 1966; while a further nine poems in *Perspectives* in 1965. The first poems to appear under Parker's new surname (as 'Patricia Parker') were in the journal *Out of Sight* in August 1966. These uncollected poems appear in the

350 NOTES

Complete Works edited by Julie Enszer. A prose piece, 'The Demonstrator', appeared in *Negro Digest* in November 1963; three essays also appeared in *Black Dialogue, Citadel,* and *Perspectives* (Parker 2016, 459).

4. An excerpt from this novel appears in the liner notes to Parker and Grahn 1976, n.p.

5. As Judy Grahn observes, Lorde had already published the overtly queer poem, 'Martha', in 1970 but was not yet widely out, and she had recently withdrawn an overtly queer 'Love Poem' from her forthcoming book *From a Land Where Other People Live* at publisher Dudley Randall's insistence (*ASR*, 188).

6. Specifically, Parker objected to the tone of Lorde's preface to *Movement in Black*, leading to a break of communication for several years (*ASR*, 244–45; Parker and Lorde, 57).

7. The poem was written in 1974: in 1976, it was published in two anthologies concerning femicide and violence against women (Russell and van de Ven, 145; *Poetry from Violence*).

8. Little published information exists on the life of the Council following this speech, though Erica R. Edwards notes that the group 'hosted workshops on liberation struggles in Puerto Rico, Eritrea, and Palestine', while Debbie Gregg recalls that 'one year, the [Eleventh Hour] Battalion printed T-shirts and Pat provided the slogan: "We are the masses and intend to kick asses"' (Edwards 2021, 200; *GCN* 1989: 12).

Chapter 10

1. Jewish lesbian (Irene 'Zee') Zahava, photographed with Kim alongside the poem, was owner of Ithaca-based lesbian bookstore Smedley's Bookshop from 1981 to 1994 (Lisa L. Moore 2013, n.p.).

2. Spatial limitations have regrettably excluded further work on Kim and Tsui in this volume. I hope to be able to present this material elsewhere.

3. For discussions of her relationship to Karen Brodine and the activities of the Berkeley Poets Co-Op and Kelsey Street Press, I am indebted to Laura Moriarty (personal conversation with Laura Moriarty, September 2020, via Zoom). Regrettably, space precludes a more detailed examination of these contexts. For published recollections, see Entrekin; La Palma; Lamott; 'Tender Benches'.

4. Brodine's poem first appeared in an issue of *Out and About: Lesbian Feminist News* by the Woman's Coalition to STOP the Green River Murders, printed opposite a poem by sex worker and poet Daisy Anarchy, a longtime Bay Area activist who toured with the band MDC (Millions of Dead Cops) in 1987: 'Like a volcano erupting / Our rage and tender love / and the Truths we know / are gonna shake the State [. . .] Us whores / are fighting back.' (Anarchy 1985, 8).

Chapter 11

1. Established in 1962 from a split in the Communist Party USA, the PL had formed part of the Worker Student Alliance Faction of SDS during the late '60s. Despite its role in

NOTES 351

SDS, it was opposed to many facets of the counterculture: it 'forbade pot-smoking, urged male students to cut their hair, and pressured couples to regularize their relationships in the belief that their doing so would make them [. . .] acceptable to the working class' (Levin and Silbar 2019, 7–8).

2. Orlando Letelier, a former member of the Allende administration in exile from Pinochet's Chile, was murdered by the Chilean secret police in Washington in 1976.

3. Despite such comments at the conference, di Prima had often been supportive of gay men: see, for instance, her friendship with John Wieners, and her book *Freddie Poems*, dedicated to her close friend, the gay dancer Freddie Herko (di Prima 1974). In turn, the Women's Press Collective purchased their first printer from di Prima, who Judy Grahn describes as 'the closest thing to a fairy godmother I have ever had' (*ASR*, 132, 171).

4. As Glück has suggested, he and Boone conceived the descriptor 'New Narrative' as a way of distinguishing their own project from that of L=A=N=G=U=A=G=E writing, with which New Narrative was often in debate (Halpern 2009; Harris 2011b, Harris 2022, 152; Tremblay-McGaw 2022, 22–23).

5. 'Shame is a kind of fear' is an unattributed quotation from Aristotle (Aristotle 1984, 1404).

6. Boone here challenges György Lukács' argument in *Theory of the Novel* that the novel inherited the community praxis of archaic epic poetry (Boone 1979, 1–4).

7. I write more extensively about Daniels and her relation to New Narrative elsewhere (Daniels 2020; Grundy 2021).

8. Entitled 'Disease Rumors Largely Unfounded', the article in question, by the *Native*'s health correspondence Dr Lawrence Mass, drew on an interview with a doctor from the New York Department of Health to suggest that reports of 'an exotic new disease [that] had hit the gay community in New York' had been exaggerated (Mass 1981a). The following month, Mass's 'Cancer in the Gay Community' appeared on the front page of *New York Native*, sounding a new note of caution, whilst also insisting that what was at the time labelled a "gay cancer" was by no means a gays-only disease. (Mass 1981b) Along with Larry Kramer, Edmund White, Paul Rapoport, Paul Popham and Nathan Fain, Mass co-founded the long-running AIDS information service Gay Men's Health Crisis the following year, authoring the organisation's booklet *Medical Answers about AIDS* in 1984. On the official adoption of the name AIDS, see Kher 2003, n.p.

9. Drawing on interviews with Bellamy, Breu's analysis of *The Letters of Mina Harker* remains one of the most in-depth and incisive in print to date.

Coda

* See here Fassbinder's *Faustrecht der Freiheit* (*Fox and his Friends*) (1975) and von Praunheim's *Nicht der Homosexuelle ist pervers, sondern die Situation, in der er lebt* (*It Is Not the Homosexual Who Is Perverse, but the Society in Which He Lives*) (1971).

1. Of note, too, is that the excerpt from Robert Glück's *Jack the Modernist* discussed in the preceding chapter—'The Sky Looked Bruised, and That's the Way the Air Felt,

352 NOTES

Achey'—appears in the same issue (7–18), alongside a lengthy interview of Judy Grahn by Dodie Bellamy and Steve Abbott (46–60).

2. Shurin's generosity in sharing his recollections in person in early 2022 was gratefully welcomed: though I have been unable to address his work in detail this book, an interview arising from our meeting appeared in *The Poetry Project Newsletter*, #275 in March 2024, as 'Making the World: An Interview with Aaron Shurin'.

3. A Selected Poems, edited by Julie R. Enszer, went to print as this manuscript was being prepared for publication. (*Fire-Rimmed Eden: Selected Poems by Lynn Lonidier*. New York: Nightboat Books, 2023.)

Works Cited

Abbott, Steve. 'Soup Intro'. *Soup*, No. 2 (1981): 1.

Abbott, Steve. 'The Politics of Gay Poetry'. *The Advocate*, May 13, 1982, 23–27.

Abbott, Steve. 'Chatting with Radical Women'. *The Sentinel*, Vol. 15, No. 8 (1987).

Abbott, Steve. *View Askew: Postmodern Investigations*. San Francisco: Androgyne Books, 1989.

Abbott, Steve. *Beautiful Aliens: A Steve Abbott Reader*. Ed. Jamie Townsend. New York: Nightboat, 2019.

Abel, David. 'Edward H. Marshall (1932–2005)'. *The Text Garage*, May 22, 2013, https://web.archive.org/web/20130707134228/http://thetextgarage.com/2013/05/edward-marshall/

Abel, David. Interview with the author. September 14, 2020. Zoom.

Abel, David. 'Leave the Word Alone: Report from the Field'. Essay for *Lost and Found*, City University, New York. 2020. Unpublished.

'Actress Is Slain at Michigan Audition'. *New York Times*, April 11, 1978, 13.

Adisa, Opal Palmer. 'Undeclared War: African-American Women Writers Explicating Rape'. *Women's Studies International Forum*, Vol. 15, No. 3 (1992): 363–74.

Agamben, Giorgio. *The Coming Community*. Trans. Michael Hardt. Minneapolis: University of Minnesota Press, 1993. (Original 1990)

Aguilar-San Juan, Karin. 'Landmarks in Literature by Asian American Lesbians'. Theorizing Lesbian Experience. *Signs*, Vol. 18, No. 4 (Summer 1993): 936–43.

Alarcón, Norma. 'The Theoretical Subject(s) of *This Bridge Called My Back*'. In Héctor Calderón and José David Saldívar (eds.), *The Postmodern Turn: New Perspectives on Social Theory*. Durham, NC: Duke University Press, 1991, 140–52.

Alexander, Dan, Chase Peterson-Withorn, and Michela Tindera. 'The Net Worth of Every 2020 Presidential Candidate'. *Forbes*, August 14, 2019, https://www.forbes.com/sites/danalexander/2019/08/14/heres-the-net-worth-of-every-2020-presidential-candidate/#c6bd69637c58

Allen, Donald (ed.). *The New American Poetry, 1945–1960*. New York: Grove Press, 1961.

Allen, Paula Gunn. 'Lesbians in American Indian Culture'. *Conditions*, No. 3 (1981): 67–87.

Allen, Paula Gunn. 'some like indians endure'. *Common Lives / Lesbian Lives*, No. 3 (Spring 1982): 75–78.

Alta (Gerrey), and Irene Reti. *Alta and the History of Shameless Hussy Press, 1969–1989*. University Library, UC Santa Cruz, 2001, https://escholarship.org/uc/item/1fx8d588

Altman, Dennis. AIDS and the New Puritanism. London: Pluto Press, 1986

Altman, Dennis. *Global Sex*. Chicago: University of Chicago Press, 2001.

Anarchy, Daisy. [Untitled poem]. *Out and About: Lesbian Feminist News*, No. 89 (1985): 8.

Anderson, Kelly. 'Voices of Feminism Oral History Project: Cherríe Moraga Interviewed by Kelly Anderson, June 6 & 7, 2005'. Sophia Smith Collection, Smith College Libraries, https://www.smith.edu/libraries/libs/ssc/vof/transcripts/Moraga.pdf

Anderson, Larry. 'No Cosmic Ribbon: An Aborted Dialogue'. *Fag Rag*, No. 12 (Spring 1975): 6–7.

354 WORKS CITED

Anonymous. 'GINO AND CARLO'S / A COUNTRY DANCE /—for Gordon Neal'. *J*, No. 6 (1960): n.p.

Anonymous. ['Dear Senior Poet']. Attrib. to 'Willaim [*sic*] Morris'. *J*, No. 2 (1959): n.p.

Anzaldúa, Gloria, and Cherríe Moraga (eds.). 1981. *This Bridge Called My Back: Writings by Radical Women of Color.* 4th ed. New York: SUNY Press, 2015. (Cited as *This Bridge*)

Aristotle. *The Complete Works of Aristotle: The Revised Oxford Translation*, Vol. 2. Ed. Jonathan Barnes. Princeton, NJ: Princeton University Press, 1984.

Arobateau, Red Jordan. *My Continuing Journey into Artistic, Spiritual, and Revolutionary Thoughts.* Oakland, CA: Red Jordan Press, 2009.

Avicolli Mecca, Tommi (ed.). *Smash the Church, Smash the State!: The Early Years of Gay Liberation.* San Francisco, CA: City Lights, 2009.

Avi-ram, Amitai F. 'The Politics of the Refrain in Judy Grahn's *A Woman Is Talking To Death*'. *Women and Language*, Vol. 10, No. 2 (March 31, 1987): 38–43.

Backus, Margot Gayle. 'Judy Grahn and the Lesbian Invocational Elegy: Testimonial and Prophetic Responses to Social Death in "A Woman Is Talking to Death" '. *Theorizing Lesbian Experience. Signs*, Vol. 18, No. 4 (Summer 1993): 815–37.

Baker, Robert. 'The Metaphysics of Gerrit Lansing'. *Rain Taxi*, Fall 2001, https://www.raintaxi.com/the-metaphysics-of-gerrit-lansing/.

Baldwin, James. *The Evidence of Things Not Seen.* New York: Holt, Rinehart, and Winston, 1985.

Baldwin, James. 'Preservation of Innocence'. In Toni Morrison (ed.), *Collected Essays.* Library of America Series. New York: Penguin, 1998, 594–600. (Original 1949)

Baldwin, James. 'Go the Way Your Blood Beats' [Interview by Richard Goldstein]. In *The Last Interview: And Other Conversations.* New York: Melville House, 2014, 59–74. (Original 1984)

Baldwin, James, and Nikki Giovanni. *A Dialogue.* New York and Philadelphia: J.B Lippincott, 1973.

Baraka, Amiri. *The Autobiography of LeRoi Jones/Amiri Baraka.* Chicago: Lawrence Hill Books, 1997. (Original 1984)

Barolini, Teodolinda. *Dante's Poets: Textuality and Truth in the Comedy.* Princeton, NJ: Princeton University Press, 1984.

Bartlett, F. Lewis. 'Institutional Peonage: Our Exploitation of Mental Patients'. *Atlantic Monthly*, June 1964.

Beckwith, Caleb. 'Spicer and His Critical Reception: A Review of Daniel Katz's *The Poetry of Jack Spicer*'. *Journal of Modern Literature*, Vol. 37, No. 4 (Summer 2014): 166–70.

Bellamy, Dodie. 'Working Notes'. *HOW(ever)*, Vol. 3, No. 1 (January 1986), https://www.asu.edu/pipercwcenter/how2journal//archive/print_archive/bellamy.html

Bellamy, Dodie. *The Letters of Mina Harker.* Madison: University of Wisconsin Press, 2004. (Original 1998)

Bellamy, Dodie. 'My Mixed Marriage'. *The Village Voice*, June 20, 2000, https://www.villagevoice.com/2000/06/20/my-mixed-marriage/

Bellamy, Dodie. *Academonia.* San Francisco: Krupskaya, 2006.

Bellamy, Dodie. 'One Final Long Tracking Shot'. *Open Space*, June 8, 2010, https://openspace.sfmoma.org/2010/06/one-final-long-tracking-shot/

Bellamy, Dodie, and Sam D'Allesandro. *Real: The Letters of Mina Harker and Sam D'Allesandro.* Hoboken, NJ: Talisman House, 1994.

Bellamy, Dodie, and Kevin Killian (eds.), *Writers Who Love Too Much: New Narrative 1977–1997.* New York: Nightboat, 2017.

WORKS CITED 355

Benjamin, Daniel. *On Lyric's Minor Commons*. Unpublished PhD Dissertation, University of California, Berkeley, 2019.

Benjamin, Meredith. '"An archive of accounts": *This Bridge Called My Back* in the Feminist Movement'. *Tulsa Studies in Women's Literature*, Vol. 40, No. 1 (Spring 2021): 45–68.

Bense, Buzz. 'LDG: Sex Panic—The Real History Behind the SF Bathhouse Closures'. YouTube, May 27 2015, https://www.youtube.com/watch?v=WGfbJbruR_Y&has_verified=1.

Bergman, David (ed.). *Camp Grounds: Style and Homosexuality*. Amherst: University of Massachusetts Press, 1993.

Bertholf, Robert J., and Ian W. Reid (eds.). *Robert Duncan: Scales of the Marvellous*. New York: New Directions, 1979.

Berkson, Bill. *Since When: A Memoir in Pieces*. Minneapolis: Coffee House Press, 2018.

Bersani, Leo. 'Sociability and Cruising'. *Australian and New Zealand Journal of Art*, Vol. 2/3, No. 2/1 (2002): 11–31.

Bérubé, Allan. 'The History of Gay Bathhouses' *Journal of Homosexuality*, Vol. 44, No. 3–4 (2003): 33–53. (Original 1984)

Bérubé, Allan. *Coming Out Under Fire: The History of Gay Men and Women in World War Two*. New York: Free Press, 1990.

Bérubé, Allan. Introduction to reprint of Robert Duncan, 'The Homosexual in Society'. *Outlook*, Vol. 4, No. 2 (Fall 1991): 67.

Bérubé, Allan. *My Desire for History: Essays in Gay, Community, and Labor History*. Ed. John D'Emilio and Estelle B. Freedman. Chapel Hill: University of North Carolina Press, 2011.

Bettcher, Talia M. 'A Conversation with Jeanne Córdova'. *TSQ: Transgender Studies Quarterly*, Vol. 3, No. 1–2 (May 2016): 285–93.

Bieschke, Marke. 'Enola Gay and the Witchy Origin of the first AIDS Protest'. *48 Hills*, September 19, 2019, https://48hills.org/2019/09/enola-gay-first-aids-protest/.

Bilge, Sirma. 'Recent Feminist Outlooks on Intersectionality'. *Diogenes*, No. 225 (2010): 58–72.

Bilge, Sirma. 'Intersectionality Undone: Saving Intersectionality from Feminist Intersectionality Studies'. *Du Bois Review: Social Science Research on Race*, Vol. 10, No. 2 (Fall 2013): 405–24.

'Biographical Sketch'. Gloria Evangelina Anzaldúa Papers, Benson Latin American Collection, University of Texas at Austin, https://legacy.lib.utexas.edu/taro/utlac/00189/lac-00189.html.

Black Scholar, The. 'The Black Sexism Debate'. Vol. 10, No. 8/9 (May/June 1979).

Blaser, Robin. *The Fire: Collected Essays*. Ed. Miriam Nichols. Berkeley, Los Angeles, and London: University of California Press, 2006.

Blaser, Robin. *The Astonishment Tapes: Talks on Poetry and Autobiography with Robin Blaser and Friends*. Ed. Miriam Nichols. Tuscaloosa: University of Alabama Press, 2015.

Blažek, Petr, 'The Deportation of the King of May: Allen Ginsberg and the State Security'. Trans. Ian Willoughby, *Behind the Iron Curtain*, No. 2 (2012): 34–47.

Boddy, Kasia. 'A Conversation with Robert Glück'. New Narrative Special. *Textual Practice*, Vo. 35, No. 8 (2021): 1257–71. (Original 1996)

Boldenweck, Bill. 'Hospice Founder Issan Dorsey Dies of AIDS'. *San Francisco Examiner*, September 1990.

Boone, Bruce. 'Castro and Market Dialectics (or, Discussing Our Growing Consumerism)'. [1977] Poetry TS Folder, Box 2, BBP.

356 WORKS CITED

Boone, Bruce. 'Note to the Reader'. May 16, 1977. Unlabelled Folder, Box 2, Literary Papers (Labelled), BBP.

Boone, Bruce. Letter to Fredric Jameson 9/7/79. Fredric Jameson Folder, Box 1, Correspondence (Labelled), BBP.

Boone, Bruce. *Century of Clouds*. New York: Nightboat, 2009. (Original 1980)

Boone, Bruce. 'Robert Duncan and Gay Community: A Reflection'. Robert Duncan Special. *Ironwood*, No. 22 (1983): 66, 82.

Boone, Bruce. 'For Jack Spicer: And a Truth Element'. *Social Text*, No. 7 (Spring–Summer 1983): 120–26. Reproduced in Boone 2020, 282–90.

Boone, Bruce. *Dismembered: Poems, Stories, and Essays*. Ed. Rob Halpern. New York: Nightboat, 2020.

Boone, Bruce. 'Writing Projects Notebook' [n.d.]. Box 4, Unsorted loose literary papers & journals 1960s–2000s, BBP.

Bost, Darius. *Evidence of Being: The Black Gay Cultural Renaissance and the Politics of Violence*. Chicago: University of Chicago Press, 2019.

'Boston GLF's 10-Point Demands Presented to the Democratic Convention in Miami Beach, July 1972'. Reproduced in Shively 2012, 103–104.

Boston Newsletter. (Robin Blaser, Joe Dunn, Stephen Jonas, Jack Spicer, and John Wieners). Self-published, 1956.

Bowles, Juliette (ed). *In the Memory and Spirit of Frances, Zora and Lorraine: Essay and Interviews on Black Women and Writing*. Washington, DC: Howard University Institute for the Arts and Humanities, 1979.

Bradshaw, Joseph. 'Reviving Jack Spicer: An Interview with Kevin Killian'. *Rain Taxi*, Winter 2008/2009, Online Edition, https://www.raintaxi.com/reviving-jack-spicer-an-interview-with-kevin-killian/.

Brandt, Kate. *Happy Endings: Lesbian Writers Talk About Their Lives and Work*. Tallahassee, FL: Naiad Press, 1993.

Branton, Ruby. 'On Being Unlikeable in Your Work'. *The Creative Independent*, March 4, 2019, https://thecreativeindependent.com/people/writer-kevin-killian-on-being-unlikeable-in-your-work/kap

Bredbeck, Gregory. 'The New Queer Narrative: Intervention and Critique'. *Textual Practice*, Vol. 9, No. 3 (1995): 477–502.

Breines, Winifred. *The Trouble Between Us: An Uneasy History of White and Black Women in the Feminist Movement*. New York: Oxford University Press, 2016.

Breu, Christopher. 'Disinterring the Real: Dodie Bellamy's *The Letters of Mina Harker* and the Late-Capitalist Literature of Materiality'. *Textual Practice* Vol. 26, No. 2 (2012): 263–91.

Briggs, Laura. 'Benefit Yields "Important Springboard" for Organizing Within Communities of Color'. *Gay Community News*, Vol. 17, No. 41 (May 6–12, 1990): 1, 10.

Brodine, Karen. 'Old Journal' [June 1973]. Box 3, KBP.

Brodine, Karen. 'Woman and Machines'. Notebook, September 30, 1973–February [1974], Box 1, KBP.

Brodine, Karen. Notebook, 1975, Box 1, KBP.

Brodine, Karen. *Slow Juggling*. Berkeley, CA: Berkeley Poets Co-Operative, 1975.

Brodine, Karen. Notebook, December 1976–77, Box 1, KBP.

Brodine, Karen. Notebook, June–December 1977, Box 1, KBP.

Brodine, Karen. *Work Week*. San Francisco, CA: Kelsey Street, 1977.

Brodine, Karen. Notebook, January–December. 1978, Box 2, KBP.

WORKS CITED   357

Brodine, Karen. 'Censorship and Red-Baiting in the Women's Movement'. 1980, Box 2, KBP.

Brodine, Karen. Letter to Judy Grahn. May 2, 1980, Box 3, KBP.

Brodine, Karen. 'Mainstream Exiles: A Weekend of Gay and Lesbian Poetry and Music'. November 1980, Box 3, KBP.

Brodine, Karen. *Illegal Assembly*. New York: Hanging Loose Press, 1980.

Brodine, Karen. '*Illegal Assembly* Bookparty [Untitled script, 1980]'. Box 2, KBP.

Brodine, Karen. Teaching Writing—Notebook, June 1980–February 1981, Box 1, KBP.

Brodine, Karen. Notebook October 28, 1981–October 1983, Box 2, KBP.

Brodine, Karen. 'A Conversation with Nellie Wong and Merle Woo, Poet-Radical Feminists'. *Freedom Socialist*, Spring 1981, 5.

Brodine, Karen. 'Ideas Banned at Berkeley'. *Freedom Socialist*, Fall 1982: 5.

Brodine, Karen. 'Merle Journal Notes 10/7'. [c. 1983], Box 3, KBP.

Brodine, Karen. [Untitled poem, 12/1985]. Looseleaf MS, Box 3, KBP.

Brodine, Karen. 'Cancer Need Not Be a Losing Battle'. *San Francisco Chronicle*, July 1986.

Brodine, Karen. 'Women Writers: Telling the Truth from all Sides'. August 22, 1986, Typescript, Box 3, KBP.

Brodine, Karen. [Untitled poem]. November 1986, Looseleaf, Box 3, KBP.

Brodine, Karen. *Woman Sitting at the Machine, Thinking*. Seattle: Red Letter Press, 1990.

Brodine, Karen. 'Sabotage'. [c. 1980]. Tripwire, No. 14 (2018): 219.

Brodine, Karen. 'Teaching Writing—Notes Folder'. [n.d.], Looseleaf, Box 2, KBP.

Brodine, Karen, and Meridel Le Sueur. Poetry Reading, November 5, 1981. [Video]. Poetry Centre Digital Archive, https://diva.sfsu.edu/collections/poetrycenter/bundles/239446.

Bronski, Michael. *A Queer History of the United States*. Boston: Beacon Press, 2011.

Bronski, Michael. 'Queers Against Hate'. *Boston Review*, August 2016, http://bostonreview.net/books-ideas/michael-bronski-faderman-downs-shepard-gay-liberation.

Bronski, Michael. 'The Last Gay Liberationist'. *Boston Review*, December 2017, http://bostonreview.net/gender-sexuality/michael-bronski-last-gay-liberationist.   [Also printed as a pamphlet by Temporal Drag (London), 2019.]

Bronski, Michael. 'Zines from a Revolution'. *The Poetry Foundation*, June 2019, https://www.poetryfoundation.org/articles/150351/zines-from-a-revolution.

Bronski, Michael. Interview with author. December 2020, Zoom.

Bronski, Michael. 'The Rise and Future of a Queer Polity of Literature in Six Scenes (part two)'. Polity of Literature. *ArtsEverywhere*, No. 48/51 (November 18, 2021), https://www.artseverywhere.ca/queer-polity-of-lit-part2/.

Brookie, Scott. 'Blood and Money: Gay Men Protest Military Spending'. *Gay Community News*, Vol. 12, No. 14 (October 20, 1984): 3.

Bruchac, Joseph. 'New Leaves on the Trees of Our Nations: Five Native American Chapbooks'. *American Indian Quarterly*, Vol. 9, No. 4 (Autumn 1985): 473–76.

Bruchac, Joseph. *Survival This Way: Interviews with American Indian Poets*. Tucson: University of Arizona Press, 1987.

Bulkin, Elly. 'Kissing / Against the Light'. *Radical Teacher*, No. 10 (December 1978): 7–17.

Bulkin, Elly. 'Introduction'. *Lesbian Poetry: An Anthology*. Ed. Bulkin and Joan Larkin. Watertown, MA: Persephone Press, 1981, xxi–xxxiv.

Bullins, Ed. Pat Parker Papers, 1944–1998; Letter to Pat Parker, March 22, 1967. MC 861, Folder 2.12. Schlesinger Library, Radcliffe Institute, Harvard University, Cambridge, MA.

358 WORKS CITED

Butterick, George. 'Editing Postmodern Texts'. *Sulfur* No. 11 (1981): 129–30.

Butterick, George. 'Edward Marshall'. In Ann Charters (ed.), *Dictionary of Literary Biography*, Vol. 16: *The Beats: Literary Bohemians in Postwar America, Part 2: M–Z*. Detroit: Gale Research, 1983, 371–76.

Byrd, Stephanie [Stephania]. *25 Years of Malcontent*. Boston: Good Gay Poets, 1976.

Byrd, Stephanie [Stephania]. *A Distant Footstep on the Plain*. Boston: Self-published, 1981.

Byrd, Stephanie [Stephania]. 'A Peck for a Peck' [First version], *Sinister Wisdom*, No. 9 (Spring 1979): 44.

Byrd, Stephanie [Stephania]. 'A Peck for a Peck' [Second version]. *Sojourner*, Vol. 15, No. 2 (October 1989): 23.

Byrd, Stephanie [Stephania]. *Two Chapbooks by Stephania Byrd: 25 Years of Malcontent and A Distant Footstep on the Plain*. Ebook, Lesbian Poetry Archive, 2012, http://www.lesbianpoetryarchive.org/sites/default/files/StephaniaByrd.pdf.

Campion, Nicholas. 'The Age of Aquarius: A Modern Myth'. In Joan McEvers (ed.), *The Astrology of the Macrocosm*. Saint Paul, MN: Llewellyn, 1990, 195–231.

Campion, Nicholas. *Prophecy, Cosmology and the New Age Movement: The Extent and Nature of Contemporary Belief in Astrology*. Unpublished PhD Dissertation, Bath Spa University, 2004.

Campion, Nicholas. *Astrology and Popular Religion in the Modern West: Prophecy, Cosmology and the New Age Movement*. Farnham, Surrey: Ashgate, 2012.

Caples, Garrett. 'Casting Spells: The Quietly Mythic Life of Gerrit Lansing'. *The Poetry Foundation*, December 2018, https://www.poetryfoundation.org/articles/148770/casting-spells.

Caprio, Frank Samuel. *Female Homosexuality: A Psychodynamic Study of Lesbianism*. New York: Citadel Press, 1954.

Carastathis, Anna. *Intersectionality: Origins, Contestations, Horizons*. Lincoln: University of Nebraska Press, 2016.

Case, Mairead. 'ONE: The First Gay Magazine in the United States'. *JSTOR Daily*, July 2020, https://daily.jstor.org/one-the-first-gay-magazine-in-the-united-states/.

Castells, Manuel. *The City and the Grassroots: A Cross-Cultural Theory of Urban Social Movements*. London: Edward Arnold, 1983.

Castro, Michael. *Interpreting the Indian: Twentieth-Century Poets and the Native American*. Albuquerque: University of New Mexico Press, 1991.

Catalogue of Free Print Shop Productions (August 1968–December 1972). San Francisco, CA: Scott Street Commune, 1973. Available online at Eric Noble (ed.), Diggers.org, https://www.diggers.org/fps_catalog.htm.

Chamberlin, Judi. *On Our Own: Patient Controlled Alternatives to the Mental Health System*. New York: Haworth Press, 1978.

Chisholm, Diana. *Queer Constellations: Subcultural Space in the Wake of the City*. Minneapolis: University of Minnesota Press, 2004.

Clark, Damion. 'Adrian Stanford'. In Emmanuel S. Nelson (ed.), *Encyclopedia of Contemporary LGBTQ Literature of the United States*, Vol.1. Santa Barbara, CA and Denver, CO: Greenwood Press, 2009, 593–94.

Clarke, Cheryl. 'Black, Brave, and Woman, Too' [Rev. of *All the Women Are White, All the Blacks Are Men, But Some of Us Are Brave*]. *Sinister Wisdom*, No. 20 (1983): 89–99.

Clarke, Cheryl. *After Mecca: Women Poets and the Black Arts Movement*. New Brunswick, NJ: Rutgers University Press, 2005.

WORKS CITED 359

Clay, Steven, and Rodney Phillips. *A Secret Location on the Lower East Side: Adventures in Writing, 1960–1980.* New York: New York Public Library/Granary Books, 1998.

Cleaver, Eldridge. *Soul on Ice.* New York: Dell, 1968.

Clendinen, Dudley, and Adam Nagourney. *Out for Good: The Struggle to Build a Gay Rights Movement in America.* New York: Touchstone (Simon and Schuster), 1999.

Cohen, Sacha. 'Lessons From a New History of ACT UP: An Interview with Sarah Schulman'. *The New Enquiry,* September 13, 2021, https://thenewinquiry.com/lessons-from-act-up/.

Coleman, Sandy. 'The Chronicles of a Culture: Roxbury Afrocentric Store Offers the Words of a Legacy'. *The Boston Globe,* March 12, 1995, 249, 258.

Coleman, Victor. 'The Berkeley Poetry Conference' (from 'Art Is My Middle Name: A Memoir'). *17 seconds (a journal of poetry and poetics),* No. 10 (Summer 2014): 20–27.

Combahee River Collective. *Six Black Women: Why Did They Die?* Boston: Combahee River Collective, 1979.

Combahee River Collective. 'Combahee River Collective Statement' (1977). In Keeanga-Yamahtta Taylor (ed.), *How We Get Free: Black Feminism and the Combahee River Collective.* Chicago: Haymarket Books, 2017, 15–27. (Original 1977)

Commonwealth v. Delrue Lafayette Anderson. 404 Mass. 767. February 7, 1989–May 1, 1989. Suffolk County. Massachusetts Cases: Published opinions from Massachusetts courts, http://masscases.com/cases/sjc/404/404mass767.html.

Conroy, J. Oliver. 'An Apocalyptic Cult, 900 Dead: Remembering the Jonestown Massacre, 40 Years On'. *The Guardian,* November 17, 2018, https://www.theguardian.com/world/2018/nov/17/an-apocalyptic-cult-900-dead-remembering-the-jonestown-massacre-40-years-on.

Cooper, Dennis. 'Gay Life and Literature as a Constant Experiment'. *The Advocate Review of Books: A Literary Supplement,* No. 4 (Autumn, 1986): 51,123.

Corman, Cid. *The Gist of Origin: An Anthology.* New York: Grossman, 1975.

Cornum, Lou. 'Desiring the Tribe'. *Pinko,* No.1 (November 2019): 34–45.

Cornwell, Anita. 'Pat Parker Poet from San Francisco'. *Hera,* Vol. 1, No. 4 (Summer 1975): 40–41. [Subsequent parts of the interview are available in edited form at http://www.amusejanetmason.com/Pat_Parker4.htm.]

Cortez, Jayne. *Pissstained Stairs and the Monkey Man's Wares.* New York: Phrase Text, 1969.

Cortez, Jayne. *Coagulations: New and Selected Poems.* New York: Thunder's Mouth Press, 1984.

'Cost of Living Index for Selected U.S. Cities, 2005'. Information Please Database, Pearson Education, 2007, https://www.infoplease.com/business/consumer-resources/cost-living-index-selected-us-cities-20051

Crenshaw, Kimberlé. 'Demarginalizing the Intersection of Race and Sex: A Black Feminist Critique of Antidiscrimination Doctrine, Feminist Theory and Antiracist Politics'. *University of Chicago Legal Forum,* Vol. 1989, No. 1, article 8: 139–67.

Culley, Margo (ed.), *A Day at a Time: The Diary Literature of American Women from 1764 to the Present.* New York: Feminist Press, 1985.

Cummings, Christine. [Judy Grahn]. 'A Lesbian Speaks her Mind'. *Sexology Magazine,* October 1966; republished in *The Ladder* Vol. XI, No. IV (January 1967): 3.

Cummings, John. 'Faggot Femininity'. *Fag Rag,* No. 11 (Winter 1974): 25.

D'Allesandro, Sam. *The Zombie Pit.* Freedom, CA: Crossing Press, 1989.

Damon, Maria. *The Dark End of the Street: Margins in American Vanguard Poetry.* Minneapolis: University of Minnesota Press, 1993.

360   WORKS CITED

Dandridge, Rita B. 'A Selected Bibliography of Ann Allen Shockley'. *Black American Literature Forum*, Vol. 21, No. 1/2 (Spring–Summer 1987): 133–46.

Daniels, Gabrielle. *Something Else Again: Poetry and Prose, 1975–2019*. London: Materials, 2020.

Dash, Danielle. 'Opinion: "Nicole Smallman and Bibaa Henry Were Denied Dignity in Death. Don't Tell Me the UK Doesn't Need Black Lives Matter."' *Stylist*, July 1, 2020, https://www.stylist.co.uk/opinion/nicole-smallman-bibaa-henry-murders-police-sel fie/403603.

Davidson, Adenike Marie, 'Ann Allen Shockley'. In Emmanuel S. Nelson (ed.), *Contemporary African American Novelists: A Bio-Bibliographical Critical Sourcebook*. New York: Greenwood Press, 1999, 433–37.

Davidson, Jeanette R. 'Danny Glover: Memories from 1968'. In Jeanette R. Davidson (ed.), *African American Studies*, Edinburgh: Edinburgh University Press, 2021, 17–25.

Davidson, Michael. 'Incarnations of Jack Spicer: *Heads of the Town up to the Aether*'. Jack Spicer. *boundary 2*, Vol. 6, No. 1 (Autumn, 1977): 103–34.

Davidson, Michael. *The San Francisco Renaissance: Poetics and Community at Mid-Century*. Cambridge: Cambridge University Press, 1989.

Davidson, Michael. 'Marginality in the Margins: Robert Duncan's Textual Politics'. American Poetry of the 1980s. *Contemporary Literature*, Vol. 33, No. 2 (Summer 1992): 275–301.

Davidson, Michael. *Guys like Us: Citing Masculinity in Cold War Poetics*. Chicago: University of Chicago Press, 2004.

Davies, Alan. 'An Hardness Prompts Literature'. *Poetry Project Newsletter*, 1976. Repr. in *Mirage: John Wieners Issue* (1985): 30–37.

Davis, Jack. 'Enola Gay, Faggot Affinity Group. "I was there . . ."' *Found SF*, 2017, https://www.foundsf.org/index.php?title=Enola_Gay,_Faggot_Affinity_Group&oldid= 27967.

Davis, Kathy. *The Making of Our Bodies, Ourselves: How Feminism Travels Across Borders*. Durham, NC: Duke University Press, 2007.

Day, Emma. *Out of the Silence: Women Protesting the AIDS Epidemic, 1980–2020*. Unpublished D. Phil Dissertation, University of Oxford, 2020.

De Gruttola, Raphael. [Letter concerning Stephen Jonas]. *First Offense*, No. 4 (Jazz) (Autumn 1988): 30–31.

De Lauretis, Teresa. 'Queer Theory: Lesbian and Gay Sexualities'. *Differences: A Journal of Feminist Cultural Studies*, Vol. 3, No. 2 (Summer 1991): iii–xvii.

Dearborn, Carrie. '"Mothers" and "Daughters" Share Poetry'. *Gay Community News*, Vol. 8, No. 43 (May 23, 1981): 14, 16.

Dejanikus, Tacie, and Janis Kelly. 'roxbury: women organizing against violence'. *off our backs*, Vol. 9, No. 8 (August–September 1979): 14.

Del Rio, Chelsea Nicole. *'That Women Could Matter': Building Lesbian Feminism in California, 1955–1982*. PhD Dissertation, University of Michigan, 2016.

Delany, Samuel. *The Motion of Light in Water: Sex and Science Fiction Writing in the East Village, 1957–1965*. New York: William Morrow, 1988.

Delmont, Matthew F. *Why Busing Failed: Race, Media, and the National Resistance to School Desegregation*. Berkeley: University of California Press, 2016.

D'Emilio, John. 'Capitalism and Gay Identity'. In Ann Snitow, Christine Stansell, and Sharan Thompson (eds.), *Powers of Desire: The Politics of Sexuality*. New York: Monthly Review Press, 1983, 100–13.

WORKS CITED 361

D'Emilio, John. *Making Trouble: Essays on Gay History, Politics, and the University.* New York: Routledge, 1992.

D'Emilio, John. 1983. *Sexual Politics, Sexual Communities.* 2nd ed. Chicago: University of Chicago Press, 2012.

D'Emilio, John, and Estelle Freedman. *Intimate Matters: A History of Sexuality in America.* New York & Cambridge: Harper and Row, 1988.

Deming, Barbara. *We Cannot Live Without Our Lives.* New York: Grossman, 1974.

Deroze, Phyllisa Smith. *Womanist Restorative Drama: Violence, Community, and Healing by Contemporary Black Women Playwrights.* Unpublished PhD Dissertation, Pennsylvania State University, 2010.

Devall, Cheryl R. 'From a Woman's Eye'. *Harvard Crimson*, July 13, 1979, https://www.the crimson.com/article/1979/7/13/from-a-womans-eye-pin-a/

DeVeaux, Alexis. *Warrior Poet: A Biography of Audre Lorde.* New York: Norton, 2004.

Deveney, John Patrick. *Paschal Beverly Randolph: A Nineteenth-Century Black American Spiritualist, Rosicrucian, and Sex Magician.* Albany: State University of New York Press, 1997.

Dewhurst, Robert. 'On John Wieners and *Measure* Magazine'. *Let the Bucket Down: A Magazine of Boston Area Writing*, No. 1 (2013): 7–22. [Ed. Joseph Torra]

Dewhurst, Robert. 'John Wieners: A Career Biography, 1954–1975'. Part 1 of *Ungrateful City: The Collected Poems of John Wieners.* Unpublished PhD Dissertation, University of Buffalo, State University of New York, 2014, 1–150.

Dewhurst, Robert. 'Ode to the Instrument: Liner Notes for a John Wieners Recording'. Woodberry Poetry Room, October 28, 2015, http://woodberrypoetryroom.com/?p=2127.

'Direct Action to Stop the War, Berkeley CA'. June 20, 2005, http://www.actagainstwar.org/article.php?id=14.

Dong, Arthur (dir.). *Out Rage '69.* (TV Film, 1995).

Douglas, Cindy. 'Pat Parker: Interview with a Poet'. *Woman's Journal-Advocate*, Vol. 4, No. 3 (April 1985): 3; and Vol. 4, No. 2 (May 1985): 5.

duCille, Anne. 'The Occult of True Black Womanhood'. In Michael A. Elliott and Claudie Stokes (eds.), *American Literary Studies: A Methodological Reader.* New York: New York University Press, 2003, 211–35.

Dunagan, Patrick James. 'Take Holding the Crackling Power'. *Open Space*, June 11, 2019, https://openspace.sfmoma.org/2019/06/take-hold-the-crackling-power/.

Duncan, Robert. 'Letter (1st of a Series)'. *Measure*, No. II (1958): 62–63.

Duncan, Robert. *Bending the Bow.* New York: New Directions, 1968.

Duncan, Robert. Poetry Reading and Remarks. Gay Liberation Day Reading, Poetry Center, San Francisco, CA, 1971. [Privately circulated recording]

Duncan, Robert. 1976. 'Conversation with Robert Duncan' [Part 2]. [Conducted by Robert Peters and Paul Trachtenberg]. *Chicago Review*, Vol. 44, No. 1 (1998): 92–116.

Duncan, Robert. *The Collected Writings of Robert Duncan: The H.D. Book.* Ed. Michael Boughn and Victor Coleman. Berkeley and Los Angeles: University of California Press, 2012.

Duncan, Robert. *The Collected Writings of Robert Duncan: The Collected Early Poems and Plays.* Ed. Peter Quartermain. Berkeley and Los Angeles: University of California Press, 2012.

Duncan, Robert. *The Collected Writings of Robert Duncan: The Collected Later Poems and Plays.* Ed. Peter Quartermain. Berkeley and Los Angeles: University of California Press, 2014.

362 WORKS CITED

Duncan, Robert. *The Collected Writings of Robert Duncan: The Collected Essays and Other Prose.* Ed. James Maynard. Berkeley and Los Angeles: University of California Press, 2019.

Dunn, Carolyn. *Eye Witness: From Black Mountain to White Rabbit. Carolyn Dunn Interviewed by Kevin Killian.* New York: Granary Books, 2015.

Dunn, James C. (Jim). 'The Mesmerizing Apparition of the Oracle of Joy Street: A Critical Study of John Wieners' Life and Later Work in Boston'. Master's Thesis, Harvard Extension School, 2017.

Echols, Alice. *Daring to Be Bad: Radical Feminism in America, 1967–1975.* Minneapolis: University of Minnesota Press, 1989.

Edwards, Brent Hayes. 'Ear Work, Cock Drill' [Rev. of Stephen Jonas, *Selected Poems* (1994)]. *Hambone*, No. 12 (Fall 1995): 253–61.

Edwards, Erica R. *The Other Side of Terror: Black Women and the Culture of US Empire.* New York: New York University Press, 2021.

Egerton, John. 'Why So Few US Blacks Comes Here'. *AMEX*, Vol 2, No. 7 (December 1970): 13–15.

Elbaum, Max. *Revolution in the Air: Sixties Radicals Turn to Lenin, Mao and Che.* London: Verso, 2001.

Elliott, Jeffrey M. 'Ntozake Shangé: Genesis of a Choreopoem'. *Negro History Bulletin*, Vol. 41, No. 1 (January 1, 1978): 797–800.

Enke, Finn. 'Collective Memory and the Transfeminist 1970s: Toward a Less Plausible History'. *TSQ: Transgender Studies Quarterly*, Vol. 5, No. 1 (February 2018): 9–29.

'Enola Gay: Affinity Group'. Shaping San Francisco, January 29, 2020. Archive.org, https://archive.org/details/enolagayaffinitygroupjanuary292020.

Enszer, Julie R. 'Spoken Miracle: On Publishing, Lesbian Poetry, and Making Meaning. Stephania Byrd Interviewed by Julie R. Enszer'. *The Poetry Foundation*, 2012, https://www.poetryfoundation.org/articles/69798/spoken-miracle.

Enszer, Julie R. *The Whole Naked Truth of Our Lives: Lesbian-Feminist Print Culture from 1969 Through 1989.* Unpublished PhD Dissertation, University of Maryland, 2013.

Enszer, Julie R. 'What Remains: Remembering Michelle Cliff, Beth Brant, and Stephania Byrd'. *Lambda Literary*, August 2016, https://www.lambdaliterary.org/2016/08/what-remains-remembering-michelle-cliff-beth-brant-and-stephania-byrd/.

Enszer, Julie R. 'Dead Lesbian Poets: A Mediation in Six Parts'. *Lambda Literary*, July 8, 2020, https://lambdaliterary.org/2020/07/lesbian-poets/.

Enszer, Julie R., and Elena Gross (eds.). *Outwrite: The Speeches That Shaped LGBTQ Literary Culture.* Newark, NJ: Rutgers University Press, 2022.

Entrekin, Charles (ed.). *The Berkeley Poets Cooperative: A History of the Times.* Orinda, CA: Hip Pocket Press, 2013.

Eshleman, Clayton. 'The Lorca Working'. Jack Spicer. *boundary* 2, Vol. 6, No. 1 (Autumn 1977): 31–50.

Espinoza, Dionne, María Eugenia Cotera, and Maylei Blackwell (eds.). *Chicana Movidas: New Narratives of Activism and Feminism in the Movement Era.* Austin: University of Texas Press, 2018.

Evans, Arthur. *Witchcraft and the Gay Counterculture.* Boston: Fag Rag Books, 1978.

Evergreen Review. 'San Francisco Scene'. Vol. 1, No. 2 (March 1957).

Faas, Ekbert. *Young Robert Duncan: Portrait of the Artist as a Homosexual in Society.* Santa Barbara, CA: Black Sparrow Press, 1983.

WORKS CITED 363

Fag Rag. [Anonymous Contribution]. 'Let there be a Vietnam in our hearts'. *Fag Rag* [No. 1] (June 1971): 7.

Fag Rag. '3rd World Gay Revolution'. *Fag Rag*, No. 2 (Fall 1971): 8.

Fag Rag. 'Behind Bars'. *Fag Rag*, No. 2 (Fall 1971): 9.

Fag Rag. 'essay on liberation'. *Fag Rag*, No. 2 (Fall 1971): 13–14.

Fag Rag. 'I am a Black Faggot'. *Fag Rag*, No. 4 (January 1973): 20.

Fag Rag Collective. 'open letter to gay brothers'. *Fag Rag* [No. 1] (June 1971) [Back page].

Fag Rag Collective. 'Open Letter to *The Advocate*'. *Fag Rag*, No. 6 (Fall–Winter 1973).

'Featured Organization: Cantíl'. *Open Space, SF Moma*, June 2018, https://openspace.sfm oma.org/2018/06/featured-organization-cantil/.

Federal Writers' Project of the Works Progress Administration of Northern California. *San Francisco in the 1930s: The WPA Guide to the City by the Bay*. Berkeley: University of California Press, 2011.

Feinberg, Leslie, 'Two-Line Struggle Tore Apart 1950s Gay Movement'. *Workers World*, January 6, 2006, https://www.workers.org/2006/us/lavender-red-50/.

Feminist Writers' Guild: National Newsletter, Vol. 1, No. 1, January–April 1979.

Fenderson, Jonathan. *Building the Black Arts Movement: Hoyt Fuller and the Cultural Politics of the 1960s*. Champaign: University of Illinois Press, 2019.

Ferris, Stephan. 'Out of the Tubs, and into the Streets! Tracing the History of Bathhouse Regulations in San Francisco, CA'. *LGBTQ Policy Journal*, May 2021, https://lgbtq.hksp ublications.org/2021/05/22/out-of-the-tubs-and-into-the-streets-tracing-the-history-of-bathhouse-regulations-in-san-francisco-ca/.

Field, Douglas. *All Those Strangers: The Art and Lives of James Baldwin*. Oxford: Oxford University Press, 2015.

Fiorenza, Mary. 'Persephone: Revolution in Process'. *Sojourner*, August 1981, 15, 17.

Fisher, Clive. *Hart Crane: A Life*. New Haven and London: Yale University Press, 2002.

Fisher, Simon D. Elin. 'Pauli Murray's Peter Panic: Perspectives from the Margins of Gender and Race in Jim Crow America'. *Transgender Studies Quarterly*, Vol. 3, No. 1–2 (2016): 95–103.

Flannery, Kathryn. '"Life's Disguise Doth Keep Flies Off": Teaching Lynn Lonidier's Poetry'. *Feminist Teacher*, Vol. 22, No. 2 (2012): 137–57.

Flannigan Saint-Aubin, Arthur. '"Black Gay Male" Discourse: Reading Race and Sexuality Between the Lines'. African American Culture and Sexuality. *Journal of the History of Sexuality*, Vol. 3, No. 3 (January 1993): 468–90.

Foerster, Jennifer Elise. 'The Dream of Suspension: A Conversation with Cedar Sigo'. *Poetry Northwest*, November 2017, https://www.poetrynw.org/interview-the-dream-of-suspension-a-conversation-with-cedar-sigo/.

Formisano, Ronald P. *Boston Against Busing: Race, Class, and Ethnicity in the 1960s and 1970s*. Chapel Hill: University of North Carolina Press, 2012.

'Francis Coppola Plans Epic Film on AIDS Epidemic'. *Tulsa World*, July 28, 1992.

Freeman, Elizabeth. 'Time Binds, or, Erotohistoriography'. *Social Text*, Vol. 23, No. 3–4 (Fall–Winter): 84–85. 'What's Queer About Queer Studies Now?', eds. by David Eng, Judith Halberstam, and José Esteban Muñoz, 57–68.

Garber, Linda. *Identity Poetics: Race, Class, and the Lesbian-Feminist Roots of Queer Theory*. New York: Columbia University Press, 2001.

Gardner, Callie. *Poetry & Barthes: Anglophone Responses 1970–2000*. Liverpool: Liverpool University Press, 2018.

Gay Community News, Vol. 17, No. 8 (September 3–9), 1989. (Cited as *GCN*)

364   WORKS CITED

'Gay Fem Lib Set'. *Berkeley Barb*, Vol. 10. No. 3 (January 16–22, 1970): 7.

'Gay Women's Liberation Presented the Following Statement . . .' *It Ain't Me, Babe*, Vol. 1, No. 11 (August 6–20, 1970).

Gengel, Dean. 'Reclaiming The Old New World: Gay Was Good with Native Americans'. *The Advocate*, No. 182 (January 28, 1976): 40–41.

Gibson, Scott (ed.). *Blood and Tears: Poems for Matthew Shepard*. New York: Painted Leaf Press, 1999.

Gidlow, Elsa. 'Footprints in the Sands of the Sacred'. Lesbian History. *Frontiers: A Journal of Women Studies*, Vol. 4, No. 3 (Autumn 1979): 47–51.

Ginsberg, Allen. 'Notes on Young Poets'. *Big Table*, No. 4 (1960): 124–26.

Ginsberg, Allen. 'Kral Majales'. [Broadside]. Berkeley, CA: Oyez Press, 1965.

Ginsberg, Allen. *Planet News*. San Francisco: City Lights, 1968.

Ginsberg, Allen. 'Marshall's Service'. 1972. Published as introduction to Marshall, *Leave the Word Alone*. New York: Pequod Press, 1979.

Ginsberg, Allen. *Collected Poems 1947–1980*. New York: Harper Perennial, 1988.

Ginsberg, Allen. 'Literary History of the Beat Generation, a Class Taught by Allen Ginsberg November 18, 1982 at Naropa'. The Allen Ginsberg Project, January 2014, https://allenginsberg.org/2014/01/allen-ginsberg-on-john-wieners-part-one/.

Gioia, Ted. 'How Lester Young Invented Cool'. *The Daily Beast*, Apr. 12, 2015, https://www.thedailybeast.com/how-lester-young-invented-cool

Giovanni, Nikki. *The Collected Poetry of Nikki Giovanni*. New York: Harper Collins, 2003.

Glave, Thomas, *Words to Our Now*. Minneapolis: University of Minnesota Press, 2005.

Glück, Robert. Postcard to Bruce Boone, December 8, 1972. Robert Glück Folder, Box 1, Correspondence (Labelled), BBP.

Glück, Robert. *Elements of a Coffee Service*. San Francisco: Four Seasons Press, 1982.

Glück, Robert. 1985. *Jack the Modernist*. New York: Serpent's Tail, 1995.

Glück, Robert. *Communal Nude*. Pasadena, CA: Semiotext(e), 2016.

Glück, Robert. *Margery Kempe*. New York: New York Review of Books, 2020. (Original 1994 and cited as)

Glück, Robert. 'A Dream Journal of the HIV/ AIDS Crisis'. *Frieze*, April 2020, https://www.frieze.com/article/dream-journal-hivaids-crisis.

Goodman, Paul, and Percival Goodman. *Communitas: Means of Livelihood and Ways of Life*. Rev. ed. New York: Vintage, 1960. (Original 1947)

Goldberg, Ariel. *The Estrangement Principle*. New York: Nightboat Books, 2016.

Grahn, Judy. 'The Cell'. n.d. Folder 448, Box 55, P CMS-0049, Manroot/Paul Mariah Collection, 1989–1996, Poetry Collection, University at Buffalo, State University of New York.

Grahn, Judy. 'Lesbians as Bogeywomen'. *Women*, No. 1 (Summer 1970): 36–38.

Grahn, Judy. 'On the Development of a Purple Fist'. *Gay Flames*, No. 12 (1971): 1–5.

Grahn, Judy. *The Work of a Common Woman*. London: Onlywomen Press, 1985.

Grahn, Judy. *The Judy Grahn Reader*. San Francisco: Aunt Lute Books, 2009.

Grahn, Judy. *A Simple Revolution: The Making of an Activist Past*. San Francisco: Aunt Lute Books, 2012.

Greene, Meg. *Henry Louis Gates, Jr.: A Biography*. Santa Barbara, CA: Greenwood, 2012.

Grundy, David. Review of Steve Abbott, *Beautiful Aliens*. *Chicago Review*, July 9, 2020, https://www.chicagoreview.org/steve-abbott-beautiful-aliens/

WORKS CITED 365

Grundy, David. 'Queer Shoulders at the Wheel' [Review of John Wieners, *Yours Presently*]. *Boston Review*, May 21, 2021, http://bostonreview.net/arts-society/david-grundy-queer-shoulders-wheel.

Grundy, David. '"A Gay Presence": Publication and Revision in John Wieners' *Behind the State Capitol*'. In Leila Kassir and Richard Espley (eds.), *Queer Between the Covers: Histories of Queer Publishing and Publishing Queer Voices*. London: University of London Press, 2021, 7–32.

Grundy, David. 'New Narratives in Gabrielle Daniels and Ishmael Houston-Jones'. *Journal of Narrative Theory*, Vol. 51, No. 3 (2021): 296–325.

Grundy, David. 'John Wieners and "the only one who ever mattered"'. In Michael Kindellan and Alex Marsh (eds.), *Utter Vulnerability: Essays on the Poetry of John Wieners*. Presses Universitaires de la Méditerranée. Forthcoming.

Guide to the Irving Rosenthal papers, c. 1950–1996. Libraries Department of Special Collections and University Archives. Stanford University.

Gumbs, Alexis Pauline. *We Can Learn to Mother Ourselves: The Queer Survival of Black Feminism 1968–1996*. Unpublished PhD Dissertation, Duke University, 2010.

Gumbs, Alexis Pauline. *Spill: Scenes of Black Feminist Fugitivity*. Durham and London: Duke University Press, 2016.

Gunn, Thom. 'Homosexuality in Robert Duncan's Poetry'. In Robert J. Bertholf (ed.), *Scales of the Marvellous: On Robert Duncan's Poetry*. New York: New Directions, 1979, 143–60.

Hall, Joan Wylie (ed.). *Conversations with Audre Lorde*. Jackson: University Press of Mississippi, 2004.

Halley, Catherine, '"We Couldn't Get Them Printed," So We Learned to Print Them Ourselves' [Interview with Julie Enszer]. *JSTOR Daily*, June 2020, https://daily.jstor.org/julie-enszer-we-couldnt-get-them-printed-so-we-learned-to-print-them-ourselves/.

Halberstam Jack. *Female Masculinity*. Durham, NC: Duke University Press, 1998.

Halpern, Rob. 'Recovering "China"'. *Jacket 2*, No. 39 (2009), http://jacketmagazine.com/39/perelman-halpern.shtml.

Halpern, Rob. 'Coda: The "Queen Under the Hill," or, Robert Duncan's Lesson in Essential Autobiography'. *Sillages Critiques*, No. 29 (2020), http://journals.openedition.org/sillag escritiques/10777

Halpern, Rob. *Hieroglyphs of the Inverted World*. Berkeley, CA: Kenning Editions, 2021.

Halpern, Rob, and Robin Tremblay-McGaw (eds.). *From Our Hearts to Yours: New Narrative as Contemporary Practice*. Oakland, CA: ON Contemporary Practice, 2017.

Hanegraaf, Wouter J. *New Age Religion and Western Culture: Esotericism in the Mirror of Secular Thought*. Albany: State University of New York Press, 1998.

Hanhardt, Christina B. *Safe Space: Gay Neighborhood History and the Politics of Violence*. Durham, NC: Duke University Press, 2013.

Harris, Bertha. 1972. *Lover*. New York: New York University Press, 1993.

Harris, Duchess. *Black Feminist Politics from Kennedy to Trump*. London: Palgrave MacMillan, 2019.

Harris, Kaplan. 'The Small Press Traffic School of Dissimulation'. *Jacket 2*, April 7, 2011, https://jacket2.org/article/small-press-traffic-school-dissimulation. (Harris 2011a)

Harris, Kaplan. 'Avant-Garde Interrupted: New Narrative After AIDS'. *Contemporary Literature*, Vol. 52, No. 4 (Winter 2011): 630–57. (Harris 2011b)

366 WORKS CITED

Harris, Kaplan. 'Causes, Movements, Theory: Between Language Poetry and New Narrative'. In Mary McAleer Balkun, Jeffrey Gray, and Paul Jaussen (eds.), *A Companion to American Poetry*. Hoboken, NJ: Wiley, 2022, 146–57.

Hartman, Saidiya. *Scenes of Subjection: Terror, Slavery, and Self-Making in Nineteenth Century America*. Oxford: Oxford University Press, 1997.

Hartman, Saidiya. *Lose Your Mother: A Journey Along the Atlantic Slave Route*. New York: Farrar, Straus and Giroux, 2007.

Hartman, Saidiya. *Wayward Lives, Beautiful Experiments: Intimate Histories of Social Upheaval*. New York: W. W. Norton, 2019.

Haslewood, Dave. Announcement card for *Hellan, Hellan*. 5 x 7 letterpress broadside, Auerhahn Press, 1960. [Text by Dave Haslewood. Poem by Edward Marshall.]

Haslewood, Dave. Interview by Steve Luttrell. *The Café Review, Auerhahn Press Tribute*, Summer 2012, https://www.thecafereview.com/summer-2012-interview-with-dave-haselwood/.

Haslewood, Dave. Interview by David Abel. November 1, 2013, Cotati, California. Unpublished. Typescript provided by David Abel.

Hay, Harry. *Radically Gay: Gay Liberation in the Words of Its Founder*. Boston: Beacon Press, 1997.

Heller, Nathan, 'Bay Watched—How San Francisco's New Entrepreneurial Culture Is Changing the Country'. *The New Yorker*, October 2013, https://www.newyorker.com/magazine/2013/10/14/bay-watched.

Heller, Steven. *Merz to Emigré and Beyond: Avant-Garde Magazine Design of the Twentieth Century*. London: Phaidon, 2014.

Hemphill, Essex (ed.). *Brother to Brother: Writings by Black Gay Men*. Washington, DC: Redbone Press, 1991. [Anthology conceived by Joseph Fairchild Beam.]

Henderson, David. 'Wolfbane—Berkeley Trees'. In *Poets Read their Contemporary Poetry: Before Columbus Foundation*. New York: Folkways Records, 1980, 9–12.

Hernton, Calvin C. Introduction to Janheinz Jahn, *Muntu: African Culture and the Western World*. New York: Grove Weidenfield, 1990.

Hester, Diarmuid. *Wrong: A Critical Biography of Dennis Cooper*. Iowa City: University of Iowa Press, 2020.

Higashida, Cheryl. *Black Internationalist Feminism: Women Writers of the Black Left, 1945–1995*. Urbana: University of Illinois Press, 2011.

Hill, Monica. 'Memorial Tribute to Karen Brodine, November 22, 1987'. FSP Files, Box 2, KBP.

Hill Collins, Patricia, and Sirma Bilge. *Intersectionality*. 2nd ed. Hoboken, NJ: Wiley: 2020.

The History Project. *Improper Bostonians: Lesbian and Gay History from the Puritans to Playland*. Boston: Beacon Press, 1998.

Hobson, Emily. *Lavender and Red: Liberation and Solidarity in the Gay and Lesbian Left*. Berkeley and Los Angeles: University of California Press, 2016.

Hocquenghem, Guy. *Homosexual Desire*. Trans. Daniella Dangoor. Durham, NC: Duke University Press, 1993. (1972; translation 1978)

Hoddersen, Guerry. 'FSP Dropout Clique Excuses Self-Exile with Anti-Party Hysteria'. *Freedom Socialist*, Vol. 13, No. 4 (August 1992): 6.

Hoffman, Amy. *An Army of Ex-Lovers: My Life at the Gay Community News*. Amherst: University of Massachusetts Press, 2007.

Hogan, Kristen. *The Feminist Bookstore Movement: Lesbian Antiracism and Feminist Accountability*. Durham, NC: Duke University Press, 2016.

WORKS CITED 367

Hogan, Mary Ann. 'Chinese American Women Seek to Unbind Ideas at Foot of Stereotypes About Them'. *Oakland Tribune*, 1980. Cited in Ordona, 135.

Holladay, Hilary. *Herbert Huncke: The Times Square Hustler Who Inspired Jack Kerouac and the Beat Generation*. Tucson, AZ: Schaffner Press, 2015.

Holland, Walter. 'The Calamus Root'. *Journal of Homosexuality*, Vol. 34, No. 3–4 (1998): 5–25. Co-published in Sonya L. Jones (ed.), *Gay and Lesbian Literature Since World War II: History and Memory*. Philadelphia: Haworth Press, 1998, 5–25.

Holliday, J. S. *Rush for Riches: Gold Fever and the Making of California*. Berkeley: University of California Press, 1999.

Holt, Kelly. '*In the Sense of a Lasting Doctrine': Ernst Kantorowicz's Historiography and the Serial Poetics of the Berkeley Renaissance*. Unpublished PhD Dissertation, University of California, Santa Cruz, 2009.

Homer, Sean. 'A Brief History of the MLG'. *MLG*, n.d., http://www.marxistliterary.org/a-brief-history-of-the-mlg.

Hong, Grace Kyungwong. *The Ruptures of American Capital: Women of Color, Feminism and the Culture of Immigrant Labor*. Minneapolis: University of Minnesota Press, 2006.

hooks, bell. 'Selling Hot Pussy: Representations of Black Female Sexuality in the Cultural Marketplace'. In *Black Looks: Race and Representation*. Boston: South End Press, 1992, 61–77.

Hull, Gloria T. *Color, Sex and Poetry: Three Women Writers of the Harlem Renaissance*. Bloomington: Indiana University Press, 1987.

Honey, Maureen. *Shadowed Dreams: Women Poets of the Harlem Renaissance*. Newark, NJ: Rutgers University Press, 1989.

Hull, Gloria T., Patricia Bell Scott, and Barbara Smith (eds.), *All the Women Are White, All the Blacks Are Men, but Some of Us Are Brave*. Black Women's Studies. Old Westbury, NY: Feminist Press, 1982.

'I Hate Women: A Diatribe by an Unreconstructed Feminist'. *The Ladder*, Vol. 9, No. 5 and 6 (February/March 1965): 7–12.

Ikas, Karin Rosa (ed.), *Chicana Ways: Conversations with Ten Chicana Writers*. Reno and Las Vegas: University of Nevada Press, 2002, 5.

Irwin, Catherine. 'Dispossession and the 1970s Trans-Genre: A Reading of Judy Grahn's "The Psychoanalysis of Edward the Dyke"'. *Contemporary Women's Writing*, Vol. 13, No. 1 (March 2019): 70–88.

J, No. 6 (1960).

Jackson, Don. 'Dachau for Queers'. *Gay Sunshine*, Vol. 1, No. 3 (November 1970).

Jackson, Earl. 'Scandalous Subjects: Robert Glück's Embodied Narratives'. *Differences: A Journal of Feminist Cultural Studies*, Vol. 3, No. 2 (Summer 1991): 112–34.

Jackson, Earl. 'Bruce Boone'. In Emmanuel S. Nelson (ed.), *Contemporary Gay American Novelists: A Bio-Bibliographical Critical Sourcebook*. Westport, CT: Greenwood Press, 1993, 25–27.

Jackson, Isaac. Review of Michael J. Smith (ed.), *Black Men/White Men: A Gay Anthology*. The Prison No. *Blackheart: A Journal of Writing and Graphics by Black Gay Men*, No. 2 (1984): 48–50.

Jahn, Janheinz. *Muntu: An Outline of Neo-African Culture*. Trans. Marjorie Greene. New York: Grove, 1961. (Original 1958)

Jane, Jessie. 'Lord! What Kind of Child Is This: A Poet Passing Through'. *Gay Community News*, Vol. 2, No. 49 (May 31, 1975): 10.

368 WORKS CITED

Jarnot, Lisa. *Robert Duncan, The Ambassador from Venus: A Biography*. Berkeley and Los Angeles: University of California Press, 2012.

Jet. 'Words of the Week'. *Jet*, January 14, 1971, 32.

Johnson, Georgia Douglas. *An Autumn Love Cycle*. Freeport, NY: Books for Libraries Press, 1928.

Jonas, Stephen. Letters to Ed Marshall, 1953–1957. Unpublished. Typescripts from manuscripts in Jack Spicer papers, the Bancroft Library, University of California, provided by David Abel.

Jonas, Stephen. 'Michael Poem'. *Boston Newsletter*, 1956. Repr. as Jonas 1957.

Jonas, Stephen. *Love, The Poem, The Sea and Other Pieces Examined by Steve Jonas*. San Francisco: White Rabbit Press, 1957. Repr. from *Boston Newsletter*; repr. in Jonas 1966, 1994, and 2019.

Jonas, Stephen. 'Word on Measure'; 'Expanding Word on Measure'. *Measure*, No. 1 (1957): 24–27. Repr. in Jonas 1994 and 2019.

Jonas, Stephen. 'A Long Poem for Jack Spicer Because He Needs It (Books 3 and 4)'. *Measure*, No. 2 (1958): 53–61.

Jonas, Stephen. Letters to Gerrit Lansing, 1961–1967. Unpublished. Series VI. Stephen Jonas papers, 1958–2001. Box 12, Letters from Stephen Jonas to Gerrit Lansing, 1961–1963. Gerrit Lansing Papers, YCAL MSS 469, Yale Collection of American Literature, Beinecke Rare Book and Manuscript Library, Yale University.

Jonas, Stephen. *Transmutations*. London: Ferry Press, 1966.

Jonas, Stephen. *Exercises for Ear*. London: Ferry Press, 1968.

Jonas, Stephen. Letter to Andrew Crozier. November 29, 1968.

Jonas, Stephen. '75 Poems & a Narration'. *Caterpillar* No. 15/16 (April–July 1971).

Jonas, Stephen. 'A Long Poem for Jack Spicer Who Needs It [Books 1 and 2]'. Jack Spicer. *Manroot*, No. 10 (Fall–Winter 1974): 67–73. (Original 1958)

Jonas, Stephen. 'White Rabbit Press'. *Fag Rag*, No. 10 (1974): 11.

Jonas, Stephen. 'A Poet's Word to a Blue Painter'. *Fag Rag*, No. 15 (February–March 1976): 14–15. (Original 1966)

Jonas, Stephen. 'take the next chorus we're in A flat'. *First Offense*, No. 4 (Autumn 1988): 34–35.

Jonas, Stephen. *Three Poems*. Berkeley, CA: Rose Books, 1989.

Jonas, Stephen. 'Poems' [From an Untitled Sequence]. *Talisman*, No. 11 (Fall 1993): 17–21.

Jonas, Stephen. *Selected Poems*. Ed. Joseph Torra. Hoboken, NJ: Talisman House, 1994.

Jonas, Stephen. *Arcana: A Stephen Jonas Reader*. Ed. Garret Caples, Derek Fenner, David Rich, and Joseph Torra. San Francisco: City Lights, 2019.

Jordan, June. *Passion: New Poems 1977–1980*. Boston: Beacon Press, 1980.

Jordan, June. *Civil Wars: Observations from the Front Lines of America*. New York: Touchstone, 1995. (Original 1985)

Jordan, June. *Directed By Desire: The Collected Poems of June Jordan*. Ed. Jan Heller Levi and Sara Miles. Port Townsend, WA: Copper Canyon Press, 2007.

Joris, Pierre. '"How to Manage the Heat": On Gerrit Lansing'. *Chicago Review*, 2018, https://www.chicagoreview.org/how-to-manage-the-heat-on-gerrit-lansing/.

J.P., 'For Men Only?' *ONE Magazine* Vol. 1, No. 8 (August 1953): 3.

Jung, Carl Gustav. *Collected Works*, Vol. 6: *Psychological Types*. Trans. H. G. Baynes and R. F. C. Hull. Princeton, NJ: Princeton University Press, 1971. (Original 1923)

Kaplan, Amy. 'Manifest Domesticity'. No More Separate Spheres! *American Literature*, Vol. 70, No. 3 (September 1998): 581–606.

WORKS CITED   369

Karr, John F. 'Triple Play'. *Bay Area Reporter,* December 1989, 89.

Karuka, Manura, *Empire's Tracks: Indigenous Nations, Chinese Workers, and the Transcontinental Railroad.* Berkeley: University of California Press, 2019.

Katz, Daniel. *The Poetry of Jack Spicer.* Edinburgh: Edinburgh University Press, 2013.

Katz, Jonathan Ned. *Gay American History: Lesbians and Gay Men in the U.S.A. A Documentary History.* London and New York: Meridian/Penguin, 1992. (Original 1976)

Katz, Jonathan Ned. *The Invention of Heterosexuality.* New York: E.P. Dutton, 1995.

Katz, Sue. 'Consenting Adult'. June 2009, https://suekatz.typepad.com/sue_katz_c onsenting_adult/2009/06/hey-to-any-new-york-friend-can-you-shoot-me-under-glass.html.

Kaufman, Erica. 'The End of Gender'. *Boston Review,* May 2016, https://www.bostonrev iew.net/articles/erika-kaufman-eileen-myles-i-must-be-living-twice/.

Keenaghan, Eric. 'Vulnerable Household: Cold War Containment and Robert Duncan's Queered Nation'. *Journal of Modern Literature,* Vol. 28, No. 4 (Summer 2005): 57–90.

Keenaghan, Eric. 'Queer Deep Songs: American Cold War Poets' Disinterment of Federico García Lorca'. In David A. Powell and Tamara Powell (eds.). *Queer Exoticism: Examining The Queer Exotic Within.* Newcastle Upon Tyne: Cambridge Scholars, 2010, 3–14.

Kearney, Larry. *Testamentality, Transcryption: An Emotional Memoir of Jack Spicer.* New York: Spuyten Diyvil, 2019.

Kelly, Catherine. '(Archive Fever) Martha Shelley and Digital Traces of Lesbiana—Part 1'. *Spamzine,* April 12 2022, https://www.spamzine.co.uk/post/archive-fever-martha-shel ley-and-digital-traces-of-lesbiana.

Kelley, Robin D. G. *Freedom Dreams: The Black Radical Imagination.* Boston: Beacon Press, 2002.

Kennedy, Evan. 'Bruce Boone by Evan Kennedy'. *BOMB,* April 2020, https://bombmagaz ine.org/articles/bruce-boone/

Kenny, Maurice. 'Tinselled Bucks: An Historical Study in Indian Homosexuality'. *Gay Sunshine,* No. 26–27 (Winter 1975–76): 17–48. Repr. in Roscoe 1989.

Kenny, Maurice. *Only as Far as Brooklyn.* Boston: Good Gay Poets, 1979.

Kenny, Maurice. 'Maurice Kenny: Gay Native American Poet' [Interview by Charley Shively and Clover Chango]. *Gay Community News,* Vol. 7, No. 47 (June 21, 1980): 10–11.

Kenny, Maurice. 'Boston Tea Party'. *Soup,* No. 2 (1981): 32–33.

Kenny, Maurice. *Last Mornings in Brooklyn: Poems by Maurice Kenny.* Norman, OK: Point Riders Press, 1991.

Kenny, Maurice. *On Second Thought: A Compilation.* Norman, OK: University of Oklahoma Press, 1995.

Kenny, Maurice. *Angry Rain: A Brief Memoir.* Ed. Derek C. Maus. New York: State University of New York Press, 2018.

Khanna, Ranjana. *Dark Continents: Psychoanalysis and Colonialism.* Durham and London: Duke University Press, 2003.

Kher, Unmesh. 'A Name for the Plague'. *80 Days That Changed the World, Time,* Monday, Mar. 31, 2003, https://content.time.com/time/specials/packages/article/0,28804,1977 881_1977895_1978703,00.html

Killian, Kevin (ed.). 'Symposium: Twelve Writers Watch & Discuss Montgomery Clift and Jennifer Jones in the rediscovered *Terminal Station aka Indiscretions of an American Wife.' No Apologies: A Magazine of Gay Writing,* No. 2, Spring, 1984, 68–91.

370 WORKS CITED

Killian, Kevin. *Argento Series*. San Francisco: Krupskaya, 2001.

Killian, Kevin. 'Spicer and the Mattachine'. In Vincent 2011, 16–35.

Killian, Kevin. 'Activism, Gay Poetry, AIDS in the 1980s'. *Paideuma*, Vol. 41 (2014): 3–19.

Killian, Kevin. Personal email, May 2019.

Killian, Kevin, and Lewis Ellingham. *Poet Be Like God: Jack Spicer and the San Francisco Renaissance*. Middletown, CT: Wesleyan University Press, 1998.

Kim, Willyce. *Eating Artichokes*. Oakland, CA: The Women's Press Collective, 1972.

Kost, Ryan. 'Bathhouse Ban Revoked: Amid One Pandemic, SF Confronts Legacy of Another'. *San Francisco Chronicle*, September 11, 2020, https://www.sfchronicle.com/bayarea/article/Bathhouse-ban-revoked-Amid-one-pandemic-San-15558609.php

Koven, Mikel J. *La Dolce Morte: Vernacular Cinema and the Italian Giallo Film*. Oxford: Scarecrow Press, 2006.

Kyper, John. '"A member of the prohibited class of persons . . . ": Or, My Modest Contribution to the Queering of Canada'. *Left History*, Vol. 13, No. 2 (Fall/Winter, 2008): 151–61.

Kyper, John. 'Coming Out and into the GLF: Banned No More in Boston'. In Avicolli Mecca 2009, 31–39.

The Ladder, Vol. 13, No. 3–4 (December–January 1968–69).

LaPalma, Marina. 'Statement by Marina De Bellagente LaPalma'. Memorial Commemorations, FSP Files, Box 2, KBP.

Lamott, Kenneth. 'Poetry Here! Hot Off the Press!' *New York Times*, August 29, 1976, 169.

Lamoureux, Mark. 'What Gerrit Gives Us'. Mass: Gerrit Lansing. Ed. Jim Dunn and Kevin Gallagher. *Jacket 2*, December 2012, https://jacket2.org/article/what-gerrit-gives-us.

Landers, Dale. '["Felicitations"]'; 'The Hipster's Lamentation'. *Mithrander*, 1963. n.p.

Lansing, Gerrit. 'Gay Talk/Writing' [Handwritten and typed draft]. Gerrit Lansing Papers, YCAL MSS 649, Box 6, F, Yale Collection of American Literature, Beinecke Rare Book and Manuscript Library, Yale University. (n.d.).

Lansing, Gerrit. 'The Burden of SET # 1 (editorial)'. *SET 1*, Winter 1961–1962: 8–12.

Lansing, Gerrit. 'The Burden of SET # 2 (editorial)'. *SET 2*, Winter 1963–1964: 38–44.

Lansing, Gerrit. *The Heavenly Tree Grows Downward*. Annandale-on-Hudson, NY: North Atlantic Books, 1966.

Lansing, Gerrit. 'The Preface to the Reader'. In Stephen Jonas, *Exercises for Ear*. London: Ferry Press, 1968, 5–6.

Lansing, Gerrit. 'Amazing Grace and a Salad Bowl'. *Caterpillar*, No. 17 (1971): 20. Repr. in in Leyland 1975 and Lansing 2009.

Lansing, Gerrit. 'from BREVETS: aesthetic meditations'. *Credences*, No. 5/6 (March 1978):125. [Early version of Lansing 1983.]

Lansing, Gerrit. *Analytic Philosophy, or the Soluble Forest is Swimming Across [Curriculum of the Soul no. 23]*. Buffalo, NY: Institute of Further Studies, 1983. Rev. and repr. in Lansing 2009.

Lansing, Gerrit. *Heavenly Tree, Northern Earth*. Berkeley, CA: North Atlantic Books, 2009.

Lansing, Gerrit. 'Gerrit Lansing on Close Listening'. [Lansing in discussion with Charles Bernstein and Susan Howe]. *Jacket 2*, December 9, 2012, http://jacket2.org/commentary/gerrit-lansing-close-listening.

Lansing, Gerrit. 'WPR RECORDING SESSION: Gerrit Lansing | Woodberry Poetry Room'. Harvard University Channel, YouTube, December 10, 2015, https://www.youtube.com/watch?list=ULbr0ZYTGuW9M&v=1ndMXtufX4o.

WORKS CITED 371

Lapsley, Hillary. *Margaret Mead and Ruth Benedict: The Kinship of Women*. Amherst: University of Massachusetts Press, 1999.

Lauria, Mickey and Larry Knopp. 'Towards an Analysis of the Role of Gay Communities in the Urban Renaissance'. *Urban Geography*, Vol. 6, No. 2 (1985): 152–64.

Lecklider, Aaron. *Love's Next Meeting: The Forgotten History of Homosexuality and the Left in American Culture*. Berkeley: University of California Press, 2021.

Left Write: Edited Transcripts of 1981 Left Write Conference. San Francisco, CA, 1982.

Lepson, Ruth. 'Thirteen Ways of Looking at Gerrit Lansing'. *Stylus: The Poetry Room Blog*, Woodberry Poetry Room, February 10, 2015, https://woodberrypoetryroom.com/?p=628.

LeRud, Elizabeth (Lizzy). *Antagonistic Cooperation: Prose in American Poetry*. Unpublished PhD Dissertation, University of Oregon, 2017.

LeRud, Lizzy. 'Radical Revision: Rewriting Feminism with *This Bridge Called My Back* and Kate Rushin's "The Bridge Poem"'. *Tulsa Studies in Women's literature*, Vol. 39, No. 2 (Fall 2020): 303–27.

Leong, Russell. 'In Memoriam: Janice Mirikitani'. *Amerasia Journal*, Vol. 47, No. 1 (2021): 172–76.

Levertov, Denise. 'To Write Is to Listen'. [Review of *Ace of Pentacles*]. *Poetry*, Vol.105, No. 5 (February 1965): 326–39. Collected in *The Poet in the World*. San Francisco: New Directions, 1973, 227–30.

Levin, John F. Levin and Earl Silbar (eds.). *You Say You Want a Revolution: SDS, PL, and Adventures in Building a Worker-Student Alliance*. San Francisco, CA: 1741 Press, 2019.

Lewis, Sophie. 'How British Feminism Became Anti-Trans'. *New York Times*, February 7, 2019, https://www.nytimes.com/2019/02/07/opinion/terf-trans-women-britain.html.

Lewis, Sophie. *Abolish the Family: A Manifesto for Care and Liberation*. London: Verso, 2022.

Leyland, Winston (ed.). *Angels of the Lyre: A Gay Poetry Anthology*. San Francisco: Panjadrum Press/Gay Sunshine Press, 1975.

Leyland, Winston. *Gay Sunshine Interviews*, Vol. 2. San Francisco: Gay Sunshine Press, 1978.

Lim, Genny, Him Mark-Lai, and Judy Yung (eds.) *Island: Poetry and History of Chinese Immigrants on Angel Island 1910–1940*. San Francisco: Hoc-Doi Project, 1980.

Lisette, Francesca. 'Spirits his wife speaks of / in the singular': Voice and Ventriloquy in the Poetry of John Wieners. Unpublished Master's Thesis, University of Sussex, 2010.

'Lives of the Poets # 3'. Group conversation: Stephen Jonas, John Wieners, Rene Ricard, with the participation of Scott Reichard and Gerard Malanga, Friday 30/01/1970, Boston. *Fag Rag*, No. 10 (Fall 1974): 10–12.

Lo, Malinda. 'Finding Queer Asian America in the Margins'. *Lo & Behold*, May 26, 2021. https://www.malindalo.com/blog/2021/5/26/finding-queer-asian-america.

Lonc, Christopher. 'Genderfuck and its Delights'. *Gay Sunshine*, No. 21 (Spring 1974): 4,16.

London, Catherine. 'Women's Words Fight Racism'. *Sojourner*, July 1981, 32.

Lonidier, Lynn. *A Lesbian Estate*. San Francisco: Manroot Books, 1977.

Lorca, Federico García. *Deep Song and Other Prose*. Trans. Christopher Maurer. New York: New Directions, 1980.

Lord Kinross [Patrick Balfour]. *The Innocents at Home*. London: Readers Union/John Murray, 1961.

Lorde, Audre. 'Need'. *Third World Women*. *Heresies*, Vol. 2, No. 4 (1979): 112–13.

372 WORKS CITED

Lorde, Audre. 'Need: A Choral for Black Women's Voices'. *Chosen Poems: Old and New*. New York: W. W. Norton, 1982, 111–15. Repr. in *The Collected Poems of Audre Lorde*. New York: W.W. Norton, 1997.

Lorde, Audre. *Need: A Chorale for Black Woman Voices*. New York: Kitchen Table Press, 1990.

Lorde, Audre. *Zami* (1982) / *Sister Outsider* (1984) / *Undersong* (1982). New York: Triangle Classics, 1993.

Lorde, Audre. *The Cancer Journals: Special Edition*. San Francisco: Aunt Lute Books, 1997. (Original 1980)

Love, Barbara, and Sidney Abbott. *Sappho Was a Right-On Woman: A Liberated View of Lesbianism*. New York: Stein and Day, 1972.

Lovelock, Molly. 'Persephone Press: Why Did It Die?' *Sojourner*, Vol. 9, No. 1 (September 1983): 4, 18.

Lowe, Lisa. *Immigrant Acts: On Asian American Cultural Politics*. Durham, NC: Duke University Press, 1996.

Lowe, Lisa. 'Transcript: In Conversation with Lisa Lowe'. Sarah Parker Remond Centre, UCL, July 19, 2021, https://www.ucl.ac.uk/racism-racialisation/transcript-conversat ion-lisa-lowe.

Mackey, Nathaniel. 'Cante Moro'. In *Paracritical Hinge: Essay, Talks, Notes, Interviews*. Iowa City: University of Iowa Press, 2018, 181–98.

Madan, A.C. *Swahili-English Dictionary*. Oxford: The Clarendon Press, 1903.

Manroot. No. 1, August 1969.

Marshall, Edward. 'Leave the Word Alone'. In Donald M. Allen (ed.), *The New American Poetry*. New York: Grove Press, 1960, 323–33. [First printed in *Black Mountain Review*, 7 (1957). Repr. as a pamphlet by Pequod Press, New York, 1979.] (1960a)

Marshall, Edward. *Hellan, Hellan*. San Francisco: Auerhahn Press, 1960. Drawings by Robert Ronnie Branaman. (1960b)

Marshall, Edward. 'Sept. 1957'. *Yugen*, No. 7 (1961): 54–58.

Marshall, Edward. 'Memory as Memorial in the Last'. *Yugen*, No. 8, (1962): 57. (1962a)

Marshall, Edward. 'Times Square'. *Measure Three: The City*, Summer 1962, 15–19. (1962b)

Marshall, Edward. *Transit Glory*. New York: Carp & Whitefish, 1966. Drawings by William Heine.

Marshall, Edward. 'Dramatic Silence'; 'A Love Poem / Forfeited'; 'Last of Jonas Cycle'. *Mulch*, Vol. 1, No. 2 (October 1971): 74–95.

Martin, Del, and Phyllis Lyon. *Lesbian/Woman*. New York: Bantam Books, 1972.

Martin, Robert K. *The Homosexual Tradition in American Poetry*. Austin: University of Texas Press, 1979.

Mass, Lawrence. 'Disease Rumors Largely Unfounded'. *New York Native*, 18 May 1981: 7.

Mass, Lawrence. 'Cancer in the Gay Community'. *New York Native*, 27 July 1981: 1, 21, 3.

Math, Mara. 'There's a Certain Kind of Woman'. In Avicolli Mecca 2009, 88–73.

'Mattachine Breaks Through the Silence'. *The Ladder*, Vol. 4, No. 1 (October 1959): 19.

Maud, Ralph. 'Background to Berkeley-II'. *Minutes of the Charles Olson Society*, No. 3 (October 1993): 15–16.

Maus, Derek C. 'Giving Something Back: An Interview with Maurice Kenny (1929–2016)'. In Laura Alonso Gallo (ed.), *Voice of America: Interviews with American Writers* Cádiz: Aduana Vieja, 2004. [Published in parallel English and Spanish language editions. PDF accessed via *Academia.edu*, https://www.academia.edu/7143576/Giving_Something_Back_An_Interview_with_Maurice_Kenny_1929_2016_].

WORKS CITED 373

Maye, Kristen. 'Black and White Men Together in North Carolina'. LGBT Identities, Communities, and Resistance in North Carolina, 1945–2012, *Out History*, n.d. http://outhistory.org/exhibits/show/nc-lgbt/pride-visibility/bwmt.

McDowell, Tara. *The Householders: Robert Duncan and Jess*. Cambridge, MA: MIT Press, 2019.

McKnight, Jennie. 'Black Lesbian Poet Pat Parker Dies'. *Gay Community News*, Vol. 16, No. 48 (June 25–30, 1989): 3.

McRruer, Robert. 'Boys' Own Stories and New Spellings of My Name: Coming Out and Other Myths of Queer Positionality'. In Carol Siegel and Ann Kibbey (eds.), *Eroticism and Containment—Notes from the Flood Plain*. New York: New York University Press, 1994, 260–84.

'Memorandum on the Gay Liberation Movement'. *SWP Discussion Bulletin*, Vol. 31, No. 3 (May 1973), 7–10, https://www.marxists.org/history/etol/document/swp-us/idb/swp-1970-76-db/v31n03-may-1973-disc-bul.pdf.

Messerli, Douglas. 'Between Visions: John Wieners'. [Orig. published as 'John Wieners and a "Post-Modernist" Quandry'.] *Sun & Moon: A Quarterly of Literature & Art*, No. 2 (Spring 1976): 86–104. Repr. online, *Project for Innovative Poetry*, July 2011, http://pippoetry.blogspot.co.uk/2011/07/between-visions-on-john-wieners.html.

Mieli, Mario. 1977. *Towards a Gay Communism*. Trans. David Fernbach and Evan Calder Williams. London: Pluto Press, 2017.

Mill, John Stuart. *Dissertations and Discussions. Political, Philosophical, and Historical. Reprinted Chiefly from the Edinburgh and Westminster Reviews*. Vol. 1. London: Parker and Son, 1859.

Miller, Adam David (ed.). *Dices or Black Bones: Black Voices of the Seventies*. Boston: Houghton Mifflin, 1970.

Miller, Edie. 'Why Is British Media so Transphobic?' *The Outline*, November 5, 2018, https://theoutline.com/post/6536/british-feminists-media-transphobic.

Mitchell, James. 'Writing Gay Liberation in San Francisco, 1968–1972: James Mitchell and Eric Sneathen in Conversation'. *Open Space*, July 2018, https://openspace.sfmoma.org/2018/07/james-mitchell-and-eric-sneathen-in-conversation/.

Mitchell, James (ed.). *Gay Sunrise: Writing Gay Liberation in San Francisco 1968–1972*. San Francisco: Ithuriel's Spear, 2019.

Mitts, Adam. 'Elegiac Citationality in Kevin Killian's "The Inn of the Red Leaf"'. *Journal of Narrative Theory*, Vol. 51, No. 3 (Fall 2021): 269–95.

Mockus, Martha. *Sounding Out: Pauline Oliveros and Lesbian Musicality*. New York: Routledge, 2008.

Monte, Bryan R. 'The Political as Personal: My Memoir of Steve Abbott, 1980–1990'. *Amsterdam Quarterly*, No. 15, https://www.amsterdamquarterly.org/aq_issues/aq15-war-peace/bryan-r-monte-the-political-as-personal-my-memoir-of-steve-abbott/

Moore, Lisa L. 'The Dream of a Common Bookstore'. *LA Review of Books,* April 2013, https://lareviewofbooks.org/article/the-dream-of-a-common-bookstore/.

Moore, Lisa L. 'It Is an Apple: An Interview with Judy Grahn'. *LA Review of Books*, August 23, 2013, https://lareviewofbooks.org/article/it-is-an-apple-an-interview-with-judy-grahn/.

Moore, Patrick. *Beyond Shame: Reclaiming the Abandoned History of Radical Gay Sexuality*. Boston: Beacon Press, 2004.

Moraga, Cherríe. *Loving in the War Years*. Boston: South End Press, 1983.

374 WORKS CITED

Moravec, Michelle. 'A Narrow History of Feminism Impoverishes Activism'. *Medium*, October 11, 2018, https://professmoravec.medium.com/a-narrow-history-of-femin ism-impoverishes-activism-565161d62dcd.

Morgensen, Scott Lauria. *Spaces Between Us: Queer Settler Colonialism and Indigenous Decolonization*. Minneapolis and London: University of Minnesota Press, 2011.

Moxley, Jennifer. 'A Deeper, Older O: The Oral (Sex) Tradition (in Poetry)'. In Julie Carr and Jeffrey C. Robinson (eds.), *Active Romanticism: The Radical Impulse in Nineteenth-Century and Contemporary Poetic Practice*. Tuscaloosa: University of Alabama Press, 2015, 70–90.

Mumford, Kevin J. 'Opening the Restricted Box: Lorraine Hansberry's Lesbian Writing'. Lorraine Hansberry: A Museum Show and Opening the Archive. *OutHistory*, 2014, outhistory.org/exhibits/show/lorraine-hansberry/.

Mumford, Kevin J. *Not Straight, Not White: Black Gay Men from the March on Washington to the AIDS Crisis*. Chapel Hill: University of North Carolina Press, 2016.

Myles, Eileen. *Cool for You: A Novel*. New York: Soft Skull Press, 2000.

Myles, Eileen. 'Gay Sunshine'. *The Poetry Foundation*, June 16, 2009, https://www.poetry foundation.org/harriet-books/2009/06/gay-sunshine.

Myles, Eileen. 'Gay Sunshine, 1971'. *Animal Shelter*, No. 2 (Spring 2012): 187–95.

Myles, Eileen. 'ABOUT BOSTON: Reading & Conversation with Eileen Myles'. Woodberry Poetry Room Harvard University YouTube Channel, July 6, 2016, https://www.youtube.com/watch?v=01k_evEtM_w.

Myles, Eileen. 'Eileen Myles on Writing with Political Meaning'. *Literary Hub*, November 2022, https://lithub.com/eileen-myles-on-writing-with-political-meaning.

Nancy, Jean-Luc. *The Inoperative Community*. Ed. Peter Connor. Trans. Peter Connor, Lisa Garbus, Michael Holland, and Simona Sawhney. Minneapolis: University of Minnesota Press, 1991.

Nangeroni, Nancy. 'The Chanelle Pickett Story'. Gendertalk.com, May 17, 1997, https://gendertalk.com/articles/victims/chanelle-revisit.shtml

Ndugu, (Prince) -Eusi. 'Black Draft Dodger Speaks Out in Canada'. *AMEX: The American Expatriate in Canada*, Vol. 2, No. 2 (January 1970): 22.

Ndugu, (Prince)-Eusi. [Poems]. *Fag Rag*, No. 11 (Winter 1974): 6. Selection repr. in Smith 1983.

Nealon, Christopher. 'Queer Tradition'. *GLQ: A Journal of Lesbian and Gay Studies*, Vol. 14, No. 4 (2008): 617–22.

Nealon, Christopher. *The Matter of Capital: Poetry and Crisis in the American Century*. Cambridge, MA: Harvard University Press, 2011.

Nersessian, Anahid. *The Calamity Form: On Poetry and Social Life*. Chicago, IL: Chicago University Press, 2020.

Nestle, Joan. 'Butch-Femme Relationships: Sexual Courage in the 1950's'. *Heresies*, No. 12 (1981). Repr. in Joan Nestle. *A Restricted Country*. Ithaca, NY: Firebrand, 1987, 100–109.

Neville, Gwen Kennedy. *Kinship and Pilgrimage: Rituals of Reunion in American Protestant Culture*. Oxford: Oxford University Press, 2005.

Neville, Tové. 'Impressions from an "Estranged" Poet'. *San Francisco Chronicle*, August 29, 1965, 33. Repr. in Spicer 1998, 242–44.

Nichols, Miriam. *A Literary Biography of Robin Blaser: Mechanic of Splendour*. London: Palgrave Macmillan, 2019.

Nichols, Rachael L. Review of *Whitman Noir: Black America and the Good Gray Poet*. *Nineteenth-Century Contexts*, Vol. 37, No. 5 (2015): 503–506.

WORKS CITED 375

Nielsen Aldon, Lynn. *Reading Race: White American Poets and the Racial Discourse in the Twentieth Century*. Athens: University of Georgia Press, 1988.

Nielsen Aldon, Lynn. *Integral Music: Languages of African-American Innovation*. Tuscaloosa: University of Alabama Press, 2004.

Nielsen Aldon, Lynn. 'Nation Times'. *The Black Scholar*, Vol. 47, No. 1 (2017): 3–15.

Noda, Barbara, Kitty Tsui, and Z. Wong. 'Coming Out: We Are Here in the Asian Community'. *Bridge: An Asian American Perspective*, Vol. 7, No. 1 (Spring 1979): 22–24.

Norton, Robert E. *Secret Germany: Stefan George and His Circle*. Ithaca and London: Cornell University Press, 2002.

Notley, Alice. *Doctor Williams' Heiresses*. San Francisco: Tuumba Press, 1980.

Ordona, Trinity. *Coming Out Together: An Ethnohistory of the Asian and Pacific Islander Queer Women's and Transgendered People's Movement of San Francisco*. Unpublished PhD Dissertation, University of California, Santa Cruz, 2000.

Otto, Herbert A. (ed.). *Love Today: A New Exploration*. New York: Association Press, 1972.

'Our History: Making History and a Difference'. Lawrence Livermore National Laboratory, 2020, https://www.llnl.gov/archives/1950s#event-the-founding-of-the-laboratory-at-livermore.

Our Vision into Words, Our Words into Action: An Historical Perspective on the Women Writers Union Stand Against Racism. San Francisco, CA: Women Writers Union, September 1980.

Parker, Pat. Pat Parker Papers, 1944–1998; Letter to Carolyn Burney, March 31, 1967. MC 861, Folder 2.13. Schlesinger Library, Radcliffe Institute, Harvard University, Cambridge, MA.

Parker, Pat. *Child of Myself*. Oakland, CA: The Women's Press Collective, 1972.

Parker, Pat. *Pit Stop*. Oakland, CA: The Women's Press Collective, 1973.

Parker, Pat. *Movement in Black: The Collected Poetry of Pat Parker 1961–1978*. Ithaca, NY: Firebrand Books, 1978.

Parker, Pat. *An Expanded Edition of Movement in Black*. Ed. Nancy K. Berneano. Ithaca, NY: Firebrand Books, 1999.

Parker, Pat. *The Complete Works of Pat Parker*. Ed. Julie R. Enszer. Brookville, NY and Dover, FL: Sinister Wisdom/A Midsummer Night's Press, 2016.

Parker, Pat, and Judy Grahn. *Where Would I Be Without You: The Poetry of Pat Parker and Judy Grahn* (LP). Olivia Records, 1976.

Parker, Pat, and Audre Lorde. *Sister Love: The Letters of Audre Lorde and Pat Parker, 1974–1989*. Introduction by Mecca Jamilah Sullivan; ed. Julie R. Enszer. Brookville, NY and Dover, FL: Sinister Wisdom/A Midsummer Night's Press, 2018.

Parkinson, Tom. 1991. 'Thomas Parkinson on Jack Spicer: An Interview' [Interview by Jack Foley]. *Talisman: A Journal of Contemporary Poetry and Poetics*, No. 10 (Spring 1993): 102–107.

Perry, Imani. *Looking for Lorraine: The Radiant and Radical Life of Lorraine Hansberry*. Boston: Beacon Press, 2018.

Persky, Stan. 'Proposition' [Editorial]. *Open Space*, No. 0: A Prospectus. (January 1964): n.p.

Persky, Stan. 'Alibi' [Editorial]. *Open Space Valentine* (February 1964): n.p.

Persky, Stan. 'Horns' [Editorial]. *Open Space Taurus*, No. 4 (April 1964): n.p.

Persky, Stan. 'A Change' [Response to Jack Spicer, 'A Protestant Letter']. *Open Space*, No. 7 (July 1964), n.p.

Persky, Stan. '[Untitled]' [aka 'Slaves']. The Jack Spicer Issue. *Manroot*, No. 10 (Fall–Winter 1974): 89. [Poem dated August 21, 1973.]

376 WORKS CITED

Persky, Stan. [Letter, March 5, 1976]. New Voices of the Seventies (1972–1976). *Manroot*, No. 11 (Spring–Summer 1977): 120–21.

Petro, Pamela. 'The Hipster of Joy Street'. *Boston College* Magazine, Fall 2000, http://bcm. bc.edu/issues/fall_2000/ft_wieners.html .

Peters, Leila. *In Spite of Everything: For the Women She Loved*. Bloomington, IN: AuthorHouse, 2010.

Peterson, Trace. 'Being Unreadable and Being Read: An Introduction'. In Peterson and T. C. Tolbert (eds.). *Troubling the Line: Trans and Genderqueer Poetry and Poetics*. New York: Nightboat Books, 2013, 15–22.

Peucker, Brigitte (ed.). *A Companion to Rainer Werner Fassbinder*. London: Wiley & Sons, 2012.

Philip, M. NourbeSe Philip. *Zong!* Middletown, CT: Wesleyan University Press, 2008.

Phillips, Frank Lamont. '[Review of] *Loving Her'. Black World*, Vol. 24, No. 11 (September 1975), 89–90.

Pisano, Claudia Moreno (ed.). *Amiri Baraka and Ed Dorn: The Complete Letters*. Albuquerque: University of New Mexico Press, 2014.

Podgurski, Robert. 'Mercurial in Nature: An Interview with Gerrit Lansing'. *Dispatches*, May 2014, https://www.dispatchespoetrywars.com/wpcontent/uploads/2018/11/ Podgurski-Interview-May-26-transcription-1-cor.pdf.

Poetry from Violence: San Francisco Conference on Violence against Women. San Francisco: Lighthouse, 1976.

Pollack, Howard. *The Ballad of John La touche: An American Lyricist's Life and Work*. Oxford: Oxford University Press, 2017.

Porter, Veneita. '. . . an evening of taking to the stage together'. *Gay Community News*, Vol. 8, No. 48 (June 27, 1981), 7–9.

Prima, Diane di. *Freddie Poems*. Point Reyes, CA: Ediolon Editions, 1974.

Prosser, Jay. *Second Skins: The Body Narratives of Transsexuality*. New York: Columbia University Press, 1998.

Puar, Jasbir K. *Terrorist Assemblages: Homonationalism in Queer Times*. Durham and London: Duke University Press, 2007.

Quarles, David. 'Robert Duncan: Poet of the Light and Dark' [Interview]. *The Advocate*, July 28, 1976, 195, 31.

Quinn, Ben. 'Family of Murdered Sisters Considering Suing Met Police'. *The Guardian*, July 7, 2021, https://www.theguardian.com/uk-news/2021/jul/07/family-murdered-sisters-bibaa-henry-nicole-smallman-considering-suing-met-police-london.

Raha, Nat. 'A Queer Excess: The Supplication of John Wieners'. *The Critical Flame*, No. 38, (September–October 2015), https://criticalflame.org/a-queer-excess-the-supplicat ion-of-john-wieners/

Raha, Nat. *Queer Capital: Marxism in Queer Theory and Post-1950 Poetics*. Unpublished PhD Dissertation, University of Sussex, 2018, https://sro.sussex.ac.uk/id/eprint/86259/ 1/Raha%2C%20Natalia.pdf.

Raha, Nat. 'Queer Labour in Boston: The Work of John Wieners, Gay Liberation and Fag Rag. In Jo Lindsay Walton and Ed Luker (eds.), *Poetry and Work: Work in Modern and Contemporary Anglophone Poetry*. London: Palgrave Macmillan, 2019, 195–243.

Rauvolf, Josef. 'The King of May Revisited'. *The Allen Ginsberg Project*, May 1, 2018, https://allenginsberg.org/2018/05/may-day-kral-majales/.

Reed, Jeremy. 'To Celebrate This Broken Man (for John Robinson)'. In *Heart on My Sleeve*, Paris and London: Alyscamps Press, 1996, 47–57.

WORKS CITED   377

Reid-Pharr, Robert. 'Tearing the Goat's Flesh: Homosexuality, Abjection, and the Production of a Late Twentieth-Century Black Masculinity'. *Studies in the Novel*, Vol. 28, No. 3 (Fall 1996): 372–94.

Reid-Pharr, Robert. *Once You Go Black: Choice, Desire, and the Black American Intellectual*. New York: New York University Press, 2007.

'Research Fact Sheet'. National Center for Victims of Crime and Crime Victims Research and Treatment Center. *New York City Alliance Against Sexual Assault*. (Site no longer operational.)

Rexroth, Kenneth. *One Hundred Poems from the Chinese*. New York: New Directions, 1971.

Reyes, Kathleen M. 'Freed Speech: Poet Karen Brodine'. *The Alliance*, December 1985.

RFD Collective. 'We Are Not the Enemy'. *RFD*, No. 14 (Winter 1977): 51.

Rich, Adrienne. 'The Transformation of Silence into Language and Action'. *Sinister Wisdom*, No. 6 (Spring 1978): 4–25 (23).

Rich, Adrienne. 'The Problem with Lorraine Hansberry'. *Freedomways*, Vol. 19, No. 4, (Fourth Quarter, 1979): 247–54.

Rich, Adrienne. *Poetry and Commitment*. New York: W. W. Norton, 2007.

Rich, David. Email correspondence with author concerning Stephen Jonas and Gerrit Lansing, September 2020.

Rieckmann, Jens (ed.). *A Companion to the Works of Stefan George*. Rochester, NY: Camden House, 2005.

Rimbaud, Arthur. *Illuminations*. Trans. Louise Varèse. San Francisco: City Lights, 1957.

Roberts, Luke. 'Lyric Audibility: In Public'. *Textual Practice*, Vol. 32, No. 5 (2018): 785–98.

Rosa, Francesca. 'From the Angels of Light to New Narrative and Labor Activism'. *XPoetics*, February 2009, http://xpoetics.blogspot.com/2009/01/from-angels-of-light-to-new-narrative.html.

Rosenthal, Irving. 'Publisher's Note' to *Transit Glory* (Marshall 1966).

Rosenthal, Irving. 'Deep Tried Frees'. *Kaliflower, New Series* No. 3 (April 30, 1978). [Text available online at Eric Noble (ed.), *Diggers.org* https://www.diggers.org/kaliflower/dtf.htm.]

Roscoe, Will. *Living the Spirit: A Gay American Indian Anthology*. New York: St. Martin's, 1989.

Ross, Loretta. 'Voices of Feminism Oral History Project: Barbara Smith Interviewed by Loretta J. Ross, May 7–8, 2003'. Sophia Smith Collection, Smith College Libraries, https://findingaids.smith.edu/repositories/2/archival_objects/89295.

Roy, Camille. *Honey Mine: Collected Stories*. Ed. Lauren Levin and Eric Sneathen. New York: Nightboat, 2021.

Ruddy, Sarah. *This Fact Which Is Not One: Differential Poetics in Transatlantic American Modernism*. Unpublished PhD Dissertation, Wayne State University, 2012.

Rumaker, Michael. *Black Mountain Days*. New York: Spuyten Duyvil, 2012.

Rumaker, Michael. *Robert Duncan in San Francisco*. San Francisco: City Lights/Grey Fox Press, 2013. (Original 1996)

Rushin, Kate. 'Pat Parker: Creating Room to Speak & Grow'. *Sojourner*, October 1985, 28–9.

Rushin, Kate. *The Black Back-Ups*. Ithaca, NY: Firebrand Books, 1993.

Russell, Diane E. H., and Nicole van de Ven (eds.). *Crimes Against Women: Proceedings of the International Tribunal*. Millbrae, CA: Les Femmes, 1976.

Saidenberg, Jocelyn. 'What's Wrong with the World Now!: An Interview with Bruce Boone'. *On Contemporary Practice*, 2017, https://static1.squarespace.com/static/52010

378 WORKS CITED

d47e4b0eefc5e9e9bf0/t/59ebda1e4c326dcab886e775/1508629022885/Saidenberg_Boone_Interview_Final.pdf

Sanders, Ed. 'Bio note for Ed Marshall'. *Fuck You: A Magazine of the Arts,* Vol. 1, No. 5 (December 1962): n.p.

sands, aimee. 'rape and racism in boston: an open letter to white feminists'. *off our backs,* Vol. 11, No. 1 (January 1981): 16–17.

Saxe, Susan. *Talk Among the Womenfolk.* Milwaukee, WI: Common Woman Press, 1976.

Scott, Cam. 'Extreme Remedies'. *Social Text,* May 28, 2020, https://socialtextjournal.org/periscope_article/extreme-remedies/.

Shand-Tucci, Douglas. *The Crimson Letter: Harvard, Homosexuality, and the Shaping of American Culture.* New York: St. Martin's Press, 2003.

Shange, Ntozake. 1978. *Nappy Edges.* New York: Bantam Books, 1980.

Shively, Charley. 'Cocksucking as an Act of Revolution'. *Fag Rag,* No. 3 (June 1972): 8–9, 20.

Shively, Charley. 'Letters on Gay Subjects, One . . . ' *Great Speckled Bird,* July 31, 1972, 9.

Shively, Charley. 'The Wild Tulip Shall Outlast the Prison Wall'. *Fag Rag,* No. 5 (Summer 1973): 11, 14.

Shively, Charley. 'Poetry, Cocksucking and Revolution'. *Fag Rag,* No. 10 (Fall 1974): 3–5.

Shively, Charley. 'Stephen Jonas'. Stonewall 5th Anniversary. *Fag Rag,* No. 9 / *Gay Sunshine,* No. 22 (Summer 1974): 19.

Shively, Charley. 'Beyond the Binary: Race and Sex'. *Fag Rag,* No. 12 (Spring 1975): 8–10. Repr. in Smith 1983.

Shively, Charley [and others]. 'dear cocksucker'. *Fag Rag,* No. 13 (Summer 1975): 30–35.

Shively, Charley. 'Cosmetics as an Act of Revolution'. *Fag Rag,* No. 19 (Spring 1977): 15–19. Repr. in Pam Mitchell (ed.), *Pink Triangles: Radical Perspectives on Gay Liberation.* Boston: Alyson, 1980.

Shively, Charley. 'To Speak the Unspeakable'. *Fag Rag,* No. 23/4 (Fall 1978): 9–11.

Shively, Charley. 'Sequins and Switchblades: In Extremis Exegesis. A Reading of John Wieners' *Selected Poems, 1958–1984'. Fag Rag,* No. 44 (1984): 28–33.

Shively, Charley. 'JohnJob: Editing Behind the State Capitol or Cincinnati Pike'. *Mirage: John Wieners Issue* (1985): 78–82.

Shively, Charley. 'Prescott Townsend (1894–1973): Bohemian Blueblood—A Different Kind of Pioneer'. In Vern L. Bullough (ed.), *Before Stonewall: Activists for Gay and Lesbian Rights In Historical Context.* New York: Harrington Park Press, 2002, 41–47.

Shively, Charley. 'Fag Rag: The Most Loathsome Publication in the English Language'. In Ken Wachsberger (ed.), *Insider Histories of the Viet Nam Era Underground Press, Part 2.* Ann Arbor: Michigan University Press, 2012, 97–120.

Shockley, Ann Allen. *Loving Her.* Boston: Northeastern University Press, 1997.

Shockley, Ann Allen. 'A Meeting of the Sapphic Daughters'. *Sinister Wisdom* No. 9 (Spring 1979): 54–59

Shelley, Martha. *Crossing the DMZ.* Oakland, CA: Women's Press Collective, 1974.

Shoptaw, John. *On the Outside Looking Out: John Ashbery's Poetry.* Cambridge, MA: Harvard University Press, 1994.

Short, Kayann. 'Coming to the Table: The Differential Politics of *This Bridge Called My Back'.* In Ann M. Kibbey and Carol Siegel (eds.), *Eroticism and Containment: Notes from the Flood Plain.* New York: New York University Press, 2004, 3–44.

Shurin, Aaron. Interview with author. February 9, 2022, San Francisco, CA.

WORKS CITED 379

Sigo, Cedar. 'Behind the State Capitol: Or Cincinnati Pike'. *The Poetry Foundation*, November 4, 2010, https://www.poetryfoundation.org/harriet-books/2010/11/behind-the-state-capitol-or-cincinnati-pike.

Sigo, Cedar. *Royals*. New York: Wave Books, 2017.

Singh, Amardeep. *Asian American Little Magazines, 1968–1974*. Lehigh University, 2019, https://scalar.lehigh.edu/asian-american-little-magazines/index.

Slater, Anne. 'Gloria Martin Remembered'. *Freedom Socialist*, December 2006, https://socialism.com/fs-article/gloria-martin-remembered/.

Solange. *When I Get Home*. Columbia Records, 2019.

Smith, Barbara. 'Naming the Unnameable: The Poetry of Pat Parker'. *Conditions*, No. 3 (Spring 1978): 99–103. (1978a)

Smith, Barbara. 'Towards a Black Feminist Criticism'. *The Radical Teacher*, No. 7 (1978b): 20–27.

Smith, Barbara. 'A Separate Struggle.' [Letter] *Sojourner*, September 1979, 2.

Smith, Barbara. *Ain't Gonna Let Nobody Turn Me Around: Forty Years of Movement Building with Barbara Smith*. Ed. Alethia Jones and Virginia Eubanks with Barbara Smith. New York: State University of New York Press, 2014.

Smith, Dale. 'On Poetry and the Occult' [Review of Gerrit Lansing, *A February Sheaf* and Jaime Saenz, *Immanent Visitor*]. *Possum Pouch*, August 2003, http://www.skankypossum.com/pouch/archives/000058.html#000058.

Smith, Michael J. (ed.). *Black Men/White Men: A Gay Anthology*. San Francisco: Gay Sunshine Press, 1983.

Sneathen, Eric. 'Earlier Selves, Strangers: A Conversation with Robert Glück'. *Open Space*, June 2018, https://openspace.sfmoma.org/2018/06/earlier-selves-strangers-a-conversation-with-robert-Glück/. (Sneathen 2018a)

Sneathen, Eric. 'The Sense of Utopia: Bruce Boone and Eric Sneathen in Conversation'. *Open Space*, July 2018, https://openspace.sfmoma.org/2018/07/bruce-boone-and-eric-sneathen-in-conversation/. (Sneathen 2018b)

Sneathen, Eric. 'Utopian Gossip: "The Homosexual in Society" from Robert Duncan to New Narrative'. Unpublished conference paper, originally presented at Passages: The Robert Duncan Centennial Conference in Paris. Sorbonne Université, June 12–14, 2019.

Sneathen, Eric. 'Nothing Ever Just Disappears: Remembering Queer Theory's New Narrative'. *Social Text*, May 2020, https://socialtextjournal.org/periscope_article/nothing-ever-just-disappears-remembering-queer-theorys-new-narrative/.

Snediker, Michael. 'Jack Spicer's *Billy The Kid*: Beyond the Singular Personal'. In Vincent 2011, 177–94.

Sneed, Pamela. *Funeral Diva*. San Francisco: City Lights Books, 2020.

Solomon, Sam. 'Offsetting Queer Literary Labor'. *GLQ: A Journal of Lesbian and Gay Studies*, Vol. 24, No. 2 (2018): 239–66.

Songolo, Aliko, 'Muntu Reconsidered: From Tempels and Kagame to Janheinz Jahn'. *Ufahamu: A Journal of African Studies*, Vol. 10, No. 3 (1981): 92–100.

Sontag, Susan. 'Fascinating Fascism'. *New York Review of Books*, February 6, 1975: 23–30.

Somerville, Siobhan B. *Queering the Color Line: Race and the Invention of Homosexuality in American Culture*. Durham and London: Duke University Press, 2000.

Soong, Jennifer. 'The Minor Poet: A Case of John Wieners'. *Textual Practice*, December 2022, ttps://doi.org/10.1080/0950236X.2022.2150296.

380 WORKS CITED

Spencer, Taronda, Brenda S. Banks, and Kerrie Cotten Williams. 'Finding Guide, the Audre Lorde Papers, ca. 1950–2002'. Spelman College Archives, 2012, https://www.spel man.edu/docs/archives-guides/audre-lorde-collection-finding-aid-(2012)be59fb34f 9bd6490bbe9ff0000b1c0f4.pdf?sfvrsn=b8e49f50_0.

Spicer, Jack. 'Notebook 4, 1956'. Folder 4, Series 2:2, Box 8. Books, Collected and Serial Poems 1948–1966 [1975], Jack Spicer Papers, BANC MSS 2004/209, The Bancroft Library, University of California, Berkeley.

Spicer, Jack. 'Hokkus'. *J*, No. 1 (1959): n.p. Repr. in Spicer 1980.

Spicer, Jack. 'Epilog for Jim'. *J*, No. 2 (1959): n.p. Repr. in Spicer 1980.

Spicer, Jack. ['New Beaches']. *J*, No. 2 (1959): n.p. Repr. in Spicer 1980.

Spicer, Jack. 'Fifth Elegy'. *J*, No. 5 (1960): n.p. Repr. in Spicer 2008, 230–31.

Spicer, Jack. 'Sixth Elegy'. *J*, No. 5 (1960): n.p. Repr. in Spicer 2008, 231–32.

Spicer, Jack. ['Lack of oxygen puzzles the air']. Attrib. to 'Mary Murphy'. *J*, No. 6 (1960): n.p. Repr. in *Manroot*, No. 10 (Fall–Winter 1974).

Spicer, Jack. 'A Protestant Letter'. *Open Space* No. 7, n.p.

Spicer, Jack. 'Letters to Graham Mackintosh'. *Caterpillar* 12 (1970): 83–114.

Spicer, Jack. *The Collected Books*. Ed. Robin Blaser. Santa Barbara, CA: Black Sparrow Press, 1975.

Spicer, Jack. *One Night Stand and Other Poems*. Ed. Donald Allen, with a preface by Robert Duncan. San Francisco: Gray Fox Press, 1980.

Spicer, Jack. 'Jack Spicer's Letters To Allen Joyce'. *Sulfur*, No. 10 (1984): 140–53.

Spicer, Jack. 'Letters to Robin Blaser, 1955–1958'. *line*, No. 9 (Spring 1987): 26–55.

Spicer, Jack. *The Tower of Babel*. Hoboken, NJ: Talisman House, 1994.

Spicer, Jack. *The House that Jack Built: The Collected Lectures of Jack Spicer*. Middletown, CT: Wesleyan University Press, 1998.

Spicer, Jack. *My Vocabulary Did This to Me: The Collected Poetry of Jack Spicer*. Ed. Peter Gizzi and Kevin Killian. Middletown, CT: Wesleyan University Press, 2008.

Spicer, Jack. *Be Brave to Things: The Uncollected Poetry and Plays of Jack Spicer*. Ed. Daniel Katz. Middletown, CT: Wesleyan University Press, 2021.

Spicer, Jack, and Robert Duncan. *An Ode and Arcadia*. Berkeley, CA: Ark Press, 1974.

Springer, Kimberly. *Living for the Revolution: Black Feminist Organizations, 1968–1980*. Durham, NC: Duke University Press, 2005.

Stanford, Adrian. *Black and Queer*. Boston: Good Gay Poets, 1977.

Stanley, Eric. 'Near Life, Queer Death: Overkill and Ontological Capture'. *Social Text*, Vol. 29, No. 2 (Summer 2011): 1–19.

Stanley, George. 'An Apparition of the Late J' [Cover Art]. *J*, No. 6 (1960).

Staples, Robert. 'The Myth of Black Macho: A Response to Angry Black Feminists'. Human Rights U.S.A. *The Black Scholar*, Vol. 10, No. 6/7 (March/April 1979): 24–33

Stefans, Brian Kim. *Word Toys: Poetry and Technics*. Tuscaloosa: University of Alabama Press, 2017.

Stehlin, John. 'The Post-Industrial "Shop Floor": Emerging Forms of Gentrification in San Francisco's Innovation Economy'. *Antipode*, Vol. 48, No. 2 (2016): 474–93.

Stein, Marc. 'Ray Daniels'. Philadelphia LGBT History Project, *Out History*, June 1993, http://outhistory.org/exhibits/show/philadelphia-lgbt-interviews/interviews/ray-daniels.

Stein, Marc. 'Anita Cornwell (born 1923), Interviewed October 6, 1993'. Philadelphia LGBT History Project, *Out History*, 2017, https://outhistory.org/exhibits/show/phila delphia-lgbt-interviews/int/cornwell.

WORKS CITED 381

Stern, Alexandra Minna. *Eugenic Nation: Faults and Frontiers of Better Breeding in Modern America*. Berkeley: University of California Press, 2005.

Stern, Alexandra Minna. 'Eugenics, Sterilization, and Historical Memory in the United States'. *História, Ciências, Saúde—Manguinhos* (Rio de Janeiro), Vol. 23 (2016): 195–212.

Stryker, Susan. *Transgender History*. Berkeley, CA: Seal Press, 2008.

Stryker, Susan, and Stephen Whittle (eds.). *Transgender Studies Reader*. Vol. 1. London: Routlege, 2006.

Tatonetti, Lisa. 'Two-Spirit Images in the Work of Maurice Kenny'. In Penelope Myrtle Kelsey (ed.), *Maurice Kenny: Celebrations of a Mohawk Writer*. New York: State University of New York Press, 2012, 119–33.

Tatonetti, Lisa. *The Queerness of Native American Literature*. Minneapolis and London: University of Minnesota Press, 2014.

Teare, Brian. 'Positively Not: A Talk About Poets and Traditions'. In Jim Elledge and David Groff (eds.), *Who's Yer Daddy? Gay Writers Celebrate Their Mentors and Forerunners*. Madison, WI and London: Terrace Books/University of Wisconsin Press, 2012, 82–89.

Temple, John. 'Haven of the Heart: The Poetry of John Wieners'. *Jacket Magazine*, No. 34, (October 2007), http://jacketmagazine.com/34/temple-wieners.shtml.

'Tender Benches: Making the Park & HAIR-RAISING (1976)'. *Kelsey Street Press Blog*. March 12, 2014, http://www.kelseyst.com/news/2014/03/12/tenderbenches-making-the-park-hair-raising-1976/.

Third World Women. San Francisco: Third World Communications, 1972.

Thomas, Hugh. *The Spanish Civil War*. New York: Harper & Brothers, 1961.

Thuma, Emily. *All Our Trials: Prisons, Policing, and the Feminist Fight to End Violence*. Chicago: University of Illinois Press, 2019.

Tilchen, Maida. 'Getting to Know Who We Are: The Lesbian Poetry Tradition, An Interview with Joan Larkin and Elly Bulkin'. *Gay Community News*, Vol. 9, No. 3 (August 1, 1981), 9–12.

Torra, Joseph. Interview with the author. September 22, 2020. Zoom.

Townsend, Jamie. '*Honey Mine* and the New Narrative Form: An Interview with Camille Roy'. *Lambda Literary*, March 2022, https://lambdaliterary.org/2022/03/honey-mine-interview-with-camille-roy/ (2022a)

Townsend, Jamie. 'An Interview with Gabrielle Daniels'. *Social Text*, May 6, 2022, https://socialtextjournal.org/an-interview-with-gabrielle-daniels/. (2022b)

Trachtenberg, Alan. *Shades of Hiawatha: Staging Indians, Making Americans, 1880–1930*. New York: Hill and Wang, 2005.

Treichler, Paula A. 'AIDS, Homophobia, and Biomedical Discourse: An Epidemic of Signification'. AIDS: Cultural Analysis/Cultural Activism. *October*, Vol. 43 (Winter 1987): 31–70.

Tremblay-McGaw, Robin. 'Torquing the Erotics of Attention: An Interview with Camille Roy'. *X Poetics*, November 7, 2008, http://xpoetics.blogspot.com/2008/11/torquing-erotics-of-attention-interview.html.

Tremblay-McGaw, Robin. *Community and Contestatory Writing Practices in the San Francisco Bay Area, 1970–Present*. Unpublished PhD Dissertation, University of California, Santa Cruz, 2009.

Tremblay-McGaw, Robin. '"A Real Fictional Depth": Transtexuality & Transformation in Robert Glück's *Margery Kempe*'. In David Hadbawnik (ed.), *Postmodern Poetry*

WORKS CITED

and Queer Medievalisms: Time Mechanics. Boston: Medieval Institute Publications, 2022, 17–44.

Troyan, Cassandra. 'Spitting Venom: An Interview with Elana Chavez & Tatiana Luboviski-Acosta' [Two Parts]. *The Poetry Foundation*, April 2015, https://www.poetryfoundation.org/harriet/2015/04/spitting-venom-an-interview-with-elana-chavez-tatiana-luboviski-acosta-part-1.

Tsui, Kitty. 'harvey milk / we burn these words let them ascend in clouds of incense'. *Bridge: An Asian American Perspective* Vol. 6, No. 4 (Winter 1978–9): 4.

Tsui, Kitty. *The Words of a Woman Who Breathes Fire*. Argyle, NY: Spinsters, Ink, 1983.

Tsui, Kitty. 'Breaking Silence, Making Waves and Loving Ourselves: The Politics of Coming Out and Coming Home'. In Jeffner Allen (ed.), *Lesbian Philosophies and Cultures*. Albany: State University of New York Press, 1990, 49–62.

Tye, Larry. *Demagogue: The Life and Long Shadow of Senator Joe McCarthy*. New York: Houghton Mifflin Harcourt, 2020.

Unamuno, Miguel de. *The Tragic Sense of Life*. Trans. J. E. Crawford Flitch. London: Macmillan, 1921. (Original 1912)

Unterceker, John. *Voyager: A Life of Hart Crane*. New York: Farrar, Straus and Giroux, 1969.

Van Ausdall, Mimi Iimuro. '"The Day All of the Different Parts of Me Can Come Along": Intersectionality and U.S. Third World Feminism in the Poetry of Pat Parker and Willyce Kim'. *Journal of Lesbian Studies*, Vol. 19, No. 3 (2015): 336–56.

Vanderkhove, August ('S.U. Zahn'). '*Traditions Occidentales et Orientales*'. *La Fronde, Février* 26, 1899, 6.

Various. 'Remembering Maurice Kenny'. *Dawnland Voices 2.0*, No. 4 (2017), https://dawnlandvoices.org/remembering-maurice-kenny-a-tribute/.

Yalom, Marilyn (ed.). *Women Writers of the West-Coast: Speaking of Their Lives and Careers*. Santa Barbara, CA: Capra, 1983.

Wade, Julie Marie. 'Poetry That Makes You Nearly Miss the Plane: The Complete Works of Pat Parker Edited by Julie R. Enszer'. *The Rumpus*, June 9, 2017, https://therumpus.net/2017/06/09/the-complete-works-of-pat-parker/.

Walker, Julia M. *Medusa's Mirrors: Spenser, Shakespeare, Milton, and the Metamorphosis of the Female Self*. Newark: University of Delaware Press, 1998.

Walters, Quincy. 'Remembering Rita: The 20th Transgender Day of Remembrance is Painfully Personal for Boston'. WBUR, November 20, 2019, https://www.wbur.org/news/2019/11/20/rita-hester-trans-women-vigil-boston-murders.

Ward, Geoffrey. 'Stephen Jonas'. *Bete Noir* No. 8/9 (Autumn 1989/Spring 1990): 284–88.

Ward, Geoffrey. *Statutes of Liberty: The New York School of Poets*. London: Palgrave MacMillan, 1993.

Ward, Geoffrey. *The Writing of America; Literature and Cultural Identity from the Puritans to the Present*. Cambridge: Polity Press, 2002.

Warner, Michael. *Fear of a Queer Planet: Queer Politics and Social Theory*. Minneapolis: University of Minnesota Press, 1993.

Warren, Calvin. 'Onticide: Afro-Pessimism, Queer Theory, & Ethics'. [s.I.]: Ill Will Editions, 2015, https://illwilleditions.noblogs.org/files/2015/09/Warren-Onticide-Afropessimism-Queer-Theory-and-Ethics-READ.pdf

'We Have to Be Our Own Spark: An Interview with "Gente" Third-World Lesbian Softball Team'. *The Lesbian Tide*, July 1974, 6–7, 25–28.

Weeks, Kathi. *The Problem with Work: Feminism, Marxism, Antiwork Politics, and Postwar Imaginaries*. Durham, NC: Duke University Press, 2011.

WORKS CITED 383

Wei, William. 1993. *The Asian American Movement*. Philadelphia: Temple University Press.

Weller, Adrienne. 'Memorial Tribute to Karen Brodine, November 22, 1987'. Box 2, KBP.

'Wembley Park Murders: Emotional Interview with Mum of Sisters Found Dead'. *BBC News*, June 26, 2020, https://www.bbc.co.uk/news/av/uk-53200019.

'What's Happening'. *It Ain't Me Babe*, Vol. 1, No. 7 (May 21–June 10, 1970): 15.

White, Evelyn C. (ed.). *The Black Women's Health Book: Speaking for Ourselves*. Seattle: Seal Press, 1994.

Whitman, Walt. *Leaves of Grass*. Ed. Jerome Loving. Oxford: Oxford University Press, 1998.

Wieners, John. *Ace of Pentacles*. New York: James F. Carr & Robert A. Wilson, 1964. Repr. in Wieners 1986.

Wieners, John. 'Ballade'; 'You Can't Kill These Machines'; 'That Old Gang of Mine'. *Boston Newsletter*, 1956, n.p. Repr. in Wieners 1961, n.p.; Wieners 1965, n.p.; Wieners 1988, 21.

Wieners, John. 'You Can't Kill these Machines'. *The Floating Bear*, No. 10 (June 1961), n.p.. [Printed alongside twelve other early poems by Wieners.]

Wieners, John. 'Ballade'. *Magazine of Further Studies*, Vol. 2 (1965) n.p. Repr. in Leyland 1975, 216–17.

Wieners, John. 'The Bridge Word (on brown paper)'. *Chicago Review*, Vol. 12, No. 1 (Spring 1958): 13–14.

Wieners, John. 'Cocaine'. *Fuck You: A Magazine of the Arts*, No. 4 (1962): n.p. Repr. in Wieners 1986: 76.

Wieners, John. *The Hotel Wentley Poems*. San Francisco: Auerhahn Press, 1958. Repr. in Wieners 1986.

Wieners, John. 'Road of Straw'. (Essay draft, 1965.). In Wieners 2015, 124–29. Also published online as 'From *Blaauwildebeestefontein* 1965'. John Wieners Feature. *The Volta, Evening Will Come: A Monthly Journal of Poetics*, No. 60 (December 2015), https://thevolta.org/ewc60-jwieners-p2.html.

Wieners, John. '1930s Jazz'. *Intrepid*, No. 8 (June 1967): 12.

Wieners, John. *Selected Poems*. London and New York: Jonathan Cape, 1972.

Wieners, John. *Playboy (We Were There: A Gay Presence at the Miami Democratic Convention)*. Boston: Good Gay Poets, 1972.

Wieners, John. '1972–3'. *Fag Rag*, No. 5 (Summer 1973): 13.

Wieners, John. 'Ailsa's Last Will and Testament'. *Fire Exit*, No. 3 (1973): 29.

Wieners, John. 'Address of the Watchman to the Night'. In Donald Allen and Warren Tallmann (eds.), *Poetics of the New American Poetry*. New York: Grove Press, 1973, 351–35. Repr. in *Manroot*, No. 10 (Fall–Winter 1974) (The Jack Spicer Issue) (Original 1963)

Wieners, John. *Behind the State Capitol: Or Cincinnati Pike*. Boston: Good Gay Poets, 1975.

Wieners, John. 'Midas, Methuselah, Solomon: An Essay on Stephen Jonas by Jackie J. Wieners'. *Fag Rag*, No. 15 (February/March 1976): 16.

Wieners, John. *Selected Poems, 1958–1984*. Ed. Raymond Foye. Santa Barbara, CA: Black Sparrow Press, 1986.

Wieners, John. *Conjugal Contraries and Quart*. New York and Madras, India: Hanuman Books, 1987.

Wieners, John. *Cultural Affairs in Boston: Poetry & Prose, 1956–1985*. Ed. Raymond Foye. Santa Rosa, CA: Black Sparrow Press, 1988.

Wieners, John. *The Journal of John Wieners Is to Be Called 707 Scott Street for Billie Holiday*. Los Angeles: Sun & Moon Press, 1996. (Original 1959)

384 WORKS CITED

Wieners, John. *A Book of PROPHECIES*. Ed. Michael Carr. Lowell, MA: Boostrap Press, 2007.

Wieners, John. 'For the Voices': *The Letters of John Wieners*. Ed. Michael Seth Stewart. CUNY Academic Works,2014, https://academicworks.cuny.edu/gc_etds/292.

Wieners, John. *Stars Seen in Person: Selected Journals*. Ed. Michael Seth Stewart. San Francisco: City Lights Books, 2015a.

Wieners, John. *Supplication: Selected Poems of John Wieners*. Ed. Joshua Beckman, C. A. Conrad, and Robert Dewhurst. New York: Wave Books, 2015b.

Wieners, John. *Yours Presently: The Selected Letters of John Wieners*. Ed. Michael Seth Stewart. Albuquerque: University of Mexico Press, 2020.

Wilkinson, John. *The Lyric Touch: Essays on the Poetry of Excess*. Cambridge: Salt, 2007.

Wilson, Ivy G. *Whitman Noir: Black America and the Good Gray Poet*. Iowa City: University of Iowa Press, 2014.

Williams, James S. *Jean Cocteau*. Manchester: Manchester University Press, 2006.

Williamson Terrion L. 'Why Did They Die? On Combahee and the Serialization of Black Death'. *Souls*, Vol. 19, No. 3 (2017): 328–41.

Wintz, Sara, 'On Authenticity and Community'. *The Creative Independent*, May 8, 2019, https://thecreativeindependent.com/people/poet-and-artist-robert-gluck-on-authe nticity-and-community/.

Wittman, Carl. *Refugees from Amerika: A Gay Manifesto*. New York: Red Butterfly, 1970.

Wolverton, Terry. 'Variant Verse'. [Review of Stephanie Byrd, *25 Years of Malcontent*, et al.]. *Lesbian Tide*, Vol. 7, No. 6 (May–June 1978): 32–33.

Women Writers Union (WWU). 'Statement of Purpose'. n.d. Teaching Writing–Notes Folder, Box 2, KBP.

Wong, Nellie. 'When You Type, Do You Read What You're Typing?' Typescript, 5/15/ 1980. Nellie Wong Folder, Box 2, KBP.

Wong, Nellie. 'Opening Remarks—International Women's Day,' 3/8/1980. n.p. Box 2, KBP.

Wong, Nellie. 'Asian American Women, Feminism and Creativity'. *Conditions*, No. 7 (1981): 177–84.

Wong, Nellie. 'What's a Nice Secretary Like You Doing in Politics Like This?' June 16–20, 1982. Nellie Wong Folder, Box 2, KBP.

Wong, Nellie. *The Death of Long Steam Lady*. New York: West End Press, 1986.

Wong, Nellie. 'When My World Opened'. *Freedom Socialist*, August 2019, https://social ism.com/fs-article/when-my-world-opened/.

Woo, Hyo Kyung. 'Korean American Poetics in Willyce Kim's *Eating Artichokes*'. *Studies in Modern British and American Poetry*, Vol. 24, No.1 (2018): 183–211.

Woo, Merle. 'For International Women's Day, 1981'. Typescript. Merle Woo Folder, Box 2, KBP.

Woo, Merle. 'Merle Woo on Feminism and Free Speech'. *Freedom Socialist*, Winter 1983, https://socialism.com/fs-article/merle-woo-on-feminism-and-free-speech/.

Woo, Merle. Letter to Karen Brodine, May 21, 1985. Box 3, KBP.

Woo, Merle. *Yellow Woman Speaks*: Exp. ed. Seattle, WA: Radical Women Publications, 2003.

Woo, Merle. 'Stonewall Was a Riot—Now We Need a Revolution'. In Avicolli Mecca 2009, 282–95.

Woman to Woman: A Book of Poems and Drawings by Women. 2nd ed. Oakland, CA: Women's Press Collective. 1971.

Women's Press Collective. *Woman to Woman: A Book of Poems and Drawings by Women*. Oakland, CA: The Women's Press Collective, n.d.

Woodwoman, Libby. 'Pat Parker Talks About Her Life and Her Work'. *Margins*, No. 23, (August 1975): 60–61.

w.s. 'my body aches from unseen beating'. *off our backs*, Vol. 9, No. 5 (May 1979): 17.

'Varied Voices of Black Women: Reading Room Entry'. *Because of a Song: An Archival Gallery*, n.d., https://becauseofasong.com/project/varied-voices-of-black-women/.

Vector: A Voice for the Homosexual Community, Vol. 5, No. 9 (September 1969).

Vincent, Ben, Sonja Erikainen, and Ruth Pearce (eds.). *TERF Wars: Feminism and The Fight For Transgender Futures*. *The Sociological Review Monograph Series*, Vol. 68, No. 4 (2020),

Vincent, John Emil. 'The End of the Line: Spicer in Love'. In *Queer Lyrics*. New York: Palgrave Macmillan, 2002, 149–76.

Vincent, John Emil (ed.). *After Spicer: Critical Essays*. Middletown, CT: Wesleyan University Press, 2011.

Young, Alex Trimble. '"The Queen of the Mad Frontier": Settler Colonialism and Jack Spicer's Queer Politics'. In Gioia Woods (ed.), *Left in the West: Literature, Culture, and Progressive Politics in the West*. Reno, NV: University of Nevada Press, 2018, 254–74.

Zimmerman, Laura. 'Taking Care of Business: New Words Collective Changes'. *Feminist Bookstore News*, Vol. 15, No. 2 (August 1992): 39–41.

Index

For the benefit of digital users, indexed terms that span two pages (e.g., 52–53) may, on occasion, appear on only one of those pages.

AAF (Asian-American Feminists), 283, 284
Abbott, Steve, 22, 31, 257, 298, 304–307, 310,
   320–322, 333
Abi-Karam, Andrea, 326
abortion, 213, 252, 274, 282
academia, 1, 11, 14, 15, 17, 22, 26, 27, 32, 58,
   65, 110, 160, 163, 166, 233, 259, 278,
   280–282, 331
Acker, Kathy, 307, 310, 312, 320
Ackerman, Jerry, 51, 53, 54, 57, 58
Adam, Helen, 15, 78, 333
addiction, 3, 110, 116, 118, 139, 152, 157,
   240, 269
   alcoholism, 31, 61, 95, 148, 205
   drug use, 31, 108, 123, 126, 139, 151, 165
   heroin, 123, 139, 151
Advocate, The, 22, 30, 161, 187
Age of Aquarius, 146, 147, 149, 342 n.15
AIDS, 5, 6, 31, 177, 219, 257, 278, 295, 296, 305,
   307, 312–325, 327, 330, 332, 333
Allen, Donald, 3, 20, 21, 84, 88, 99, 198
American Indian Movement (AIM), 179, 198,
   199, 204, 209, 326
Amnasan, Mike, 306, 333
anarchism, 6, 10, 14, 36, 37, 40, 49–51, 55, 56,
   78, 79, 86, 90, 91, 150, 157, 159, 162–
   165, 206, 247, 250, 300, 330
Anarchy, Daisy, 350 n.4
Anderson, Larry, 162, 178, 179, 186
anthologies, 19–21, 25–27, 165, 250
anti-Blackness, 17, 322
anti-Semitism, 42, 66, 76, 90, 113, 114, 126, 129,
   348 n.25
anti-war activism, 10, 92, 100, 160, 162, 213, 314
   Vietnam War, 59, 65, 92, 93, 152, 178, 182,
   261, 265, 273, 285, 320
Anzaldúa, Gloria, 19, 211, 225, 226, 229, 232–
   234, 282, 306
Arobateau, Red Jordan, 247, 249
Asian-American lesbian writing, 228, 255, 281–
   285, 290, 291
Auden, W. H., 162

Aulerich-Sugai, Ed, 299, 314

Baldwin, James, 29, 36, 46–49, 184, 234, 269
Bambara, Toni Cade, 233
Baraka, Amiri, 21, 126, 128, 148, 158, 184, 185,
   199, 224, 309
bathhouses (gay), 1, 2, 8, 77, 78, 89, 182, 314–
   316, 330
'bathroom problem, the' (Halberstam), 242,
   243, 265
Bay Area, 5, 7, 9, 16, 22, 31, 67, 239, 247–249,
   254, 255, 266, 277, 284, 301, 304, 325,
   326, 330, 333
Beam, Joseph, 26, 29, 30, 180
Bellamy, Dodie, 3, 6, 22, 32, 298, 299, 306–308,
   310–312, 314, 317–319, 321, 326
   works by
      Letters of Mina Harker The, 308, 311, 312,
      317–319
      *Real: The Letters of Mina Harker and Sam
      D'Allesandro,* 317, 318
beloved, the; beloveds, 60, 80, 81, 84, 88, 111,
   123–125, 135
Bergé, Carol, 282
Berkeley Renaissance, 6, 9, 12, 14, 16, 38, 49–52,
   54, 56–58, 60, 61, 63, 65–67, 69, 72,
   73, 79, 97, 101
   Throckmorton Manor, 49, 51, 60
Bérubé, Allen, 36, 48, 314, 315
Bethel, Lorraine, 214, 218
Blackberri (singer-songwriter), 260
Black Mountain College, 10, 20, 69, 91, 100, 132,
   136, 137, 143, 201, 202, 207, 290
Black Panther Party for Self Defense (BPP), 11,
   14, 16, 161, 178, 213, 247, 260, 330
'Black Sexism Debate, The,' 346 n.9
Blaser, Robin, 1–3, 8–11, 21, 38, 50, 51, 54, 58,
   63, 65, 66, 68–70, 73, 76, 77, 79–81,
   83, 87, 92, 93, 97, 99, 101, 113, 132,
   137, 337 n.9
blowjob, 116, 117, 142, 143, 152, 162,
   279, 321

388 INDEX

bohemia, 6, 36, 38, 49, 58, 60, 65, 67, 69, 70, 73, 97, 98, 100, 109, 117, 119, 132, 136, 143, 144, 151, 152, 165, 166, 198, 262, 330
Boone, Bruce, 42, 57, 95, 96, 257, 298–313, 324, 326, 331
  works by
    'Castro and Market Dialectics,' 300
    Century of Clouds, 298, 301–303, 311, 313, 316, 322, 331
    'Toward a Gay Theory for the ' 80s,' 298, 301, 304, 305
Bost, Darius, 17, 26, 29
Boston, 9–12, 100, 115, 117, 121, 129, 133, 138, 139, 152, 157–159, 207–215, 218–220, 222, 223, 225–228, 230, 323, 325, 328–331
  Beacon Hill, 97–98, 110, 126, 132, 330
  Boston College, 132, 138, 168, 171, 225
  Boston Common, 10, 97, 100, 101, 152, 209
  busing, 212, 228, 230, 330
  Fenway (cruising spot), 117, 166, 343 n.8
  Playland (bar), 10, 138, 330
  Roxbury, 121, 133, 152, 211, 213, 215, 224, 226, 228, 229, 234, 330
  Scollay Square, 229
Boston Gender Violence Campaign (1979), 211, 218, 219, 223, 224, 226, 227, 230, 234, 330, 331
Boston Newsletter, 69–73, 122, 131, 132, 134, 135, 137, 338 n.4
Brodine, Karen, 31, 245, 278, 280–283, 285–297, 306, 307, 310, 332, 333
  works by
    'No One Immune,' 294, 295
    Slow Juggling, 287
    Woman Sitting at the Machine, Thinking, 286–289, 292, 295, 319
    Work Week, 106, 216, 242, 278, 285, 287, 296
Bronski, Michael, 3, 7, 13, 19–21, 70, 157, 158, 160, 161, 172, 182, 323
Bryant, Anita, 273
Bulkin, Elly, 19, 25, 225
Bullins, Ed, 260–262, 270
Burton, Deryck, 146, 148, 149
Byrd, Stephania (Stephanie), 6, 17, 31, 155, 177, 179, 191–197, 215
  works by
    'I Many,' 192–193
    'Love Poem,' 195
    'Quarter of a Century,' 193–196, 215
    25 Years of Malcontent, 191–193

Cadden, Wendy, 19, 246–251, 253

Cambridge, MA, 132, 159, 160, 191, 212, 213, 215, 232
camp, 36, 40, 41, 75, 76, 89, 120, 173
canon-formation, canons, 7, 24, 26, 27
carceral system, carcerality, 9, 17, 35, 119, 120, 133, 134, 150, 151, 157–159, 169, 173–176, 178, 182, 192, 213, 216, 218, 246, 247, 254, 257, 266, 269, 278, 285, 296, 333
care work, 175, 239, 250, 266, 278, 287, 310, 313, 314
celebrities, 169, 172, 173, 188, 321
censorship, 18, 140, 148, 174
Chamberlin, Judi, 175
childcare, 212, 277
Christianity, 52, 53, 98, 99, 101, 205, 206
Clarke, Cheryl, 17, 214, 226, 232, 268, 269, 279, 303
class, 10–12, 25, 32, 40–43, 69, 110, 121, 125, 158, 160, 164, 166, 169, 173–175, 178, 206, 211, 213, 216, 233–234, 240–241, 244, 249, 251–255, 259, 278–279, 282–283, 286, 293, 300, 305–306, 312, 330, 331
closet, 8, 98, 106, 165, 170, 184, 205, 260
coalitions, coalition-building, 68, 115, 161, 182, 211–216, 223, 227, 231–233, 248, 275, 276, 282, 307
Cocteau, Jean, 82–84
colonialism, 45, 55, 200, 202, 207, 240, 275
Combahee River Collective, 17, 196, 210–219, 223–226, 232, 234, 268, 295, 331
coming out, 4, 36, 165, 170, 214, 262, 286, 329
commodification, 36, 42, 82, 172, 190, 300, 304
communism, 35, 41, 67–68, 90, 93, 164, 283, 305, 315
Compton's Cafeteria Riot, 152, 245
consciousness-raising, 157, 161, 216, 227, 247, 266
Corman, Cid, 69, 109, 110, 137
Cornwell, Anita, 259–263
coterie, 18, 40, 57, 58, 69, 71, 78, 86, 87, 92, 125, 130, 131, 139, 159, 163, 303, 313, 331
counterculture, 146, 148, 206, 299, 300, 330
  hippies, 100, 186, 299–301
Crane, Hart, 24, 41, 49, 72, 124, 135–137, 204
Creeley, Robert, 102, 109, 152, 246
Crenshaw, Kimberlé, 234
Crosby, Harry, 135–137
cruising, 10, 39, 65, 69, 71, 77–78, 99–101, 106, 107, 117, 145, 152, 161, 166, 198, 203, 205, 207

D'Allesandro, Sam, 317–320

INDEX 389

Daniels, Gabrielle, 282, 305, 306, 310, 333
Dante Alighieri, 38, 50, 56, 61–63, 79–81, 84,
    111, 124, 148
Daughters of Bilitis, 3, 15, 16, 98, 241, 249, 282
    Ladder, The, 15, 18, 98, 241, 247, 262, 263
Davidson, Michael, 7, 39, 53, 57, 82, 84, 141, 142
Davis, Angela, 259, 265, 276, 325
De Lauretis, Teresa, 15, 16
D'Emilio, John, 7, 8, 11, 41, 47, 292
Dickinson, Emily, 24, 73
domestic, domesticity, 38, 57–61, 63, 65, 77,
    141, 143, 149, 185, 191, 215, 255, 261,
    316, 327, 333
domestic labour, 103, 232, 293, 294
domestic violence, 58–61, 63, 65, 77, 103, 132–
    134, 141, 143, 149, 191, 215, 232, 255,
    261, 272, 293, 294, 316, 327
drag, 120, 122, 132, 140, 161, 167, 169–171, 178,
    186–190, 244, 245, 311, 329
    drag queens, 140, 161, 167, 169, 171, 178,
        187–190, 245, 311
Duncan, Robert, 5–6, 8–9, 15, 35–67, 69, 76–80,
    83, 87, 89, 92, 93, 101, 132, 138–140,
    144, 148, 157, 161–163, 176, 184, 245,
    247, 251, 307, 308, 325, 327
    works by
        'An African Elegy,' 35, 43, 45, 46, 51, 52, 55
        Dante Sonnets, 62–64
        Heavenly City, Earthly City, 51–53
        'Homosexual in Society, The,' 3, 5, 21, 35–
          42, 48, 49, 62, 64, 144, 148, 161, 327
        'A New Poem for Jack Spicer,' 61–62
        Venice Poem The, 8, 53–55, 57, 58, 67
Dunn, Carolyn, 15, 69, 72, 73, 78, 132
Dunn, Jim, 148, 166, 176
Dunn, Joe, 69–73, 78, 80, 97, 99, 100, 109–111,
    125, 126, 128, 132, 139
Durham, Sukey, 281, 283, 286
Durkee, Dana, 132, 134, 135, 139–143

Edwards, Brent Hayes, 10, 120, 121
Ellingham, Lew, 31, 61, 72, 79–81, 88, 113,
    123, 331
Ellis, Havelock, 74, 171
Enola Gay Faggot Affinity Group, 298, 312, 313,
    314, 325
Enszer, Julie, 13, 20, 31, 195, 197, 231, 259
Eros, 57, 59, 63, 71, 78, 327. *See* Thanatos
Evans, Arthur P. (*Witchcraft and the Gay
    Counterculture*), 206
Everson, Landis, 8, 9, 50, 58, 101

Faas, Ekbert, 36, 37, 47, 49, 50, 53, 54, 64

Fag Rag, 5, 6, 10–14, 18, 19, 21, 22, 71, 78, 86,
    108, 155, 157–163, 165–206, 210, 250,
    257, 299–300, 325, 329
Fassbinder, Rainer Werner, 328
feminism, 3, 14, 19, 144, 191, 211–217, 222–
    228, 237, 239, 244–247, 255–257,
    261–262, 275, 280–281, 286, 303,
    310, 330
Floating Bear, The (magazine), 338 n.3
Foye, Raymond, 135, 172, 176
Frazier, Demita, 17, 211, 213, 214
Freedom Socialist Party (FSP), 281, 283–286,
    292, 295
Freeman, Elizabeth, 131, 153
Freud, Sigmund, 35, 45
Fuck You: A Magazine of the Arts, 100–101, 162,
    167, 171

Gabriel, Kay, 326
Garber, Linda, 15, 242, 244
Garbo, Greta, 162, 169, 172, 173, 203
García, Inez, 213, 266
Gay Activists Alliance (GAA), 161, 162
gay-bashing, 320
Gay Liberation Front (GLF), 161, 162
Gay Pride, 4, 60, 96, 159, 177, 205, 244, 283, 329
Gay Sunshine, 3, 18–22, 48, 158, 160–162, 169,
    170, 174, 180, 197, 200, 204–206, 299,
    308, 329, 333
gender, 4, 7, 12–28, 31, 44, 47, 56, 68, 120–121,
    125, 127, 131, 142, 147–148, 157–
    159, 162–176, 178–179, 184, 186,
    193, 198, 199, 206, 207, 209, 214,
    216–222, 227–233, 240–249, 254,
    257, 261, 271, 273, 279, 285–289,
    291, 295, 296, 305, 310–312, 321,
    324–326, 328–333
    androgyny, 67, 147, 240
    butch, 68, 105, 187, 241, 242, 244, 311
    effeminacy, 171, 206, 244
    femme, 170, 171, 187, 244, 305, 311
    gender-bending, 158, 245
    'gender-critical,' 245
    gender-fluidity, 168, 170
    genderfuck, 166, 170
    hermaphrodite, 147, 148, 245, 342 n.16
    transgender, 17, 27, 169–172, 240–245, 249,
        310, 321–333
Genet, Jean, 21, 118
gentrification, 18, 117, 159, 300, 326, 330
George, Stefan, 10, 50, 81, 337 n.10
    George-kreis, 10, 56, 324
giallo, 319–321

390 INDEX

Ginsberg, Allen, 8–9, 24, 66, 67, 88, 93–95, 99–
101, 107–108, 137, 139, 140, 323
works by
'Howl,' 8, 9, 67, 70, 101, 102, 140
'Kaddish,' 100, 102
'Kral Majales,' 93
Giovanni, Nikki, 48, 184, 185, 269–270
Gizzi, Peter, 332
Gladman, Renee, 19, 326
Glide Memorial Church, 251, 281, 294
Gloucester, MA, 84, 102, 145, 148, 151
Glück, Robert, 3, 6, 11, 22, 57, 257, 298–300,
302, 304–316, 318, 322, 326, 331
works by
Jack the Modernist, 315–317
Margery Kempe, 312
'Sanchez and Day,' 308–309, 313, 316
Goldberg, Ariel, 326
Gomez, Jewelle, 232, 259, 268
Good Gay Poets, 6, 18, 21, 27–30, 158, 165–169,
176, 177–183, 191, 197, 200–202, 333
gossip, 57, 303, 308
Grady, Panna, 151
Grahn, Judy, 3–6, 14–15, 19–26, 31, 237, 239–
257, 263, 264, 270, 271, 279, 280, 285,
294, 305, 307, 323–325, 332–334
works by
'Cell, The,' 246
Common Woman Poems, The, 31, 217,
250–253, 258, 268, 309
'Psychoanalysis of Edward the Dyke, The,'
4, 12, 21, 173, 240–245, 250–258
She Who, 254
A Simple Revolution, 240, 244–246, 257
A Woman is Talking to Death, 253–256
Gruttola, Raffael de, 108–110, 116, 123, 126, 129
Gumbs, Alexis Pauline, 27, 219, 225
Gunn, Thom, 52, 200
Gunn Allen, Paula, 25, 199, 200

Halberstam, Jack, 242
Halpern, Rob, 59, 302, 325–328
Hammonds, Evelyn, 325
Hansberry, Lorraine, 262, 263
Harlem Renaissance, 180, 263
Harrington, Imani, 325
Hartman, Saidiya, 13, 27, 47, 336 n.13
Harvard University, 10, 69, 129, 137, 143, 159,
160, 165, 212, 219, 329
Hay, Harry, 67, 68, 205–207
Hemphill, Essex, 26, 29, 30, 180, 186
Herndon, Fran, 79, 84
HIV, 314, 316, 322, 324
Hobson, Emily, 11, 13, 274, 301, 306, 325

Holiday, Billie, 15, 120, 169, 172, 188
Hollibaugh, Amber, 305
Hollywood, 15, 114, 172, 173, 282, 309, 320, 332
homonationalism, 327, 330
homophile organisations, 3, 14, 16, 29, 67, 98,
145, 161, 166, 184, 241, 243, 246, 248
homophobia, 1, 10, 17, 28, 31, 42, 44, 51–58, 61,
83, 90, 98, 101, 113–115, 134–135,
139, 142, 148–149, 152, 158, 166, 173,
179, 181–185, 193, 198–200, 203, 204,
216, 251, 265, 273, 275, 283–285, 298,
301, 304–306, 310, 318, 321
Horne, Lena, 188–190, 345 n.5
Howard University, 109, 215, 240, 241
Hughes, Langston, 180, 260, 265, 279
humanism, 35, 36, 40, 49, 56, 96, 163
Huncke, Herbert, 100, 144
hustling, 30, 81, 101, 124, 125, 144

identity, 4, 6–9, 12, 15, 16, 22, 26–29, 31, 36–38, 42–
44, 47–49, 57, 65–69, 71, 73–77, 79–83,
85, 87, 89, 91–93, 95, 96, 108, 114, 120–
122, 129, 131, 134, 145, 146, 158, 161,
164–167, 169–173, 175, 179, 182, 184,
185, 193, 197–200, 206, 210, 230, 231,
241–246, 253, 256, 259, 261, 268–270,
292, 293, 304, 309–311, 321, 327, 328
immigration, 181, 282, 284, 290, 291
imperialism, 37, 38, 54–56, 60, 62, 92, 93, 158,
159, 165, 178, 182, 207, 265, 275, 276,
322, 324–326
incarceration. *See* carceral system, carcerality
'Indian'. *See* Native American and Indigenous
Queerness
in-group, 71, 120, 129, 182
'insanity'. *See* mental health
institutionalization. *See* mental health
internationalism, 11, 14, 91, 166, 295, 325
interpellation, 39, 48, 49, 96, 105, 114,
152, 175
intersectionality, 234
irony, 54, 113, 279, 280, 321, 322
Isherwood, Christopher, 144

Jahn, Janheinz (*Muntu*), 147, 342 n.17
jail. *See* carceral system, carcerality
Jameson, Fredric, 301, 303, 304, 309
Jarnot, Lisa, 43, 54, 55
Johnson, Helene, 215, 329, 331
Johnson, Marsha P. 161, 245
Jonas, Stephen, 10, 16, 17, 69–71, 78, 97–101,
105, 108–132, 143, 146, 148, 152, 153,
160–162, 329, 331
conspiracy theories and, 108, 126, 127, 129

INDEX 391

magic evenings, 71, 98, 110, 126, 127, 148
works by
   'Cante Jondo for Soul Brother Jack Spicer,'
      114–115
   Exercises for Ear, 108, 117–129, 148
   Love, The Poem, The Sea, 1, 78,
      110–112
   'A Poem for Dale Landers,' 123–124
   Orgasms/Dominations, 109, 127–129
   Transmutations, 108, 152
Jordan, June, 220, 224, 269, 270
Jung, Carl Gustav, 146–148

Kael, Pauline, 37, 49
Kantorowicz, Ernst, 10, 11, 50, 54, 56, 58
Kastan, Denise, 257, 304, 306
Katz, Daniel, 8, 76
Katz (Sue), 158
Kaufman, Bob, 113, 119, 262
Kelsey Street Press, 6, 18, 283, 285
Kennedy, Jackie (Jacqueline Bouvier Kennedy
     Onassis), 162, 169, 172
Kenny, Maurice, 6, 17, 162, 179, 180, 197–205,
     207–209, 305, 307
works by
   'Boston Tea Party,' 207, 209
   Only as Far as Brooklyn, 200–204, 207
   'Tinselled Bucks,' 200, 201
   'United,' 200–201, 209
   'Winkte,' 201, 209
Killian, Kevin, 13, 31, 61, 72, 80, 81, 92, 113,
     158, 298, 299, 306, 307, 311, 314, 317–
     323, 326, 331, 332
   Jack Spicer scholarship of, 31, 73, 331–333
works by
   Argento Series, 299, 319–322
Kim, Willyce, 251, 283, 284–285, 292, 333
Kinsey Report (*Sexual Behavior*), 58, 74, 76
Krafft-Ebbing, Richard von, 39, 74, 76, 171
Ku Klux Klan, 195, 196, 216, 275, 277
Kyger, Joanne, 15, 79, 139, 326

labour, 11, 67, 103, 174, 175, 197, 203, 204, 209,
     233, 240, 248, 252, 279, 286–288, 290,
     291, 293, 302, 305
landlords, 139, 140
language, 13, 16, 20, 32, 41, 48, 50, 53, 58, 62,
     77, 79–82, 84, 87, 88, 109, 111, 116,
     118, 120, 126, 129, 138, 146, 149,
     157, 159–161, 163–165, 168, 169,
     183, 186, 189–191, 194, 195, 200,
     203, 209, 217, 220, 222, 242, 243,
     288, 289, 292, 293, 326, 328, 329,
     332, 334

Lansing, Gerrit, 10, 69, 70, 96–99, 110, 117, 119,
     122–126, 131, 143–150, 152, 153
works by
   'Burden of *SET,* The,' 131, 143, 145, 146
   Heavenly Tree Grows Downward, The,
     148–150
Larkin, Joan, 19, 225
La Touche, John, 143–145
Lavender Scare, 11, 37, 66, 141, 169, 240
Lavender Vision, 21, 158
lesbian separatism, 191, 212, 228, 239, 248, 257,
     264, 275, 276, 285, 294
Leyland, Winston, 19, 162, 299, 333
Lindsay, Vachel, 46, 55
Little, Joann, 251, 266
Lonidier, Lynn, 245, 333, 342 n.16
Lorca, Gabriel García, 1, 35, 44, 45, 77–79,
     113–116
Lorde, Audre, 184, 194, 197, 211–224, 226, 227,
     232–234, 257, 263, 267–278
works by
   'Need,' 211, 218–224, 234, 267, 268, 271,
     347 n.18
lyric poetry, 15, 63, 73, 88, 168, 176, 233, 255,
     256, 259

Mackintosh, Graham, 67, 71, 73, 79, 80, 86, 92,
     339 n.5
Malanga, Gerard, 127, 129, 162
Manroot (magazine), 21, 201, 204, 205, 248, 333
Maoism, Mao Tse-tung, 92, 253, 265, 283, 301
Mariah, Paul, 246, 247, 333
marriage, 39, 58, 103, 123, 172, 185, 248, 254,
     260–263, 272, 282–285, 287, 292,
     293, 311
Marshall, Ed, 10, 69, 96–109, 123, 125, 131, 132,
     152, 153
   Lena Marshall (mother), 100, 102–104
   Rhoda Straw (grandmother), 104, 107
works by
   Hellan, Hellan, 98, 100, 105, 106
   'Leave the Word Alone,' 99, 102–104
Marxism, 90, 91, 213, 293, 298, 300, 301,
     303, 326
masochism. *See* sexuality: sado-masochism
Mass, Lawrence, 351 n.8
Mattachine Society, The, 3, 10, 13–16, 29, 31,
     65–68, 73–76, 83, 92, 95, 98, 162, 183,
     205, 206, 241, 248
Matthews, Tede, 170, 275, 284, 305, 333
McCarthyism, 67, 86, 91, 141, 158, 169, 294
Measure (magazine), 6, 18, 21, 71, 98, 100, 106,
     109, 116, 122, 131, 137–139, 143, 146,
     148, 152

392 INDEX

mental health, 31, 44, 51, 98, 100, 102–104, 107,
    117, 126, 128, 130, 140, 151, 157, 165,
    169, 173–176, 219, 240, 249
  asylums, 103, 104, 106, 151, 165, 169,
    174, 175
  electroshock, 151, 165, 173, 244
Miles, Josephine, 10, 58
Milk, Harvey, 11, 18, 274, 298, 300, 301
Mirage (magazine), 19, 22, 158, 298, 307, 317
misogyny, 16, 39, 76, 98, 163, 216, 217, 294
Mitchell, James, 9, 299, 306
Mitzel, John, 157, 168, 176
modernism, 4, 15, 36, 40, 45, 60, 69, 109, 117,
    120, 135, 209, 298, 308, 315, 316
Moraga, Cherríe, 19, 211, 225–230, 232, 254, 299
  works by
    'La Jornada,' 228, 230, 254
Morgan, Robin, 244
Murphy, Mary, 85, 340 n.16
Myles, Eileen, 7, 148, 320, 328, 329, 331
  works by
    'Gay Sunshine, 1971,' 329
myth, 37, 52, 56, 58, 80, 82–84, 146, 186, 188,
    194, 257, 258, 333

narcissism, 42, 55, 56, 134
Native American and Indigenous Queerness,
    25, 104, 179, 180, 197–209, 269
nature, 8, 42, 48, 68, 159, 206
Nazism, 42, 50, 82, 84, 277, 315
  Neo-Nazism, 275, 295
Ndugu, Prince-Eusi, 6, 17, 177, 179–183, 195,
    345 n.1
Nealon, Chris, 23, 66
negativity, 42, 54, 57, 66, 72, 90, 91, 94, 96, 184,
    307, 310, 319
New Narrative, 5, 6, 14–16, 19, 20, 22, 23, 28,
    57, 59, 83, 95, 129, 176, 204, 205, 207,
    233, 237, 254, 257, 276, 280, 298, 299,
    301–303, 305–307, 309–315, 317–
    322, 325, 326, 332, 333
  text-metatext, 302, 308, 312, 316, 320
Newton, Huey P. 247, 265, 276
Nielsen, Aldon Lynn, 46, 121, 122, 142

Oakland, CA, 11, 21, 38, 67, 68, 92, 203, 247,
    249, 251, 255, 268, 274, 275, 278, 282,
    284, 285, 302, 330
O'Brien, Alice. *See* Wieners, John: 'Ballade'
Occult School of Boston, 5, 6, 10, 12, 14, 18, 65,
    69, 73, 78, 96–99, 101–153, 157, 163
O'Hara, Frank, 21, 69, 101, 132–134, 136, 137,
    140, 299, 300, 303

Okazawa-Rey, Margo, 214
Oliveros, Pauline, 245, 333
Olivia Records, 244, 257, 266
Olsen, Tillie, 281, 305
Olson, Charles, 10, 60, 69, 84, 97, 99, 100, 102,
    116, 117, 129, 132, 137–139, 145, 146,
    148, 151
One (magazine), 18, 29, 70, 98, 183–186
Open Space (magazine), 84, 87–92, 94, 95,
    159, 230
Orpheus, 44, 52, 80, 82–84, 147
Othello, 44, 46, 54
outsiders, 54, 74, 113, 120, 142, 167, 176,
    296, 331
OutWrite (conference), 239, 245, 323
O'Hara, Frank, 21, 69, 101, 132–134, 136, 137,
    140, 299, 300, 303

pacifism, 10, 53, 67, 93, 162, 223
paranoia, 45, 66, 79, 80, 83, 98, 113, 126, 129,
    139, 151, 312
Parker, Pat, 3, 5, 6, 12, 14, 15, 17, 21, 31, 32, 36,
    39, 69, 184, 195–197, 218, 220, 224,
    237, 239, 244, 245, 250, 251, 253, 257–
    280, 282, 285, 294, 303, 325, 332–334
  publication history, 349–350 nn.3–4, 350 n.7
  Revolutionary Black Women's Council, 275,
    350 n.8
  works by
    'Gente,' 266–267
    'Group,' 267
    'I have a dream, too,' 264–266
    Jonestown and Other Madness, 265, 276–277
    'Movement in Black,' 32, 220, 242, 267–
      270, 273, 333, 347 n.17), 348 n.24
    'Revolution: It's Not Neat or Pretty or
      Quick,' 275–276
    Womanslaughter, 196, 220, 253, 266, 270–
      273, 277, 282
pathologisation, 47, 74, 167, 243, 244
patriarchy, 26, 28, 103, 104, 165, 190–193, 225,
    255, 284, 291, 293, 295, 302
peonage, institutional. *See* carceral system,
  carcerality
Persephone Press, 211, 224–226, 228
Persky, Stan, 61, 65, 66, 77, 79, 80, 84, 87–92, 94–96
perversion, 41, 75, 122, 124, 152, 327
pinkwashing, 275
police, 17, 39, 70, 105, 117, 129, 132, 133, 140,
    141, 159, 169, 188, 215–217, 221, 222,
    228, 234, 243, 247, 254–256, 265, 271,
    275–277, 301, 302, 308, 309, 313, 315,
    326, 330

pornography, 6, 14, 22, 70, 173, 190, 292, 298, 310, 326
Pound, Ezra, 60, 69, 108, 111, 126–130, 145, 256
poverty, 25, 151, 160, 166, 173, 175, 212, 239, 248, 271, 302
Powers, Jack, 11, 232
Praunheim, Rosa von, 299, 300, 328
Prima, Diane di, 148, 151, 250, 262, 305, 326, 351 n.3
printing, 84, 105, 146, 168, 181, 196, 217, 226, 250, 251, 254, 257
prisons and prison activism. *See* carceral system, carcerality
private property, 6, 57, 70, 110, 150, 158, 253, 332
procreation. *See* sexuality: heterosexuality
prophecy, 29, 106, 109, 189, 194, 208
prose, 2, 22, 40, 79, 82, 84, 86, 90, 116, 136, 146, 161, 162, 168, 178, 204, 214, 225, 233, 241, 243, 257, 261, 281, 283, 290, 298, 301, 306, 308, 310, 311, 319, 322
prosody, 94, 124
prostitution, 116, 122, 152, 246
psychiatry, 21, 35, 103, 151, 152, 157, 158, 165, 167, 169, 174, 175, 243, 245, 249, 255
psychoanalysis, 14, 21, 39, 45, 67, 173, 240, 241, 245, 250
Puar, Jasbir, 327
publication, 1–4, 7–9, 13, 18–23, 29, 30, 35, 43, 49, 70, 71, 78, 88, 90, 108, 111, 126, 134, 151, 157, 161, 162, 165, 167–169, 176, 179–182, 184, 187, 191, 198, 204, 212, 282, 333
small-press publishing, 1, 18, 168

queens, 16, 100, 120, 121, 182, 186
queer bars, 3, 8, 14, 61, 65, 68, 77, 78, 81, 84, 141, 144, 152, 186, 187, 249, 265, 266, 299, 304, 314, 330
queer-bashing, 170, 308, 309, 321
queer theory, 6, 15, 26, 27, 145, 311

racism, 10, 42–45, 48, 55, 66, 108, 113, 121, 159, 163, 179–181, 185, 190, 193, 196, 203, 212, 215, 216, 220, 225, 227, 230, 231, 265, 271, 275, 282, 285, 291, 299, 302, 305, 314, 316
Radicalesbians, 214, 250
Radical Faeries, 158, 205–207, 299
Raha, Nat, 13, 16, 157, 158, 167, 169, 170, 174–176, 326
Randolph, Pascal Beverly, 144
Ransom, John Crowe, 35, 36, 38, 43, 44, 58

rape. *See* sexual assault
Raymond, Janice, 244
Reagan, Ronald, 239, 258, 277, 280, 295, 300
religion, 3, 29, 42, 53, 83, 87, 99–104, 106, 108, 129, 145, 149, 187, 194, 301
reparation, 82, 130, 176
resurrection, 52, 104, 108, 151
Rexroth, Kenneth, 49, 116, 117
RFD (journal), 205, 206, 299
Ricard, René, 127, 129, 162
Rich, Adrienne, 24, 25, 194, 195, 219, 257, 263
Rimbaud, Arthur, 79, 123, 138–140, 152, 342 n.7
Rivera, Sylvia, 161, 244, 245
Röhm, Ernst. *See* Nazism
Rosenthal, Irving, 99, 100
Roy, Camille, 3, 306, 310, 311, 320
Rumaker, Michael, 60, 101, 132, 134, 135, 137, 139, 141, 152
Rushin, Kate, 155, 219, 226, 227, 230–233, 259, 261, 263, 273, 278, 280
works by
'Black Back-Ups, The,' 232–233, 268
'Bridge Poem, The,' 227, 230–231, 233–234
Ryan, John Allen, 67, 71, 78–80

Sade, Marquis de, 118, 327
sailors, 8, 11, 87, 112, 124, 135, 145, 146, 149
Sam, Canyon, 283, 294
Sanchez, Sonia, 184, 250
Sandburg, Carl, 252
Sanders, Ed, 101, 162, 167
San Francisco, 1, 2, 4–12, 14, 18, 19, 21, 24, 25, 42, 53, 57, 59–61, 65, 67, 68, 70, 71, 73, 77, 78, 84, 87, 90–92, 97, 100–105, 119–125, 137–143, 152, 157, 162, 170, 180, 199, 200–203, 225–229, 235–257, 260, 262, 266, 268, 281, 282, 285, 286, 290, 291, 296, 298, 299, 301, 304–306, 308, 310, 313, 314, 323, 325, 326, 329, 330, 332, 333
Castro, The (district), 330, 335
San Francisco Renaissance, 6–9
San Francisco State University (SFSU), 281–283, 285, 287
Sappho, 4, 247, 251, 257, 262, 326
scholarship, 7, 13, 14, 31, 157, 170, 200, 219, 232, 234, 326
Sebastian Quill (journal), 21, 299, 300
secretarial labour, 250, 282, 286, 289–292
seduction, 56, 106, 123
segregation, 98, 133, 152, 212, 228, 329, 330
settler colonialism, 200, 202, 206, 207, 340 n.18
sexism, 164, 189, 220, 283, 284, 291, 296, 305

394   INDEX

sexual assault, 187, 188, 190, 192, 197, 198, 205,
    209, 215–217, 220–222, 249, 255,
    272, 331
sexuality, 1–3, 7, 12, 18, 19, 21, 26, 31, 37, 39–48,
    50, 51, 59, 60, 65–67, 74–76, 78, 79,
    89, 93–95, 98, 99, 106, 116, 124, 143,
    145, 157, 158, 164, 178–181, 184, 185,
    189, 190, 195, 198, 200, 202, 205, 207,
    209, 214, 216, 233, 240, 241, 243, 245,
    248, 262, 274, 281, 284, 286, 287, 292–
    294, 303, 311, 319, 324–326, 328, 329
  bisexuality, 68, 75, 76, 123, 147, 148, 184, 215,
    292, 333
  heterosexuality, 9, 15, 21–25, 27, 28, 39, 42,
    47–49, 56, 57, 59, 60, 63, 67, 68, 72,
    75, 76, 79, 103, 104, 123, 138, 146,
    151, 152, 164, 166, 173, 178, 184, 185,
    189, 190, 200, 202, 205, 206, 209, 211,
    218, 222, 223, 244, 247–249, 253, 262,
    271, 283, 284, 287, 291, 292, 303, 306,
    309–311, 313, 324, 329, 333
  homoeroticism, 2, 30, 54, 68, 106, 183
  homosexuality, 5, 16, 17, 35–37, 39, 41–43,
    45, 47–49, 51–53, 55–57, 59, 61, 63,
    65, 74, 75, 80, 91, 132, 158, 159, 162,
    169, 207, 215, 240, 243, 244, 248, 249,
    273, 283, 292, 331
  interracial relations, 178, 180, 310
  lesbianism, 25, 36, 158, 181, 195, 200, 203,
    206, 213, 214, 219, 224, 228, 240, 241,
    244, 245, 247–251, 253, 261, 262, 266,
    268, 282–286, 289, 293, 294, 301, 311
  monogamy, 77, 88, 143, 243, 339 n.10
  pansexuality, 150
  polygamy, 35, 78, 143, 339 n.10
  polymorphous perversity, 47, 94, 143, 149, 292
  promiscuity, 6, 78, 143, 242, 243, 325
  queerness, 23, 28, 47, 57, 64, 68, 72, 74, 82, 88,
    136, 138–140, 142, 150, 160, 161, 176,
    184, 200–202, 204, 209, 263, 303, 305,
    311, 326, 334, 335 n.5
  sado-masochism, 44–46, 144, 164, 208, 209
  sex-positivity, 158, 159, 163, 203
Shakespeare, William, 44, 50, 54, 55, 80, 191
shamanism, 206–208
shame, 55, 60, 141, 150, 159, 175, 188, 190, 192,
    193, 203, 294, 307
Shange, Ntozake, 217, 218, 220, 223, 224, 227,
    251, 254, 268, 333
  works by
    for colored girls who have considered suicide
      when the rainbow is enuff, 217, 268
    'with no immediate cause,' 217–220

Shelley, Martha, 250, 333
Shepard, Matthew, 320–322
Sherrod, Tony, 123, 124
Shively, Charley, 6, 10, 97, 100, 108–121, 129,
    155, 157–170, 174, 176–178, 182,
    189–199, 205, 210, 324
  works by
    'Cocksucking as an Act of Revolution,'
      164–154
    'Poetry, Cocksucking and Revolution,' 162,
      164–154
Shurin, Aaron, 60, 307, 333
Sigo, Cedar, 326
Silliman, Ron, 305
Simone, Nina, 252
slavery, 17, 47, 129, 181, 189, 194, 214, 261, 263,
    268, 269
Small Press Traffic Bookstore, 11, 257, 298, 306
Smith, Barbara, 17, 19, 25, 169, 199, 200, 211–
    213, 215, 218–220, 223, 225–230, 241,
    247, 259, 262, 263, 268
Smith, Beverly, 17, 211, 213, 218, 219, 230, 325
socialism, 5, 42, 86, 91, 206, 212, 213, 225, 248,
    252, 276, 280, 281, 283, 285, 286, 291,
    294, 301, 302, 304, 332
sodomy, 35, 62, 67, 132
solidarity, 16, 31, 63, 82, 121, 141, 142, 165,
    176, 182, 183, 205, 209, 213, 229, 235,
    245, 247, 274, 275, 285, 294, 301, 309,
    325, 330
sonnets, 38, 61–63, 80, 193, 252
Sontag, Susan, 88, 89
Soup (magazine), 19, 22, 207, 298, 307, 308
Spicer, Jack, 1–6, 8–16, 18, 21, 22, 31, 33, 38, 50,
    51, 54, 56–58, 61, 63–101, 112–116,
    119, 122, 123, 126, 128–130, 132, 134,
    136, 137, 148, 153, 157, 159–163, 184,
    306, 324, 325, 331–333
  Martians, 4, 65, 79, 84, 112, 113,
    339 n.12
  Outside, The, 79, 80, 82, 84, 85, 96, 113,
    339 n.12
  Pacific Nation, The, 66, 91, 92, 340 n.18
  serial poem, 1, 2, 5, 66, 71, 77–79, 83, 87, 88,
    234, 339 n.10
  Spicer Circle, 2, 14, 65, 66, 71, 78, 79, 84, 86–
    88, 90, 91, 95, 331
  works by
    Admonitions, 1–2, 77
    Book of Magazine Verse, 92–95
    'Goodnight,' 72, 73, 75, 77, 82, 136
    Heads of the Town up to the Aether,
      The, 79–84

Open Space poems
    'Be Brave to Things,' 88
    'Love Poems,' 88–89
    'Three Marxist Essays,' 90–91
    'A Prayer for Pvt. Graham Mackintosh on
        Halloween,' 71–72
    'Unvert Manifesto and Other Papers of
        Oliver Charming Found in the Rare
        Book Room of the Boston Public
        Library, The,' 73–77, 84, 91, 148
Stalinism, 35, 42, 90, 93, 286, 301
Stanford, Adrian, 27–31, 183, 185–190, 195
    works by
        Black and Queer, 27–28, 183–190
        'Black and Queer,' 185
        'Psalm of the Visionary,' 188–189
        'Remembrances of Rittenhouse Square,'
            186–187
        'Sacrifice,' 27–28
        'tina turner (after hearing her sing),'
            189–191
Stanley, George, 78, 86, 90, 92, 123
Stein, Gertrude, 15, 25, 26, 38, 45, 58, 60, 242,
        243, 250, 257, 324
sterilization, 35, 212, 337 n.1
Stone, Sandy, 242–244
Stone Soup series, 11, 232
Stonewall, 7, 8, 14, 15, 19, 20, 108, 152, 153, 160,
        161, 166, 171, 184, 284
Stryker, Susan, 14, 243, 244
Students for a Democratic Society (SDS), 14,
        213, 247, 298
sublimation, 37, 75, 124
submission. *See* sexuality: sado-masochism
suicide, 35, 44, 69, 72, 104, 129, 132, 134–137,
        151, 197, 198, 217, 239, 254, 268, 269,
        276, 277, 317, 321
surrealism, 35–37, 39–41, 43, 144
surveillance, 25, 60, 70, 83, 117, 139–141, 315
survival, 26, 28, 55, 60, 75, 94, 102, 104, 105,
        132, 135, 137, 157, 158, 165, 167, 172,
        174, 175, 177, 185, 187–189, 197, 201,
        217, 233, 234, 252, 264, 269, 271, 276,
        281, 302, 305, 309, 319–328

Tangents (magazine), 29, 184
Tatonetti, Lisa, 180, 197, 198, 200–202, 204
temporality, 5, 6, 39, 45, 131, 152, 153, 189, 217,
        218, 229, 234, 240, 241, 279, 309
textuality, 2, 29, 79, 329
Thanatos, 57, 184, 255, 319. *See* Eros
This Bridge Called My Back, 225–232, 267, 275,
        290–292, 333

tragedy, 105, 107, 112, 129, 132, 176, 188,
        228, 277
Trans Day of Remembrance, 331
transsexual. *See* gender: transgender
Trotskyism, 92, 283, 285, 286, 330

unconscious, 43, 45, 49, 264, 288
unemployment, 240, 254, 255
unions, unionization, 6, 249, 281–283, 287, 288,
        295, 301, 304, 305, 311
universalism, 36, 42, 43, 59, 64, 95, 149
unpublished texts, 13, 72, 113, 137, 152, 167,
        171, 219, 263, 273, 296, 298, 300,
        301, 312
Uranian, 75, 147
utopianism, 37, 101, 104, 111, 112, 122, 148–
        150, 176, 187, 203, 204, 209, 270, 288,
        302, 309, 314, 322, 326

Valentine's Day, 88
Valli, Alida, 173
Vancouver, 92, 199, 287, 304
Vaughan, Sarah (drag queen), 186, 187
vigils, 167, 247, 249

Waldman, Anne, 166, 307
Wallace, George, 127
Washington, DC, 226, 240, 241, 265, 278, 325
welfare, 67, 212, 248, 276
Welsing, Frances Cress, 215, 220
Weston, Carol, 110, 126
White Night Riots, 11, 274, 301, 304
White Rabbit Press, 1, 9, 11, 18, 21, 78, 85, 111
Whitman, Walt, 1, 5, 9, 24, 75, 113, 145, 146,
        160, 167, 175, 183, 192, 204, 269, 327
    adhesiveness, 146–147
    amativeness, 146–147
    Calamus, 5, 160
Wieners, John, 3–6, 9–16, 18, 21, 22, 31, 69, 71,
        72, 96–102, 106, 109, 110, 116, 125–
        127, 129–144, 146, 148, 151–153, 155,
        157, 158, 160–162, 165–177, 184, 188,
        199, 229, 324, 326, 329–331
    publication history, 343 n.2, 343–344 nn.8–
        9, 13, 19
    reception history, 342–343 n.2
    works by
        Behind the State Capitol, 167–177
        'Children of the Working Class,'
            173–175
        'Yours to Take,' 171–172
        Boston Newsletter poems
            'Ballade,' 132–4, 137, 171, 330, 341 n.5

396 INDEX

Wieners, John (*cont.*)
    'That Old Gang of Mine,' 135–137
    'You can't kill these machines,' 134–135
    Hotel Wentley Poems, The, 139–141, 151,
      152, 329
    'With Meaning,' 153
    'A Poem for Cocksuckers,' 141–142
    'A Poem for Record Players,' 140–141
Williams, William Carlos, 24, 40, 60, 84, 109, 125
Wilson, Carol, 247–249
Winfrey, Oprah, 296
Wittman, Carl, 7, 8, 159
woman-identified, 170, 214
A Woman's Place Bookstore, 249, 251, 285
Women Writers' Union (WWU), 281–283, 286,
    287, 295, 306, 310

Wong, Nellie, 5, 6, 237, 280–286, 289–292, 294,
    295, 297, 305, 332
    works by
      'When You Type, Do You Read What
      You're Typing?,' 289–290
Woo, Merle, 5, 6, 17, 22, 226, 237, 280–286, 288,
    291–297, 304, 305, 310, 325, 332
    works by
      'Polymorphously Perverse,' 292–294
Woolf, Virginia, 35, 44, 312
workplace, 73, 286, 289, 292, 295, 304, 307
world-historical, 50, 90, 92

Yeats, W. B., 145, 146
Young, Lester, 120
Yūgen (magazine), 100, 109